Subjects to Groups

RANDOM ASSIGNMENT
(Experimental Designs)

One Dependent Measure per Subject		Two Dependent Measures per Subject		More than Two Dependent Measures per Subject	
Two levels of the independent variables actually included in the study	More than two levels for one or more independent variables	Two levels of the independent variables actually included	More than two levels for one or more independent variables	Two levels of the independent variables actually included	More than two levels for one or more independent variables
2x2, 2x2x2, etc. FACTORIAL	2x3, 4x3, 2x2x4, etc. FACTORIAL	2x2, 2x2x2, etc. SPLIT–PLOT FACTORIAL SOLOMON** FOUR–GROUP	2x3, 2x4, 2x3x5, etc. SPLIT–PLOT FACTORIAL	SINGLE– SUBJECT COMPONENT ANALYSIS	2x3, 3x4, 3x4x5, etc. SPLIT–PLOT FACTORIAL
CHAPT. 10	CHAPT. 10	CHAPT. 10	CHAPT. 10	CHAPT. 11	CHAPT. 10
RANDOMIZED TWO–GROUP ANCOVA	MULTILEVEL ANCOVA	BEFORE– AFTER TWO–GROUP ANCOVA	MULTILEVEL WITH PRE– TEST ANCOVA		MULTILEVEL WITH RE– PEATED MEASURES ANCOVA
CHAPT. 8, 21	CHAPT. 10, 21	CHAPT. 8, 21	CHAPT. 10, 21		CHAPT. 10, 21
RANDOMIZED TWO–GROUP	MULTILEVEL	ONE–GROUP BEFORE– AFTER CHAPT. 7 BEFORE– AFTER TWO–GROUP	MULTILEVEL WITH PRE– TEST	TIME SERIES COUNTER– BALANCED EXPERIMEN– TAL CONDI– TIONS CHAPT. 7 SINGLE–SUBJECT A–B, A–B–A, A–B–A–B, DRO Changing Criter- ion Multiple Baseline CHAPT. 11	REPEATED MEASURES MULTILEVEL
CHAPT. 8	CHAPT. 10	CHAPT. 8	CHAPT. 10		CHAPT. 10

EXPERIMENTAL PSYCHOLOGY

Research Design and Analysis

THIRD EDITION

DOUGLAS W. MATHESON
University of the Pacific

RICHARD L. BRUCE
University of Alaska

KENNETH L. BEAUCHAMP
University of the Pacific

HOLT, RINEHART AND WINSTON   New York   Chicago   San Francisco   Dallas
Montreal   Toronto   London   Sydney

Note: The endpapers at the front and back of the book carry a complete tabular summary of research designs.

Library of Congress Cataloging in Publication Data
Matheson, Douglas W   1939–
      Experimental psychology.

      First-2d ed. published under title: Introduc-
tion to experimental psychology.
      Bibliography: p. 379
      1. Psychology, Experimental. 2. Psychological
research. I. Bruce, Richard Loren, 1938–
joint author. II. Beauchamp, Kenneth L.,
joint author. III. Title.
BF181.M33 1978   150′.7′24   77-25185
ISBN 0-03-089891-9

PREFACE

More than the two previous editions, the third edition of this text focuses on the procedural approach to experimental psychology rather than on presenting a representative survey of experimental research in learning, motivation, perception, and social psychology. We introduce the experimental psychologist's approach to answering questions about behavior, describe data-description techniques, describe in detail the various kinds of research designs that may be employed in the study of behavior, provide sample practical problems encountered in the conduct of experiments, show how research proposals and final reports are written, and present examples of statistical analysis techniques that may be employed.

In keeping with our past efforts to keep abreast of general trends in research methods, we have included a new chapter (11) on single-subject or $N = 1$ designs. We are grateful for the advice and constructive criticism of Professor Roger Katz, who reviewed the first draft of this chapter.

Another new development in the third edition is the change in the title of the book. The new title, *Experimental Psychology: Research Design and Analysis,* is a modest change from the former title *(Introduction to Experimental Psychology)* that reflects our focus on research methods and strong emphasis on research design. Consistent with this focus, material that was partially included in previous chapters has been expanded to a new chapter on the problems of experimental artifacts. This new chapter (14) reviews research and theory concerning the effects the experimenter and experimental situation might have on the behavior studied. These reactive effects of experimentation are always present in an experiment and we have provided increased guidance on how to cope with them.

Another new feature of this edition is the emphasis on understanding the nature of data, the observations that we accumulate in an experiment. Students often have little or no background in the basic procedures and systems of measuring behavior. A new chapter (4) introduces the elements of measurement and provides descriptions of how data are created.

As is often the case, the third edition retains and expands the pedagogical devices designed to facilitate learning. In addition to the boldface type used to emphasize major new terms as they are first defined and italic typeface used to emphasize critical procedural details, we include a glossary of terms to allow the reader easier access to key terms. The text continues the use of marginal notations that call attention to important concepts, label subsections, and emphasize major terms and critical points. We include chapter outlines at the beginning of each chapter along with a brief overview of the chapter. As in previous editions, each chapter closes with a point-by-point summary and a brief list of suggested readings.

We have made a major effort to delete sexist language in accordance with the policy of the American Psychological Association described in the *Guidelines for Nonsexist Language in APA Journals* (APA, 1977). Considerable effort was spent in simplifying the language; we expect that the text is more readable than ever before. In line with our emphasis upon the importance of the APA *Publication Manual* in writing research proposals and reports, we have taken care to conform to its rules in editorial style.

We deleted the section that contained student research projects. Users of the second edition reported that students, while finding the material very interesting, tended not to use it. The former unit on research equipment also was deleted because of reported lack of use. Also, we modified the length and content of some of the statistics chapters. We assume that students taking a first course in experimental psychology have taken or are taking a course in statistics. Therefore some of the material on the binomial and sign tests was deleted and the Wilcoxon-Mann-Whitney test and Spearman Correlation Coefficient were deleted. The extended description of the underlying model of the analysis of variance and the probability chapter were relocated in the new *Student Manual* authored by Dr. Edwin G. Brainerd, Jr., and Dr. Bernard Caffrey of Clemson University.

The *Student Manual* will be of great assistance to students. The *Student Manual* includes behavioral objectives, key terms, sample test questions, exercises, problems to solve, and class projects. These practice sets certainly will help the student acquire a stronger understanding of the material.

We sincerely appreciate the efforts of all who in various ways contributed to the production of this edition. The comments of students who used the first and second editions as a text have been very helpful. Similarly, the comments and criticisms of colleagues were useful and encouraging. We are particularly indebted to: Sachio Ashida, State University of New York, Brockport; Wayne Bartz, American River College; Edwin G. Brainerd, Jr., Clemson University; L. M. Gustafson, California State University, Los Angeles; Gary Meunier, Ball State University; Robert Prytula, Middle Tennessee State University; Mark Sanders, California State University, Northridge; Charles L. Sheridan, University of Missouri, Kansas City; and Ronald Suiter, Eisenhower College. Johnna Barto and Brian Heald of Holt, Rinehart and Winston, with great good humor and patience criticized our work and kept the production close to schedule. Also we appreciate the work of Sharlvne Nomellini and Bill Kearns on the *Instructor's Manual*. Equally important were the patience and encouragement of members of our families, Judy, Karen, and Jeff Beauchamp, Sally, Karyn, Marian, and Linda Bruce, and Sandy and Richy Matheson. They had to put up with us during the long and not always pleasant revision task.

Stockton, California   D.W.M.
Anchorage, Alaska   R.L.B.
Stockton, California   K.L.B.

CONTENTS

section one

The Scientific Process

1

Approaches to Knowledge

We are all involved in the search to discover and understand more about ourselves and our environment. Although we may not be conscious of it, we conduct simple experiments daily. We also take other approaches toward knowledge. By learning more about science, we improve our informal, habitual ways of acquiring knowledge. This chapter outlines the basic characteristics of scientific methodology and provides a background for understanding research.

A compelling "need to know" is a dominant characteristic of human beings as well as of other species. The surreptitious swipe of a finger along a surface marked with the sign "Wet Paint" shows the compulsive tendency to confirm for ourselves the truth of the statement. Science is an extension of this confirming process. We are all like scientists at such moments, although many of us have never learned scientific terminology or the formal steps of scientific research. To illustrate, we will describe the "Wet Paint" example in formal scientific terms.

The "Wet Paint" sign represents a statement by the painter about the condition of the paint. It leads us to guess (or *hypothesize*) that the paint is in fact wet or dry, and curiosity impels us to test that *hypothesis*. An *experiment* is conducted by swiping the fingertip across the paint. Thus we obtain *data:* the surface is smooth or sticky. The hypothesis is either confirmed or denied by this empirical (or verifiable) test. Usually, we assume that other "Wet Paint" signs nearby reflect the same conditions found on the first test. In other words, we use our first test as a *sample* from which we *generalize* to similar situations.

Our test of the sign meets the criteria of a crude scientific experiment. Unfortunately, we are often confronted with information too extensive or too complicated to test so easily. It is necessary to establish some procedural rules for investigating these more complex circumstances. The "rules" of science are a formalized set of procedures for collecting, organizing, and evaluating knowledge. They help us separate right information from wrong information. The scientific process is very useful in areas such as physics, chemistry, and biology, and the process has been applied profitably to the study of behavior.

The history of science shows that the scientific method itself has changed. Nineteenth-century science was different from the science of today. Moreover, there are other approaches to the selection and accumulation of knowledge. These alternative approaches overlap considerably, and they share certain characteristics with the scientific approach.

THE METHOD OF AUTHORITY

Common sense says that a "Wet Paint" sign should be placed only where paint *is* wet. Some people test the information on the sign while others accept it as conclusive. The second group, relying on the sign's authority, is using one of the oldest approaches to "knowing." In so-called primitive cultures taboos and laws often declare the seeking of certain knowledge to be off limits. Similarly, certain religions prescribe the boundaries of inquiry. Frequently, the authority for these rules rests in a shaman or priest who interprets the environment for the group.

A statement from an authoritative source can be one useful source of information. In many cases, folklore, superstitions, taboos, and religious strictures have prescribed actions that have great pragmatic value. They represent accumulated wisdom that aids in coping with the environment.

Parents often resort to authority in dispensing (or avoiding dispensing) knowledge to children. Certain dangers ought to be identified and avoided without confirmatory tests. For this reason, parents declare automobiles, appliances, and poisons dangerous. Frequently, however, parents make authoritative statements that children eventually challenge and find wanting.

Authorities are found in the scientific world too. Individual scientists rise to positions of authority on the basis of their professional performance. Their names become synonymous with expertise (B. F. Skinner in behavioral psychology, Paul Erlich in ecology, Paul Samuelson in economics, Linus Pauling in chemistry) and they wield considerable power in the development of a science.

Reliance on authorities is probably inevitable: No one of us can test all the information that surrounds us. An authority rigid and unresponsive to new developments will hinder the quest for knowledge. For example, sixteenth-century church authorities charged Copernicus with heresy when he proclaimed that the sun (not the earth) was the center of the universe. On the other hand, an authority accounting for information in a cogent, coherent fashion may provide a valuable guide to the development of knowledge.

THE ARTISTIC APPROACH

Art emphasizes the process of perceiving truth intuitively. A masterpiece in painting, sculpture, poetry, literature, music, or drama, captures and portrays a view of the world that can be recognized and shared by the observer and the creator. The sculptures of Michelangelo are well known examples of the artistic approach. In his *Moses* (Figure 1.1), for example, Michelangelo went beyond realism. He transformed the written, biblical description of Moses into a fascinating marble statement. The intense expression of the face, particularly of the eyes, and the wild flow of hair and beard dramatically convey Michelangelo's interpretation of Moses' strength of character. The artist's product represents a new source of knowledge, organized in a new way and unavailable to us in any other form.

A work of art, in addition to being a highly individualistic, subjective organization of knowledge, may be an expression of a particular philosophical point of view. Michelangelo's sculptures illustrate the Renaissance conception of humanity. During the Middle Ages, a human being was regarded as a "frail creature, in need of God's grace and salvation" (Palmer, 1958, p. 52). The Renaissance brought with it a sense of human individuality, creativity, and power. Much of the spirit of the Renaissance may be perceived in the artistic works of that time.

The artist, like the scientist, is an observer and interpreter of the world. Sometimes the artist's interpretation is direct and literal, as in Audubon's bird paintings. Other

FIG. 1.1
Michelangelo's *Moses*
(c. 1513–1515).
(Alinari-ARB, Ancram,
N.Y.)

artists convey their message in more abstract or less realistic ways, as in the paintings of Picasso or Dali. Scientific observations and descriptions are more constrained than the observations and descriptions of most artists. The appeal of a masterpiece is often—perhaps usually—multidimensional and different persons may have different interpretations of it. Such ambiguity is not compatible with the scientific approach. However, the artist's ability to observe closely and to organize observations into a coherent total package is a valuable scientific skill. Similarly, the use of intuition in interpreting observed events is one means of developing scientific theories.

THE RATIONALISTIC APPROACH

Whereas the artist concentrates on the process of observation, the rationalist emphasizes the consistency of nature and its underlying universal "laws." To the rationalist, the artistic stress on the extreme example misses the order and organization that underlie all knowledge. Instead, a rationalist looks for universal principles that encompass many different specific examples. When confronted with observations that do not fit these "laws," the rationalist is inclined to dismiss them as deviations—as "exceptions that prove the rule."

For a period of time it was believed that all that could be known was implicit in laws known already. The researcher's task was to "discover" new knowledge through the appropriate rearrangement of these basic truths. The following incident, real or fictional, is an extreme example of the rationalistic approach.

> In the year of our Lord 1432, there arose a grievous quarrel among the brethren over the number of teeth in the mouth of a horse. For thirteen days the disputation raged without ceasing. All the ancient books and chronicles were fetched out, and wonderful and ponderous erudition, such as was never before heard of in this region, was made manifest. At the beginning of the fourteenth day, a youthful friar of goodly bearing asked his learned superiors for permission to add a word, and straightway, to the wonderment of the disputants, whose deep wisdom he sore vexed, he beseeched them to unbend in a manner coarse and unheard-of, and to look in the open mouth of a horse and find answer to their questionings. At this, their dignity being grievously hurt, they waxed exceedingly wroth; and joining in a mighty uproar, they flew upon him and smote his hip and thigh, and cast him out forthwith. For, said they, surely Satan hath tempted this bold neophyte to declare unholy and unheard-of ways of finding truth contrary to all the teachings of the fathers. After many days of grievous strife the dove of peace sat on the assembly, and they as one man, declaring the problem to be an everlasting mystery because of the grievous dearth of historical and theological evidence thereof, so ordered the same writ down. (Francis Bacon, quoted in Mees, 1934, p. 17)

This anecdote illustrates the potential danger of relying on rationalist authority to the point of shunning empirical observation. When a universal law becomes so authoritative that it is unchallengeable, it should be most suspect.

Although we are not always aware of the process, we are continually forming general impressions (principles) on the basis of our experiences (observations). In science, the rationalistic approach leads to the use of theories, models, rules, hypotheses, hunches, and guesses to guide the making of empirical observations.

THE SCIENTIFIC APPROACH

Each of the above approaches is committed to the search for truth. Our world has been greatly enriched by these quests. In a sense, the scientific approach makes a more limited approach to truth: It is concerned with discovering what the world *is* rather than what it *ought to be*.

The scientist borrows some of the perceptiveness of the artist to observe the world, some of the logical commitment of the rationalist to combine these observations into a coherent explanatory system, and some trust in authority to provide guidance in the overall process. In each case, however, the borrowed element is limited by the practical question, "Am I adequately describing and explaining some aspect of the world?" In other words, the ultimate criterion of the scientific approach is the extent to which theory matches the real world.

All scientists work to simplify, organize, and generalize knowledge by constructing theories. Initial observations are organized into descriptive categories. Tentative generalizations (simple hypotheses) are formed and tested. All valid generalizations in a particular area are related in an explanatory model. A theory consists of the organizing model, established generalizations (supported hypotheses), and further hypotheses that predict observations yet to be made. Predictions from the theory determine when and where subsequent observations are made. Predictions also provide a further testing of the theory. If the subsequent observations confirm the predictions, then the theory is supported, at least until another test. This continuous process of observing, testing, organizing, inferring, predicting, testing, reorganizing, and so on constitutes the scientific approach.

The sciences differ in their basic subject matter. The techniques and procedures used by individual scientists depend on the nature of their current research problem; for example, physiologists studying nerve conduction and geologists studying petrochemical processes are engaged in very different activities. However, all scientists make the same basic assumptions, seek to answer similarly restricted kinds of questions, and share the same general goals.

Assumptions of the Scientific Approach

In order for the scientific approach to work, three basic assumptions must be made about the nature of the world: order, determinism, and discoverability.

Order

Scientists assume that **order** pervades the universe. Events do not occur in a chaotic, random manner; there is a basic pattern to their occurrence. The ability to formulate general theories that summarize and predict events is impossible without the assumption of order.

Determinism

Determinism is an extension of the assumption of order. It is the belief that there are preceding events that determine the nature of each event. Psychologists assume that at least theoretically, it is possible to trace the chain of "reasons" for any particular behavior.

Discoverability

The third assumption, that of **discoverability,** is implied by the proviso of the last sentence, "at least theoretically." The scientist is convinced that each step in the causal chain can eventually be traced and measured. The assumption of discoverability dismisses the use of "magic" or "unknowables" in an explanatory system. As technology advances, our power to observe improves. Sometimes, however, we may hypothesize that certain processes are in action before we have the capacity to confirm their existence. To do so is not a violation of discoverability because the presumed processes must be confirmed in the long run.

Restrictions on Scientific Observation

The observations used to confirm or deny a hypothesis are the key to the scientific process. No matter how compelling the argument for how it "ought to be," the whole system depends on observational evidence. Because the confirming of observations is so vital to the development of science, there are constraints on what constitutes a legitimate scientific observation. One of the reasons for these restrictions is that science is a cooperative process: we rely on the observations of others as an extension of our own senses. Two people may use different observational procedures that lead to problems of interpretation. For example, a high gloss paint may appear wet to the eye but dry to the fingertip. In order to interpret observations made by someone else, we need a clear specification of the observation procedure. With any scientific observation, the more careful and thorough the observational process, the more useful the observation. In addition, there are some universal restrictions on what constitutes a scientific observation.

Empirical

First, the observations must be **empirical.** "Empirical" means that the phenomena are "real," "objective," and not a figment of the observer's imagination. The restriction to empirical observation creates some interesting interpretation problems in science. Many things that have not been observed directly (such as atoms, gravity, learning, and emotion) are nonetheless empirically established entities. In the case of these constructs, it is sufficient to measure their *effects*. For example, the results of many experiments indicate that physical matter behaves *as if* it were made up of atoms. As research continues, some of the distinguishing characteristics of different atoms are surmised.

Public

The second restriction on scientific observations is that they must be **public.** That is, another observer must be able to agree that the event has occurred (eliminating the need to rely on the authority of the first observer). Under ideal conditions, the event should be so obvious that it can be observed without special training. However, part of the training of many scientists requires learning how to make accurate observations. When the special skills for observing are possessed only by a certain category of observers (such as those who can see "ghosts") the data become suspect. Many of the elaborate controls imposed on behavioral experiments are intended to increase the reliability of the observer's reports.

Repeatable

A third requirement is that observations must be **repeatable.** For most scientific observations, this requirement simply involves setting up the conditions so that the events will occur again. Occasionally, however, the conditions are so rare that they may never recur in a lifetime. If such an event can be anticipated (as solar eclipses can be) simultaneous and complementary observations can provide a means of confirmation. At other times, similar events provide corroborative (confirming) data for the observations in question. If an event is truly unique it will not be rejected flatly from the body of scientific fact, but addressed with skepticism.

Goals of the Scientific Approach

Understanding

Scientists are interested in **understanding** the world and the phenomena that occur in it. To understand an event, we must first describe what happened. Then we must trace the sequence of events that led to this event, in order to know why it happened. As our explanation becomes complete, we recognize the contributing conditions at progressively earlier stages, until it is possible to predict the event.

Prediction

Successful **prediction** is an important goal of any scientific endeavor. It provides considerable leverage in dealing with the world. For example, the increasing capacity of seismologists to anticipate the occurrence of earthquakes will have significant social consequences. Much of the terror and destructiveness of an earthquake is the result of its unexpectedness. If an earthquake is predicted in time, citizens can be evacuated or at least warned to take protective measures that will minimize destruction. In addition, prediction facilitates further scientific study. It enables scientists foreseeing an earthquake to set up special instruments to make more precise observations. Such observations will provide better information for subsequent predictions. Thus, knowledge provides an increasing capacity to obtain better knowledge.

One of the eventual consequences of this accumulation of knowledge is that events can be controlled. That is, if the causal chain is traced sufficiently well, it becomes possible to manipulate the environment so that the event occurs at a time and place determined by a scientist. On a small scale, this kind of control occurs in many scientific experiments; for example, certain forms of electrical brain stimulation are given to reinforce bar-pressing behavior. On a larger scale, this control may provide benefit or harm to human beings, as when airplanes "seed" clouds to cause rain. The basic scientific process consists of describing, explaining, and predicting; the application and exploitation of knowledge is more in the realm of applied research or engineering. For example, engineers are using the facts and principles of theoretical nuclear physics to create alternative energy-generating systems.

Eventually, scientists group their accumulated observations into categories in terms of common features, eliminating unimportant or irrelevant aspects. This process of **induction** yields a descriptive summary of the observations made so far.

The process of induction is followed by a sequence of **deduction.** (1) The systematically organized inductive descriptions are examined for gaps, similar events not yet observed. (2) If gaps exist, generalizations are made about them. These generalizations represent tentative predictions (or deduced hypotheses) about how the world is organized. They serve to test the validity of the organizing system. (3) On the basis of subsequent observations, the deductions (hypotheses) are sometimes flatly rejected, frequently substantially altered, or occasionally confirmed as stated.

The accumulated valid hypotheses are organized into general principles. These general principles may be related to a model[1] that provides an organizing framework for the principles. The model, related principles, accumulated valid hypotheses, and untested deductions form a theory. In each field, the established theories as well as isolated principles and unorganized but confirmed generalizations represent the present status of scientific knowledge. Together they constitute the **organized body of knowledge** that is the major goal of the scientific approach. The entire inductive/deductive cycle is known as the **hypothetico-deductive** process.

Induction
Deduction

Organzed Body of Knowledge
Hypothetico-deductive Process

An Example of the Scientific Approach

Let us trace the scientific process at work on an actual research problem. Recently, the human eye has received considerable attention as a source of information about thought. Hess (1965) has suggested that pupil diameter may be used as an accurate indicator of the degree of interest a scene has for the viewer.

Hess's discovery of the phenomenon is a good example of an almost accidental stimulus to the scientific process. One evening, as he was examining a book of

---

[1]We will discuss the meaning of the term "model" later in this chapter.

unusually attractive animal photographs, Hess's wife commented that the lighting must be poor, because Hess's pupils were dilated. Hess believed that the light level was more than adequate at the time. Therefore, Hess thought, his pupil size seemed not to be a function of light level only.

Changes in pupil size had been observed and tested scientifically before. Experiments had shown that pupil size seemed to be determined by level of illumination. Hess's wife's observation, however, seemed to reflect a situation in which the light-level hypothesis was inadequate. Hess mulled over the alternatives and recalled that some research had shown pupillary size was also affected by extreme emotion. The situation in question, however, hardly involved terror or euphoria, merely a high degree of interest. Therefore he formed an alternative hypothesis: Perhaps pupil size changed in accordance with the degree of the viewer's interest.

To test this new, intuitive hypothesis, Hess devised a rough, one-shot, pilot experiment. The next morning he selected a number of relatively innocuous photographs and added one seminude female pinup picture. He asked a male laboratory assistant (Jim) to look at each picture as they were shown one at a time. Hess found that Jim's pupils suddenly dilated when the pinup came into view. This simple experiment supported the hypothesis that pupil size reflects interest and was sufficient to justify a much more thorough research program.

THE ROLE OF THEORIES

Model

Theory

A **model** consists of a set of assumptions, an organizational framework, and a set of rules for manipulating the details of the model. The construction of a theory involves relating the details of a model to empirical events in the real world. A **theory** consists of a model and the established general principles organized in terms of the model.

New hypotheses are generated through the manipulation of the elements of the theory according to its rules. Each new hypothesis is a prediction of what ought to be observed in a new situation. Much of the research process involves the testing of these new hypotheses; Hess's experiment followed such a sequence.

If a theory successfully passes the criterion of predicting a phenomenon, we strongly tend to assume that the theory reflects the sequence of events in the real world. That is, the lawfulness in the theoretical model that leads to a successful prediction is the same orderliness in operation in the environment. Such is not necessarily the case. Figure 1.2 illustrates the relationship between the model world and the real world. The two worlds are separate entities, with an occasional bridge between the two to coordinate the abstract statements in the model with the specific environmental conditions of the experiment. Essentially, an experiment is an attempt to match the antecedent conditions specified by a model with antecedent conditions in the real world. The results of the experiment should be analogous to (correspond with) the consequent conditions deduced according to the rules of the model.

The pupil-dilation experiment required that Hess make some assumptions and identifications between his theoretical statement and the real conditions of the experi-

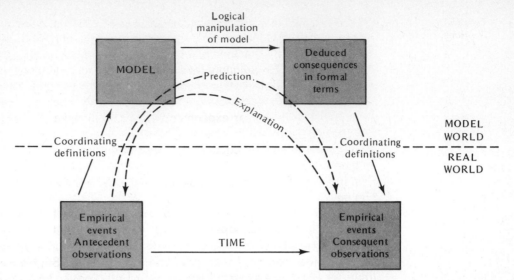

FIG. 1.2
Schematic presentation of the structure of a theory. (Modified from "Some views on mathematical models and measurement theory" by C. H. Coombs, H. Raiffa, and R. M. Thrall, *Psychological Review*, 1954, 61, 132–144, and from *Psychology: The Science of Behavior* by R. L. Issacson, M. L. Hutt, and M. L. Blum, New York, Harper & Row, 1955.)

ment. The hypothesis suggested that pupillary size reflects degree of interest.[2] The experiment involved observing the response to a pinup picture. In order to connect hypothesis and experiment, Hess had to assume that the laboratory assistant would be more interested in the pinup picture than in the remainder of the photographs. The experiment was a test of a much-restricted hypothesis: "Jim's eyes will dilate when he sees the pinup picture and not when he sees the other photographs."

Experimental Hypothesis

An **experimental hypothesis,** the first formal step of an experiment, consists of a specific, suggested explanation for the occurrence of an event. An experimental hypothesis must (1) potentially answer a specific question, (2) be stated as clearly and simply as possible, and (3) be capable of being directly supported or refuted by the results of an experimental test. Hess hypothesized that the pupils of Jim's eyes would dilate when Jim saw the pinup. Such an experimental hypothesis does potentially provide an answer to a specific question, is clearly and simply stated, and is capable of direct support or refutation by experimentation.

Operational Definitions

The requirements that an experimental hypothesis be clearly stated and directly testable are not easily met. Even the apparently simple concept of "hunger" may not be defined identically by behavioral scientists. Bridgman (1927) introduced the idea of

[2]It must be noted that Zuckerman (1972) strongly suggests that the great sensitivity of the eye to changes in illumination was not adequately controlled in Hess' pilot study. It has been demonstrated that the pupil may contract 1% to 5% when gaze shifts from relatively dark to relatively bright areas (Woodmansee, 1966). Zuckerman maintains that since visual reactions to emotionally arousing stimuli rarely exceed a change of 5% pupil diameter, the change in pupil diameter may be due to the subject's shift of fixation. Other variables that may affect pupil size are novel stimuli such as stimulus change, near vision reflex, high variability of spontaneous pupillary activity, and experimenter effects. Zuckerman also points out that most of Hess's pupil work was done with small numbers of subjects.

Operational Definition

using **operational definitions** to delineate the meaning of an experimental hypothesis clearly. Operational definitions specify the terms of an experimental hypothesis according to the actions (operations) taken in making the observations. Thus, you may operationally define a hungry rat as one that has been deprived of food for 23 hours. There are a number of other possible definitions for the term "hunger," but with this operational definition established, everyone knows what the term means within the context of the particular experiment. Operational definitions provide a precise and replicable definition of a given term. In the purest, simplest sense, the concept of operational definition requires that every element in a researcher's procedure be defined in terms of how it was measured, and the elements have no more meaning than that specified in the definition. In actual practice, we don't let this pure interpretation get in our way.

Consider some other examples. Suppose you are interested in anxious behavior. Anxiety may be defined operationally in terms of cigarette smoking: A highly anxious person is one who smokes six or more cigarettes per hour, while an unanxious person is one who smokes less than one cigarette per hour. Studying creativity, you may operationally define a creative answer as any that is given by no more than 5% of your subjects. In the Hess study, the operational definition of an interesting photograph was the pinup picture chosen by Hess.

Coordinating Definition

Coordinating definitions are operational definitions used to bridge the gap between the model world and the real world. They specify the actions of the scientist in measuring (observing) the key terms in a conceptual hypothesis. When coordinating definitions are provided for a conceptual (theoretical) hypothesis, the researcher has created an experimental hypothesis. There are many possible coordinating definitions for the terms in a conceptual hypothesis. An experimental research hypothesis is often called a **working experimental hypothesis,** because it is subject to revision with each change the experimenter makes in the coordinating definitions as the research progresses.

Working Experimental Hypothesis

Partial Outline of a Theory

To clarify the elements of a theory (Figure 1.2) let us consider again the pupil-dilation experiment. Not all aspects of the model and theory are included. The material is presented in outline form to facilitate understanding; obviously, most psychological theories are not presented in this way. Most psychological theories are not as extensively, formally developed as this admittedly incomplete example. The example is fictionalized; we do not mean to imply that Hess necessarily followed precisely this process in testing the pupil-dilation hypothesis.

I. Some elements of the model
  A. Primary proposition
     Animal physiological (bodily) processes are influenced by external stimulus events.
  B. Secondary propositions
     1. The heredity, history, and current state of an organism affect the relationship between environmental stimulus intensity and the physiological response.
     2. Members of the same species tend to exhibit similar physiological reactions to a class of stimulus events.

3. At any one time, for each individual a multiplicity of conditions influence the specific response to a stimulus.

C. Conceptual hypothesis

Pupil dilation is a function of the interest value of a stimulus.

1. Some limiting conditions and assumptions
   a. This conceptual hypothesis is limited to human beings.
   b. The diameter of any human pupil has physical limits.
   c. Environmental illumination is constant, because pupil dilation is known to be a function of brightness.
   d. The human subjects are in a normal body state, not under the influence of substances or conditions that affect the pupil-dilation response.
   e. The subjects' eyes are open and adapted to the level of room illumination.
   f. The pupil-dilation response is involuntary; the subjects do not attempt to exercise active control of the response.

2. Derived conceptual hypotheses
   a. Increasing the interest value of a stimulus will lead to increase in pupil diameter (within limits).
   b. Decreasing stimulus interest value will lead to decrease in pupil diameter (within limits).

3. Range of stimulus values
   The conceptual hypothesis is assumed to be correct for many different definitions of stimulus interest value; interest value is defined in terms of human choice behavior.

II. Sample antecedent conditions (coordinating definitions, operationally defined)

A. Jim is a physiologically and psychologically normal human being.

B. Jim is in a normal body state: not under the influence of drugs affecting pupil dilation, not suffering from a recent brain concussion, not suffering from an eye defect, and so on.

C. Room illumination is normal (light switch on) and Jim has adapted to the room illumination for at least 15 min.

D. The female pinup picture has high interest value to most adult male human beings, including Jim.

E. The other pictures have medium to low interest value to adult males, including Jim.

F. Measurement of pupil diameter shall occur through visual inspection of the subject's eyes, later confirmed by inspection of photographic recordings.

III. Deduced consequences in formal terms

It is given that all propositions, assumptions, limitations, and hypotheses apply and are correct. If a stimulus of high interest value is presented in a series of stimuli of medium to low interest value to a representative human being, then the diameters of the person's pupils will increase upon viewing the high-interest stimulus.

IV. Consequent observations (coordinating definitions, operationally defined)

A. All items under point II apply again (IIA – IIF).

B. When the partially nude female pinup picture is encountered in the sequence of other, innocuous pictures shown to Jim, a detectable increase in pupil diameters occurs (*experimental hypothesis* confirmed).

The experiment could have failed to confirm Hess's experimental hypothesis in a number of ways. First, of course, the pupillary response might not be related to interest. One or more of the supposedly uninteresting pictures might have been very important to the subject. Alternatively, Jim might not have been particularly interested in pinup pictures. Either of the latter reasons would account for a "false" reading from

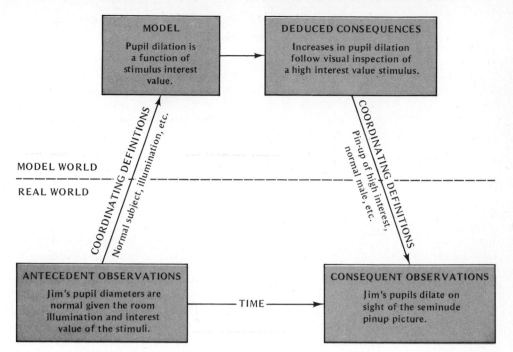

FIG. 1.3
The correspondence between a theory and the real world, using the Hess (1965) pupil-dilation theory.

that particular experiment even though the *conceptual hypothesis* was correct. In Hess's case, everything worked.

Hypothesizing played an important role in the events leading up to the Hess experiment. The existing explanation for the adjustment of pupil size was related to light level. Thus, Mrs. Hess's first response to the observation that Hess's pupils were dilated was to explain it in terms of a low light level. **Explanation,** then, is the process of working backward from the consequent event through the theoretical framework to the antecedent situation. In other words, explanation goes backwards in time while prediction is the same process moving forward in time.

Explanation

Although explanation and prediction are essentially the same process, the direction in time is a powerful difference. The saying, "Hindsight usually has 20–20 vision," illustrates the difference. Theories are therefore useful as explanatory devices, but a critical test of a theory is whether it successfully predicts events before they occur. Research is conducted to test such theoretical predictions.

Hess used Jim as a representative of the human species. Theories are typically stated in general terms and are intended to account for an entire category of individuals, while experiments are typically conducted on a relatively small number of these individuals. It is assumed that the individuals actually observed in an experiment form a representative collection.

Sample
Population

This collection of individuals actually observed is known as a **sample** of a much larger population. The **population** is technically the collection of all of the items (subjects) of interest, while the sample is the collection of all of the items actually observed. Observations made on the sample allow us to draw conclusions (**generalizations**) regarding the characteristics of the population. Jim's pupillary response was

Generalizations

highly representative (generalizable), but it could have been unique, which would have limited the generality of the results. Therefore an important part of the scientific approach to knowledge is considerable repetition of observations in order to confirm the generality of the results from a sample.

To summarize, the scientific approach is an extension of our everyday interactions with the world. We observe, infer, predict, test the inference and prediction, and continually acquire changing information about the world around us. Scientists share information with one another. In order to make their communication effective, a number of assumptions and rules establish the kinds of data that are admissible as scientific. However, scientists do not live by a very restrictive, static set of rules. In actuality, our daily attempts to understand behavior are quite sloppy. The scientific approach is dynamic; we constantly discover new directions. New hypotheses, new guesses, new techniques, new data all lead to revised conceptions that mark the advancement of the scientific process.

SUMMARY

1. We all conduct crude scientific experiments to find out more about our environment, although we may have been unaware of the scientific nature of the process.
2. The method of authority is a simple, often useful, but potentially stifling way to evaluate and accumulate ideas.
3. The artistic approach to knowledge is an intuitive, perceptual, and extremely subjective way of interpreting the world.
4. The purely rationalist approach to knowledge represents an antiempirical means of generating universal principles to explain all phenomena.
5. The scientific approach is concerned with discovering what the world is rather than what it ought to be. The approach uses both inductive and deductive logic (the hypothetico-deductive process) in making observations, forming hypotheses, predicting outcomes, testing predictions, relating valid generalizations to theoretical models, forming deductions, testing deductions, and so forth.
6. The general assumptions of the scientific approach include the universality of order, determinism or causation, and the discoverability of answers to research questions.
7. Scientific observations must be empirical, public, and repeatable.
8. The goals of the scientific approach include understanding, prediction, and the building of an organized body of knowledge.
9. Models consist of assumptions, organizational frameworks, and sets of rules for manipulating the abstract details of the models. A theory consists of a model and the established general principles organized in terms of the model. Theories specify the probable relationships between antecedent and consequent events.
10. An experimental hypothesis consists of a specific explanation for the occurrence of an event. Experimental hypotheses must be capable of being directly supported or refuted by the results of an experiment.
11. Operational definitions clearly delimit the terms of an experimental hypothesis according to the observational operations of the scientist. Coordinating definitions are operational definitions that relate the abstract terms of the model to the real, empirical world. A conceptual hypothesis is a theoretical hypothesis without coordinating definitions.
12. Scientific observations allow us to make generalizations from a sample population to the larger population of all the subjects of interest.

SUGGESTED READINGS

Bachrach, A. J., *Psychological research: An introduction* (3rd ed.). New York: Random House, 1972.

Bergmann, G., & Spence, K. W. Operationism and theory in psychology. *Psychological Review,* 1941, *48,* 1–14.

Bridgman, P. W. Remarks on the present state of operationalism. *Scientific Monthly,* 1954, *79,* 224–226.

Conant, J. B. *On understanding science: An historical approach.* New Haven: Yale University Press, 1947.

Coombs, C. H., Raiffa, H., & Thrall, R. M. Some views on mathematical models and measurement theory. *Psychological Review,* 1954, *61,* 132–144.

Deese, J. *Psychology as science and art.* New York: Harcourt, Brace, Jovanovich, 1972.

Kerlinger, F. N. *Foundations of behavioral research* (2nd ed.). New York: Holt, Rinehart and Winston, 1973.

Kuhn, T. S. *The structure of scientific revolutions* (2nd ed.). Chicago: University of Chicago Press, 1970.

Miller, N. W. Comments on theoretical models: Illustrated by the development of a theory of conflict behavior. *Journal of Personality,* 1951, *20,* 82—100.

Sanford, F. H., & Capaldi, E. J. (Eds.) *Advancing psychological science. Vol. 1. Philosophies, methods, and approaches.* Belmont, Calif.: Wadsworth, 1964.

Siever, R. Science: Observational, experimental, historical. *American Scientist,* 1968, *56,* 70–77.

Townsend, J. C. *Introduction to experimental method.* New York: McGraw-Hill, 1953.

Turner, M. B. *Philosophy and the science of behavior.* New York: Appleton, 1967.

2

Basic Elements of Research

This chapter presents and defines key, elementary scientific terms. We must know these terms in order to understand what research is all about. Most research is involved with apparently insignificant questions; however, they are really pieces of much larger and more important questions. In our attack on researchable questions, we attempt to eliminate potential explanations until only one remains. The process of eliminating alternative explanations is disorderly, haphazard, chancy—and fascinating.

Students frequently fall asleep in lecture classes. As a researcher, you might ask why that happens. The research process often begins with such a question. In seeking to answer the question, your first task is to define the behavior of interest. In this case the behavior is sleeping under certain environmental conditions, lecture classes. You define sleeping as a state in which a person with closed eyes is not responsive to normal classroom stimulation. The subjects are students, and in order to have ready access to a pool of subjects, you limit the study to students at your college. For expediency you further limit the population to those in a particular class in which lectures are regularly given.

You speculate about the possible causes of the sleeping behavior. Your fellow students may sleep because of internal body conditions such as fatigue, drug-induced somnolence, or digestion of a large meal. On a given day each body condition varies among the students—some may be very fatigued and others not at all. Each body condition is a potential variable to study in the research on sleeping in class. Environmental conditions also may contribute to the sleeping behavior. For example, the room temperature may be too high, the students' chairs may be softly padded, or the lecturer may speak in a dull monotone. Each of these conditions may facilitate or cause sleeping. Your task is complicated by the large number of potential causes of sleeping behavior.

The way to attack such a research question is to devise ways of eliminating most potential causes so that only one or two are left, or at least to eliminate the minor causes, leaving only the most important ones. Ideally, sleeping in class would have a single cause, but unfortunately in research behavior seldom, if ever, has a single cause. One way to determine the importance of a potential causative variable is to change the value of the variable and see whether the behavior changes. For example, you can change the room temperature during a lecture to see whether more or fewer students fall asleep at different temperatures. If there is no noticeable change in number of students sleeping, then temperature probably may be eliminated from the list of potential causes. (Of course, you must make sure that behavior is not influenced by succession of temperatures, by the temperature outdoors that day, by how early or late in the lecture the change occurred, and so on.) To determine the importance of other variables you could vary the time relationship between the potential cause and the behavior. For instance, you may arrange to have the scheduled 1:00 p.m. lecture take place at a later hour or before the lunch period so that the effect of full or empty stomachs may be examined. (A hidden problem here is that not everyone eats at noon.) If there is no change in sleeping frequency, then the effects of a recent meal probably may be eliminated. (Note that variable eating habits make that conclusion uncertain.) In a similar fashion you may examine the effects of all the potential causes that you can think of, until finally you come to a statement about which variables seem to have the greatest effect on frequency of sleeping behavior in class. (In the examination of potential variables you probably will follow at least one misleading trail, spending tremendous amounts of time on a potential explanation that eventually turns out to be erroneous!)

When your sleep project is finally completed, your friends might ask, "Who cares?" After all, frequency of sleeping in a particular introductory psychology class is hardly a fascinating topic, except, perhaps, to the ego-threatened instructor of the class. The answer is of greater concern than might be obvious. You will attempt to generalize the results of your research to all college lecture classes. Such a generaliza-

Replication tion itself constitutes a research question that requires testing by repetition (**replication**) with different lecture classes. There is an even more general question behind this little study: What are the most effective means of teaching? An answer to the apparently insignificant research question about sleeping in a particular class can provide a bit of information toward answering the much bigger and obviously important question of the most effective means of transmitting information and motivating students to learn.

Research is the process of attempting to answer researchable questions. Unfortunately, not all questions of interest to people are experimentally researchable questions. Most questions that seem worthy of our effort are too complex, too vague, and too all encompassing for any one researcher to handle. The question, "Why do human beings engage in organized warfare?" is an example of an important question that is too complex for even a group of researchers to handle. Realistic researchers therefore pick out a small segment of the question and work on it. For example, current research on the effects of watching aggression in films and TV programs may yield some information that will help us to understand and predict the complex group of behaviors we label "war." Frequently, research questions are suggested by theories about the behavior of interest. At other times the research question is generated by a hunch, an intuitive guess about the reason for a behavior. In either case, the experimenter examines the effect of certain antecedent variables on the behavior of interest.

The term "variable" plays an elementary but crucial role in the language of scientists. As the scientific approach has matured, a number of terms have become comparatively standardized. One obvious benefit is that scientists can communicate with each other more quickly and effectively. An unavoidable side effect is that science students must memorize the standard terminology to participate in this communication process. To complicate matters further, each science has developed its own particular terminology, and even subareas of a science have developed their own special terms. The bulk of this chapter will be devoted to the presentation of key terms, both general scientific terms and terms specific to experimental psychology.

VARIABLES

Variable

A **variable** is any condition in a scientific investigation that may change in quantity and/or quality: for example, room temperature, time of day, amount of food consumed, size of a crowd, flavor of a wine, and so on. In contrast to a variable, a **constant** is any condition that does not change. If you decide in the sleeping-in-class study that the same professor will deliver all the lectures, this factor (the lecturer) is a constant.

Constant

Two types of variables are studied in experimental science: independent and dependent variables. **Independent variables** are controlled or manipulated by an experimenter. The experimenter chooses different levels of an independent variable to use in an experiment. An independent variable must be assigned at least two levels (also called treatments). For example, a subject may smoke a marihuana cigarette or a placebo (in this case, a placebo is a cigarette that supposedly contains marihuana but does not); a subject may look at pictures of buildings or a pinup; the thermostat in a lecture room may be set at 65°F or at 75°F.

Independent Variables

In psychological research, independent variables fall into two general categories. An **environmental variable** is any characteristic of an organism's total environment that may influence its behavior. For example, room temperature is an environmental variable. An **organismic variable** is any physiological or psychological characteristic of an organism. Sex, blood type, intelligence, degree of fatigue, and shoe size are all examples of organismic variables.

Dependent Variables

The second type of variables studied in experimental science are **dependent variables.** In psychology, dependent variables are measures of behavior. Dependent variables are so named because their measures are expected to depend on the value of the independent variable. In the preceding example, the number of people sleeping during lectures was counted to measure the dependent variable; in the study discussed in chapter 1, pupil dilation, obtained by measuring pupil diameter, was the dependent variable. In any experiment the experimenter manipulates independent variables and measures their effects on dependent variables.

The example of a social psychological study of human aggressive behavior (Baron, 1976) may clarify the meanings of the terms, independent and dependent variables, as used in experimental research. The general question motivating the researchers was how to control or prevent human interpersonal aggressive behavior. A major proposition of their theoretical model is that organisms are incapable of engaging in two incompatible responses simultaneously. The main conceptual hypothesis is that inducing responses or emotional states incompatible with either aggression or overt violence against persons will prevent or at least reduce the likelihood of aggressive behavior.

One of the *independent variables* manipulated in the study was the stimulus condition serving to induce feelings or emotional states incompatible with anger or overt aggression. The five levels or treatment conditions of this independent variable were: (1) distraction control, with no incompatible emotional arousal, (2) empathy arousal, (3) amusement arousal, (4) mild sexual arousal, and (5) no-distraction control and no incompatible emotional arousal. The research was conducted in a naturalistic field setting (see chapter 6) in which the subjects were unaware of the experiment.

FIG. 2.1
The treatment conditions of Baron's experiment on human aggressive behavior. (Photographs courtesy of Dr. Robert A. Baron.)

Aggression and annoyance were induced in passing male motorists by a male experimenter who failed to move his car at a street intersection for 15 sec. after the traffic light changed to green. Just prior to the annoying delay, the subjects in the three incompatible emotion groups (Groups 2, 3, and 4) and in the distraction control group (Group 1) were exposed to their respective experimental treatments. The subjects in the no-distraction control (Group 5) experienced the annoyance but no other manipulation by the experimenters. There were 12 male drivers per treatment group; each driver was alone in his car. Figure 2.1 shows the treatment conditions.

The five treatment conditions (instituted during the period when the light was still red) were operationally defined as follows. In the distraction-control condition (Group 1), a female experimenter carrying a notebook and dressed in jeans and a blouse crossed the intersection by passing between the male experimenter's car and the subject's car. She walked quickly down the street, passing from view before the street light turned green. In the empathy-arousal condition (Group 2), the same experimenter, dressed in the same clothes, followed the same route but hobbled along on crutches with a bandage on her leg. In the amusement-arousal condition (Group 3), she crossed the street wearing the same clothes as in the distraction condition, but she also wore an incongruous, humorous clown mask. In the mild sexual-arousal condition (Group 4), she followed the same route, but was dressed in extremely brief, revealing clothes of unusual design. In the no-distraction control condition (Group 5), the female experimenter did not appear.

One of the *dependent variable* measures of aggressive behavior was the frequency of horn-honking behavior in each group. In other words, aggressive behavior was operationally defined as honking in the situation. Observers in a nearby parked car deduced from several cues whether the subjects' cars were air-conditioned, and tape-recorded the subjects' horn-honking behavior during the 15-sec delay. For each group, the proportion of subjects in non-air-conditioned cars who honked is presented in Table 2.1. (Under all treatment conditions, the outside temperature was in the mid-80°F range.) As indicated in Table 2.1, a greater proportion of subjects honked under the two control conditions than under the three incompatible emotional-arousal conditions. The experimenters concluded that, under uncomfortably warm conditions, the experimental manipulations designed to induce empathy, amusement, or mild sexual arousal tended to reduce the incidence of aggression against an annoying person.

TABLE 2.1 Proportion of Subjects Honking under Various Arousal Conditions (Dependent Variable)

Experimental Treatment (Independent Variable)				
1 Distraction control	2 Empathy arousal	3 Amusement arousal	4 Sexual arousal	5 No-distraction control
.9[a]	.6	.5	.5	.9

Note. Adapted from "The reduction of human aggression: A field of study of the influence of incompatible reactions" by R. A. Baron, Journal of Applied Social Psychology, 1976, 6, 260–274. Copyright 1976 by Scripta Publishing Co., Inc. Reprinted by permission.
[a]Data to nearest tenth.

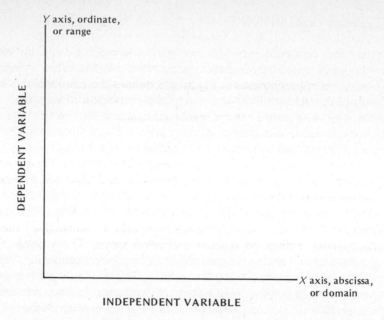

FIG. 2.2
Components of a graph. (On rare occasions the labeling of the X and Y axes is reversed.)

Another easily understood way of presenting experimental data is by means of a graph. The components of a graph are shown in Figure 2.2. The data of the aggression experiment are plotted on the graph shown in Figure 2.3. (*Data* is the plural form of the Latin noun, *datum.*) The levels of the independent variable (Groups 1–5) constitute a set of symbols or numbers (X) that is placed on the X axis. The values of the dependent variable (proportions) represent another set of numbers (Y) that is plotted on the Y axis.

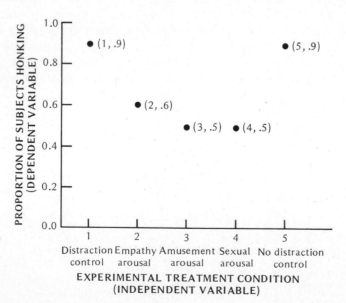

FIG. 2.3
Date from the aggression study plotted on a graph. The levels of the independent variable were three incompatible emotional arousal conditions and two control conditions. The dependent variable was the proportion of subjects who honked per group. (Adapted from "The reduction of human aggression: A field study of incompatible reaction" by R. A. Baron, *Journal of Applied Social Psychology*, 1976, 6, 260–274. Copyright 1976 by Scripta Publishing Co., Inc. Reprinted by permission.)

RELATIONSHIPS AND FUNCTIONS

Relationship

Somewhat differently from the common meaning, in science **relationship** is defined as the set of paired values of the independent and dependent variables. The set of five data points in parentheses in Figure 2.3 defines the relationship between the various levels of the independent variable and the proportion of subjects honking under each level. The relationship can be briefly summarized thus: Aggressive behavior (proportion of honkers) was greater under the control conditions than under conditions of induced emotional responses incompatible with aggression.

Another example of a relationship is presented in Figure 2.4. Many colleges routinely ask students to evaluate teachers, and they often assume that teaching effectiveness is measured by scores on the student evaluation forms. Rodin and Rodin (1972) examined the relationship between an "objective" measure of teaching effectiveness (what the students learned) and a "subjective" measure of teaching effectiveness, ratings on teacher-evaluation forms. There were 293 students in an undergraduate calculus course with 11 teaching assistants, "instructors" for the course, each with one recitation section. The students were required to learn 40 specific procedures and were tested with a specific problem for each procedure. The final grade in the course was solely determined by the number of problems solved. The students graded the instructors at the end of the quarter, using the usual letter grade system in the usual way with A = 4, B+ = 3.5, B = 3, and so on. The average course grade of the students in each section was paired with the average student rating of the section instructor. The relationship between the two sets of measures is graphed in Figure 2.4. The three instructors with the lowest subjective scores had the highest objective scores, and the instructor with the highest subjective score had the lowest objective score. Student evaluations of instructors probably do measure the social

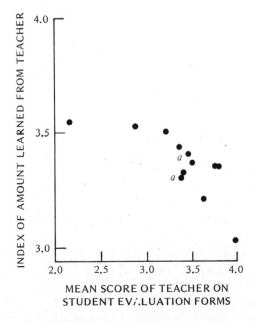

FIG. 2.4
Relationship between objective and subjective evaluations of teaching. The points labeled *a* are two sections taught by the same instructor. (Data from "Student evaluations of teachers" by M. Rodin and B. Rodin, *Science*, 1972, *177*, 1164–1166. Copyright 1972 by the American Association for the Advancement of Science. Reprinted by permission.)

skills and personal qualities of an instructor; however, this observed relationship indicates that student evaluations do not measure how much students learn from a course. Note that this study is not an experiment, because there is no independent variable controlled by the researchers. It is a correlational study (chapter 21).

Function

One special type of relationship is called a **function.** The conclusion of a study may state that the dependent variable, Y, is a function of the independent variable, X. Mathematically, a function is defined as follows: if for *every* element in the domain (X axis) there exists *one and only one* element in the range (Y axis), the relationship between X and Y is a function. A relationship that is *not* a function can have more than one element in the range for each element in the domain.

Psychologists usually use the term "function" with much less precision than mathematicians do. In general, we tend not to worry much about whether quantitative or qualitative variables are represented on the X axis. We also summarize variables by group averages rather than by portraying all of the individual Y scores for subjects in each treatment condition or X-axis value. If we did graph all these scores, we would rarely find data that satisfy the mathematical definition of a function. The subjects in each treatment condition rarely have identical dependent-variable measures. We avoid imprecision by graphing group average scores under each treatment condition and referring to the results as depicting functional relationships, even though the same precise function does not describe the behavior of all subjects.

In the aggression experiment, you can say that the horn-honking behavior was a function of the incompatible emotional arousal treatments, since the plot of the proportions fits the mathematical definition of a function. In the study of the relationship between student evaluations and amount learned, the plot of the data does not satisfy the mathematical definition of a function. In Figure 2.4 there is more than one element in the *range* (X axis) for each element in the *domain* (Y axis). Figure 2.4 does illustrate a relationship between two dependent variables.

THE DEVELOPMENT OF CONCEPTUAL HYPOTHESES

Deciding which variables to manipulate and measure in an experiment depends on the experimental hypothesis. In turn, the experimental hypothesis depends on the conceptual hypothesis. This section is concerned with the origin of conceptual hypotheses.

If the real world were as orderly as textbooks would have us believe, describing the development of conceptual hypotheses would require a simple expansion on the hypothetico-deductive process discussed in chapter 1. However, reality is not so convenient. McGuire (1973) provides a well-written, entertaining description of the many ways in which scientific hypotheses are created. The following paragraphs describe some of McGuire's categories.

Many research hypotheses develop as a consequence of the experimenter being alert to naturally occurring, curious events. Observing behavior that does not fit into some readily available explanatory model, the alert researcher is stimulated to speculate why the happening occurred the way it did. Why did Hess's eyes dilate while looking at animal photographs? Why didn't a large group of New York City citizens come to the assistance of a young woman who was repeatedly stabbed in their sight and/or hearing until she finally died? Why do people continue to smoke cigarettes when there is clear, uncontestable evidence of the relationship between smoking and lung cancer? Why do obese people cheat on their own self-created diets? Such *paradoxical events* have stimulated researchers to seek explanations of the curious behavior.

Reasoning by *analogy* is another common method of approaching the explanation of behavior. Researchers once theorized that the brain's information storage system operates as if it were a telephone switchboard; a later theory was that it operates as if it were a computer; and a more recent theory is that it works on principles similar to those underlying holographic projections by laser technology. Some of McGuire's own research was based on the application of a medical/biological analogy to social behavior. He developed an "attitude inoculation" model suggesting that in order to immunize people against propaganda, they should be exposed to bits of counterpropaganda to let them build up defenses. The preceding sentence should be recognized as a conceptual hypothesis derived from the inoculation analogy.

Conflicting results, or results that do not support our theories, provide important sources of further theorizing and conceptual hypotheses about behavior. We are committed to the search for negative evidence. As scientists, we are taught to confront the painful facts that inconveniently do not fit our theories and explanatory models. We also learn that negative cases disconfirming a theory are always more powerful than positive cases supporting the theory. If a theory predicts that some event will happen and the event does happen, the theory may or may not be the best explanation of the event, for other theories may also predict the occurrence of the same event. However, if the predicted event does *not* happen, we can be confident that something is wrong with our theory. Therefore as we conduct research in a given area, we are continually seeking ways to disconfirm our hypotheses. Confirmation with appropriate tests provides good support for a hypothesis about behavior.

B. F. Skinner (1956) provides a detailed "case history" of his own early research, which had a profound effect on the history of experimental psychology, including the development of new research devices, research procedures, and theoretical structures. Skinner's main argument is that research is a "dirty" process, best described as the disorderly, accidental stumbling about of the persistent, but often vague, unfocused researcher. Skinner summarized his description of the real messiness of the scientific process in four "Informal Scientific Principles." Principle No. 1: "When you run into something interesting drop everything else and study it." Principle No. 2: "Some ways of doing research are easier than others." Principle No. 3: "Some people are lucky." Principle No. 4: "Apparatuses sometimes break down." The humorous description of the events that led to the formulation of each principle is well·worth reading. Skinner's case history shows that a major development within scientific psychology occurred because of a series of accidental, fruitful findings while the researcher was seeking the order behind observed behavior. *Serendipity* (the aptitude for making fortunate, accidental discoveries) is a source of important conceptual hypotheses in scientific research.

The stereotypical description of the research scientist carefully formulating clear conceptual hypotheses about behavior and subjecting these hypotheses to precise, careful examination in highly formalized experimental procedures is a reassuring, comfortable description of a process that rarely happens. Actually, the process of doing research includes a lot of floundering, developing some ideas somehow, often wasting a lot of time on a badly formulated idea, but persistently, doggedly muddling through with the occasional result that a significant positive contribution is made to the science (Taylor, Festinger, Garner, Hebb, Hunt, Lawrence, Osgood, Skinner, & Wertheimer, 1959). However, we ask undergraduates to learn the hypothetico-deductive stereotype in order to get started doing research in a generally correct and productive way.

THEORETICAL CONSTRUCTS

Theoretical Constructs

Psychologists often use terms such as "learning," "motivation," "perception," and "thinking" to describe relationships between variables. These terms, called **theoretical constructs,** symbolize or label the relationship between at least two measured variables. The relationship illustrated in Figure 2.3 may be labeled "aggression reduction" and the relationship illustrated in Figure 2.4 may be labeled "teaching evaluation and effectiveness."

The abstract terms and phrases we call theoretical constructs are not definable in a fixed, dictionary sense. Rather, they are fluid, dynamic terms that are "ideal fictions." As indicated by the process of operational definition, constructs are related to events in the real world, but they are not identical with real world events. In a sense, a theory consists of a set of created abstractions that are tenuously related to real world events. The specific nature of that tenuous relationship is constantly subject to change as the results of thought, observation, and exploration suggest change. On the other hand, these abstractions and the theoretical relationships between them do lead to predictions and the predictions sometimes do get supported. Each time a theoretical prediction is supported, the theory becomes a little bit more credible. Because of the demonstrated utility of theories in the physical sciences, experimental psychologists have continued to use the approach of creating theories, developing coordinating/operational definitions, testing the research hypotheses that result, modifying the definitions and the theory, retesting, and so forth. Although this process involves "messing around" and muddling through, "messing around" is not a fault; rather a major reason why research is pleasurable is that there is so much room for creative, intuitive guessing and groping.

VARIANCE

In the impossible "ideal experiment" all the observed measures of the dependent variable are attributable to the manipulations of the independent variable. In the opening paragraphs of this chapter, several possible factors that might influence the observed sleeping behavior were suggested. There are innumerable factors, organismic and environmental, contemporary and historical, that may affect the behavior of a subject at a given time. All of these factors working together, in addition to the independent variable, may elevate or depress the scores obtained by subjects in an experiment. It is the experimenter's task to discriminate between changes in behavior due to the independent variable and other sources of change.

The differences between the observed scores on the dependent variable are called **variance.** Variance may arise from three general sources: (1) *Organismic or subject factors* (the heredity, history, and present state of the subject), (2) *environmental factors* (the nature of the physical and social environment), and (3) *experimentation factors* (the characteristics of the experimental arrangement, the experimenter, and the measuring devices used). Factors in any of the three categories may be manipulated as independent variables in behavioral experiments. Once the factor or factors of interest have been selected, we must try to control and minimize the effects of *all* other factors that contribute to the variance of the dependent variable. Our attempt to control the sources of variance in an experiment is a major feature of experimental research. In order to understand methods of control, you must first understand the basic characteristics of variance in the dependent variable measures.

Primary Variance

An experimenter manipulates an independent variable in order to observe certain changes in a dependent variable. The observed, *consistent* variation in behavior related to the independent variable is called **primary variance.** (It is also called systematic variance, experimental variance, or **between-groups variance.**) As implied by the term, primary variance is the major reason for conducting the experiment. Another way to think about it is that primary variance is predicted by the experimenter; it is "wanted" or expected variance, while all other variance is unwanted noise that confuses the situation.

The unwanted variation in the dependent variable measures may be divided into two categories. If the measure of the dependent variable is changed in a *consistent* fashion by some factor other than the independent variable, the change is called **secondary variance,** or sometimes extraneous variance. The other category of unwanted variance results from factors affecting the observed data in an *inconsistent* fashion. This category is termed **error variance;** it is also called **within-group variance,** random variance, or random error.

Secondary Variance

Secondary variance is a product of an unrecognized, unexpected variable that changes the dependent measure in a *consistent* way. A magician depends on secondary variance, deliberately misdirecting the audience about the processes of each trick. To experimenters, however, secondary variance adds a problem in determining relationships. In the Hess (1965) study of the relationship between interest and pupil dilation, if the "innocuous" pictures had all been photographs of pleasure boats and if Jim had been interested in boating, then the difference in pupil dilation between the boats and the pinup picture might have been severely reduced. As another example, if the Baron (1976) aggression study had been conducted between 4:30 and 6:00 p.m. instead of between 2:30 and 4:00, it is possible that all the subjects would have been in a hurry, and therefore more likely to exhibit aggressive behavior. If that had been the case, the proportion of subjects honking under all conditions might have been so close to 1.0 that no treatment effect would have been observed.

Secondary variance can be the result of a variable that elevates or depresses all of the measures by a constant amount without altering or interfering with the desired relationship. For example, the length of a maze directly affects the time it takes the subject to run the maze. It is more common, however, to find that an extraneous variable *interacts* with the independent variable to enhance or reduce the effect of the independent variable. An **interaction** occurs when the observed effect of one variable changes because of the effect of a second variable. If in the agression study, the control groups had been tested at 5:15 p.m. each day and the incompatible emotional arousal groups at 2:30 p.m. each day, then the secondary variable of time of testing might have interacted with the treatment variable to enhance the observed treatment effect. Whenever such an interaction occurs, it is difficult to determine how much of the observed effect is due to the independent variable and how much is due to the extraneous secondary variable.

The terms "primary" and "secondary" refer to the *intent* of the experimenter when designing the research. Both types of variance result from antecedent events. Either type of variable can be the major source of variance in any given experiment. The same variance in behavioral data may be labeled primary or secondary by two different experimenters depending on their research orientations. During the course of an experiment, an alert researcher may find that altering the research plan to pursue a source of secondary variance is more interesting than further investigation of the original hypothesis (Skinner's "Principle Number 1"). Thus Secondary variance can become primary variance to a researcher who switches to another experimental hypothesis.

Error Variance

The second category of unwanted variance, error variance or within-groups variance, results when some factor affects the observed data in an inconsistent fashion. Error variance is the result of many factors that decrease the accuracy of a dependent variable measure. One source of error variance is the use of an inappropriate measuring instrument. For example, inconsistent data may result from using a 30-cm ruler to measure a city block or using a bathroom scale to measure small quantities of chemicals. In general, unreliable or unstable measurement procedures or tests increase error variance. Another source of error variance is the use of inconsistent experimental procedures. Any changes in the treatment of individual subjects will increase inconsistencies in the observed data. Individual scores may vary considerably if some subjects are allowed 8 to 9 sec. to perform a task, and others get 11 to 12 sec. for the same "10-second task." The effect of any error source is to increase the variability of the data, making it difficult to isolate the effect of the independent variable as noise interferes with receiving a signal.

The primary problem facing an experimenter is to arrange the experimental conditions so that research data clarify the relationship between the independent variable and the dependent variable. The key to obtaining such data is the use of

Interaction (margin note)

Error Variance (margin note)

adequate and appropriate control procedures (see chapter 3). Kerlinger (1973) says of control:

Principle of Control

> According to this principle [control] by constructing an efficient research design the investigator attempts (1) to maximize the [primary] variance of the variable or variables of his . . . research hypothesis, (2) to control the variance of extraneous or "unwanted" [secondary] variables that may have an effect on his experimental outcomes but in which he is not interested, and (3) to minimize the error or random variance including so-called errors of measurement (p. 306).

MAXIMIZING PRIMARY VARIANCE

A well-designed experiment provides good control of irrelevant factors. However, you cannot eliminate secondary and error variance completely. Good research is that which yields the desired information, not just superb control of secondary and error variables. If the noise level in a dormitory is so high that you cannot hear a favorite radio or TV program, it may be more satisfactory to turn up the volume than to attempt other control procedures. Similarly, there are certain methods available to an experimenter that enhance the effects of the primary variance so that it is more easily discerned from the background variance.

Extreme Values of the Independent Variable

One way to increase the effect of an independent variable is to choose extreme values of the variable. Occasionally a variable automatically falls into two diverse classes, such as male – female. In other cases, the experimental conditions represent a selection of the extreme values on a continuum.

A classic example of this technique is found in a study by Tryon (1940) in which a large number of animals were run in a particular maze task. Selecting animals in terms of maze-learning ability, Tryon mated the top 5% (maze-bright) with one another and the bottom 5% (maze-dull) with one another. The top 5% of the offspring from the maze-bright group were mated and the bottom 5% of the offspring from the maze-dull group were likewise interbred. After several generations of selective breeding, Tryon produced two strains of animals with extremely different abilities for learning a particular type of maze. Note that the selection of extreme values resulted in the loss to this experiment of 90% of the available subjects; in some cases the extreme-values method may be too extravagant to be seriously considered.

An example of selecting extreme values of an environmental factor would be to condition animals to discriminate between black and white instead of shades of gray. Of course, if extreme values are used, the effects of intermediate values of the primary variable are not determined in the study.

Optimal Values of the Independent Variable

Occasionally the choice of extreme values of the primary variable will not maximize the observed effect. Animals that have not been deprived of food probably will not run in a maze to find food. Animals that have been deprived of food for 30 days may not run in the maze either! It is not uncommon to find that as the measure of the independent variable is increased, the measure of the dependent variable will increase, level off, and then decrease (see Figure 2.5). If a variable yields such an "inverted-U" relationship you should choose an intermediate value and an extreme value of the independent variable in order to maximize the effect of the primary variable.

If other research indicates that particular values of the independent variable will maximize primary variance, use these optimal values. By this means you will maximize the chance of detecting an effect if it exists.

Several Values of the Independent Variable

Usually you do not know the optimal values of the independent variable. The arbitrary choice of two values may lead to the conclusion that the variable has no effect on behavior. For example, if you had chosen to use the A and B values of the food-deprivation variable in the maze-running experiment in Figure 2.5 you would have found all animals running at the same speed. Your conclusion would have been that food deprivation does not affect running speed; however, the whole curve in Figure 2.5 reveals a strong relationship between the two variables. If possible, use several values of an independent variable when conducting an experiment.

FIG. 2.5
An example of an "inverted-U" function. The independent variable is hours of food deprivation and the dependent variable is maze-running speed. At A and B values of food deprivation yield identical dependent-variable scores, concealing primary variance.

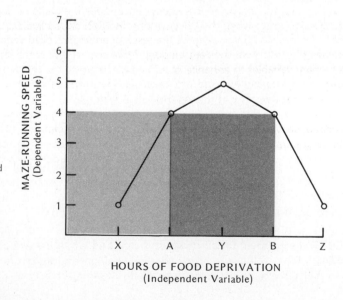

HOURS OF FOOD DEPRIVATION
(Independent Variable)

Multivalent Research

When many values of the variable are included in a study, it is sometimes called **multivalent research.** An advantage of a multivalent approach is that it increases the probability of choosing values of the independent variable that will have an effect on the dependent variable. Most importantly, you can determine the full nature of the relationship between the independent and dependent variables.

SUMMARY

1. Research is the process of attempting to answer researchable questions. Not all questions that interest people are experimentally researchable.
2. Specialized scientific terminology has developed because of the need for clear, efficient communication between scientists.
3. An experimenter manipulates independent variables, organismic or environmental, and observes their effects on dependent variables. In psychology, dependent variables are measures of behavior.
4. A relationship is a set of scores formed by pairing the measures on one variable with the measures on another variable. A function is a special type of relationship in which each pair of scores is unique in the sense that there is only one Y score for each X score.
5. Among other ways, conceptual hypotheses are developed by examining paradoxical events, reasoning by analogy, examining conflicting results, being alert for interesting, accidental events (serendipity), and formulating explanatory ideas on the basis of research results.
6. A theoretical construct is a label based on the observed relationship between independent and dependent variables.
7. The differences among observed behavioral measures are called variance. Variance is a result of organismic or subject factors, environmental factors, and experimentation factors.
8. Variance can be divided into three categories: primary variance due to the experimental treatment, secondary variance due to the consistent effects of extraneous factors, and error variance due to the inconsistent effects of uncontrolled, extraneous factors.
9. An interaction exists when the effect of one variable depends on the level of a second variable. Secondary variance can be the result of an uncontrolled variable that elevates or depresses all scores by a constant amount. More commonly, secondary variables interact with primary variables to enhance or reduce the effect of the primary variables.
10. Two sources of error variance are unreliable, unstable measurement procedures and inconsistent experimental procedures across subjects.
11. Experimental control is the arrangement of variance sources so that primary variance is maximized, secondary variance is controlled, and error variance is minimized.
12. Maximizing primary variance can be accomplished by choosing extreme values, optimal values, or several values (multivalent research) of the independent variable.

SUGGESTED READINGS

Kerlinger, F. N. *Foundations of behavioral research* (2nd. ed.). New York: Holt, Rinehart and Winston, 1973.

Plutchik, R. *Foundations of experimental research* (2nd ed.). New York: Harper & Row, 1974.

Selltiz, C., Wrightsman, L. S., & Cook, S. W. *Research methods in social relations* (3rd ed.). New York: Holt, Rinehart and Winston, 1976.

Skinner, B. F. A case history in scientific method. *American Psychologist,* 1956, *11,* 221–233.

Taylor, D. W., Festinger, L., Garner, W. R., Hebb, D. O., Hunt, H. F., Lawrence, D. H., Osgood, C. E., Skinner, B. F., & Wertheimer, M. Education for research in psychology. *American Psychologist,* 1959, *14,* 167–179.

3

Control and Generalization

This chapter presents more basic terms and the concepts of control and generalization. Fortunately, scientific definitions of these terms are close to their everyday meanings, reflecting the relatively recent development of most experimental research methodology. The chapter presents an overview of the procedures for controlling plausible secondary-variance sources and minimizing the effects of error-variance sources. We need to select proper samples and to focus more on replicating important studies, if we are to determine how far to generalize results. Unchecked overgeneralization is a trap that may delude us into believing we know more than we actually do.

The ability to control sources of variance is a major feature of experimental research. The more we can control secondary variance and minimize error variance, the clearer will be our estimate of the effects of an independent, primary variable on a dependent variable. Only then are we in a position to try to generalize the results of our research from the sample observed to the population from which the sample was drawn. Much of the effort of designing a research project is devoted to the problems of controlling plausible secondary-variance sources.

CONTROLLING SECONDARY VARIANCE

Organismic or subject factors such as age or past experience obviously can have an effect on data, but often they are not controlled. Other subject factors may not be so obvious. For instance, male rats will press a bar more often than females in a brightly illuminated environment (Sackett, 1963). The uncontrolled sex factor may be a source of confused results in bar-pressing studies. The term "laboratory rat" conceals another important potential source of secondary variance. There are differences between the behavior of pigmented and albino rats in laboratory situations (Beauchamp, 1968). Moreover, some experimental laboratories establish and maintain their own highly inbred animal colonies; it might be interesting to compare the behaviors of these strains. Strain differences probably might explain some differences in results between similar experiments run in different laboratories.

Diverse environmental factors such as time of day, amount of sleep, blood-sugar level, or an impending examination may markedly affect a subject's performance. Also, subjects are remarkably adept at picking up cues from the experimenter. Animals' utilization of experimenter feedback is illustrated by a study that found that rats learned a difficult maze discrimination in a suspiciously short time. Subsequent investigation revealed that the animals were learning to run to the side of the maze by which the experimenter was standing—which was always the correct side. A different experimenter-related secondary variable is encountered in research interviews of human subjects; the responses of each subject may differ depending on the sex of the interviewer (Rosenthal, 1967).

Bias

Secondary variance also occurs when a measuring technique is biased. <u>A **biased measure** is one that yields scores that are distorted in a consistent way.</u> For example, biasing can occur in a difficult discrimination situation in which you must decide which object the subject looked at first. If you *expect to find* a certain phenomenon, then you are more likely than an unbiased observer to find evidence for this phenomenon.

Rosenthal (1966, 1969) discusses several examples of the **experimenter expectancy bias effect.** Any researcher should be especially careful to guard against inadvertently introducing a bias because of personal expectations, engaging in "self-fulfilling prophecy" (see chapter 14).

Several control procedures may be employed once an extraneous factor is identified as having a real chance of affecting the experimental data. Such secondary variables are termed "plausible" sources of secondary variance.

Control

In a chapter written just before his death, psychology historian E. G. Boring (1969) traced the history of the scientific meanings of the term "control." Originally the word "control" meant "counter-roll," a master list against which subsequent special lists could be checked. The word is still used in this sense to mean an assessment for accuracy. In science, the word "control" has four distinct meanings.

Maintaining Constancy

(1) In its oldest scientific use, the term "control" means maintaining constancy of conditions. This meaning applies in the discussions of eliminating a secondary variable and holding a secondary variable constant (pp. 40–41).

Calibration

(2) In the late nineteenth century, the use of the control experiment, control test, or control series was introduced to psychology and biology. The idea was to standardize research equipment and the human subject as a measuring device. *Calibration,* checking the accuracy of measuring tools, is a commonplace aspect of control in any experiment. Checking the accuracy of human subjects' judgments, particularly perceptual discrimination judgments, is also a standard feature of experiments in which such judgments are involved. Frequently, we check a subject's accuracy by including within the regular experimental trials certain *probe trials* in which no actual physical stimuli are presented or only one stimulus is presented when two are expected.

(3) There is a third, engineering meaning to the word "control" in applied behavior analysis. Here the terms "control of behavior" and "stimulus control" refer to the conscious manipulation of behavior. School teachers utilize this type of control.

Control Groups

(4) Finally, an important meaning of the term "control" is embodied in the term "control group." Much of the section on research design (chapters 6–11) is concerned with the advantages and disadvantages of various kinds of groups in controlling secondary variance. In its simplest form, a control-group experiment involves two groups of subjects. One group (the experimental group) is given some form of treatment, and the other group (the control group) is not given the treatment. Boring presents the dramatic example of a study in 1890, in which the effect of immunization was demonstrated by injecting the experimental group of mice with tetanus antitoxin, whereas the control group was not injected. Both groups were then given tetanus toxin; the experimental group lived and the control group died. The independent variable, immunization, clearly affected the dependent variable, staying alive.

Sources of Secondary Variance

In chapter 2, we indicated that dependent-measure variance may arise from three general sources: subject factors, environmental factors, and experimentation factors. As sources of secondary variance, these three categories can be labeled individual

Internal Validity

differences, outside influences, and experimental contamination, respectively. The first two categories, individual differences and outside influences, relate to the **internal validity** of the research (Campbell & Stanley, 1963). When the experimental setting, measurement procedures, sample of subjects, and treatment levels are properly controlled, then a study has the needed internal validity.

External Validity

The third category, experimental contamination, affects the **external validity** of the research. To what extent may the observed treatment effects in the particular research setting, with the particular measurement procedures and sample of subjects, be generalized to other levels of the treatment variable, other environmental settings, other measurement procedures, and the population you have sampled? External validity is the *generalizability* of the research results.

Individual Differences

Individual differences that are sources of secondary variance include:

1. The **maturation** of each subject as time passes during the study; subjects grow older, more tired, more frustrated, hungrier, and so on. If a study requires people to continue a boring task for a long period of time, their dependent variable scores (for example, accuracy) might be very low regardless of the treatment condition.
2. The effects of an initial **testing** upon performance on a second test (pretest or **sequence** effect).
3. The **biased selection** of subjects for research groups; for example, differences in species or differences in past-experience may not be controlled when subjects are assigned to groups. If all the "smart" people are in the experimental group and all the less "smart" in the control group, then the test scores of the experimental group will be higher than the control-group scores, regardless of the experimental treatment.

Internal Validity Confounding

4. In complex research designs (chapter 10), the interaction **(confounding)** of two or more sources of individual difference; for example, **group selection bias by maturation** or **testing interaction.** Suppose you conducted a year-long study of the effects of an assertion-training course on the social self-confidence of high school students using the junior class as the control group and the freshman class as the experimental-treatment group. If the one-year average gain in self-confidence for the freshman class were greater than that of the junior class, it might be due to a lower initial level of self-confidence and/or a faster maturation rate for freshmen, rather than to the assertion-training course.
5. The effect of **statistical regression,** particularly when groups are selected on the basis of extreme scores on some test. *Regression toward the mean* ("mean" is another word for average) is a statistical concept referring to the case when two measures taken at different times are obtained from each subject. We may compare the two test scores from a particular subject with the group average scores for each testing time. When the two measures (tests) are not perfectly related (that is, when both of the subject's scores are not identical), the subject's second test score will be as close or closer to the second test average than the subject's first score was to the first test average. Regression toward the mean is frequently observed in the repeated measurement of organismic characteristics. Suppose we were to create two groups of subjects on the basis of their extreme scores on a measure such as anxiety, aggressiveness, or hypertension. Without exposing either group to any treatment, if we retest the two groups with the same test at a later date, we can expect that the previous high-scoring group will have a lower average score because of regression. Statistical regression is a direct function of the correlation (degree of relationship; see chapter 21) between the two measures. It occurs whether the same or different tests are given at different times to the subjects, but the smaller the correlation between the two measures, the greater the regression effect (Furby, 1973).

Outside Influences   Outside influences that are sources of secondary variance include:

1. **History,** or the effects on the dependent measure of all events, other than the independent variable, that occur between the first measure (pretest) and a second measure after the independent-variable treatment occurs. For example, in a study about the perceived attractiveness of certain foods, if only some of the subjects eat lunch between the first and second measurement of attractiveness, the dependent variance is likely to be increased compared to the case where none of the subjects eats lunch.
2. **Experimental mortality,** the differential loss of subjects between experimental groups due to factors other than the independent variable. If for any reason other than the experimental treatment, most of the experimental group subjects do not complete the experiment and most of the control subjects do complete it, then the difference between the average dependent scores of the two groups may be due to the experimental mortality factor rather than the treatment.
3. Differences in **time** or **place of testing** of groups. If the control group is tested at night and the experimental group in the morning, the group differences on the dependent measure may be due to the time of testing variable rather than the treatment.
4. Any other intervening factors or events not part of the independent-variable that affect the subjects in the groups differentially. For example, the experimenter might pinch an animal's tail in the door of the testing maze, inadvertently feed some animals that were supposed to be deprived, or try to "make time" with one of the subjects.

Experimental Contamination   Experimental contamination as a source of secondary variance includes:

1. **Pretest sensitization** to treatment. Giving a test before the independent-variable manipulation can alert or sensitize the subjects to the independent variable so that they react differently to the treatment than they would have if there had been no pretest. For example, measuring peoples' attitudes before showing a propaganda film may alert the subjects to the manipulative nature of the film, leading them to resist the propaganda. Pretest sensitization is not the same as the testing effect we listed under individual differences as sources of variance. In the testing effect, the pretest, the first dependent variable measure, directly raises or lowers scores on the next test, the second dependent variable measure; it does not interact with the treatment. In pretest sensitization, the pretest does interact with the treatment, and that interaction in turn affects subsequent dependent measures.
2. **Interaction of selection bias with the treatment,** confounding the effects of the independent variable with the effects of the selection bias. For example, if the group selection bias led to placing all the smarter persons in the experimental training group, and if the experimental group (getting the treatment) learns more, then is the better learning due to the selection bias, the experimental treatment, or the interaction of both? We listed group-selection bias under individual differences as sources of variance also. There the bias directly affects the dependent measures, producing differences between the groups' measures that are not due to the independent variable; the bias does not interact with the treatment. Here, however, an interaction with the treatment affects the subsequent dependent measures.

External Validity Confounding

3. **Reactive effects of experimental arrangement.** If aware that they are being observed by an experimenter, human subjects may behave atypically. Other features of the experimental situation also may interact with the independent variable, so that the results of the experiment can be generalized only to subjects who undergo a similar testing procedure.

FIG. 3.1
Psychophysiological research with human beings involving extensive response recording and amplifying equipment is particularly susceptible to the reactive effects of experimental arrangement. (Photograph by D. W. Matheson.)

For example, the results of an experiment run in a laboratory may not successfully generalize to a normal environment (Fig. 3.1). People who learn to relax in a biofeedback laboratory may not be able to relax at home.

4. The occurrence of **multiple-treatment interaction.** In certain complex research designs that involve exposing each subject to several levels of an independent variable, the effect of having experienced one level of a treatment may affect the subject's response to the second level of the treatment. For example, if drug X produced an aftereffect, then the subject's response to drug Y may be affected by the response to drug X when the drugs are taken in the sequence X–Y.

The goal of experimental psychology is the generation of theories that specify functional relationships between variables. There are so many different, plausible, potential sources of secondary variance that some individuals assume the goal is impossible to reach. These pessimists perceive the variety and number of secondary variance sources as overwhelming. Practicing experimental psychologists perceive the magnitude and complexity of the problems instead as an incentive to ingenuity. The following section outlines many tactics for dealing with plausible sources of secondary variance. The procedures were developed in response to the challange of research problems. The word *plausible* is worth emphasizing; it is easy to overlook the fact that not all possible sources of secondary variance are plausible or likely sources in a given study.

Eliminating a Secondary Variable

A highly desirable control technique is to eliminate a secondary factor from the experimental situation. For example, you can hang a sign on the laboratory door stating, "Quiet Please, Experiment in Progress." With luck, people will not barge into the experiment room during data collection. With even more luck, people will try to be quiet outside the laboratory room, eliminating the effect of extraneous noise. Likewise, much of the experimenter's influence can be eliminated in some research by placing a screen or one-way viewing mirror/window between the subject and experimenter.

In a study of human behavior, one potential source of secondary variance is the subjects' knowledge of the experimental hypothesis and treatment conditions. One means of controlling for this potential source of variation is to arrange the experimental conditions so that the subjects are "blind" to (ignorant of) the purpose of the study **Single-Blind** and the particular treatment they are receiving. This arrangement is called a **single-blind** technique. A version of this technique appropriate to drug studies is to let all the subjects think they are receiving some amount of a drug, while some subjects in fact are receiving an inert substance or one that is known to have no effect on the dependent measure (such as a sugar pill). The inert or ineffective substance is called a **Placebo** **placebo.** The use of placebo-control groups is routine in many psychophysiological studies. For example, in any relatively novel study it is standard practice to use **sham-operation** groups in which all the procedures of a real operation are followed, except for the presumably critical step of removing specific tissue or implanting a foreign object or substance.

It is possible to eliminate or at least decrease the effect of experimenter expectancy bias by having a laboratory technician collect the data. If the technician is not informed as to which subjects are in the experimental condition, the technician is less likely to bias the results because of personal expectations. This method is another form of the *single-blind* technique. If neither the human subjects nor the researchers or technicians that work directly with the subjects know which subjects are receiving which **Double-Blind** treatment at which time, then the experimental technique is called a **double-blind** procedure. In a double-blind experiment, only one person, who is not directly involved with data collection, has access to the code that identifies which subjects experienced which treatment conditions.

Holding a Secondary Variable Constant

Some secondary factors, such as gravity, temperature, or time of day, cannot be eliminated from the experimental situation. Since any variation in these factors could alter the experimental results, the alternative is to hold them constant. Treating all subjects in the same manner will sometimes allow the secondary factors to affect performance equally. If temperature affects the performance of students on an anxiety test, you can control the temperature variable by holding it constant. If room illumination might affect the manual-dexterity scores of a group of children, you can control room illumination by holding it constant for all subjects. Recall that maintaining constancy of conditions is the oldest scientific meaning of the term "control."

Matching Subjects on a Secondary Variable

Suppose you wish to determine which of two study conditions facilitates learning. You must take into account the relative intelligence of the subjects in each learning condition. The hold-constant method of control would require all subjects to have the same score on an IQ test. As a result, you would have to reject a large number of potential subjects.

It is possible to utilize more of the available subjects by selecting several pairs of subjects, *matched* on IQ score. One person in each pair may be assigned to the first study group and the other subject to the second study group. The IQ factor will contribute equally to the scores of each group, and any consistent difference between the groups will be the result of the treatment conditions. Unless each person in the original sample can be matched, some subjects must be rejected, or the matching procedure must be made less rigid. The last alternative weakens the effectiveness of the control. Matching on one variable does not control for other possible sources of differences between matched subjects. Matching is discussed in greater detail in chapter 9.

Using Subjects as Their Own Controls

A major form of the matching method uses subjects as their own controls. In general, the procedure consists of obtaining more than one measure of behavior from each subject and comparing behaviors over time. Using subjects as their own controls may involve obtaining a measure before and after the introduction of the experimental treatment. The purpose of the procedure is to reduce the influence of subject factors on the total variance. The observed difference between a subject's behaviors at two times is not affected by differences between subjects. Fewer subjects are required than with the usual matching method. This procedure is described in greater detail in chapters 7 and 11.

Randomizing a Secondary Variable

Suppose you have no IQ measures. Then your best procedure for reducing the influence of intelligence as a secondary factor is to assign the subjects to groups by a random method, such as flipping a coin. With a random-assignment procedure, both groups have an equal chance of getting bright subjects and dull ones. Random assignment *theoretically* will equate the groups not only on average intelligence, but also on any other factor. This procedure is used in most experiments because it controls for the effects of unmeasurable and/or undiscovered secondary factors.

Random assignment is accomplished by means of a table of random numbers such as Appendix C or one of the random-number generating programs contained in many electronic calculators. A **random-number table** consists of the numbers from 0 to 9 arranged in a random sequence. There is no known pattern or rule that will account for the sequence of numbers shown. Human beings do not make good random-number generators, primarily because they cannot bring themselves to call out the same number several times in succession, an event that does occur in a random sequence.

The table in Appendix C presents numbers in groups of five for easy reading. To use the table in assigning subjects to treatment conditions, you begin reading the table at any point. This point is usually chosen by closing your eyes and placing a pencil tip somewhere on the page, but more exotic or superstitious methods work equally well.

Random Assignment

Using a Random-Number Table

Then read a sequence of digits in any direction at all. After a sequence is obtained, alphabetically list the subjects' names, one beside each digit. Assign all subjects paired with even numbers to one condition, and subjects with odd numbers to the other group. Assigning numbers from 0 to 4 to one condition, and from 5 to 9 to the other works as well.

The method of obtaining a random-number sequence is unimportant provided you do not always enter at the same point or collect the numbers in the same direction. Similarly, when using a calculator, start with a new "seed number" to generate each new sequence of random numbers. If you require more than 10 digits in the assignment scheme, you can list the numbers in pairs or larger groups.

Value of Random Assignment

Suppose you have four subjects whom you wish to assign at random to an experimental group and a control group. You decide that the even-numbered subjects will be assigned to the control group and the odd-numbered to the experimental group. After listing the four subjects in some order, you enter on the second page at Row 20 and Column 09 of the first thousand numbers of the Table of Random Numbers (Appendix C). Each column is denoted by a two-digit number. The columns of random numbers are grouped in sets of five, and Column 09 is at the end of the second set of five. In other words, Column 09 is the tenth column of digits from the left. Reading down the column, you assign the following numbers to the list of subjects in order: 8,9,8,3. Thus the first and third subjects on your list are assigned to the control group. The choice of the second page, Row 20, and Column 09 was determined in some chance manner, as was the decision to read down the column. The point of this elaborate, seemingly ridiculous ritual is to be sure that in no way can the assignment of one subject to a group affect the assignment of the other subjects. This method establishes the *independence* of the two groups and the *unbiased* assignment of subjects to groups.

Uses of Random-Number Tables

The preceding completely random assignment procedure could result in three or four subjects in one group and one or none in the other. If the research requires an equal number of subjects in each group, you continue to sample until one group is full; then the other group, if there are only two groups, is automatically filled with the remaining subjects. If there are three groups in the experiment, the rule might be that the numbers 1–3 constitute the first group, 5–7 the second group, and 8–0 the third group. Note that the number 4 is ignored because 10 cannot be evenly divided by three. Four groups can be created by first obtaining two groups, and then randomly dividing them in two. If the research required that the groups be balanced to contain equal numbers of each sex in each group, then you randomly assign subjects to groups one sex at a time. The number of ways to select a random sample is limited only by the researcher's ingenuity. A coin or dice can be used to select a random sample, but a table of random numbers is the best, most likely to be *unbiased,* method.

A table of random numbers may be used to *select* subjects, *assign* subjects to conditions, determine the *order* of subject appearance in the experiment, *choose* stimuli, establish the *sequence* of stimuli in the experiment, and govern the *pattern* of reinforcement to the subjects.

Note that it is still possible to assign randomly only bright subjects to one group and only dull subjects to the other. Such an event is more likely with small groups than with large groups. Therefore, <u>as the sample size increases, randomization becomes more effective as a control procedure for both selection of subjects and assignment of subjects to groups.</u>

Systematizing a Secondary Variable

Another method of dealing with a secondary variable is to make it an independent variable. Suppose you wish to determine whether rats are more active in a brightly illuminated environment or a dark environment. As previously mentioned, male and female rats differ in activity when exposed to short test periods of light and dark. You must choose some method of controlling the effect of the organizmic variable, sex. You could hold the variable constant by working with only one sex. Not only is that less fun, but the research conclusions could not be generalized to both sexes. You could assign both sexes to each group randomly, or you could balance the groups by randomly assigning an equal number of males and females to each experimental condition, making sex an independent variable. By manipulating sex as an independent variable, you recover more information than by randomization or holding constant.

For example, suppose that you have 10 males and 10 females, divided into two groups of five males and two of five females. The proper method of assigning each individual male or female to a group is to use a table of random numbers. This plan for assigning subjects to groups and groups to experimental conditions is called a *research design.* The design is summarized in Figure 3.2. You have four groups of subjects: five females in the light condition (1); five females in the dark condition (2); five males in the light condition (3); and five males in the dark condition (4). In order to evaluate the effect of the brightness variable, you combine the data from Groups 1 and 3 and compare the result with the combined data from Groups 2 and 4. The comparison is

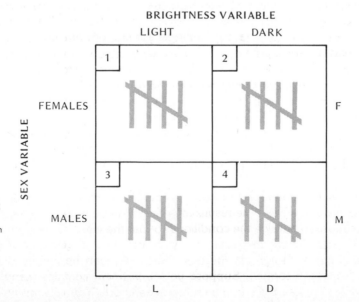

FIG. 3.2
A 2 X 2 matrix showing four groups of five subjects each. Sex is an organismic, independent variable. Each tally mark represents a single subject.

Table 3.1 Comparison of Northern and Southern Men and Women in Tolerance of Nonconformists

	Number of Subjects Interviewed				Percentage Tolerant		
	Male	Female	Total		Male	Female	Total
North	1416	1655	3116	North	39	32	35
South	647	768	1415	South	17	13	15
Total	2108	2423	4531	Total	32	26	29

Note. From Communism, conformity, and civil liberties *by S. Stouffer (Garden City, N.Y., Doubleday, 1955). Copyright 1955 by Doubleday. Reprinted by permission.*

represented in the table by contrasting column L, which represents all of the subjects in the light condition, with the data from column D, or all the subjects in the dark condition. You now have the desired comparison of the two environmental conditions with the secondary factor, sex, systematized.

You also can compare activity differences between males and females. By comparing the data from Groups 3 and 4 (all male subjects) with the combined data from Groups 1 and 2 (all female subjects), you can determine the effect of sex difference under matched environmental conditons. Sex and brightness both become independent variables, in the same experiment! Furthermore, you can determine whether the combination of the two variables produces an interaction effect. That is, you can see whether the activity difference between the light and dark conditions depends on the sex of the subject. An interaction occurs when the effect of one independent variable depends on another independent or secondary variable.

Interaction

Stouffer (1955) describes a study that illustrates one of the values of systematizing secondary variables. In that study, a large sample of men and women were interviewed and classified as being either tolerant or intolerant of nonconformists. The main variable of interest was sex; however, the secondary variable, residence in a northern or southern state of the United States of America, was included as a systematized variable. Table 3.1 shows the number of subjects interviewed in each category and the percentage of subjects tolerant of nonconformists. The table shows there was a *main effect*[1] of sex (males were more tolerant of nonconformists); there was also a regional main effect (northerners were more tolerant than southerners); the sex effect seemed *not* to interact with the regional effect. That is, the males were two or three percentage points higher than the total and the females two or three percentage points lower than the total for each region and for both regions combined. The author safely generalized the sex main effect to both regions of the United States.

Conservatively Arranging a Secondary Variable

Occasionally you may not care whether a secondary variable is uncontrolled in an experiment, so long as the results are not confused by the effects of the variable. You may choose to arrange the conditions so that the effect of the secondary variable can only weaken the primary variance. Since such an arrangement consists in deliberately stacking the cards *against* the hypothesis, you can be even more confident if the hypothesis is supported. Suppose your apartment contains many cockroaches and you decide to use them in a learning experiment. You can put the "subjects" in an

[1]This term is explained in chapter 10.

apparatus where they can choose between a light or a dark compartment. You can make either compartment light or dark. Whenever the bugs enter the dark compartment, they are given a shock. According to theory, after several shocks, the cockroaches should learn to stay in the light compartment. They should run to the other compartment when the brightness is changed. This learned response is opposite to cockroaches' normal preference for dark places. Therefore, it they do learn, you can conclude that the results are due to learning and not to the cockroaches' natural preference. Since any other procedure for controlling the secondary variable would produce even stronger results, the technique is known as conservatively arranging the secondary variable.

MINIMIZING ERROR VARIANCE

As you learned in chapter 2, error variance is any inconsistent variation in the dependent measure. It is the product of many factors, each of which may change a particular score at the instant of observation. Error variance constitutes the ever-present background noise out of which the primary variance "signal" must be discerned. To guarantee that the observations are as accurate and meaningful as possible, you must try to minimize error variance.

Individual-Differences Error

The first component of error variance reflects individual differences. Because of differences in the heredity and past history of experimental subjects, variability in responses must be expected. Individual differences also result from uncontrolled and uncontrollable factors in the environment that affect each subject differently. Inconsistent effects of individual differences produce error variance; individual differences that are consistent between groups produce secondary variance. As indicated in chapter 2, error variance can also arise from experimental procedures inconsistently applied to subjects. In all, the individual-differences component of error variance can arise from subject factors, environmental factors, and experimentation factors. The effect of individual differences can be minimized by (1) random assignment of subjects to the levels of the independent variable, and (2) increasing the total sample size, thus increasing the likelihood that the sum of all uncontrolled individual differences will cancel each other.

Random Assignment

Increased Sample Size

A second component of error variance results from the methods employed to gather data. As indicated in chapter 2, unstable or unreliable measurement procedures are a source of error variance. No matter how elegant the experimental procedures, the results of an experiment may be inconclusive if the measurement is sloppy. In all cases, instrumentation error or **measurement error** must be minimized. The measurement technique should be able to discriminate between the performances of subjects. Using a creativity test that yields equivalent scores for all subjects would be silly. On the other hand, too fine a measure produces "noise" that can confound the interpretation of a relationship. Measuring running time in a maze to the nearest ten-thousandth of a second would also be ridiculous.

Measurement Error

Psychologists are often faced with the problem of deciding how to score a particular observation. A wrong decision can produce measurement error. For example, in research on conditioning psychologists are sometimes faced with the question, "Did the response occur or not?" Frequently the same problem is encountered in observational studies concerned with small movements. For example, in studies involving the measurement of infants' visual fixation time, the measuring device is often an adult's judgment about the direction of the gaze of each subject.

Data Analysis Errors

A third component of measurement error involves data analysis. Several different statistical procedures may be used in analyzing the results of an experiment. If you use an inappropriate statistical procedure or make errors in calculation, the conclusions will be inaccurate. We are all too familiar with the tedium involved in checking and rechecking the calculations involved in statistical analysis. To our knowledge, we have never published an erroneous conclusion but we have all had the experience of making errors, thinking that the results indicated a particular conclusion, announcing that to our associates, and then, on rechecking, discovering some foolish calculation error.

The principle of control requires the experimenter to *minimize* error variance, because it is impossible to eliminate error variance in any real study. The multifaceted nature of error variance "noise" includes an infinite variety of possible, plausible, essentially random sources of minute variation in the observed data. The resultant uncertainty involved in all of our hypothesized functional relationships leads us to view all hypotheses as tentative, probabilistic statements. Persons who find uncertainty too worrisome should avoid experimental psychology!

SAMPLING

Population

When designing a research project, we intend to generalize the conclusions to the behavior of organisms that will never be in an experiment. This larger group of individuals, the set of all possible subjects of interest, is called the **population.** The attributes defining the population should be specified for each experiment. Examples of populations are: all living organisms, all mammals, all humans, all United States citizens, all United States college students, all students at a particular college, all students taking a particular class, students who sit in the front row of that class, and so on. The population is the larger group about which we are trying to draw conclusions.

Sample
Statistic
Parameter

The group of individuals selected by the experimenter constitutes a sample of the population. A **sample** is defined as a part or subset of the population. The descriptions of the data obtained from a sample (such as the average score) are called **statistics,** while the corresponding descriptions of a population are called **parameters.** Statistics are used to estimate values of the population parameters. The accuracy of such an estimate depends, among other things, on the nature of the sample.

How well the sample statistics estimate the parameters of the population is of vital concern to both the experimenter and to the person reading the experimental results. Both the experimenter and the reader are interested in generalizing from the sample to the population. To use a sample statistic with confidence, you must ascertain that it is both valid and reliable.

Validity of the Sampling Technique

Validity is the degree to which a measure actually reflects what it is supposed to measure. A sample statistic is valid if it closely approximates the population parameter.

Sample Bias

The validity of a statistic is reduced if the sample is **biased** in one of two ways. First, the sample may include individuals who are not members of the population. Inadvertently including a few married college students in a study about premarital sexual behavior might alter the conclusions. Your conclusions may be accurate, but there is no way in which you can extend them legitimately to the population of interest if the sample is not properly a subset of that population.

Second, a sample is biased when it is not representative of the total population. If you want to study the effects of height on the self-concept of adult Canadians, you do not study only short women from Montreal. Another example is the now legendary *Literary Digest* American presidential poll of 1936, which predicted the landslide election of Landon as president of the United States. The *Literary Digest* questionnaires were sent only to persons whose names appeared in telephone directories. Later it was discovered that an important segment of the population, people who did not have telephones, voted overwhelmingly for Roosevelt. The conclusions of the poll were probably correct—for people with telephones. None of the population elements should be excluded by the sampling technique.

Representative Sample

A biased or invalid sample yields data that are altered in some consistent fashion away from the parameter values. Obviously, large random samples are more likely to be valid than small samples. A valid sample is often referred to as a **representative sample.** The concept of validity, when applied to sample statistics, is similar to the concept of secondary variance, because consistent deviation (bias) yields inaccurate results in both cases.

Reliability of the Sampling Technique

Reliability is defined as consistency, or obtaining the same results, time after time. A sampling technique is reliable when several samples from the same population yield similar data. In most cases, sampling technique reliability is directly related to the size of the sample. If it were possible to eliminate the sources of secondary and error variance in behavioral data, a one-subject sample would suffice. Most behavior, however, is highly variable. It would be unwise to draw conclusions concerning the characteristics of a child based on a single, 15-min. sample. The conclusions from such data might be correct but you cannot be sure.

Sample Size

Proper size depends on two major factors. First, the amount of work and expense involved in collecting the data usually increase directly with the sample size. By contrast, a "rule of thumb" is that the reliability of the obtained data increases only proportionally to the square root of the number in the sample (Cantril, 1944). Therefore, each additional subject in the sample contributes a decreasing amount to the reliability of the data. There are no fixed upper or lower limits to the acceptable size of a sample. The usual approach is to establish how much time and money you feel the study is worth and to collect the largest sample within these limits.

Second, the nature of the research design may dictate the minimum number of subjects required. For example, certain statistical analyses require that at least two subjects be measured under each experimental treatment. Within cost limitations, the larger the sample size the better.

Reliability can be defined also in terms of amount of error—the more error the less the reliability. That is, if measurement error is high in an experiment, the data are not likely to provide good population parameter estimates. Suppose there is some "true" measure of a variable, and this value is unknown to you. Through observation you obtain a measured score composed of the true score and an error score. In other words, the observed score equals the true score plus or minus error. The smaller the error, the closer the observed score approximates the unknown true score.

Sampling Techniques

There are several sampling techniques available. The following techniques vary in their usefulness to experimental psychologists.

Bellwether samples   Occasionally a social psychologist discovers that particular subsets of a population are unusually accurate in reflecting the behavior of the entire population. A case in point is national voting behavior. Broadcasting companies hire professional polling organizations to select certain "bellwether precincts," based on the similarity of their voting patterns to that of the nation as a whole. By analyzing the vote of the selected precincts, the networks usually can predict election winners before all the votes are collected.

Quota samples   In most cases, we don't have the necessary information to select bellwether samples. We may, however, have knowledge concerning the characteristics of the population that help to select a representative sample. For example, in studying human behavior, in general a sample containing approximately the same number of males and females will be more valid than a sexually biased sample (such as a sample that is 90% female). If the sample is selected in such a manner that it matches certain characteristics of the population, it is known as a **quota sample**, **stratified sample**, or **representative sample**.

One method of quota sampling is to divide the population into *strata,* subgroups sharing different characteristics, then to sample from these subgroups so that the proportions of the sample match the population. Voter-prediction pollsters are careful to obtain samples that match the population in terms of socioeconomic status, political affiliation, urban–rural environment, and since 1936, possession of a telephone. A good stratified sample may be almost as valid and reliable as a total census would be; however, the technique demands a very large expenditure of time and effort. Even if a sample is stratified along a single dimension, such as income level, you should select from each subgroup at random.

Random samples   If the entire population is potentially available to the experimenter, the table of random numbers can be used to select the sample. That way, each subject in the population is equally likely to be chosen. As indicated previously, random selection makes it highly unlikely that a large sample will be biased.

Available samples Most of the psychological data on human behavior are generated from samples of college students who happen to be available to experimenters. Animal psychologists rely most on the laboratory rat as a source of data. It has been charged that if we discover another life form in the exploration of outer space, experimental psychologists will not be able to tell much about the life form's behavior patterns unless they can study its equivalents in the laboratory rat and college student!

Experimental psychologists usually find it difficult to select a representative sample from a population. Cost and time factors often dictate using the elements of the population that are readily available. You should be careful in drawing conclusions from research, because the actual population sampled usually differs from the population that the experimenters would like to have sampled.

The bellwether, quota, and random sampling procedures all apply to sampling from a very large (approaching infinitely large) population. Such sampling procedures are, in general, more characteristic of public opinion polls and sociological research than of experimental psychology. In the typical experiment run by a research psychologist, all or nearly all of the available subjects are utilized in the study.

GENERALIZING

In good experimental research (chapters 7–10), there is a great emphasis on random assignment of subjects to groups or random selection of subjects for groups, but there is too often little or no concern for random sampling of subjects from any population. The dominant concern of experimental psychologists is for the validity and reliability of the procedures internal to the research study; unfortunately there is often too little concern for the representativeness of the sample (external validity).

Similarly, we do not spend a great deal of time and effort worrying about the representativeness of tasks, actions, choices, or, in general, the behaviors we observe in our research projects. For example, we generally don't worry about the possibility that maze-running behavior in a Dashiel maze will require a different explanatory model to that of maze-running behavior in a multiple-T maze. In this respect, experimental psychological research is more similar to experimental physics research than to sociological or anthropological research. In experimental physics the result of a single nineteenth-century experiment on the speed of light in a particular place and time with a particular apparatus was presumed to hold true for all apparatuses and all places on earth. Psychologists and physical scientists act as if the results of research with particular equipment, subjects, environments, and time frames apply universally until shown otherwise. This is great presumption on our part! However, we take for granted that this potentially dangerous presumption will be checked by theory-guided research on the limits to our generalization from single studies on available samples. Such a presumptuous position strongly underlines the need for replications of each major study to be sure that the original, broadly generalized results are reliable. As the

Easy Generalization

Replication

science progresses, we learn more and more about the potential and actual limits to generalizing from a study of available subjects. Much of the increased interest in experimental field studies (experimental research in nonlaboratory settings) and naturalistic field research derives from this growing awareness of the limits to generalization.

One way to look at the sampling process is to think of the experimenter as using a small ladle (the sample selector) to dip into a very large pot full of beans (the population), removing a ladleful of beans (the sample), testing the sample, and returning the sample to the pot. The test results are generalized to the entire pot. While it is commonly recognized that the beans are a sample of the potential population of research subjects, it is not as frequently recognized that the testing situation and the behaviors measured are also samples from a potential population of situations and behaviors. We emphasize the need for replication in order to deal with the problem of representativeness of the sample. Replication means not only that alternative dippers of subjects must be tested, but also that alternative dippers of environmental situations (social context, physical environment, mode of stimulus presentation, apparatus, and so forth) and alternate means of measuring behavior, including obtrusive and unobtrusive measures, should be selected in order to test the ecological validity and measurement generality of an hypothesis.

Experimental research has a particular problem with generalization because of the reactive nature of experimentation. In a sense we ask our subjects to play a role in the experimental setting. In the standard laboratory experiment, all subjects, human and otherwise, are aware at some level that they are involved in an experiment. In effect, the subjects are asked to act as if they didn't know they were in an experiment and to behave as they would if they were in a natural (nonexperimental) setting. From this point of view, the experimenter is simultaneously manager, set designer, theater technician, director, and producer of a play in which the subjects are the actors. The experimenter's job is then to produce a play that is a good simulation of real life. To the extent that the experimenter is a good producer, the results of the research can be generalized to behavior in a nonstaged, natural setting. Although we don't wish to push this metaphor too far, there is some truth to the idea that experimental psychologists are dramatic artists.

SUMMARY

1. In science, "control" means calibrating measuring devices, manipulating behavior, maintaining constancy of research conditions, and establishing different groups of subjects that are exposed to various treatment conditions.
2. Threats to the internal validity of a research project arise from secondary variance from sources of individual differences and outside influence. Threats to external validity arise from secondary variance due to experimental contamination. External validity refers to the generalizability of the research findings.
3. Individual differences that are general sources of secondary variance include maturational processes over time, the effects of a pretest on later tests, group-selection bias on the part

of the experimenter or by maturation or testing interactions (confounding), and statistical regression of repeated measurements.

4. Outside influences that are general sources of secondary variance include the effects of events intervening between pretest and posttest, differential experimental mortality between groups, differences in time or location of testing between groups, and any other factors or events differentially experienced by groups.

5. Experimental contamination as a general source of secondary variance includes pretest sensitization to treatment, the interaction of selection bias with the treatment (confounding), the reactive effects of experimentation, and multiple-treatment interaction (confounding).

6. The single-blind control technique involves arranging experimental conditions so that the subjects do not know the purpose of the study or which treatment they receive. A placebo is an ineffective substance that the subjects are led to believe is effective. The double-blind technique involves hiding the purpose and assignment to treatment groups from both the subjects and the data collector.

7. Secondary variance is controlled by manipulating extraneous factors so that their effect is eliminated, made constant, matched, randomized, systematized, or conservatively arranged with respect to the dependent variable.

8. Matching requires a larger potential sample size than other methods of control. Using subjects as their own controls is a form of matching that reduces the impact of individual differences on the dependent measure.

9. Random assignment of subjects to groups theoretically equates the groups on known as well as unknown secondary variance factors. Increasing the sample size increases the effectiveness of random assignment.

10. Systematizing a secondary variable has the advantage of providing direct information about the effect of the variable and the interaction of the variable with the primary variable. The cost of systematizing is the increased complexity of the research design.

11. Minimizing error variance is accomplished by minimizing the effect of individual differences, reducing measurement error, and eliminating errors of data analysis.

12. A sample is a subset of a population; the statistics calculated from a sample are estimates of the parameters of the population.

13. Samples are described in terms of their validity, how accurately they reflect characteristics of the population, and their reliability, how consistent the measures would be if several samples were taken.

14. Sampling techniques include bellwether samples, quota samples, random samples, and available samples. Most experimental research uses available subjects. We pay close attention to internal validity, but relatively much less attention to the external validity of our research. There is a strong need for systematic replication of major studies to test the external validity of their findings.

SUGGESTED READINGS

Boring, E. G. Perspective: Artifact and control. In R. Rosenthal & R. L. Rosnow (Eds.), *Artifact in behavioral research.* New York: Academic Press, 1969.

Campbell, D. T., & Stanley, J. C. *Experimental and quasi-experimental designs for research.* Skokie, Ill.: Rand McNally, 1963.

Kerlinger, F. N. *Foundations of behavioral research* (2nd ed.). New York: Holt, Rinehart and Winston, 1973.

Rosenthal, R., & Rosnow, R. L. (Eds.). *Artifact in behavioral research.* New York: Academic Press, 1969.

Rosenthal, R., & Rosnow, R. L. *Primer of methods for the behavioral sciences.* New York: Wiley, 1975.

Selltiz, C., Wrightsman, L. S., & Cook, S. W. *Research methods in social relations* (3rd ed.). New York: Holt, Rinehart and Winston, 1976.

Sheridan, C. L. *Fundamentals of experimental psychology* (2nd ed.). New York: Holt, Rinehart and Winston, 1976.

4

Data: The Measures of Behavior

Although you may not devote any time to thinking about it, we spend much of our daily lives in making and using measurements. However, the concept of measurement often appears to be very abstract and complex. In this chapter we will try to demystify the concepts of measurement and data. Apparently complex questions of "How much?", "How Long?", and "How strong?" can be reduced to questions of "How many?" and even difficult-to-work-with continuous variables can be converted to countable, discrete variables.

Each day we make measurements, varying from simple to complex and from casual to precise. We make both rough, approximate estimates of distances in kilometers and precise length measurements in centimeters. We use various simple and complex gauges such as temperature, wind speed, and barometric pressure gauges. We classify people as large or small, attractive or unattractive, good or bad. All these activities are forms of measurement.

Measurement

Measurement is defined as the assignment of symbols (usually numbers) to objects, organisms, or events according to a set of rules (Stevens, 1946). A story may help to illustrate this definition. Kershner and Wilcox (1950), in a delightful chapter on the development of mathematics, relate how the concepts of number and measurement might have started. Imagine that an ancient tribal chieftain and his faithful warriors had an intense need to conquer several neighboring tribes. The problem was that those tribes had many warriors. To the chief, the word "many" meant "more than two"; so that a tribe might have one, two, or many warriors. Consequently, if all tribes had many warriors, all tribes might be considered equal on the battlefield.

Early in his position as head of the tribe our expansionist chief learned that in a battle "many" did not always mean the same thing. In fact, occasionally tribes with many warriors were soundly trounced by other tribes with many warriors. Our chief was sharp enough to want to discriminate between many in one tribe and many in another tribe without losing a battle. He recalled several clashes when his troops lined up one-to-one with the enemy and the enemy still had warriors standing around with no one to fight. These extra warriors proceeded to wreak havoc on the chief's already busy warriors. The chief determined that the tribe that had extra warriors would be more than likely to win a skirmish. He sat back to discover a way to determine which tribe had more warriors.

According to Kershner and Wilcox (1950), the original concept of "more" was that "collection A has 'more' than collection B if each of the things in B can be matched with one of the things in A without exhausting A" (p. 20). Our scheming chieftain sent a spy out to hide along the trail. The spy was told to break a twig every time one of the enemy ran by. The spy, bored with his assignment, began to grunt as each enemy sped by. In the course of time, these grunts evolved into the words we now say when counting, "one," "two," "three," "four,". . . .

As Kershner and Wilcox point out, some genius observed that the broken twigs were no longer necessary, since the question of how many could be answered by the final grunt or "number." Thus, measurement consists of a collection of symbols—twigs, grunts, or numbers—representing actual things or events, and a rule for the use

55

of the symbols—the final grunt or count must be associated consistently with a pile of twigs and a corresponding tribe of warriors. The question of "many" or specifically, "How many?" was resolved without the loss of blood; and the one-to-one correspondence between counting and measurement was firmly established.

The development of measurement did not stop with answers to questions of "How many?" (the frequency of occurrence of a particular event or thing). People went on to determine answers to questions like "How long?" (the duration of an event) and "How strong?" (the intensity of an event). As you will see, the question of "How much?" is closely related to the question of "How many?" These questions—or rather, the answers to these questions—constitute the beginning of scientific measurement.

Mathematicians have developed a system whereby complex problems are reduced to other problems for which we already have solutions. For example, if you have a candle on one table and a book of matches on another table, how do you light the candle? Obviously the solution is to pick up the matches, walk over, and light the candle with a match. Now change the problem slightly. The matches have fallen to the floor and your task is to light the candle. An acceptable procedure would be first to pick up the matches and place them on their table, and then to apply the solution to the first problem that you know works. A rather silly example, but that really is the way mathematicians and scientists often proceed, solving complex problems by reducing them to problems that already have been solved.

WHAT ARE DATA?

Attribute

An **attribute** is a single feature of a particular person, thing, or event. For example, a college freshman might have hundreds of attributes. An important one is intelligence. Other attributes are analytical ability, running speed, and size. All these attributes contribute to a description of the person and all of them can be reduced to measures of *"How much?"* We don't measure the freshman; we measure how much of his various attributes exist at a particular time. So to describe the freshman, we measure his intelligence, speed, size, analytical ability, and so forth.

Attributes and Variables

The terms "variable" and "attribute" are related. A variable is any condition that may change in quantity or quality. An organismic variable is any physiological or psychological characteristic of an organism. The organismic attribute of human size has two gross dimensions, height and weight. Each dimension is an organismic variable. The attribute of running speed has one dimension; and therefore the attribute is a variable. In general, multidimensional attributes vary along two or more dimensions, and unidimensional attributes are variables.

In Hess's (1965) study relating interest to pupil dilation (see chapter 1), the dependent variable was operationally defined as change in pupil diameter. The crucial measurement question was whether or not Jim's pupils dilated on sight of the pinup picture. That simple question has only two possible answers, yes or no. Even though we may ask sophisticated questions about the universe and our behavior in it, we always reduce the complex questions to simpler ones like "Did it occur?", "How much?'', ''How strong?'', and ''How long?'' Measurement is really always concerned with ''How many units?'' of a particular feature or attribute of an object, event, or thing are present at the time of measurement.

Discrete and Continuous Measurement

Discrete Variables

Discrete measurement involves counting events, things, or units that are clearly separated or demarcated. Just as your house number is different from your neighbors', your social security number is supposed to be unique (unfortunately, not all are), and your driver's license had better be unique. Your age can be measured as a discrete attribute if you define it as 18, 19, 25, or whatever whole number of years is appropriate. The number of correct responses in a learning study is a discrete measure.

Continuous Variables

There are some variables that do not have a clear demarcation between measures. For example, if your wristwatch has a second hand you can note that time is continuously changing. Variables such as time are called **continuous variables** because the changes in the measure are infinitely small and therefore invisible. Compared to discrete variables, continuous variables are more difficult to measure. For example, it is impossible to know exactly what time it is because time, like a moving atomic particle, is continuously changing. You have to allow for a little error in your measurement and assume that the measure obtained is the best available.

The technology of digital watches illustrates this solution. In these watches, time is divided into very small units that are grouped into ''bunches'' of time. If a second is divided into 32,000 parts or pulses, the mechanism adds the number of bunches of 32,000 pulses to obtain seconds, adds the number of 60-sec intervals to obtain minutes, and so forth. The finer the initial division, the better the measure of time and the more accurate the watch.

When a continuous variable is broken into small, discrete parts and the parts are added, the process is called *analog-to-digital conversion;* in the jargon of science, it is called ''A to D conversion.'' The process of changing a continuous measure into a discrete measure is an example of changing a complex problem into a simpler one. Maybe we should say that we really don't measure time, but rather an attribute of time.

Scales of Measurement

There is close similarity between the process of addition or counting and measurement; that is, measurement has a mathematical basis. According to Stevens (1975), the process of measurement has at least two parts. The first is a *mathematical model*—the system of numbers and rules for combining them—and the second is the actual, physical or empirical manipulations, measurement, carried out in the act of measuring. The one-to-one correspondence between the model and measurement is not surprising.

Given a model to represent an attribute of the real world (a clock is a model for the concept we call time and a meter stick is a model for the concept of length) the potential operational definitions for the terms of the model and the various rules for the manipulation of the model provide for different kinds of measurements. For example, suppose you want to measure the surface area of your kitchen floor. If it is square, it would be relatively simple to measure the length of one side in meters and square that number to determine the number of square meters. The model $L^2 = A$ is used where L is the length of one side and A is the area in square meters. Note that the mathematical model used to obtain the answer involved multiplication, and that the empirically observed objects were the number of meter sticks laid end-to-end to make up the length L, a measure of "How many?" again. Thus we engage in the physical activity of measurement, relate the observed measure to the model, and from the model arrive at an estimated measure of the floor area. You could use a yardstick, a 30-cm ruler, and so forth; if you did, the resultant measures of area would be expressed differently.

Measurement Scales

The various relations among objects and the relations among the symbols or numbers assigned to them are called **scales of measurement.** A measurement scale consists of a mathematical system associated with a specific, empirical measurement procedure. The numbers represent attributes of real persons, objects, or events. The process of measurement involves specifying coordinating operational definitions for the abstract symbols of the mathematical model. Therefore, to develop a scale you must identify the empirical, operational measurement procedures that put the numbers in one-to-one correspondence with attributes of real persons, objects, or events. The close similarity of scale development and theory development is no accident. Indeed, developing a theory often involves developing a measurement scale.

According to Stevens (1946), there are at least four kinds of measurement relations: (1) identity relations, in which numbers label and identify items or classes; (2) order relations, in which numbers reflect the rank order of items or objects; (3) interval relations, in which numbers reflect differences or distances between items or objects; and (4) ratio relations, in which numbers reflect ratios among items. Corresponding to these four measurement relations are scales called nominal, ordinal, interval, and ratio scales, respectively. Table 4.1 illustrates these four scales of measurement, the operations one can perform, permissible transformations, appropriate statistics, and a few examples for the use of each scale. The critical issue to remember here is that we are using numbers to represent empirical operations.

The key that defines the type of scale lies in the permissible transformations, the ways in which we can alter the numbers and still represent all the empirical information. Operations permissible for nominal scales are also permissible for ordinal, interval, and ratio scales; operations permissible for ordinal scales are also permissible for internal and ratio scales, and so on. For example, in the nominal scale the transformation rule, substitution of numbers, involves maintaining the identification of the objects. Any direct substitution that preserves identity is permissible. For example, males could be consistently labeled "1" and females "2," or vice versa. The ordinal transformation rule allows any change that preserves the order. Thus, frequencies of 8, 58, and 103 could be relabeled "1," "2," and "3," respectively, because distance between points is not specified in an ordinal scale. The interval transformation rule allows multiplication (or division) by a constant or addition (or subtraction) of a constant, operations which preserve order and identity. For example, if you have an

**TABLE 4.1
Scales of
Measurement**

Scales	Operations Used for	Permissible Transformations	Some Appropriate Statistics	Examples
Nominal	Identify and classify	Substitution of any number for any other number	Number of cases Mode	Numbering football players Sex Psychiatric classification
Ordinal	Establish rank order	Any change that preserves order	Median Percentiles	Preference lists Hardness of minerals Rank order of performance on a course exam
Interval	Find distances or differences	Multiplication or division by a constant Addition or subtraction of a constant	Mean Standard deviation Pearson product-moment correlation	Temperature (Fahrenheit or Celsius) Calendar time Standard scores on achievement tests
Ratio	Find ratios, fractions, or multiples	Multiplication by a constant only	Percent variability	Length, weight, numerosity, duration, and most physical scales Temperature (Kelvin)

Note. *Adapted from* Psychophysics *by S. S. Stevens, 1975, p. 49. Copyright 1975 by John Wiley & Sons, Inc. Reprinted by permission. Adapted from "On the theory of scales of measurement" by S. S. Stevens,* Science, *1946, 103, 677–680. Copyright 1946 by the American Association for the Advancement of Science. Reprinted by permission.*

interval scale composed of the CEEB Scholastic Aptitude Test Scores 450, 490, and 590, you could add 100 to each score without changing the identity, order, or distance relationships among the three scores. The permissible transformation for ratio scales is limited to multiplication by a constant.

Nominal scales   Nominal measurement is nothing more than naming discriminable classes of events. If you ran several rats for one trial each in a T maze and noted whether each rat turned right or left on the first trial, the classification would be nominal because all you would be doing is labeling the response. In the end you would have the number of right turns and the number of left turns. These data are commonly called *frequency data.* Only certain kinds of statistical manipulations can be done on frequency data; chi-square (χ^2) tests are one kind (chapter 17). The nominal level rules specify that the total set of observations must be partitioned into at least two subsets and that all the elements or observations of a subset must be assigned the same symbol (Guilford, 1965).

Ordinal scales   In ordinal scales the observations are rank ordered from most to least on some attribute (Nunnally, 1967). There is no information provided on how far apart the objects are in an ordinal scale. For example, Miss America wins the roses and the crown and she has her jealous first, second, and third runners-up (and Bert Parks), but based on the rank information the runners-up do not know how close they came to winning. The person who records the first, second, and third finishes in an automobile race is using an ordinal level of measurement. An ordinal scale is also a nominal scale, since it is possible to identify a driver uniquely as "the one who finished first." In addition, the smaller the number or ranking, the faster the driver must have been. The ordinal ranking does not, however, tell us how far apart the first and second finishers were.

Interval scales In an interval scale the rank ordering of observations is shown with respect to some attribute, and we know also how far apart from one another the observations or objects are on that attribute. Thus, we can indicate the amount of difference with an interval scale whereas we cannot do so with an ordinal scale. In the automobile race an interval scale would be obtained if the fastest car were given a score of 0, the second fastest car a score of 0 plus the number of seconds between first place and second place, and so forth. Another way to obtain an interval measure would be to record the average time for all cars that finish, and then subtract the average from each car's time. That way a car that was 20 sec slower than the average would receive a score of +20 (20 sec longer to finish), while a car finishing 15 sec faster than the average would receive a score of −15 (15 sec earlier). Note that there is no necessary reference to a zero point or starting time, and an average "running time" can be determined from many arbitrary starting points, such as the approximate midpoint of the race.

With an interval scale we do not know the absolute magnitude of a particular observation. That is, we do not know with scores such as +20 and −15 the actual time-to-finish of an individual car. All we know is the relative distance or difference between cars. An interval scale is also called an *equal interval scale,* since the basic units or intervals on the scale are equal. In the car race example, the difference between scores of +20 and +25 is the same as the difference between +5 and +10 (25 − 20 = 10 − 5).

Another example of an interval scale is provided when we measure scholastic achievement using a nationally administered achievement test and express individual scores in terms of the difference from the national average for a given grade level. The student who earns a score of +10 achieved 10 more correct answers than the national average. Three other students who got scores of +20, −10, and −20 can be compared with the +10 student. The student with a +20 score is not "twice as smart" as the +10 student; the +20 student only scored 10 points better. The difference between +20 and +10 is the same as the difference between −20 and −10 (10 points or 10 correct answers).

Ratio scales A ratio scale has all the properties of the other three scales plus one other: it has an *absolute zero point.* That is, (1) different numbers represent different things; (2) there is a rank order on some attribute being measured; (3) the distance between observation units is known; and (4) the distance from some absolute zero point is known. In the car race example, if the starting time is known, one can use the running time to provide comparisons between cars. In a ratio scale, a car moving at 60 kmph is going twice as fast as a car going 30 kmph. It is obvious that the ratio scale of measurement provides more information about the cars' performance than does an interval or ordinal scale. Another example of a ratio scale is provided by the number of errors on a learning task. If you count number of errors, then "no errors" is a nonarbitrary, real zero point (you cannot have fewer than zero errors). Similarly, 20 errors is twice as many as 10 errors, and 20 errors is four times as many as 5 errors. However, on an ability test it is unlikely that a person with a score of zero errors has the maximum possible amount of the ability tested. Thus, it is unlikely that the set of test scores as a psychological measurement scale forms a ratio scale.

The order of presentation of scales from nominal to ratio might seem to imply that ratio scales are the best scales. Such is not the case. The various levels of measurement are merely different; what is best depends on the theory, research question, research context, and behaviors involved.

The Importance of Measurement Scales

You cannot make ordinal statements about nominal data. That is, you can label a bunch of things A or B, but you cannot say anything about one set being better than the other. The numbers on football players' jerseys label them according to position. Quarterbacks are numbered from 1 to 19, flankers are numbered in the 20's, fullbacks in the 30's, and so on. Experience tells us that backs are faster than defensive linemen, but we can't tell that from the numbers on the jerseys. It would take another indicator on the jersey to tell us about the player's speed; and then we would no longer have a nominal scale.

The rules of measurement protect researchers from saying more about data than is safe. For example, according to Table 4.1, in order to maintain a ratio scale we are allowed only one kind of transformation of the data. We can multiply by a constant only. For example, the United States of America is planning to switch from the English system of measurement to the metric system. The conversion will maintain the integrity of the ratio scales involved. That is, we can multiply by a constant (2.54) to change inches to centimeters [(2.54) (number of inches) = number of centimeters]. (Dividing is permissible because division is the same as multiplying by a constant equal to or less than one; that is, dividing 10 by 2 is the same as multiplying 10 by .5.) Both inch and centimeter measures of length provide ratio scales. Any transformation other than multiplication by a constant would stretch and distort the picture the original ratio scale served to portray (Stevens, 1975).

One final example is appropriate. Notice in Table 4.1 that both Fahrenheit and Celsius (centigrade) temperature scales are listed as interval scales. Suppose that you were in Anchorage, Alaska, and flew nonstop to Stockton, California. When you took off in Alaska, the temperature was 10°C. When you landed in Stockton, the temperature was 20°C. Was it twice as hot in Stockton as it was in Anchorage? No, because Celsius temperature is an interval scale, and the statement "twice as hot" is a ratio scale statement.

THE BASIC KINDS OF DATA

When all the smoke clears and the dust settles, there are only three major kinds of data. They are: (1) frequency data, (2) intensity data, and (3) duration data. Each kind of data is gathered by answering the question, "How much?" The question is converted to "How many?" by converting all continuous variables to discrete units.

Frequency Data

**Frequency
Distribution**

Whenever an experimenter is counting discrete events or objects there is an automatic accumulation called a frequency distribution. A **frequency distribution** illustrates the number of observations falling into each category (chapter 5). The data recording can be as simple as marking down whether a rat turned right or left in a T maze, or as difficult as deciding whether a brain-wave pattern is an "alpha wave" or a "beta wave." Frequency data are discrete and can be placed in a table or on a graph so that conclusions may be made by visual inspection.

The act of partitioning groups of people, objects, or events into various categories for counting is the foundation of data description and analysis. The most important consideration in obtaining frequency data is to arrange the categories of data to answer research questions adequately. Suppose we have a hypothesis that states, "Blonds have more fun." To test the hypothesis we must first operationally define what we mean by "blond" and then what we mean by "fun." Then to answer the question you might set up a four-class table before collecting the data (Table 4.2). If the operational definitions are clear, filling in the frequencies should be easy.

**Categorization
Rules**

The categories should satisfy the following rules:

(1) The categories should be appropriate to the research problem and purpose.
(2) The categories should be exhaustive. Each observation should fit into a category and all categories should account for all observations.
(3) The categories should be mutually exclusive and *independent*. That is, every observation or measure must be assigned to one cell and one cell only and its assignment to that cell must in no way affect the assignment of any other observation to that cell or any other cell.
(4) Each category should be derived from only one classification principle. You must not involve more than one attribute in a simple two-category classification. The category "blond and female" in Table 4.3 mixes hair color and sex, violating this rule.

In order to avoid violating Rule 4 for the data in Table 4.3, you could create two 2 × 2 tables, one for males and one for females; otherwise the data could be very confusing. Nominal, ordinal, interval, or ratio data can be cast into a frequency table but you must take care not to draw conclusions beyond the information contained in the scale of measurement.

Intensity Data

Intensity data are usually continuous data representing measures of a variable's strength. In all cases intensity data are converted into discrete units for purposes of analysis. The four rules for frequency data must be satisfied for intensity data also.

TABLE 4.2 An Example of a Four-Class (2 × 2) Data Table

	Having Fun	Not Having Fun
Blond	A FREQUENCIES	B
Other	C	D

TABLE 4.3   An Incorrect, Mixed-Attribute Classification System

	Having Fun	Not Having Fun
Blond and Female	A *FREQUENCIES*	B
Other	C	D

Examples of intensity data are measures of brightness (light), measures of loudness (sound), measures of effort to overcome a barrier (a rat crossing an electric grid to get to a goal), measures of physical strength (squeezing a grip dynamometer), psycho-physiological measures of voltage levels or potentials (brain waves and muscle potentials), and measures of temperature (changes in skin surface temperature). Intensity measures provide ratio scales. *ratio scale* *skin temp reading-int scale*

Clear, well-thought-out operational definitions aid the conversion of continuous intensity data to discrete data. For example, suppose you want to train a person in shoulder relaxation. An electromyograph may be used to measure muscle tension, and relaxation may be operationally defined as any measure below 10 microvolts (μV). You place an electrode on the subject's skin at the muscle site and take a series of measurements (Fig. 4.1). Even though the muscle voltage is continuously changing, by defining "relaxation" as any measure below 10 μV, you can convert to a discrete measure. Each time the voltage drops below the criterion, one "relaxation" event is counted, contributing to a frequency distribution.

Duration Data — *Time*

Obviously, duration data are measured in terms of time. Although time is considered a continuous variable, it is converted into discrete bundles for processing.

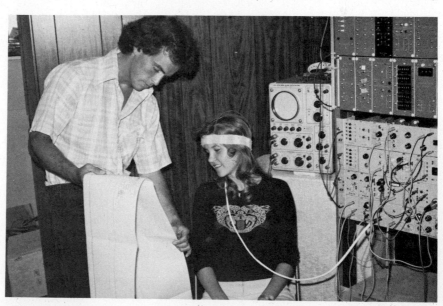

FIG. 4.1
Electromyographic and electroencephalographic measures can be recorded as continuous data or converted into digital, frequency data. The polygraph record that the experimenter is holding provides a continuous record of responses over time. (Photograph by D. W. Matheson.)

Duration measures form a ratio measurement scale and are a favorite choice of experimental psychologists. Stopwatches, digital timers, and counters divided by a time base are all used to measure duration.

CHOOSING A MEASUREMENT PROCEDURE

As we showed in chapter 1, a number of coordinating, operational definitions are possible for any conceptual hypothesis. Different operational definitions may eventually lead to different research conclusions. This fact applies to the operational definition of dependent variables, and therefore to the choice of a dependent measurement scale. For example, in chapter 2, part of Baron's study of the effect of induced incompatible emotional responses on human aggressive behavior was briefly described (pp. 21–23). The proportion of each treatment group that engaged in horn-honking behavior was presented in Table 2.1. In this case the operational definition of aggressive behavior provided frequency data converted to proportions by dividing each group's frequency by the size of the group. The experimenters also employed a duration measure of aggression. This measure, "latency of horn-honking," was operationally defined as the interval between the moment when the traffic light turned green and the subject's first honk. The proportion measure formed a nominal scale, and the latency measure formed a ratio scale.

The conclusions from the duration data were generally similar to but not identical with the conclusions from the frequency data. In the approximate-frequency data the two control-group proportions were identical; the three emotional-arousal group proportions were much lower and lay close to one another. In the "latency-of-horn-honking" data, the no-distraction control group (average = 7 sec) honked sooner than the empathy group (average = 11 sec), the humor group (average = 12 sec), and the sexual-arousal group (average = 12 sec). On the average, the distraction-control group (average = 8 sec) was a little slower to begin honking than the other control group; the empathy group was slightly faster than the other two incompatible-emotion groups. The duration data did not lead to as clear and simple an interpretation as the frequency data did.

In summary, the type of measurement observations you make in a psychology experiment determines the scale of measurement, the kinds of data analysis possible, and the scope of the conclusions you can make about your data. In many cases the choice of measurement procedure is dictated by the research question, the available equipment, and other factors. However, it is important that you carefully consider the limitations and advantages of each kind of measurement procedure before you start your experiment.

SUMMARY

1. Measurement is the assignment of symbols to objects, organisms, or events according to a set of rules. The rules are usually part of a standard mathematical number system.
2. Complex problems can be resolved by reducing them to sets of simpler problems or by reducing them to problems that already have been solved.

3. An attribute is any specific feature of a person, object, or event. We measure attributes of a person, object, or event; we don't measure the person, object, or event itself.

4. Single-dimension attributes are variables. An attribute may have more than one dimension, each of which is a variable.

5. Each unit of a discrete variable or attribute is distinctly different from every other unit. In contrast, continuous variables or attributes do not have periodic, defined units. Rather, continuous variables exist in a smooth, uninterrupted progression of values.

6. Changing a continuous variable to a discrete measure is called analog-to-digital conversion.

7. Scales of measurement consist of a mathematical number system identified with an operationally defined, empirical measurement process.

8. Nominal scales consist of persons, objects, or events categorized into discrete named classes. Ordinal scales are nominal scales with the classes placed in sequence or rank order. Interval scales are ordinal scales with information on the distance between ranks. Ratio scales are interval scales with absolute, nonarbitrary zero points.

9. The three major categories of data are (1) frequency data (counts of discrete variables), (2) intensity data (continuous measures of strength), and (3) duration data (continuous measures of time). Because continuous variables are converted to discrete approximations, each form of data consists of counts of discrete units.

10. Research measurement operations determine the scale of measurement, the kinds of data analysis possible, and the scope of possible conclusions.

SUGGESTED READINGS

Anderson, N. H. Scales and statistics, parametric and nonparametric. *Psychological Bulletin,* 1961, *58*, 305–316.

Guilford, J. P., & Fruchter, B. *Fundamental statistics in psychology and education* (5th ed.). New York: McGraw-Hill, 1973.

Kerlinger, F. N. *Foundations of behavioral research* (2nd ed.). New York: Holt, Rinehart and Winston, 1973.

Kershner, R. B., & Wilcox, L. R. *The anatomy of mathematics.* New York: Ronald Press, 1950.

Nunnally, J. C. *Psychometric theory.* New York: McGraw-Hill, 1967.

Stevens, S. S. On the theory of scales of measurement. *Science,* 1946, 103, 677–680.

Stevens, S. S. *Psychophysics.* New York: Wiley, 1975.

5

Presenting the Data: Summaries and Graphs

The research process yields data, and deciding what to do with the data often presents a problem. Often summarizing your data in a chart or graph makes it easier to understand what has happened in your experiment. This chapter tells you how to handle masses of data in the most efficient way.

Even before you select the first subject for your psychology experiment you should answer the question, "How will I present the data so that others understand what happened in the experiment?" The question may seem premature and unimportant, because we seldom worry about graphs—some of us worry so little about them that we don't read them when they are presented in research articles. Of course that is a mistake, because graphs generally summarize and represent a collection of *raw data,* the dependent measures recorded from the experiment. The form into which the raw data will be cast may affect the manner in which you gather them.

FREQUENCY TABLES

Suppose you are a fan of the popular TV series *Star Trek,* and you wish to know who the more popular character in the show is, Captain James Kirk or Lieutenant Commander Spock. Before you start the experiment you devise Table 5.1, on which you will record the data.

You realized before collecting the data that a simple recording of the choices would constitute measurement at the nominal level, so the table would be little more than a list. Now if you count the number of responses by male respondents you see that $N = 7$ for Spock and $N = 3$ for Kirk, while for female respondents $N = 7$ for Kirk ($N = 3$ for Spock). When one counts in this fashion an ordinal-level scale of measurement is derived, and certain comparisons may be made. For example, look at Table 5.2.

TABLE 5.1 Responses of 20 College Students to the Question, "Which Character Do You Prefer on the TV Show *Star Trek,* Capt. James Kirk or Lt. Spock?"

Male	Female
Spock	Kirk
Spock	Spock
Kirk	Kirk
Spock	Spock
Kirk	Spock
Spock	Kirk
Spock	Kirk
Spock	Kirk
Spock	Kirk
Kirk	Kirk

TABLE 5.2   Frequency Table (Matrix) of Responses of Males and Females to the Question, "Which Character Do You Prefer on the TV Show *Star Trek,* Capt. James Kirk or Lt. Spock?"

	Male	Female
Spock	7	3
Kirk	3	7

2 × 2 Matrix

This type of table is called a **2 × 2 matrix,** because it consists of two rows and two columns. Here the columns denote the sex of the subjects and the rows indicate their preference. The number in each cell of the matrix represents the frequency of occurence of that event.

A frequency table may be made up with any size of matrix, as long as the categories along any dimension are arranged so that each score can be located in one appropriate cell without ambiguity. Frequency tables are preferred to lists because they convey information more efficiently and briefly.

ORDERED LISTS

Some raw scores are more meaningful, however, when they are arranged in an ordered list. When the data are ordinal, comparisons can be made among them. Table 5.3 lists data recorded from a parapsychology experiment. Two people in Los Angeles who were supposed to be highly sensitive telepathists were each asked to flip at random through a deck of 52 cards twice, sending telepathically the name of each card, at the rate of one card every 30 seconds. The two sent the messages at separate times. Meanwhile 52 people in New York City, acting as receivers, recorded their thought-impressions every 30 seconds. The researchers in charge of the experiment knew the order of the card names and the number of correct "hits" by the receivers. The number of hits for each receiver out of 208 trials is illustrated in Table 5.3.

The receivers' scores have been ordered in Table 5.3 from highest to lowest. The ordered list immediately provides information on the range of scores involved and on gaps in the data.

FREQUENCY DISTRIBUTIONS

An ordered list is inappropriate and cumbersome for large masses of data. Rather than listing each score, a procedure has been developed to summarize the main features of the data. A *frequency distribution* shows the number of cases falling within each class interval or range of scores. To summarize the scores from the telepathy experiment, the number scores usually would be divided into 10–15 *class intervals.* Class intervals are arbitrary divisions of data into groups of scores. When the data are integers (whole numbers) the intervals are described in integers. For example, suppose we want 10 intervals from the ordered list in Table 5.3. The scores from 1 to 49 can be divided into 10 equal intervals by assigning the scores that fall into the interval 1–5 to the first interval, the scores that fall into the interval 6–10 to the next interval, and so forth until

TABLE 5.3						
Ordered Scores	49	34	29	25	21	12
from 52 Receivers	44	33	29	24	19	11
in a Telepathy	43	33	28	24	18	10
Experiment	40	33	28	23	17	9
	39	32	27	23	17	7
	39	31	26	23	16	5
	38	30	26	22	15	1
	37	29	26	22	14	
	36	29	25	21	13	

Note. *Highest possible score = 104.*

all scores have been assigned to class intervals of 5. The intervals are 1–5, 6–10, . . . , 46–50. The scores then can be tallied and summed for each interval (Table 5.4).

The first interval, 1–5, has an apparent upper limit of 5, and the next interval, 6–10, has an apparent lower limit of 6. The *apparent* limits of a class interval are the highest and lowest scores of the interval. The *real* limits of a class interval are defined as one-half of the smallest measurement unit above the highest score and one-half of the unit below the lowest score. The distinction between the apparent and real limits is illustrated in Figure 5.1. The apparent width of the interval 21–25 is 4 $(25 - 21 = 4)$. The real width of the interval is 5 $(25.5 - 20.5 = 5)$.

It is convenient to have a real class-interval width that is an odd number. Such real widths guarantee that the midpoint will be an integer. In our example the real interval $20.5 - 25.5$ is five units in width with a midpoint of 23. We make the assumption that the midpoint of an interval is the best *single value* to represent all the values of that interval. Note also that a real zero point exists in the frequency distribution, so it is a ratio scale. From a frequency distribution it is easy to construct a graph.

GRAPHICAL PRESENTATION

Histograms

A histogram or bar graph is probably the easiest way to present data graphically. The X axis represents the midpoints of class intervals and the Y axis represents frequency. A histogram derived from the data in Table 5.3 is shown in Figure 5.2.

TABLE 5.4				
Frequency	Class Intervals	Tally Marks	Frequency (f)	Midpoint of Each Interval
Distribution of the	46–50	I	•1	48
Data Shown in	41–15	II	2	43
Table 5.3	36–40	₩ I	6	38
	31–35	₩ I	6	33
	26–30	₩ ₩ I	11	28
	21–25	₩ ₩ I	11	23
	16–20	₩	5	18
	11–15	₩	5	13
	6–10	III	3	8
	1–5	II	2	3

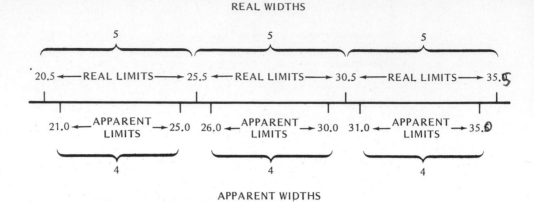

REAL WIDTHS

APPARENT WIDTHS

FIG. 5.1
An illustration of the relationship between real and apparent class-interval limits.

The central tendency of the distribution is easily seen in Figure 5.2: The scores tend to pile up in the middle of the distribution. (Central-tendency statistics will be discussed later in the chapter.) The height of each bar represents the frequency of the scores in that interval, and the width represents the real width of each class. Since the edges of each bar are determined by real limits, there are no gaps between adjacent bars. Instead of frequencies, percentages may be labeled on the Y axis by dividing the frequency in each bar by the total frequency of all of the bars. For example, interval 1 –5 = 2 out of 52, or 3.8%.

Histograms
or bar graph

Histograms can be used deceitfully. If the bars change widths as well as heights while representing a single factor such as frequency or percentage of a measure of behavior, they can easily be misleading. Also, if the ordinate does not begin at zero, then the meaning of the relative heights of the bars is difficult to determine. The use of such tactics to deceive the reader is described amusingly by Huff (1954).

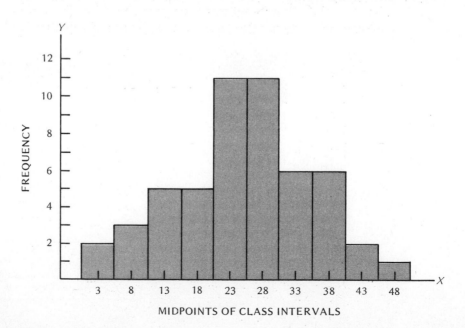

FIG. 5.2
Histogram of the data from Table 5.3. The real limits of each class interval determine the edges of each bar.

Frequency Polygons

Frequency Polygon

A frequency polygon is another method of portraying data graphically. The axes are labeled as in the histogram: The midpoint scores are plotted on the X axis and frequency or percentage scores are plotted on the Y axis. A frequency polygon of the data in Table 5.4 is shown in Figure 5.3. The midpoints of adjacent bars are connected by a solid line.

A frequency polygon indicates the general shape of a distribution. In many psychological experiments, it is important to compare the data with a hypothetical distribution called the "normal distribution" or "bell-shaped curve." A normal curve is a theoretical distribution of a very large amount of data. A major feature of the normal distribution is that it is symmetrical; that is, there are an equal number of both high and low scores in the distribution. By drawing a frequency polygon, we can estimate whether data tend to be normally distributed or skewed. By *skewed* we mean that there are more scores on one end of the distribution than on the other (see Figures 5.4 and 5.5).

Skewed Distribution

DESCRIPTIVE STATISTICS

Let us return to the frequency polygon in Figure 5.3. As mentioned earlier, if a distribution is symmetrical as in a normal distribution, there are an equal number of scores above and below the middle. A psychologist would be interested in knowing whether there are an equal number of scores above and below the central part of the distribution. Not all distributions are symmetrical; in fact, most are not.

After measuring the dependent variable, the data must be arranged in a way that shows their meaning. If the number of observations is small, the individual data points may be presented best in tabular form or in graphical form. As the number of data points increases these presentations become unwieldy. For example, data from a large sample, such as the United States census, are overwhelming without some kind of

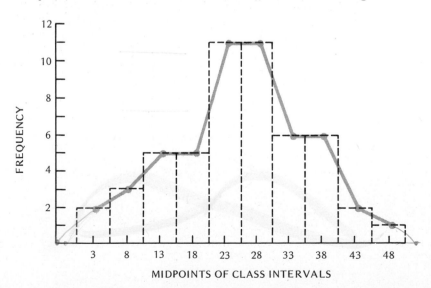

FIG. 5.3
A frequency polygon of data from Table 5.4

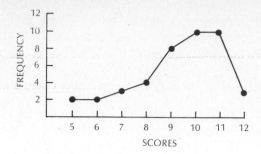

FIG. 5.4
Frequency polygon skewed left or negatively. While most of the scores are clustered at the right, a few stragglers "pull" the curve toward the left.

shorthand method of describing their essential features. We will examine three common types of descriptive statistical measures: measures of central tendency, measures of variability, and measures of individual comparison. Slope, a measure of relationship, is discussed at the end of this chapter.

Measures of Central Tendency

An easily understood method of summarizing many scores is to report the value of a "typical" score. In most frequency distributions, there is a tendency for the scores to cluster around the middle values of the distribution rather than at either end. A value that would be most representative of all of the measurements would be most likely to come from the central part of the distribution. *Measures of central tendency* describe the most typical values of the distribution of scores.

Measures of Variability

Measures of central tendency vary in their descriptive value according to the amount of variation or scatter in the summarized scores. It is quite possible to have two distributions with the same typical score differ greatly because one set of scores clusters tightly together, while the other is widely scattered. *Measures of variability* describe the dispersion or variation in the scores. When used appropriately, a measure of central tendency and a measure of variability together summarize the major features of a large sample distribution.

Measures of Individual Position

In certain situations we need to compare the performance of two individuals on some measure or compare an individual's performance with that of the group. For example, as Blommers and Lindquist (1960) state, "a single score such as is derived from most educational and psychological tests has little, if any absolute significance— that is, it is not capable of meaningful interpretation when considered alone" (p. 67). *Measures of individual position* are used in comparing the performance of an individual with other performances.

All the descriptive statistics mentioned above involve a group of scores collected along a single variable. In other words, we have been concerned with a single

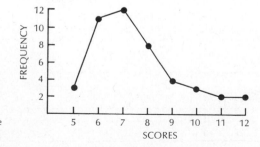

FIG. 5.5
Frequency polygon skewed right or positively. While most of the scores are clustered at the left, a few stragglers "pull" the curve toward the right.

distribution. Occasionally we are concerned with the relationship between two differ-ent distributions. We may decide that grade-point average (GPA) is related to hours spent in the library. We then measure each variable for a large number of students; the resulting pairs of GPAs and hours represent the observed relationship. The relation-ship can be numerically summarized by a single number called a *measure of relation-ship* or correlation.

Measure of Relationship

Measures of Central Tendency

There are three basic measures of central tendency: the mode, median, and mean.

Mode   A mode (Mo) of a frequency distribution of scores is a score with a frequency that is the largest compared to neighboring scores. Suppose that a test is given to a 20-student experimental psychology class. The resulting scores on the hypothetical test are presented in Table 5.5. The mode for the distribution in Table 5.5 is 17, since that is the score with the highest frequency.

Occasionally, there will be two points in a frequency distribution where the frequencies are relatively large. In such cases, there will be two modes (a bimodal distribution). The two modes need not have the same frequency. It is also possible to have more than two modes in a distribution. For example, the results of the test might have been distributed as in Table 5.6, in which case the three modes would be 13, 16, and 20.

Bimodal Distribution

Trimodal Distribution

Although a mode is simple to calculate, there are several limitations to using it as a measure of central tendency. First, in the case of multimodal distributions, the determination of which high-frequency points are modes is somewhat arbitrary. Second, the mode is more sensitive to *sampling fluctuations* than is any other measure of central tendency. If the psychology test were repeated, we might obtain a different mode or modes. Third, when the frequency distribution is grouped, the use of different class intervals may lead to different modes for the same data. As a conse-quence of these limitations, the mode is seldom used in psychology as a measure of central tendency.

Median   The median (Mdn) of a distribution is defined as the midpoint (50% point) of that distribution. Half the scores are greater and half are less than the median. For a frequency distribution, the median may be determined by arranging the scores in order and determining the value of the middle score for an odd number of subjects, or the value that lies midway between the two middle scores for an even number of

TABLE 5.5   Tabular Presentation of a Hypothetical Frequency Distribution

Scores (number correct)	11	12	13	14	15	16	17	18	19	20
Frequency (numbers of students)	0	0	0	2	4	4	5	3	2	0

TABLE 5.6   Tabular Presentation of a Trimodal Distribution

Scores	11	12	13	14	15	16	17	18	19	20
Frequency	1	0	5	0	0	4	1	1	2	6

TABLE 5.7   Hypothetical Frequency Distribution with Ties

Scores	3	4	5	6	7	8	9	10	11	12
Frequency	1	2	3	2	3	3	3	2	3	2

subjects.[1] In Tables 5.5 and 5.6, both medians are 16.5 (the midpoint between 16 and 17).

In some distributions, there are tied scores around the midpoint (Table 5.7). In such a case, the calculation of the median requires the use of the arbitrary rule that the discrete value of a single score represents the midpoint of an interval of length 1 unit. For example, the score value 8 represents the midpoint of the interval with real limits of 7.5 to 8.5. In the example presented in Table 5.7, the midpoint of the distribution lies somewhere in the interval between 7.5 and 8.5, since there are eleven scores below 8 and ten above. Since the median is defined as the midpoint, we could decide that the median is 8.0. However, such a conclusion conflicts with the above definition, since the frequencies above and below the score of 8 are not equal. In order to reduce the discrepancy, we decide that the value of the median is really 7.83. We obtained this figure by dividing the interval 7.5–8.5 into thirds. Three people received a score of 8, each accounting for one-third of the interval (Figure 5.6). By counting one of the scores as below the median and the other two as above, we meet the criterion of 12 scores above and 12 scores below the median. The median is therefore located one-third of the way into the interval (7.5 + 1/3 = 7.83). Calculation of the median is usually not so complicated.

Advantages of Median

The median is less subject to sampling fluctuation than the mode. Also, the median is not affected by the values of the scores at either end of the distribution. For example, two distributions might have equal medians when the lowest score is 11 in one distribution and 14 in the other (see Tables 5.5 and 5.6).

Limitations of Median

There are three disadvantages of the median as a measure of central tendency. First, the calculation of the median in the case of grouped or tied distributions is complicated and can be confusing. Second, two quite dissimilar distributions can have equal medians, which may lead to erroneous conclusions. Third, the median, as an ordinal statistic, does not allow algebraic manipulation. For example, if we determined the medians for two distributions and combined the data into a single distribution, we could not calculate the median of the new distribution by averaging the medians of the original two.

[1]See McNemar (1969, p. 15) for the procedure used in calculating the median for grouped distributions.

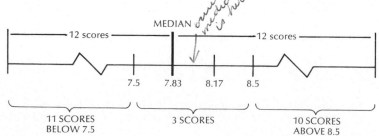

FIG. 5.6
Determination of the median for the distribution presented in Table 5.7. The three scores between 7.5 and 8.5 each occupy one-third of the interval.

Mean   The *arithmetic mean,* $\overline{Y}$, of a distribution is equivalent to what is commonly called the "average." The arithmetic mean is defined as the algebraic sum of the scores divided by the number of scores. If there are any negative scores, the negative signs are taken into account when the scores are added together. Symbolically,

$$\overline{Y} = \frac{\Sigma Y}{N} \tag{5.1}$$

where Y equals each individual score value, N equals the total number of scores, and Σ (the summation sign) indicates that all N scores must be added together. (The rules for handling summation signs are contained in Appendix A.) To calculate the mean of the scores in Table 5.5, add the 20 scores to yield a sum of 329 and divide the sum by 20 to yield a mean of 16.45. Unlike the median and mode, the value of the mean depends on the value of every score in the distribution.

The definition of the mean has a number of important implications. First, if a constant amount is added to each of the scores in a distribution, the mean of this new distribution is equal to the original mean plus the added constant. If each of the scores is multiplied by a constant, the mean of the new distribution is equal to the mean of the original distribution multiplied by that constant. If a set of subgroups each contains the same number of scores, then the mean of the combined subgroups is equal to the mean of the subgroup means. Finally, if we subtract the mean from each score in the distribution, we obtain a set of differences whose sum is zero.

Another advantage of the mean is that for approximately normal distributions, it is the measure of central tendency least subject to sampling fluctuations. The mean is the most frequently used measure of central tendency in psychology. Often two or more means from different groups are compared.

When you have an extremely skewed distribution, the median is preferred to the mean, because the value of the mean is affected by extreme scores. Table 5.8 provides a comparison of the three measures for three sets of scores.

Advantages of Mean *(margin note)*

Measures of Variability

Measures of variability describe the dispersion or variation in a group of scores. Such measures include range, variance, and standard deviation.

Range *(margin note)*

Range   The range (R) is the crudest measure of variability. It is defined as the difference between the smallest and largest scores in a distribution:

$$R = Y_H - Y_L \tag{5.2}$$

where Y_H is the upper real limit and Y_L is the lower real limit. For example, in Table 5.9, $R = 19.5 - 13.5 = 6$. The range is determined by only two points in the distribution. The main advantage of this measure is simplicity of calculation; however, R is a weak measure that tells us only the maximum possible difference between the scores in a distribution.

TABLE 5.8
Measures of
Central Tendency
for Hypothetical
Data

		Measures	
Data	Mode	Median	Mean
Table 5.5	17	16.5	16.45
Table 5.6	13, 16, 20	16.5	16.65
Table 5.7	None	7.33	7.79

Variance

Variance   The variance (S^2) provides another measure of dispersion. It is defined as the average squared deviation from the sample mean. Each score is subtracted from the mean, the difference (deviation) is squared, the squared differences are summed, and the total is divided by the number of scores. The formula for the variance is derived from the definition:[2]

$$S^2 = \frac{\Sigma Y^2 - \frac{(\Sigma Y)^2}{N}}{N - 1} \qquad (5.3)$$

The data in Table 5.5 are reorganized in Table 5.9 to facilitate the calculation of variance. Using these data, the calculation consists of seven steps:

1. Sum all the scores: $(\Sigma Y) = 329$.
2. Square the sum of the scores: $(\Sigma Y)^2 = (329)^2 = 108{,}241$.
3. Divide $(\Sigma Y)^2$ by N: $108{,}241 \div 20 = 5{,}412.05$.
4. Square each of the individual scores (Y^2): $14^2 = 196$; $15^2 = 225$; ... $19^2 = 361$.
5. Sum the squared scores: $\Sigma Y^2 = 196 + 196 + 225 + \cdots 361 = 5{,}455$.
6. Subtract $(\Sigma Y)^2/N$ from ΣY^2: $5{,}455 - 5{,}412.05 = 42.95$.
7. Divide $\Sigma Y^2 - [(\Sigma Y)^2/N]$ by $N - 1$: $S^2 = 42.95/19 = 2.26$.

[2]The denominator of Equation 5.3 uses $N - 1$ rather than N. We use $N - 1$ because when we sample from a population, the extreme values in the population are not likely to be included in the sample. Using $N - 1$ corrects for this restricted sampling effect, yielding an *unbiased estimate* of the variance. The biased variance equation involves division by N rather than $N - 1$. We are presenting only the unbiased version used in inferential statistics (chapter 15) because of the rare use of the biased version for purely descriptive purposes and the common use of the unbiased version as a population parameter estimate.

TABLE 5.9
Frequency
Distribution from
Table 5.5
Organized for the
Calculation of S^2

Scores (Y)	Frequency (f)	fY	Y²	fY²
14	2	28	196	392
15	4	60	225	900
16	4	64	256	1024
17	5	85	289	1445
18	3	54	324	972
19	2	38	361	722
Sums:	N = 20	ΣY = 329		ΣY² = 5,455

Since the variance is an algebraic quantity (as is the mean), the variance of the combination of two distributions can be determined by averaging the variance of both.[3] Also, adding or subtracting a constant amount from each score in the sample does not change the value of S^2, and when each score is multiplied or divided by a positive constant (C), the new variance is equal to C^2S^2 or S^2/C^2, respectively. The variance is the major statistic used in inferential statistics and the most frequently used measure of variability.

A disadvantage of the variance is that its value is not expressed in the same unit of measurement as the set of scores. For example, if the measurement unit of the set of scores is errors, then the value of the variance is expressed in "square errors," which is meaningless.

Standard deviation   In order to have a measure that is expressed in the units of the sample distribution, the square root of the variance is computed. The standard deviation (S) is defined as the square root of the variance ($S = \sqrt{S^2}$). While the most frequently used measure of variability is the variance, the standard deviation is used more often for purely descriptive purposes. Table 5.10 compares all three measures for three sets of scores.

When descriptive statistics are used to characterize a distribution, both a measure of central tendency and the corresponding measure of variation are presented. Consequently, the median and the range, and the mean and standard deviation are usually presented together. Given these two distribution characteristics, a reader quickly can grasp some of the major features of the distribution. If the sample size is large ($N > 30$) and the data form at least an interval scale of measurement, some precise conclusions can be drawn. Figure 5.8 illustrates the major features of the normal curve in terms of standard deviation units. The normal curve is a theoretical distribution that should result if an infinitely large sample of randomly distributed scores were collected. Therefore the characteristics of the normal curve are only approximated by a finite sample. In many cases, however, the approximation is sufficiently close with samples greater than 30 for the normal curve to be used to interpret the statistics. For example, if we collect examination scores from a class of 400 students and find that the distribution appears normal with a mean score of 84 and a standard deviation of 15, we can conclude that approximately 68% (272 students) scored between 69 and 99 on the exam.

[3]When determining the combined variance of two or more unequal distributions, you must take the number of subjects in each distribution into account; see McNemar (1969; p. 24).

TABLE 5.10
Measures of
Variability for
Hypothetical
Data

Data	Range	Variance	Standard Deviation
		Measures	
Table 5.5	6	2.26	1.5
Table 5.6	10	9.50	3.1
Table 5.7	10	7.13	2.7

Measures of Individual Position

Measures of individual position describe the position of an individual score within the distribution of a group of scores.

Uniqueness   When the scale of measurement is nominal, the corresponding measure of individual position is called uniqueness. For example, the statement that a woman is the only one with a 16-foot alligator in her swimming pool provides information about her uniqueness. Occasionally, the important factor is that the individual position is shared by many other individuals, as when more people choose Brand X than any other brand.

Rank   If we have ordinal measurement and wish to compare the performance of one subject with that of the total sample, we can use the rank of the individual's score. The rank of a score is its location when all the scores are arranged in order of magnitude. The direction of rank ordering must be specified. For example, a score with a rank of six is the sixth highest or sixth lowest score in the distribution.

Percentile rank   Obviously, the meaning of rank value depends on the number of scores in a distribution. A test score with a rank of 6 has a different meaning in a class of 7 students than it does in a class of 50 students. Percentile rank provides more information about the relative position of the individual within the sample. The percentile rank indicates the position of a score in terms of the percentage of the sample that had smaller scores.

In a sample of 10 subjects, a rank of third is the 30th percentile rank. Occasionally, we must use the arbitrary rule we discussed in the computation on the median (p. 74). For example, in determining the percentile rank of the score of 16 in Table 5.5, we observe that 30% of the scores lie below 16 and 50 percent above (6 out of 20 and 10 out of 20 respectively). Therefore, the percentile rank for 16 is 40%, the midpoint between 30% and 50%. The median has the percentile rank of 50% in all distributions.

Standard score   A standard score is a score defined in terms of the mean and standard deviation of the distribution. The most commonly used type of standard score is called the relative deviate or z score. It is defined as the deviation of a score from the sample mean, divided by the standard deviation, or

$$z = \frac{Y - \overline{Y}}{S} \tag{5.4}$$

where Y is an individual score. For example, if $\overline{Y} = 10$ and $S = 2$, a score of 5 would yield a z score of $(5 - 10)/2 = -5/2 = -2.5$.

A z-score distribution has the following properties: (1) the mean of the distribution is zero, (2) the algebraic sum of the z scores is zero, (3) the variance and standard deviation of the distribution are both equal to one, and (4) the sum of the squared z scores equals N (the number of scores).

z Score

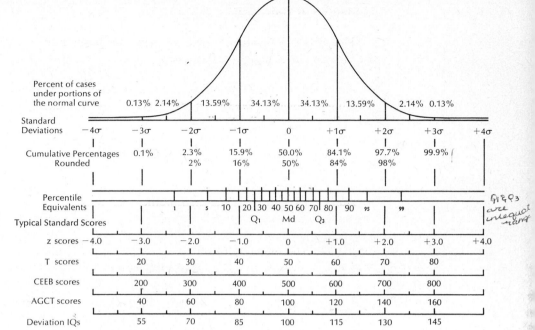

FIG. 5.7
The major characteristics of a normal distribution in terms of standard deviations, percentiles, and selected standard scores. A T score = $10z$ + 50. CEEB stands for College Entrance Examination Board tests. AGCT stands for the Army General Classification Test.

The other standard scores listed in Figure 5.7 are z scores that have been transformed into other numerical values. For example, the IQ measure is a distribution in which $\bar{Y}$ is 100 and S is 15. With this information, if you know your measured IQ is 120 you should be able to conclude that you are within the top 10% of IQ scores.

The z scores are pure or abstract numbers. Abstractness is the chief value of standard scores. Pure numbers can be compared directly. For example, your z score on a test of one ability, such as typing speed, may be compared directly with your z score on a test of another ability, such as spelling accuracy. Positive z scores indicate that you scored above the mean and negative z scores that you scored below.

GRAPHS DEPICTING TWO OR MORE VARIABLES

Measures of Relationship

A histogram and a frequency polygon graphically summarize data along one attribute or dimension of an attribute; they are graphic counterparts to an ordered list and a frequency distribution. Many times, however, it is important to illustrate two variables simultaneously, showing how one varies with the other. In most experimental situations, more than one variable is recorded at a particular time. As different measures are taken, time itself (a variable) changes, and consequently two variables change together or *covary*. A scatterplot is used to illustrate the "relationship" between two or more variables.

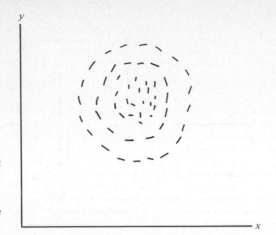

FIG. 5.8
A "scatterplot" of a shot in which no variable (other than the barrel and the distance from the target) influences the data.

Scatterplots

A physical analogy to a scatterplot is the effect of firing a shotgun straight at a large piece of cardboard. If the shotgun is properly designed and built, the shot leaves a fairly circular pattern on the cardboard. This pattern means that no variable, such as a flaw in the barrel of the gun, has affected the trajectories of the shot (see Figure 5.8). If the pattern tends to be elliptical, or have any shape other than circular, it indicates that some variable has influenced the pattern (Figure 5.9). A gun expert looking at the pattern of the shot can deduce what variable or variables influenced it. Now if you labeled axes adjacent to the pattern with the names of the attributes of two variables influencing the shot, you could determine their effect (see Figure 5.8). You would have a crude scatterplot, a graph showing the relationship between two variables, one on the X axis and one on the Y axis.

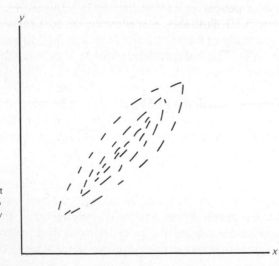

FIG. 5.9
A "scatterplot" of a shot in which X and Y, two variables such as a flaw in the barrel and the shape of the bullet, influence the data.

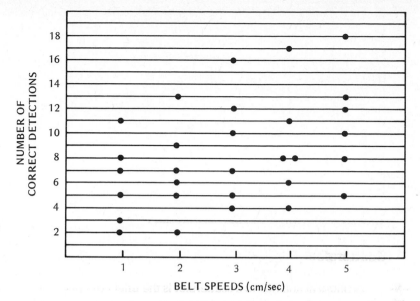

FIG. 5.10
A scatterplot of the data
on a detection of
defective pills for
various belt speeds.
Each dot represents the
score of a single subject.

The tabular analogy to a scatterplot is a frequency table (Table 5.2) in which one variable is represented by the row and the other variable is represented by the columns of the table. By plotting the pairs of scores on a graph, we obtain a visual representation of a relationship. Frequency, percentage, errors, number of correct responses, or any other measure of the dependent variable is usually plotted on the ordinate, and the levels of the independent variable, such as trials, drug level, age, or time are plotted on the abscissa. (There are exceptions to this general arrangement.)

Drug companies hire people to inspect pills on a moving belt and remove the defective ones. Figure 5.10 illustrates a scatterplot of hypothetical data from an industrial psychologist's study of the relationship between belt speed and accuracy of detection of defective pills. The independent variable is belt speed; the dependent variable is the number of correct detections. The position of each dot on the graph precisely locates an ordered pair with respect to the independent and dependent variables. (Ties, two scores having the same value, must be approximated by placing two dots, bracketing their correct position.) The pattern formed by the data points in a scatterplot is the relationship between the independent and dependent variables.

Line Graphs

The relationship between an independent and dependent variable is approximated graphically by a line graph. A line graph uses the average score for each level of the independent variable. Therefore it is a *concise* (rather than *precise*) description of the relationship between two variables. Figure 5.11 shows a line graph derived from

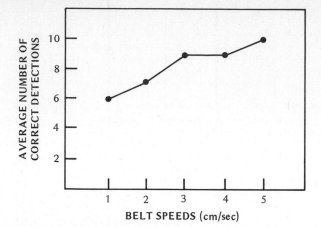

FIG. 5.11
A performance curve derived from the data in Figure 5.10. Each point is the average score of the six subjects in each group.

the scatterplot data in Figure 5.10. Each point on the line represents the average score of one treatment group.

A learning curve frequently shows the *trend* of the average performance of a group across learning trials. Such a line graph is presented in Figure 5.12. The curve starts at the lower left corner and rises to the upper right corner. This figure illustrates a negatively accelerated growth curve. The average number of correct responses increases rapidly for the first few trials, but slows as the number of trials increases. Figure 5.13 shows a negatively accelerated decay curve. It is based on the same data as Figure 5.12, but the dependent variable is the number of *errors* instead of the number of correct responses.

Figure 5.14 illustrates positively accelerating growth (curve *A*) and positively accelerating decay (curve *B*). In positively accelerating curves, the behavior changes slowly at first and then faster as the number of trials increases. The steepest part of a positively accelerated curve is where the greatest rate of change of behavior occurs. It is possible to get various combinations of positive and negative growth and decay

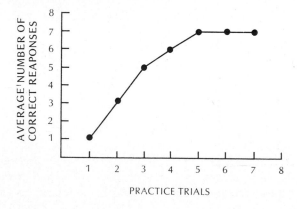

FIG. 5.12
A negatively accelerated growth curve.

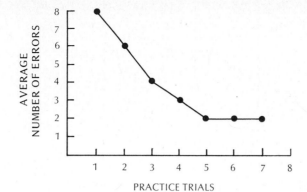

FIG. 5.13
A negatively
accelerated decay
curve.

curves. Some of these curves are called sigmoidal or S-shaped curves. An example is shown in Figure 5.15. The S shape indicates that the measured behavior changes slowly at first, then changes faster, then reaches a high, more stable rate.

When there is a zero line on the ordinate, and both axes of the line graph are in proportion, the line graph provides a very simple, clear picture of the relationship between the independent and dependent variables. However, if you eliminate the zero line by chopping off the bottom of the graph and so expand or contract the *Y* axis relative to the *X* axis, you can imply any relationship you wish. Thus the line graph is capable of deceiving (Huff, 1954). The use of deceptive graphs is mainly encountered in advertising and politics. To quote the old adage: "Statistics don't lie, but liars use statistics." Fortunately, legitimate researchers do not knowingly play such games.

Line graphs are frequently used in behavior-modification studies to indicate the course and results of treatment. For example, Christophersen, Arnold, Hill, and Quillitch (1972) set up a token reinforcement program to be used by parents to modify the problem behavior of their children. The children were required to earn points in order to "buy" basic privileges such as watching television as well as special rewards such as movies or picnics. They earned points by performing typical household chores

**Misuse of Line
Graphs**

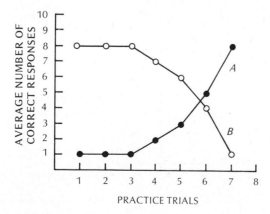

FIG. 5.14
Positively accelerated
curves: *A* shows
positively accelerated
growth; *B* shows decay.

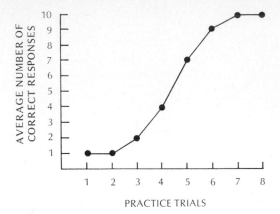

FIG. 5.15
An S-shaped curve.

and lost points for engaging in disruptive, problem behavior, such as bickering or whining. Figure 5.16 is one of 14 graphs presented in the research report. It is obvious that the 10-point fine had a dramatic effect on the girl's jumping on furniture.

Two-Way Interaction

An experiment was performed recently (Matheson, Edelson, Hiatrides, Newkirk, Twinem, & Thurston, 1976) that utilized two independent variables: time and vibrotactile stimulation from a vibrating chair to facilitate muscle relaxation (measured by electromyographic recordings from the forehead). The results of the experiment are shown in Figure 5.17. On the X axis, the first independent variable, time, is presented as B_1 and B_2; the dependent variable (average EMG in microvolts) is presented on the Y axis. Notice, however, that the two lines in the body of the graph intersect (are nonparallel) and that each line represents one level of the second independent variable, vibrotactile stimulation. The line that rises slightly from left to right (A_1) shows the results from the control group. The line that sinks from left to right (A_2) shows the effect of the other level of the independent variable, vibrotactile stimulation. When two levels of one independent variable (vibrotactile stimulation) act differentially on another independent variable (time) the effect is called a *two-way interaction*. The two

FIG. 5.16
Effects of a 10-point fine on the social behavior of an 8-year-old, mildly retarded girl. (Graph from Christerophersen, Arnold, Hill, and Quillitch, *Journal of Applied Behavior Analysis*, 1972, 5, 491. Copyright 1972 by the Society for the Experimental Analysis of Behavior, Inc.)

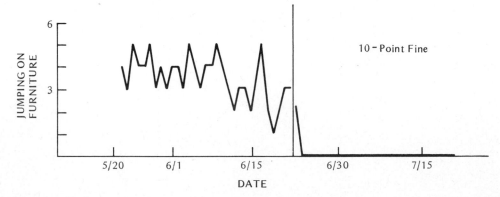

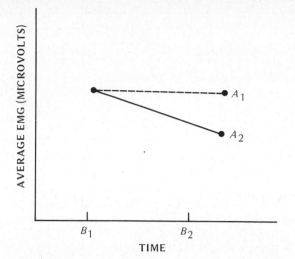

FIG. 5.17
Graph of a two-way interaction. A_1 and A_2 represent different levels of vibrotactile stimulation; a second independent variable interacts with time.

lines represent the effect of one independent variable on another independent variable in terms of the dependent variable. It is important to remember that the dependent variable goes on the Y axis, one independent variable goes on the X axis, and the other independent variable is identified by labeling the two lines in the body of the graph.

Three-Way Interaction

A three-way interaction is represented graphically by four lines (assuming two levels of each variable): two lines for variable B_1, and two for variable B_2, with each pair showing the effects of the two conditions of variable C. Variable A is on the abscissa (Figure 5.18).

Figure 5.18 is a concise but complicated way of showing a three-way interaction. Another way is to show two separate figures in which two independent variables (A

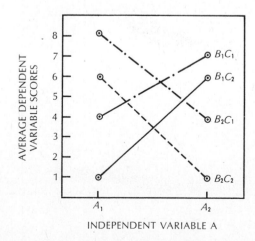

FIG. 5.18
A hypothetical three-variable (ABC) interaction. The ABC interaction is that the effect of variable B depends on the levels of variables C and A. The interaction is indicated by four nonparallel lines.

and B) are illustrated first under one level of the third independent variable (C_1) and then under the second level of the third independent variable (C_2). The two graphs in Figure 5.19 illustrate this alternative. Notice that they conform to the same rules of construction as a two-way interaction: dependent variable on the Y axis, one independent variable on the X axis, and one independent variable in the body of the graph. The only difference is that the third independent variable (C) requires two graphs to show it. If C had three levels, then three graphs would be required, one for C_1, one for C_2, and one for C_3.

We present a hypothetical example to illustrate the interpretation of graphed interactions. Suppose your roommate is a great fisherman. Knowing that you are a student of behavior, he asks you to train some fishing worms to be very active so that they wriggle on the end of a hook to attract fish. You decide that you will study the effects of three independent variables on wriggling: (1) time of day (A_1 is daytime and A_2 is night), (2) the medium in which the worms are stored (B_1 is coffee grounds and B_2 is plain dirt), and (3) stimulation of the worms (C_1 is a mild electric shock and C_2 is no shock). The dependent variable is wriggling for a 10-min period. Figure 5.18 might represent the results of such an experiment if we assume that activity is on the Y axis, time of day on the X axis, and the other two independent variables are identified by the different lines of the graphs. The two graphs in Figure 5.19 present the data from Figure 5.18, partitioned according to the stimulation variable (C). Notice on the left that during daytime hours (A_1) fishing worms are more active in plain dirt (B_2) when given an electric shock (C_1) than when given shock during the evening (A_2). Further, notice that during nighttime hours (A_2) worms are more active in coffee grounds (B_1) with mild shock (C_1) than during the daytime (A_1). There are eight different combinations of these three variables, and these combinations all must be considered when accounting for a triple interaction. What additional findings can you determine from

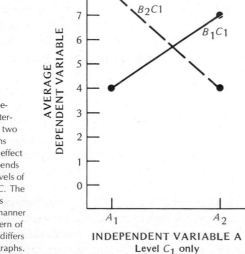
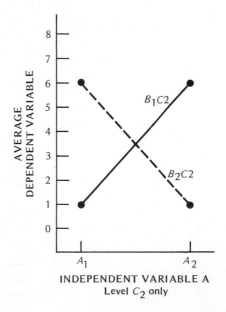

FIG. 5.19
Hypothetical three-variable (ABC) interaction plotted on two graphs. The graphs illustrate that the effect of variable B depends on the different levels of variables A and C. The ABC interaction is indicated by the manner in which the pattern of the crossed lines differs between the two graphs.

Figure 5.19? Remember, the data are simplified, but you should be able to write down how these three independent variables differentially affect the dependent variable measure.

STRAIGHT LINES AND SLOPES

Two sets of ordered pairs, (X_1, Y_1) and (X_2, Y_2), are depicted in Figure 5.20. A line, L, is drawn through the two ordered pairs. In order to determine the slope of line L, a vertical line is dropped from the point (X_2, Y_2) to the X axis, and a horizontal line is drawn through the point (X_1, Y_1) and extended until it intersects the vertical line. The distances ΔY and ΔX are given by the following statements: $\Delta Y = Y_2 - Y_1$ and $\Delta X = X_2 - X_1$. The symbol Δ (delta) indicates the difference between two values of a variable. The ratio of ΔY to ΔX, $\Delta Y/\Delta X = (Y_2-Y_1)/(X_2-X_1)$, is equal to the *slope* (*b*) of the line L. That is, $b = (Y_2-Y_1)/(X_2-X_1)$. The slope indicates how the variable Y changes with respect to X. In behavioral terms, the slope represents the rate at which the dependent variable (behavior) changes with respect to the independent variable (treatment): The steeper the slope, the greater the rate of change in the behavior. The values of X and Y in Figure 5.20 are $X_1 = 4$, $X_2 = 6$, $Y_1 = 2$, $Y_2 = 4$. Therefore $b = (4-2)/(6-4) = 2/2 = 1$. The slope of 1 indicates that 1 unit of increase on the X axis is associated with an increase of 1 unit on the Y axis. If $X_1 = 4$, $X_2 = 6$, $Y_1 = 4$, $Y_2 = 8$, then $b = (8-4)/(6-4) = 4/2 = 2$.

In Figure 5.21, a slope of 2 indicates that the dependent variable measure here is increasing twice as fast as that depicted in Figure 5.20, where the slope is 1. In the two preceding examples, suppose the straight lines represent two different learning curves. The second example with a slope of 2 indicates the rate of learning was twice as fast as in the first case (slope of 1). The slopes just mentioned were all positive; the lines ran from the lower left to the upper right of the graph. A slope may also have a negative sign. A negatively sloped line runs from the upper left to the lower right. An example is shown in Figure 5.22. The ordered pairs are (X_1, Y_1) and (X_2, Y_2). In Figure 5.22, $\Delta Y = Y_2 - Y_1 = 1 - 2 = -1$, and $\Delta X = X_2 - X_1 = 2 - 1 = 1$. The value of $b =$

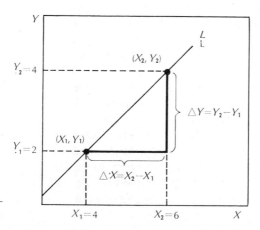

FIG. 5.20
Example of a straight line L with a slope $b = \Delta Y/\Delta X = (Y_2 - Y_1)/(X_2 - X_1) = 1$.

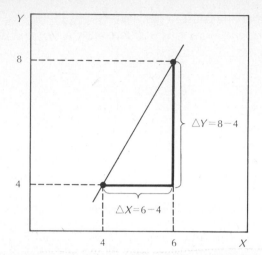

FIG. 5.21
Example of a straight
line with a slope $b = 2$.

$\Delta Y/\Delta X = -1/1 = -1$. The concept of a negative slope is similar to the concept of a negative correlation coefficient (see chapter 21). In both cases, as the value of the independent variable increases, the value of the dependent variable decreases.

Measurement of slopes of lines is important for determining how rapidly one variable changes with respect to another. For example, if you are on a diet, plotting your weight over time and calculating a slope tells you you how fast you are losing weight (negative slope) or gaining (positive slope). The steeper the slope, the more rapidly your weight is changing. Changes with respect to time are commonly analyzed by a slope analysis, assuming that the same units of time are used in each case. Testing the slope of a line against a hypothesis of zero slope is a powerful statistical test of significance.

Slope Analysis

Later in this book, we will discuss various statistical techniques that measure the strength of relationship between two variables. The techniques come under the heading of "correlation coefficients," and "regression." Generally, the strength of

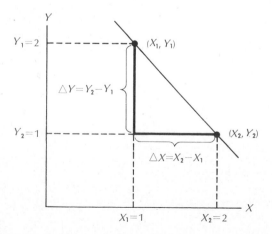

FIG. 5.22
Example of a straight
line with a negative
slope ($b = -1$).

relationship varies with how closely a set of variables fits a straight or curved line. The more closely the variables fit the line, the stronger the relationship. Chapter 21 will provide the details of these techniques.

SUMMARY

1. Raw data may be presented in lists or frequency tables. A frequency table is more economical than a list.
2. Ordered lists or frequency distributions are used with large masses of data. They consist of arbitrary divisions of the data into class intervals.
3. The apparent limits of a class interval are the highest and lowest numbers of the interval. The real limits are one-half of the smallest unit above the highest number and one-half of the unit below the lowest number of the interval. The midpoint of a class interval is assumed to be the most representative score for that interval.
4. A histogram is a graphical presentation of a frequency distribution. A frequency polygon consists of lines connecting the midpoints of the class intervals. Frequency polygons may be skewed or approximately normal in shape. Frequency polygons vary in kurtosis; they may be flat or peaked compared with a normal curve.
5. The relationship between two measures may be displayed in a scatterplot. Usually, the dependent variable is plotted on the Y axis and the independent variable is plotted on the X axis.
6. In addition to measures of relationship, measures of central tendency, measures of variability, and measures of individual position describe masses of data. The mean, median, and mode are measures of central tendency; the range, variance, and standard deviation are measures of variability; uniqueness, ranks, percentile ranks, and standard scores are measures of individual position.
7. A line graph summarizes the relationship between two variables. The average dependent variable measure for each level of the independent variable is plotted in a line graph. The trend of the data is indicated by the direction of the graph.
8. Two or more variables "interact" when the effect of one variable depends on the effect of the other variables. Graphically, an interaction is indicated by nonparallel lines.
9. If the relationship between two measures is approximately linear, then the slope of a straight line drawn through the data summarizes the relationship in terms of one number. The slope is defined as the ratio of the change in the dependent variable measure (Y) to the change in the independent variable (X). Slopes may be positive or negative and may be used to test the significance of a change in behavior.

SUGGESTED READINGS

Edwards, A. L. *Statistical analysis* (4th ed.). New York: Holt, Rinehart and Winston, 1974.

Huff, D. *How to lie with statistics.* New York: Norton, 1954.

Schutte, J. G. *Everything you always wanted to know about elementary statistics but were afraid to ask.* Englewood Cliffs, N.J.: Prentice-Hall, 1977.

Young, R. K., & Veldman, D. J. *Introductory statistics for the behavioral sciences.* New York: Holt, Rinehart and Winston, 1977.

section two

Research Design

6

Naturalistic Observation

Experimental scientific research involves manipulative control of the situation being studied. Naturalistic scientific research lacks manipulative control. Often the type of behavior studied determines the choice of naturalistic or experimental observation. Naturalistic observation is generally less susceptible to experimental contamination than is experimental research, but it makes inferring causal relationships more difficult. However, both are useful, complementary methods that aid the understanding of behavior.

One of the unsolved mysteries of nature was the disappearance of the bright golden-orange monarch butterfly in the winter. These beautiful butterflies live in fields and gardens from Texas to New England and from Florida to Minnesota, but when the weather gets cold they migrate, apparently to escape the cold and to reproduce. A Canadian zoologist (Urquhart, 1976) has spent his life studying the mysterious yearly disappearance of the eastern monarch butterfly. Urquhart developed a method of tagging a butterfly for identification. He released thousands of tagged butterflies, and all over the United States and Canada people caught the migrating butterflies and returned them to his laboratory. One butterfly was captured, tagged, released, and captured again the next day, 80 miles away! Although the trail of the butterflies led to Texas and on to Mexico, the zoologist did not find its end.

Then he received a telephone call from Mexico; the excited caller claimed to have found the butterfly colony in the Sierra Madre mountains. Urquhart traveled to Mexico; in the mountains, 9,000 feet above sea level, he found millions of butterflies covering the trees and plants. Among them was a butterfly that had been tagged in Minnesota. While in Mexico, Urquhart tagged over 10,000 butterflies, and several months later two of them were recovered 1,000 miles away in northern Texas. The location of the monarch's winter home had been discovered by naturalistic observation.

NATURALISTIC VERSUS EXPERIMENTAL OBSERVATION

Naturalistic Observation

The observation of events in their natural settings is called **naturalistic observation.** Naturalistic observers examine empirical, public events. Theoretically, these observations are repeatable, given that the events "naturally" occur more than once. The occurrence of the events is independent of the observer's behavior. For example, astronomers are naturalistic observers. The movements of the stars are not under the control of the observer; they are empirical, public events that usually recur within a time span that allows a second observation. Similarly, many zoologists and some geologists primarily use naturalistic observation methods. In contrast, the observation of events in a restricted setting is called **experimental observation.** Experimental observers also make empirical, public, repeatable observations. In addition, experimental observations are made under controlled conditions in which you manipulate the environment so that the critical events occur at a specified time and place.

Experimental Observation

94

Manipulation allows you to be prepared for precise observation. You also are assured that the events will occur a second time, allowing verification of your observations under approximately the same conditions. Finally, you can vary the physical conditions systematically to discover what changes in the events ensue.

Naturalistic observation is not casual observation. Casual observation, while often helpful in initiating further probing into the what, how, and why of behavior, cannot answer all these questions completely. Systematic observation is essential for answering them. By systematic observation we mean observation that is planned to provide organized, interpretable records of behavioral measures.

Research Design

An organized plan for obtaining these useful measures is called a research design. A **research design** is a fundamental plan for research, including the assignment of subjects to levels of the independent variables, the specification of the independent variables (and manipulation of them in experimental research), and the operational definition of the dependent variable measures. The research design specifies how most of the sources of variance are controlled in a study. Different designs are appropriate to experimental and nonexperimental (naturalistic observation) research. In this text we primarily are concerned with experimental research; however, we explore naturalistic research designs in this chapter.

Quasi-experimental Research

We call naturalistic observation "quasi-experimental" research because it fails to meet the strictest requirements for experimental control. According to B. F. Anderson (1971), experimental research "begins with a situation in which all variables are controlled and allows variation to be introduced one variable at a time. . . . [Naturalistic research] begins with a situation in which all variables are free to vary and allows control to be introduced one variable at a time. This means that in [naturalistic research] you control only the variables you are aware of, while in [an experimental study] you control many variables of which you are not even aware. It also means that there are inevitably far fewer controls, and a much greater possibility of confounding, in a [naturalistic study]" (pp. 40–41). Independent variables are measured in naturalistic research. The difference between naturalistic and experimental research is the degree of control of the independent variables by the researcher. The levels of the independent variables occur naturally, without the researcher's help, in naturalistic research, but are selected and made to occur by the experimenter in experimental research.

The research designs in this chapter present a problem to the authors of a textbook in experimental psychology. Usually emphasis is placed on the elegance of the control procedures, and a basic requirement for most experimental psychologists is that there be some control group or control score to compare with the experimental group. Technically speaking, the naturalistic observation procedures that are presented in this chapter often lack this vital feature of a corresponding group for the purpose of comparing the effects of the primary variance source. Although elegance and cleverness in devising appropriate controls in experimental research is desirable, do not be fooled by our relatively brief treatment of the naturalistic observation procedures. In some cases, these are the only ways that it is possible to collect data that are meaningful.

For example, the migratory patterns of wild fowl, or some of the courting and mating behaviors of many species, can only be observed in a natural setting without manipulated independent variables. In other cases, you may prefer to use a nonexperimental or quasi-experimental research design after deciding that the manipulation of an independent variable may create an artificial situation that significantly affects the validity of the subjects' behavior. That is, behavior of a particular species, including human beings, in a laboratory situation may be directly affected by the fact of observation under controlled conditions. As indicated in chapter 3, the reactive effect of experimentation is a source of secondary variance that is a threat to the external validity or generalizability of the research results. For example, college students who are aware of being subjects in a study many, under certain conditions, modify their behavior either to please the experimenter, particularly if the researcher is their instructor, or to mislead the experimenter, which sometimes happens when the subjects and experimenters are all students. In addition, you may decide to use a naturalistic design because of a concern for the ecological generality of the results. The behavior of captive animals in a zoo or laboratory setting probably differs in significant ways from the behavior of the same species in a natural, wild setting. For example, the frequency of overt homosexual behavior in laboratory monkeys appears to be considerably higher than the related frequency in the natural setting.

Advantages of Naturalistic Research

There are several forms of naturalistic observation, which vary in the number of subjects involved and degree of control of the subjects' environment. Naturalistic observation studies include at least four kinds of research plans: (1) case studies, (2) natural-environment studies, (3) contrived natural-environment studies, and (4) correlational studies. All four kinds can involve a single subject observed over a period of time under different conditions, or several subjects as a group observed over time and perhaps under varying conditions.

CASE STUDIES

Longitudinal Studies

A case study is a longitudinal study of a specific individual's behavior. **Longitudinal studies** involve repeated observation of the same subject or subjects over a relatively long period of time. Case studies commonly are used by clinical psychologists; however, they also have been used to determine the normal trend of changes in behavior. For example, Lenneberg (1962) conducted a case study of a boy with a congenital disability in the acquisition of motor speech skills. The medical and family histories of the boy were examined. Physical examinations and psychological tests were given and the boy's vocalizations were recorded for four years. The boy learned to comprehend English fully, yet could not speak it. The case study demonstrated that comprehension of a language does not require babbling in infancy or imitation of adult speech. Other examples of case studies include almost any biographical report.

Case studies may also be used with nonhuman species. For example, Jones and Kamil (1973) describe a study of tool making and tool using by the northern blue jay. Laboratory-reared jays were kept in a large suspended cage with newspapers beneath the wire floor. By chance, food pellets collected on the ledges formed by wooden supports at the sides of the cage. One jay was observed tearing pieces of paper from the pages of newsprint and using the pieces of paper as tools to rake the otherwise unreachable food pellets close enough to eat. The bird had been maintained under food deprivation conditions several times during its 16 months of life. Jones and Kamil speculated that the jay acquired its tool-making and tool-using behavior because of the combination of three factors: food deprivation, food pellets just out of reach, and available newspapers. They recorded many instances of the tool-using behavior on film. Subsequently, they manipulated the presence or absence of food and the food-deprivation state of the animal and verified that the tool-using behavior was dependent on hours of deprivation and the presence of food pellets on the ledges. Incidentally, five other jays in their colony have been observed making and using the paper rakes; apparently they learned by imitation of the first jay.

The blue-jay and mute-boy studies demonstrate three essential elements of case studies: (1) the focus on one subject, (2) the collection of multiple observations of behavior over a relatively long period, and (3) the examination of the data for generalizations that may apply to other members of the species.

NATURAL-ENVIRONMENT STUDIES

Field Studies

The second form of naturalistic research plan is a natural-environment study, field study, or field-research study, in which the behavior is observed in the wild or home environment. No deliberate changes are made in the environment, except that attempts may be made to hide the observer. Observations may be made continuously, or a sequence of observations may be collected either at fixed or at random time intervals. Goodall (1963) spent several years living with a group of chimpanzees near Lake Tanganyika. She observed them using straws to get termites out of rotten trees, the first recorded observation of tool usage by animals in their natural environment. She also has studied cranes in their natural environment (van Lawick-Goodall, 1968). She observed cranes using tools also: They picked up rocks and hurled them in order to break the shells of ostrich eggs.

Fawl (1963) observed 16 children for a complete day in their normal, natural surroundings. Among other things, he found that the children averaged about 16 frustrations (blocks to attaining a goal) per day. In previous laboratory research, when children were frustrated they displayed marked aggressive behavior. In Fawl's study the children's usual response to naturally occurring frustration was mild or no response at all. The children usually did not exhibit aggression when frustrated in their normal environment.

The monarch butterfly study described in the opening paragraphs of this chapter is another example of a natural-environment study of behavior. In both of van Lawick-Goodall's studies, Fawl's study, and Urquhart's study, the researchers did not hide themselves from the subjects studied. If the presence of an observer is suspected of disrupting the natural behavior of the subjects, you may choose to hide, or to bring a sample of subjects to a contrived natural environment.

CONTRIVED NATURAL-ENVIRONMENT STUDIES

In contrived natural-environment studies, the subjects are brought to a constructed facsimile of their home environments. With the exception of insects, the facsimile is, of course, necessarily smaller than the home environment. The ant colonies available in any pet shop, and modern zoos, represent contrived naturalistic environments. Because of the reduction in size of the environment, and the consequent limitations on the freedom of the organisms, you must be careful in generalizing observations to uncaptured organisms in their home environment. In addition to providing a means of controlling for observer interference (an experimental-contamination source of secondary variance), contrived environments are developed to allow the greater possibility of observation. For example, nocturnal animals that are insensitive to red light may be placed in a contrived environment illuminated by red light at night.

Klopfer (1963) placed sparrows in a room containing pine and oak foliage on perches. The chipping sparrows preferred the pine perches and the white-throated sparrows showed no preference. Because Klopfer controlled or manipulated the type and number of perches, the study is really an experimental study, rather than a naturalistic study. It is included here as a good research example of a contrived natural environment.

CORRELATIONAL STUDIES

The fourth form of naturalistic research plan is called a correlational study. These studies are designed to determine the degree of relationship between two or more variables (chapter 21). At least one and usually both of the variables are free from control by the researcher. Such uncontrolled variables could be organismic variables such as personality introversion, or environmental variables such as phases of the moon. Bradburn (1963) found that "father dominance" was negatively associated with need for achievement in male Turkish junior executives. The measure of the organismic variable, father dominance, was the age at which the subject was separated from his father (by death or choice). The older the subject at the point of separation, the lower his later need for achievement.

Correlational studies may involve the case-study technique and natural or contrived natural environments. In addition, when an experimental research study includes variables that are not manipulated by the experimenter, the subpart of the experimental research project that is concerned with the relationship between an uncontrolled independent variable and the dependent variable or variables may be designated a "correlational study."

Correlational studies may be much less complicated than the Bradburn example. Sechrest (cited in Webb et al., 1966) found that there are more erotic graffiti in men's than in women's rest rooms. The difference was less in the Philippines than in the United States. Ross and Campbell (cited in Webb et al., 1966) found that a crackdown on speeding in Connecticut was not related to the number of traffic fatalities. Blomgren and Scheuneman (1961) found that a scare promotional campaign was less effective in selling seat belts than a "macho" ad featuring a professional race-car driver. In all three of these studies neither of the two variables involved in each study was controlled by the researchers.

"If sanity and insanity exist, how shall we know them?" (Rosenhan, 1973, p. 250). For many people, this is an important question, and the answer is certainly not obvious. There is a substantial confusion about the meanings of the terms "sanity," "insanity," "mental illness," and "schizophrenia." Unusual behaviors do exist but when are these terms reliable and valid and when should they be applied? To work on this question, Rosenhan (1973) studied mental hospital admission procedures, psychiatric diagnosis, and the perception of life in a mental hospital. The observations consisted mostly of the anecdotal description of the experiences of eight people in 12 mental hospitals. Rosenhan's study has flaws, but it is an interesting example of a crude correlational study.

Eight "sane" people, including Rosenhan, sought voluntary admission at different times to 12 mental hospitals. Each person told the admitting psychiatrist of hearing voices saying "empty," "hollow," and "thud." Other than false names and, occasionally, fake occupation descriptions, the fake auditory hallucinations plus the request for voluntary commitment were all the information they offered. In all cases except Rosenhan's, the purpose and nature of the research were unknown to the entire hospital staffs. All the psuedopatients were admitted to the hospitals: In 11 cases the admitting diagnosis was schizophrenia and in the remaining case, manic-depressive psychosis. From this experience one can conclude that those who seek voluntary admission to mental hospitals probably will be admitted. Further, the behavior of seeking admission may be sufficient to yield the diagnosis of schizophrenia.

Length of hospitalization ranged from 7 to 52 days, and the average confinement was for 19 days. The pseudopatients were told by Rosenhan that they would have to get out by their own devices, except that they could not tell the truth about being part of a research project. The pseudopatients stopped "hearing voices" immediately after entering the hospital and behaved as "sanely" as they could from that point. Their one "abnormal" behavior consisted of constantly keeping notes on their experiences. During their hospitalization, the eight were given nearly 2,100 tranquilizers (which they threw in the toilet, the way some of the other residents also disposed of their pills).

The pseudopatients reported that the experience of being in the hospital was very unpleasant. It was boring and frightening because of the depersonalization and powerlessness involved in most hospital settings. Staff members often acted as if the patients were not really there. While a large number of the other patients voiced suspicions about the pseudopatients ("You're not crazy. You're a journalist or a professor."), none of the hospital staff verbally or in writing questioned their diagnosis. Not one of the patients was released from the hospital on the basis of mistaken diagnosis. All were released with a diagnosis of schizophrenia "in remission."

Rosenhan concluded that this diagnosis means the patient is still schizophrenic, but no longer exhibits symptoms. There is some confusion about this conclusion as well as other points, as indicated in 15 letters criticizing the study (Fleischman et al., 1973). However, it seems safe to conclude that if a person volunteers for admission to a mental hospital, lies in order to get in, and subsequently does not reveal the lie, then that person probably will stay in the hospital for a while.

The Rosenhan study is fascinating and should have led to further research; however, a cursory review of the literature has not revealed any follow-up. The major dependent variables were the diagnostic labeling of the eight subjects and their subsequent treatment by the hospital staff. Since no independent variables were involved, this correlational study has limited scientific value, which may account for the lack of follow-up. However, the study did provide a significant, extensive description of the experience of life in a mental hospital from the point of view of a patient.

MEASUREMENT TECHNIQUES IN NATURALISTIC OBSERVATION RESEARCH

The monarch butterflies were tagged to make it possible to identify them after they had migrated. Birds and other animals living in their natural environments have been tagged to facilitate finding them again at a later time. It is hoped that the tags do not affect the behavior of the organisms in their natural environments. Arranging the measurement procedures so that they do not affect the subjects' natural behaviors is a major concern in naturalistic research.

Unobtrusive Measures

The important feature of natural-environment observation is that it allows the observation of naturally occurring behavior without the restraints and limitations of a laboratory setting. In order to maintain the naturalness, researchers often must resort to unusual measurement techniques that do not alter normal patterns of behavior. Wildlife photographers may use telephoto lenses and elaborate camouflage, and may spend several months to record the ongoing behavior of wildlife species. Radar has been used to study bird migration. Using this technique, it has been discovered that birds do not drift in crosswinds when flying over land in the daytime (Schmidt-Koenig, 1965). Webb, Campbell, Schwartz, and Sechrest (1966), discuss a number of unobtrusive measurement techniques that may be applied to human behavior without the subject's awareness of the observation process.

The note-taking behavior by the "Rosenhan eight" is an example of unobtrusive measurement. The notes were records of patient and staff behaviors. Patient writing behavior is not uncommon on a mental hospital ward. The hospital staff paid no attention to the note taking except to record occasionally that the pseudopatients were writing a lot.

As another example of unobtrusive measurement, students of human behavior occasionally dress to fit in with a skid-row environment. In their disguises they observe the "drunks and bums" loitering on the streets. One common observation is that the people carrying small brown paper bags are most frequently engaged in conversation by others. Also, little action takes place in the middle of the blocks; street corners are the site of skid-row social activity.

Inventories and Questionnaires

You may use inventories and questionnaires if you feel that they will not alter the ongoing behavior. Usually, however, they are very obtrusive; any assumption to the contrary must be carefully examined.

Many ready-made, published inventories are available as measurement devices. Ready-made inventories have the advantage of being constructed by someone sophisticated in test and measurement theory. Published inventories have been field tested, which provides some normative data for comparison with other groups. Many published inventories have evolved from earlier instruments that were improved. Buros's *The Seventh Mental Measurements Yearbook* (1972) contains information on many current mental tests. Anastasi (1976) also presents information and criticism on many types and kinds of tests. In addition, new inventories are continually being presented in psychological journals.

Disadvantages of Questionnaires

The construction of an adequate questionnaire or inventory is a difficult, time-consuming process. We have seen many students attracted to the questionnaire approach because of its apparent simplicity, ease of data handling, and relevance to their research question. These apparent positive characteristics of questionnaires are often misleading.

If the only way to collect the data relevant to a research question is to construct an inventory or questionnaire, then first consult a reference such as Nunnally (1970), Oppenheim (1966), or Selltiz, Wrightsman, and Cook (1976). The high probability of erroneous wording of questions by the beginner and the excessive amount of work involved in analyzing the data from a questionnaire lead us to recommend strongly that the beginning student avoid the questionnaire technique.

Likert Scale

Generally speaking, a questionnaire yields better results if the respondent is allowed a variety of choices (a **summated scale**) rather than a yes–no answer scale. A widely used type of summative scale is a *Likert-type scale.* Each test item offers the respondent several degrees of agreement and disagreement. For example, if an item on an anxiety scale states, "I always perspire during tests," the possible answers could be, (1) "strongly agree," (2) "agree," (3) "undecided," (4) "disagree," and (5) "strongly disagree." This scale permits the use of items that are not manifestly related to the attitude or behavior being studied (Selltiz et al., 1976). For example, a question such as "Do you like cut flowers?" is ostensibly concerned with gardening, but it may be scored in terms of aggressive tendencies. The numerical values of responses to items concerned with a trait are summarized to obtain a single measure of that trait. Summated scales are simple to construct and usually provide reliable results when the questions or statements are devised properly. The choice of certain words or phrases is crucial to the subject's response. For example, questions with "should" or "ought to" provide an indication of the idealized policies of an individual. Questions phrased "Would you do . . . ?" involve a personal prediction of the subject's behavior in a specific situation. Consequently, great care should be taken in making up test items in questionnaires. (See *Newsweek,* July 8, 1968, pp. 23–27 for errors often encountered.)

Advantages of Questionnaires

Questionnaires and inventories have certain advantages over other means of obtaining dependent variable measures. For example, interviews are often very expensive in time and money. Inventories can be administered to large groups of subjects at the same time and usually can be machine scored. Also, tests and questionnaires can be sent through the mail, which provides subjects that otherwise cannot be obtained. One problem, however, with mail-outs is that many people do not respond to a mail-out test. In order to ensure a large enough sample, it is a good idea to send out about three times as many questionnaires or tests as you need replies. Otherwise your sample would probably be too small. A third advantage comes from the standardized and impersonal nature of tests. Subjects will respond more honestly on a test when they are sure that their identity is protected. Psychological testing is considered by many to be an invasion of privacy (Ruch, 1967). It is the tester's moral and legal responsibility to protect the person who takes the test by keeping scores anonymous. Once in a while you may wish to obtain information about how certain groups will respond to an anonymous test. Suppose you had a mail-out test that measured racial attitudes, and you wanted to know how plumbers, doctors, lawyers, and engineers would respond to the test. You could print the test in four different colors and send a different color to each group. Using this procedure you could determine the score of each and still maintain each individual's anonymity.

In summary, naturalistic observation studies are sometimes necessary. Quite often submitting subjects to a laboratory situation can change their responses significantly. Furthermore, the confounding source of variability associated with the laboratory situation cannot be separated from the variability due to the primary variable, making it hard to assess the effect of the independent variable. On the other hand, the results of naturalistic-observation case studies, many natural-environment or contrived natural-environment studies, and some correlational studies cannot be generalized to the population because the studies do not involve random sampling. The following chapters describe experimental research designs that provide greater control of the sources of variance that threaten the internal validity of research studies.

SUMMARY

1. Naturalistic observation is the observation of organisms and events in their natural settings. The observed events are empirical, public and, at least theoretically, repeatable.
2. Experimental observation is the observation of organisms and events in restricted, controlled settings. The experimenter manipulates the environment to control the time and place of occurrence of the events. The observed events are empirical, public, repeatable, and controlled.
3. A research design is an organized plan for systematic observation, including assignment of subjects to treatments, definition and manipulation of independent variables, and definition of the dependent variables.
4. Scientific research includes experimental and naturalistic or quasi-experimental research.
5. Naturalistic research is conducted when there is no other alternative, or when the reactive effects of experimentation seriously threaten the external validity of the research.
6. Naturalistic research studies include four different kinds of research plan: case studies, natural-environment studies, contrived natural-environment studies, and correlation studies.
7. Case studies are longitudinal studies of a single individual's behavior.
8. Natural-environment studies, field-research studies, and field studies are studies in which behavior is observed in the organism's natural "home" environment.
9. Contrived natural-environment studies involve constructing simulated natural environments and observing a sample of organisms in the contrived environment.
10. Correlational studies are designed to determine the degree of relationship between two or more variables; at least one of the variables is not controlled by the researcher.
11. In naturalistic observation research there is much concern about minimizing the effects of the measurement procedures. Unobtrusive measurement procedures do not significantly affect the behavior observed.
12. Inventories and questionnaires may be unobtrusive measures under special, limited

circumstances. Published inventories are preferable to the home-made variety; they provide empirically based estimates of reliability and validity.

13. Summated scales provide more information than yes–no scales. The phrasing of questions in an inventory or questionnaire is crucial to its validity.

SUGGESTED READINGS

Anastasi, A. *Psychological testing* (4th ed.). New York: Macmillan, 1976.

Buros, O. K. *The seventh mental measurements yearbook.* Highland Park, N.J.: Gryphon Press, 1972.

Nunnally, J. C. *Introduction to psychological measurement.* New York: McGraw-Hill, 1970.

Oppenheim, A. N. *Questionnaire design and attitude measurement.* New York: Basic Books, 1966.

Selltiz, C., Wrightsman, L. S., & Cook, S. W. *Research methods in social relations* (3rd ed.). New York: Holt, Rinehart and Winston, 1976.

Webb, E. J., Campbell, D. T., Schwartz, R. D., & Sechrest, L. *Unobtrusive measures: Nonreactive research in the social sciences.* Skokie, Ill.: Rand McNally, 1966.

7

Introduction to Group Designs: One-Group Designs

Studying people individually provides information that is difficult to generalize to large groups. We get a better picture of how people in general behave if we look at group behavior. This chapter deals with the control of factors that help us get a better picture of group behavior and outlines procedures for the study of behavior of a single group.

Chapter 6 described naturalistic research methods that do not involve manipulative control of research variables. Many problems in the social and behavioral sciences do not lend themselves to experimental inquiry. The major reason is that often we do not have control over the sources of variation that might influence the data. For example, many variables, such as home environment, intelligence, or blood type, are impossible to control in some situations,and difficult at best to control in others.

Naturalistic observation research suffers from three major weaknesses. (1) In naturalistic observation the researcher cannot manipulate an independent variable. (2) A naturalistic study does not utilize randomization of subjects to groups, and therefore by chance a disproportionate number of bright people, fast animals, or hypertensive men is likely to end up in a group. (3) Because random sampling is not likely to be included, generalizing the results of the study to other groups is prohibited. The risk of an improper interpretation is high in naturalistic studies.

In order to reduce these kinds of problems, experimental designs were developed so that independent variables could be manipulated, random sampling would be done, and more precise interpretations of the data might be performed. Generally, an experimental design includes some procedures for controlling secondary variance as well as manipulating an independent variable. Experimental designs exist in two general forms: single-subject designs (chapter 11) and group designs (chapters 7 – 10).

CONTROL IN GROUP DESIGNS

To illustrate the advantage of an experimental design over naturalistic observation, imagine a television commercial (a highly restricted form of naturalistic observation in a contrived naturalistic setting). A man is shown applying a certain preparation to his hair and, immediately after, is shown in the embrace of a pretty girl. The manufacturer of the preparation wishes the viewer to infer that there is a relationship between the independent variable (application of hair tonic) and the dependent variable (attention from girls). Is such an inference justified in this case? It is impossible to tell. A number of alternative hypotheses could account for the ovserved behavior of the girl. The young man may be kissed by many girls, no matter what the condition of his hair. Some other product (after-shave lotion, mouthwash, elevator shoes, black velvet jacket, and so on) might be the real cause for the observed behavior. It is also possible that the girl is very friendly. It could be that the entire sequence was performed at the request of an advertising agency. Thus, although hair tonic might be the important variable, we cannot eliminate any of the alternative hypotheses without additional information. If we could determine that the young man is only attractive to girls when he uses the hair preparation, or the girl is attracted only to men who use the preparation, we could be more confident in our conclusions. We need a reference point, a control, in order to evaluate our results. An ideal reference condition would be to observe the same individuals under the same conditions, except that the young man would not apply the hair preparation. If the observed behavior were different, we could attribute the change in behavior to the change in the independent variable.

It is impossible to make the two observations under identical conditions. The fact that the observations cannot be made at the same time and in the same place forces the experimenter to make comparisons under less than optimal conditions. Any condition other than the independent variable that is different between the two observations may serve as a source of secondary variance and invalidate inferences drawn from the data.

As you learned in chapter 2, variations in behavior measures arise from three general sources: subject factors, environmental factors, and experimentation factors. An experimenter uses a research design to control for potential secondary variables. The choice of a design is based on data-collection limitations and the secondary variables that seem most likely to be relevant.

Control of Subject Factors

The first source of secondary variance is labeled individual difference. Two methods of controlling for the effect of individual differences in an experimental design are (1) to make the treatment groups (if there is more than one) equivalent on some measure of behavior and (2) to provide that the subjects in a single group are similar with respect to some variable before treatment. When more than one group is used, random assignment theoretically equates all groups with respect to all variables, so that the average score of one group should equal the average score of another. Matching groups of subjects (chapter 3) also increases the likelihood that the averages will be equal. As indicated in chapter 2, any difference between the group averages is called *between-groups variance*. Within groups, control of individual difference is achieved by matching the subjects on some variable. The effect of matching is to minimize the *within-group variance*. Before the treatment is administered, between-groups variance and within-group variance should be minimized. The independent variable should produce a difference between previously equivalent groups. In most studies, after the treatment is administered, between-groups variance should increase, and within-group variance should remain unchanged.

Measurement Decisions

Notice that the important dimension of research is to make *comparisons* and not to describe the behavior in numerical form. There is a common misconception that the ability to express any observed behavior in some precise numerical form makes the observation much more scientific than less quantitative description. The important factor is not "What is the most precise measure that can be obtained from my observation?" but rather "What level of measurement gives the most useful information?" The observation that an animal learned to choose the maze path that led to food may be much more informative than the observation that it traversed the maze in exactly 140 paces.

Research designs do not necessarily solve the problem of measurement error. The choice of a measurement device, whether it is a counter, recorder, or human observer, is not a function of the research design. It should be obvious, however, that the observations taken in any experiment will be more useful if an appropriate measuring technique is used. Similarly, multiple observations are more likely to be representative than a few observations.

Control of Environmental Factors

The second source of secondary variance is the effect of environmental factors. As mentioned in chapter 3, these factors are anything in the environment which inadvertently causes a change in behavior: a noise in the lab, a room that is too hot or cold, a short in the electrical measurement equipment. As mentioned earlier, a sign over the lab door saying "Quiet, experiment in progress" is helpful (especially if you take it down when the experiment is not in progress). The general rule on the control of environmental factors is that, if anything other than the independent variable can affect the data, get rid of it, or hold it constant across subjects. Methods for doing so were outlined in chapter 3.

Control of Experimentation Factors

Most students and professional researchers want to have their research studies come out just the way they predicted. Unfortunately, results that do not support a hypothesis are rarely published, unless the study is a replication of one previously published. The unconscious motivation to make things occur as predicted overwhelms people at times and can influence the outcome of research.

Currently there is considerable controversy surrounding the results of Wallace and Benson's (1972) study on transcendental meditation. The study strongly supports the contention that transcendental meditation facilitates the relaxation response and its attendant physiological responses, such as lowered oxygen consumption, decrease in blood lactate, increase in electrical resistance of the skin, increased alpha brain waves, and decreased respiratory rate. The results of the study were indeed striking: All the physiological parameters studied during transcendental mediation indicated relaxation and reduced stress. However, some scientists suggested that the effect of experimenter expectancy bias is evident in the study. They do not argue that TM has no effect; it is the extent of the effect that they question. The Public Broadcasting System has shown a movie in its *Nova* series entitled "Meditation and the Mind," which raises the same question. Because both Wallace and Benson were personally involved in transcendental meditation, they may have somehow influenced the results. Their influence on the highly motivated TM-trained subjects may have enhanced the effects of meditation.

Rosenthal (1969) has stressed the importance of controlling for experimenter expectancy bias. An obvious solution to the problem lies in having the experimenter

Single-Blind Method

Double-Blind Method

unaware of whether the subject is in the experimental group or control group. Recall that the experimental group gets the treatment or independent variable while the control group does not. As indicated in chapter 3, when the subjects do not know to which group they belong, this method is called the "single-blind" method. When both the experimenter and the subjects do not know who is in the experimental group, the method is called the "double-blind" method. Rosenthal (1966) reported in a review of nearly 100 drug studies utilizing placebos that the placebos always work better when a double-blind study is used. Apparently when a physician does not know that the drug given a patient is a placebo, the physician expects to get results and does! The placebo is a powerful clinical tool, but it must be controlled in an experiment.

ONE-GROUP DESIGNS

One-group designs involve the observation of a single group of subjects under two or more experimental conditions. *Each subject serves as his or her own control* by contributing experimental and control scores. One-group designs are intended to control for individual differences. An experimenter primarily interested in the change in the behavior of each individual due to the experimental treatment should consider a one-group design.

We do not recommend all types of one-group studies. For example, the hair-preparation commercial discussed earlier in the chapter is an example of a **one-shot case study.** Such a study is not an experimental design and should not be used under any circumstances. We describe it in order to suggest that students not waste their time with such a study. The hair-preparation example is summarized in Table 7.1. The symbol *X* represents the experimental condition; *Y* represents an after-observation (measurement of the dependent variable). No pretreatment measure (before-observation) was taken, and time moves from left to right. The treatment was the application of the hair preparation and the after-observation was the embrace.

A one-shot case study provides a very weak basis for inferring any relationship. Data comparison is a crucial aspect of the research process; consequently, the one-shot case study is not included as a legitimate research design, because it does not permit comparison.

For illustrative purposes, each of the following legitimate designs is presented in terms of a specific model, and the model is evaluated. You can use these models as a basis for developing a design that is best suited to your research hypothesis. The addition of certain control procedures will increase the value of a given design. Similarly, two or more of the designs presented here as separate entities can be combined for a more controlled test of a hypothesis. Such modifications are encouraged, since no model is intended to serve as an arbitrary standard for good research.

Guide to Research Design Descriptions

TABLE 7.1   One-Shot Study Case

Group	Before-Observation	Treatment	After-Observation
1	—	X	Y

Before–After Design

A one-group before–after design consists of observing the subjects at some time prior to the onset of the experimental condition *(W)* and comparing that performance with a similar observation made during or after the treatment *(Y)*. The term "before–after design" refers to the temporal relationship of the observations to the experimental condition. The data are analyzed by comparing the before and after scores for all subjects.

TABLE 7.2   One-Group Before–After Design

Group	Before-Observation	Treatment	After-Observation
1	W	X	Y

Function   A before–after design provides a direct measure of the change in the behavior of each subject under two observation conditions. It may be used when you know that the experimental condition will occur, and that you can observe subjects before and after its occurrence. Before–after designs occasionally are employed experimentally to evaluate the effect of propaganda on attitudes. Subjects are randomly sampled from a population.

It is not necessary for a researcher to create the experimental condition. It is possible to use this design naturalistically, for example, to observe the effectiveness of national advertising campaigns on political attitudes throughout an election year campaign.

Advantages   The difference between the before and after scores, in the absence of a treatment effect, should be minimal. Because subjects serve as their own controls in a one-group before–after design, additional subjects for a control group are not required. If the subjects are continuously available for observation (as zoo animals are) or periodically available (school children or weekly sensitivity group meetings), a before–after design is particularly convenient. If the experimenter has access to a before measure, and the experimental condition includes all available subjects, a one-group design will be useful.

Limitations   A one-group before–after design leaves a large number of secondary variables uncontrolled. Any outside influence that occurs between the two observations may account for an observed difference. For example, measurement of racial attitudes before and after a documentary film on race relations may be changed substantially if a race riot occurs between the observations. If one observation is made on a Friday and the other on the following Sunday, the different days of observation may also account for the observed differences in behavior. If the time between two observations is more than a few days, the intervening learning and maturational processes may produce a change in behavior. Moreover, before–after designs are particularly vulnerable to experimental contamination.

The process of collecting the before data also may alert the subjects so that they are more sensitive or resistant to the experimental condition. If the subjects have just

TABLE 7.3   Potentially Relevant Secondary Variance Sources Not Controlled in a One-Group Before–After Design

Individual Differences	Outside Influences	Experimental Contamination
Maturation	History	Pretest sensitization to treatment
Testing or sequence		Reactive effects of experimental arrangement

completed a questionnaire on racial attitudes, they might be cynical about any attempts to alter those attitudes with a propaganda film, or they might be particularly susceptible to the arguments presented in the film. A before–after design requires that two observations be made for each subject. If the subject is not available during one of the observation periods, the other observation must be discarded. If the subjects are not selected at random, then any observed difference between measures may be due to some unknown factor (Table 7.3).

Statistical analysis   The phrase "subjects as their own control" means that the behavior of the one group of subjects, measured before administration of the treatment, is compared with the measure obtained after treatment. That is, the subjects' behavior after the treatment is compared with the control measure of their behavior before encountering the treatment. The comparison of the two sets of measures may be accomplished with a significance-of-changes χ^2 test if the data consist of frequency counts of subjects falling into two categories before and after the treatment (chapter 18). Alternatively, the sign test may be used if the dependent variable measure consists of ranking the subjects before and after treatment (chapter 17). Finally, the related-groups t test (where the two related "groups" are the before scores and after scores of the subjects) or randomized-blocks analysis of variance (chapters 20 and 21, respectively) may be used if the measures are at least interval-level numbers (chapter 4).

Comments   A one-group before–after design is relatively weak because it does not control many secondary variables. Probably the most important problem is the effect of being observed. If the data can be collected without the awareness of the subject, this design may be somewhat useful. However, a one-group before–after design seldom is used unless supplemented with additional control procedures, for example, matching or counterbalancing with matching.

Time-Series Design

A time-series design consists of collecting multiple observations before treatment and comparing them with observations made during or after treatment. A time-series design is an extended form of the before–after design.

TABLE 7.4   Time-Series Design

Group	Before-Observation	Treatment	After-Observation
1	W_1, W_2, W_3	X	Y_1, Y_2, Y_3

Function   The experimenter measures the change in the behavior of the subjects under at least three observation conditions at fixed time intervals. Once a trend, called a *baseline,* has been established, the experimental treatment is introduced and the experimental observations are continued. Any discontinuity in the observations that occurs after the onset of the experimental treatment is attributed to the treatment.

A discontinuity may occur in one of two ways. First, it may be that the observations change consistently over time, in which case the experimenter must examine the data for any deviation from the expected trend. We might record the performance curve of human subjects solving long addition problems. We announce that scores on this task are related to the intelligence of the subject. Performance may level off for a few problems. We would conclude that the announcement impaired arithmetic performance, since the observed performance did not increase at the same rate as before the treatment.

You may notice a strong similarity between the time-series group design and the repeated-measures single-subject designs in chapter 10. Indeed, the before-observations correspond directly to a baseline period. Once the baseline is stable for the group, the introduction of a treatment effect (independent variable) may reveal an effect in the after-observations (dependent variable measures).

Advantages   Time-series experiments utilize relatively few subjects because the subjects serve as their own control. The fact that multiple measures are obtained from each subject, both before and after the treatment, reduces the probability of a single erroneous observation. The fact that the subjects are observed several times prior to the treatment also reduces the probability that the subject is behaving atypically because of being observed. The trend provides a measurement of the maturational and learning effects occurring during the period of the experiment. These effects can then be controlled statistically by measuring the departure from the established trend created by the independent variable. A well-conducted time-series experiment yields data that can be interpreted clearly.

Limitations   A time-series design does not control for the effect of outside influences (secondary variables) that occur in the same time interval as the experimental condition. Therefore the experimenter must be alert for any such coincident events. Because several before measures are made, there is an even greater possibility for experimental contamination than in a before–after design.

Since multiple observations are made, the experimenter must schedule more time for the collection of data. It also means that all of the subjects must be available for several observations, which usually results in the loss of a higher proportion of subjects. In addition, if the before condition is too rigorous or too monotonous, performance may be altered due to fatigue or boredom. (See Table 7.5.)

Statistical analysis   The average before scores and average after scores or selected, representative before and after scores may be compared with the same techniques listed under the one-group before–after design. Sometimes the data from a time-series study may be statistically analyzed with the ''goodness of fit'' slope

TABLE 7.5 Potentially Relevant Secondary Variance Sources Not Controlled in a Time-Series Design

Individual Differences	Outside Influences	Experimental Contamination
Maturation	History	Pretest sensitization to treatment
Testing or sequence		Reactive effects of experimental arrangement

analysis technique outlined in chapter 21. A straight line is fitted to the average before measure and average after measure and the slope of the straight line is tested to see if it is reliably different from zero.

An important problem in a time-series experiment is to determine which scores to analyze. In the case of a trend of changing scores, Campbell and Stanley (1963) suggest comparing the before and after trend at the point where the treatment occurred. In some cases, a graphical presentation may illustrate the discontinuity and help in analysis. If the data consist of a constant pretreatment baseline and a different posttreatment level of performance, the experimenter may find comparing an average score in each condition is adequate.

Care must be taken in analyzing time-series data, since the effect of the treatment must occur within the time period being analyzed. If you were to conduct a drug study with a time sample every 10 min., it would be important to your data analysis to know when the drug becomes effective.

Comments Time-series experiments are best applied to behavior that occurs periodically. Many industrial settings, school settings, and hospital or other institutional settings provide ideal situations for time-series studies.

Counterbalanced-Experimental-Conditions Design

Rather than collecting all observations in one block, it is sometimes possible to intersperse the treatment and observation conditions. The subject is first given treatment 1 and an observation (Y_1) is made, then the procedure is repeated for treatment 2, repeated again with 2, and again with 1 (see Table 7.6). In this case, we obtain two measures under treatment 2 and two measures under treatment 1. The sequence of administration of treatment is sometimes referred to as an ABBA sequence. Our version involves a 1221 sequence in which the 1s and 2s are subscripts of the treatments X_1 and X_2. "Counterbalanced" means balanced sequences or orders of treatments or experimental conditions. In a 1221 design, the sequence of treatments 1,2 in that order occurs once and the sequence of treatments 2,1 in that order occurs once. Thus the sequences are balanced. The counterbalanced design is not a before–

TABLE 7.6 Counterbalanced-Experimental-Conditions Design

Treatment	X_1	X_2	X_2	X_1
After-Observation	Y_1	Y_2	Y_3	Y_4

after design, rather it is an after–after–after–after design in which there are two levels of the independent variable.

Function   A counterbalanced design provides a different kind of experimental control from other one-group designs, while retaining the feature of subjects serving as their own control. If you suspect that experimental-contamination factors such as learning or fatigue may systematically alter successive observations, you may use the trend-estimation technique of the time-series design, or you may counterbalance your experimental conditions so that they are more likely to be affected equally by the contaminating factor. By arranging conditions in a 1221 pattern, and computing an average score for both observations in each condition, you cancel the sequential factor.

To counterbalance even more thoroughly, half of the subjects may serve under the 1221 sequence, while the other half experiences a 2112 sequence. Using both counterbalance orders provides control for any peculiar effects which may result from a particular presentation order. The data from the two presentation orders may be combined (by treatment) for analysis.

Advantages   Being a one-group design, counterbalanced presentation uses fewer subjects than two-group experiments, and the subjects provide their own control data. Time-related variables such as maturation, learning, outside events, frustrations, and fatigue are controlled by the data-collection sequence rather than by later statistical manipulation. A counterbalanced design usually is concerned with relatively short-term experimental variables; all four observations can be made in a short period of time. A single data-collection session results in less data loss due to subject defection (experimental mortality). A counterbalanced design requires fewer observations than the time-series design.

Limitations   A counterbalanced design is based on the assumption that *all time-related secondary variables are essentially linear* in nature. That is, the effect of the change from trial 1 to trial 2 will be the same as between all other adjacent trials. If the actual effect of these time-related variables is a nonlinear relationship to the behavior, they are not adequately controlled. Sufficient time must be allowed between observations, otherwise the data will be contaminated by *carry-over* from the previous trial condition (Gaito, 1958). Suppose a study involves measuring eye-hand coordination under two stress conditions, and that performance on the experimental task normally improves with practice. In order to control the practice effect, the experimenter uses a counterbalanced-conditions design. The experimental task is also tiring. If the experimenter failed to allow the subjects to recover from the fatigue encountered in trial 1 (under treatment X_1), then performance on trial 2 (under treatment X_2) would be affected by the treatment and fatigue. Obviously, the comparison of the effects of the two treatments would be contaminated by such carry-over. (See Table 7.7.)

Carry-over

Statistical analysis   The average performance under experimental condition X_1 is calculated and the average under X_2 is also calculated. The two averages are

TABLE 7.7 Potentially Relevant Secondary Variance Sources Not Controlled in a Counterbalanced-Experimental-Conditions Design

Individual Differences	Outside Influences	Experimental Contamination
Maturation	History	Pretest sensitization to treatments
Testing or sequence		Reactive effects of experimental arrangement
		Multiple-treatment interaction

compared to determine the differential effect of the two conditions. The specific statistical technique depends on the level of measurement of the dependent variable. The techniques to be used are the same as those for the one-group before–after design.

SUMMARY

1. An experimental design is a plan or program for research, including the assignment of subjects and manipulation of the independent variable.
2. Three general sources of secondary variance are individual differences, environmental influences, and experimental contamination.
3. Any differences between the average scores of the treatment groups is called between-groups variance. Within-group variance refers to the amount of individual differences among the subjects within a group. Before administration of the experimental treatment, both between-groups and within-group variance should be minimized. After the treatment, between-groups variance is expected to be increased.
4. A design must allow the experimenter to make comparisons, otherwise it is not an experimental research design.
5. A poor method is the one-shot case study, which does not allow comparison.
6. One-group experimental research designs all involve the use of subjects as their own controls.
7. A one-group before–after design consists in the administration of a pretest (before measure), treatment, and posttest (after measure) to one group of subjects. The subjects may be randomly selected or naturalistically observed. The design does not control for several possible sources of outside influence and experimental contamination.
8. A time-series design consists in collecting several measures of a behavior before the treatment is given and several measures after the treatment is given, and subsequently comparing the before and after measures.
9. A counterbalanced design controls for order effects. Given that the subjects are going to be observed under at least two treatment conditions, you can counterblance the order of the conditions. A counterbalanced design is used when you suspect that experimental contamination will affect the scores of the subjects.

SUGGESTED READINGS

Campbell, D. T., & Stanley, J. C. *Experimental and quasi-experimental designs for research.* Skokie, Ill.: Rand McNally, 1963.

Gaito, J. Statistical dangers involved in counterbalancing. *Psychological Reports,* 1958, *4,* 463–468.

Johnson, H. H., & Solso, R. L. *An introduction to experimental design in psychology: A case approach.* New York: Harper & Row, 1971.

Kerlinger, F. *Foundations of behavior research* (2nd ed.). New York: Holt, Rinehart and Winston, 1973.

Selltiz, C., Wrightsman, L. S., & Cook, S. W. *Research methods in social relations* (3rd ed.). New York: Holt, Rinehart and Winston, 1976.

8

Independent Two-Group Designs

This chapter discusses the "classic" prototype of the psychology experiment: the independent two-group design. The two static-group comparisons presented before the classic two-group design are approximations to the classic design. These approximations frequently are employed in naturalistic research. The inability to assign the subjects to the groups randomly is a significant flaw in each of these static comparison studies. The remainder of the designs in this chapter are possible improvements that are added to the classic design to control specific sources of extraneous variance. In many cases when researchers discuss their data, they reduce the research problem to a two-group comparison, although the design itself may be more complex than a two-group design. Thus, careful study of the differences among the two-group designs will provide useful cues to understanding more complicated designs.

An independent two-group design involves the observation of two separate groups of subjects under different levels of the independent variable. The design requires that the two groups be independently constituted in the sense that the probability of each subject being assigned to a group is not affected in any way by the nature of the other members of either group. In contrast, in a related two-group design (chapter 9) the method of assignment of subjects to groups requires that subjects be matched on some attribute.

Typically, two-group designs consist of one group experiencing a particular treatment and a nontreated comparison group. The researcher tries to arrange the research conditions so that the experience of the two groups does not differ in any other important way (minimal secondary variance). It is common among researchers to label the group that experiences the treatment the "experimental group" and the group that does not experience the treatment the "control group." Technically speaking, we should refer to both groups as "experimental groups," since they both are created for an experiment. However, the traditional terms are apparently a permanent part of research terminology, even though they can lead to confusion. As you read this text you will find other examples of terms that might be revised for the sake of clarity, but our traditions are established too firmly to permit casual change. (This resistance to change may indicate that the science of psychology is maturing.) New terms and new units, such as the metric system, must overcome considerable resistance to displace established systems that still work.

Experimental and Control Groups

As an example of a two-group design, suppose that the experimental group is shown a propaganda film (nonzero level of the independent variable, or the treatment) and the control group does not view the film (zero level of the independent variable, or no treatment). The independent variable is the viewing of the film. The researcher might measure the attitudes of both groups to see if the propaganda film produced any difference. The dependent variable is the attitude measurement. The research question is, "Will the propaganda film have an effect on attitudes?" or, in plain language, "Will the film work?"

Two-group designs provide a strong basis for measuring the effect of an independent variable. The two groups are designed to be essentially equivalent on all variables except the independent one. The equivalence is achieved by assigning the subjects independently to the two groups and by maintaining, as far as possible, identical research conditions for both groups except for the treatment. In all independent two-group experimental designs, the subjects are *randomly assigned* to the groups. (Random assignment does not mean the same thing as random selection of a sample from a population.)

Random Assignment

When compared with one-group designs, two-group designs have two significant advantages. First, the observations on the two groups can be made at essentially the same time so that time-related secondary-variance sources such as aging, weather, or current events are controlled. Second, in a one-group, before–after design, the pretreatment observation sometimes can contaminate the posttreatment observation. That is, the fact of having been observed before the treatment can affect the way the subjects respond to the after-observation (see chapter 2). In a two-group design, this pretest or sequence effect can be either eliminated by not using a before-observation or controlled by using the same pretreatment observation procedure for both groups.

The two static-comparison procedures discussed next are only approximations to experimental designs. Their weakness lies in uncontrolled secondary variables, while their strength is in their utility in nonexperimental settings. They are described here to alert you to their existence (in both the positive and negative senses). Here especially, the terms "experimental" and "control" groups are technical misnomers although descriptively convenient.

STATIC-GROUP COMPARISON

The static-group comparison procedure provides for the comparison of one group of subjects that has experienced a treatment condition with a similar group that has not experienced the treatment. Observation conditions for the two groups are kept as similar as possible to provide a basis for comparison.

TABLE 8.1
A Typical
Static-Group
Comparison Study

Group	Before-Observation	Treatment	After-Observation
1 (Experimental)	—	X	Y_1
2 (Control)	—	—	Y_2

Function

A static-group comparison is an ex-post-facto design; the comparison is made after the unplanned occurrence of the "treatment". In ex-post-facto research the independent variable is not manipulated. Consequently, the static-group comparison is *not an experimental research design.* The independent variable is the occurrence of some natural event experienced by a group of subjects (Group 1). The researcher then tries to locate a group of subjects (Group 2) who have not experienced the event but who are apparently equivalent in other respects. Subjects are *not* randomly assigned to groups.

Comparing behaviors of the same species of animal in a zoo and in the wild exemplifies a static-group design. Static-group comparison might allow a researcher to comment on the effect of captivity on behavior. As another example, suppose that you were given the task of evaluating the success of a drug-addiction program such as methadone therapy for heroin addicts. The program has been discontinued, but you still have access to most of the participants. At that point you might measure the drug consumption of the remaining members of the treatment group and of a nontreatment group of addicts located by the local law-enforcement authorities.

Advantages

The static-group comparison is sometimes the only way to study certain kinds of behavior. If the researcher has collected data from a number of subjects who have experienced a treatment condition and does not have access to any before-observations, the static-group design will provide a crude basis for comparison. When, for example, "treatment" involves exposure to a cataclysmic event (flood, earthquake, or A-bomb explosion), an experimental research design is impossible. If the control condition involves denying needed therapy, such as treatment for syphilis, an experimental research design is unethical.

Limitations

A static-group comparison depends entirely on the equivalence of subjects in the two groups except for the treatment-induced differences. If the groups are different at the beginning of a study due to selection bias, any differences between their behavior after the treatment occurs may be due either to the treatment or to the initial differences. Because the static-group comparison is an ex-post-facto design, there is no way for the researcher to be sure that the two groups were equivalent. For example, at least one obvious initial difference between the animals in a zoo and the animals in the wild is the ability to avoid capture. In the case of the drug-addiction research, many differences probably exist between the two groups besides the treatment difference. One of many possible problems with the example is that there **Experimental** may be a differential drop-out rate between the two groups, or *experimental mortality,* **Mortality** due to factors other than the therapy treatment. Campbell and Stanley (1963) provide an amusing example of such a problem. Supposedly, studies aimed at ascertaining the effects of a college education by comparing measures on freshmen with measures on seniors have shown that freshmen women tend to be more beautiful than senior women. One legitimate interpretation is that a college education is debeautifying; an alternative interpretation is that beautiful women tend to get married, and marriage tends to interrupt college careers. Without equivalent groups, any conclusions drawn from a static-group comparison are questionable. Because the static-group comparison is an ex-post-facto design, it is possible that the subjects who received the "treatment" are aware of their unique status, and that this awareness flavors their responses in the dependent measures. This reactive effect will lead to a spurious difference that will be attributed to the treatment. Thus, the "treatment" effect can be confounded by subject awareness.

In addition to their separate effects, the sources of secondary variance also **Interactions** combine to complicate interpretation further. Combined effects, called *interactions* (chapter 2), are described more fully in chapters 10, 14, and 21. These chapters deal with multiple treatments in a single study, and the analysis of the interactions between

**TABLE 8.2
Potential Sources
of Secondary
Variance Not
Controlled in a
Static-Group
Comparison Study**

Individual Differences	Outside Influences	Experimental Contamination
Selection bias	Experimental mortality	Interaction of selection bias with treatment Reactive effect of experimental arrangement (can be less than in an experimental design)

treatments is an important component of statistical decision procedure. For the present, a single example must suffice. One might become involved in measuring the political attitudes of individuals who had been victims of police abuse. If, however, the involvement with police occurred because of political demonstrations, there is an obvious selection bias *combined with* a biased attitude towards the police response.

In the basic two-group designs, interactions involve secondary variance sources, and the fine nuances of statistically analyzing them are not possible. Therefore we list them in the Tables 8.2 and 8.4 without extensive additional treatment. After you understand the concept of interaction better, the tables will acquire additional meaning.

Statistical Analysis

Descriptive statistical comparisons of the two groups may be made using graphical techniques or measures of central tendency or variability (chapter 5). When the groups contain 30 or fewer subjects, inferential statistical analysis for the purpose of generalizing the results of the study to a larger population of subjects is not appropriate. Small-sample inferential statistical theory is applicable only to experimental studies involving random sampling and random assignment to groups. Logical, but nonstatistical, analysis and generalization is permissible with small static-group comparison studies. With large samples (the larger the better), simple large-sample statistical methods may be used to interpret the data (chapters 5 and 16). The interpretation of a naturalistic study such as a two-group, static-group comparison tends to be more difficult than the analysis of randomized designs; however, the problems are not computational. The major difficulty lies in deciding which factors are most likely to account for the differences observed. This decision process does not involve statistical significance tests; rather it is based on "educated guesses."

Comments

Except for preliminary studies or some naturalistic observations, the static-group comparison design should be avoided. Although any observed group difference may be related to the experimental conditions, it is difficult to separate this relationship from naturally occurring differences between groups. You may use a static-group comparison design inadvertently. By collecting subjects for the treatment and control conditions under different circumstances of time, place, or group membership, you may be creating static groups. Even when subjects are all selected randomly from a common population, if some factor other than random assignment dictated the research-group membership, then the student has conducted a static-group comparison study rather than an experimental research study. Suppose that someone proposes to compare methods for teaching reading by using the "look–say" method at one grammar school and the "phonics" method at another school. There are a number of obvious possible sources of differences in the dependent measure (reading achievement test scores) other than the two teaching methods, so definitive conclusions cannot be drawn.

BEFORE–AFTER STATIC-GROUP COMPARISON

The before–after static-group comparison (Table 8.3) involves a combination of the elements of the one-group before–after design and the static-group comparison. It is not an experimental design. A before–after static-group comparison study is used when the researcher cannot assign the subjects randomly to the experimental and control groups; thus, a randomized one-group before–after design is not possible. However, the experimenter wishes to use a more powerful procedure than static-group comparison. The initial observations (W) made on each group are compared to determine whether the two groups are initially equivalent on the measured variable.

If the two groups measure the same on the before-observation, then a direct comparison of the after-observations (Y) is appropriate. If, on the other hand, the before-observations (W) reveal an initial difference between the two groups, any posttreatment comparison must include a correction for the initial difference.

Function

A before–after static-group comparison is intended to provide some measure of group differences when the researcher cannot assign the subjects to equivalent groups, that is, when randomization or matching is impractical. The study allows the researcher to estimate the equivalence of the two groups and provides the opportunity to correct for initial differences. The before–after static-group comparison requires that the researcher have access to both the control and treatment group subjects before and after the treatment; and, therefore, the design can be used only in cases where the researcher can anticipate the treatment condition or be able to rely on measurements collected before the study was contemplated.

Advantages

Outside influences (secondary variables) should affect both groups equally, because the dependent-variable measures are taken during the same time interval.

TABLE 8.3
A Typical
Before–After
Static-Group
Comparison Study

Group	Before-Observation	Treatment	After-Observation
1 (Experimental)	W_1	X	Y_1
2 (Control)	W_2	—	Y_2

Experimental contamination is measured by comparing the difference between W and Y scores of the control group, and this measure may be used to correct the experimental group data.

Limitations

Table 8.4 summarizes limitations of this type of study. The subjects are not assigned randomly to the two groups. Even though the before-measures are equivalent, uncontrolled consistent differences (selection bias) could create differences in the after-observations. The before-observations may introduce experimental contamination by sensitizing the subjects to the independent variable. For example, in a learning experiment, the before-measures may make the subjects more motivated to pay attention to the treatment. The potential pretest sensitization to treatment will not be controlled by the presence of the control group since the control group does not receive the treatment.

The potential interaction of a selection bias with maturation, history, or testing is a particularly significant problem with this design and its traditional application in educational or clinical research. Suppose the treatment group consists of clients who have sought group therapy and the control group consists of a collection of "normals." It is likely that any before-treatment measurement of psychological adjustment will reveal a significant between-groups difference. If there is no longer a difference between the two groups after the therapy treatment, then there are at least four possible explanations for the large change in the client group. First, the therapy could be responsible for the difference. Second, the client group may have experienced spontaneous remission of symptoms (selection bias × maturation interaction). Third, as a consequence of being involved in group therapy a number of other changes may have occurred in the personal lives of the treatment group that led to the large change in personal adjustment (selection bias × history interaction). Fourth, the initial large difference in adjustment scores between the two groups would probably be diminished regardless of any intervening events between before and after measures. As noted in chapter 3, regression towards the mean can be expected to occur for the extreme group whether or not the therapy is effective (statistical regression). If the control group is chosen to match the extreme scores of the treatment group, statistical regression will operate for both groups, and the effect of the treatment will be masked by the regression effect. Such studies have been published in the history of psychological and educational research; they are less likely to be published now.

Regression towards Mean

TABLE 8.4
Potential Sources of Secondary Variance Not Controlled in a Before–After Static-Group Comparison Study

Individual Differences	Outside Influences	Experimental Contamination
Statistical regression	Experimental mortality	Pretest sensitization to treatment
Selection bias		Interaction of selection bias with treatment
Selection × maturation, selection × history, or selection × testing interaction		Reactive effect of experimental arrangement

Statistical Analysis

The statistical analysis described for the static-group comparison design is appropriate here. The researcher calculates the difference between the average before- and after-scores of each group $(Y - W)$, then examines the difference between the two differences. Again, small-sample inferential statistical analysis is inappropriate because of the lack of random sampling and random assignment. In particular, the covariance analysis (chapter 21) is unlikely to be appropriate to this design, since most of the assumptions underlying covariance analysis are likely to be violated.

Comments

The before–after static-group comparison design is frequently employed when the experimental and control groups are already formed and available to the researcher. Many educational studies involve the introduction of a new curriculum to a class or to an entire school. Suppose a school introduces a language laboratory in the Spanish program. The school may evaluate the effectiveness of the laboratory by comparing the language skills gained by students using the laboratory with the skills shown by similar students in another school not using the language laboratory. Many factors may dictate that a certain type of student is enrolled in one school or the other and may contribute a biasing effect. In addition, any differential treatment as a result of group membership, such as differences in curriculum or teachers, will also contaminate the results.

RANDOMIZED TWO-GROUP DESIGN

The essential feature of all randomized two-group designs is that the experimenter assigns the subjects randomly to the experimental and control groups. (Randomization is indicated by R in Table 8.5.) Inferences about the effects of the independent variable are drawn by comparing the dependent-variable scores of the two groups.

Function

A randomized two-group design contains a major control feature not employed in the two comparisons we have just discussed. The fact that the experimenter randomly assigns subjects to the two conditions and creates the two conditions means that this design is truly an *experimental design*. As you learned in chapter 2, randomization controls for the effects of a large number of potential secondary variables. An ancient example of the utilization of this design is provided by Jones (1964; cited in Rosenthal

TABLE 8.5
A Typical
Randomized
Two-Group Design

Assignment	Group	Before-Observation	Treatment	After-Observation
R	1 (Experimental)	—	X	Y_1
	2 (Control)	—	—	Y_2

	died	lived
cont no citron	25	0
exp fed citron	0	25

& Rosnow, 1975). A magistrate in Egypt had sentenced a group of convicted criminals to execution through contact with poisonous snakes. As the criminals were being conducted to the place of execution, out of pity a market woman gave the criminals some citron to eat. All the criminals were bitten; however, none died. (Since death is the usual occurrence, we now have a static-group comparison.) Learning of the charitable gift of citron, the magistrate decided to test the hypothesis that the citron was an antidote. The magistrate had the group divided (randomly?) into two subgroups; the experimental group was fed citron, the control group was not. The sentence was carried out a second time. None of the experimental group died while all of the control group died instantly. The fanciful nature of this story does not detract from the fact that it is an example of a simple, good research design written over 2,100 years ago.

Advantages

The random-assignment procedure allows the experimenter to *assume* the initial equality of the two groups prior to the treatment. Since only one observation is made on each subject and the subjects are randomly assigned to groups, the experimental-contamination sources of secondary variance are well controlled in this design. Of course, other variance-control procedures may be employed with randomization in a simple randomized two-group design. For example, various potential sources of secondary variance may be held constant, as when experimental lighting conditions are the same for all subjects; various potential sources may be eliminated, as when only subjects of one sex are included in the study; or they may be conservatively arranged, as when college students are used as subjects even though the treatment is less likely to be effective with a college population than with a sample from the general population.

Limitations

The experimenter must be able to assign the subjects to the experimental and control groups before treatment. If the two groups are observed at different points in time, there is a possibility that intervening events occurring outside of the experiment may affect the dependent variable measures. Time of observation also should be controlled.

It is possible with strict random assignment to create two groups of very unequal size (for example, 4 in one group and 16 in the other). The small group's mean score on the after-observation would be relatively unreliable compared to the mean of the larger group. It is generally true that the inferential-statistical analysis computations are simplified and the inferences more powerful if there are equal numbers of subjects in each group. For these reasons, most experimenters utilize a limited form of random assignment so that equal numbers of subjects are assigned to the two groups. These unbiased assignment procedures are usually called "random assignment" or "random assignment within the limits of equal sample size," although they do not meet the strict requirements of totally random assignment. One example of these procedures is random assignment of subjects using the Table of Random Numbers (chapter 2) with the provision that as soon as half the subjects are assigned to one group, all remaining subjects are assigned to the other group.

The effect of random assignment, including the limited form, in controlling sources of secondary variance is increased as the total sample size increases. Two groups of two subjects each, even though randomly assigned, will not be equal in average score on many of the characteristics that are sources of individual differences between people. However, if 100 people are randomly assigned to two groups, you can be confident that at the outset, the two groups will be approximately equivalent on most sources of individual differences.

TABLE 8.6   Potential Sources of Secondary Variance Not Controlled in a Randomized Two-Group Design

Individual Differences	Outside Influences	Experimental Contamination
None if time of testing is controlled	None if time of testing is controlled	Reactive effects of experimental arrangement

Statistical Analysis

For the purpose of describing and summarizing the data, the appropriate tabular and graphic techniques and the appropriate measures of central tendency and variability (chapter 5) may be used. The inferential statistical analysis (chapter 16) depends on the level of measurement and other characteristics of the dependent variable measure. The two independent-groups median χ^2 tests (chapter 18), the two independent-groups t test (chapter 19), or a two-group analysis of variance (chapter 20) may be used. On rare occasions, the observed differences between the two groups will be so obvious and clear that no inferential statistical test is necessary.

Comments

The major difference between the randomized two-group design and the static-group comparison design is random assignment of the subjects. Although the randomized two-group design is commonly used in the laboratory to obtain maximum control of environmental conditions, it is also used for experimental field studies.

Half of a study by Traynham and Witte (1976), a replication of a previous study with 5-year-old children, is an example of a randomized two-group design. Previous research indicated that racial attitudes could be manipulated by changing the positive and negative evaluations given to color concepts (that is, changing "black is bad" and "white is good" to neutral: "black is good or bad"). Preschool children who were administered a reinforcement procedure reduced their subsequent racial concept attitude scores. The 1976 study replicated the previous research, conducted in North Carolina, with 40 Caucasian kindergarten children in Arkansas. The subjects were randomly assigned to an experimental group and a control group within the limitations that equivalent numbers of each sex were assigned to each group. Both groups received 24 training trials in each of two training sessions. The Color Meaning Test (CMT II; Williams, 1971) consists of 12 cards depicting two animals, identical except for their color—one black, the other white. The experimenter told a short story about each card and then asked the child a question, such as, "Here are two ducks. One of them is a *happy* duck. It swims all day in the pond. Which is the *happy* duck?" The children in the experiment group were "punished" for "guessing wrong" (choosing a white animal in response to a positive-adjective story or a black animal in response to a negative-adjective story). "Punishment" was defined as taking away 2 pennies from a stock of 50 provided at the beginning of the experiment. "Guessing right" did not result in a "reward" or "punishment." The pennies were traded for candy at the end of each session. The control group children received the same test without pennies or punishment. (Actually, all children received the same amount of candy at the end of each session.) The training session produced a reliable difference in responding by the two groups. The "punishment" group tended to pick black and white animals equally often for both the positive- and negative-adjective questions; the control group tended consistently to pick black animals for negative-adjective questions.

The Preschool Racial Attitude Measurement picture-story test (PRAM II; Williams, Best, Bostwell, Mattson, & Graves, 1975) is used to assess attitudes toward blacks and whites. The PRAM II consists of 24 cards depicting drawings of two human beings of the same age and sex but different color. A story-question procedure similar to the CMT II procedure is used with the same set of positive and negative adjectives. Traynham and Witte administered the PRAM II test to the children two weeks after the training session on the animal pictures. As in the previous research, the experimental, "punished" subjects tended to pick drawings of black and white persons for both positive- and negative-adjective questions with equal frequency. The control subjects tended to pick drawings of black persons for the negative-adjective and of white persons for the positive-adjective questions. Therefore the treatment, modification of the children's color-meaning concept, led to a modification of the dependent variable, their racial attitudes as measured by the PRAM II test two weeks after the treatment.

BEFORE–AFTER TWO-GROUP DESIGN

A before–after two-group design offers the power of random assignment of the subjects along with a measure of some initial behavior of each group. If the before scores (W) indicate that the two groups are equated, a comparison of the after scores (Y) is sufficient. If, however, the W scores are different, adjustments can be made in the data analysis.

TABLE 8.7 A Typical Before–After Two-Group Design

Assignment	Group	Before Observation	Treatment	After Observation
R →	1 (Experimental)	W_1	X	Y_1
R →	2 (Control)	W_2	—	Y_2

Function

As we have mentioned, random assignment is a control method that theoretically equates the two groups of subjects. However, the two groups may not be well equated with respect to the relevant variables operating in the experiment. Nonequivalence is more likely to occur with small sample studies. The before-observation in the present design allows you to test the initial equivalence of the two groups on one measure of the subjects' behavior. Usually, the before-measurement procedure is the same as the after-measurement (the dependent variable of the study). The experimental research question is usually of the form, "Does the treatment produce difference between the groups where there was initially little or no difference?" The use of random assignment here (as with the randomized two-group design) means that the design is truly an experimental design.

Advantages

The before–after two-group design provides a measure for between-group differences. It also provides a check on the effectiveness of the random-assignment procedure. The effect of the W measure on the Y measure is controlled by being held constant for both groups. Thus, the individual-differences sources of secondary variance are well controlled with this design. Outside influences are minimized between groups, since the W and Y observations occur at the same time for each group. The effects of outside influences that occur between the W and Y measures may be estimated by the differences between the W_2 and Y_2 scores for the control group. As indicated for the randomized two-group design, additional variance-control procedures may also be employed in this design.

Limitations

The experimenter must assign the subjects to the two groups. Most experimenters use limited random assignment, as discussed in the randomized two-group design section. The major limitation of the before–after two-group design is that it requires a fairly large sample of subjects in order for the procedure to be effective. The W and Y measures for both groups should occur simultaneously. The W measure is used to examine the initial equivalence of the two groups on the dependent variable. Even if they are equivalent on that measure, they could be different on other variables. These secondary variables may interact with the treatment to affect the dependent measures.

A second limitation is that the W observation may sensitize the experimental group to the treatment (experimental contamination: pretest sensitization effect). Therefore the observed effect or lack of effect of the treatment may be due to the W-measure procedure.

TABLE 8.8 Potential Sources of Secondary Variance Not Controlled in a Before–After Two-Group Design

Individual Differences	Outside Influences	Experimental Contamination
None if time of testing is controlled	None if time of testing is controlled	Pretest sensitization to treatment Reactive effects of experimental arrangement

Statistical Analysis

The statistical techniques indicated for the randomized two-group design are also appropriate for the randomized before–after two-group design. The W measures for each group are compared first. If there are no differences between the two groups (two sets of W scores), then the Y measures for the two groups may be directly compared. However, if there are differences between the two sets of W measures, some statistical correction should be made. The simplest correction is to subtract the W scores from the Y scores for each subject, then analyze the resulting two groups of difference scores ($d = Y - W$, where d = difference). The appropriate statistical tests are: the two independent-groups χ^2 test, median χ^2 test, t test for two independent groups, or analysis of variance (chapters 18–20). There are other, usually more appropriate, statistical ways to handle the existence of before-measure group differences (covariance analysis, for example); however, they are beyond the scope of this text. One common, but erroneous, method of analyzing the data is to compute a related t test separately on each group's set of before- and after-scores. The data to be analyzed are all of the Y scores, or all of the $Y - W$ difference scores for both groups simultaneously.

A Misapplication

Comments

A before–after two-group design controls for individual differences by both randomization and measurement. The two-group aspect of the design controls outside-influence sources of secondary variance. The design also provides partial control for experimental contamination.

Sloan, Love, and Ostrom (1974) studied the phenomenon of political heckling. "Heckling" was defined as jeers and jibes directed at a speaker under conditions that did not allow the speaker to be aware of, or respond to, the attacks. Part of this study represents a before–after, two-group design. The subjects were 217 Ohio State University undergraduates who completed a pretest questionnaire (W) that included the question: "In general, do you agree with Richard Nixon's policy views?" (For approximately half the subjects, the politician was Senator Muskie.) The subjects responded on a seven-point Likert scale ranging from "strongly disagree" to "strongly agree." The students then watched 6 min. of a videotaped speech (X) by the politician (Nixon or Muskie), which had been broadcast the night before the November 1970 election.

The students were randomly assigned to the experimental and control groups. For the experimental group, during the presentation of the tape, two male, confederate students delivered five hecklings each (such as "Shoot a few more students, Dick!" and "Bullshit!"). For the control group (in another room), no heckling was arranged.

After the conclusion of the taped speech, the students were given a posttest questionnaire (Y measure) that repeated the key pretest question concerning agreement with the speaker.

The main results were: (1) in general, heckling did not reduce or augment the effectiveness of each speaker; (2) students in the nonheckled control group who were initially neutral toward the speaker (rating of 4) tended to become more favorable after the speech (48% more, 10% less); (3) initially neutral students in the experimental group tended to become *less* favorable toward the speaker (24% less, 12% more);

and (4) of the students with initially extreme positive or negative attitudes toward the speakers, the students in the experimental group tended to give more neutral ratings after the treatment than did the students in the control group. In summary, there was no simple main effect (chapter 10) of heckling; rather, heckling produced opposition to the speaker in initially neutral students and change toward neutrality in students with initially extreme opinions in either direction.

RANDOMIZED-BLOCKS DESIGN

A logical extension of the randomized two-group design is the randomized-blocks design. The purpose of the design is to make the groups more homogeneous prior to the treatment. At the outset of an experiment the design controls both the between-groups and within-group variance. Suppose, for example, that we wish to study the perception of a visual illusion. Visual acuity can be controlled by assigning subjects to blocks. A randomly selected group of 24 subjects is given a visual acuity test. On the basis of the test, the subjects are assigned to three blocks: "good," "average," and "poor." Half the subjects in each block are assigned randomly to the experimental group. The other half are assigned to the control group (Group 2). Consequently, each group contains equal numbers of "good" subjects, "average" subjects, and "poor" subjects.

TABLE 8.9
A Typical Randomized-Blocks Design

Assignment	Group	Before-Observation	Treatment	After-Observation
BR →	1 (Experimental)	—	X	Y_1
→	2 (Control)	—	—	Y_2

Function

The effect of the acuity premeasure is evenly distributed between treatment groups by the assignment procedure, thus ensuring similarity of the groups on that measure. The between-groups and within-groups variance is thus controlled before the introduction of the treatment. In an ideal independent two-group design, the likelihood of a subject being assigned to a group is not affected by the characteristics of any other subjects. In a randomized-blocks design, the subjects *within each block,* are assigned randomly to the treatment and control groups. Although this procedure is very similar to that for matched-group designs (chapter 9), the randomized-blocks design does not involve individual matching of subjects. This fact qualifies the design as an independent two-groups design even though it has some of the features of the related two-groups designs.

The randomized-blocks design is appropriate when you have reason to believe that the value of the dependent variable will be affected by a secondary variable which you can measure. The secondary variable usually is some naturally occurring organismic characteristic such as sex, age, race, intelligence, pulse rate, agility, or visual acuity. Matching the distribution of scores (within-group variance) enhances the possibility of detecting a statistically significant treatment effect. You also can see whether the treatment has a comparable effect over all blocks. Outside influences are well controlled in the design, provided that the normal precaution of controlling time of testing (Y measure) is followed.

Limitations

The randomized-blocks design requires additional experimenter effort in assigning subjects. To be effective, the blocking variable must be related significantly to the dependent measure; the greater the correlation between the blocking variable and the dependent variable, the greater the reduction of the within-groups variance and the stronger the statistical test. If there is little or no relationship between these two variables, then the experimenter wastes research time and undermines the randomization procedure. Ideally, each block should contain a large population to be sampled, and a large number of subjects should be assigned randomly to each group.

TABLE 8.10 Potential Secondary Variance Sources Not Controlled in a Randomized-Blocks Design

Individual Differences	Outside Influences	Experimental Contamination
None if time of testing is controlled and the blocking variable is related to the dependent variable	None if time of testing is controlled	Reactive effects of experimental arrangement

Statistical Analysis

The statistical-analysis techniques appropriate to the randomized two-group design are appropriate here. They include the two independent-groups χ^2, median χ^2, t test for independent groups, and multilevel analysis of variance (chapters 18–20). If the dependent variable is measured at the interval or ratio level (chapter 4), the most appropriate inferential-analysis technique is the randomized-blocks analysis of variance (chapter 20).

Comments

A randomized-blocks design offers considerable control for individual differences. *If the blocking variable is highly related to the dependent variable and a sufficient number of subjects is available,* the design is extremely useful.

A portion of a study by Herman (1974) represents a randomized-blocks design. Male Columbia University students (108) were assigned to two blocks: heavy smokers (20 or more cigarettes per day) or light smokers (15 or less cigarettes per day), based on the blocking variable, their self-reported rate of smoking. The subjects within each block were randomly assigned to two groups, with the limit that average daily consumption of cigarettes was balanced across the two groups. The subjects were engaged in a task that prevented them from smoking for 30 minutes. They were then required to listen to quiet music alone in a setting in which six cigarettes were available. The independent variable was external cue salience. For the high-salience group, the cigarettes were brightly illuminated in an otherwise dark room; for the low-salience group, the cigarettes were not specially illuminated. The students were explicitly told they could smoke the cigarettes at their leisure. The time before smoking the first cigarette and the total number of cigarettes smoked were recorded through a one-way viewing mirror.

The principal results for the time-to-first-cigarette measure were: (1) the external cue did not significantly affect the heavy smokers (a mean of approximately 1 min.); (2) the external cue had a strong effect on the light smokers (a mean of 11 min. to the first cigarette for the low-salient condition vs. a mean of 2 min. for the high-salient condition; and (3) the heavy smokers chose to smoke a cigarette much more quickly, on the average, than the light smokers (mean of about 1 min. vs. mean of about 6 min.). The results for the number of cigarettes smoked were parallel to the results for the latency measure.

It is clear that the blocking variable (reported rate of smoking) was highly related to the dependent variables (number of cigarettes smoked in the experimental setting and latency to the first cigarette). Thus, the randomized-blocks procedure worked for the experimenter. In summary, the study showed that the external cue condition significantly affected the smoking behavior of light smokers but had no effect on the smoking behavior of heavy smokers.

SUMMARY

1. Independent two-group designs involve two levels of an independent variable, or, in other words, varying treatments.
2. The terms "experimental" and "control" group are frequently used to refer to the two groups.
3. In order to provide effective control of secondary variance sources, two-group designs must involve random assignment of the subjects to the two groups.
4. The nature of random assignments is such that the larger the number of subjects in each group, the more powerful the technique.
5. A static-group comparison is a pseudo-design without random assignment. They are employed when the nature of the treatment is such that it cannot be manipulated in an experiment. Static-group comparisons may be the only way to collect information on an event which has already occurred (ex-post-facto research).
6. If you can anticipate the occurrence of a nonexperimental treatment event, it helps to take a before measure on the group of subjects who will experience the event. Still, without random assignment of subjects, the data are difficult to interpret.
7. Small-sample two-group inferential statistical tests are not appropriate for static-group comparisons because the tests assume random assignment.
8. The randomized two-group design is the basic independent group design. It is worth contrasting this design with the basic related-group designs in order to appreciate a vital difference in statistical tests.
9. The before–after two-group design adds a before measurement to assure that the random assignment was effective along the dimension of interest to the experimenter.
10. The randomized-blocks design uses an extremely limited form of random assignment in order to equate the groups even closer. Still, because the subjects are not matched one-by-one, this design is considered to be an independent design and not a matched design.
11. Note that the appropriate statistical tests for all three of the true independent-group designs are the same.

SUGGESTED READINGS

Campbell, D. T., & Stanley, J. C. *Experimental and quasi-experimental designs for research.* Skokie, Ill.: Rand McNally, 1963.

Hills, M. *Statistics for comparative studies.* London: Chapman & Hall, 1974.

Kerlinger, F. N. *Foundations of behavioral research* (2nd ed.). New York: Holt, Rinehart and Winston, 1973.

Scott, W. A., & Wertheimer, M. *Introduction to psychological research.* New York: Wiley, 1962.

Selltiz, C., Wrightsman, L. S., & Cook, S. W. *Research methods in social relations* (3rd ed.). New York: Holt, Rinehart and Winston, 1976.

9

Related Two-Group Designs

The related two-groups designs combine the advantages of the two-group designs with the logic of the one-group designs. Measuring the control treatment and experimental treatment behavior of different subjects prevents contamination from previous experience, a problem particularly vexing in some of the single-subject and one-group designs. At the same time, the related two-group designs match the experimental and control groups on a subject-by-subject basis. Thus, it is possible to establish the difference between each pair's behaviors directly. In contrast, the independent-groups designs involve assigning subjects to the groups in such a way that the average group scores are equivalent without paying attention to the individual subjects within the group. The related designs require more effort in setting up the experiment; but frequently the results yield a generous return.

Related two-groups designs involve the observation of an experimental group and a control group that have been *matched* (chapter 2) on some variable. Because of the matching, each individual in the experimental group may be identified with his or her counterpart in the control group on some measure. Therefore, the dependent scores may be thought of as occurring in pairs, with matched subjects each contributing one half of a pair under each condition. The matching procedure minimizes between-groups variability at the outset of the experiment. The random assignment of the members of each pair to the two groups controls for unknown and/or unmeasurable secondary-variance sources. The combination of matching with random assignment of matched pairs usually results in a more precise statistical analysis of the effect of an experimental treatment than does random assignment alone. The advantages of two-group designs over one-group designs (chapter 8) apply also to the related two-group designs.

MATCH-BY-CORRELATED-CRITERION DESIGN

A match-by-correlated-criterion design involves two groups that are matched in pairs on a measure that is related to the dependent variable. The term "correlated criterion" refers to the criterion measure that is available before the experiment begins and is known to be or assumed to be correlated (chapter 21) with the dependent variable (Y) measure. (Matching pairs with subsequent random assignment of individuals is signified by MR in Table 9.1.)

Function

Matching by correlated criterion allows you to compare the scores of matched subjects in the experimental and control conditions. The design requires that you have access to records that allow matching the subjects prior to the experiment. For example, you might wish to equate two groups in terms of physical ability before

**TABLE 9.1
A Typical Match-by-Correlated-Criterion Design**

Assignment	Group	Before-Observation	Treatment	After-Observation
MR ⟶	1 (Experimental)	—	X	Y_1
⟶	2 (Control)	—	—	Y_2

evaluating a new physical-education program (under the assumption that physical ability is correlated with Y). If the school records include physical-ability scores, you could use these records to match pairs of students before assigning the members of each pair to the old and new physical education programs. The old program is one level (control) and the new program is the other level (experimental) of the independent variable. The dependent measure (Y) would be the rate of learning or the final competency level of each group. Since you randomly assign the members of each pair to the two conditions, the assignment procedure is unbiased.

Advantages

Matching of subjects plus random assignment of subjects to groups is efficient in controlling individual differences. Outside influences such as changes in the weather are controlled by taking the experimental and control Y observations at the same time. If the correlated-criterion measure has been collected in a different context, it is not likely that the correlated-criterion measure will sensitize the subjects to the treatment. In addition to matching the subjects in pairs between the two groups, the subjects *within* each group also may be matched, reducing the within-group variability. Thus, this design has an advantage over any other before–after design.

In general, experimental contamination is controlled in this design. Each individual Y measure is compared with its matched counterpart. Within the limits of measurement error, the differences between the matched scores are presumed to be due to the experimental treatment. A matching design is more sensitive to small differences in levels of the independent variable than are designs without matching.

Limitations

The matching measure must be at least moderately related to the Y measure or the procedure will not accomplish its objective. As a rough rule of thumb, a moderate correlation is approximately .40 to .70. If the experimenter matches subjects on a noncorrelated criterion, his or her research time will be wasted and the effects of random assignment will be diminished. In the statistical analysis, a matching procedure costs degrees of freedom (chapter 16). This cost is offset by the gain in precision, provided that the matching criterion and dependent variables are sufficiently correlated. As indicated in chapters 2 and 8, the effect of random assignment is increased as the total sample size increases. Matching subjects on a correlated criterion can be wasteful because subjects without a match must be discarded. Depending on how closely the pairs of subjects are matched, it is usually the case that many more than 40 subjects must be sampled in order to create two matched groups of 20 each. An extreme example occurred in a study in which 96% of the subjects and the data already collected on them were discarded for lack of a nontreated match, to achieve a final sample of only 23 matched pairs (cited in Althauser & Rubin, 1970, and Campbell & Stanley, 1963). Experimenters usually do not match on a correlated criterion unless they know that the criterion is highly correlated with the Y measure and that they have access to a relatively large population of subjects.

Another limitation is that the correlated criterion and the independent variable should not interact. Such an interaction will increase the within-groups variance of the Y measures, masking the effect of the independent variable.

TABLE 9.2   Potential Sources of Secondary Variance Not Controlled in a Match-by-Correlated-Criterion Design

Individual Differences	Outside Influences	Experimental Contamination
None if time of testing is controlled	History	Pretest sensitization to treatment
		Reactive effects of experimental arrangement

Statistical Analysis

Inferential analysis (chapter 16) of this design depends on the level of measurement and other characteristics of the dependent measure. At the ordinal level of measurement with both groups' scores ranked, the sign test (chapter 17) may be used. At the interval or ratio level use the t test for related groups (chapter 19) or the randomized-blocks analysis of variance (chapter 20). In the analysis of variance each pair of matched subjects forms a "block," so there are as many blocks as there are subjects in a group.

Comments

If a matching criterion that is highly related to the dependent variable exists, and if there is an ample supply of potential subjects, then use this design. In general, the dependent measure is the best bet as a potential matching criterion variable.

A study concerned with methods of increasing academic achievement in primary-grade children (Walker & Hops, 1976) used a complex form of match-by-correlated-criterion design. The 48 children were sampled in pairs from grades one, two, and three. The pairs were matched simultaneously on several criteria. Each pair had to be of the same sex, from the same classroom, of average or above-average intelligence, at or below 60% observed appropriate behaviors in their regular classrooms, and below grade level in mathematics and reading. One child from each pair was randomly assigned to the experimental group and the other to the control group.

The control-group students remained in their regular classrooms throughout the study. The experimental group was removed to an experimental classroom setting for 10 weeks. The experimental group was divided into three groups of eight children each. Each of the three subgroups was reinforced with verbal praise from teachers and points to be exchanged for games, toys, and so on, for academic survival skills, such as paying attention and volunteering, and for direct academic performance. The dependent measures were standardized reading and mathematics test scores and observations of appropriate classroom behaviors. The three subgroups with different reinforcement conditions showed no differential effect on any of the dependent measures.

However, the experimental group as a whole made greater gains in achievement test scores and appropriate classroom behavior than did the matched control group.

A number of studies have been concerned with relating maternal child-rearing attitude and maternal behavior to child development. One variable of interest is prematurity of birth; it has been suggested that mothers become anxious and guilty and develop a "china-doll" attitude toward their premature offspring. Goldstein, Taub, Caputo, and Silberstein (1976) used a match-by-correlated-criterion design to examine this hypothesis. For healthy premature infants born during a 39-month period on Staten Island, New York, a control group was selected by matching with nonpremature infants on sex, race, hospital of birth, socioeconomic status, parity (first-born, second-born, and so on), and date of birth. The sample of 322 babies (161 pairs) received a pediatric examination within 72 hours of birth and a psychiatric/developmental examination at 12 months of age. Between 24 and 48 hours after delivery the mothers were interviewed to collect demographic and IQ data, child-rearing attitudes, and ratings of each baby's activity and potency (size, strength, and ruggedness). Within two weeks of each child's first birthday, the mothers were reinterviewed to secure further child-rearing attitude measures, and their ratings of their children's activity and potency.

Multiple-regression analysis (chapter 21) of the many variables involved in this longitudinal developmental study indicated that a child's premature or nonpremature birth was not related to the mother's child-rearing attitude at 12 months. The overall findings were that maternal child-rearing attitudes at 12 months are related to attitudes at birth and to demographic variables such as parental education, age, and IQ, but not to child-status variables such as prematurity, sex, size, potency, activity, and so on. Maternal controlling attitudes and hostile attitudes toward the child were associated with lower socioeconomic level, lower IQs of the mother, and older fathers. The "china doll" hypothesis was not supported; at least for the first year of the baby's life, maternal attitudes do not seem to be related to characteristics of the child.

BEFORE–MATCH–AFTER DESIGN

In the before–match–after design, a before-observation is made with the specific intent of using the data to match the experimental and control subjects. As opposed to the less intrusive matching of the preceeding design, in the before–match–after design the pretest measurement occurs because the experimenter needs the data to match subjects. As in the match-by-correlated-criterion design, each pair of matched subjects is assigned randomly to the two treatments (symbolized by MR in Table 9.3).

TABLE 9.3
A Typical Before–Match–After Design

Before-Observation	Assignment	Group	Treatment	After-Observation
W	MR →1 (Experimental)		X	Y_1
	→2 (Control)		—	Y_2

Function

Matching the groups allows you to compare the scores of matched subjects under the experimental and control conditions directly. The design requires that you pretest the groups on a W measure before the administration of the treatment and collection of the Y measures. The statistical analysis is then applied to the Y data. The random assignment of subjects in each pair to the two groups means that the assignment procedure is unbiased.

Advantages

A before–match–after design has most of the advantages of the match-by-correlated-criterion design. Individual differences are specifically controlled by the design. The effect of the W measure on the Y measure (testing or sequence effect) is held constant for both groups. Outside influences are controlled by collecting the W measures for each group simultaneously and the Y measure for each group simultaneously or nearly so. The before–match–after design is more powerful than the before–after independent two-group design because of the greater reduction in between-group variability before the treatment is administered. Therefore, the before--match–after design is more likely to detect a small treatment effect than the before–after two-group design.

Limitations

The before-matching procedure introduces one possible experimental-contamination factor: The before-observation might alter the experimental subjects' responses to the experimental treatment. That is, in contrast to the match-by-correlated-criterion design, it is more likely that the W-measurement procedure may interact with X.

The experimenter must administer a before-measure to the subjects and, within each matched pair of subjects, randomly assign them to the two groups. The same limitation with respect to the correlation between the criterion and Y in the match-by-correlated-criterion design applies to the before–match–after design.

In both the match-by-correlated-criterion design and the before–match–after design, the matching procedure must not include discarding a few subjects from one or both groups in order to make the experimental and control groups more similar (for example, in group means) before the treatment begins. Such an erroneous procedure has several defects: (1) group-assignment bias is introduced in that the subjects are no longer strictly randomly assigned to groups or randomly assigned within matched pairs; (2) if the sample was randomly selected from a population, the elimination of "deviant" subjects in order to make more equivalent groups means that the sample is no longer representative of the population; and (3) the usual way that subjects are discarded to make group means similar is to delete the extreme high W-score subjects from one group and the extreme low W-score subjects from the other group; the effect of such a procedure is to introduce statistical regression as an uncontrolled source of individual differences. The group means may shift because of upward regression of the group with deleted high scores and downward regression of the group with deleted low scores.

The problem of statistical regression is particularly hazardous in naturalistic studies in which extreme groups are compared on a Y measure or in studies in which a W measure is used nonrandomly to select extreme groups to compare on a Y measure. There are legitimate ways to accomplish such matching with static-group observational studies (Althauser & Rubin, 1970; Rubin, 1973a,b).

TABLE 9.4 Potential Sources of Secondary Variance Not Controlled in a Before–Match–After Design

Individual Differences	Outside Influences	Experimental Contamination
None if time of testing is controlled	None if time of testing is controlled	Pretest sensitization to treatment
		Reactive effect of experimental arrangement

Statistical Analysis

Since the subjects and groups are matched on the basis of the before-measure, there is no purpose in statistically examining the W measures. The Y measures may be examined with exactly the same techniques listed for the match-by-correlated design: sign test, t test for related groups, or randomized-blocks analysis of variance (chapters 17, 19, and 20 respectively).

Comments

If used inappropriately the control procedures themselves may interfere with the interpretation of the data. In order to maximize the generalizability of the results, the entire population should be given the W measure; a subpopulation of matched pairs then would be created and the experimental sample of pairs would be selected randomly from that population. Such an ideal procedure would allow the clear generalization of results from the sample to a precisely known population. Unfortunately, such a procedure is seldom technically or financially feasible. To the extent that subjects are discarded because matches cannot be found, the sample is biased in an unknown way. However, when a large sample is available, an appropriate W measure is feasible, and matching results in the discarding of no more than a few cases, the before–match–after design is a powerful one.

A before–match–after design was used in a recent study of social influences on person perception. It has often been suggested that a fundamental human need is to achieve a sense of control or mastery over one's environment. Kelley (1971) proposed that a person will tend to modify his or her social perceptions in such a way as to bolster feelings of personal control, and the desire to maintain a sense of control may serve as an important source of bias in attributing characteristics to others. For example, research has shown that persuaders will be assigned greater intelligence by someone who yields to their persuasive arguments than by disinterested bystanders.

Likewise, persuaders see an easily persuaded target as more intelligent than an unyielding target. Cialdini and Mirels (1976) used a before–match–after design with 112 subjects in a study of these social processes. Pairs of subjects were matched on sex, pesonal-control scores (Rotter Internal–External Scale), attitudes, and degrees of interest in two social issues (taxation of churches, legalization of marijuana). A confederate of the experimenters stated a pro or con "opinion" on each of the two issues (always opposite to the opinion shared by the pair of subjects). One of each pair was randomly assigned the role of "persuader" (stating his/her opinion and trying for at least 30 sec. to persuade the confederate to change his opinion); the other member of each pair was the "observer" who did not publicly reveal an opinion. At the conclusion of each persuasive argument, the confederate announced whether or not his or her opinion had been changed.

Several independent and dependent variables were involved in the study. One independent variable was the role played by the subject (persuader or observer). One of the dependent measures was the rating of intelligence of the confederate (target of persuasion). As predicted, the intelligence of the yielding target was rated higher by the persuader than by the matched observer. (This portion of the study provides an example of before–match–after, two-group design.)

The most interesting results of the study, which involved a very complex multivariate, matched-groups, factorial design, were: (1) among subjects who strongly believed in their ability to control their own lives, a yielding target was viewed more positively and a resister more negatively by persuaders than by observers; and (2) among subjects who strongly believed that they did not control their fates, persuaders regarded the resister more positively and yielder more negatively than did the matched observers. Those with low belief in their own power evaluated other people in a pattern opposite to those who had a strong belief in their own power.

YOKED CONTROL-GROUP DESIGN

A yoked control-group design consists of manipulating the environment (X') of a control subject so that the stimulus conditions correspond to those of an experimental subject. Occasionally subjects in an experimental group encounter different exposures to a treatment due to their own performance. For example, if a subject must learn to avoid electric shock, a subject who learns the task quickly experiences less total shock. In human verbal-retention experiments, a major problem is to control for differences in the original level of learning. There is a need to match the subjects in terms of the amount of practice and particular sequence of learning experiences. This matching may be accomplished by "yoking" pairs or triples of subjects together. The yoking may occur through physical means (as in the case of oxen yokes) or through more indirect procedures such as the programmed sequence of experiences two subjects receive. For example, if the experimental subject controls the reinforcement conditions received by pushing a bar or level, then a record of the exact frequency and rate of bar pressing can be kept. The yoked-control subject can be exposed to the identical reinforcement conditions according to that record. The yoked control-group design matches the subjects in terms of time and stimulus events (symbolized by X' in Table

TABLE 9.5
A Typical Yoked
Control-Group
Design

Before-Observation	Assignment	Group	Treatment	After-Observation
—	R ⟶	1 (Experimental)	$X(X')$	Y_1
—	⟶	2 (Control)	(X')	Y_2

9.5). A control-group subject is exposed to the same quantity of experimental conditions as an experimental subject. The difference between the treatment and control subjects is the contingent relationship between the subject's behavior and environmental events. The experimental group controls the occurrence of stimulation; the control group does not. Statistical analysis is applied to the differences between the Y scores of matched (yoked) subjects.

Function

A yoked control-group design specifically controls for secondary variables introduced as a result of the subject's actions in the experiment. Brady's (1958) experiment on "executive monkeys" provides a good example of a yoked control-group design. Brady found that monkeys receiving electric shock on a fixed time schedule could learn to avoid the shock by pressing a bar before the shock was due to be given. He also found that prolonged exposure to this situation caused the animals to develop massive stomach ulcers. Brady could not be sure whether the ulceration was the result of the "responsibility" for turning off the shock or a natural physiological response to being shocked. Brady attacked the problem with a yoked-control design. The experimental animals were placed in a shock-avoidance situation with a lever, which if pressed would terminate the shock. The control animals were placed in an identical apparatus; however, manipulation of the lever did not control the shock. The two apparatuses were interconnected so that both animals experienced the same sequence and number of shocks (X'). (Brady named his experimental animals "executives" and the control animals "employees," describing the different roles in the decision-making process.) The "executive" animals all developed ulcers, while the corresponding "employees" did not. Since the only *known* important difference between the yoked pairs was the "executive" monkey's ability to control onset of shock, Brady concluded that ulceration was indeed an "executive" malady.

Instead of randomly assigning the members of each yoked pair to the two treatment conditions, Brady assigned the four monkeys to the "executive condition" that exhibited the highest rate of avoidance responding on a pretest. The remaining four were the control or "employee" monkeys. This assignment procedure has subsequently been shown to be an unfortunate choice; rate of avoidance responding is a variable that is related to the rate of ulceration under shock avoidance learning conditions. Weiss (1971a,b,c) conducted replications and several variations of the Brady study with a large number of rats in a series of yoked triplet design studies. In those situations most analogous to the Brady study, the randomly chosen "executive" rats developed *less* ulceration than their yoked "employee" rats. Weiss developed a theory that accounts for both his results and those of Brady. The contrast between the two studies illustrates the importance of random assignment of subjects to groups and the fact that research "facts" are only temporarily established until new information leads to new (and sometimes quite different) "facts."

Advantages

When the experimental situation involves a number of environmental-change factors that cannot be preprogrammed, a yoked control-group design may be necessary to isolate a significant factor. Individual differences are controlled by randomly assigning one member of each yoked pair to the experimental group and the other member to the control group. Outside influences are controlled by testing the pairs of subjects at approximately the same time (Brady and Weiss tested them at exactly the same time). The yoked control-group design also controls for experimental contamination.

Limitations

The manipulations necessary to create a yoked control-group condition increase the costs involved in research. Often these manipulations require the construction of complicated equipment, as in the Brady and Weiss studies. On the other hand, the yoked control-group design is a less costly design in terms of subject selection than either of the preceding matching designs. The subjects are matched (yoked) on experimental conditions, not on the basis of a correlated criterion or pretest; therefore, no subjects need to be discarded because matching scores are not available.

You must be able to assign subjects to the experimental conditions. The effect of random assignment in controlling sources of secondary variance is increased as the total sample size increases.

TABLE 9.6   Potential Sources of Secondary Variance Not Controlled in a Yoked Control-Group Design

Individual Differences	Outside Influences	Experimental Contamination
None if time of testing is controlled	None if time of testing is controlled	Reactive effects of experimental arrangement

Statistical Analysis

The statistical analysis is exactly the same as that for the match-by-correlated-criterion and before–match–after designs. The possible techniques include: the sign test (chapter 17), the t test for related groups (chapter 19), and the randomized-blocks analysis of variance (chapter 20). In the analysis of variance, each yoked pair of subjects forms a block.

Comments

A yoked-control design should be employed whenever it is technically feasible. To be even more effective, it could be combined with one of the subject-matching procedures we have described.

Bloom and Esposito (1975) studied the effects of response-dependent (contingent) social stimulation and response-independent social stimulation on infant vocalization. Previous research indicated that infant vocalization was controlled by contingent social stimulation such as smiling, touching, and adult speech. However, informal, anecdotal reports indicated that young infants' vocalization rates did not depend directly on contingent adult behaviors.

A yoked control-group design was used with 16 three-month-old infants studied in their own homes. Baseline rates of vocalization (chapter 11) were established for each child with the adult experimenter present but not providing any social stimulation. Then the eight response-dependent (experimental group) subjects received a smile, a touch on the abdomen, and "tsk, tsk, tsk" for each vocalization. For two of these subjects the timing of the experimenter's social stimulation was recorded. Five of the response-independent subjects were yoked to one of these two children and the remaining three were yoked to the other child. That is, for the eight control subjects, the adult experimenter smiled, touched the infant's abdomen, and said "tsk, tsk, tsk" according to the tape-recorded sequence established for the two response-dependent children. (Taped cues were presented through earphones.) Thus, the adult's social responses did not depend on the child's behavior for the response-independent control group. Instead of a simple yoked-pairs design, the experimenters chose to yoke groups of control subjects with two of the experimental subjects. The rate of infant vocalization (dependent measure, Y) was recorded with a second tape recorder.

Infant vocalization increased when the adult subjects responded to the children. However, contrary to the findings of previous research, there was no difference in rate of responding between the experimental and control subjects. That is, the infants' vocalization responses did not depend on a contingent relationship between the child and adult behaviors. Merely having an adult present and smiling and so on was sufficient to produce infant vocalization regardless of the timing of the adult's behaviors.

A very old theory is that vision develops as a result of spontaneous movement in a physical environment. Held and Hein (1963) tested this theory using a yoked control-group design. They reared kittens in total darkness until they could walk with fair proficiency. Yoked pairs were then assigned to an active movement condition and a passive movement condition respectively. A "kitten carousel" physically yoked each pair together so that one kitten had its feet on the ground (the active kitten) and the other was carried in a cradle (the passive kitten). Whenever the active kitten moved, the passive kitten moved in a corresponding manner. The carousel, which permitted circular movement around its central axis, was placed inside a large cylindrical arena with vertically striped walls. The amount and kind of visual experience was the same for each yoked pair, but the active kitten controlled the sequence of visual stimulation while the passive kitten passively experienced it.

The kittens received their visual experience only in the carousel. When mature they were given a variety of visually guided behavior tests. The active cats performed well on all tests; the passive cats acted as if they were blind. The researchers concluded that active movement is necessary to the development of visually guided behavior.

Pay particular attention to the difference between the independent-group procedures (chapter 8) and the procedures under the matched-groups designs. The independent-groups designs involve assigning subjects to the groups in such a way that the average group scores are equivalent, without paying attention to the individual subjects within the group. The matched designs, on the other hand, match individual subjects, with one each in the experimental and the control group. Each subject observed under the experimental condition has a corresponding subject in the control group generating control data. Although the difference may seem trivial at the present time, it becomes a very important factor when you analyze data. In order to select the right statistical technique for data analysis, the researcher must understand the difference between related-groups designs and independent-groups designs. The precision of the related-groups designs frequently justifies the extra costs incurred by their use.

SUMMARY

1. Related two-group designs involve an experimental group and control group that are matched subject-for-subject.
2. The matching procedure involves more complicated experimental procedures than for independent-group designs, but it provides a more sensitive basis for data analysis and interpretation.
3. The reason for the matching procedure is to make the subjects in the experimental and control groups as similar as possible on the dependent variable. If the procedure does not accomplish this, the effort is a waste of time and effort.
4. The match-by-correlated-criterion design uses a measure other than the dependent variable as a basis for matching. The stronger the correlation between the criterion measure and the dependent variable, the more effective the procedure.
5. The before–match–after design uses a measure of the dependent variable as the criterion of matching. This matching procedure is more likely to be effective, but it may introduce secondary variance due to the premeasurement procedure.
6. The yoked-control design matches the subjects in terms of their interaction with the treatment condition. In many training procedures, the experimental subjects create different sequences of treatment conditions because of their own behavior. The yoked control exposes a control subject to exactly the same sequence.
7. The data from these related designs are treated as if each pair of observations were from the same hypothetical subject. Thus, the statistical tests involve examining the difference observed on a subject-by-subject basis.

SUGGESTED READINGS

Campbell, D. T., & Stanley, J. C. *Experimental and quasi-experimental designs for research.* Skokie, Ill.: Rand McNally, 1963.

Scott, W. A., & Wertheimer, M. *Introduction to psychological research.* New York: Wiley, 1962.

Selltiz, C., Wrightsman, L. S., & Cook, S. W. *Research methods in social relations* (3rd ed.). New York: Holt, Rinehart and Winston, 1976.

10

Multiple-Treatment Designs

Multiple-treatment designs solve the limitations of two-group designs by simultaneously conducting two, three, four, or more two-group designs in a single experiment. In other words, the elements of one- and two-group designs are the "building blocks" of multiple-treatment designs. Sometimes the additional groups are used to investigate various levels of a treatment. In other studies several treatments are simultaneously investigated. When groups experience combinations of two or more treatments simultaneously, you can measure the interaction between them. More than half of published research studies examine potential interactions. Multiple-treatment designs begin to approach the complexity of the multiple causes of behavior.

The designs presented in the three preceding chapters vary in complexity, but they are all relatively simple. Unfortunately for the beginning student, most research reported in professional journals does not employ these designs. Rather, it involves the use of multiple treatments in various combinations, usually with multiple measures of behavior. This chapter introduces the simpler forms of multiple-treatment designs.

A multiple-treatment design involves more than two levels of the independent variable or more than one independent variable in a single experiment. Multiple-treatment designs usually require more subjects but yield more information than one- or two-group designs. The number of variables and the number of levels of each variable in a single experiment are determined by the research hypotheses, the experimenter's imagination, the available research tools, and the availability of subjects. The subjects in various groups may be randomized, matched, or both. The dependent variable(s) must be the same over all treatments. The research may involve multiple measures on a single dependent variable or measures on several dependent variables. For example, people may be tested on reading comprehension several times; or, they may be tested on reading comprehension, reaction time, and typing skill in the same experiment. Clearly, multiple-treatment designs can be complex. In this chapter we present three main types of multiple-treatment design: multilevel design, factorial designs, and the Solomon four-group design. Two special forms of the factorial design—the randomized-blocks factorial design and the repeated-measures factorial design— also are discussed.

MULTILEVEL DESIGN

In one sense, a multilevel design is several two-group designs run simultaneously. To illustrate this complex situation, let us examine an example from research on speech anxiety.

Speech anxiety may be measured in two ways: (1) objective, behavioral measures in a speech-giving situation, such as mannerisms, number of words spoken per unit of time, duration of silences, and number of "ahh" and "duh" utterances; and (2) subjective measures of fear in a speech-giving situation, such as self-reports of confidence and ability in making a speech before an audience, and self-report inventories of social avoidance and fear of negative evaluations. There are two forms of therapy that have been applied successfully to cases of speech anxiety: group insight and group desensitization. **Group insight therapy** involves attempting to increase the client's awareness of self-verbalizations and internalized sentences that contribute to the maladaptive behavior. The client is encouraged to examine possible incompatible self-instructions and other behaviors incompatible with negative verbalizations. The therapy is based on the assumption that maladaptive self-verbalizations are instrumental in producing anxiety. The clients discuss the irrational and self-defeating aspects of such verbalizations and internalized sentences emitted while thinking about the speech situation. **Group desensitization therapy** involves group training in relaxation techniques, constructing a group hierarchy of the anxiety-provoking speech-giving and of other social situations (ranging from least anxiety-provoking to most anxiety-provoking), group training in visualizing (imagining) each of these elements, and pairing the relaxation experiences with the imagined speech-making scenes, slowly moving from the least anxiety-provoking scenes to the most anxiety-provoking scenes in the hierarchy. The group should come to be less sensitive (desensitized) to the anxiety-producing situation, as a function of associating relaxation, which is incompatible with anxiety, with the imagined speech-making scene. The theory behind desensitization is that a person cannot be both anxious and relaxed at the same time.

Meichenbaum, Gilmore, and Fedoravicius (1971) conducted a well-controlled study of the relative effectiveness of the two therapies on speech anxiety. A combined desensitization-insight treatment condition was employed with a desensitization treatment condition and an insight treatment condition in a *multilevel design*. In addition a

Placebo

"speech-discussion" *placebo* control group was employed; the control group met with the therapist and discussed neutral (nonanxiety-provoking) topics. The placebo group was included to control for nonspecific group-treatment factors such as expectation of relief, suggestion, therapist-patient relationships, and group spirit resulting from frequent group meetings. Another control group was placed on a "waiting list" and measured for any improvement over the period of the study while waiting for treatment. Thus, a total of five groups were involved in the study. All five received both objective and subjective measures of speech anxiety before and after receiving eight weeks (1 hr per week) of group treatment.

Several dependent measures of both types were used. In brief, the results indicated that the insight and desensitization therapies were about equally effective on all measures. The combined desensitization-insight therapy and the speech-discussion placebo "therapy" were about equally effective as measured by behavioral measures of mannerisms and a self-report anxiety checklist, and both were less effective on these measures than insight or desensitization alone. Except with the "ahh" mannerism, the combined desensitization-insight therapy was as effective as either therapy alone in all other measures, and the speech-discussion treatment was less effective. Being on a waiting list did not lead to any improvement.

The Meichenbaum et al. (1971) study is a good example of a multilevel design. The use of two control groups, two primary treatment groups, and the combined-therapies treatment group provided more information than any two-group design could possibly provide. The use of the placebo control group with the waiting-list control group was a powerful procedure. The results indicate the usefulness of these two control groups.

Multilevel Design

As our example shows, a **multilevel design** uses several levels of the independent variable. Usually several independent groups are exposed to different levels of treatment, including a zero level (no-treatment control group). Occasionally, one

TABLE 10.1
A Multilevel Design with Four Independent Groups

Group	Assignment	Before-Observation	Treatment	After-Observation
1	R	(W_1)	—	Y_1
2	R	(W_2)	X_1	Y_2
3	R	(W_3)	X_2	Y_3
4	R	(W_4)	X_3	Y_4

Repeated-Measures Multilevel Design

group of subjects is exposed to each level of the design (**repeated-measures multilevel design**). In the independent-groups version, the subjects are assigned randomly to groups, and the groups are assigned randomly to the levels of the treatment (Table 10.1).

There may be pretests of each group, indicated by W_i in Table 10.1. As is the case in the before–after two-group design, initial differences between the groups complicate data analysis. If you have time, the groups may be matched on the pretest measures, or you may subtract the before-score from the after-score for each subject, then analyze the remaining difference score. Before-measures are not necessary to a multilevel design; however, as indicated in the preceding chapters, pretests normally improve a design.

Function

Multivalent Research

A multilevel design allows you to evaluate several levels of the independent variable under comparable conditions. You can determine whether or not the treatment affects behavior, and the effect of varying levels of the treatment. As indicated in chapter 2, a multilevel design is used for *multivalent* research. Multilevel design research indicates the presence of a linear (straight line) or nonlinear (curved) relationship between the independent and dependent variables. A graph of the average score for each group usually portrays the main feature of the data.

The following study is an example of a *repeated-measures multilevel design* that illustrates the value of a multilevel design in detecting the form of the functional relationship between the independent and dependent variables. Haber (1958) studied affective judgments as a function of deviations of temperature from the adaptation level. Male college students adapted both hands to water of a given temperature. Then

FIG. 10.1
A hypothetical M-shaped curve. The ordinate contains the observed rank of affect, and the abscissa presents the measure of difference in degrees C from adaptation level.

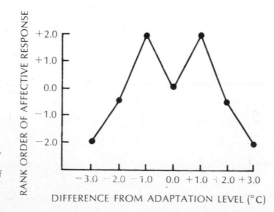

they placed each hand in different buckets containing water at different temperatures. Each man removed his hand from the least pleasant temperature. The students were tested several times with various degrees of difference in temperature. Slight increases or decreases in temperature from the adaptation level were preferred. Greater differences, either colder or hotter, were felt to be unpleasant. In summary, while there were differences between individuals, the graphed mean data points tended to form a "butterfly" or "M-shaped" curve similar to the theoretical curve of Figure 10.1. Clearly, the relationship is not linear, and such information could not be obtained with a two-group or two-level design.

Advantages

Multilevel designs are extensions of the randomized two-group designs (see chapters 8 and 9). The advantages of the corresponding two-group designs generally apply to multilevel designs. These include the value of random assignment in controlling for individual differences and three more optional advantages: the value of before-observations in checking for initial equivalence of groups; the value of matching (repeated measures on the same subject, groups matched on a correlated criterion, or groups matched on a before-measure) in controlling for between-groups variance; and the value of yoking as a control for individual differences. Outside influences as a source of secondary variance are normally controlled by controlling the time of testing of all groups.

TABLE 10.2 Potential Sources of Secondary Variance Not Controlled in the Various Forms of Multilevel Design

Form of Multilevel Design	Source of Secondary Variance		
	Individual Differences	Outside Influences	Experimental Contamination
Randomized, No Before-Measures	None if time of testing is controlled	None if time of testing is controlled	Reactive effects of experimental arrangement
Randomized, Before-Measures	None if time of testing is controlled	None if time of testing is controlled and correlated-criterion measures are not too old	Pretest sensitization to treatment Reactive effects of experimental arrangement
One-Group, Repeated Measures	None if time of testing is controlled	None if time of testing is controlled	Reactive effects of experimental arrangement Multiple-treatment interaction—Confounding

Limitations

The limitations of the corresponding two-group designs generally apply to multilevel designs. You must be able to assign the subjects to the various groups prior to the treatment; therefore ex-post-facto studies are excluded. The larger the treatment groups, the more likely random assignment will control for individual differences. All

W and Y measurements must be administered simultaneously or as close to simultaneously as possible. If a W measure is used, it is possible there will be a pretest sensitization effect; if groups are matched on a correlated criterion, the criterion must be moderately to highly related to the Y measure; and if groups are matched on a before-measure, the before-measure may interact with the treatment (pretest sensitization effect). In addition, multilevel designs usually require more subjects than simpler designs.

Statistical Analysis

The analysis of variance (chapter 20) is most appropriate to the multilevel design, given an interval or ratio level of measurement. In the analysis of variance of a multilevel design, the effects of all levels of a variable such as type of therapy can be assessed simultaneously. If the dependent variable is measured at the nominal level the multiple-group χ^2 test (chapter 18) is appropriate. If the dependent variable is measured at the ordinal level, use the Kruskal-Wallis one-way analysis of variance by ranks (Kirk, 1968; not included in this text).

Comments

A multilevel design can be used in a pilot study where you are primarily interested in finding the most effective treatment levels for subsequent experiments, called "optimal values" (chapter 2). It is also useful for determining more precisely the functional relationship between a dependent and independent variable that two-group design research has shown to be effective.

FACTORIAL DESIGNS

Suppose you want to investigate the effect of the combination of lack of sleep and lack of food on final examination scores in an experimental-psychology class. (This example can only be hypothetical; the ethical problems associated with such a study are numerous and prohibitive.) You would assign a different group of persons randomly to each specific combination of the two variables. Variable A might be the number of hours of food deprivation (24 and 48) and variable B might be the number of hours without sleep (36 and 72) (see Table 10.4). The students in Group I would not be allowed to eat for 24 hours or sleep for 36 hours. The students in Group II would not be allowed to eat for 24 hours or sleep for 72 hours. Students in Group III would not be allowed to eat for 48 hours or sleep for 36 hours, and those in Group IV would not be allowed to eat for 48 hours or sleep for 72 hours (the really unpleasant condition). You now have a factorial design.

TABLE 10.3
A 2 × 2 Factorial Design

		Variable B	
		B_1	B_2
Variable A	A_1	I	II
	A_2	III	IV

TABLE 10.4
Hypothetical
Example of a 2 × 2
Factorial Design

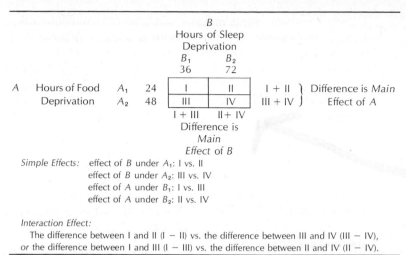

Simple Effects: effect of B under A_1: I vs. II
effect of B under A_2: III vs. IV
effect of A under B_1: I vs. III
effect of A under B_2: II vs. IV

Interaction Effect:
The difference between I and II (I − II) vs. the difference between III and IV (III − IV),
or the difference between I and III (I − III) vs. the difference between II and IV (II − IV).

Randomized
Factorial Design

A **factorial design** involves all possible combinations of the levels of two or more independent variables. Thus, the effects of two or more independent variables can be measured in a single experiment. A factorial design may be a related design, in which each subject experiences all of the treatment conditions; it may be an independent design, in which different groups of subjects experience a single treatment; or it may be a mixed design, in which a subject experiences all levels of one treatment, but only one level of another treatment. In Table 10.3, each independent variable (A and B) has two levels (1 and 2). There are four combinations of the two levels of each variable (the four quadrants: I, II, III, and IV). The example is called a 2 × 2 (read "two by two") factorial design. A given factorial design may involve more levels of each variable, for example, 3 × 5, or 2 × 4, or more variables than two, for example, 2 × 2 × 2, or 2 × 2 × 2 × 2. Or a factorial design may involve any combination of levels and variables, for example, 2 × 3 × 5, or 3 × 2 × 9. The hypothetical food- and sleep-deprivation example is an independent-groups, 2 × 2, factorial design (Table 10.4).

Function

Factorial designs are *efficient* since data concerning the effects of two or more variables are collected simultaneously from each subject. To evaluate the effect of variable A, compare all the scores under treatment A_1 with all the scores under treatment A_2. Combine the scores of quadrants I and II to determine the average performance under treatment A_1, and combine the scores in quadrants III and IV to determine the average for A_2. The effects of the two levels of B are equally represented in the two combinations of quadrants (I-II and III-IV). To determine the effect of variable B, compare all of the B_1 scores with all of the B_2 scores. Add the exam scores of quadrants I and III to determine the average score for 36 hours without sleep, and add the scores for quadrants II and IV to find the average score under 72 hours of sleep deprivation. The average effects of the independent variables are called the

Main Effects

main effects of the design.

Simple Effects

The effects of the two levels of B under *each level of A,* and the effects of the two levels of A under each level of B are called the **simple effects** of the design. You can determine the effect of different hours without sleep when the students have gone without food for 24 hours, and also when they have gone without food for 48 hours. In the same fashion, you can determine the differential effect of food deprivation under each level of sleep deprivation.

Interaction Effect

The effect of both levels of B under both levels of A is called the **interaction effect.** It could also be worded as the effect of both levels of A under both levels of B. As indicated in chapter 3, an interaction effect occurs if the effect of one variable, for example, food deprivation, depends on the level of another variable, for example, sleep deprivation. The presence or absence of an interaction is determined by comparing the effect of the B variable at the first level of the A variable ($1 - \text{II} = $ effect of B at A_1) with the effect of the B variable at the second level of the A variable ($\text{III} - \text{IV} = $ effect of B at A_2). In other words, you examine the data to find any *difference between differences,* or compare the two simple effects of B to see whether they are approximately equal.

2×2 Randomized Factorial Design

This section presents one real research example involving a factorial design. The example is included to facilitate your understanding of the basic, randomized factorial design.

On a scale ranging from short-term, small, local-community efforts to long-term, huge, international efforts, great amounts of human and financial resources are spent annually on various aid and human-care service programs. The general goals of these efforts include alleviating the suffering of the aid receiver, promoting general good-will and brotherhood, and encouraging people to become self-sufficient. There have been a number of studies on the receiver's reaction to such aid; most have dealt with the effects of aid on the receiver's evaluation of the donor. Some research has focused on the self-perception of the receiver.

In general, research on receiver evaluation of the donor indicates that the evaluation depends on the conditions associated with the aid. Under certain conditions the receipt of aid may be perceived as a supportive or threatening experience to the receiver. Free aid may be perceived as supportive by the receiver since it serves to overcome natural or personal disasters and convey positive information about the giver's liking and concern. On the other hand, aid may be perceived as threatening by the receiver since it may suggest the failure and relative inferiority of the receiver, which has led to a state of dependency. For example, state welfare aid to parents with dependent children may seem threatening to them. The donor's level of resources also may affect the receiver's evaluation of the donor; relatively poor donors get more favorable receiver responses than do relatively wealthy donors. Aid may have a more positive attributional value when it is seen as being a large sacrifice than when it is seen as a small sacrifice. That is, the receiver infers the degree of caring and concern of the donor from the degree of effort or sacrifice represented by the aid.

Fisher and Nadler (1976) hypothesized that receipt of aid representing a relatively high cost to the donor should be seen as a supportive experience by the receiver, since the gift conveys donor liking and concern and does not stress failure and dependency cues. In contrast, a gift that is of relatively low cost to the donor should be seen as threatening to the receiver since it stresses the failure and dependency of the receiver without providing the supportive cues of liking and concern. To oversimplify, a $100 gift to a poor family from a very rich person may serve to make the poor family evaluate themselves as cheap, relatively worthless, helpless persons; however, the same gift from a poor neighbor may cause the poor family to evaluate themselves as good people because the giver obviously cares for and is concerned about them.

Fisher and Nadler conducted a complex research study designed to test these two hypotheses. The design was essentially a 2 × 2 factorial design with several dependent measures. The two independent variables were (1) receipt of aid (aid or no-aid) and (2) resources of the donor offering the aid (high or low). College males were assigned randomly to each of the four experimental conditions of the 2 × 2 factorial design (Table 10.5). The students were tested in groups of 8–12 in individual soundproof cubicles containing a television monitor with earphones. Each student was told he was matched with a "pair-mate" with whom he would later interact in the experiment. (The pair-mate didn't really exist.) All instructions were videotaped.

The experiment was described as a stock market simulation (the "Stock Market Game"), supposedly consisting of four playing periods. The first period was designed to involve the students in the game and enhance the deception that the game really was a stock market simulation. The second period was an investment period in which the students were led to believe that they could accumulate resources through investment policies. The projected third and fourth periods, which did not actually occur, were also supposed to be investment periods. At the beginning of the second period, the students were given 30 poker chips for investment and were motivated to accumulate a large collection of chips by cleverly using the investment information provided. Actually, the investment outcomes were preprogrammed for each person. The students were informed that during the projected fourth period they would invest jointly with their pair-mate.

During each trial of the second period, the students were notified how many chips they could invest in any company they chose. Following each decision, they received a computer print-out containing the results of their choice and the choices of all of the other 11 supposed participants in the game, listed by player number. (All subjects were actually always Number 6.) At the end of the second period, all students had only four chips left while apparently the fictitious other players had experienced varying degrees of success and failure. All students thus faced the danger of being eliminated from the game at the beginning of the third period, since they needed 3–5 chips to invest on each trial and anyone who did not have enough to invest would be eliminated from the game.

TABLE 10.5
Experimental Design of Fisher and Nadler (1976) Study

		Receipt of Aid	
		No Aid (0)	Aid (4)
Resources of "Pair-Mate"	Low (16)	15[a]	17
	High (60)	17	15

[a]The numbers within each cell indicate the number of subjects under each combination of conditions.

At the end of the second period of play, the "high-resource" imaginary pair-mate had 60 chips, setting him among the most successful fictitious players, and the "low-resource" pair-mate had 16 chips, setting him among the least successful apparent players. All students in the aid condition received an envelope from their pair-mate containing four chips as a donation, representing a low cost to the high-resource person and relatively high cost for the low-resource person. Students in the no-aid condition received no envelopes.

Following the receipt or nonreceipt of aid, all students were asked to fill out an "interim report" questionnaire containing several sections. Three of these sections were: (1) a measure of situational self-esteem, how intelligent and self-confident the person perceived himself to be relative to the other players; (2) a measure of self-evaluation, summed bipolar Likert descriptive adjective scales; and (3) a measure of evaluation of the pair-mate, similar to Measure 2.

Measure of situational self-esteem. The results for the self-esteem measure are presented in Figure 10.2. It was hypothesized that higher self-esteem should result from receiving aid from a relatively poor donor than from a relatively rich donor. In other words, this hypothesis is that the variables of donor resources and aid will interact. For the self-esteem measure, there was no reliable *main effect* of either independent variable. The aid mean did not significantly differ from the no-aid mean, and the high-resource donor mean did not significantly differ from the low-resource donor mean. There was a reliable *interaction effect*. An interaction effect is most clearly comprehended when the data are presented in graphic form. As can be seen in Figure 10.2, the students who received aid from a low-resource donor tended to have higher ratings of their own self-esteem in the situation than students who did not receive aid from their poor pair-mate. In contrast, students who received aid from a high-resource donor tended to have lower situational self-esteem than men not receiving aid from the rich pair-mate. The hypothesis that the effect of aid on self-esteem would depend on donor resources, or that the two variables would interact, was clearly supported by the results of the self-esteem measure. The data are presented in the graph by placing one independent variable (aid–no aid) on the

Significant Interaction with No Main Effects

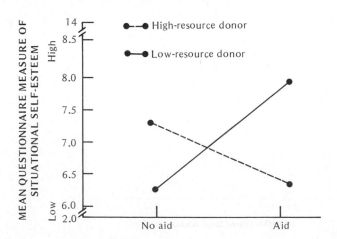

FIG. 10.2
Aid-by-resources interaction for questionnaire measure of situational self-esteem. (From "Effect of donor resources on recipient self-esteem and self-help" by J. D. Fisher and A. Nadler, *Journal of Experimental Social Psychology*, 1976, *12*, 139–150. Copyright 1976 by Academic Press, Inc. Reprinted by permission.)

horizontal axis and the dependent variable on the ordinate. The two levels of the second independent variable (donor resources) are represented by the two lines on the graph. (See the discussion of graphing procedures in chapter 5.) The interaction is denoted by the fact that the two lines are not parallel.

In order for an interaction to exist, the two lines in the graph do not have to cross on the graph. This crossed-lines form of an interaction is a special case that vividly illustrates the value of a factorial design (Figure 10.2). If the experimenters had made a test of the effect of aid using only one level of donor resources (such as rich donors), they would have made one kind of conclusion (for example, receiving aid lowers self-esteem). If the same experimenters had tested the aid variable using the other level of donor resources, they would have made the opposite conclusion (aid increases self-esteem).

Measure evaluating pair-mate. The questionnaire section on the evaluation of the pair-mate yielded a reliable main effect of resources, a reliable main effect of aid, and a reliable interaction. These results are presented in Figure 10.3. The high-resource pair-mate was evaluated more favorably than the low-resource person; persons who gave aid were evaluated more positively than pair-mates who did not give aid; both of these main effects were qualified by the reliable interaction effect,

"Crossed-Lines" Interaction

Significant Main Effects and Interaction Effect

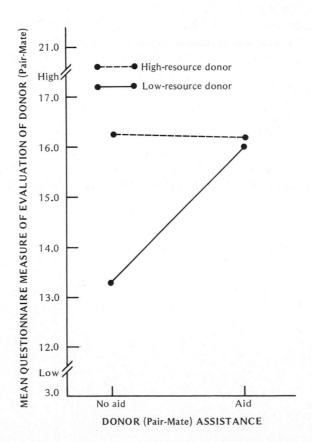

FIG. 10.3 Aid-by-resources interaction for questionnaire measure of evaluation of pair-mate. (From "Effect of donor resources on recipient self-esteem and self-help" by J. D. Fisher and A. Nadler, *Journal of Experimental Social Psychology,* 1976, *12,* 139–150. Copyright 1976 by Academic Press, Inc. Reprinted by permission.)

indicating that the major reason for the main effects was due to the nonaiding, low-resources person receiving a much lower evaluation than the other three types of persons/conditions (high-resource and low-resource donors and high-resource nondonors).

These results indicate the value of a factorial design in interpreting the significance of reliable main effects. If the resource variable had been examined in a simple, independent two-groups design with both high- and low-resource persons providing aid, the researchers would have concluded that level of resource had no effect on evaluation of the donor. Similarly, if the resources variable had been examined in a simple, independent two-groups design, with no aid given, the researcher would have arrived at the opposite conclusion: that evaluation depended strongly on the level of resources of the pair-mate. Whenever there is a significant interaction effect, the meaning of any reliable main effects must be interpreted in the light of the reliable interaction effect. Without a factorial design, you have no way of determining the existence of reliable interaction effects.

Measure of self-evaluation. In the analysis of the questionnaire data about evaluation of self, there was no reliable interaction effect, no reliable main effect for resources, but a reliable main effect for aid. Subjects who received aid evaluated themselves more favorably ($\bar{X} \approx 15.3$) than subjects who did not receive aid ($\bar{X} \approx 13.7$). The lack of interaction should be indicated by approximately parallel lines in Figure 10.4. Visually the lines do not appear to be approximately parallel; in fact the interaction came close to being statistically significant. However, the interaction was not significant at $\alpha = .05$; by comparing Figures 10.3 and 10.4 you can see the greater *lack* of parallelness in the significant interaction of Figure 10.3. The difference between the two resource group means under the no-aid condition is numerically greater than the difference under the aid condition. However, the differences are not appreciably greater than could be expected on the basis of chance. Therefore, as indicated by the lack of a reliable interaction effect in the data analysis, the two lines in the graph can be considered to be approximately parallel (differing from parallelness only by chance factors). Another way of describing the lack of interaction is to say that there is an *additive relationship* between the two variables. That is, the effect of aid vs. no-aid is to add approximately ½ to 2 points to self-evaluation for both the high-resource and low-resource pair-mate conditions. If there had been a reliable interaction, then the relationship would have been described as *nonadditive*.

In summary, the results of the study generally supported the hypothesis. Aid from a poor donor was viewed as relatively supportive while aid from a rich donor tended to be a relatively threatening experience for the receiver. The data on evaluation of the donor indicated that students receiving aid from a poor donor evaluated him positively, while students receiving or not receiving aid from a rich donor did not evaluate him differently.

As the experimenters suggest, great care should be taken in attempting to generalize these results to complex real-life situations. In this study, neither the receiver's need state nor the giver's aid were as critical as in most real-life helping relationships. Many other variables that intervene in such relationships in a real-world setting were

One Significant
Main Effect with No
Interaction

Additive
Relationship

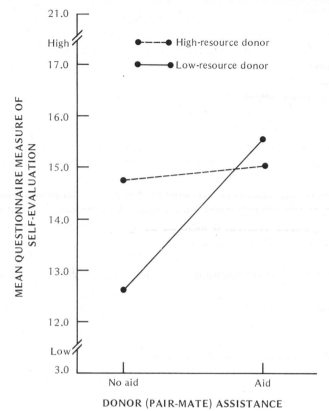

FIG. 10.4
Aid-by-resources interaction for questionnaire measure of self-evaluation. (Unpublished data from J. D. Fisher and A. Nadler by personal communication January 24, 1977. Copyright 1977 by J. D. Fisher and A. Nadler. Reprinted by permission.)

controlled by elimination or by being held constant in this study. The study does provide a good set of examples of the value of factorial designs, particularly since the major research hypothesis predicted the interaction of two variables and a factorial design is the only design that could provide data directly relevant to the hypothesis.

$2 \times 2 \times 2$ Randomized Factorial Design

In order to illustrate the comparative complexity of analysis involved when three or more independent variables are included in a single experiment, we describe another study briefly.

Dillon, Graham, and Aidells (1972) studied the effects of videotape training, practice, and individual vs. group brainstorming on the number of different problem-solving ideas generated. Male and female students from the University of California at Berkeley volunteered in 1970 to participate in the study. The problem used in the study was the then current escalation of the Vietnam War, what individuals could do to effect a change in the situation, and what general changes the students would suggest.

The three independent variables were: (1) viewing or not viewing a 10-min. videotape of the performance of a smoothly functioning, rapid idea-generating brainstorming group working on a problem; (2) practicing or not practicing brainstorming as a technique for generating ideas for 10 min; and (3) "real" brainstorming four-person

TABLE 10.6
Mean Number of Ideas Generated under Different Training and Practice Conditions

Group	Videotape Training		No Videotape Training	
	Practice	No Practice	Practice	No Practice
Nominal	39.67	50.00	74.67	51.33
Real	16.33	13.67	18.33	12.67

Note. From "Brainstorming on a 'hot' problem: Effects of training and practice on individual and group performance" by P. C. Dillon, W. K. Graham, and A. L. Aidells, Journal of Applied Psychology, 1972, 56, 487–490. Copyright 1972 by the American Psychological Association. Reprinted by permission.

groups vs. "nominal" brainstorming groups. In nominal groups the ideas from four individuals working alone were pooled as if they had worked as a group. The design was a 2 × 2 × 2 factorial design with 8 independent groups of 12 students each. The dependent measure was the total number of different ideas generated by each real group of four and each nominal group of four. The data are presented in Table 10.6.

In a 2 × 2 × 2 factorial design, there are three possible main effects, three possible two-variable interactions, and one possible three-variable interaction. The following list summarizes the results for each possible effect.

1. *Main effect: videotape training*—significant effect. Training reduced the mean number of ideas generated.
2. *Main effect: nominal group vs. real group*—significant effect. Nominal groups of individuals working alone produced more ideas than brainstorming groups.
3. *Main effect: practice*—no significant effect. Practice did not reliably increase the number of ideas generated.
4. *Two-variable interaction effect: videotape training and practice*—significant effect. The mean number of ideas produced was greater when the students practiced without receiving videotape training; under the no-practice condition there was no effect of training.
5. *Two-variable interaction effect: videotape training and individual vs. group brainstorming*—significant effect. Training had no differential effect on the real groups, but decreased the number of ideas generated by the nominal groups.
6. *Two-variable interaction effect: practice and individual vs. group brainstorming*—no significant effect.
7. *Three-variable interaction effect: training, practice, and individual vs. group*—no significant effect.

Figure 10.5 presents the data of Table 10.6 in graphic form. The three-variable interaction is nonsignificant; the four lines in the graph (Figure 10.5) are approximately parallel or differ from parallel only by chance.

The overall pattern of results for the study indicates that: (1) as previously observed, four individuals working alone produce more different ideas using brainstorming procedures than a group of four working together; (2) contrary to the prediction, the videotape training inhibited rather than facilitated performance; (3) practice did help for both nominal and real groups when it was *not* preceded by videotape training; (4) watching the videotape inhibited nominal group performance more than real group performance; and (5) the most effective combination of procedures was the no-videotape training with 10-min practice for a nominal group of four individuals using brainstorming procedures.

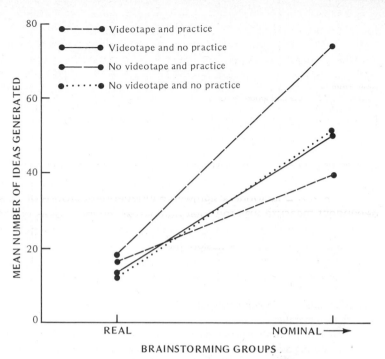

FIG. 10.5
Interaction of three variables—videotape training, practice, and real or nominal brainstorming groups —as measured by the mean number of different ideas generated. (From "Brainstorming on a 'hot' problem: Effects of training and practice on individual and group performance" by P. C. Dillon, W. K. Graham, and A. L. Aidells, *Journal of Applied Psychology*, 1972, 56, 487–490. Copyright 1972 by the American Psychological Association. Reprinted by permission.)

Randomized-Blocks Factorial Design

One form of a factorial design is the randomized-blocks design (see chapter 8). Sometimes you wish to control for individual differences between subjects, but do not have the necessary facilities for subject-by-subject matching. Using the randomized-blocks factorial design, you can match the experimental and control groups in terms of groups (blocks) of subjects. Suppose that you want to study the effects of two methods of teaching on the learning performance of college sophomores. You expect that the intelligence of the subjects might affect your dependent variable. You therefore divide your subjects into two blocks: a high-intelligence block and a low-intelligence block. Subjects in each block are randomly assigned to each treatment group. Thus, you have a 2 × 2 factorial with one "blocking" variable, intelligence, and one treatment variable, method of teaching. The advantages of the design are similar to those obtained with matching techniques, but since individual subjects are not matched, an independent-groups statistical test is used with the data.

An interesting study by Sprafkin, Liebert, and Poulos (1975) provides a real example of a simple, randomized-blocks factorial design. The study examined the hypothesis that regularly broadcast, commercial, entertainment television shows can facilitate positive social behavior in children. A 3 × 2 factorial design was employed; the three levels of the main independent variable being observation of a prosocial "Lassie" show, a neutral "Lassie" show, and a neutral "Brady Bunch" show. The blocking variable was the sex of the children; 15 boys and 15 girls were randomly sampled from the pool of four first-grade classes. Five children of each sex were randomly assigned to the three treatment conditions. (This study is a rare example of both random sampling and random assignment to groups.)

The children were individually escorted from the classrooms to a television viewing room where they watched the videotaped programs. In the prosocial "Lassie" program, one of Lassie's puppies fell onto a ledge in a mine shaft. Lassie brought the boy, Jeff, to the scene and Jeff risked his life to save the puppy, a prosocial, helping behavior. In the neutral "Lassie" program, the theme was Jeff's attempts to avoid taking violin lessons. The show featured the dog in a positive way, but contained no example of a human helping a dog. In the other neutral control condition, a *Brady Bunch* program was shown. No dogs were included in the story and no cues were provided concerning human or canine heroics.

The assessment of the effect of the three shows on the children's prosocial behavior involved placing each child in a conflict situation requiring a choice between continuing to play a game for personal gain or trying to get help for puppies in distress. After the televised program had been viewed, each child was taken to a second room. There, the child was invited to play a game in which points could be earned by pressing a button that lit a bulb and started a digital timer. The number of points earned was the number displayed on the timer. The more points earned, the better or bigger the displayed prize that could be traded for the points. The experimenter in this room, who was blind to the treatment condition, also explained that the child could help her by listening to some earphones. The earphones were ostensibly connected to a distant kennel full of puppies. The puppies were alone and were judged to be "O.K." if no barking could be heard. If the puppies were to bark, pressing the "Help" button (on a different table from the game) would call the experimenter's helper to see about the puppies. The child was asked to wear the phones while playing the point game and told: "If you hear barking you can help the puppies if you want by pressing the help button" (p. 123). Also, there was a better chance that the helper would hear the signal the longer the help button was pressed. Then the children were told to try to get as many points as they could and that if the puppies started barking, they would have to choose between helping the puppies and getting more points.

After leaving the room, the experimenter turned on a tape recorder that provided 30 sec of silence followed by 120 sec of increasingly frantic barking. After the end of the barking (the "helper" had finally arrived), the experimenter reentered the room and awarded the prize. The total seconds of help-button pressing was the dependent measure.

The analysis of variance (chapter 20) indicated that there was no reliable main effect of sex, a reliable treatment effect, but no reliable treatment-by-sex interaction effect. The subjects who saw the prosocial "Lassie" program helped more than those who saw the two neutral programs; average helping times were 93 sec for the prosocial "Lassie" show, 52 sec for the neutral "Lassie," and 38 sec for the "Brady Bunch." The experimenters concluded that a televised example of prosocial helping behavior can increase a child's willingness to engage in helping behavior. Further, the prosocial behavior of the human protagonist, Jeff, was the critical ingredient, since the alternate dog show and warm "Brady Bunch" program produced less helping. The mere presence of a canine heroine was not sufficient to produce prosocial behavior in the subjects. Further, the results generally were the same for both sexes, as indicated by the lack of a sex main effect and lack of a reliable interaction effect. (There was a slight tendency for the girls to be more affected by the prosocial model; and for the boys to be more helpful generally.) The randomized-blocks design allowed the experimenters to generalize the support for the experimental hypothesis safely to both sexes.

Repeated-Measures Factorial Design

Split-Plot Design

Another particular form of a factorial design is called a repeated-measures factorial design (sometimes called a **split-plot design**). In the repeated-measures factorial design, the subjects each experience all the levels of at least one variable. That variable usually consists of learning trials or some similar variable under which several measures of the subjects' behavior are taken. The simplest example of a repeated-measures factorial is a 2 × 2. For example, subjects might be given two trials at learning a motor task. One group would attempt to learn under a high-motivation condition (50 dollars) while the other group would attempt to learn under a low-motivation condition (50 pennies). The change in performance of the task across the two trials would be determined. The trials variable is the repeated, related-groups variable; the motivation variable is a nonrepeated, independent-groups variable. The design combines the advantages of one-group designs with the advantages of independent-groups designs.

The following study is a real research example of a 3 × 3 repeated-measures factorial design. A technique known as time-out from positive reinforcement has been used by parents and teachers as an effective means of controlling undesirable behaviors of children. **Time-out from positive reinforcement** is defined as a period of time following the occurrence of an undesired response in which a variety of reinforcers is no longer available to the child. A study by Scarboro and Forehand (1975) involved five-year-old children and their mothers. The mother–child pairs were observed in a laboratory playroom containing different toys. Unobtrusive visual and auditory monitoring occurred through a one-way mirror and microphone. The pairs were observed for nine different experimental sessions spread over four days. The first three sessions were baseline observation periods, the middle three sessions involved training mothers in the use of time-out, and the last three sessions involved posttraining observation of each mother's performance.

During each experimental session, three types of maternal behaviors and two types of child behavior were observed. The three maternal behaviors were: (1) giving commands to play with a specific toy every 3 min; (2) giving warnings for failure to obey a command within 5 sec or failure to maintain compliance with the command for any 5-sec period; and (3) executing the appropriate time-out procedure whenever the child failed to comply within 5 sec of a warning. Two time-out procedures were used in the study: out-of-room time-out, in which the mother took the toys and left the room for 2 min, and within-room time-out, in which the mother moved away from the child and withdrew all attention for 2 min. The warnings consisted of informing the child of the specific type of time-out maternal behavior that would occur. There were three time-out treatment groups—out-of-room, within-room, and control (no time-out used)—with three boys and five girls randomly assigned to each group. The observed children's behaviors were: (1) initiated compliance, doing what he or she was commanded to do within 5 sec, and (2) oppositional behavior, failure to comply with a command within 5 sec, or failure to continue to play with the specified toy for any 10-sec period in the 3 min between each new maternal command. The main dependent measures were the frequency of initial compliance with a command and the percentage of oppositional behavior by each child for each session. The number of time-outs and warnings issued by each mother were also recorded.

The research design was a 3 × 3 repeated-measures factorial. The between-subjects variable was the three time-out treatment conditions with different children in each condition. The repeated-measures variable was the nine training sessions experienced by all children: (1) baseline—Sessions 1–3, in which the mothers were cued as to which command to give every 3 min but were asked to play with their children otherwise in their usual manner; (2) training—Sessions 4–6, in which the mothers in each of the two time-out conditions were trained in using time-out, including cuing when time-out was appropriate and when to cease time-out, and were reinforced verbally for carrying out the appropriate procedure; and (3) posttraining—Sessions 7–9, in which the mothers used the time-out procedure on their own and were not reinforced. The control group essentially experienced nine sessions of baseline. The cuing was accomplished with a short-range radio receiver and speaker placed in the mother's ear allowing the experimenter to communicate directly with each mother without the child hearing.

The analysis of variance indicated a reliable time-out treatment-groups effect, a reliable training-session effect, and a reliable treatment-by-training-session interaction effect for both dependent measures, child compliance and oppositional behavior (Figures 10.6 and 10.7). In summary, for both measures, the three groups did not differ during baseline. The control condition differed reliably from the two time-out conditions during both training and posttraining; however, the two time-out conditions did not differ from each other under any of the three training conditions. Both time-out procedures were effective in increasing the rate of initial compliance and decreasing

FIG. 10.6
Mean number of initiated compliances for the Out-of-Room Time-Out (OUT-TO), Within-Room Time-Out (IN-TO), and Control groups during each of the three experimental conditions or groups of sessions. (From "Effects of two types of response-contingent time-out on compliance and oppositional behavior of children" by M. E. Scarboro and R. Forehand, *Journal of Experimental Child Psychology*, 1975, *19*, 252–264. Copyright 1975 by Academic Press, Inc. Reprinted by permission.)

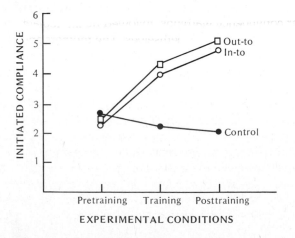

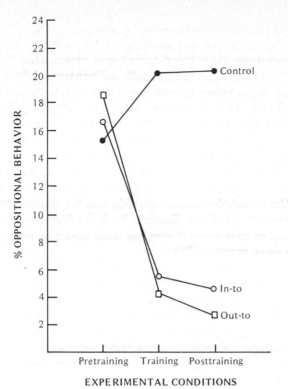

FIG. 10.7
Mean percentage of oppositional behavior for the Out-of-Room Time-Out (OUT-TO), Within-Room Time-Out (IN-TO), and Control groups during each of the three experimental conditions or groups of sessions. (From "Effects of two types of response-contingent time-out on compliance and oppositional behavior of children" by M. E. Scarboro and R. Forehand, *Journal of Experimental Child Psychology*, 1975, 19, 252–264. Copyright 1975 by Academic Press, Inc. Reprinted by permission.)

the percentage of time spent in oppositional behaviors. The mothers were able to use both time-out procedures effectively on their own during the posttraining sessions. The within-room time-out procedure required the mothers to use more time-outs during both training and posttraining than the out-of-room time-out procedure; this was not an unexpected result as it is difficult to control the withdrawal of attention completely when the mother is still in the room with the child. The observed effective control of the childrens' behavior was probably due to the extremely consistent and detailed procedures of issuing commands consisting of simple, direct statements, followed by clear contingency warnings, followed by immediate time-out procedures, as well as the time-out procedures themselves. The mothers and children appeared to learn the "rules of the game" quickly, producing dramatic results.

The experimenters hypothesized that the time-out training variable would interact with the sessions variable, since they expected all mother–child pairs to perform about the same during baseline, but differently during the training and posttraining sessions. The repeated-measures factorial design eliminated the possibility of individual differences confusing the estimate of the between-sessions effect. In addition, the reliability of the interaction effect was determined by comparing the training-by-sessions between-groups variance with the individuals-by-sessions within-group variance. This means that the over-all-sessions individual differences did not enter into the computations for testing the reliability of the interaction effect. In this way the repeated-measures factorial design minimizes the effects of error variance (chapter 20).

Advantages and Limitations

Factorial designs increase the amount of information provided by each response. In a factorial design, each measure of behavior provides information about at least two variables. *Only* factorial designs allow the experimenter to study all possible interactions between variables. Other designs not covered in this text provide some information about certain interactions, but other interactions are confused (confounded) with main effects.

In order to evaluate the interaction effect clearly in a factorial design, *at least two* measures of behavior should be observed under each combination of variables. Usually, this means that at least two subjects are included in each cell of the design table. As the number of variables increases, the number of possible interactions rapidly increases. With two variables, only one interaction is possible. With three variables (*A, B, C*) four interactions are possible: an *AB* interaction, an *AC* interaction, a *BC* interaction, and an *ABC* interaction.

**TABLE 10.7
Potential Sources
of Secondary
Variance Not
Controlled in the
Various Forms of
Factorial Designs**

Form of Factorial Design	Source of Secondary Variance		
	Individual Differences	Outside Influences	Experimental Contamination
Randomized	None if time of testing is controlled	None if time of testing is controlled	Reactive effects of experimental arrangement
Randomized-Blocks	None if time of testing is controlled and the blocking variable is related to the dependent variable	None if time of testing is controlled	Reactive effects of experimental arrangement
Repeated-Measures	None if time of testing is controlled	None if time of testing is controlled	Reactive effects of experimental arrangement Pretest sensitization to treatment

Statistical Analysis

Given an interval or ratio level of measurement of the dependent variable, the most appropriate statistical technique is the analysis of variance for a factorial, randomized-blocks factorial, or repeated-measures design described in chapter 20. At the nominal level of measurement, the multiple independent-group χ^2 test (chapter 18) is appropriate for a factorial design but not a randomized-blocks factorial or repeated-measures factorial.

Comments

A casual survey of research published in psychological journals during 1976 indicated that the modal design choice was some version of a factorial design. Clearly, both the users and producers of research must understand the basic nature of factorial designs. A factorial design is often considered an indicator of "sophisticated" research. However, if the data-collection techniques are inadequate or the statistical analyses inappropriate, the fact that a factorial design was used will not save the research.

SOLOMON FOUR-GROUP DESIGN

The Solomon (1949) four-group design uses additional groups to control for the effects of additional secondary variables. It is a particular form of the factorial design in which one independent variable is the administration of pretests. The four-group design is presented in Tables 10.8 and 10.9. The subjects are assigned randomly to the four groups.

We will introduce the Solomon design by briefly summarizing a real research study. As discussed in chapters 3, 7, 8, 9, and 14, it is possible that a before-measurement may sensitize subjects to the experimental treatment so that they respond differently than they would have if they had not been pretested. All designs involving a before-measurement are subject to this form of potential experimental contamination that may reduce the generalizability of the results. The pretest-interaction source of secondary variance is thought to be particularly relevant to attitude research in which opinions are measured before and after an experimental treatment such as a persuasive communication. However, according to Rosnow, Holper, and Gitter (1973), there has been "surprisingly little documented evidence of this pretest-treatment interaction in laboratory opinion-change research" (p. 7). Two alternative hypotheses have been offered to explain the failure to observe the interaction effect: the "demand-characteristics hypothesis" and "the subject-commitment hypothesis."

Pretest Sensitization Effect

The demand-characteristics hypothesis assumes that the subjects are aware of the experimenter's manipulatory intent. When questionnaires are followed by a persuasive communication and subsequent questionnaires containing virtually the same questions as the pretest, people recognize the similarity of the questions and infer the experimenter's manipulatory intent; whether or not they then comply with the experimenter's demands depends on certain situational and personal variables. For example, volunteers tend to play the role of "good subject" while nonvolunteer or "captive" persons tend not to play the role of "good subjects." In studies employing captive subjects, some of whom would have volunteered and some not, the negative and positive reactions of these two groups tend to cancel each other out, masking a pretest-by-treatment interaction.

Testing Effect

The subject-commitment hypothesis suggests that people become strongly committed to a position on a serious issue when they have to reveal it publicly. Therefore a pretest may cause a person to "freeze" in a position so as not to appear "gullible." If this hypothesis is correct, then a pretest-by-treatment interaction could not occur, since the hypothesis specifies a pretest or testing effect *independent* of the nature of the treatment.

It is possible that these two hypotheses may both be correct. The subject-commitment hypothesis may operate in personally significant, motivational conflict situations, while the demand-characteristics hypothesis may operate in the artificial

**TABLE 10.8
The Solomon Four-Group Design (Standard Presentation Form)**

Groups	Before-Observation	Treatment	After-Observation
I	W_1	X_1	Y_1
II	—	X_1	Y_2
III	W_2	X_2	Y_3
IV	—	X_2	Y_4

TABLE 10.9   The Solomon Four-Group Design (Factorial Presentation Form)

		Pretest	
		Yes	No
Treatment	X_1	I	II
	X_2	III	IV

laboratory context with its minimal personal involvement. In a laboratory context, Rosnow, Holper, and Gitter (1973) tested the conflicting predictions that: (1) nonanonymous subjects would be more likely to be committed to their pretest opinions—and therefore less responsive to a persuasive communication—than anonymous subjects (no pretest-treatment interaction under conditions of nonanonymity, a pretest-treatment interaction under conditions of anonymity); and (2) nonanonymous subjects, identifiable as "good" or "bad," would be more likely to comply with a persuasive-communication demand than anonymous subjects (a pretest-treatment interaction under conditions of nonanonymity, no pretest-treatment interaction under conditions of anonymity).

Students were randomly assigned to the cells of a Solomon four-group design. The procedure involved presenting each student with one of four forms of a test booklet. (The four cells of the design, Table 10.9, define the four forms.) That is, Group I's booklet contained a pretest and the persuasive communication, Group II's booklet did not contain a pretest but did contain the persuasive communication, Group III's booklet contained the pretest but an irrelevant control communication, and Group IV's booklet contained only the control communication. The experimenters expected the following functional relationships to occur in the after-scores:

The mean of Group I is a function of pretest, treatment, pretest × treatment interaction, and extraneous error.
The mean of Group II is a function of the treatment and error.
The mean of Group III is a function of the pretest and error.
The mean of Group IV is a function of error.

From these expectations it follows that a pretest × treatment interaction is the mean of Group I minus the mean of Group II, minus the mean of Group III, plus the mean of Group IV $[\overline{Y}_1 - (\overline{Y}_2 + \overline{Y}_3 - \overline{Y}_4)]$. A positive outcome of the arithmetic would indicate a facilitative interaction effect of pretesting; a negative outcome would indicate a depressive pretest × treatment interaction, and a zero outcome would indicate no interaction.

In addition to the basic Solomon four-group design, approximately half of each group completed the test booklet anonymously and the other half nonanonymously. (Actually the experimenters lied to the students; after they had finished the test all students had to put their names on the test booklet.)

The pretest and posttest questionnaires were identical. There were four questions concerning the person's opinion about the effect of continued nuclear research on world destruction, the responsibility of nuclear scientists, the subject's willingness to sign a petition protesting government support of nuclear research, and the relationship

TABLE 10.10
Composite Posttest Means Corresponding to the Predicted Interaction of Pretest × Persuasion Treatment × Anonymity

Anonymity Condition	Treatment Groups (Solomon Four-Group Design Designation)				
	I	II	III	IV	I − (II + III − IV)
Anonymous	23.04	22.34	22.21	21.73	0.22
Nonanonymous	23.35	23.97	20.18	21.71	0.91

Note. *From "More on the reactive effects of pretesting in attitude research: Demand characteristics or subject commitment?" by R. L. Rosnow, H. M. Holper, and A. G. Gitter,* Educational and Psychological Measurement, 1973, 33, 7–17. Copyright 1973 by the publisher of the journal. Reprinted by permission.

between the funding of nuclear research and the standard of living. The persuasive communication was purported to be an editorial from the *New York Times* which forecast the horrible effects of further nuclear research and the likelihood of inflation resulting from federal support of nuclear research. The control communication, also represented as an excerpt from the *Times*, dealt with sexual promiscuity among college students.

The analysis of variance of the after-opinion scores indicated a reliable pretest × treatment × anonymity interaction and the nonexistence of a pretest × treatment interaction. These results, consistent with earlier findings, support the concept that pretest sensitization to treatment depends on situational factors such as the voluntary or nonvoluntary participation. The data for the triple interaction are presented in Table 10.10.

The reliable triple interaction does not, by itself, indicate which of the two competing factors, subject commitment or demand compliance, was the more influential in the study. The last column of Table 10.10 provides the crucial data. If compliance with the experimenters' demands were the determining influence, a smaller positive number should occur under the anonymous condition (since the "good" and "bad" subjects could not be discriminated) than under the nonanonymous conditions. The reverse effect should occur if the commitment variable were determinative, since the nonanonymous precommitment to a position should yield no facilitative pretesting interaction effect. The observed smaller number (.22) under the anonymous condition indicates that the demand-characteristics hypothesis received greater support than the subject-commitment hypothesis. Perhaps most interesting was the finding that the pretest sensitization effect (pretest × treatment interaction) depended on the third variable, subject anonymity. That portion of the research design discussed here was a factorial combination of a Solomon four-group design with a third variable to create a 2 × 2 × 2 factorial design.

Function

The Solomon design is an outstanding example of careful control of secondary variables through multiple "control" groups. Each individual group was discussed in chapters 8 and 9. The Solomon four-group design consists of the before–after two-group design combined with the randomized two-group design. The limitations of each two-group design are handled by the combination of the two into a four-group design. You can determine the effects of the before-measure (pretest), the effects of the experimental treatment, the effects of the treatment uncontaminated by the pretest, and the effects of the pretest by treatment interaction. The pretest performance of Groups I and III can be *combined* to estimate the scores of Groups II and IV had they been pretested. The effects of pretesting can be discovered by analyzing the differences between the after scores of Groups I and II and the differences between the after scores of Groups III and IV. Finally, the interaction between pretest and the treatment variables can be determined.

Solomon and Lessac (1968) maintain that this design is the "minimum design" required for a study of the effects of deprivation or enrichment on the development of behavior. The effects of environmental restriction or enrichment may be due to the deterioration or enhancement of already-developed capacities, or to the retardation or acceleration of the rate of development of behavioral capacities. Using a two-group design, it is not possible to discriminate between the alternative explanations, as can be done with the Solomon design. For example, suppose you hypothesize that early environmental stress affects later emotional stability. You test the hypothesis by exposing half of the subjects to a series of electric shocks (X_1) and the other half of the subjects to no shock (X_2). Half of the shocked and nonshocked subjects are pretested on emotionality, and all four groups are given the after-measure of emotional behavior. A high score indicates emotional instability or excitability. Suppose that the average *pretest* emotionality scores were: Group I = 15, and Group III = 15. The average *after-treatment* emotionality scores are presented in Table 10.11.

The shock experience led to a decrease in emotionality (average of Groups I and II compared to average of Groups III and IV). If you had used only Groups I and III, you would have made the erroneous conclusion that the shocks had little effect on emotionality. If you had used only Groups II and IV, you would have overestimated the effect of the shock. The pretest performance of Groups I and III was less than the after performance of Group II, indicating that the shock experience contributed only part of the decrease. The pretest served to decrease the later measures of emotionality as indicated by the difference between: (1) the combined average of Groups I and III versus the combined average of Groups II and IV, (2) the difference between the posttreatment averages of Groups I and II, and (3) the difference between the posttreatment averages of Groups III and IV. Finally, an interaction between pretesting and shock treatment occurred. That is, the pretest decreased the effect of the shock (the greater difference between Groups II and IV compared to Groups I and III), but both shock and the pretest combined to decrease the measure of emotionality. The fictitious data indicate that early shock retards the development of emotionality to the usual high level.

TABLE 10.11
Average Emotionality Scores in the Hypothetical Early Experience Study

| | | Pretest | | |
		Yes	No	Average
Treatment	Shock	I 10	II 20	15
	No Shock	III 12	IV 30	21
	Average	11	25	

Advantages and Limitations

For a study of a two-level independent variable, a four-group design provides a great deal of control of secondary variables, particularly the before-observation variable. The four-group design can be generalized to a factorial design with more than two levels of the primary variable, or a factorial design with more than one primary variable. A four-group design requires more subjects than a two-group design. If a pretest is meaningless or not possible, then a four-group design is inappropriate.

TABLE 10-12 Potential Sources of Secondary Variance Not Controlled in a Solomon Four-Group Design

Individual Differences	Outside Influences	Experimental Contamination
None if time of testing is controlled	None if time of testing is controlled	Reactive effects of experimental arrangement

Statistical Analysis

The techniques listed for the factorial design are appropriate here, since the Solomon four-group design is a factorial design. These include: the multiple-independent-group χ^2 test (chapter 18) and analysis of variance for factorial designs, randomized-blocks factorial, and repeated-measures factorial (chapter 21).

Comments

You should examine the advantages of a four-group design over one of the two-group designs closely. If the additional control warrants the increase in complexity, a four-group design should be employed. It is particularly appropriate in the case of developmental research where a pretest is meaningful, and in attitude-manipulation research where a pretest is standard procedure.

SUMMARY

1. Most current research involves multiple-treatment designs, usually with multiple behavioral measures.
2. Multiple-treatment designs contain more than two levels of an independent variable, more than one independent variable, or both.
3. A multilevel design contains several levels of a single independent variable. In a repeated-measures multilevel design, all subjects experience all levels of the independent variable. Multilevel designs may include pretests and/or matching. Multilevel designs are useful for determining the precise functional relationship between a dependent and an independent variable.
4. A randomized factorial design contains all possible combinations of the levels of two or more independent variables. A factorial design may be a related- or repeated-measures design in which all subjects experience all combinations of levels of treatments, an independent design in which different subjects experience each combination, or a mixed

design in which a subject experiences all levels of one treatment and only one level of the other treatment.

5. A factorial design may involve any combination of number of levels and number of treatment variables. Factorial designs are efficient since data concerning the effects of two or more variables are simultaneously collected from each subject.

6. The main effects of a factorial design are the averaged effects of each independent variable.

7. The simple effects of a factorial design are the effects of one independent variable under one level of another independent variable.

8. Two variables interact when the effects of one variable depend upon the effects of the other variable. Graphically, an interaction is indicated by nonparallel lines.

9. In a given study using a factorial design, no main effect or interaction effect may be significant, all effects may be significant, or some of each may be significant.

10. The crossed-lines graphical depiction of a significant interaction illustrates the value of a factorial design particularly well. The presence of a significant interaction between variables is also called a nonadditive relationship between the variables.

11. Only factorial designs allow the analysis of all possible unconfounded interactions.

12. A randomized-blocks design is a special case of a factorial design. The blocking variable is used to control for an individual-differences, secondary source of variance and serves as an independent variable.

13. A repeated-measures factorial design is a special case of a factorial design. It is also called a "split-plot" design. The subjects are repeatedly measured under the levels of at least one variable (subjects-as-their-own-control) and at least one other independent-groups variable is included in the design.

14. A Solomon four-group design is a combination of a before–after two-group design and a randomized two-group design. A Solomon four-group design is a factorial design.

15. A Solomon four-group design allows the estimation of the effect of the primary independent variable, the effect of before observations, the effect of the primary variable uncontaminated by a before measure, and the interaction effect.

16. A Solomon four-group design is the minimum necessary design for developmental studies of the effects of enriched or impoverished environments when pretests are possible; the design is particularly appropriate to attitude-manipulation or propaganda research where a pretest is a standard procedure.

SUGGESTED READINGS

Campbell, D. T., & Stanley, J. C. *Experimental and quasi-experimental designs for research.* Skokie, Ill.: Rand McNally, 1963.

Edwards, A. L. *Experimental design in psychological research* (4th ed.). New York: Holt, Rinehart and Winston, 1972.

Hays, W. L. *Statistics for social scientists* (2nd ed.). New York: Holt, Rinehart and Winston, 1973.

Kerlinger, F. N. *Foundations of behavioral research* (2nd ed.). New York: Holt, Rinehart and Winston, 1973.

Kirk, R. E. *Experimental design: Procedures for the behavioral sciences.* Belmont, Calif.: Brooks/Cole, 1968.

Lindquist, E. F. *Design and analysis of experiments in psychology and education.* Boston: Houghton-Mifflin, 1953.

Myers, J. L. *Fundamentals of experimental design.* Boston: Allyn and Bacon, 1966.

Selltiz, C., Wrightsman, L. S., & Cook, S. W. *Research methods in social relations* (3rd ed.). New York: Holt, Rinehart and Winston, 1976.

Solomon, R. L. An extension of control group design. *Psychological Bulletin,* 1949, *46,* 137–150.

Solomon, R. L., & Lessac, M. S. A control group design for experimental studies of developmental process. *Psychological Bulletin,* 1968, *70,* 145–150.

11

Single-Subject Designs

In many cases, group experimental designs are not appropriate in answering questions about a certain person, or about a person's specific behavior. Single-subject designs are most applicable when matching subjects in a large group would be too expensive, when ethical considerations prevent you from withholding treatment from some subjects, and when group differences may be due to a small number in an experimental group showing large changes while others show little or no change. These and other details of single-subject designs are discussed in this chapter.

Although psychologists utilize statistics such as the mean, median, and standard deviation to describe group data, these statistics may not describe the behavior of any one particular person adequately. The individual is very important to psychologists. With the rise in popularity of behavior therapy, behavior modification, and biofeedback, studies involving only single subjects have increased. In a single-subject experimental design, repeated measures are taken across time on one particular individual. The subject serves as his or her own control.

Single-subject designs were introduced in chapter 7 under the heading of time-series designs. In a time-series design, multiple observations are taken on a group of subjects before the independent variable is administered, yielding *baseline measures*. After the independent variable is administered, several more measures are taken to examine its effect on the behavior of the subjects in the group. An important difference between the time-series and the single-subject design is that instead of a group, we use only one subject. Therefore single-subject designs are an extension of the before–after design.

Although single-subject designs are not new (Sidman, 1960) they have gained in popularity with applied researchers, who have made many clinical contributions through use of such designs. These researchers maintain, rightfully, that group designs often are impractical or impossible to use. According to Barlow and Hersen (1973), there are several advantages of single-subject designs over group designs: (1) matching large groups of subjects is difficult and expensive at times; (2) withholding clinical treatment from control subjects while giving treatment to others has negative moral implications; and (3) between-group differences may be due to a small number of subjects in the experimental group who show large changes, while other subjects in that group may not change at all or may change in a direction opposite to that of the group. Group results may not help in applied clinical situations because the individual's behavior may be masked by the group average. Furthermore, in single-subject designs, unlike most group designs, continuous measurements are made so that subtle changes in behavior may be noted.

In group designs, an independent variable is declared effective if a statistical test shows a greater effect on the experimental group than on the control group. In clinical research, statistically significant findings may be useless (Barlow & Hersen, 1973), since the differences may not be large. Conversely, a treatment that does not produce statistically significant group differences may have an important effect on one or a few individuals.

Research Example The following study is an example of a single-subject design. Sterman (1973) reported novel and potentially important results using biofeedback in the control of seizure disorders in human beings. Utilizing electroencephalography (EEG), Sterman and his associates studied brain activity from the area just over the sensorimotor cortex. Earlier, Sterman had noted that cats trained to stay very still exhibited a high percentage of brain waves in this area in the 12–14 Hz range. Such brain-wave activity is called sensorimotor rhythm. Sterman further noted that cats trained to emit the sensorimotor rhythm also stayed still. These cats were also highly resistant to drug-induced seizures. Sterman turned his efforts to human beings with severe seizure problems including epilepsy.

Five different persons who suffered seizures were available as subjects. A group type of experiment would have been inappropriate since the variables contributing to each subject's behavior were so different that it would have been impossible to control for them. The obvious design was a form of single-subject design. Detailed data from one case were presented in the report. Seizure activity was recorded for some time before the experimental procedure was administered. This time period, called baseline, is labeled "A." After enough baseline measures were taken, sensorimotor-rhythm feedback training was given the subject for a period of 6 mo. during which time seizure activity decreased. The treatment period, called "B," was terminated after 6 mo. and the situation returned to baseline (A) for approximately 9 weeks. In behavior modification terms, terminating the treatment (the independent variable) and returning to baseline conditions is called a **reversal.** During Sterman's reversal phase, which lasted 4 to 5 weeks, seizure-activity manifestations were exacerbated (increased). When biofeedback technique (B) was resumed the subject's symptoms returned to their improved clinical state.

The experiment was a controlled single-subject design with one reversal phase, sometimes called an A–B–A–B design. The results were highly encouraging for the successful behavioral treatment of epilepsy: The data provided clear evidence that the independent variable affected behavior. Control was demonstrated because behavior changed with changes in the level of the independent variable.

The subject in the Sterman experiment practiced sensorimotor rhythm behavior both in the lab and at home. Most single-subject designs are adaptable to natural settings outside the formal laboratory situation.

IMPLICATIONS OF SINGLE-SUBJECT DESIGNS

Sampling and Control

Single-subject designs do not always lend themselves to clear statistical analysis. The experimenter looks at a graph of the behavior and notes any change in behavior as a function of change in the independent variable. Because there is no between-groups variance, few statistical tests can be made, a fact which distresses many proponents of group designs. However, since the subject is his or her own control and reversals usually provide clear evidence of the effect of the independent variable, control can be demonstrated.

Although single-subject designs use extremely small samples, they are appropriate for many situations of clinical importance. When a behavioral problem is unique to one person it is impossible to do a group study.

TABLE 11.1
A Brief Comparison between Group Designs and Single-Subject Designs

	Sampling	Control	Hypothesis Testing	Reliability
Group Designs	Random	Random assignment	Formal	Larger sample size
		Matching	Rejection of null	Careful measurement to reduce error
		Manipulating variables	Statistical test	
Single-Subject Designs	Available	Subjects as own controls	Informal	Replication
	Clinical	Reversal effects	Convincingness of data	Careful measurement to reduce error

Hypothesis Testing and Reliability

Hypotheses are not formally tested in single-subject designs. More often than not a hypothesis is advanced prior to the beginning of the experiment, but a formal statistical test of the data is not done afterwards. Most often the experimenter relies on the convincingness of the data (Bickett, 1975). If the data on line graphs change as a function of the independent variable, then the data are convincing. Recently techniques have been suggested for analyzing single-subject design data with analysis-of-variance techniques (Gentile, Roden, & Klein, 1972). However, Michael (1974) regards statistical tests of single-subject data as unnecessary and perhaps harmful. He points out that individual-organism research has been going on for over 30 years, and that if the need for statistical techniques were great, they would have been developed. He maintains that statistical tests of single-subject data lead to inflexibility and distract from the researcher's primary interest, analysis of behavior.

Single-subject designs can be very open and flexible. In a clinical situation, when a hypothesis fails to be supported, it is still important to solve the clinical problem to which it pertains. If one independent variable does not work, another is tried until a solution is found. Because of their flexibility, single-subject designs stimulate researchers to try out new hypotheses.

In order to make single-subject research more accountable, replication of experimental procedures on different subjects is encouraged. If a procedure works for several individuals its reliability is increased. A brief comparison of group designs and single-subject designs is presented in Table 11.1. The designs are compared with respect to sampling, control, hypothesis testing, and reliability, and the manner in which these aspects are achieved.

SINGLE-SUBJECT PARADIGMS

The Baseline

We have mentioned that in a single-subject design the subject serves as his or her own control. This means that the measures taken during baseline are compared with measures taken during or after the administration of the independent variable.

Obviously, the baseline measures are critical. **Baseline** is defined as a measure of behavior (often a frequency or rate of occurrence of a well-defined behavior) taken before the introduction of the independent variable. Conventionally, at least three measures or data points are taken per experimental session in order to obtain some measure of variability in each session.

Baseline measures should be taken over a period long enough for the behavior in question to become stable (Bickett, 1975). Changes during baseline should be in a direction opposite to that predicted by any hypothesis. If changes take place naturally in the direction predicted by the experimental hypothesis, the effect of the independent variable cannot be analyzed. Finally, the baseline conditions must be described carefully and clearly in any experimental write-up so that they may be replicated.

The A–B Design

An A–B design involves a baseline period (A), and an experimental period during which the independent variable is manipulated (B). Notice that this pattern occurs twice in the Sterman experiment. While the A–B is the basic and simplest of all single-subject designs, it represents an improvement over uncontrolled one-shot case studies. The changes in behavior over a period of time are illustrated effectively by a graph. Single-subject experiments usually follow a form similar to Figure 11.1.

Research Example

According to Barlow and Hersen (1973), the A–B design must be considered a correlational design, since the introduction of the independent variable does not necessarily mean that it alone had an effect. Other variables associated with the experimental period may have brought about the changes. For example, Leitenberg, Agras, and Thomson (1968) performed an experiment on a female suffering from anorexia nervosa, a pathological condition of extreme underweight and no appetite from psychic causes. They kept track of her weight and caloric intake for 50 days (Figure 11.2). During that period the subject was given 30 min. to eat one of four 1000-calorie meals per day. At the end of the baseline period, they began to reinforce the subject at meal time with praise for consuming food. Figure 11.2 shows a dramatic increase in both weight and caloric intake. At first glance it appears that the increases were due to the reinforcement; they probably were, but they also could be due to the phase of the moon, mood, attitude, or any other secondary variable correlated with

FIG. 11.1
The basic design and graph format for a single-subject A-B design.

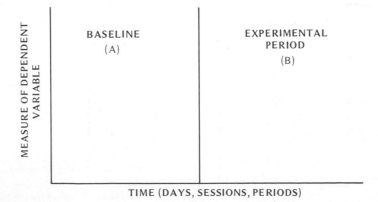

FIG. 11.2
Effects of
nonreinforcement and
reinforcement in a case
of anorexia nervosa for
subject 1. (From "A
sequential analysis of
the effect of selective
positive reinforcement
in modifying anorexia
nervosa," by H.
Leitenberg, W. S. Agras,
and L. Thomson,
*Behavior Research and
Therapy,* 1968, 6, 211–
218. Reprinted by
permission.)

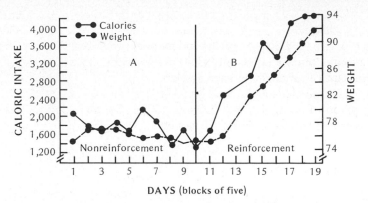

the subject's behavior. In order to be sure that the results were due to the treatment, the reinforcement would have to be removed in a return to baseline, or reversal, to see if the weight and caloric intake dropped. That extension of the A–B design is called an A–B–A design.

The A–B–A Design

The A–B–A design is illustrated in Figure 11.3. If the behavior returns to baseline level during the reversal, then a strong possibility of causality has been demonstrated. The independent variable is most likely to account for the change in behavior.

There is a potential ethical problem in using the A–B–A design. When a patient ends the experiment on a reversal, it is possible that he or she could be left with the undesired clinical condition of the beginning of the experiment. If, for example, biofeedback in an experiment lowers diastolic blood pressure in a hypertensive person, it would be rather sad to return that person to baseline high blood pressure as the last stage of the experiment. A solution to this problem is the A–B–A–B design.

The A–B–A–B Design

We described earlier in the chapter Sterman's (1973) A–B–A–B study. This design is the A–B–A plus a return to treatment after the reversal. The A–B–A–B design is good in that it includes a reversal but does not end with it. Two demonstra-

	BASELINE	TREATMENT	RETURN TO BASELINE REVERSAL
MEASURE OF DEPENDENT VARIABLE	A	B	A

TIME

FIG. 11.3
A–B–A design, which
includes a reversal
phase to ensure control.

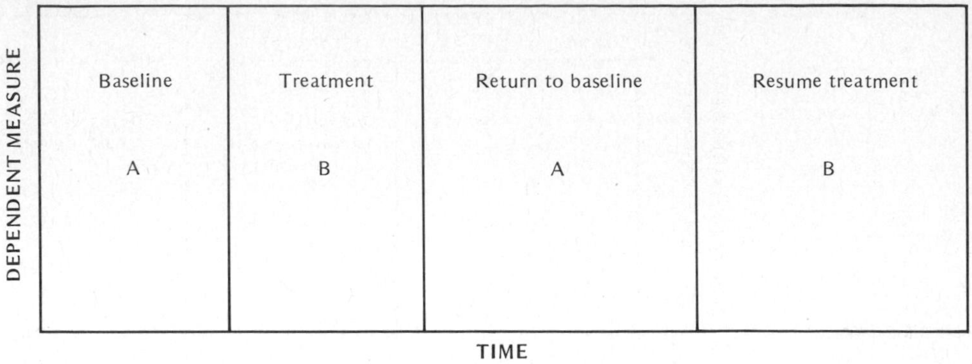

FIG. 11.4
A–B–A–B design,
which solves the ethical
problem of ending on
reversal and allows
good control.

tions of control with the independent variable plus a reversal make this one of the more powerful single-subject designs. Figure 11.4 illustrates the A–B–A–B design.

One of the major problems encountered with any single-subject design that includes a reversal phase is the fact that a true return to baseline is not always possible. For example, a person trained to reduce his or her blood pressure through a relaxation technique may not desire to return to a hypertensive state. Consequently the person consciously or unconsciously may resist returning to baseline, and blood pressure may not rise even when the independent variable presumably has been withdrawn. It is possible that other response-producing stimuli are conditioned during the learning phase and that these responses somehow continue to be reinforced during the reversal. In other words, it may be that once the reinforcement has done its job, the behavior (lower blood pressure) may be irreversible. It is important to note, however, that without a reversal it is hard to know what produced the change in the first place.

VARIATIONS ON SINGLE-SUBJECT DESIGNS

In order to cope with the difficulty of returning some behaviors to baseline once they have been learned, several variations on single-subject designs have been developed. We will discuss four of these designs: D.R.O., changing-criterion, multiple-baseline, and component-analysis designs.

D.R.O. (Differential Reinforcement of Other) Design

In D.R.O. design, a baseline period (A) is followed by a treatment phase (B), during which the target behavior is reinforced. Next, instead of a regular reversal, the experimenter begins to reinforce any and all behavior other than the target behavior (phase C). The experimenter not only fails to reward the target behavior during C, but also rewards the learning of new responses competing with the target behavior. Even when a target behavior is difficult to extinguish, the behavior usually changes quickly under this reinforcement contingency.

Suppose, for example, that a schoolteacher wanted to test the effect of verbal reinforcement on the study habits of a particular child. The teacher could record the frequency of study responses during baseline, then begin reinforcing study behavior

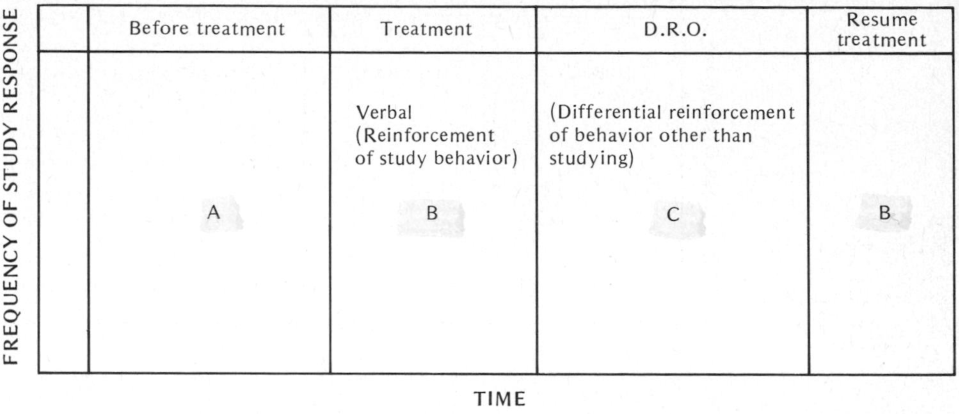

FIG. 11.5
A D.R.O. design to
study the effect of
verbal reinforcement on
study behavior.

with verbal praise. After establishing a rate of studying, the teacher could change to a D.R.O. phase (C) in which study behavior was no longer reinforced, but all other behaviors, such as talking, shuffling feet, and out-of-chair behavior, were reinforced. Still measuring study behavior, the teacher would now have an effective measure of the effect of verbal praise on the target behavior. Study behavior should drop in frequency. Of course, the big drawback is that the D.R.O. techniques are not facilitating the academic purpose of the child's education, and it would be inappropriate to leave the child at the D.R.O. phase. The teacher must return to reinforcing study behavior. This A–B–C–B design is shown in Figure 11.5.

Changing-Criterion Design (Shaping)

The changing-criterion design (Kazdin, 1975) involves establishing a baseline for a certain period of time and then introducing reinforcement dependent upon level of performance of a certain behavior. Once the level of performance reaches the stated criterion, the criterion is raised to a new level, more difficult to reach. The effect of the reinforcement is demonstrated if the behavior continues to match the criterion as it is changed.

Suppose a man who recently had had a stroke and was semiparalyzed on the right side was referred to a psychologist. A neurologist had determined that there was a possibility that the patient could regain the use of his right arm if biofeedback training was used. The psychologist hooked the patient up to an EMG machine (a device that measures muscle activity) and established a baseline level of muscle activity. Subsequently, a criterion for increased activity was selected slightly above baseline so the patient would have to tighten his muscles slightly to obtain a reinforcement (a tone indicating the criterion had been reached). In this way, the patient's muscles could be reeducated by continually increasing the muscle-tightening criterion until the muscle function was restored. This procedure, analogous to "shaping" used in operant-conditioning animal experiments, is exceptionally helpful when the target behavior is weak or does not exist.

Use of the changing-criterion design to control smoking behavior was reported by Axelrod, Hall, Weis, and Rohrer (1974). A 23-year-old female graduate student averaged 16.6 cigarettes per day over a 17-day baseline period (A). The treatment

Research Example

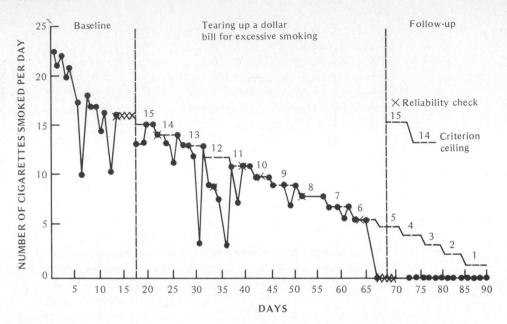

FIG. 11.6
Record of the number of cigarettes smoked per day in a changing criterion design. (From "Use of self-imposed contingencies to reduce the frequency of smoking behavior," by S. Axelrod, R. V. Hall, L. Weiss, and S. Rohrer. In M. J. Mahoney and C. E. Thomsen (Eds.), *Self-control: Power to the person*. Copyright © 1974 by Wadsworth Publishing Company, Inc. Reprinted by permission of the publisher, Brooks/Cole Publishing Company, Monterey, California.)

condition consisted of having the subject destroy a dollar bill for each cigarette over 15 (the specified daily criterion) she smoked. In a few days the criterion was lowered to 14, then to 13, 12, 11, 10, 9, and so forth. Figure 11.6 illustrates her progress. It would appear that the smoking behavior was successfully controlled in about 66 days by changing the criterion for avoiding punishment, the loss of money.

The changing-criterion design is well suited to responses that are gradually acquired rather than quickly learned (Kazdin, 1975). The design does not provide as much control as reversal designs, since a change in behavior may be the result of extraneous or secondary factors other than the reinforcement contingency. A change in life style or the mere fact that time has passed may be the cause of the behavior change. Nevertheless, the design can be very helpful in demonstrating control, especially if a stable baseline is established.

Multiple-Baseline Designs

There are three types of multiple-baseline designs: (1) across behaviors, (2) across settings, and (3) across subjects. A multiple-baseline design does not rely on reversal to show an effect. Rather, at least two behaviors, subjects, or behaviors in various settings (the more the better) are sampled to determine stable baselines. The treatment effects are introduced sequentially. If a change in behavior is observed when each treatment is introduced, and only then, this fact provides a convincing demonstration of control. Let us first look at multiple-baseline design across behaviors of one individual.

Multiple-baseline design across behaviors In this version, more than one behavior is modified. Two or more behaviors are sampled simultaneously so that reliable baselines may be obtained. After the behaviors reach a stable baseline rate, an experimental treatment is introduced for one of the behaviors but not the others. It is expected that the behavior for which the reinforcement is given will be modified but that other behaviors (still being sampled) will remain stable and at baseline. When the reinforced behavior reaches a new stable level, the reinforcement is administered for the second behavior and the first behavior together. One would expect both behavior 1 and behavior 2 to show the effect of the reinforcement. After behavior 1 and 2 are stable (at some new level) a third behavior could be worked into the contingency. Behavioral control (the effect of the independent variable) is demonstrated if each behavior changes only when treatment is introduced. In this case no reversal is required to demonstrate a cause-and-effect relationship. If all three behaviors change as the result of reinforcing behavior 1, then the causal relationship is clouded, but if only one behavior changes with respect to the contingency at a time, it is highly probable that the reinforcement affected the behavior.

Research Example

Schwartz and Hawkins (1970), used a multiple-baseline technique with a 12-year-old girl who was having trouble in school. It was reported that she had a "poor self-image," had trouble in mathematics, made her numerals too small, slouched in her chair with her face only 3 or 4 in. from her work (an eye test revealed normal vision), frequently touched her face irritating her acne, and spoke so quietly that she could not be understood. It was decided that four target behaviors would be modified: (1) size of subject's written numerals; (2) frequency of touching her face; (3) amount of time spent in excessively low posture; and (4) loudness of voice during the class period. The experiment was divided up into three periods: a baseline phase, a control phase, and three sections of an experimental phase. During baseline, measures were collected on all four behaviors for 12 days. No attempt was made to modify any of them. All experimental phases occurred during school hours.

CONTROL PHASE During the control phase (days 13–22), baseline measures continued, except that the experimenter met with the subject after school for ½ hr. and worked with her on making her numerals larger. In effect the control phase served as an experimental phase for numeral size. When appropriate, poker chips were used as a reinforcer. The chips were redeemable for items such as a bracelet, a pen, a trip to the beauty shop, and so forth. Other behaviors were not reinforced. The results of the control phase are shown in Figure 11.7.

EXPERIMENTAL PHASE 1 After numeral size had increased, experimental phase 1 began (days 22–26). This phase was designed to modify face touching. The subject was shown a videotape of her behavior in that day's mathematics class. She was given a stopwatch and instructed to start the watch whenever she was not touching her face and to reset the watch whenever she touched it. For reducing face-touching behavior she was rewarded with poker chips. By day 26 face touching was reduced to zero. Results of phase 1 are shown in Figure 11.8.

EXPERIMENTAL PHASE 2 During phase 2 (days 27–33) the subject was rewarded for reducing slouching behavior. She was given a chip for every consecutive 10 sec. she sat with her head above a line drawn on a blackboard behind her. The results are shown in Figure 11.9.

FIG. 11.7
Baseline and control
phases of a multiple-
baseline design across
behavior, showing
changes in size of
numerals. Behavior
remained stable for the
remainder of the
experiment. (Figures
11.7–11.10 are from
"Application of delayed
conditioning
procedures to the
behavior problems of
an elementary school
child," by M. L.
Schwartz and R. P.
Hawkins. In R. Ulrich,
T. Stachnik, and J.
Mabry (Eds.), *Control of
human behavior: From
cure to prevention* (Vol.
2). Copyright 1970 by
Scott, Foresman.
Reprinted by
permission.)

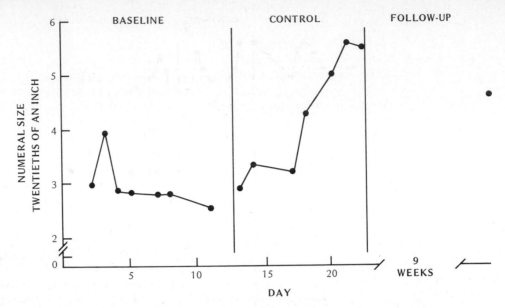

EXPERIMENTAL PHASE 3 In experimental phase 3, a loudness indicator on the voice track of the videotape recorder was monitored. The subject monitored the needle deflections during the replay of her recitations in mathematics. She received poker chips whenever the needle rose above a specified criterion. This procedure continued until day 51. The results are shown in Figure 11.10.

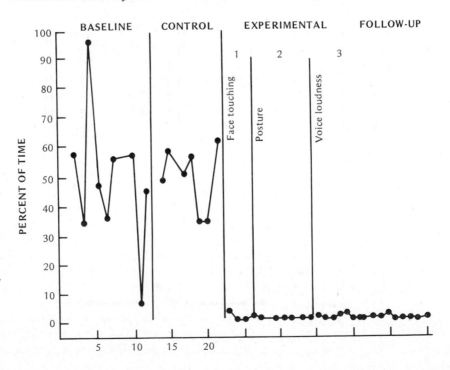

FIG. 11.8
Face-touching behavior
in Schwartz and
Hawkins' experiment.
In experimental phase I,
the purpose was to
modify face-touching
with videotape
feedback. Notice the
dramatic drop in face-
touching responses.

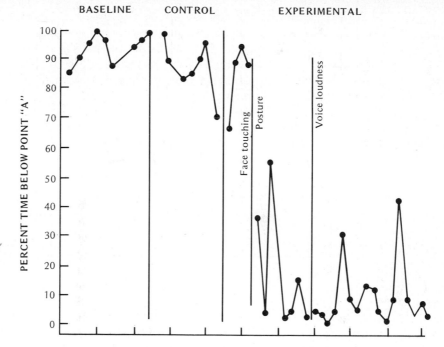

FIG. 11.9
Slouching behavior in Schwartz and Hawkins' experiment. In experimental phase 2, subject was rewarded for reducing slouching behavior. Note that a decrease in slouching begins at this phase.

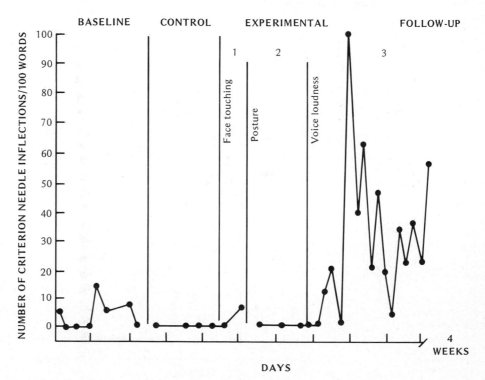

FIG. 11.10
Voice level in Schwartz and Hawkins' experiment. Experimental phase 3 was designed to increase voice level. Notice the increase when reinforcement was given.

Notice that each behavior did not change until the experimental variable was introduced. Also note that the subject was not informed what the subsequent target behaviors would be. Figure 11.7 shows that numeral size increased after the control phase was in force for several days; but as Figures 11.8–11.10 show, face touching, posture, and voice did not change then. In phase 1, face touching responded very well almost immediately, but slouching and voice level were unaffected. Similarly, during phase 2, posture improved but loudness of voice did not. Finally, during the last phase, loudness of voice improved somewhat. Once the treatment effect had been introduced, the target behavior remained at the desired level. The follow-up data (4 weeks later) indicated that all behaviors were still improved.

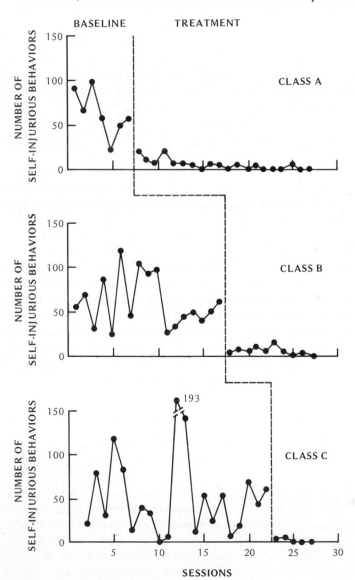

FIG. 11.11
Results of a multiple-baseline study across settings. (From "Reducing self-injurious behavior with a retardate in three classrooms by facial screening," by J. R. Lutzker. Reprinted by permission.)

The multiple-baseline technique across behaviors in this study illustrates the dramatic effect of the treatment on behaviors. This powerful tool can be used with great success in single-subject experiments.

Research Example **Multiple-baseline design across settings** Lutzker (1977) utilized a multiple-baseline study across settings with a 20-year-old profoundly retarded resident of a state hospital. The subject exhibited a high rate of self-injurious behavior, such as face slapping and hitting. The subject attended classes for severely retarded persons for 3 hrs. each morning. Baseline measures of self-injurious behavior were taken for eight sessions. Subsequently, teachers in each of three one-hr classes were instructed to flip a bib over the subject's face and head and hold it for 3 sec. each time self-injurious behavior was observed. During this facial screening, the teacher said "No!" in a loud voice. Five teachers participated in three separate classroom settings.

The data are shown in Figure 11.11. Notice that the treatment facial screening was begun in class A and continued until the self-injurious behavior decreased, then the treatment was given in class B. Shortly after the self-injurious behavior dropped to a very low level in class B, the procedure was introduced in class C. The data illustrate an immediate and relatively permanent change in the frequency of response as a function of the punishment.

Research Example **Multiple-baseline design across subjects** In the third type of multiple-baseline design, baseline data are collected for a particular behavior across two or more individuals. Once the behaviors have reached a fairly stable rate, the treatment effect is given to one of the subjects while baseline continues for the others. According to the design, the behavior of the subject undergoing the treatment effect should change while the behavior of the untreated subjects should not change. Hall, Cristler, Cranston, and Tucker (1970) studied three high school students who were doing poorly in class, receiving Ds and Fs on daily quizzes. After ten days of baseline the first student was given tutoring after school if he earned a poor grade (Figure 11.12). The other two students were not offered tutoring at this time. Once the behavior changed for the first student, the second student was put on the contingency. Similarly, after the second student showed a change the third student was put on the contingency. Behavior changes with changes in treatment effects strongly suggest control due to the reinforcement schedule and not due to secondary factors.

Component-Analysis Design

Research Example The last in our series of single-subject designs is component analysis, in which the experimenter assesses the effects of two or more independent variables separately and in combination. One type is labeled an A–BC–B–BC design. The A level is baseline, BC is a combination of two treatment levels, and, of course, B is one treatment effect alone. Realon (1976) studied an agoraphobic male. Agoraphobia is an intense fear of going outside or of open spaces. Realon recorded both the distance the subject would travel away from his residence and time away in minutes (Figure 11.13).

Two independent variables were utilized in the study: reinforcement in the form of social praise (B) and modeling by the experimenter (C). Baseline was taken for six

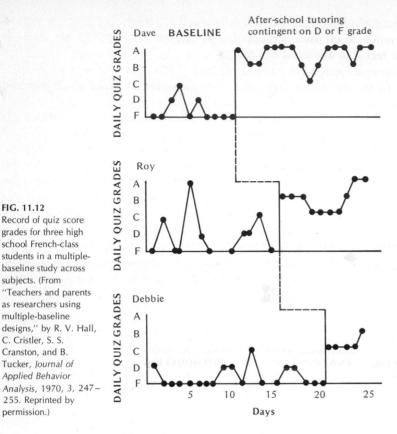

FIG. 11.12
Record of quiz score grades for three high school French-class students in a multiple-baseline study across subjects. (From "Teachers and parents as researchers using multiple-baseline designs," by R. V. Hall, C. Cristler, S. S. Cranston, and B. Tucker, *Journal of Applied Behavior Analysis*, 1970, 3, 247– 255. Reprinted by permission.)

sessions, followed by nine sessions when treatments B and C were combined. Sessions 16 and 17 were done with only B as reinforcement, followed by nine more sessions of B and C in combination. Figure 11.13 shows a relatively stable baseline followed by a rapid increase in both distance and time for the BC condition. Notice, however, that in the following B condition, both distance and time rapidly decrease back to baseline levels. This finding would strongly indicate that B (praise) alone was not an effective treatment. In the last nine sessions, when B and C are recombined, the behaviors return to their previous high levels. The results do not indicate what the effect of modeling (C) by itself would be, only the effect of the combination of the two variables. Clearly, order effects are not well controlled in this design, and the multiple-treatment interaction effects may be unclear. The solution to this problem is to replicate the treatment effects under a different order with another subject.

LIMITATIONS AND ADVANTAGES

It is apparent that single-subject designs cannot answer all the questions we need to have answered, but these designs do provide a basis for understanding the effects of some independent variables in clinical settings. Single-subject designs are limited when more than one independent variable is involved in a treatment program. If more than one treatment is to be used, a group design may be more appropriate. Another limitation is the fact that statistical hypothesis testing is, in most cases, impossible. However, Barlow and Hersen (1973) and Michael (1974) maintain that a treatment does not have to be statistically better than no treatment in order to be clinically preferable.

Another limitation of single-subject designs is the confounding effects of sequential or order effects. Once a treatment has been given, it is impossible to isolate or get rid of that effect later in the experiment. For example, suppose a subject has been taught to relax by means of transcendental meditation as a treatment effect. It is impossible for an experimenter to partial out the effect of that training in subsequent reversal trials—or any other trials for that matter. If a person takes a test, the effects of taking it can influence the scores on a second test. In other words, some treatment effects may be irreversible. In group designs, sequence effects can be controlled.

A final limitation of single-subject designs is the limited ability to generalize the results of an experiment. In group designs, the goal is to be able to generalize from the sample to the population at large. In single-subject designs, the sample subject may not be representative of the population.

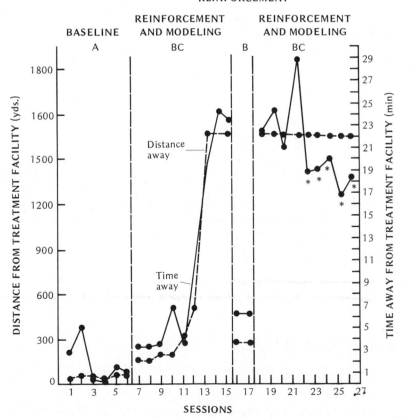

FIG. 11.13
Data from a component analysis experiment. Two variables are illustrated: time away from treatment facility and distance away. Notice the changes in behavior as a function of different reinforcement strategies. Fading of the experimenter's presence is denoted by the stars. (From "Reinforcement and participant modeling in the modification of agoraphobia," by R. E. Realon. Reprinted by permission.)

The advantages of single-subject designs outweigh the disadvantages in clinical settings, where flexibility in applying treatment effects is desirable. The ability to run a single-subject experiment inexpensively makes the designs "cost effective," especially if several replications of the experiment add little to the cost.

Some psychologists (Gottman, McFall, & Barnett, 1969) have suggested that a new technique, "time-series analysis," might prove helpful in determining whether variations in data are due to an independent variable. According to Gottman et al., time-series designs involve successive observations throughout an experiment. The analysis provides a description of changes in data not due to noise (chance occurrences) in the system. Noise or uncontrolled sources of variation thus may be accounted for. A time-series analysis investigates how well a series of numbers "remembers" what it did in the past. That is, one measures the autocorrelation function (correlation with itself) by testing the correlation of data at time t with data at time $t + 1$, and so forth. Obviously, this technique is very complex and beyond the scope or intent of this book. Michael (1974, p. 29) points out: "in the case of the autoregressive techniques that seem to be 'just around the corner,' their understanding will surely require a good deal of graduate instruction time and their proper usage could easily become the main concern from the point of view of data analysis—clearly a case of the tail wagging dog."

SUMMARY

1. Single-subject designs are appropriate when large groups are difficult to match or otherwise too expensive in terms of time and money.
2. Single-subject designs are an outgrowth of applied clinical research, especially behavior modification.
3. Single-subject designs do not lend themselves to clear statistical analyses.
4. Hypothesis testing is not formalized in single-subject designs. The experimenter relies on the "convincingness" of the data.
5. The single-subject design usually has a baseline phase where the target behavior is recorded until it stabilizes. The baseline is followed by a treatment phase. Once the behavior changes in the desired direction, a return to baseline or reversal is performed. If the behavior returns to baseline levels, the treatment is said to be effective, and behavioral control has been established. This basic design is called the A–B–A design.
6. Because there are some ethical considerations about leaving a subject at baseline, most experimenters resume the treatment phase after the reversal, resulting in an A–B–A–B design.
7. The D.R.O. design is used by experimenters when a behavior does not return to baseline readily. During the D.R.O. the experimenter reinforces all behaviors other than the target behavior.
8. There are several variations of more complex single-subject designs. The changing-criterion design utilizes a shaping procedure to gain control over behavior. The multiple-baseline designs do not rely on a reversal to show an effect; rather, at least two behaviors, subjects, or behaviors in different settings are studied sequentially. If a change in behavior is observed when each treatment effect is introduced, and only then, a convincing demonstration of control is provided.

9. The component-analysis design assesses the effects of two or more independent variables separately and in combinations. Order effects are not well controlled in this design.
10. Single-subject designs do not provide a good basis for generalization and do not control for order effects. They do, however, provide a very "cost-effective" method for the study of behavior. They also provide a basis for information that is not always obtainable in group designs.

SUGGESTED READINGS

Barlow, D. H., & Hersen, M. Single-case experimental design: Uses in applied clinical research. *Archives of General Psychiatry,* 1973, *29,* 319–325.

Davidson, P. O., & Costello, C. G. *N = 1: Experimental studies of single cases.* New York: Van Nostrand Reinhold, 1969.

Hersen, M., & Barlow, D. H. *Single case experimental designs: Strategies for studying behavior change.* New York: Pergamon, 1976.

Kazden, A. E. Methodological and assessment considerations in evaluating reinforcement programs in applied settings. *Journal of Applied Behavior Analysis,* 1973, *6,* 1–23.

Statistical inference for individual organism research. *Journal of Applied Behavior Analysis: Monograph Number 4,* 1975.

section three

The Research Process

12

The Research Proposal

Where do you look for ideas? How do you evaluate ideas? How do you describe a proposed research project formally? These are the questions broached in this chapter. Too often, both experienced and novice researchers launch a research project without adequately thinking through the entire process. A well-done research proposal can prevent wasted effort. Whether written for a psychology class project or for a fund-granting agency, a proposal serves as a model for the entire experiment. A carefully written proposal can illuminate previously unseen problems, provide a guide for the actual experiment, and serve as a model for organizing the final research report.

We hope the material in this chapter will help you avoid becoming enmeshed in a research project without knowing what should happen next. The chapter is concerned with some of the practical problems that you encounter in the course of selecting a project, specifying the research hypothesis, determining a detailed research procedure, and writing the entire, formal proposal. At the end of the chapter, a suggested outline for a research proposal and a student's proposal should serve as helpful models.

FINDING POTENTIAL TOPICS

All too often when students are assigned a research project for a psychology class, they don't have any idea what to research, let alone how to do it! The research proposal is often cause for a lot of head-scratching and consternation.

If you need a promising source of instant ideas, you should consider reading a number of general reference books, jotting down ideas as they occur. For example, almost any introductory psychology textbook is rich in researchable ideas. If your interests are restricted to a specific research area, concentrating on the relevant chapters in an introductory text or reading a general book about that area should unearth many research possibilities.

As you gain experience in the research process you begin to realize that the really difficult aspect is to *limit* the number of ideas, variables, and hypotheses to be empirically tested. While you read the literature, ideas keep popping up such as: "I wonder how that relates to . . . ?" or "What if the experimenter had . . . ?" Each of these questions can lead to a potential research project. However, unless you write down the ideas as they occur, you are likely to forget many of them.

Idea Logbook as in text

You may find an idea logbook helpful in recording research ideas. An **idea logbook** contains ideas briefly jotted down as they occur to you while you read. It provides a permanent record of potential research topics that you may evaluate at a later time. If you have established and maintained an idea logbook, the problem of choosing a research topic becomes one of selecting the most interesting questions.

As you become acquainted with an area, you rely more on primary sources that communicate new developments to people involved in research. Journals such as *Psychological Review* and *Psychological Reports* publish articles concerned with theories and theoretical issues in psychology. *Behavioral Science* provides a similar function for all behavioral disciplines. Theoretical articles are rich sources for research ideas.

There are a few publications that include research from a broad spectrum of psychological areas. The editors of these journals try to select articles that are contemporary and stimulating, and these articles provide good raw material for research ideas. *Human Behavior* and *Psychology Today* attempt to keep their readers informed of recent developments throughout the area of psychology. *The Sciences* and *Scientific American* serve a similar function for all scientific fields. All four publications usually present background research as well as new findings.

Psychonomic Science and its replacement, the *Bulletin of the Psychonomic Society,* publish two-page research reports from all areas of psychology. *Science* magazine provides a similar service for those interested in all fields of science. Both of these publications sample the latest empirical discoveries. Articles in these journals are characterized by a short time period between manuscript submission and publication.

For the student interested in generating research hypotheses, any of the above publications are suitable. In addition, there are a large number of professional journals (Figure 12.1) devoted to publishing research in specific areas. These sources provide empirical data for understanding an area or expose the reader to novel experimental techniques. The articles published in these journals are often so technical that the reader must have some prior acquaintance with the field, especially its particular terminology, in order to understand and evaluate them. If you have some background in an area, these publications also provide a rich source for research ideas.

Searching the literature is not the only way to generate research hypotheses. Listening to a lecture on a topic can lead to research possibilities. Involving the lecturer in a subsequent informal discussion may be even more productive. Also, you may find that a "rap session" with other interested students exposes many research possibilities.

SELECTING THE TOPIC

Once you have succeeded in locating a few research possibilities, you then have the task of evaluating and selecting the most promising one. You should first ask yourself, "Would this experiment be a waste of my time?" If the initial answer is "No," the next step in the selection process is to formulate the conceptual hypothesis and develop a tentative research proposal. Reading published research reports may assist you in forming the conceptual hypothesis, in designing the research, in specifying the procedure, and in choosing the appropriate data-analysis procedure.

Bibliographic Publications

There are several publications for the person seeking research articles in specific behavioral areas, providing relevant and sometimes comprehensive bibliographic sources. The reference librarians at any college or university library can provide invaluable assistance in locating the appropriate bibliographic resources.

Psychological Bulletin contains articles that summarize and integrate the research findings on specific research topics. *Review of Educational Research* and *The Annual Review of Psychology* provide a similar service, emphasizing research that has been published within the past three to four years. *Current Contents* (Behavioral, Social, and Management Sciences edition) is a weekly publication that lists the table of

	Animal Subjects	Human Subjects	Theory and Systems	Research Technology and Statistics	Perception and Sensation	Motivation and Emotion	Learning and Thinking	Physiological Psychology	Pharmacology	Genetics	Developmental and Child Psychology	Educational Psychology	Social Psychology	Personality	Mental Retardation	Clinical Psychology
American Educational Research Journal		■									■	■				
American Journal of Clinical Hypnosis		■	■			■								■		■
American Journal of Mental Deficiency	■	■					■	■		■	■	■	■	■	■	■
American Journal of Orthopsychiatry	■	■				■					■	■	■	■	■	■
American Journal of Psychiatry, The	■	■				■		■	■		■		■	■	■	■
American Journal of Psychology, The	■	■	■	■	■	■	■	■			■		■	■		
American Psychologist	■	■	■	■	■	■	■	■	■	■	■	■	■	■	■	■
American Scientist	■	■	■	■	■		■	■	■	■			■			
American Statistical Association Journal				■												
American Statistician				■												
Animal Behaviour	■		■		■	■	■	■		■	■					
Animal Learning and Behaviour	■				■	■	■	■								
Annual Review of Physiology	■	■			■	■	■	■	■	■						
Annual Review of Psychology	■	■	■	■	■	■	■	■	■	■	■	■	■	■	■	■
Archives of General Psychiatry	■	■				■		■	■	■			■	■		■
Australian Journal of Psychology		■			■	■	■				■		■	■		■
Behavior	■		■		■	■	■	■		■						
Behavior Research and Therapy	■	■				■	■									■
Behavior Research Methods and Instrumentation	■	■		■												
Behavior Therapy		■				■	■							■		■
Behavioral Science	■	■	■	■		■	■	■					■			
Biofeedback & Self-regulation		■				■		■								
Biometrics				■												
Biometrika				■												
British Journal of Educational Psychology		■				■	■				■	■	■	■	■	
British Journal of Medical Psychology		■											■	■		■
British Journal of Psychiatry		■						■					■			■
British Journal of Psychology	■	■	■	■	■	■	■	■		■	■		■	■		
Bulletin of the Psychonomic Society, The	■	■		■	■	■	■	■	■	■	■		■	■		

FIG. 12.1
A partial listing of professional journals publishing psychological research. The column headings present an approximate guide to the usual contents of a journal.

	Animal Subjects	Human Subjects	Theory and Systems	Research Technology and Statistics	Perception and Sensation	Motivation and Emotion	Learning and Thinking	Physiological Psychology	Pharmacology	Genetics	Developmental and Child Psychology	Educational Psychology	Social Psychology	Personality	Mental Retardation	Clinical Psychology
Canadian Journal of Psychology	■	■	■		■	■	■	■	■						■	■
Canadian Psychologist	■	■	■	■	■	■	■	■	■	■	■	■	■		■	■
Child Development		■			■	■	■			■	■	■	■	■		
Cognitive Psychology		■	■	■	■		■									
Developmental Psychobiology	■	■			■	■	■	■		■	■					
Developmental Psychology		■			■	■	■			■	■	■	■	■		
Dissertation Abstracts	■	■	■	■	■	■	■	■	■	■	■	■	■	■	■	■
Educational and Psychological Measurement		■		■			■				■	■	■	■		
Genetic Psychology Monographs	■	■		■	■	■	■	■		■	■	■	■	■		■
Human Behavior		■	■			■					■		■	■		■
Human Relations		■	■			■						■	■	■		
Journal of Abnormal Child Psychology		■				■	■				■			■	■	■
Journal of Abnormal Psychology		■	■		■	■	■						■	■		■
Journal of the Acoustical Society of America	■	■		■	■											
Journal of Applied Behavior Analysis		■				■	■				■	■	■		■	■
Journal of Applied Behavioral Science, The		■	■			■							■	■		
Journal of Applied Psychology		■		■	■	■	■					■	■	■		
Journal of Applied Social Psychology		■				■							■	■		
Journal of Auditory Research	■	■		■	■											
Journal of Autism and Childhood Schizophrenia		■			■	■	■				■			■	■	■
Journal of Biological Psychology	■				■	■	■	■	■	■						
Journal of Child Psychology and Psychiatry		■			■	■	■			■	■	■		■	■	■
Journal of Clinical Psychology		■		■							■		■	■	■	■
Journal of Comparative and Physiological Psychology	■	■			■	■	■	■	■							
Journal of Consulting and Clinical Psychology		■	■			■					■		■	■	■	■

FIG. 12.1
(Continued)

	Animal Subjects	Human Subjects	Theory and Systems	Research Technology and Statistics	Perception and Sensation	Motivation and Emotion	Learning and Thinking	Physiological Psychology	Pharmacology	Genetics	Developmental and Child Psychology	Educational Psychology	Social Psychology	Personality	Mental Retardation	Clinical Psychology
Journal of Counseling Psychology		■		■							■	■	■	■		■
Journal of Educational Measurement		■		■								■				
Journal of Educational Psychology		■	■								■	■				■
Journal of the Experimental Analysis of Behavior	■			■	■	■	■		■		■					■
Journal of Experimental Child Psychology		■									■					
Journal of Experimental Psychology: Animal Behavior Processes	■															
Journal of Experimental Psychology: General	■	■			■		■				■					
Journal of Experimental Psychology: Human Learning and Memory		■					■									
Journal of Experimental Psychology: Human Perception and Performance		■		■	■											
Journal of Experimental Research in Personality	■	■									■		■	■		
Journal of Experimental Social Psychology											■		■			
Journal of General Psychology	■	■	■	■	■		■				■		■			
Journal of Genetic Psychology	■	■								■	■					
Journal of Mathematical Psychology	■	■	■	■												
Journal of Mental Deficiency Research	■	■		■							■				■	
Journal of the Optical Society of America	■	■	■		■											
Journal of Personality		■				■							■	■		■
Journal of Personality and Social Psychology	■	■											■	■		■
Journal of Psychology, The	■	■	■		■	■	■	■	■	■	■	■	■	■	■	■
Journal of Social Issues, The		■	■										■	■		
Journal of Social Psychology, The		■											■			
Journal of Verbal Learning and Verbal Behavior		■					■				■					
Learning and Motivation	■					■	■									
Memory and Cognition		■		■	■		■				■	■		■		

FIG. 12.1
(Continued)

	Animal Subjects	Human Subjects	Theory and Systems	Research Technology and Statistics	Perception and Sensation	Motivation and Emotion	Learning and Thinking	Physiological Psychology	Pharmacology	Genetics	Developmental and Child Psychology	Educational Psychology	Social Psychology	Personality	Mental Retardation	Clinical Psychology
Perception and Psychophysics	■	■		■	■											
Perceptual and Motor Skills	■	■		■	■	■		■	■		■	■	■	■	■	■
Physiology and Behavior	■	■			■	■	■	■	■	■						
Physiological Psychology	■	■		■	■	■	■	■	■	■						■
Professional Psychology		■										■	■	■	■	■
Psychological Abstracts	■	■	■	■	■	■	■	■	■	■	■	■	■	■	■	■
Psychological Bulletin	■	■	■	■	■	■	■	■	■	■	■	■	■	■	■	■
Psychological Record, The	■	■	■	■	■	■	■	■	■	■	■	■	■	■	■	■
Psychological Reports	■	■	■	■	■	■	■	■	■	■	■	■	■	■	■	■
Psychological Review	■	■	■		■	■	■	■	■	■	■		■	■		
Psychology Today	■	■	■		■	■	■	■	■	■	■	■	■	■	■	■
Psychometrika		■	■	■								■				
Psychopharmacology	■	■			■	■	■	■	■							
Psychophysiology	■	■		■	■	■	■	■	■							■
Quarterly Journal of Experimental Psychology	■	■		■	■	■	■	■	■							
Review of Educational Research		■	■	■		■	■				■	■	■	■	■	
Scandinavian Journal of Psychology	■	■	■	■	■	■	■	■			■	■	■	■		■
Science	■	■	■	■	■	■	■	■	■	■						
The Sciences	■	■	■	■	■	■	■	■	■	■						
Scientific American	■	■	■	■	■	■	■	■	■	■	■	■	■	■	■	■

FIG. 12.1

(Continued)

contents for a large number of behavioral science journals. The publishers of *Current Contents* also offer a special service that lists all article titles containing certain key terms. *Science Citation Index* provides quarterly lists of journal articles and book reviews.

A literature search is a crucial aspect of a behavioral research project. It would be stupid not to take advantage of the accumulated wisdom and observations of previous researchers. Knowing where to look in the research journals is important since there is such a large number of psychological journals (Figure 12.1). The best single tool to help find relevant research articles is *Psychological Abstracts,* containing "nonevaluative summaries of the world's literature in psychology and selected disciplines." Brief summaries or abstracts of research articles, technical reports, and books as well as titles of dissertations and theses are presented in *Psychological Abstracts.* There is an index at the end of each monthly issue and a cumulative index for each semiannual, consolidated volume (Figure 12.2). Since each set of six issues contains approximately 13,000 abstracts of material from over 400 journals, these indexes are essential. By reading the abstract, you can decide if the material is relevant enough to your proposed project to justify taking the time to find and read the original source.

Suppose you are interested in behavior therapy for mentally retarded people. You are a volunteer at a local institution for retarded persons, and you have observed a person there who vomits frequently. You wish to know if anyone has done any work on controlling such behavior. In the January–June, 1976, semiannual index to *Psychological Abstracts,* on page 1006, you find the heading "Vomiting." The article listed under the heading is circled in Figure 12.2. Since the article seems to be related directly to your interest, you search for article number 5082 in the January–June monthly issues. The article number is not a page number; however, there is a running head at the top of each *Psychological Abstracts* page that gives the volume number and the range of article numbers included. For instance, page 515 in the March issue has the heading 55: 5071–5083, indicating that articles 5071–5083 are included on that page. Page 515 contains the subheading "Behavior Therapy and Behavior Modification," and article 5082 is the third article listed under that heading (Figure

Using *Psychological Abstracts*

FIG. 12.2
A section of a page from the cumulative, semiannual subject index for *Psychological Abstracts*. The target article is circled. (From the *Author and Subject Index to Psychological Abstracts,* 1976, 55 (Jan.–June), 1006. Copyright 1976 by the American Psychological Association. Reprinted by permission.)

Vomiting · SUBJECT INDEX · Water Intake

volunteer recruitment & training program, community mental health center, 7864
Volunteers (Experiment) [See Experiment Volunteers]
Vomit Inducing Drugs [See Emetic Drugs]
Vomiting
self correction & positive practice procedure, nonmedically-caused habitual vomiting, profoundly retarded 36 yr old female inpatient, 5082
Voting Behavior
correspondent inference theory analysis, attitude attribution in voting behavior, black & white Ss, 9795
demographic determinants & ethnic basis of political behavior, white voters in South Africa, 2290
Guttman scale analysis vs factor analysis as applied to legislative roll call votes, 5950
media & message & interpersonal influence, perception of political figures, college students, 12144
private competitive market & simple majority rule, decision rules in social choice space, 12048
propositional inventory & stepwise regression analysis, voter behavior in school financial elections, 13013
validity & reliability of Thurstone's Attitude toward Capital

season of birth, schizophrenic & neurotic patients, England & Wales, 12399
suicide ascertainment procedure, accuracy of reported suicide rates, England vs Denmark & Wales, 4796
suicide rates, England vs Wales vs Scotland, 10038
Walking
behavioral techniques, walking & social interaction & oral hygiene, 58–88 yr old geriatric patients in residential nursing home facility, 5121
mechanical disturbance caused by winds, skilled performance & semantic assessments, 19–59 yr old females, 8545
War
cognitive style, personality characteristics & vocational choice, Vietnam era veterans & comparison of schizophrenic & nonschizophrenic veterans, 4602
evaluation of Army experience & service in Vietnam vs other than Vietnam, anomie & self concept & socialization in readjustment, male Army veterans, 9909
grief stages & coping model, war widows in Israel, implications for professional caregiver, 5231
interpretation & analysis, Rorschach responses, Nazi leaders tried at Nuremberg book, 12061

FIG. 12.3
A section of a page from a monthly issue of *Psychological Abstracts*. The target summary and portions of two other summaries are included (From *Psychological Abstracts*, 1976, *55*, 515. Copyright 1976 by the American Psychological Association. Reprinted by permission.)

the discrimination control of rectal pressure for elimination. Social and material reinforcers were added for appropriate toileting behavior. A 6-mo follow-up showed that the behavior was maintained.

5082. **Azrin, N. H. & Wesolowski, M. D.** (Anna State Hosp, Behavior Research Lab, IL) **Eliminating habitual vomiting in a retarded adult by positive practice and self-correction.** *Journal of Behavior Therapy & Experimental Psychiatry*, 1975(Aug), Vol 6(2), 145–148.—A combination of self-correction and practice in the correct manner of handling the urge to vomit entirely eliminated the nonmedically-caused vomiting, of many years standing, of a profoundly retarded 36-yr-old female inpatient.

5083. **Barton, Elizabeth S.** (Meanwood Park Hosp, Leeds, England) **The problem of generalization in the operant conditionings of social speech in the severely subnormal: Use of reversal to establish generalizability.** *British Journal of Psychiatry*, 1975(Oct), Vol 127, 376–385.—Conducted 3 studies with 6 retarded 27–46 yr old (IQ range, 34–42) Ss who were reinforced for talking to each other. Reinforcement (tokens) was delivered in a reversal design (baseline, reinforcement, no reinforcement, reinforcement). Whether social speech would continue to occur without external reinforcement was examined by observing Ss through a 1-way mirror in an

12.3). The abstract indicates that the article is indeed relevant to your interests, so you next find Volume 6, issue 2 of the 1975 *Journal of Behavior Therapy and Experimental Psychiatry* to read the entire article.

Sometimes you may begin a literature search with a very specific, limited topic in mind. Such a topic may be too precise to be listed as an index heading in *Psychological Abstracts*. If you do not know the appropriate more general terms under which your topic would be likely to be included, your instructor can help you.

Personal Communication and Reprints

If a person has done considerable work in your area of research interest, it is often profitable to contact that researcher directly. While their supply lasts, people who have published research articles are willing to send article reprints, or copies to anyone requesting them. You fill out a reprint request postcard with the title, date, author, and journal name, and send it to the first author of the article. In most recent articles, the senior author's current address is footnoted on the first page. Be sure you include your name and return address on the postcard. Psychological conventions provide an excellent opportunity for direct communication with researchers working in your area of interest.

EVALUATING A TENTATIVE PROPOSAL

A tentative research proposal usually is modified during the proposal-evaluation process. Assuming a proposed experiment appears meaningful, is it feasible? Can the problem be attacked successfully within the limitations of available resources? Limited resources can become a major factor in the design of your experiment.

One of the most important, yet least often considered, limitations is the time necessary to conduct the research. Completing a relatively small research project is

Time Limitation

more valuable than leaving a more comprehensive effort unfinished because of lack of time. Sufficient time must be allotted to set up the experimental conditions, collect the data, analyze the data, and write the research report. Also, time should be set aside for mulling over the research results before you prepare the final report.

Subject Availability

Another limitation is associated with the type of subjects used in the experiment. Animal subjects must be acquired, housed, and properly cared for. All experimental animals should be given the best possible care for two reasons. First, healthy animals are more likely to yield valid behavioral data than unhealthy animals; second, you should avoid violating the ethical standards established by research psychologists, state law, and local humane societies (chapter 13). Human subjects may require payment, are often less convenient than other animals, and are frequently undependable. In contrast, rats almost always show up for their experiment.

Time and Effort Cost

A third limitation is the potential cost in subject and experimenter time and in experimenter effort. The final decision to conduct an experiment should be based on a very simple rule: *Will the utility of the expected data justify the cost required to collect it?* Sometimes a projected, magnificent expenditure of time and money may look like it will yield trivial conclusions with little or no practical or theoretical value. In this case, you should consider more profitable uses for your research. On the other hand, the anticipated results may look so promising that the expense is justifiable. Evaluating the utility of anticipated data is a highly subjective process. The same potential research conclusion will generate different degrees of enthusiasm in different investigators.

Pilot Study

Sometimes it is wise to look at a sample of the dependent variable measures to estimate their usefulness. You can perform a **pilot study,** an abbreviated experiment using a few subjects, to obtain a sample of the research results. A pilot study allows you to make an evaluation of potential data before investing significant amounts of time and money on a full-blown project. An additional advantage of a pilot study is that it often reveals the need for additional control procedures. In chapter 1 we discussed a pilot study performed by Hess (1965).

WRITING THE FORMAL PROPOSAL

When you conclude that your research plans are both useful and feasible, you should prepare a formal research proposal. A research proposal is a written statement of the procedures you intend to follow. Most of the procedures should have been designed in the research-evaluation process. However, stating them in written form forces you to face any remaining ambiguities. A thorough and well-organized research proposal requires considerable effort. It is an important step in the process of translating an abstract idea into empirical observations. Because of the intrinsic value of a research proposal and because it is often required by individuals who must evaluate the research, we shall suggest a form for written research proposals. The *Publication Manual of the American Psychological Association* (1974) is the standard for the style of writing research reports. It is also helpful in writing a research proposal since the final report generally follows the format of the proposal. If you do not already own a copy of this manual, you should order one from your local bookstore or directly from APA headquarters in Washington, D.C.

Except for the discussion of previous research and background theories, a research proposal is written in the future tense. The following outline is presented in formal outline style. An actual research proposal is not written in outline form, but in narrative form. Again, the APA manual provides definitive information on organization, writing style, and the styling of details such as headings, quotations, citations, footnotes, and abbreviations.

Outline of a Research Proposal

I. Title of the research proposal   The title of a research proposal should convey briefly the content of the proposed study. The title should specify the relationships to be studied in the experiment. For example, "Behavior of light- and dark-reared rats on the visual cliff" briefly details what the experiment is about. "Behavior . . . on the visual cliff" is the dependent variable, "light- and dark-reared" constitutes the independent variable, and "rats" are the subjects. It does not take a lot of imagination to discern the content of this experiment. Similarly the title, "Behavioral study of obedience" succinctly conveys the area of Milgram's (1963) landmark study. The important concept to remember is that the title should tell the reader what to expect. Try not to make the title so dull that the reader loses interest in the proposal; but on the other hand, do not make the title so gaudy, vulgar, or ribald that it is offensive.

II. Introduction   The first part of a proposal introduces the general context of a research problem. Include theoretical and empirical background that pertains to your research idea. Indicate why you feel your research should be conducted. It is not enough to say that it sounds interesting. Your review of the relevant literature should be organized logically to show the importance of the proposed research in its theoretical or practical implications. The references you cite should be clearly relevant to your proposed study. If someone has completed a study of the effect of "macho" movies on the reproductive success of chimpanzees in a zoo, you would not use that study as a reference for a study in rote memory. On the other hand, if you were interested in the study of college males' attitudes with regard to sexual mores, then it might be appropriate.

III. Statement of the problem

A. CONCEPTUAL HYPOTHESIS   A conceptual hypothesis is a brief, theoretical statement of the expected relationship between the independent and dependent variables. The conceptual hypothesis is derived from the researcher's model, the background research, and relevant theories. The terms of the conceptual hypothesis are operationally definable. For example, if your experiment is concerned with the relationship between sex and intelligence, your conceptual hypothesis might be, "Women trained in karate are more intelligent than men, on the average."

B. IDENTIFICATIONS   In order to develop an experimental hypothesis, each concept in the conceptual hypothesis must be defined operationally. For example, in the conceptual hypothesis above:

1. Women—those college students who mark an X in the box after Female at the top of the intelligence test form.
2. Men—those college students who mark an X in the box after Male at the top of the intelligence test form.
3. Intelligence—the score on the Lorge-Thorndike intelligence test.
4. Karate—an oriental martial art form involving smooth muscle movements, speed, strength, and self-discipline.

C. INDEPENDENT AND DEPENDENT VARIABLES   You must specify the levels of the independent variables and dependent variables in terms of how you measure them. For example, the independent variable for the conceptual hypothesis above is karate training. You may require a minimum of one year of training at a certified school as your operational definition of the term. The dependent variable has been defined as the score on a specific intelligence test.

D. EXPERIMENTAL HYPOTHESIS   The experimental hypothesis must be stated in terms of the identifications and specifications of the independent and dependent variables. You must state each element explicitly in terms of the operational manipulations. The conceptual hypothesis restated as an experimental hypothesis might read: "College students who checked 'Female' on the Lorge-Thorndike test form and who have trained for a minimum of one year in the martial art of karate will, on the average, show higher scores on the intelligence test than will college students who checked 'Male' on the test."

The experimental hypothesis is much less general than the conceptual hypothesis. Confirmation of the experimental hypothesis can only be said to be a confirmation of the conceptual hypothesis if the female and male students who participated in the experiment are a random sample of women and men and if the operational definitions are appropriate.

IV. Method

A. *Subjects*
The method of sampling, the number, and the relevant descriptive characteristics of the subjects are described.
B. *Design and method of assignment of subjects.*
The specific type of research design to be used is stated and clearly illustrated. The method of assigning subjects to treatments is specified.
C. *Equipment*
The equipment to be used in a study is described, including mazes, paper and pencil tests, response recorders, or stimulus pictures.
D. *Procedure*
The step-by-step order of the events of a proposed experiment is carefully described. A clear description of procedures includes such things as where the subjects are contacted,

how they are pretrained, and/or when they are exposed to a treatment. Sometimes a description of the experiment as if seen by a subject is the clearest way to describe the procedure.

E. *Control of secondary and error variance*
The relevant, plausible, potential sources of secondary and error variance are specified and the procedures used to control these sources are described.

V. Proposed data analysis

A. *Measures of the dependent variable*
The operational definition of a dependent variable specifies precisely how behavior is measured. The means of recording the data should also be specified.

B. *Statistical tests*
How the experimental data will be organized in the final report is briefly indicated. Generally, how the data will be statistically evaluated should be specified.

VI. References   In this section you include all of the reference material cited in the proposal; you do not include sources that were consulted but did not prove to have direct relevance to your study. As indicated in the *Publication manual of the APA,* when citing previous research within the text of a proposal, the authors' names and the year of publication are presented as follows: "Jones and Clarke (1985) reported . . ." These references are listed completely in your reference section in alphabetical order. For guidance on form, look at the *Publication manual,* any recent APA journal, or chapter 15 of this book.

If the research proposal is done well, data collection consists of following your written procedures. However, you should be alert to any unusual or unexpected behavior that may occur in the course of the experiment. Pursuing accidental phenomena may lead to interesting findings. As indicated in chapter 2, you should cultivate serendipity, the capacity to recognize the potential implications of an unexpected observation and pursue it (Skinner's Principle Number 1).

A Sample Research Proposal

The following research proposal is a draft of a real proposal presented to one of us by a junior psychology major at the University of the Pacific. The proposal is not perfect; it contains statements that are difficult to understand, but it provides a good example of what undergraduates can do. The comments in the margin indicate improvements that could be made or points where clarification is needed.

Massage vs. Progressive Relaxation in the Reduction of Muscle Tension in the Trapezius Muscle

Kathy O'Connell
University of the Pacific

First "muscle" is redundant.

Needs an opening paragraph introducing area, scope and general purpose of the study. "Tension, or" is redundant.

What evidence? Sub. "is not aware" for "does . . . know."

Delete "very"

Delete "as such."

No transition between paragraphs. Missing page number of quote.

Quoted sentence awkward, too long; could be broken into two sentences.

Location of "again" leads to misunderstanding of the sentence.

"Noted" should be "recorded."
What stimuli?

Purpose of paragraph is unclear.

"has pointed out" should be "summarized."

Tension, or muscle tension, is a stiffness or tightening of the muscles and the connective tissue beyond the amount of tonus needed for normal healthy functioning (Downing, 1972). There is evidence that the average person does not actually know when he is tense. Psychological experiments have indicated that sensations of tenseness or contraction constitute some of the very essence of the processes of thinking and attention (Malmo, 1975), but this is not to say that the thinker is aware of the sensations as such.

Holmes and Wolff (1950) noted that, "a pattern of skeletal muscle hyperfunction characterized by a generalized and sustained increase in motor and electrical activity was a common accompaniment to the reaction of subjects exhibiting the backache syndrome to situations which threatened their security and engendered apprehension, conflict, anxiety and feelings of resentment, hostility, humiliation, frustration and guilt." The individuals involved may not again be aware of their own muscle tenseness. Gottschalk (1950) reported

that varying muscular reactions were noted electromyographically to the stimuli presented and yet most of the patients were unaware of muscular movement or changes in muscular tension in respect to these stimuli.

Acute muscle strain in the neck region may affect the neck muscles of the upper back or dorsal spine, causing pain and muscle tension (Kraus, 1949). Martin (1960) has pointed out the evidence for the relationship between electromyographic measures and muscle tension.

Massage, according to Kovacs (1944), is one of the most simple and effective forms of physical treatment of muscle "variety" does not "exert."

tension. The variety of movements in massage exerts various effects on the structures of the body and upon the general organism itself. General massage affects the circulation of the whole body by speeding up the flow of the blood in the skin, the subcutaneous tissue, and muscles. Muscles are among the chief objects of treatment by massage. Kovacs (1944) states that physiological experiments are on record

Delete "proving," sub. "indicating."

proving that massage applied to a resting muscle increases its power for work and retards fatigue. Massage stimulates the nutrition of muscle tissue and restores the tone and strength of muscles if they have weakened or are tense.

Final prepositional phrase is confusing.
No transition between paragraphs.
Why capital "P" and "R"?

As stated by Borkovec, Kaloupek, and Slama (1975), training in Progressive Relaxation involves "a) instructions to focus attention on pleasant, relatively monotonous

Missing page number

internal feelings, thus precluding cognitive intrusions, and b) systematic tension—release of gross muscle systems to reduce physiological arousal". Paul (1969) has indicated

Delete "has indicated through his studies," sub. "found." "produces" should be "produced."

through his studies that Progressive Relaxation produces greater reduction in physiological arousal than hypnotic and self—relaxation techniques.

Sub. "the present" for "this."
Delete "that of."

The conceptual hypothesis of this study is that massage will be more effective in reducing muscle tension than that of Progressive Relaxation. The independent variables are (a)

Why massage more effective?
How does this definition relate to the definition in the preceding paragraph?

Progressive Relaxation, which is a technique based primarily on systematically tensing and releasing various muscle groups in order to eliminate muscle contractions and experience a feeling of deep relaxation; and (b) massage,

Delete semicolon.
The independent variable is the relaxation technique which has two levels: progressive relaxation and massage.
Write in future tense.

which is the manipulation of tissues, as by rubbing, stroking, kneading, or tapping with the hand in order to reduce body tension. The dependent variable is the amount of tension measured from the area of the Trapezius muscle in the upper back and neck. This will be measured in microvolts by an electromyograph, placing the electrodes on the surface area of the skin over the Trapezius muscle. A reduction in

"Trapezius" should not be capitalized.
Delete "determined by," sub. "defined as."

muscle tension will be determined by a decrease in the amount of tension registered on the electromyograph as compared to that of baseline.

"than Progressive Relaxation" should follow "more effective."

The experimental hypothesis is that the technique of massage will be more effective in reducing the amount of muscle tension in the Trapezius muscle than Progressive Relaxation as measured by the electromyograph in comparison to baseline measurements of tension.

Why should this research be done?

METHOD

Capitalize M only.

Delete "to be used."

What kind of "patients"?

Why will the subjects participate? "connected with" is the wrong verb.

Chosen how? What "available population"? Delete "to be used." Delete "best."

Should be "Figure 1." Why this design? Future tense should always be used.

What is a "stable region"?

Should be "15 min."

What does "once stable," mean? Should be "Phase 1." Should be "Figure 1." What is S1? What are S2 and S3?

How are subjects assigned to the S1, S2, and S3 conditions? Should be "Phase 2" and "Phase 3." Where is "Here"?

The experimental and conceptual hypotheses refer to comparison of massage vs. progressive relaxation, but this design compares massage vs. massage *and* progressive relaxation. Should be "Phase 4" and "Phase 5."

Capitalize "model."

Subjects. The subjects to be used in this experiment will be three male patients suffering from muscle tension of the Trapezius muscle in the upper back and neck. Males will be used in order to eliminate any modesty problems connected with female subjects when disrobing in front of strangers. The subjects will be chosen from an available population at the University of the Pacific.

Design. The design to be used will be a Component Analysis Design. This design can best be labeled as A–BC–B–BC (see figure one). The A level is baseline, BC is a combination of two treatment levels, Progressive Relaxation and massage, B is one treatment alone, massage, and BC is again the two treatments together. Baseline, which is the recording of a behavior (i.e., muscle tension in the Trapezius muscle) prior to treatment, will be taken until a stable region of muscle tension has been established. Each subject will receive three fifteen–minute baseline sessions on successive days. Once stable, all subjects will begin phase one of the experiment (see figure one) in which S1 receives both treatments, Progressive Relaxation and massage, while S2 and S3 remain at baseline level. When S1 shows a decrease in muscle tension, phase two will begin. Here S2 begins both treatments, while S1 receives the massage treatment. Meanwhile S3 continues with baseline. Again, when a decrease in S2's muscle tension has occurred phase three will begin. Now S3 receives both treatments, S1 returns to both treatments, and S2 receives the massage treatment alone. When another decrease in muscle tension in S3 has been established, phase four begins. In this phase S2 receives both treatments, while S3 is given the massage treatment. Finally S3 receives phase five of the experiment, in which both treatments, Progressive Relaxation and massage, are given.

Apparatus. The equipment to be used will be a table or cot for massage, a comfortable chair for Progressive Relaxation, a Biofeedback Technology Inc. (BFT) model 410 electromyograph, a BFT model 215 timeperiod integrator, silver/silver chloride electrodes, a cassette tape containing Progressive Relaxation instructions, and graph paper.

How long are the cassette instructions?
On what basis are subjects to be chosen?
Delete "Here."

Should be "Figure 2."

Procedure₃ After all three subjects are chosen, baseline sessions will begin. Here silver/silver chloride electrodes will be placed unilaterally on the Trapezius muscle of each side of the back. (See figure two.) The skin will first be prepared by briskly rubbing the area on which the electrodes will be placed with an alcohol solution. When a stable baseline reading has been established, after approximately three fifteen minute sessions for each subject, phase one will begin. Here S1 receives both treatments, Progressive Relaxation by use of a cassette narrative and massage for

Should be "15-min."
Should be "Phase 1."
Will all 3 subjects be in the same room at the same time? Delete "Here." Should be "10 to 15 min." Use Future tense. How much of a decrease in μV is "a decrease"?
Should be "Phase 2."
Delete "where."

ten to fifteen minutes, while S2 and S3 remain at baseline. Phase two will begin when a decrease in S1's muscle tension

Should be "Phase 3."

Delete "Here."

has occurred, where S1 receives massage alone, S2 receives both treatments and S3 continues with baseline. When a decrease in S2's muscle tension has been established, phase three begins. Here S1 again receives both treatments, S2 receives massage alone and S3 receives both treatments. Again when a decrease in S3's muscle tension has been

After baseline, does this all take place in one day?
Should be "Phase 4."

Who gives the massage?

indicated phase four will begin. In this phase S2 receives both treatments and S3 receives massage alone. Finally, S3 receives both treatments, Progressive Relaxation and massage. This is phase five. Measurements from the electromyograph will be recorded at each session on a graph.

Should be "Phase 5."

Use future tense. Are measurements automatically recorded by the machine?
Delete "on a graph."
Delete "for." Can susceptibility to the relaxing effects of massage and progressive relaxation be measured and employed to match subjects?
What is a "basic level"?

Delete "for."

Controls₃ Secondary variance, such as the subjects' differing degrees of tenseness on the days of each treatment session, will be controlled for by only starting treatment after a stable baseline has been established. In this way it would seem probable that the amount of tenseness is at a

basic level. Another form of secondary variance to be controlled for will be the elimination of outside environmental distraction during the Progressive Relaxation treatment sessions. This will be accomplished by providing a quiet atmosphere for the subject.

Last two sentences can be combined into one.

Delete "for."

What does the 2nd observer observe? How is this a control for error variance?

Error variance will be controlled for by checking the reliability of the measurements through the use of a second observer present at each session.

Analysis of Results

The data will be collected at each session and recorded on a graph. When the treatments have been completed the graphs will be compared (i.e., the effects of Progressive

All data analysis will be by graphical comparison (interocular trauma test)? Parenthetical material should be a complete sentence and should replace the entire sentence.

Last sentence is unnecessary.

Relaxation and massage together or massage alone). From this observation a reliable approximation of the effects of massage as compared to Progressive Relaxation on the reduction of muscle tension in the Trapezius muscle will be concluded.

References

Capitalize only first letter of first word in this title.

Don't include month.

Borkovec, T., Kaloupeck, D. G., & Slama, K. The Facilitative Effect of Muscle Tension—Release in the Relaxation Treatment of Sleep Disturbance. Behavior Therapy, May 1975, 6, 302–309.

Period after title of book. Colon after New York.

Downing, G. The massage book, New York, Random House, 1972.

Gottschalk, L. A., Serota, H. M., & Shapiro, L. F. Psychological conflict and neuromuscular tension in life stress and bodily disease, Baltimore: Williams & Wilkins, 1950.

Ampersand between authors' names.

Holmes, T. H., and Wolff, H. G. Life situations, emotions and backache in life stress and bodily disease. Baltimore: Williams & Wilkins, 1950.

Reverse order of place of publication and publisher.

Kovacs, R. M. A manual of physical therapy, Lea & Febriger, Philadelphia: 1944.

Kraus, H. Principles and practices of therapeutic exercise. Springfield, Illinois: Charles C Thomas, 1949.

Abbreviate publisher's name to C. C Thomas.

Malmo, R. B. On emotions, needs and our archaic brain. New York: Holt, Rinehart and Winston, 1975.

Put editor's initials in front of surname. Do not include page numbers.

Martin, I. Somatic reactivity. In Eysenck, H. J. (Ed.), Handbook of abnormal psychology. London: Putnam, 1960, pp. 417–487.

Include volume number and page numbers of the article.

Paul, G. L. Physiological effects of relaxation training and hypnotic suggestions. Journal of Abnormal Psychology, 1969.

Delete comma after R. W.; underline volume number. Don't include Sperry as he is not cited in the proposal.

Sperry, R. W., Neurology and the mind—brain problem, American Scientist, 1952, 40, 291–312.

	BASE LINE	PHASE 1	PHASE 2	PHASE 3	PHASE 4	PHASE 5
S_1	A	BC	B	BC	—	—
S_2	A	A	BC	B	BC	—
S_3	A	A	A	BC	B	BC

A = Baseline
BC = Progressive relaxation and massage
B = Massage only

Figure 1. Component analysis design for the study. S1 is subject number 1, S2 is subject 2 and S3 = subject 3.

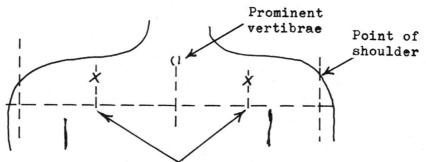

Figure 2. Diagram of subject's back showing approximate electrode placements on the skin over the trapezius muscles, at points labeled X.

SUMMARY

1. There are several potential sources of research topics. These include articles published in research journals, general references such as introductory textbooks, lectures, discussions with other students, and conventions of psychological associations.
2. There are a large number of psychological journals. Some of these are devoted to new developments, some cover a broad spectrum of research areas, and some are devoted to specific research areas.
3. Selecting a topic among alternative research possibilities includes deciding on the relative worth of the topics and then drafting a conceptual hypothesis and tentative research proposal for the most promising one.
4. Reviewing the published literature assists in formulating the conceptual hypothesis and tentative research proposal. *Psychological Abstracts* is the best tool for finding the relevant research literature quickly.
5. A tentative proposal should be evaluated in terms of time feasibility, equipment availability, subject availability, and cost in terms of subject and experimenter time and effort.
6. A pilot study is a brief, inexpensive, prerun of an experiment. A pilot study is used to estimate the potential value of a complete study and to examine the effectiveness of control procedures.
7. A research proposal is a formal, written statement of the plan for an experiment. A proposal includes a statement of the problem, the theoretical and research background, the conceptual and experimental hypotheses, a description of the subjects, design, procedures, and data analysis to be used, and the references.
8. The *Publication manual of the American Psychological Association* should be consulted for all questions on organization, form, and style of the research proposal.

SUGGESTED READINGS

Allen, E. M. Why are research grant applications disapproved? *Science,* 1960, *132,* 1532–1534.

American Psychological Association, Council of Editors. *Publication manual of the American Psychological Association* (2nd ed.). Washington, D.C.: Author, 1974.

Bell, J. E. *A guide to library research in psychology.* Dubuque, Iowa: W. C. Brown, 1971.

Turabian, K. L. *A manual for writers of term papers, theses, and dissertations* (3rd ed.). Chicago: University of Chicago Press, 1967.

13

Pragmatic and Ethical Issues

Rats or people, worms or monkeys—what kinds of subjects will you use in your experiment? The present chapter deals with some of the ''mechanical'' details of selecting, recruiting, and treating research subjects. It also deals with guidelines for ethical treatment of your subject.

Apart from the "nuts and bolts" of the research process—the control of variables, minimization of error, and research design—other practical factors must be considered: obtaining subjects and equipment, and dealing with subjects ethically. If like most researchers, especially college students, you do not have much money, there are constraints on your "research behavior." Other constraints are equally binding. For example, there are procedures you obviously cannot undertake with human beings that maybe you can with animals. Certain kinds of experimentation must proceed with caution. Consider the following example.

Until recently, college students were highly interested in "drug" experimentation as a research topic, primarily because they were not sure whether certain drugs that made them feel good were harmful. Marijuana was one drug that fascinated them, young and old alike. Undergraduate researchers wanted to perform research projects concerned with studying the effects of marijuana on everything from learning, memory, sex life, appetite, and visual perception to its effect on sleep onset and its interaction with hypnosis, wine, and beer. The students who proposed the research were, for the most part, sincere, bright, well-intentioned people who had a genuine interest in the effects of marijuana. The problem was, they were proposing to experiment with an illegal drug at a college or university that could not condone such research unless underwritten and suported by the federal government and controlled by qualified researchers. We are not saying that marijuana research should not be done, but that it should be done only with the appropriate approval of the college, university, or faculty supervisor, and especially with the written permission of the intended human subjects. Unless student researchers consider all possible aspects of their proposed research, they could find themselves in difficulty.

We know that human subjects may do almost anything under the guise of "research" (Milgram, 1963, 1964). As a result of this consideration and others, we present some guidelines for the choice of subjects, treatment of subjects, and the ethical considerations that need to be clarified before you take on a research project. Particular attention should be paid to the ethical issues related to the treatment of subjects.

The discussion here is fairly brief, since volumes of information are available. The student needing additional information should consult the selected readings at the end of this chapter.

SELECTION AND TREATMENT OF SUBJECTS

There are approximately a million and a quarter animal species remaining on earth. About ten species have been studied extensively by psychologists: flatworms, goldfish, pigeons, mice, rats, cats, dogs, rhesus monkeys, chimpanzees, and human beings. The number of studied species is appallingly large or small depending on your belief as to whether psychologists should understand human behavior or all behavior. Irrespective of that issue, however, the selection of subjects is important to the success of the experiment.

Animals

There are at least two reasons why researchers observe animal behavior. In most cases, the animal species presents a unique means of investigating a universal behavioral trait; it gives a *clue to understanding human behavior.* The other reason for studying animal behavior is that the animal or the behavior is *intrinsically interesting.* Although the choice of a species is often a matter of circumstance and not consciously considered by the researcher, some illustrative discussion may make the reader aware of the process.

Darwin's theory of evolution holds that the acquisition of behaviors and structures is necessary to the continued survival of the evolving species. Inherent in this view is the idea that the "more advanced" species share a common basis with the "less advanced." If we are interested in one of these early, common traits, it is sometimes advantageous to study it in a species where it is not overridden by later developments. For example, the foundation for the behavior-modification techniques now extensively applied to humans (see chapter 11) was established in Skinner's laboratory using rats and pigeons.

Drug companies invest substantial amounts of money in animal research before releasing a new compound for use by human beings. Similarly, psychological experiments on animals are giving us information on the potentially harmful and helpful effects of certain environments. Harlow's (1959, 1962, 1969) studies on early socialization in monkeys, Calhoun's (1962) studies on overcrowding in rat colonies, Held and Hein's (1963) investigation of the effects of early sensorimotor experience on cats, and the wide variety of studies indicating the superiority of animals raised in an enriched early environment (such as Krech, Rosenzweig, & Bennett, 1962) have far-reaching implications for the human condition.

In addition to providing a substitute for human beings in some research programs (particularly when the experiment involves conditions that cannot be ethically employed with humans, such as experimental brain surgery), animals occasionally provide a *unique combination of circumstances* for research. For example, the fruit fly combines a rapid breeding rate, an unusually small number of chromosomes, and chromosomes large enough to observe directly. All these factors make it easier to research the hereditary transmission of traits. Although human chromosomes are far more numerous, complex, and too small for direct observation, the laws of genetic transmission in the fruit fly are equally applicable in human genetics.

Other animal species offer unique traits that provide rich research opportunities. The nerve cells in the squid are giant compared with those found in a human being. Experiments on this relatively easily observed cell have yielded much information concerning the functioning of nervous systems. The normally neat, geometric pattern of a spider web is converted into a chaotic, almost random pattern when the spider eats a fly dosed with LSD. Whether the disruption of the normal web spinning is due to bizarre perceptual effects, as reported by humans, or represents a general disruption of the spider's system, the web spinning provides an easily observed indicator of deviation from normal. Hibernating animals provide interesting possibilities for a comparison between hibernation and normal sleep, and for studies of the effects of passage of time (in the active and passive state) on phenomena such as learning and memory.

It would be a mistake to attempt to justify all animal behavioral research in terms of its direct application to understanding human behavior. Many animal species have behavior capabilities that are interesting for their own sake. The echo-locating ability of bats in avoiding trees and catching moths is well documented. The similar ability of the dolphin not only is interesting, but has been put to practical use in training dolphins to locate objects under water.

There is a large group of researchers who observe and write about animal behavior simply "because it is there." Most of these animal books are a direct offshoot of the efforts of a naturalist who has chosen to do a careful study of that particular species. The fact that such books are profitable shows that the interest is shared by the public. Walt Disney Enterprises have also found animal behavior to be profitable, both in nature and in whimsy.

Sometimes the efforts of the naturalist are extrapolated (extended) to apply to human behavior even when that was not the original intent. The work of the European ethologists began as the careful observation of common species in their normal environments. From this work came such terms as "innate behavior patterns," "pecking orders" (and the corresponding "alpha animal"), and "territoriality." Now a number of books by such authors as Desmond Morris and Robert Ardrey argue that human beings are equally locked into certain innate behavior patterns, and that the explanation for much human behavior lies in the genetic heritage passed on by our Darwinian ancestors.

There are a number of practical reasons for using animals in a behavioral experiment instead of people. A major one is that it is possible to establish considerable *control over the heredity* of experimental laboratory animals. The experimenter can obtain "maze-bright" or "maze-dull" animals from commercial suppliers. Based on the work by Tryon (1940), special strains of laboratory rats have been bred through several generations specifically for their learning ability in a particular maze situation. The "maze-bright" animals are from stock all of which learned a standard maze task quickly. The "maze-dull" animals derive from slow-performing ancestors. Thus, the experimenter can specify the abilities of the rats, depending on the type of maze study to be run. For example, if it is a study of learning phenomena, the researcher may specify "maze-dull" so that the learning process can be extended for better observation. If, on the other hand, the researcher is interested in how a task is remembered, then the training time may be shortened by using "maze-bright" animals. [It is interesting to note that "maze-dull" and "maze-bright" animals do not differ on tasks other than mazes and do not differ in other kinds of mazes (Searle, 1949).]

Since animal species such as mice and rats have faster reproduction rates than humans and the individuals mature relatively rapidly, the effects of *heredity and maturation* are more conveniently studied in animals. Multiple births also provide opportunities to test simultaneously several individuals with common genetic characteristics or identical early environments up to the time of testing.

Animals provide another obvious and unique contribution to behavioral research. There is a class of experiments that cannot be *ethically* conducted using human subjects. The effects of certain drugs, destruction of certain regions of the brain, extreme environmental stresses, or years in a restricted environment cannot be determined using human subjects. One of the major reasons the rat is found so frequently in physiological laboratories is because of its fantastic degree of tolerance to surgical insult.

Probably more important to many behavioral researchers is the opportunity to exercise almost complete *control over environmental factors.* This control cannot be accomplished in most human studies. Experience between laboratory sessions can be manipulated according to the design of the experimenter. Animals can be raised from birth in a specified environment, either as part of a specific research effort, or as a means of standardizing the animals in a colony. Even dietary supplements or deficiencies are utilized as a part of animal research.

As we said earlier in this chapter, the history of experimental psychology has consisted mainly of the study of ten species. Of these, rats, pigeons, and human subjects (especially college students) have made the largest contribution to our knowledge of behavior. A great deal is known about the morphology and behavior of these animals. The *background of available knowledge* promotes the use of these species in preference to other animals. Most frequently, these animals are used in graduate and undergraduate curricula. Consequently, each new scientist builds up a repertoire of research skills and knowledge in terms of one or two species. This means that in selecting any new species we should compare carefully the contribution of the new species with the behavioral information base we already have on often-used species.

Laboratory animals all share one important virtue: they are available on demand. People are not so dependable. A relatively large colony of small animals such as rats, mice, chickens, or pigeons may be maintained inexpensively. In the case of a large, or ongoing, research effort, obtaining additional subjects for comparison is often easier with animals.

Choosing among animal species Selecting appropriate research animals requires knowledge of the morphology and behavior of the different species available. Certain animal species are particularly suited to a particular research problem. The fact that planaria can be cut in half and that each half will regenerate a whole animal allows interesting possibilities in determining the physiological location of learning and memory. The additional fact that planaria will "cannibalize" chopped-up bits of other planaria provides the opportunity to study chemical transfer of learning. If "cannibals" who have eaten other planaria trained on a task perform better on the same task, there is a possibility that the learned task is transferred somehow in the consumed tissue (McConnell, 1966).

Do not think only of stereotyped characteristics of species. Bee colonies are often considered good subjects for the study of social behavior. However, the ability of the common honeybee to orient itself using the plane of polarization of sunlight (Frisch, 1950) and the ability of the Italian honeybee to orient itself along the lines of force in an AC magnetic field (Caldwell & Russo, 1968) make these animals useful for the study of other types of behavior.

Knowledge of species characteristics also will prevent foolish research mistakes. One of the reasons little behavioral research has been conducted on snakes is the fact that snakes can go for a month without food and will exist quite well on only one meal a week. It is difficult to use food deprivation as a motivator for snakes. Similarly, desert mammals such as the kangaroo rat, and to a lesser extent the gerbil and hamster, are efficient in their use of water; therefore, water-deprivation schedules are not effective with them. However, care must be taken in generalizing about desert animals, for desert wood rats store succulent plants as a water reservoir and will die if placed on a strict 24-hour water-deprivation schedule.

In some ways, the common laboratory rat is a singularly unsuitable animal for the behavioral laboratory. Although a majority of the experiments require that the animal make some response to visual cues, rats are not primarily visual animals. In addition, many students use colored stimuli in their research without realizing that the rat is color-blind. One disadvantage of this phenomenon is that many discrimination studies require that the rat determine whether a light is on or off. If the apparatus happens to be equipped with a red discrimination light, the determination becomes very difficult for the rat, although it is easy for the experimenter.

Another major determinant of species choice is the *cost* of the subjects, both the initial cost and the cost of maintaining them. Chimpanzees are interesting research animals, but the initial cost is more than $2500 per animal, and maintenance costs are also high. A researcher may find day-old cockerel chicks at 10¢ apiece more appropriate to a limited budget.

Obtaining animal subjects   Commercial animal suppliers are the usual sources for research animals. These suppliers advertise in journals such as *Science,* and the managers of research colonies can provide the names of their suppliers. Poultry can be obtained at chicken hatcheries or through large mail-order houses. If a college is located near a farming area, poultry also may be bought directly from farms. If the research project is acceptable, it may be possible to work with animals at a zoo. Small numbers of subjects can be purchased from pet stores. However, a researcher has no control over the past history of animals obtained from pounds or pet stores. Naturalistic observations of wild animals are possible, but experimental studies of wild animals are usually beyond the economic and time resources of the beginning student. One can try trapping wild animals. However, we do not recommend that untrained students attempt trapping. Our main objection is that wild animals potentially carry various infectious diseases that can be fatal to human beings (for example, rabies, bubonic plague, tularemia, and Rocky Mountain spotted fever). A second objection is that the student may unwittingly damage the ecological balance of an area.

The biology, pharmacology, zoology, physiology, or psychology departments at a college or university may maintain animal colonies. A student may be able to obtain a small number of research animals from these colonies. First check with the instructor of the introductory research course to find out the appropriate channels for obtaining animals for student research.

Treating animal subjects   Suppose that you have decided that you want to do a research project involving food deprivation with rats. Further suppose that you have designed the study, the design has been approved by your instructor, and you have been given the requested number of rats of the appropriate age.

Your initial problem is providing an adequate living environment for the animals. You could take all 24 rats home, but your roommate may not be happy with that arrangement. Besides, state laws may not allow you to keep them in the dormitory or your roommate may be allergic to animal hair. So you choose the obvious alternative of keeping them in cages in the psychology department's rat colony room. If your department is running a legal and ethical operation, the temperature and humidity of the colony room will be closely monitored and controlled. The colony manager should provide you with manuals and tips on the care of animals as well as the standard operating procedures of the colony. Fortunately, people and laboratory rats have about the same temperature and humidity preferences and needs.

If your department has a tight budget, there may not be enough funds to provide a paid animal caretaker. You and the rest of the student researchers may be obliged to take care of the animals. If you have a small, tightly knit group of psychology majors, you might rotate the responsibility so that each one of you has to clean, feed, and water all the animals only once or twice a month. Otherwise you must care for your animals each day. This means that each day you must remove the accumulated excreta, make sure that the water bottles are full and functioning properly, and provide an appropriate amount of rat food. Fortunately, animal research is such big business in the United States that several companies supply balanced diets for the commonly used animals.

An additional element of the daily rat detail is checking each animal to be sure that it is healthy. If any animal looks sick, you should notify the person in charge of the colony room. The normal procedure in most colonies is to destroy diseased animals so that other animals do not become ill.

DEPRIVATION   In order to motivate your animals to learn a task that will provide your dependent-variable scores, you decide to put the animals on a food-deprivation schedule. Using one cage for each animal controls for crowding by holding it constant. With one animal to a cage it is fairly easy to control the food-deprivation variable also. You might make the erroneous assumption that depriving the animals of food for only one day would be sufficient to motivate them to work for food. However, while such a procedure is fairly effective with people, it is not with rats.

There are three ways you could manipulate food deprivation as a motivator: (1) control the daily hours of food deprivation, (2) manipulate the amount of food provided per day, and (3) control the body weight of the animals. The most popular method is to adapt the animal for 10 to 14 days to a deprivation schedule such as 23 hr a day of deprivation with an ample supply of dry food and water for 1 hr. When you begin to test the animals in your maze, test them just before the normal daily feeding time, when they are alert and active. Such a schedule works well for rats and pigeons and is not physically detrimental to the animals.

TAMING   In your first encounter with laboratory rats, you probably noticed immediately that they have long, sharp teeth. If the animals have never been used in a research study and have not been handled at all except when they were transferred from rearing cages to their individual cages, they probably noticed immediately how large you are. If you do not do something about the initial mutual fears, you and the rats are going to have a most difficult time getting your research project completed. In the typical case, the past history of your animals is a dull, sterile existence in which the most interesting visual environment was a blank wall seen through the bars at the front of the cage. Moving the rats' cages about will make them nervous, and nervous rats can be a problem. Experience (often sad experience) has shown that it is very important to deal with the initial fear reaction of the animals. If they are highly stressed when placed in a maze, they are likely to bite the experimenter. There are several possible solutions to this problem: (1) don't run rats in an experiment; (2) use the home cage as the testing equipment; (3) build a system so that the test maze and the home cage can be hooked together without moving the cage; or (4) adapt the animal to the experimenter and to the novel equipment and procedures involved. The purpose is to produce a comfortable, alert animal that is behaving normally.

Suppose you choose the fourth option, adaptation. The principle of adaptation procedures is to eliminate fears and to minimize the general level of stress of each individual by accustoming it to specific novel events, persons, and equipment. When the animals have been adapted to their home cages by living there for a couple of weeks, you proceed to taming the animals by handling them. *Handling* is a standard part of experimental research with laboratory animals (except adult rhesus monkeys and animals with lesions in certain parts of their brains). Wild-trapped rodents must be handled with gloves, preferably padded, but your hooded or albino rats should be handled without gloves, mainly because gloves make it difficult for you to be sure you are not holding the animals too tightly. The standard procedure is to place an animal in a large enclosed space at a comfortable height. On the first day of handling the animal is coaxed out of the cage. Then for 3 to 6 min. per animal you let them explore the enclosure with you standing near emitting gentle sounds or phrases. Continue this procedure for at least 5 days, gradually increasing the amount of hand contact. Begin with your hand near the animal, then progress to touching and stroking the animal's back, to gently picking it up, and to playing with it. At the end of the handling procedure, a well-tamed rat will tolerate being turned over in your hand so that it is lying on its back, although rats dislike being upside-down. Incidentally, if you are bitten by a laboratory-bred and raised animal, get a tetanus shot immediately. Other treatment usually is not required, although you should check with your instructor or the colony manager, because some local health laws require *all* animal bites to be reported. If bitten by a wild-trapped animal, try to keep the animal alive and isolated, immediately notify the Public Health Service, and see a physician. Each author of this textbook has been bitten by laboratory rats so many times that we have lost count.

However, the experience was edifying because it always meant we were being sloppy and in need of a reminder. Once you have gotten your animals well tamed, you should be able to reach into their cages, remove them, carry them to the experimental maze, remove them from the maze, and return them to the cages without any danger of being bitten and any fear on your or the animal's part.

The next step is to adapt the animals to your maze before testing begins. The standard procedure is to allow the animals several periods in which they can explore all parts of the maze completely. Similarly, animals are adapted to Skinner boxes and "magazine-trained" before testing. Magazine training consists of adapting each animal to the noise of the food-delivery mechanism, called the magazine, as well as letting them discover where the food is delivered. If you are using food pellets of standardized size and weight as rewards, you also need to let the animals discover before training begins that those strange little pellets are food objects. Next we will consider working with human beings.

Human Beings

The case for using human subjects in psychological research can be stated succinctly. If you are interested in explaining human behavior, then use human research subjects whenever possible. Obviously, there are a large number of behavioral phenomena that are uniquely human. Human subjects are best suited for research into language and abstract reasoning, although animal subjects have been used successfully in some instances. A case can be made for observing the "lower" behavioral functions in human subjects as well. If we follow the phylogenetic argument, the behaviors humans shared with other animals have been superseded by newer functions early in the evolutionary process. To evaluate the role of these new functions in human behavior, perhaps the human being is the only appropriate research subject.

Obtaining human subjects A researcher defines the subset of those people in the immediate vicinity that will constitute the sampling population. The defined subset will consist of people who can be grouped according to organismic variables such as sex, ethnic origin, vocation, or church affiliation. A defined sampling population will not take account of all potential grouping variables. For example, the population of all freshman students at a particular college includes the variables of sex, socioeconomic level, and ethnic group. When sampling from that population, the experimenter must make certain that the grouping variables do not influence the sampling procedure.

The researcher must decide whether to collect subjects individually or in intact groups. In order to obtain a representative sample from the population the researcher should choose names randomly from the entire list of freshmen and speak to each person individually. If, on the other hand, the researcher can assume reasonably that one or two freshman courses contain representative samples of the entire freshman class, then the researcher can save time by soliciting students from those intact groups.

Several techniques can be used when soliciting subjects individually or in intact groups. No matter what the situation, a researcher must sell a potential subject on the idea of taking part in a study. Usually, the subjects are asked to provide their time and effort for little payoff.

Make participation sound interesting. In most studies, the only payoff the subject receives is the chance to do something unusual. Appeals in terms of "doing your bit for science" have been used too frequently and do not lead people to participate in a study. Instead, emphasize any part of the procedure that would be likely to be interesting to the population sampled.

As soon as the subjects are reached, a researcher explains the general purpose of the study and why the particular subjects were selected. Do not lie to a potential subject. If the study requires misleading instructions or procedures, then do not detail these procedures.

No matter what a study is about, the subjects' anonymity outside the study must be guaranteed. The subjects must be assured that no one other than the experimenter will know how they performed. In a group research study, a researcher is not concerned with "finding out" anything about a particular individual. In some way, a researcher must convey the idea of trying to make a general conclusion about a population of people, not the individual subjects. If subjects generate interesting behavior in the experimental situation, personal identifying traits should be deleted when discussing the behavior.

When subjects must report at some time other than the initial contact period, sign-up sheets are used. A sheet lists the researcher's name, clearly directs the subject to the exact research location, indicates the time and date of participation, and offers a choice of meeting times. If behavioral observation will take place several days after the initial contact, a sign-up sheet should require the subjects to list their telephone numbers and mailing addresses. Once a person has indicated willingness to partici-pate, a researcher mails a postcard one or two days prior to the designated participa-tion date. A reminder postcard contains the name of the researcher, the location of the meeting place, and the name of the study. Among college students, about two-thirds of those people who sign up for a study are likely to appear at the proper time. You can try phoning a delinquent subject and rescheduling the meeting date. It is most important that the researcher show up at the meeting place on time. Prospective subjects get very angry when stood up. If you cannot make a scheduled meeting, call the subjects beforehand and reschedule it.

A researcher may offer to let the subjects know the results of the research. In the case of intact groups, a researcher can indicate the time of a meeting with the group. In the case of individually contacted people, a researcher can promise to mail them a summary of the research. The feedback is a simple description of the study and the general results in lay language. Unless a very small number of subjects participates, individual feedback in the form of conferences with each subject should not be promised. When the data analysis is likely to take a very long time, feedback should not be promised either.

When individual subjects are selected randomly, every effort should be made to ensure that they participate in the study. Failure to obtain participation restricts the effects of the randomization procedure, biasing the sample. Sometimes, no matter what a researcher does, a particular subject cannot be persuaded to participate. The number of such failures is recorded and included in the final report of a study. Also record the number of subjects that signed up for a study but could not participate.

Similarly, when questionnaires are mailed to people, on the average, about one-third of the questionnaires will be returned. The number mailed out and the number returned are included in a final report.

CHILDREN   You have several ways to contact children in intact groups. It is unlikely that you know enough parents to allow you to contact a sufficiently large number of children individually. Intact groups of children occur in public schools, Sunday schools, and in after-school social settings such as Cub Scout packs. Each of these groups has at least one person in a position of leadership or authority. Normally the best method is to start at the topmost authority figure and work your way down to the potential subject pool. This progression can be sidestepped safely if you have a contact person within the organization who can clear the way for you; otherwise you must present your appeal for subjects to each person in the chain of command. Your appeal should be geared to each authority position and should change as you move down the line. In general, authority figures are likely to be sympathetic if the research appears to be interesting and potentially useful to the organization. On the other hand, a research proposal that includes the use of shock or stress with nursery school children as subjects is unlikely to make it past the nursery school director's office. The undergraduate students of one of the authors have conducted more than 100 studies in public schools and nursery schools. The author has received letters from school principals thanking him for sending the students to the schools and asking that more be sent. In all these cases, the research could not be considered potentially dangerous to the subjects, and it provided a welcome, short break in routine for the children, and occasionally, useful information for the teachers.

Another problem you may face, particularly with children, are the state laws pertaining to research with human subjects. For example, in California, written permission from the parents or legal guardians of children in Grades 5 through 12 must be obtained prior to administering any questionnaire concerning the personal beliefs or practices of a child or the child's parents in the areas of sex, family life, morality, or religion.

If you have gotten the approval of the director of the organization, you may subtly enlist that person's aid in approaching subordinate authorities and the children. For example, you might ask what aspect of the proposed research project is most likely to interest the potential subjects or their immediate supervisors or teachers. Do not rely on teachers to select the subjects for an experiment. Teachers will not select children at random; rather, they select children to impress the experimenter or to find out more about particular children. Castaneda and Fahel (1961) and Mullen (1959) discuss procedures for conducting research in public schools.

ADULTS   If working with children in intact groups sounds formidable, or if you do not feel comfortable with children, you must use adults or college students. In this case, you have a real choice of contacting subjects individually or in intact groups. The advantage of contacting subjects individually is that you do not have to contend with the group membership as a potential source of secondary variance. If the defined sampling population includes strangers whom you normally would not meet, then you should provide advance notice to the potential subjects. A typed letter of introduction should include your academic affiliation, your student status, a brief description of the research project, and an explanation of how the individual was selected, and should notify the potential subject that you will phone to schedule an interview. In the interview, you should follow the techniques described on page 222. In addition, you must convince a potential subject that you are competent and serious, and that you are not trying to sell a product. Telling a subject that he or she will be helping you sometimes works, and some subjects respond to implied prestige. If a subject wants to be paid for the time spent, and if you have the funds available, then a promise of payment sometimes works. However, the promise of money works better with indigent college students than with other groups.

Opportunity to escape from participation must be provided for those people who are unwilling to participate. To decrease the incidence of escape, social pressure may be used. Social pressure may consist of calling for a show of hands of those who are willing to participate. Stooges or shills may be used to increase social pressure, but such procedures raise ethical questions.

Because of their availability, groups of college students are often used. When dealing with college students, you should schedule more subjects than you need. When any sizable group is scheduled, you can count on some of the subjects not showing up. Captive audiences such as introductory psychology classes provide a large supply of subjects, but it may seem unethical if the students are *required* to participate in a research project. As a general rule, college instructors do not like to have strangers take class time for research. However, they usually can be persuaded to let you ask for volunteers. A psychology professor may even let you use an entire class period for research, provided that the research has educational value and is interesting to the class.

Treating human subjects   You should run through the entire procedure as if you were a subject in order to get a first-hand understanding of how subjects will react to it. Then you can use that understanding in maintaining rapport with each subject. As with animal subjects, a researcher, within the limits of the research design, should strive to make human subjects as comfortable and calm as possible. We shall describe the adaptation of subjects to the experimenter and their treatment throughout one experiment.

Research Example

Since she was already working with deaf children, one student (Phelan, 1972) decided to conduct a research project on the topic of tactual perception in deaf and hearing children. It is commonly believed that a child sensorily deprived in one area (deaf or blind, for example) will exhibit greater acuity in the remaining senses. The increased acuity might be due to increased organ sensitivity, greater attention paid to the other senses, or more efficient use of the information derived from the other senses.

From her previous work with children, Phelan knew that adaptation to an experimenter may be even more important with children than with other types of subjects. Unless children are so adapted, an experimenter will have difficulty in getting them to "play the game" voluntarily. When dealing with nursery school and kindergarten children, a researcher should spend several days at a school letting the children get used to seeing him or her. During the adaptation period, a researcher should try to talk with each child for at least a few minutes. Since Phelan had spent an entire semester with the deaf class, these children were well adapted to her. She wanted to compare the tactual-discrimination ability of the deaf children with that of a control group of normal-hearing children. Most of the children at the school were of normal hearing, and since much of her time was spent on the playground, Phelan believed that most of the normal-hearing children in the 9–12 age range were also familiar with her. For her study, she chose ten deaf children and ten of the available normal-hearing children to be the subjects. She knew that the study, necessarily, was a static-group comparison. However, the fundamental question she was asking dictated a static-group comparison.

Next, she had to design the experimental situation. As a general rule, the research situation should be as free from distracting stimuli as possible. As Stevenson and Wright (1966, p. 581) point out: "The child's attention is often diverted from the experimental task by . . . exploration of the apparatus and the experimental room, and it appears that almost any stimulus change may serve further to reinforce such activity." Children should be allowed to explore the experimental setting prior to the onset of the experiment. Such adaptation increases the likelihood of their attending to the important changes involved in the research. Phelan decided to test the children individually in an empty room at the school. This procedure was convenient for both her and the children.

Six styrofoam cups were covered completely with one of three different textures of sandpaper: fine, medium, or coarse. There were two cups of each type. The deaf and hearing children were presented with three cups, two of the same texture and one different. She hypothesized that the deaf children would be able to pick out the different one with more accuracy than the hearing children.

Each subject was tested separately. Phelan explained to each subject before testing (verbally to the hearing and in signs to the deaf) that there were six cups, and that they had three different textures. She knew that for both groups, the comprehension of verbal and signed instructions would be a critical problem. As Bijou and Baer (1960, p. 166) indicate: "If successful, this [verbal instruction] is undoubtedly an efficient technique. Too often however, the experimenter may have promoted a misunderstanding in the child by only the use of verbal instruction." Particular care was taken to use elementary terms. Asking each child whether he or she understands instructions can be misleading. Young children usually will nod their heads and say "yes" whether or not they comprehend what you are saying. In general, children should be pretested to see whether they understand the instructions. Phelan checked for understanding by having each subject touch each cup and indicate which were coarse, medium, and fine. She then took two fine cups and one coarse, and pointed out that one was different from the others while letting each child touch the three cups once again. Because of the hearing difference between the groups, and because of her knowledge from working with children, Phelan knew that she had to fit the instructions and pretraining procedures to each individual subject.

Finding reinforcers for behavior presented another problem. Candy as a reward for children generally leads to more problems than it is worth. Bijou and Sturges (1959) present a list of token rewards that have been shown to be reinforcing for children. If possible, the reward value of a token should be determined by pilot studies. Infants as well as older children respond positively to mild surprises or novelty.

For example, Bower (1966) successfully used "peek-a-boo" with infants. Social reinforcers such as talking with the experimenter also can be used to motivate performance. The use of the phrase "Let's go play a game" is based on the idea that game-playing is reinforcing to children. Since the teacher of the deaf class had been using candy as rewards with the children, Phelan decided to use candy in her study as a reward for a correct discrimination.

Candy was placed under the *different* cup while the subject watched. The subject was told that he or she would be blindfolded and that the cups would be mixed up. By touching, the child was to find the cup that was different and pick it up. If the child found the right one, the child would get the candy.

The test was repeated three times with each subject, using different groups of cups each time. The groups of cups were presented in the following order: fine vs. coarse, fine vs. medium, and medium vs. coarse. The easiest discrimination problem was presented first in order to avoid discouraging the subjects.

Each child could make three correct responses (3 yes), two correct responses (2 yes, 1 no), one correct response (1 yes, 2 no) or no correct response (3 no). The hearing group's correct responses were 1, 4, 4, and 1, respectively. The distribution of frequencies of correct responses by the hearing group was as close to chance as possible with 10 children. The deaf children's frequencies were 6, 1, 2, and 1. These observed frequencies were compared to the hearing group's frequencies using the two-group χ^2 test (chapter 18). The deaf group performed better than chance, and the difference between the hearing and deaf group's behaviors is not likely to be due to chance. Phelan noticed that during the instruction period, the deaf subjects paid closer attention and were more anxious to enter into the "game" physically; they always took full advantage of the opportunity to feel the cups, while often the hearing children were reluctant to do so.

As a rule, the deaf children spent more time touching the cups and did not make decisions as hastily as did some of the hearing children. Two of the deaf children and one of the hearing children touched each cup briefly and then immediately responded correctly.

Several factors might have contributed to these results. One problem with the procedure was that, because their instructions were received visually rather than aurally, the deaf children had to look at the experimenter during instructions. In almost every case, Phelan had the deaf subjects' full attention. It was not possible to determine whether the hearing subjects attended to the instructions to the same extent.

Phelan concluded from the fact that the deaf students were consistently superior to the hearing students in their responses that they were able to distinguish minor tactual differences more efficiently. However, it is impossible to determine whether this greater ability on the part of the deaf subjects was due to a more acute development of tactual perception or to a greater ability to make use of the tactual information.

If the difference is due to an ability of the deaf children to make better use of the available information, we can ask why they have this ability. It could be due to the fact that in their school projects (and maybe at home), these children are more visually and tactually oriented. For instance, in the tested subjects' classroom the teacher always makes a point of having the students feel the texture of objects introduced in the classroom. When they grow plants, they feel the seeds, dirt, and leaves, which might not be done in a class of hearing students.

Previous experience with games also might have influenced the results of the present study. The deaf group may have had more experience with tactual discrimination games. On the other hand, the hearing group may have had more experience with such games but may have treated them like "guessing games" instead of concentrating. If they had had much previous experience, they might have taken the attitude that this was "just another game," which would account for the fact that they did not spend as much time feeling the cups before making their choices. (Of course, if they could not detect any difference in textures, that also would account for the fact that they did not take the time the deaf subjects did.)

Amount of previous contact with the experimenter could have affected the performance of the subjects. She had worked with the deaf subjects, but had had only casual contact with the hearing subjects. Nevertheless, it appears that the deaf children were more accurate at detecting tactual differences than normal hearing children. Next we will turn to a discussion important to all research, ethical considerations.

ETHICAL ISSUES

Popular magazines frequently publish articles about scientific research. Occasionally one of these articles is an exposé. Of particular concern has been the issue of "invasion of privacy" by psychologists (APA, 1965). Another public issue has been the misuse and ill-treatment of animal subjects. A growing debate deals with the right of scientists to use animals as research subjects in any study involving the physiological alteration of the subjects (for example, Wade, 1976).

Any set of ethical standards in research somehow sounds like a restrictive code designed to impede the progress of science. However, such standards often are based on sound, logical research practices. For example, minimum standards in housing experimental animals not only are humane but also assure the experimenter of observing the behavior of healthy animals. For a more complete statement, see *Ethical Standards for Psychologists* (APA, 1973).

General Research Ethics

Progress in science is enhanced by making data public. A major saving in time and effort is accomplished by utilizing data from other laboratories. A basic assumption of both preceding statements is that the data are carefully and accurately recorded. If the original observations were haphazard or inaccurate, the entire structure based on them may collapse. Before offering data to the scientific community, the researcher should be absolutely certain that they are accurate.

In addition to collecting the data conscientiously, a researcher must be absolutely honest in describing the observation procedures. Accidents and unexpected contingencies often occur in the middle of an experiment. Some of these accidents may make an experimenter appear foolish. If, however, the accidents had any possible effect on the scores obtained in the research, they should be reported faithfully.

Most research projects are the result of dynamic exchanges of ideas between colleagues. Seldom is the research project entirely a one-person project. If any of the features of a research project are the result of suggestions, ideas, or the work of other individuals, they should be given credit. Major help in a study strongly suggests coauthorship. Minor help and suggestions of importance may deserve a footnote.

Ethics in Animal Research

Most states have laws regulating the use of animals in scientific research. These laws, primarily intended for medical research facilities, include standards for administering anesthesia, surgical procedures, and postoperative recovery. Because of the wording of most of these laws, they also apply to animal colonies used in behavioral research.

Legal requirements should not be the sole basis for taking good care of an animal colony. On purely pragmatic grounds, the colony is maintained to supply animals for research projects. Animals that are sick or in pain do not make good subjects in behavioral research. Fearful animals are much more likely to bite the researcher as well as behave abnormally in the research situation. Animals stressed by overcrowding or improper diet are more subject to disease and abnormal behavior. A colony of animals kept in prime condition is necessary to a research program.

For most animal researchers, neither law nor practicality is the primary reason for good care. Most individuals are interested in the welfare of their animals because they like them. It is the rare researcher who deliberately mistreats animals, although unfortunate incidents too often occur because of inattention or lack of foresight. The following paragraphs suggest some of the problems that take the fun out of conducting animal research and result in the charge of cruelty to animals (APA, 1971).

Any condition that contributes to the untimely death or unnecessary discomfort of an animal can be considered cruelty. Filthy cages and unclean colony quarters are an invitation to infection and disease (for the researchers as well as the animals). Cages that are too small may seriously impair the physical condition of the animals. Fights in overcrowded cages can result in death or injury. With some wild species, two individuals in the same cage will automatically fight to the death. Leaving an inadequate food or water supply or monitoring them infrequently can result in starved animals. New cages and new animals must be monitored carefully during the initial period, as an animal sometimes cannot reach food that appears to be abundant. (One author discovered that a squirrel's nose is shorter than that of a rat; the squirrel could not eat out of the food hopper in a rat cage.) A more common example is a clogged delivery tube on a water bottle, or the attachment of the bottle to the cage at an angle at which the water cannot flow through the tube.

A new set of problems may be introduced by the requirements of an experiment. Food deprivation, the most common method of manipulating motivation in an experiment, provides a case in point. The deprivation schedule should not be so extreme as to endanger the survival of the animal. If the schedule requires a daily feeding period, care must be taken to see that the period is not cut short and that sufficient food is available during the period. The feeding period for food-deprived animals may be ineffective if water is not also available, if several animals are expected to eat simultaneously from a single feeder, or if a different kind of food from the regular laboratory diet is used. As mentioned earlier, rats can conveniently tolerate a 24-hour deprivation of food, and even accidentally skipping one day will not be fatal. Other animal species are not always so hardy. For most animal species, water deprivation is more dangerous than an equal period of food deprivation. Water deprivation almost invariably includes food deprivation, since the animal cannot swallow the usual amount of food without water.

The other major motivational variable in animal research is the use of punishment such as electric shock. Obviously the shock must be uncomfortable in order to be effective, but precautions should be taken to see that the shock level is never too high. Extreme shocks caused by someone changing the controls between experimental sessions are preventable. Extremely painful shock may disrupt the animal's behavior completely without allowing it to learn the desired response. In addition to the cruelty, animals subjected to extreme shock levels are nasty to handle!

Occasionally an experimenter wishes to impose an extremely stressful condition on an animal deliberately. For instance, there are some studies that use survival rate as the measure of the dependent variable. Such research should be conducted only if important data are unavailable by other approaches. The decision concerning the justifiability of such research must be made in terms of the profits to be gained and the costs to be incurred. If you choose to run an experiment involving extreme stress for animals, you may become the example of why behavioral research should be sharply curtailed. Be prepared to justify your research on both scientific and humanitarian grounds.

When obtaining animals, a researcher should consider how to dispose of them at the end of the experiment. Termination is an unpleasant task, particularly to novice researchers, who frequently become attached to particular subjects. Naturalistic observers do not have such problems, because they just leave the subjects after completing the research.

Ethics in Human Research

If behavioral scientists were only interested in commonplace, everyday behavior, then research would be a relatively simple process. The behavioral researcher, however, is often interested in seeing what behavior occurs in unusual situations, such as emergencies, drug-induced states, fatigue, or other stressful situations. Since we know that behavior under stress due to natual occurrences such as theater fires, earthquakes, floods, or robbery is different from the usual, nonstress-related behavior, the ability to create stressful situations in the laboratory could provide valuable information. But is it fair to the subjects, however short the duration of the stress?

The rights of human subjects in experimentation have received much attention recently. One of the outstanding examples of violation of the rights of subjects ostensibly in the cause of science is the infamous Tuskegee study of the 1930s, in which black males known to be infected with syphilis were specifically not treated for the disease in order to ascertain the full effects of the disease. This study, along with some of the "medical experiments" conducted in Nazi concentration camps, may have provided useful information; however, the cost in terms of human suffering was far greater than the gain.

As an example of the increased concern with this problem, the Surgeon General of the United States issued a directive (Policy and Procedure Order 129, July 1, 1966) to the Public Health Service, Division of Research Grants, on the subject: "Investigations involving human subjects, including clinical research: requirements for review to insure the rights and welfare of the individuals." Under this directive, the federal government will not knowingly provide financial support for research that infringes on the rights and welfare of human subjects, occasional scandals notwithstanding.

The American Psychological Association has published a monograph (1973) on the topic of ethical considerations in the conduct of research on human subjects. The monograph contains an extensive discussion of the issues. The following list of ten ethical principles is quoted from the first two pages of the monograph. The authors recognize that not all ethical problems associated with psychological research or human beings can be solved by resort to absolute principles of right and wrong. It is understood that an ethical obligation of the psychological researcher is to conduct the best research possible. This obligation means that ethical conflict is sometimes unavoidable. Given such a conflict, the question to be answered is whether the negative effects on the participants are justified by the importance of the research. In general, priority must be given to the individual subject's welfare. Whatever the requirements of participation as a subject are, they should be requirements that the research psychologists would find acceptable if they, members of their immediate families, or other loved ones were to participate in the study. To help resolve ethical conflicts, the 1973 APA monograph provides a lengthy discussion of each of the ten principles, including reviews of incidents that exemplify problems and discussions relating each principle to specific issues, research settings, and populations of research participants.

The decision to undertake research should rest upon a considered judgment by the individual psychologist about how best to contribute to psychological science and to human welfare. The responsible psychologist weighs alternative directions in which personal energies and resources might be invested. Having made the decision to conduct research, psychologists must carry out their investigations with respect for the people who participate and with concern for their dignity and welfare. The Principles that follow make explicit the investigator's ethical responsibilities toward participants over the course of research, from the initial decision to pursue a study to the steps necessary to protect the confidentiality of research data. These Principles should be interpreted in terms of the context provided in the complete document offered as a supplement to these Principles.

1. In planning a study the investigator has the personal responsibility to make a careful evaluation of its ethical acceptability, taking into account these Principles for research with human beings. To the extent that this appraisal, weighing scientific and humane values, suggests a deviation from any Principle, the investigator incurs an increasingly serious obligation to seek ethical advice and to observe more stringent safeguards to protect the rights of the human research participant.

2. Responsibility for the establishment and maintenance of acceptable ethical practice in research always remains with the individual investigator. The investigator is also

responsible for the ethical treatment of research participants by collaborators, assistants, students, and employees, all of whom, however, incur parallel obligations.

3. Ethical practice requires the investigator to inform the participant of all features of the research that reasonably might be expected to influence willingness to participate and to explain all other aspects of the research about which the participant inquires. Failure to make full disclosure gives added emphasis to the investigator's responsibility to protect the welfare and dignity of the research participant.

4. Openness and honesty are essential characteristics of the relationship between investigator and research participant. When the methodological requirements of a study necessitate concealment or deception, the investigator is required to ensure the participant's understanding of the reasons for this action and to restore the quality of the relationship with the investigator.

Advocates of the use of deception justify it by pointing out that the subjects are informed of the real intent of the experiment before leaving the experimental situation. Thus, the effects of the misinformation are established for a limited time in a laboratory setting, and the situation is corrected as soon as possible. The effect on the subjects, however, is to make them very wary of experimental psychologists in subsequent interactions. Although subterfuge yields interesting research data, it should be used sparingly because of its negative "public image."

5. Ethical research practice requires the investigator to respect the individual's freedom to decline to participate in research or to discontinue participation at any time. The obligation to protect this freedom requires special vigilance when the investigator is in a position of power over the participant. The decision to limit this freedom increases the investigator's responsibility to protect the participant's dignity and welfare.

The use of personality tests in behavioral research involves another aspect of subjects' rights. It may be argued that the measurement of personality traits constitutes an invasion of a person's privacy (APA, 1965). In this case, subjects must be given the opportunity to refuse to serve in an experiment, or they must give permission for an experimenter to use their scores. The usual interpretation is that, if a subject voluntarily participated in an experiment, he or she implicitly gave permission for the data to be used anonymously.

Exploitation of individuals or groups of individuals is unethical. An individual's right to privacy must be respected for legal as well as moral reasons. It is not acceptable to force all members of a group such as a college class to be subjects in a research project. The use of social pressures to take part in research should be carefully considered from a moral viewpoint. Coerced subjects may cause a researcher considerable problems, including consciously or unconsciously distorted data.

6. Ethically acceptable research begins with the establishment of a clear and fair agreement between the investigator and the research participant that clarifies the responsibilities of each. The investigator has the obligation to honor all promises and commitments included in that agreement.

7. The ethical investigator protects participants from physical and mental discomfort, harm, and danger. If the risk of such consequences exists, the investigator is required to

inform the participant of that fact, secure consent before proceeding, and take all possible measures to minimize distress. A research procedure may not be used if it is likely to cause serious and lasting harm to participants.

Some experiments are concerned with behavior at the extremes of psychological or physical endurance. Other experiments may expose the subject to a short-term stress, such as a simulated emergency or a traumatic social interaction. While the data from this type of study may be quite informative, the beginning researcher *should avoid it.* There are too many things that can go wrong to risk any possible damage to the subjects. Even for established professional researchers, this type of research is of questionable value.

    8. After the data are collected, ethical practice requires the investigator to provide the participant with a full clarification of the nature of the study and to remove any misconceptions that may have arisen. Where scientific or humane values justify delaying or withholding information, the investigator acquires a special responsibility to assure that there are no damaging consequences for the participant.

    9. Where research procedures may result in undesirable consequences for the participant, the investigator has the responsibility to detect and remove or correct these consequences, including, where relevant, long-term aftereffects.

    10. Information obtained about the research participants during the course of an investigation is confidential. When the possibility exists that others may obtain access to such information, ethical research practice requires that this possibility, together with the plans for protecting confidentiality, be explained to the participants as a part of the procedure for obtaining informed consent.[1]

Finally, subjects in a control group are often disappointed that that they did not really get to "participate" in the experiment. One suggestion to consider is to make the experimental treatment available to the control subjects after the experiment is completed. The additional time spent may be prohibitive, but it does often satisfy the control subjects, and also it provides a time-related control for the real experimental group.

CHOICE OF EQUIPMENT

A researcher has two ways to acquire apparatus for the laboratory: purchase a manufactured device from a commercial supplier, or outline a description of the desired device and construct it or have it constructed. Commercial suppliers provide catalogs with descriptions of the devices they sell. For the person interested in purchasing a specific item of equipment, *buyer's guides* provide a list of the manufacturers and suppliers of different kinds of equipment. Usually, a guide is organized by the function served by the equipment, so it can be used to locate most of the sources of equipment for any specific research application. The special instrumentation issue of *American Psychologist* (Sidowski & Ross, 1969) includes a buyer's guide for psychologists. *Science* magazine publishes an *Annual guide to scientific instruments.*

Custom-built equipment ranges from elaborate units that are designed specifically for a research program to home-built devices made of cardboard and glue. There are a number of sources that provide plans and specifications for laboratory apparatus. The equipment section of any research report in a journal provides a description of the apparatus used. In addition, several behavioral research journals publish notes on new devices developed in behavioral laboratories. The journal *Behavioral Research Methods and Instrumentation* publishes articles dealing with technological developments in psychology. The March 1969 issue of *American Psychologist* provided a special section on the uses of instrumentation in psychology. The reader who wishes to find a more thorough and technical discussion of laboratory equipment may find Sidowski's *Experimental methods and instrumentation in psychology* (1966) a valuable source. Zucker's *Electronic circuits for the behavioral and biomedical sciences* (1969), Malmstadt, Enke, and Toren's *Electronics for scientists* (1963), Weber & McLean's *Electrical measurement systems for biological and physical scientists* (1975), and Diefenderfer's *Principles of electronic instrumentation* (1972) provide a similar function for electronic devices.

LEVINSON'S LAW

"Levinson's law" (also known as "Murphy's law") states, "If anything can possibly go wrong, it will" (Levinson, 1967, cited in Sheridan, 1976).

Apparatus does malfunction, producing measurement error. Equipment does break down. People do fail to show up as scheduled. Animals do jump out of mazes instead of running the correct path. Animals do discover how to short out shock grids by urinating or defecating on the bars. People do deliberately mislead experimenters, whether out of boredom, resentment, the challenges of outfoxing the researcher, or pure perversity. People do get sick at the wrong time. People do misunderstand instructions.

Sheridan (1976) describes the case of a research director who ran a study on animal learning for almost a year before he learned that two of the three assistants running the animals were defining an "error" incorrectly. One of the present authors conducted a study on people's ability to identify each other through "hugging" (while blindfolded). Midway in one experimental session the pulleys controlling the curtains separating people between trials stuck. The curtain remained open and the light was turned on by the assistant, who expected the curtains to be closed. The people at that point could all see each other, ruining the data for the entire set of subjects. We have had the experience of marking baby chicks with felt-tip pens, leaving them over the weekend, and returning to find all the individual subject markings mysteriously erased from the subjects' backs. (We still don't know how that happened.) Sheridan describes a case of monkeys escaping from complex automated research equipment, playing with the equipment, and tearing up the electrical wires for half an hour before they were discovered. The list of research incidents exemplifying Levinson's law may be infinite.

Levinson's law is an undeniable natural law that is bound to apply to everyone eventually. Therefore we urge you to play the role of a subject in your study if it involves human subjects, and to write detailed research proposals so that you can anticipate disasters before they happen. Further, you should run pilot studies to check the operation of your equipment and your procedures before committing a lot of subject and experimenter time to a full-blown version of your study. A graduate student working with one of the authors of the text spent months working on a device that would hold a small chicken in a manner similar to Held and Hein's (1963) kitten carousel (Van Dyke & Beauchamp, 1975). Eventually she was rewarded by the success of the equipment and the completion of her master's thesis. Great patience and tolerance of frustration are normally required of experimental researchers. As Sheridan suggests, the key to dealing with Levinson's law is to accept its inexorable nature, remember it, and check and double-check every aspect of your experiment.

A RESEARCH EXAMPLE

We shall conclude with an example of a research study that went to great lengths to protect the subjects from an experimental situation that could have been very embarrassing. The experimenters showed ingenuity in using limited equipment, patience in solving potential flaws in advance, and tact in handling an ethically delicate situation—qualities we have urged in this chapter. The study dealt with the topic of personal space.

There is substantial anecdotal and research evidence to support the concept that the variable of personal space determines in part how people respond to their physical and social environments. Personal space is defined as the "area with invisible boundaries surrounding a person's body into which intruders may not come" (Sommer, 1969, p. 26). People seek to maintain comfortable interpersonal distances. A person whose personal space is violated will engage in a variety of behaviors designed to reestablish the boundaries or minimize the invasion: moving away, making submissive gestures, visually ignoring the invader, or apologizing. Why do people behave this way? The common, simplistic theory is that invasions of personal space are emotionally arousing; this emotional arousal motivates the observed behavioral responses to invasion, the execution of which reduces the arousal. Unfortunately, this theory has no clear evidence to support or reject it.

If the arousal theory has merit, there must be some way to test it. The theory essentially consists of two hypotheses: (1) personal space invasion produces arousal, and (2) the arousal leads to the observed behavioral responses. A first step in testing the theory would be to test the first hypothesis. Middlemist, Knowles, and Matter (1976) carried out such a test in a clever manner. Since the theory concerns human behavior, the research had to deal with human subjects. The hypothesis that invasion produces arousal produces the first question to be answered: How can arousal be measured in human subjects? Asking people whether they are aroused (*introspective verbal report*) has several problems as a method. One problem is that the mere asking of the question may produce arousal. Another problem is that the responses are likely to be subject to all the problems associated with subjects being aware of their participation in an experiment (chapter 14). Arousal can be measured by a variety of physiological indices (heart rate, galvanic skin response, EMG, respiration rate, and so on); however, all these require that the subject be hooked up to a variety of instruments. Again the subjects would be aware of their participation in an experiment and have a good idea of its nature. An unobtrusive measure (chapter 6) of arousal would be the best answer, one that does not involve the subject's awareness of the measurement process, does not depend on verbal report, and does not require elaborate electrophysiological amplification and recording devices.

Research on urination indicates that social stressors inhibit relaxation of the external urethral sphincter, delaying the onset of urination, and increase intravesical pressure, shortening the duration of urination. A men's lavatory, in addition to providing access to measures of the micturation response, also provides a setting in which personal space violation can occur in a "natural" way. Personal space invasion in a lavatory (as opposed to a laboratory) would be minimally confounded by the compensating responses that usually occur upon invasion. For these reasons, Middlemist, Knowles, and Matter ran a pilot study to determine whether urination behavior in a men's lavatory would serve as a useful measure of arousal as a response to invasion of personal space. The pilot field-observation study involved an observer apparently grooming himself at one of the sinks in a large lavatory. When a subject approached a urinal, the observer recorded the distance between the subject and the nearest user and, with a chronograph wristwatch, recorded micturation delay and persistence as indicated by the sound of the stream of urine striking the water in the urinal. The pilot study indicated that the measurement was feasible and showed the expected relationship between interpersonal distance and micturation delay and persistence. The greater the distance between users, the shorter the delay and the longer the average micturation time.

At this point, the researchers had established a viable arousal measurement procedure but needed better control over the factor of invasion of personal space. In the pilot study, subjects selected their own level of distance between users, and the factor of subject assignment to conditions needed better control. The size of the lavatory in the pilot study made control of degree of invasion difficult; the researchers therefore found a smaller lavatory (three urinals, two toilet stalls) with sufficient normal traffic, near a large classroom. The next problem was the fact that a person standing next to a user could not hear the urine striking the urinal. Fortunately, the physical arrangement of the stalls and urinals was such that one stall, with the usual openings at the bottom of its walls, was adjacent to a urinal. This allowed direct view of the lower torso of a person using the nearest urinal. Since unobtrusive observation of the urine flow was necessary, the experimenters hid a periscopic prism in a stack of books on the floor of the toilet stall. The prism provided a view of the lower torso and direct sighting of the urine stream. The observer recording data in the stall used two stopwatches to time the delay of onset of urination and the duration of micturation. The control of degree of personal space invasion was achieved by forcing the subject to use the urinal next to the occupied stall and having a confederate apparently use the middle urinal or the far urinal, or not having a confederate present at all.

Precise measurement of the dependent variable and the independent variable were achieved at this point, but subject self-selection was yet to be controlled. Also, if the experimenters merely waited until only one subject was in the right place and no one other than the observer and the confederate were in the lavatory, they would spend an inordinate amount of time. The question was how to control traffic flow, force the subjects to the right urinal, and control subject assignment to groups. They solved that problem by using a "Don't use, washing urinal" sign accompanied by a bucket of water and a sponge. For the close-distance (high-invasion) condition, the confederate was stationed at the middle urinal and the sign, bucket, and sponge were placed in the far urinal. For the moderate-distance (moderate-invasion) condition, the sign, bucket, and sponge were placed in the middle urinal and the confederate at the far urinal. For the control (no-invasion) condition, the sign, bucket, and sponge arrangement was used for both the middle and far urinals and the confederate was not in the room.

The researchers gathered data on 60 subjects. (A subject was counted as long as no one other than the subject, confederate, and observer were present in the lavatory.) The subjects were randomly assigned to the three treatment conditions by preparing the room before the entry of each subject into the lavatory.

The results supported the hypothesis that personal space invasion produces arousal. In terms of the treatment conditions, average micturational delay increased from 4.9 seconds (control), to 6.2 seconds (moderate), to 8.4 seconds (close). Average micturation duration decreased from 24.8 seconds (control), to 23.4 seconds (moderate), to 17.4 seconds (close). The results for both variables support the hypothesis. This is a particularly interesting finding because under normal conditions delay and duration are positively correlated (chapter 21) but in the experiment the group means were negatively correlated across the three conditions for the two dependent variables.

SUMMARY

1. Nonhuman subjects are chosen for research projects for at least two basic reasons: (a) animals may provide information useful to the understanding of human behavior, and (b) the description and explanation of animal behavior is intrinsically interesting to some researchers.

2. Additional reasons for using animals rather than human beings include: (a) certain research treatments and situations cannot be ethically employed with human beings; (b) animals can provide unique structural or behavioral characteristics that facilitate the research; (c) it is possible to have greater control of the heredity of certain animals than of humans; (d) maturation rates are faster in many species than in human beings, providing greater opportunity to study developmental processes; (e) standard laboratory animals such as rats and mice offer the opportunity for almost complete control of the animal's environment; (f) a great background of available knowledge promotes the repeated use of a limited group of animal species; and (g) certain subhuman species are more available, reliable, and convenient to use than human beings.

3. Selecting appropriate animal subjects for research requires knowledge of the physiology and of some of the behavior of the chosen species. The particular research problem at hand will lead to certain types of animals being more appropriate than others. One of the most significant limitations on choice is the cost of various species.

4. If you choose to work with nonhuman animals, you will probably be responsible for providing adequate, appropriate housing conditions for the subjects.

5. One way to motivate animals to engage in appropriate behaviors in a research setting is by food or water deprivation. Appropriate schedules of deprivation have been developed for the standard laboratory animal species.

6. If you work with laboratory rats, you may need to adapt the animals to you. This involves taming or gentling the animals for several days. You also need to adapt the animals to the testing apparatus and routines.

7. Human subjects are usually selected on the basis of age. Two obvious alternatives are the choice of children or of adults, and selection by individuals or by intact groups.

★8. A standard series of procedures have been developed for soliciting research participation by human beings. These procedures include (a) explaining the real purpose of the study, (b) guaranteeing anonymity, (c) making the participation interesting, (d) providing clear directions for appointments, and (e) detailing the feedback procedures.

9. Contacting children in an intact group requires carefully planned approaches to authority figures responsible for the group. You must be aware of all legal requirements regarding the participation of children in research projects.

10. When soliciting college students as research subjects, schedule more subjects than you need.

11. Playing the role of a subject in a human experiment is one good way to anticipate problems and deal with some of the potential subject reactions to the research setting.

12. Growing issues of concern to the general public are (1) the question of invasion of privacy, (2) the misuse and ill-treatment of animal subjects, and (3) the use of animal subjects in studies that necessitate changes in the physical structure or living state of the organism.

13. It is morally and practically mandatory that scientists report their research procedures and results completely and accurately. Publication of false data is a self-evident and sufficient reason for expulsion from the research community.

14. The significant contribution of any person to a published research project requires granting credit to that person, either in the form of a footnote to the article or in the form of coauthorship.

15. Animal-research ethics, the validity of research results, generalization, and pragmatic reasons *all* dictate that research animals be maintained in as healthy and normal an environment as possible.

16. The American Psychological Association has published guidelines for both animal and human research. The experimenter's responsibilities include confidentiality, full disclosure, openness and honesty, guaranteeing individual freedom, honoring all promises, protection of individuals from physical and mental harm, full explanation after the data is collected, and removal of any untoward effects.

17. In general, whenever ethical principles and the principle of experimental control conflict, priority must be given to the welfare of the individual research participant.

18. Levinson's law (Murphy's law) states that "If anything can possibly go wrong, it will." The inexorable nature of this law suggests that every aspect of a proposed experiment should be checked and double-checked.

SUGGESTED READINGS

General

Anderson, B. *The psychology experiment: An introduction to the scientific method* (2nd ed.). Belmont, Calif.: Wadsworth, 1971.

Bell, J. E. *A guide to library research in psychology.* Dubuque, Iowa: William C. Brown, 1971.

Calfee, R., *Human experimental psychology*. New York: Holt, Rinehart and Winston, 1975.

Candland, D. K. *Psychology: The experimental approach*. New York: McGraw-Hill, 1968.

Kling, J., & Riggs, L. (Eds.). *Woodworth/Schlosberg's experimental psychology* (3rd ed.). New York: Holt, Rinehart and Winston, 1971.

Koch, S. (Ed.). *Psychology: A study of a science* (6 vols.). New York: McGraw-Hill, 1959–1963.

McGuigan, F. *Experimental psychology: A methodological approach* (2nd ed.). Englewood Cliffs, N.J.: Prentice-Hall, 1968.

Osgood, C. E. *Method and theory in experimental psychology*. New York: Oxford University Press, 1953.

Runkel, P. J., & McGrath, J. E. *Research on human behavior*. New York: Holt, Rinehart and Winston, 1972.

Selltiz, C., Wrightsman, L., & Cook, S. W. *Research methods in social relations* (3rd. ed.). New York: Holt, Rinehart and Winston, 1976.

Sheridan, C. L. *Fundamentals of experimental psychology* (2nd ed.). New York: Holt, Rinehart and Winston, 1975.

Sidowski, J. B. (Ed.). *Experimental methods and instrumentation in psychology*. New York: McGraw-Hill, 1966.

Stevens, S. S. *Handbook of experimental psychology*. New York: Wiley, 1951.

Underwood, B. J. *Experimental psychology* (2nd ed.). New York: Appleton, 1966.

Comparative Psychology

Denny, M. R., & Ratner, S. C. *Comparative psychology: Research in animal behavior* (Rev. ed.). Homewood, Ill.: Dorsey, 1970.

Dethier, V., & Stellar, E. *Animal behavior* (3rd ed.). Englewood Cliffs, N.J.: Prentice-Hall, 1969.

Dewsbury, D. A., & Rethlingshafer, D. (Eds.). *Comparative psychology: A modern approach*. New York: McGraw-Hill, 1973.

Gay, W. I. (Ed.). *Methods of animal experimentation* (5 vols.). New York: Academic Press, 1965–1974.

Lehrman, D. W., Hinde, R. A., & Shaw, E. (Eds.). *Advances in the study of behavior* (7 vols.). New York: Academic Press, 1965–1976.

Maier, N. R. F., & Schneirla, T. C. *Principles of animal psychology*. New York: Dover, 1964.

Maier, R., & Maier, B. *Comparative animal behavior*. Belmont, Calif.: Brooks/Cole, 1970.

McGill, T. E. (Ed.) *Readings in animal behavior*. New York: Holt, Rinehart and Winston, 1965.

Sluckin, W. *Imprinting and early learning*. Chicago: Aldine, 1965.

Development and Cognition

Ausubel, D., & Sullivan, E. *Theories and problems of child development* (2nd ed.). New York: Grune & Stratton, 1970.

Bandura, A., & Walters, R. *Social learning and personality development*. New York: Holt, Rinehart and Winston, 1963.

Bruner, J. S., Olver, R. R., Greenfield, P. M., Hornsby, J. R., Kenney, H. J., Maccoby, M., Modiano, N., Mosher, F. A., Olson, D. R., Potter, M. C., Reich, L. C., & Sonstroem, A. M. *Studies in cognitive growth*. New York: Wiley, 1966.

Endler, N. S., Boulter, L. R., & Osser, H. (Eds.) *Contemporary issues in developmental psychology*. New York: Holt, Rinehart and Winston, 1968.

Flavell, J. *The developmental psychology of Jean Piaget.* New York: Van Nostrand Reinhold, 1963.

Ginsberg, H., & Opper, S. *Piaget's theory of intellectual development: An introduction.* Engelwood Cliffs, N.J.: Prentice-Hall, 1969.

Hurlock, E. *Developmental psychology* (4th ed.). New York: McGraw-Hill, 1975.

Jensen, A. R., Kagan, J. S., Hunt, J. M. V., Crone, J. F., Bereiter, C., Elkind, D., Cronbach, L. J., & Brazziel, W. F. *Environment, heredity, and intelligence.* Cambridge, Mass.: Harvard Educational Review, Reprint Series, No. 2, 1969.

Klausmeier, H. G., Chatala, E. S., & Fryer, D. A. *Conceptual learning and development: A cognitive view.* New York: Academic Press, 1974.

Langer, J. *Theories of development.* New York: Holt, Rinehart and Winston, 1969.

Lipsitt, L. L., & Spiker, C. C. (Eds.). *Advances in child development and behavior* (11 vols.). New York: Academic Press, 1963–1976.

Mussen, P. H. (Ed.). *Handbook of research methods in child development.* New York: Wiley, 1960.

Mussen, P. H. (Ed.). *Carmichael's manual of child psychology* (3rd ed.). New York: Wiley, 1970.

Reese, H., and Lipsitt, L. (Eds.). *Experimental child psychology.* New York: Academic Press, 1970.

Learning

Anderson, B. F. *Cognitive psychology: The study of knowing, learning and thinking.* New York: Academic Press, 1975.

Ferster, C. B., & Perrott, M. C. *Behavior principles.* New York: Appleton, 1968.

Hergenhahn, B. R. *An introduction to theories of learning.* Englewood Cliffs, N.J.: Prentice-Hall, 1976.

Hilgard, E. R., & Bower, G. H. *Theories of learning* (4th ed.). New York: Appleton, 1974.

Horton, D., & Turnage, T. *Human learning.* Englewood Cliffs, N.J.: Prentice-Hall, 1976.

Houston, J. P. *Fundamentals of learning.* New York: Academic Press, 1976.

Hulse, S. H., Deese, J., & Egeth, H. E. *The psychology of learning.* (4th ed.). New York: McGraw-Hill, 1975.

Jung, J. *Verbal learning.* New York: Holt, Rinehart and Winston, 1968.

Kimble, G. A. *Hilgard and Marquis' conditioning and learning* (2nd ed.). New York: Appleton, 1961.

Kimble, G. A. (Ed.) *Foundations of conditioning and learning.* New York: Appleton, 1967.

Spence, K. W., & Spence, J. T. *The psychology of learning and motivation: Advances in research and theory* (10 vols.). New York: Academic Press, 1967–1976.

Motivation

Bolles, R. *Theory of motivation.* New York: Harper & Row, 1967.

Cofer, C. N., & Appley, M. H. *Motivation: Theory and research.* New York: Wiley, 1964.

Ferguson, E. D. *Motivation: An experimental approach.* New York: Holt, Rinehart and Winston, 1976.

Haber, R. N. (Ed.) *Current research in motivation.* New York: Holt, Rinehart and Winston, 1966.

Troland, L. *The fundamentals of human motivation.* New York: Hafner, 1967.

Vernon, M. *Human motivation.* New York: Cambridge University Press, 1969.

Weiner, B. (Ed.). *Cognitive views of human motivation.* New York: Academic Press, 1974.

Naturalistic Observation

Ittleson, W. H. *Environment and cognition.* New York: Academic Press, 1973.

Proshansky, H. M., Ittelson, W. H., & Rivlin, L. G. *Environmental psychology.* New York: Holt, Rinehart and Winston, 1970.

Thorpe, W. H. *Learning and instinct in animals* (2nd ed.). London: Methuen, 1963.

Webb, E. J., Campbell, D. T., Schwartz, R. D., & Sechrest, L. *Unobtrusive measures: Nonreactive research in the social sciences.* Skokie, Ill.: Rand McNally, 1966.

Willems, E., & Raush, H. (Eds.). *Naturalistic viewpoint in psychological research.* New York: Holt, Rinehart and Winston, 1969.

Wright, H. *Recording and analyzing child behavior.* New York: Harper & Row, 1967.

Sensory and Perception

Cornsweet, T. *Visual perception.* New York: Academic Press, 1970.

Corso, J. F. *The experimental psychology of sensory behavior.* Holt, Rinehart and Winston, 1967.

Day, R. *Human perception.* New York: Wiley, 1969.

Dember, W. N. *The psychology of perception.* New York: Holt, Rinehart and Winston, 1960.

Forgus, R. H., & Melamed, L. E. *Perception: A cognitive-stage approach* (2nd ed.). New York: McGraw-Hill, 1976.

Geldard, F. A. *The human senses* (2nd ed.). New York: Wiley, 1972.

Gibson, E. J. *Principles of perceptual learning and development.* New York: Appleton, 1969.

Gibson, J. J. *The senses considered as perceptual systems.* Boston: Houghton Mifflin, 1966.

Gregory, R. *Eye and brain: The psychology of seeing.* New York: McGraw-Hill, 1966.

Gregory, R. *The intelligent eye.* New York: McGraw-Hill, 1970.

Haber, R. N., & Hershenson, M. *The psychology of visual perception.* New York: Holt, Rinehart and Winston, 1973.

Murch, G. *Visual and auditory perception.* Indianapolis, Ind.: Bobbs-Merrill, 1973.

Stevens, S. S. Problems and methods of psychophysics. *Psychological Bulletin,* 1958, *55,* 177–196.

Stevens, S. S. *Psychophysics.* New York: Wiley, 1975.

Social

Aronson, E. *The social animal* (2nd ed.). San Francisco: Freeman, 1976.

Berkowitz, L. (Ed.). *Advances in experimental social psychology* (10 vols.). New York: Academic Press, 1964–1976.

Brown, R. *Social psychology.* New York: Free Press, 1965.

Eisenberg, J. F., & Dillon, W. S. *Man and beast: Comparative social behavior.* Washington, D.C.: Smithsonian Institution Press, 1971.

Gergen, K., & Marlowe, D. *Personality and social behavior.* Reading, Mass.: Addison-Wesley, 1970.

Lindzey, G., & Aronson, E. (Eds.). *Handbook of social psychology* (Rev. ed.) (5 vols.). Cambridge, Mass.: Addison-Wesley, 1967–1969.

McGinnies, E. *Social behavior: A functional analysis.* Boston: Houghton Mifflin, 1970.

Mills, J. (Ed.) *Experimental social psychology.* New York: Macmillan, 1969.

Nuttin, J. M., Jr. *The illusion of attitude change.* New York: Academic Press, 1975.

Tests and Questionnaires

Anastasi, A. *Psychological testing* (4th ed.). New York: Macmillan, 1976.

Buros, O. K. *The seventh mental measurements yearbook.* Highland Park, N.J.: Gryphon Press, 1972.

Cronbach, L. *Essentials of psychological testing* (3rd ed.). New York: Harper & Row, 1970.

Edwards, A. *The measurement of personality traits by scales and inventories.* New York: Holt, Rinehart and Winston, 1970.

Kerlinger, F. N. *Foundations of behavioral research* (2nd ed.). New York: Holt, Rinehart and Winston, 1973.

Nunnally, J. *Introduction to psychological measurement* (2nd ed.). New York: McGraw-Hill, 1970.

Oppenheim, A. *Questionnaire design and attitude measurement.* New York: Basic Books, 1966.

Summers, G. *Attitude measurement.* Skokie, Ill.: Rand McNally, 1970.

14

Artifacts of Experimentation

Among the many ways in which a research study may lead to inconclusive results are mistakes by the researcher who designs the study and mistakes by the experimenter who carries out the research. This chapter outlines a number of ways in which the social nature of research, particularly with human subjects, can involve confounding variables that destroy the internal validity of a research project. The chapter also describes how the external validity of research results can be severely limited by the unrepresentativeness of the subjects selected, the peculiarity of the research setting, the characteristics of the experimenter, and the reactive effects of the variables manipulated. A number of methods to deal with these problems are also outlined.

According to the *American Heritage Dictionary of the English Language,* an artifact is "a structure or substance not normally present, but produced by some external agent or action" (1969, p. 75). In biological and behavioral research, **artifactual behavior** is behavior shaped or produced by experimentation itself; it is behavior that would not naturally occur in a nonexperimental setting. An ever-present issue in these sciences is the concern that the observation process may generate behavioral data that are not representative of the nonobserved, "real" world. (We referred to this effect in chapter 2 as "reactive effects of experimentation.") How much of our data is artifactual and how much of the data can be *generalized* to the nonexperimental setting?

McGuire (1969) provides an excellent example of one specific artifact encountered in psychological research and of the various ways in which researchers deal with artifacts. The artifact described is most commonly referred to as **response bias** (sometimes called response set or response style). Many questions on a self-report inventory have an answer that is easily recognized as socially more desirable than the other answers. When asked to fill out a personality inventory as part of applying for a job or for entrance to an educational institution, a person may be motivated to pretend (Anastasi, 1976), choosing the answer most likely to create a favorable impression even when the answer is not an honest self-description. The tendency to choose socially desirable answers may occur as deliberate deception or without awareness on the part of the respondent. Response bias is encountered primarily in psychological testing, including ability tests, aptitude tests, and personality tests (particularly self-report inventories). Other forms of response bias include the tendency to agree (acquiescence set) or to mark positive or "yes" answers, the tendency to make noncommittal, "don't know" responses, and the less frequently encountered tendency to give unusual responses (deviation set).

According to McGuire, there is a natural progression of psychological interest in any artifact. This progression involves the three stages of *ignorance, coping,* and *exploitation.* At first, even though two researchers in 1937 and 1938 observed the existence of response sets, most researchers seemed to be unaware of the artifact. As more research and theorizing made the existence of the artifact undeniable, researchers began to devise ways of coping with it: (1) including questions designed to detect the various kinds of bias and using these "catch scales" or "lie scales" to reject data from subjects with an unacceptable bias level; (2) constructing questions or scales that provide data to correct the biased person's total test performance; and (3) changing the form of a test to prevent the occurrence of response bias. Eventually response bias became so important that some researchers began to study it in its own right. Thus, the

Artifactual Behavior

Response Bias

secondary variable that at first was creating misleading data finally came to be a primary variable. "Social desirability" and "acquiescence" are now considered to be interesting sources of individual differences. "It is a wise experimenter who knows his artifact from his main effect; and wiser still is the researcher who realizes that today's artifact may be tomorrow's independent variable. Indeed, even at a given time, one man's artifact may be another man's main effect" (McGuire, 1969, p. 13).

Artifactual bias in a research project is not limited to experimental research with human beings. For example, it has been suggested as a factor in planaria research. It is not very likely that planaria change their behavior because of being observed by a human being. It is more likely that the equipment we use to study the behavior of planaria may influence their behavior. The use of bright lights, distilled water, electric shock, plastic mazes, and so on may limit generalization of the research results to the behavior of planaria in a natural setting. As we work with more complex animals (such as rats, chimpanzees, and human beings) their behavior is subject to an expanding list of more subtle experimental artifacts.

Abandoning the experimental format will not solve the experimental artifact problem. Attempts to conceal the observer in naturalistic observation studies may also influence the behavior observed in unknown ways. Goodall's classic naturalistic observation of wild chimpanzees includes several anecdotes involving the presence of the observer. However, artifactual data are most likely to be encountered in experimental research with human beings, particularly experimental social psychology and personality research.

EXTERNAL VS. INTERNAL VALIDITY

Internal Validity

External Validity

The existense of artifactual data is one aspect of the broader problem of external vs. internal validity (Campbell & Stanley, 1963). **Internal validity** refers to the degree of control of secondary and error variance within a research study. With adequate control the observed data of the study can be interpreted as a direct function of the experimental treatment or independent variable. **External validity** refers to the generalizability of the results. It is concerned with the precise populations, sampling prodedures, types of measurement, forms of treatment, types of environment, and time frames to which the research results may be generalized. Artifactual variables may limit both the internal and external validity of a study. In research with human subjects, the subjects usually know they are involved in an experiment. Human subjects have been known to modify their behavior in order either to please the experimenter or to ruin the research project. Either reaction can disrupt the action of the primary variable, in which case internal validity suffers. In addition, the results may not be generalized to a nonexperimental setting; therefore the external validity of the data is also diminished or destroyed by the reactive nature of the experiment.

As indicated in chapter 2, we tend to use the most readily available subjects in our research, rather than systematically obtaining a representative sample. *Available* subjects may not be representative of the population to which we think we can generalize our results. The external validity of the data is limited by the degree of nonrepresentativeness of the sample. It is an empirical question whether the research-based explanations of the social behavior of United States college sophomores can be generalized to explain the social behavior of factory workers in Japan. It seems obvious and simple to say that the best way to test the generalizability is to run the same experiment with factory workers in Japan. Even disregarding the potential costs of such a project, it is not as simple a resolution of the generalization question as it appears. Not only do the location and subjects differ, but also every other aspect of the research project (including the experimenter) may affect the observed results. As we gain control of secondary variance by the experimental manipulation of variables, we also increase the possibility that the results will be artifactual. This dilemma (Jung, 1971) has always plagued (and apparently always will plague) the experimental scientist, and at the same time stimulates creative attempts to deal with it.

THE SOCIAL NATURE OF PSYCHOLOGICAL RESEARCH

The typical introductory-text description of psychological research gives the impression that the actual conduct of a research project rigorously follows the idealized principles of control (chapter 2). In fact, carrying out a research project is a form of human social behavior that exhibits all the variability characteristic of any human activity. Even when the subjects are not human beings, the experimenters engage in primitive forms of social interaction with the subjects. Each of the authors of this text has developed preferences for certain rats in rat studies and have also experienced anger or irritation toward other subjects. Early in their research on the development of affectional behavior in rhesus monkeys, the Harlows (1959, 1962, 1969) noted that some infants isolated from members of their own species developed normally. Without the awareness of the Harlows and their associate researchers, a female undergraduate research assistant was spending a substantial amount of time in daily cuddling and "mothering" of these animals.

When the subjects are human beings, social interaction is more natural and more complex; an experimenter responds differently to different subjects, and different experimenters respond differently to the same subject. Subjects likewise respond differently to different experimenters. Thus, the interaction between subject and experimenter is not the sterile, uniform, standardized procedure implied by the abstract principles of the control of variance.

Standardization

This *lack of standardization* may have either positive or negative value. First, it is possible that the lack of standardization can increase the magnitude of error variance to the point that the real effect of an independent variable is masked (decreased internal validity). Second, it is possible that the lack of standardization may interact with the treatment to enhance or depress the effect of the treatment as represented in the data (decreased external validity). Third, it is possible that the lack of standardization might result in one experimenter observing a significant effect of an independent variable while another experimenter fails to observe the effect.

The nonstandardized treatment of subjects may have a positive value in either of two ways. First, tailoring the experimenter–subject interaction to create a constant mental set may allow the same results in different settings or with different experimenters. When this occurs, the researcher could confidently generalize the results to many experimenter–subject combinations. Second, the nature of the experimental treatment may be such that the planned interaction between subjects and experimenters would produce a desirable nonuniform treatment experience for each subject. For example, most if not all applied psychological therapy requires the careful tailoring of a particular therapeutic treatment to the particular needs and circumstances of each individual. While all individuals in an experimental treatment group may receive "desensitization therapy," the precise sequence and rate of the therapy varies from individual to individual depending on the specific fears or anxieties experienced by each subject.

Subject awareness of the fact of being observed in an experiment is an important potential source of variance within and between experiments. A group of industrial psychologists (Roethlisberger & Dickson, 1939) conducted a series of studies at the Hawthorne plant of the Western Electric Company measuring the effects of working conditions (illumination, rest periods, wage rate, and so on) by recording the productivity of the workers. The most important result of their research was that any change in working conditions created an increase in the rate of production. The researchers concluded that the workers felt honored to be chosen for the study and pleased that management cared about their welfare. The mere fact of being in an experiment changed the social situation and the measured behavior. This phenomenon is called the **Hawthorne effect**. The Hawthorne effect has been treated at times as if it were a source of error that needed control by elimination in any social psychological study. However, Sommer (1968) points out that the placebo and Hawthorne effects are not "errors." The expectations, beliefs, attitudes, motivations, perceptions, values, and so on of subjects do influence their behavior, both in and out of experimental research projects. The total social milieu influences human behavior. The Hawthorne effect should be recognized as an instance of a fundamental phenomenon of human nature rather than merely an instance of lack of control.

Hawthorne Effect

Suspiciousness-of-Persuasive-Intent

McGuire (1969) indicates that "subjects' suspiciousness-of-persuasive-intent of the experimenter in attitude change research" has recently entered the third stage, "exploitation" in the life of an artifact, the stage in which the effect is interesting in its own right as a variable affecting human behavior. Jung (1971) summarizes the research and theorizing about how being experimented on may affect the behavior of human subjects. In brief, the subjects may: (1) be apprehensive about the impressions they make and try to make themselves look good; (2) be cooperative in order to please the experimenter and thus be judged "good" subjects; (3) docilely follow the instructions without attempting to discern the nature or purpose of the experiment; (4) resent being "used" and become hostile, apathetic, or uncooperative, or deliberately attempt to sabotage the experiment; (5) behave as they would if they were not involved in an experiment; or (6) generally behave in whatever way will best serve their own self-interest, which may include doing what the experimenter wants them to do. It is possible in a given experiment that different subjects may exhibit all six of these attitudes or behaviors, and that the same subject may simultaneously or sequentially hold two or more of them.

Demand Characteristics

Orne (1969) reviews the research and theorizing about the "demand characteristics" of an experiment, cues that control the subjects' perception of their roles in the experiment and of the experimenter's expectations. Rosenberg (1969) reviews the

Evaluation
Apprehension

research and theorizing about the "evaluation apprehension," anxious concern that the experimenter will evaluate some aspect of the subject's emotional adequacy, mental helath, ability, and so on typically experienced by human subjects. Rosenberg indicates that even if the experimenter's behavior does *not* provide direct cues, the subjects will construct their own personal interpretations of the "real meaning" of an experiment, which will affect their responses.

REPRESENTATIVENESS OF HUMAN SUBJECTS

Jung (1971) summarizes three surveys of the types of human subjects employed in experimental psychological research. The percentage of studies using college students ranged from 73% to 90% depending on the research journals and publication years surveyed. There appears to be a disproportionate number of male subjects, and perhaps as much as 80% of all human subjects are recruited from introductory psychology classes. It is obvious that college students from introductory psychology classes in English-speaking countries do not form a representative sample of all human beings on this planet. Specifying the degree of representativeness for humans in general would require an enormous research effort. However, for behavior significantly affected by health, age, intelligence, group membership, and any sociocultural variable, only with great caution may the research results be generalized beyond college student populations.

There are additional external validity problems with the ways in which human subjects are recruited for research projects. Jung (1969) found that most subjects from psychology courses were drafted by means of a course requirement. "Volunteers" received extra credit towards the course grade or chose research participation among optional ways to fulfill a course requirement. Less than 7% of all subjects were real volunteers (paid or unpaid) not pressured by course requirements or by implicit instructor expectations. "The true volunteer subject is primarily a mythical creature or one fast becoming extinct" (Jung, 1971, p. 27). Aside from the problem of volunteers, the scheduling of research participation appointments and choice of experiments is usually left to the subjects to select according to their own personal schedules and preferences. This fact may alter the nature of the "volunteers" and could have an effect on the observed behavior.

Rosenthal and Rosnow (1969b) review the research on the phenomenon of volunteering to be a research subject and differences between volunteers and nonvolunteers. The results of research both in laboratory and in the field seem to indicate that, as compared to nonvolunteers, volunteers for behavioral research tend to: (1) be better educated, (2) have a higher occupational status, (3) have a higher need for social approval, (4) be more intelligent (especially males), and (5) be less authoritarian. Research evidence also indicates that, of those who do "volunteer," a substantial proportion never will actually participate in the research project ("no shows"). At least in terms of personality tests, "no shows" are psychologically more like nonvolunteers than the volunteers who do actually show up for the research project.

Even though a given sample of volunteers may differ in a number of important ways from nonvolunteers, we do not know whether the status of being a volunteer makes any real difference in terms of the dependent measure of a study. It is possible

Volunteer Subjects

in a given experiment that the volunteer–nonvolunteer variable could have no effect on the results of the project. The direct experimental evidence on this issue at this point is so minimal that no conclusion is possible.

TYPES OF ARTIFACTS

Pretest Sensitization

Lana (1969) reviews the research on pretest-sensitization effects. Recall from chapter 2 that the pretest-sensitization source of secondary variance and external invalidity refers to the situation where a pretest or before-measure interacts with the experimental treatment to either enhance or depress the effect of the treatment. If a pretest does sensitize the subjects to the treatment, this interaction effect limits the generalizability of the conclusions regarding the effect of the treatment.

As indicated in chapter 10, the Solomon four-group design is uniquely suited to the empirical examination of the pretest-sensitization effect in attitude-change research. Lana's (1969) summary of the research utilizing the Solomon four-group design indicates that in attitude-change studies involving a single, persuasive one-sided argument there is an "overwhelming lack of a pretest sensitization effect" (Lana, 1969, p. 134). However, several studies have discovered a significant pretest-by-treatment interaction when the treatment involved bidirectional argument, two opposed, conflicting arguments on the same topic. In the three studies discussed, the pretest of attitude served to depress the degree of attitude change. These results were interpreted to support the subject-commitment hypothesis. This hypothesis suggests that the pretest serves to commit the subjects to their original opinion when bidirectional arguments subsequently are presented.

The Rosnow, Holper, and Gitter (1973) study described in chapter 10 indicates that the existence of pretest-sensitization effects may depend on other situational variables such as the anonymity of the subjects, the degree of seriousness of the issue to the individuals, and whether or not the subjects are volunteers. There may be a three-way interaction among the pretest, treatment, and one of these situational variables.

The Experimenter Effect

There are many ways in which an experimenter may influence the results of an experiment, and all are referred to by the term **experimenter effect**. Rosenthal (1969) reviewed the research and theorizing about the experimenter effect up to 1969. Rosenthal makes an important distinction between two types of experimenter effect: (1) a noninteractive effect that does not influence the behavior of the subjects, but rather influences the data or conclusions of the research, and (2) an interactive effect that does influence the behavior of the subjects and thus the data of the experiment. The noninteractive category includes errors in recording observational data, errors in computation, errors in interpreting the data, and intentional (fraudulent) "errors."

Observational errors range from nonselectively accepting folklore, myths, and prejudice to misjudging the borderlines in categorizing behavioral observations. A well-planned research effort avoids most of these problems by establishing clear observation categorization criteria *before* the problem arises. Criteria established after the fact can be affected by the subjects' treatment conditions. Computational errors ought to be randomly distributed; however, it is a fact of life that errors that support the hypothesis are not checked while the errors against the hypothesis are usually corrected. They thus become a biasing factor. Observational, computational, and interpretation errors, if not corrected by the researcher, are usually detected when the research report is made public. It is our belief that while intentional "errors" (cheating) exist, they are very infrequent in published research.

Rosenthal's second category, that of interactive effects in which the behavior of the subjects is affected by the behavior and characteristics of the experimenters, is more important. The sex, age, and race of experimenters have been found to affect the results of several studies. These organismic attributes of the experimenters may influence the subjects' behavior in an active way (for example, experimenters unintentionally treating male and female subjects differently); in a passive way (subjects responding differently to male and female experimenters because of their sex rather than because of differential treatment by the experimenters); or in a transactive way (male and female experimenters unintentionally treating subjects differently both because of the experimenter's sexually based behaviors and because the subjects react differently to the two sexes). Similarly, the behavioral characteristics and social attributes of the experimenters, such as anxiety, power status, warmth, experience, and so on, can have active, passive, and transactive effects on the behavior of the subjects. Additionally, the physical setting of the experiment may influence the behavior of the experimenters, which, in turn, may influence the behavior of the subjects. In general, the scattered research results so far indicate that these effects may or may not occur in a given experiment, and that the magnitude of the effects if they occur can vary from trivial to substantial. These forms of experimenter effect are not limited to studies with human subjects, although it seems probable that they are more important in studies that involve human behavior.

Experimenter-Expectancy-Bias Effect

The most substantially researched interactive experimenter effect is the experimenter-expectancy-bias effect (Rosenthal, 1966, 1969). Even when we conduct pilot and exploratory studies that seldom involve an explicitly formulated research hypothesis, we still do have casual working hypotheses or at least implicit expectations about the outcomes of the research. If we did not expect to find something, we would not expend the effort to conduct the research project. Furthermore, whenever we speculate about the causes of a behavior, we make "reasonable assumptions" about what is and what is not relevant (Beckwith & Miller, 1976). For example, if we are concerned about the stimuli that control sexual arousal in adult male human beings, we "reasonably assume" that the amount of ozone in the atmosphere, the state of the economy in Brazil, the humidity of the room (within obvious limits), and the color of the subjects' hair, among millions of other possible events, states, and behaviors, have little or no bearing on the behavior in question. Without such reasonable assumptions, we could not even contemplate beginning a research project. The expectations and assumptions of the experimenter influence the choice of research design, control procedures, variables to be considered, dependent measures, type of subjects, and so forth. Any of these choices may also bias the research outcome.

The experimenter's expectancy may directly influence the subjects' behavior. The experimenter may unintentionally bias the responses of the subjects so that the data of the study support the experimenter's predictions. Such a subtle **experimenter-expectancy-bias** effect is *not* public in nature; not only will other researchers not know whether such a bias has occurred, but even the experimenter may not know. By definition, the experimenter-bias effect, if it occurs, always differentially affects the results in favor of the prediction. Therefore it is possible that any research results may reflect the operation of a "self-fulfilling prophecy."

The basic research paradigm used by Rosenthal and his associates to study the experimenter-expectancy-bias effect is an "experiment within an experiment" (Jung, 1971). Essentially, two groups of experimenters, performing the same experiment, are given different expectations for their subjects' responses. The data are examined to see whether the observed results differ in the direction of the induced expectations. In some cases a third, "no-expectation" control group is included.

Although a number of studies have failed to find evidence for an expectancy-bias effect, the large number that have found reliable evidence of such an effect is substantial. Barber and Silver (1968) suggest that the expectancy-bias effect may be limited to relatively ambiguous tasks, such as planaria studies in which the scoring of a conditioned response (classically conditioned shock-avoidance contraction response) is highly dependent on the observer's judgment, or to person-perception studies, in which the subjects are faced with a subjective interpretation task. How the expectancy-bias effect occurs is still an open question, but it seems most likely that paralinguistic cues, such as intonation, and kinesic cues, such as facial expression or movement, provide the essential communication between experimenter and subject (Jung, 1971).

"The investigator who studies [expectancy bias] represents an interesting paradox since, in principle, he could be biasing his own results!" (Jung, 1971, p. 47). One of the major critics of Rosenthal's work, T. X. Barber (1976), has consistently failed to find evidence of a bias effect. Thus, it appears that the expectancy-bias effect is, itself, subject to experimenter-expectancy bias.

The expectancy-bias effect has reached the third stage in the life of an artifact. The concept has been shown to have theoretical and practical significance in such areas as clinical psychology and educational psychology. Rosenthal and Jacobson (1968) describe the effects of teacher expectations on the progress of individual students. Even though the effect does not appear to be as pervasive as once thought (Barber, 1976; Landon, 1976), it is one more potential factor we must at least consider when evaluating the control of secondary variance in a completed or projected study.

The Effect of Deceiving Human Subjects

Most experiments involve the use of deception in one of two forms: either the subjects are deliberately misled about the nature of the research (as often happens in social and personality research) or the subjects just are not told all of the reasons why the research is being conducted. The latter form, omission of information, is most prevalent. Obviously, it would take a great deal of the experimenter's time to explain the hypothesis, procedures, and so forth of every research project to every subject. In the great majority of cases, deception by omission causes neither experimental artifacts nor ethical problems. Deliberate deception provides artifactual and ethical concerns. (The ethical issue was discussed in chapter 13.)

Given the normal curiosity of human beings and the fact that most subjects are college students who are involved in the daily practice of figuring things out, we expect human subjects will try to discover the purpose behind the procedures as well as the overall purpose of each experiment. In many cases we provide a false description of the purpose of the study in order to provide all subjects with a uniform expectation base. If we allowed subjects to generate their own hypotheses about the real nature of the experiment, it is possible that the differences among hypotheses might reduce the internal validity of the study by increasing the variability observed (uncontrolled error variance). In other cases, we actively deceive subjects because we believe that if they knew the true purpose of a study, they would not behave in a natural, generalizable manner (reduced external validity). For example, if you told the subjects that the study was concerned with the effect of group size on the willingness of individuals to volunteer aid for persons in distress, it is doubtful that the observed voluntary behavior would be generalizable to a real-world emergency situation.

"Experimental situations which involve the use of deception are especially prone to difficulties stemming from the reactive nature of experiments" (Jung, 1971, p. 20). Studies concerned with reactions to stress, danger, inflicting of pain on others, guilt, and so forth require that the subjects be convinced of the authenticity of the situation. The experimenters may resort to clever, devious contrivance in order to create the successful deception. However, the subjects are aware that they are participating in an experiment. It is probable that most subjects assume that their introductory psychology instructor is not really going to subject them to physical danger or psychological harm. Further, since most subjects are college students, they presumably have read popular accounts of social psychology research involving deception. Whether through reading, participation in prior experiments, or conversation with other students who have participated as subjects, most college student subjects are alerted to the deceptive character of much psychological research. The plausibility or credibility of any deception procedure in a given experiment is therefore highly suspect. Indeed, McGuire (1969) suggests that the potential artifactual effect of suspiciousness exists *because of* the practice of deception by experimenters.

Debriefing

The effectiveness of deception and the role of subject suspiciousness in an experiment usually are assessed by debriefing. Essentially, **debriefing** involves individually interviewing the subjects after the data are collected; subjects are asked: (1) what suspicions they had about the study, (2) what advance knowledge they received from other subjects or literature in the area, and (3) how much they believed the experimenter's deceptive contrivances. The subjects are also informed of the real nature of the study, and any misleading information about their character, ability, and so on is corrected in the debriefing session. Jung (1971) concludes that debriefing does not occur often enough, and even when it is included, it probably leads experimenters to underestimate the amount of detected deception and prior information about the real nature of the study.

An interesting study of the impact of openness (nondeception) on the conclusion of a project was conducted by Resnick and Schwartz (1973; reported in Rosenthal & Rosnow, 1975). It has been demonstrated in hundreds of research projects that an experimenter can shape the verbal behavior of a subject by saying "good," "okay," or "mm-hm" every time the subject says the correct words. The standard paradigm is to present the subject with a sequence of individual cards with a different verb and the six personal pronouns printed on each card, and request the subject to construct a sentence containing the verb and one of the six pronouns. Verbal rewards ("good") for beginning a sentence with one of two specific pronouns (such as "I" and "we") yields an increasing probability of the use of those two pronouns over the learning trials. Subjects are ususally used as their own controls (repeated-measures, one-group, A – B, baseline design). Resnick and Schwartz manipulated the openness – deception variable by informing one group of the purpose, procedure, and expected results of the study (a prebriefing group). The second group was treated normally; they received the standard instructions about the procedure but no information about the purpose, procedure, and expected results. The uninformed, standard-procedure group yielded results consistent with the hundreds of previous studies. For the prebriefing group the results were just the opposite: the subjects tended to use "I" and "we" *less* often than during baseline. In the debriefing interviews, three subjects mentioned that they suspected an elaborate devious double-reversal manipulation in which the prebriefing procedure was employed because the experimenters really expected the subjects to *resist* conforming to the prediction openly shared and to nonconform by conforming to the prediction! Other subjects responded counter to the demand characteristics in a triple-reverse fashion. If this kind of game-playing is characteristic of college student subjects, then prebriefing subjects is no solution to the deception-artifact problem.

Ethics and Deception

The ethical aspects of deception research are particularly troublesome. Every experimenter who uses active deception of subjects must experience some doubt about the rightness of the behavior, or else the experimenter is engaging in self-deception (McGuire, 1969)! The freedom to conduct research is not an absolute right (Siekevitz, 1976). In most of Western society, the individual is deemed to have a basic right to privacy of thoughts, feelings, and personal life. While this right is also not absolute, it is generally interpreted to mean that human subjects have the right to freely choose to participate in an experiment on the basis of their own evaluation of the information provided by the experimenter ("informed consent"). The ethical dilemma is that deception is sometimes necessary to the external and internal validity of certain research, and deception precludes the possibility of honestly informed consent. Human subjects also have the right to expect protection from physical and psychological harm. Some forms of deception research have included violations of that right. For example, shock and drug studies have caused physical harm. Deception experiments involving frustration, ridicule, demeaning, or failure experiences have been accused of producing harmful psychological effects.

For most researchers, the way to resolve the dilemma is to assess the probable degree of real harm to the subjects. If the deception is so innocuous that it can create no potential harm, then the subject's right to informed consent is deemed of lower value than the broader potential benefit of the research results. No one is likely to be harmed by being told that a study of verbal learning is concerned with the effect of intertrial interval when in fact it is really concerned with the effect of meaningfulness of the material.

If the deception is likely to produce real physical harm, then the research is not possible. If the deception is likely to produce real psychological harm of a lasting nature, then the research is not possible. Between the two extremes, the experimenter must weight the potential value of the study to the advancement of knowledge against a potential, probably temporary, psychological harm to the subjects. Debriefing may serve to terminate the psychological harm produced in a study. In addition, psychologists in general must be concerned about the total public image of the discipline. No long-term good can come of the repeated experience of "cute" and sometimes crass deception at the hands of research psychologists. Subjects who learn they have been duped in a debriefing session may be particularly resentful.

According to Jung (1971), "Examination of a few studies attempting to determine the influence of past deception and suspicion of deception yields no clear-cut answer. Undoubtedly, the type of deception, the type of task, as well as the personalities of the [subjects] can produce different reactions to experimental deception" (p. 33). "We need more research aimed at the question of whether or not deception is harmful. If possible, impartial observers rather than the investigator himself should be employed for this evaluation. Similarly, more investigation of the effectiveness of debriefing is needed. It is appalling that little research has been done in these areas" (p. 63).

Intentional "Errors"

In our review of the experimenter effect, one form of noninteractive effect (not influencing the behavior of the subjects) mentioned was intentional "errors." The content and process of scientific research in any culture at any time is shaped by the social, political, and economic environment. The kinds of questions that are asked, who asks the questions, how the questions are asked, and how the data are interpreted are affected by the total social milieu (Beckwith & Miller, 1976). These subjective, social influences on scientific research can result in at least two kinds of error: (1) Researchers working on a politically or socially explosive topic may be blinded by their own prejudices and, without real awareness, fail to control for variables that could invalidate results supportive of their prejudices; and (2) researchers may consciously distort the procedure or design of an experiment or even create data that support their theories or prejudices. Three recently discovered cases apparently exemplify consciously distorted, fraudulent "research": (1) research on the effect of asbestos fibers on the health of individual workers, (2) research on the relationship between XYY chromosomes and criminal or antisocial behavior, and (3) research on the heritability of intelligence as measured by IQ tests (Beckwith & Miller, 1976; Lewontin, 1976). These kinds of willful "errors" are *not* examples of artifacts of experimentation. They do indicate that the psychology of scientists might be a fruitful field of study.

CONTROLLING ARTIFACTS

The second stage in the response of scientists to artifacts involves attempts to cope with them. At this stage we recognize that one of our "reasonable assumptions" about which variables will *not* affect an experiment is wrong. By definition, artifactual variables are initially recognized as potential defects in methodology (such as confounded designs) that lead to plausible alternative explanations for the results of our experiments. Therefore the control of artifacts requires modificaiton of research methods.

There are three general ways to approach controlling the influence of artifactual variables in a study: (1) modifying the research design; (2) controlling secondary variance by elimination, holding constant, or conservative arrangement (chapter 2); and (3) decreasing the artificiality of the research environment.

Modifying the Research Design

There are at least six specific ways to modify the basic two-group research design to control artifactual variables.

First, the experimenter may employ "**quasi-control**" groups (Orne, 1969), designed to examine the reactive effect of the experimental technique. In contrast to real control groups, quasi-control groups do not yield direct information about the independent variable. One or more groups of randomly assigned subjects are asked to play the role of subjects in one of two ways. Either they are asked to imagine that they are subjects in an experiment and produce data accordingly, or they are asked to pretend that they have been affected by a treatment (such as a drug) which they did not receive or to which they are really immune. The quasi-control subjects in their role-playing are really acting as coexperimenters or experimental assistants rather than as subjects to be manipulated. Their general purpose is to provide evidence of the demand characteristics of a given experiment. If the real experimental treatment group provides data similar to that of the quasi-control, then we know that there are at least two possible explanations of the results—the data are unaffected by artifact or an artifactual variable is operative. The pretending quasi-control group allows the separation of experimenter-expectancy bias from other demand characteristics of an experiment.

Second, the effects of awareness of being a subject (Hawthorne effect and other demand characteristics) may be controlled by using a naturalistic observation, field-study approach in which the measures are as unobtrusive as possible (chapter 6). Jenni and Jenni (1976) provide examples of this approach. Male and female college students' book-carrying behavior was observed in an unobtrusive manner in Montana, Ontario, New York, El Salvador, Costa Rica, and Tennessee. All observation showed similar, consistent sex differences. College females usually wrap one or both arms around the books, which rest on the hip shelf or at the front of the body in line with, or higher than, the hips. College males carry books in one hand away from the body or resting against the side of the body. Further observation indicated that sex differences in physical strength or load size are not consistently related to the behavior differences, and a study of weight and grasp strength failed to reveal any causal relationship. Extensive observations of subjects of every age—children through adults—revealed other consistent behaviors. The data were interpreted to show a subtle but reliable modeling effect. It is extremely unlikely that the subjects were aware of their participation in this series of studies.

Third, Campbell (1969) discusses the utility of control by **systematic, supplemental variation** where direct or complete control is not possible. Essentially, the procedure involves anticipating possible sources of observed differences *other* than the experimental treatment. Once a variable is identified, studies are designed that maximize the chance that that variable will affect the results. If the original data remain essentially unchanged, the tested alternative explanation is eliminated. An excellent example is provided by Bitterman (1965; cited in Campbell, 1969). Bitterman has conducted an extensive series of studies comparing the learning capacities of fish and rats. There is no known way to equate, for fish and rats, the sensorimotor demands of an experimental study. Neither is there a known way to equate the hunger motivation and incentive value of food for the two species. Rats show progressive improvement in the rate of learning over a series of reversal-learning trials; under similar conditions fish do not show progressive improvement. Differences in degree of hunger actually experienced might account for the differences between the species. Testing the fish under the widest possible variation in degree of hunger experienced and measuring for progressive improvement in rate of learning would shed light on this possibility. If progressive improvement is not observed, differences in hunger are not the explanation. Progressive improvement has been observed in rats under extremely varied conditions and has *never* been observed in fish under a wide variety of conditions. Thus, while direct control of various alternative causal variables has not been possible, Bitterman, through the method of systematic, supplemental variation, provides strong support for the hypothesis that the interspecies behavior differences are biologically based.

Fourth, artifacts of measurement may be controlled by using several forms of measurement. Most research studies have used a single dependent-variable measure. Each measurement device or procedure may carry with it various sources of bias or error. Measurement artifacts include response bias, halo effects in rating people (judge's bias toward rating positively in all contexts the person who has received a positive rating in one context), artificial limitation of the range of scores because the measures have ceilings lower than the actual abilities of some subjects, insufficiently precise measures, and so forth. It is possible that an observed effect is peculiar to a particular form of measurement. This is not a pretest-sensitization effect but a limitation on generalization of the test instrument itself. The solution to this general type of artifact is the systematic variation of the type of measurement used. The increasing use of multivariate analyses suggests that researchers are more and more frequently using multiple dependent measures in a given study.

Fifth, one frequently utilized method of dealing with potential artifactual variation is the addition of **expanded-content control groups** (Campbell, 1969). Essentially, a randomly assigned group of subjects experiences more of the environmental factors associated with a treatment than the no-treatment control, but does not experience the presumed crucial element of the treatment. The single-blind placebo control group in psychopharmacological research and the sham-operation control group in psychophysiological research provide two excellent examples of this procedure. In the single-blind placebo control, the subjects receive a "drug" that they expect will have various effects on their behavior; in actuality they receive an essentially inactive substance such as milk-sugar or saline solution. Similarly, the sham-operation controls experience all the aspects of a surgical operation except the supposed critical step. The sham-operation group controls for such factors as surgical shock and post-operative recovery processes. Where factors such as surgical shock have been empirically discounted as causes for an observed effect, the use of sham-operation controls is no longer needed. The most sophisticated form of the expanded-content control group is the yoked-control design described in chapter 8.

Sixth, at the third stage an artifact is studied directly as an independent variable. The randomized-blocks design and various forms of factorial design often include artifactual variables as blocking variables or primary variables in a study. As indicated in chapter 10, the Solomon four-group design is uniquely suited to the examination of pretest-sensitization effects. The cost of utilizing factorial designs is the increased complexity of the procedure and data analysis; the benefit is the clear examination of both the main and interaction effects of a suspected artifactual variable. While this approach will not control for the effect of the unnaturalness of experimental setting, it can be applied to all other aspects of the reactive nature of experimentation.

Eliminating, Conservatively Arranging, and Holding Constant Artifactual Variables

At least three types of control may be employed with a basic two-group design. First, we may use various methods to assess the degree of bias experienced by individual subjects and *eliminate* the severely biased subjects from the data analysis. The most common assessment procedure is the debriefing procedure discussed in the deception section of this chapter. Careful debriefing requires awareness of the fact that the subject may be reluctant to indicate initial suspicions about the experimenter's real intent. Further, the debriefing inquiry is highly sensitive to the experimenter-expectancy-bias effect, in that the experimenter may unintentionally cue the subject as to the appropriate things to say. Orne (1969) suggests that a "pact of ignorance" may operate in the debriefing session, in which neither party really wants to reveal the operation of artifacts. The subjects who have "caught on" to a deception may be reluctant to admit it because such an admission may result in disqualification, and thus the subjects will have wasted their time. The disqualification of subjects is painful to experimenters, for disqualification means that more subjects will have to be run. Probably it would be best to use an equal-status but blind coexperimenter to conduct postexperimental debriefing interviews.

Second, we may control the effects of suspected artifactual variables by the method of *conservative arrangement* (chapter 2). Campbell (1969) describes conservatively arranged procedures used in an anthropology study (Segall, Campbell, & Herskovits, 1966) to control for the suspected artifactual variable of different procedures by the various researchers. The study involved cultural differences in susceptibility to optical illusions. The standard procedure required the anthropologists to present pictures of visual illusions held vertically, 4 ft. from each subject's eye, and record the responses. In a control study, half the subjects were treated exactly as specified by the standard procedure, and half viewed the pictures horizontally at 1½ ft. The latter procedure was assumed to be a more extreme deviation from the proper procedure than any which might have occured with different researchers in different settings. The two procedures with the control group did produce small differences, but these differences were much less than the differences observed among the various cultures studied. The potential artifact of variation in procedure could not account for the observed cross-cultural differences.

Third, we may modify the way the treatment is administered in order to eliminate or *hold constant* the influence of potential artifactual variables. The use of single and double-blind controls to reduce the reactive nature of experimentation has been discussed in chapters 2 and 13 and in the preceding sections of this chapter. The double-blind control procedure is particularly useful for controlling experimenter-expectancy-bias effects. Another way to eliminate various experimenter effects is to eliminate the experimenter by automating the experiment. Taped or printed instructions may eliminate the direct effect of the experimenter at least during the data-collection portion of an experiment. At some point an experimenter must make some contact with the subjects, so automation cannot totally eliminate such effects. A way of dealing with the subjects' tendency to "fake good" as a response to the demand characteristics of a study is the "bogus *pipeline*" method (Rosenthal & Rosnow, 1975). The subjects are led to believe that a physiological monitoring device will detect any lying. Some reactive aspects of this procedure indicate it is not a panacea, but it may prove useful.

Modifying the Experimental Setting

Artifacts also may be controlled by at least two possible variations in experimental setting. First, we might reduce the artifactual effect of the artificial laboratory setting by moving the experiment to a natural setting. The study of the arousal effect of invasions of privacy (chapter 13) and the Western Electric Hawthorne Plant studies represent examples of this approach. As indicated by the Hawthorne effect, the conduct of experimental research in a natural, nonlaboratory environment does reduce the artifactual effect of the unnatural setting, but it does not eliminate other reactive artifacts. The combination of unobtrusive measurement with the power of random assignment and other control characteristics of a field experiment provides an especially powerful control for the reactive effects of experimentation. For example, Adams (1963; cited in Webb, Campbell, Schwartz, & Sechrest, 1966) studied the effect on productivity of subjects' belief that they are unqualified for a job. Both control-group and experimental-group subjects were hired to be interviewers (without awareness that they were part of an experiment) and were paid the same hourly wage. Members of the experimental group, who were led to believe they were not qualified, produced significantly more than the controls.

An interesting combination of unobtrusive measurement, field study, and laboratory study is described by Rosenthal and Rosnow (1975). The procedure, called "dual observation," consists of observing the critical behavior first in the laboratory and then outside the laboratory in an atmosphere which the subject does not connect with the experiment. The difference between observed laboratory data and unobtrusively obtained data provides an estimate of the artifactual bias of the experimental laboratory setting. Rosenthal and Rosnow describe a study in which a posthypnotic suggestion given to control and hypnotized subjects in a laboratory setting was tested outside the laboratory by a secretary in a waiting room, setting up appointments for future laboratory sessions.

A second approach to decreasing the unnaturalness of the laboratory setting is to utilize nonexperimental, naturalistic field-observation studies, as described in chapter 6. Here also, the unobtrusive measurement concept can be fruitfully applied.

As Jung (1971) states, "The experiment is not without its limitations. . . . The existence of such problems need not cause us to abandon the use of the experimental [approach]; rather, recognition of the limitation of experiments warns against the misuse or over-reliance on this [approach]. Such knowledge should aid us in better planning of the conduct of our experiments and lead us to continually check their results against natural observations" (p. 72). Further, as indicated previously in this chapter, we can use the experimental approach to improve the experimental approach.

McGuire (1973) criticized both the standard paradigm of experimental social psychology and the new paradigm of field experiments and naturalistic field research. He suggests that much of traditional social psychology research amounts to simulations of natural behavior conducted in laboratory settings that are carefully stage-managed by the experimenter. If the data do not support the experimenter's theory, the researcher has failed in stage-managing ability. McGuire also suggested that the flight from the laboratory to either type of field study again amounts to stage-managing. The field-study simulation amounts to finding an appropriate setting in which to demonstrate the truth of our theories. McGuire suggested that an alternative paradigm may be emerging, involving complex, multivariate theories of human behavior based on multivariate time-series designs such as the longitudinal, cross-lagged correlation approach (chapter 21). It is true that we are becoming more sophisticated about the limitations of prior approaches and employing more complex measurement and analysis procedures. It appears that the judicious use of multiple methods involving laboratory research field experiments and naturalistic research with multivariate designs will provide both a more realistic and a more comprehensive picture of behavior than the simple two-group designs of the past.

SUMMARY

1. Artifactual behavior is behavior produced as an effect of an experiment. The reactive nature of some research can produce artifactual behavior that cannot be generalized to nonexperimental conditions.
2. The three stages in the life-history of an artifact are (a) ignorance of the artifact, (b) attempts at coping with the artifact, and (c) exploitation of the artifact as an independent variable.
3. An internally valid study has good control of secondary and error variance sources. An externally valid study allows generalization to the subject population, environmental conditions, and treatment conditions sampled in the study. Artifactual variables may limit the external validity, the internal validity, or both types of validity of a study.
4. A research project is a form of human social behavior even when the subjects are not human beings. The complex nature of the social interaction between experimenter and subject can produce artifactual behavior.
5. The actual interaction pattern between subjects and experimenter never follows the rigidly standardized procedures implied by the principle of control. This lack of standardization can (a) increase error variance, (b) interact with the treatment to confound the interpretation of the results, (c) lead to the lack of replication of an effect by different experimenters, (d) increase the chances of different experimenters observing the same results, and (e) increase the uniformity of treatment as actually experienced by each subject.

6. The Hawthorne effect occurs when the subjects are aware of being in an experiment and their behavior is a function of this awareness, not of the experimental treatment. In human social psychology research, awareness of being in an experiment is an important variable that may affect the results.

7. A large proportion of the subjects of published research projects are undergraduate recruits from introductory classes. This fact means that there are severe limitations to the generalization of research results. In addition, many of the subjects are not volunteers. The effect of the volunteer/nonvolunteer variable on the generalizability of research results is unclear.

8. The interaction of a pretest with the experimental treatment is called the pretest-sensitization effect. In simple attitude-change studies, the effect does not appear to occur. The existence of such an interaction seems to depend on other situational variables.

9. All the ways that an experimenter may influence the results of an experiment are referred to by the term "experimenter effect." There are two general classes of experimenter effect, (a) a noninteraction class in which the experimenter influences the data or conclusions but not the subjects' behavior, and (b) an interactive class in which the subjects' behavior is changed. The first type includes observation errors, computational errors, data-interpretation errors, and fraud. The noninteraction type probably has little lasting effect.

10. The interactive experimenter effect includes effects due to the organismic characteristics, behavioral characteristics, and social attributes of the experimenter. Also included in this class is the experimenter-expectancy-bias effect in which the experimenter unintentionally biases the subjects' responses so that the data support the experimenter's predictions.

11. Human subjects may be deceived by experimenters in two different ways: (a) by deliberate misleading or (b) by omission of information. In most cases, omission of information is not likely to be a source of secondary variance or an ethical concern. Deliberate deception can provide both artifactual and ethical concerns.

12. Debriefing is usually used to assess the effectiveness of deceptive procedures and the role of subject suspiciousness in a research study. The debriefing procedure typically involves interviewing the subjects after the experiment to assess their suspiciousness, foreknowledge, and belief in the experimenter's deception. In addition, the subjects are informed of the real nature of the research and misleading, deceptive implications about their character, ability, and so forth are corrected.

13. The ethical dilemma posed by deception is that for certain studies, deception is necessary to the external or internal validity of the research; simultaneously, human subjects have the general right to choose to participate or not participate in the experiment on the basis of the presumed honest information about the study provided by the experimenter.

14. Conscious, fraudulent distortion of an experiment or the creation of false data that support a particular theory or prejudice are not examples of "artifacts of experimentation."

15. The second stage in the life of an artifact involves coping with the discovered artifact. There are three general approaches to controlling an artifact: (a) modifying the research design, (b) adding secondary-variance-control procedures, and (c) modifying the artificiality of the research setting.

16. The various ways to modify the research design to control an artifactual source of variance include: (a) using quasi-control groups of "subjects" that act as if they were subjects; (b) using naturalistic observation, field study procedures involving unobtrusive measures; (c) using systematic supplemental variation of the basic study in which the possible effects of identified artifactual sources are maximized so as to detect their operation; (d) using systematic variation of the measurement procedures; (e) using expanded-content control groups such as placebo groups, sham-operation control groups, and yoked control groups; and (f) including the artifactual variable as an independent variable in the study.

17. The various ways to add secondary-variance-control procedures include: (a) using techniques such as debriefing to eliminate contaminated subjects from the data analysis; (b)

using conservative arrangement of the potential artifactual variable so as to maximize its effect in a way counter to the effect of the primary independent variable; and (c) using single- or double-blind control procedures, automation, or bogus-pipeline techniques with all subjects.

18. Modification of the experimental setting can include (a) moving the experiment from the laboratory to a natural setting (the field experiment), or (b) using naturalistic observation instead of experimentation. Both of these approaches can be improved by the use of unobtrusive measures.

SUGGESTED READINGS

Barber, T. X. *Pitfalls in human research: Ten pivotal points.* New York: Pergamon, 1976.

Barber, T. X., & Silver, M. J. Fact, fiction and the experimenter bias effect. *Psychological Bulletin Monograph,* 1968, *70* (6, Pt. 2).

Campbell, D. T. Prospective: Artifact and control. In R. Rosenthal & R. L. Rosnow (Eds.), *Artifact in behavioral research.* New York: Academic Press, 1969.

Jung, J. *The experimenter's dilemma.* New York: Harper & Row, 1971.

Lana, R. E. Pretest sensitization. In R. Rosenthal & R. L. Rosnow (Eds.), *Artifact in behavioral research.* New York: Academic Press, 1969.

Orne, M. T. Demand characteristics and the concept of quasi-controls. In R. Rosenthal & R. L. Rosnow (Eds.), *Artifact in behavioral research.* New York: Academic Press, 1969.

Rosenberg, M. J. The conditions and consequences of evaluation apprehension. In R. Rosenthal & R. L. Rosnow (Eds.), *Artifact in behavioral research.* New York: Academic Press, 1969.

Rosenthal, R. *Experimenter effects in behavioral research.* New York: Appleton-Century-Crofts, 1966.

Rosenthal, R. Interpersonal expectations: Effects of the experimenter's hypothesis. In R. Rosenthal & R. L. Rosnow (Eds.), *Artifact in behavioral research.* New York: Academic Press, 1969.

Rosenthal, R., & Rosnow, R. L. (Eds.). *Artifact in behavioral research.* New York: Academic Press, 1969.

Rosenthal, R., & Rosnow, R. L. The volunteer subject. In R. Rosenthal & R. L. Rosnow (Eds.), *Artifact in behavioral research.* New York: Academic Press, 1969.

Silverman, I. *The human subject in the psychological laboratory.* New York: Pergamon, 1977.

Sommer, R. Hawthorne dogma. *Psychological Bulletin,* 1968, *70,* 592–595.

15

The Research Report

The scientific research criteria of public, replicable observation require that research projects be reported to the scientific community. The formal character of research reports stands in sharp contrast to magazine and newspaper writing. The emphasis on accuracy and completeness of research reports, the avoidance of speculation divorced from observation, and the demand for brevity diminish the literary attractiveness of research reports. However, the powerful ideas presented can motivate reading, and the egoistic pleasure of publication can keep you at the difficult task of writing a report.

Whether the data from an experiment support or fail to support the hypotheses, the information should be made available to others. Working secretly and alone, individuals such as Leonardo da Vinci and Gregor Mendel made brilliant contributions to knowledge. Their achievements at first stood outside scientific knowledge because the research was not reported so that it could be verified. Not until the research was published could their results be incorporated into organized bodies of scientific knowledge.

The printing press, whose development fostered the rapid expansion of knowledge in the physical sciences, can be considered a major development in scientific equipment. Books and scientific papers provide permanent records of observations and hypotheses, transmitting information rapidly and precisely to a large number of people. The free exchange of information provided by printed records is necessary to the growth and development of the sciences.

As a student, you may wonder how research reports and publication affect you. They affect you in several ways: first, you must read reports in order to increase your knowledge; second, you must write reports in order to satisfy requirements of certain psychology classes, and finally, you may publish a report yourself.

READING A RESEARCH REPORT

Reading a research report in the *Journal of Experimental Psychology* is quite different from reading the advice columns in *Playboy* or *Playgirl*. The most obvious difference is the content of the two kinds of publications. However, the difference that is most relevant to this discussion is the style of writing. In technical, scientific writing, stylistic devices that attract attention to words and sounds are avoided. Poetic expressions, alliteration, slang, and metaphors are appropriate to popular magazines but not to scientific writing. Students tend to describe scientific writing as difficult to read, boring, tedious, heavy, or sleep-inducing. One student commented, "This book is so dry the bookworms have to carry their own canteens" (Bartz, 1976). Too often such criticisms are justified. As a consequence, the most important requirement for reading a scientific journal is sufficient motivation to stay at the task.

The following procedure may help to increase your interest in reading scientific material or at least help you to endure the dullness often dictated by publication costs, convention, and the objectives of technical writing. First, pay close attention to the title of the article; if properly written it should summarize the main idea of the report. Then read the abstract or summary and look at the tables, graphs, and figures. This exercise may leave you with some unanswered questions. For example, an abstract might suggest that students who meditate perform better on final examinations than students who do not. Reading such an abstract may lead to questions such as: (1) What kind of meditation? (2) How long does it take to have an effect? (3) How long does the effect last? and (4) How much better do meditating students perform? It may help to write down these questions as they occur. An important question you may ask is "What are the independent and dependent variables in the experiment?" The title and abstract should give you that information.

Next read the entire article, keeping in mind your questions. As you read, stop occasionally and ask yourself what you have just read. If you can recite the main content of your reading, you are probably understanding and learning the material. If you cannot summarize what you have just read, either you are not paying attention or the writer has not presented the ideas clearly. Reread the material and test yourself again. Resist the urge to skip over unclear sections; you may accidentally miss the most important information in the report. This recitation technique, rehearsal of material for later recall, reinforces and consolidates learning.

After you have read the entire article and recited the details to yourself, review the complete study in terms of the relationship between the independent and dependent variables, the control procedures, the results, and the conclusion regarding support or lack of support for the research hypothesis. Review is essential to coding the material for long-term memory storage. Using memory games or mnemonic devices facilitates storage and recall. Lorayne and Lucas (1974) describe such memory-aiding devices.

SQ3R
The relatively simple process just described is called the SQ3R method: *Survey, Question, Read, Recite,* and *Review.* Finally, as you are reading an article and afterwards, try to relate your reading to other information you possess. The more of these associations you make, the better you will understand and the longer you will remember the material.

Critical Analysis
Once you have mastered the content of a report, the next step is to evaluate the study. A scientific report, in addition to presenting the details of a study, also presents a theoretical point of view and a research conclusion in terms of that point of view. Beyond understanding a report, your task as a reader is to analyze the research project and the research conclusion critically. You should ask questions such as these:

1. Was there a clear relationship between the conceptual hypothesis and the background research and theory?
2. Was the experimental hypothesis clearly derived from the conceptual hypothesis?
3. Were the operational definitions sufficiently precise and detailed?
4. Was the research design appropriate to the research study?
5. Were the subject selection, assignment, and treatment procedures ethical, and were they appropriate to the research question?
6. Was the entire research procedure described well enough to permit precise replication?
7. Did the research procedures adequately control for all plausible, potentially relevant sources of secondary variance?
8. Was error variance adequately minimized?
9. Were the results adequately summarized?
10. Was the statistical analysis appropriate to the research question, the research design, and the data?

11. Did the conclusion depend on or ignore the data?

12. Were the experimenter's generalizations appropriate to the sampling procedures and the reliability of the results?

Even the most sophisticated researchers occasionally make errors that journal editors and manuscript reviewers discover by asking such questions.

Critical analysis of research reports is an excellent way to learn the basic concepts of experimental design and the various techniques for implementing the principle of control. As you become proficient in reading research reports, reading for content and critical analysis occur simultaneously.

WRITING A RESEARCH REPORT

Not all students will be able to publish their research reports in an American Psychological Association research journal. However, it is good practice to write research papers in a manner closely approximating American Psychological Association publication style. The second edition of the *Publication Manual of the American Psychological Association* (1974) is *the* authoritative source of information on style and format of research manuscripts. The 136-page manual is an excellent, detailed source of information, and we will not attempt to duplicate or even summarize the highlights of that publication. The remainder of this chapter will outline some of the criteria for a research report, provide a brief outline of the format for a research report, briefly discuss oral reports, and present a sample report.

General Criteria

Research data and conclusions can be communicated in a variety of ways, ranging from a term paper to a research article in a professional journal. Whatever the vehicle of communication, you should adhere to certain general guidelines in reporting your research.

Accuracy

First, the information contained in a report must be *accurate*. Reporting erroneous research data not only wastes the time and effort spent in the laboratory, but can have major consequences for other researchers who accept the report as valid. For example, a German experimental physicist incorrectly measured the absorption cross-section of graphite. As a consequence, the German scientists working on the atomic bomb chose not to try to build a graphite-moderated reactor and focused all their efforts on a heavy-water–moderated reactor. British and Norwegian commandos managed to stop the production of heavy water; thus Hitler did not get his magic weapon (Libby, 1968).

In addition to accuracy of data, all quotations and citations must be accurately reported. It is always legitimate and often most efficient to quote from previous research reports, as long as you use quotation marks, quote accurately, and cite the source of the quoted material. Using the words of others without proper acknowledgement is called plagiarism; it is theft that is inexcusable, unethical, sometimes illegal, and at least at some schools grounds for academic probation or dismissal.

Completeness

A second general characteristic of a research report is that it be *complete* enough to allow verification. In addition to assisting replication, as research on a specific behavior progresses, more details concerning the experimental conditions are found to be relevant. If an earlier experiment is described in sufficient detail, the data can be reexamined in the light of new developments.

Brevity

A third criterion is that a research report be *concise*. Those reports which are brief and concise are more likely to be read. The attempt to be concise seems contrary to the goals of accuracy and completeness. One way to describe an experiment accurately and completely is to pour sentences into the research paper until everything is covered. It is doubtful that a reader will be willing to wade through all of the verbiage. A well-organized report can be compact without sacrificing the other goals of communication.

Clarity

A fourth criterion is that a research report should be *readable*. The other criteria place severe restrictions on literary freedom; however, within these limitations, you should write for the reader rather than simply document facts. The report should present ideas in a logical progression that facilitates understanding. You are writing for someone who does not know what you did, so review your writing from that person's point of view. The unrestricted and undefined use of jargon reduces clarity and may violate the criteria of accuracy and completeness.

Writing a research report is not an easy task; in fact, it consumes a substantial part of a researcher's time. Most research psychologists, including the authors of this text, have piles of partially analyzed data that they have not found the time to describe in a research report. It is easy to find reasons to delay the difficult task of writing a good technical report.

The first draft of a complete research report is never adequate. Often, even the third draft can be substantially improved. It is helpful to have someone else criticize your work; of course, reacting defensively to that criticism is self-defeating. We recommend that classmates get together in pairs to criticize each other's second drafts. Most professional research journals send all submitted research manuscripts to two or three acknowledged researchers in the field for critical review. In addition, the editor or editorial staff copy-edits the final drafts of research reports. Occasionally the reviewer and copy editors make only minor changes in a manuscript; more frequently substantial revisions are necessary.

Technical writing, creative writing, and standard English expository writing require some of the same basic skills: precision, clarity, conciseness, logical progression, appropriate usage, and the conventional mechanics of writing. In contrast to creative writing, technical writing focuses on accuracy and completeness of description while discounting flair, novelty, and style.

To assist both authors and readers, the format for a psychology research report has been standardized. The format allows reports to be read as rapidly and efficiently as possible so that the reader can focus on evaluating the information presented. The best way to learn the format is to read research articles and write research reports.

Format

There are eight parts or sections to a manuscript: (1) title, (2) author's name and institutional affiliation, (3) abstract, (4) introduction, (5) method, (6) results, (7) discussion, and (8) references. In addition, you may attach an appendix if it is necessary. Let us examine each section.

Title   The title should summarize the main research idea and, if possible, state clearly the relationship between the independent and dependent variables being studied. Titles such as "Effect of feedback contingencies on the control of occipital alpha" and "Covariation and temporal contiguity as principles of causal inference in young children" make a clear statement of article content for ease of indexing and retrieval and provide the reader with a preview of things to come.

Do not make any direct reference to research methods or results in the title or include redundancies such as "A study of" or "An experimental investigation of" (APA, 1974, p. 14). Do not phrase titles as questions. Try to keep the title of the paper to a maximum of 15 words. Clever or catchy titles, such as "The snark was a boojum" (Beach, 1950) or "Pigeons in a pelican" (Skinner, 1960), do not convey much information; but, they are likely to be read because of the reputation of the authors. Undergraduate students cannot afford such cleverness.

Author's Name and Institutional Affiliation   The second section is self-explanatory. Include as authors anyone who contributed substantially to the project (see APA, 1974, pp. 14–15) and state their institutional affiliation without abbreviating it. The form is illustrated in the sample report presented later in this chapter. The comparatively minor assistance of individuals other than the author is recognized in a footnote, as illustrated in the example.

Abstract   An abstract is designed to give the reader a very brief preview, in 100–175 words, of what to expect in the text of the article. The abstract immediately follows the title and assists readers in deciding whether the article is important for thém to read. An abstract provides the following information:

1. The kind of problem investigated.
2. The subjects used.
3. The name of the apparatus used.
4. An indication of the experimental procedure.
5. A statement of the major results.
6. If space permits, the major conclusions drawn from the research.

An example of an abstract is found in the article by Horvath (1977, p. 127) entitled "The effect of selected variables on interpretation of polygraph records."

Ten field-trained polygraph examiners (evaluators) made blind judgments of a stratified sample of the polygraph records of 112 criminal suspects. Correct calls averaged 63.1% ($p < .001$), 64.1% on records where ground truth was established by confessions (verified) and 62.1% on records where ground truth was not known (unverified) but where the criterion measure was the original testing examiners' judgment. Evaluators' hit rates in both situations were quite similar, averaging about 77% true positives and about 51% true negatives; the variable having the greatest effect on evaluators' errors was the type of investigation from which records were drawn. Reliability coefficients showed high interevaluator agreement on both verified and unverified records, .89 and .85, respectively.

Another example appears later in this chapter. Notice that in both abstracts there is a limited use of technical terminology in order to meet space limitations. The abstract is usually the last part of an article to be written.

Introduction   The introduction of a research article is not labeled, since it begins a new page with the title at the top and is obviously an introduction. The major purpose of the introduction is to inform the reader of the specific problem under question and the research strategy. The introduction should clearly state the purpose of the study and the relationship between the research problem and the research design. Also there should be a discussion of the theoretical implications of your study. The APA *Publication manual* (1974) extensively describes the content of the introduction.

The content of the introduction may be organized as follows:

1. Begin with the broadest conception of the problem.
2. Discuss the origin of the problem and the conceptual hypothesis of your study.
3. Indicate the theories and previous research related to your study.
4. Describe important previous relevant studies, but do not write a complete literature review. Cite your sources correctly.
5. Give a careful and precise summary of the present state of knowledge in the area of the problem, noting the most important studies.
6. Show how the present study evolved from previous knowledge in the area.

It is important to conclude with a clear, concise statement of the problem under investigation. The statement should include the experimental hypothesis being tested and the identifications relating the hypothesis to empirical events.

Method   The method section tells the reader, step by step, how the study was conducted. The detail should be sufficient to allow readers to replicate your study. The method section usually is divided into three subsections: subjects, apparatus, and procedure. In complex studies, a subsection on research design may appear after that on subjects.

SUBJECTS   The section on subjects gives all relevant demographic details about the participants in the study. It should tell who participated in the study, their sex, age, and other relevant characteristics, the total number of participants, and how they were selected from the population. The number assigned to each treatment condition may be included here or under procedure. If you used animals in your study, be sure to indicate their sex, age, genus, species, strain number, and other relevant details.

APPARATUS   The apparatus section should include a brief description of the laboratory equipment used in the study. Description of special commercial equipment should include manufacturer and model number. Drawings may be necessary for complex equipment.

PROCEDURE   The most important part of the method section is the description of procedure, a step-by-step, blow-by-blow description of what you did. It must include what you told human participants prior to the beginning of the study and the method of assignment to groups (if that was not covered in the subjects or optional research design subsections). Be sure to describe the randomization or other control procedures used. Detail each phase or step of your study from beginning to end. If human subjects are involved, state the debriefing procedure used (chapter 14). In order to ease this difficult task of description, it is helpful to keep a detailed log of events as you conduct your experiment. Your detailed research proposal also can make this task easier, as it can serve as a convenient place to note variations from the planned procedure. Do not slight the procedure section, because the reader will need this information if replication is attempted. "Remember that the method section should tell your reader *what* you did and *how* you did it" (APA, 1974, p. 18).

Results   The results section describes the data obtained in an experiment. The description should be complete enough to allow readers to examine the data in any way they wish. Here is a suggested format:

Constructing Tables and Figures

1. First describe or summarize the data. Tables, figures, and descriptive statistics may be used. In constructing tables and figures, do not use abstract codes such as "Group A," "Group B," and "Condition 1." If the size and complexity of the illustration dictate abbreviation, use codes that have some relationship to the thing coded and decode in the caption. For example, use "Group C" for control, "Group P" for punishment, and "T1" for trial 1. Do not use different colors to indicate different groups in a line graph; use dashed lines, dotted lines, or other black-and-white identification symbols. Color printing is expensive, and some of us are color-dichromatic (color-weak) and have difficulty distinguishing colors such as red and green. Each table and figure is presented on a separate page. For class papers, your instructor may direct you to insert the tables and figures in the appropriate place in the text of the report. In manuscripts to be published, figures, tables, captions, and footnotes appear at the end of the manuscript. In every case, the headings, code identifications, and captions of tables and figures should provide sufficient information for the reader to understand the illustration without having to refer to the text. In single-subject studies, all the data are presented, usually in graph form. In group studies, if your instructor requires the inclusion of all raw data measures for each subject, you may place them in an appendix.
2. Analyze the data in terms of the experimental hypotheses. Name and present the calculated values of any statistical tests. Present the probability levels obtained.
3. If observed, any interesting results not related to the experimental hypotheses may be described.
4. After presentation, the results are interpreted in the following section. If the material in the results section is relatively brief, the results and discussion sections may be combined.

The APA *Publication manual* (1974) makes an important point about results. "Caution: Do not infer trends from data that fail by a small margin to meet the usual levels of significance [chapter 16]. Such results are best interpreted as caused by chance and are best reported as such. Treat the results section like an income tax return: Take what's coming to you, but no more" (p. 19).

Discussion   In the discussion section, you interpret and evaluate the results of your research. The preceding section is concerned with the clear and accurate transmisison of empirical observations. The discussion section allows you to select, emphasize, and interpret your findings in the way you think is most informative. We suggest the following organization:

1. Discuss the results of the experiment in relationship to the alternative or conflicting theories and hypotheses presented in the introduction. Summarize the present state of knowledge with the addition of the data from your experiment. Include the limits imposed on generalization by the subject-sampling procedure and operational definitions.
2. Discuss the implications for further theorizing and research.
3. Avoid extreme speculation (leave that to other academic disciplines) and excuses. If you suggest improvements upon your experiment, make them brief. Do not succumb to the temptation to describe the flaws in your study endlessly.
4. In general, state whether or not your study answered the questions stated in the introduction. Failure to find support for your experimental hypothesis is not bad; it is information. A research study is never a failure merely because the prediction and results do not agree.

References   The proper form for listing references confuses many students because it is so different from the forms previously learned. The APA *Publication manual* (1974) is the sole authority in this regard and should be consulted when in doubt. References are listed in alphabetical order by author's last name. The format for each reference is as follows:

1. Author: Put all authors' last names and initials in reverse order. For example, Bandersnatch, J. P., & Stitts, P. L.
2. Title: article, chapter in a book, or entire book.
3. Facts of publication:
   a. for journals, the complete journal name (do not abbreviate), date of publication, volume number, and the inclusive pages;
   b. for books, city where the book was published, the publisher's name, and the date of publication.

The *Publication manual*'s punctuation rules are: "Use *periods* to separate the three major subdivisions of a reference citation: author, title, and publication data. Use *commas* within the subdivisions (e.g., between date and volume number in a journal entry). Use a *colon* between the place of publication and the book publisher. Use *parentheses* for extensions, qualifications, or interpretations of each subdivision or the entire entry" (p. 61). Note that, since most typewriters do not have italics, you underline the words that need italics.

The following examples may be used as guide for your references format:

1. Journal Article:
   Skinner, B. F. A case history in scientific method. <u>American Psychologist,</u> 1960, <u>15,</u> 28–37.
   Warkany, J., & Takacs, E. Lysergic acid diethylamide (LSD): No teratogenicity in rats. <u>Science,</u> 1968, <u>159,</u> 731–732.

2. Books:

Ornstein, R. E. <u>The mind field.</u> New York: Grossman, 1976.

Edited book:

Dohrenwend, B. S., & Dohrenwend, B. P. (Eds). <u>Stressful life events: Their nature and effects.</u> New York: Wiley, 1974.

Article in an edited book:

Stevenson, H. W., & Wright, J. C. Child psychology. In J. B. Sidowski (Ed.), <u>Experimental methods and instrumentation in psychology.</u> New York: McGraw-Hill, 1966.

3. Unpublished Manuscript:

Pardini, J. C. <u>An adroit analysis of the sex life of the sponge.</u> Unpublished manuscript, 1972. (Available from Department of Psychology, University of the Pacific, Stockton, California 95211).

For other examples and types of references, consult the APA *Publication manual* (1974).

A Published Research Report

The following paper was published in the *Journal of Experimental Psychology: Human Perception and Performance* in 1976. It is printed in typewritten format to illustrate how your papers should be typed. Note the constant use of double-spacing and the use of underlining for italics. Your instructor may request that you locate footnotes and figures at the appropriate places in the text rather than at the end as illustrated here. We hope you will be able to use the previous section and this example to construct your own research report.

The Predominance of Seven and the Apparent Spontaneity of Numerical Choices

Michael Kubovy and Joseph Psotka
Yale University

Abstract

When asked to report the first digit that comes to mind, a predominant number (28.4%) of the respondents choose 7. Three further experiments sought to establish whether this predominance is due to an automatic activation process or to a deliberate choice. The first experiment shows that the response pattern changes markedly (with 17.3% choosing 7) when the request is for a number between 6 and 15. The second experiment shows that if 7 is mentioned by the experimenter as an example of a response, its frequency drops significantly (to 16.6%). The third experiment shows that if a number in the 20s is requested, the choice pattern remains unchanged (27 is chosen by 27.7%), but if a number in the 70s is requested, 77 is chosen only by 15.5%. All these results are consistent with the idea that subjects choose the response such that it will appear to comply with the request for a spontaneous response.

Published in the *Journal of Experimental Psychology: Human Perception and Performance*, 1976, *2*, 291–294. Copyright 1976 by the American Psychological Association. Reprinted by permission. In manuscript form the title and authors' names appear on a separate page.

The Predominance of Seven and the Apparent Spontaneity of Numerical Choices

Seven Yale University undergraduates asked 558 people to give the first number between 0 and 9 that came to mind. Figure 1 shows the proportion of respondents choosing each digit from 0 to 9, together with similar data from several previous experiments (Heywood, 1972; Simon, 1971; Simon & Primavera, 1972). Although these data were collected under a variety of different conditions in a variety of places (Heywood obtained his data in England), they all show a striking prominence in the choice of the digit 7. Dietz (1933) reported a preference for 7 among 500 people choosing a number from 0 to 99 in yet another country, the Netherlands. In fact, the phenomenon is so reliable that it is reported as commonplace by Fodor (1947) and is used as the basis for parlor tricks (Gardner, 1973) and mindreading acts. In addition, the number 7 has a long history of superstition behind it.[1]

One psychologist (Heywood, 1972) commented that "the existence of such unmotivated preferences remains a bit of experimental debris that tidy psychological theories have yet to sweep up" (p. 358). The purpose of the present paper is to show that this stable and pandemic phenomenon of heptaphilia is far from being unmotivated.

The first experiment in this series is designed to establish a baseline to which we will compare later results.

EXPERIMENT 1

Method

Seven students[2] from an introductory statistics section taught by one of the authors (M. Kubovy) stopped 558 passersby on the Yale campus and said, "Please give me the first number that comes to mind between 0 and 9."

Results

Since these results were designed to establish a baseline, they are presented with the results from previous experiments cited in the introduction and are shown in Figure 1. Thirteen clusters, ranging in size from 14 to 328, were averaged: 2 (males and females) from Simon (1971), 2 (males and females) from Simon and Primavera (1972), 1 from

Heywood (1972), and 8 from Kubovy's seven students (one of whom reported separate data for males and females). In 11 of the 13 clusters, 7 was the modal choice, with an estimated percentage of 28.36%. The standard error of the percentage of 7 was calculated assuming random unequal cluster sampling (Kish, 1965, pp. 187-188); it was found to be 1.93%. The square-root design effect (the factor by which we would underestimate the standard error had we pooled our clusters and considered them as one simple random sample of the same number of elements, $\underline{n}$ = 1,770) was found to be 1.915.

In Experiments 2-4 we shall assume a design effect of 3.666 ($\sqrt{\text{deff}}$ = 1.915). That is, we shall augment the standard errors of our estimated proportions by a factor of 1.915 in order to take into account the effects of clustering.

EXPERIMENT 2

There are two ways to conceptualize the predominance of 7 in the results of Experiment 1. On the one hand, 7 could be an automatic association activated by the request. If such were the case, the frequency of the response would be resistant to subtle suggestion and context effects. On the other hand, this choice could be the outcome of a decision process which is under conscious control. In such a case, 7 might predominate because it appears to be the most "appropriate" response to the request for a spontaneous choice. It follows that the frequency of the response would change in contexts where 7 is not a spontaneous-looking response.

The following experiment was designed to demonstrate that the frequency of 7 is context sensitive. We simply chose the set of numbers from 6 to 15 as the set of responses.

Method

The experiment was conducted on 237 undergraduates in two Yale psychology classes: 30 students in introductory statistics (not the section taught by Kubovy) and 207 students in introductory psychology.[3] The students were asked to write down "the first number that comes to mind between 6 and 15."

Results and Discussion

The choice frequency distribution is shown in Figure 2. The pattern of results is strikingly different from that of Experiment 1.

There are three notable features to these data. First, 7 is not preferred over 8 and 9. Second, single digits are overwhelmingly preferred over two-digit responses. Third, numbers which have a special connotation (7, 11, 12, 13) are not chosen more often than other responses having the same number of digits (8 and 9, 10 and 14).

Seven was chosen by 17.3% (standard error: 1.85%, assuming random unequal cluster sampling) of the subjects, 11.05% less than the baseline, which is a statistically significant difference, $z = 2.75$, $p = .0035$ (after multiplying the standard error, 1.85, by 1.915).

This context sensitivity of the numerical response does not preclude its being automatically activated. It does however reduce the plausibility of such a mechanism.

EXPERIMENT 3

If 7 is not automatically activated by the request, then perhaps it predominates because it appears to be an "appropriate" response. The present experiment reduces the apparent spontaneity of 7 by suggesting to the subjects that it is on the experimenter's mind and could be a "typical" response.

Method

The experiment was conducted on 319 undergraduates in three Yale psychology classes. The students were asked to write down "the first number that comes to mind between 0 and 9, avoiding fractions, and using only whole numbers like 7."

Results

The choice frequency distribution is shown in Figure 3. As expected, the frequency of 7 is dramatically reduced: It is chosen by only 16.61% (standard error: 2.18%) of the students. Thus there is an 11.75% drop in the choice of 7, which is a statistically significant difference; $z = 2.55$, $p = .0054$ (after multiplying the standard error, 2.18, by 1.915).

EXPERIMENT 4

A second method for reducing the apparent spontaneity of 7 is employed in this experiment; it is designed to make the choice of 7 appear obvious and easily explicable. Since spontaneity implies freedom from obvious causality, we expect respondents who seek to appear to comply with the request for the first response that comes to mind to shun a trite response.

Method

Two groups of subjects were studied. The first, consisting of a class of 166 undergraduates in an introductory psychology section, was asked to give a number between 20 and 29. The other, consisting of 139 students enrolled in another section of the same class, was asked to give a number between 70 and 79.

Results

The results are shown in Figure 4. Twenty-seven was selected by 27.7% (standard error: 6.65%) of the respondents who were asked to choose in the 20s, whereas 77 was selected only by 15.5% (standard error: 6.08%) of the respondents who were asked to choose in the 70s. Thus, 27 was chosen .7% less often in the 20s than 7 was chosen among the single digits; this difference is not significant with the design effect factor (z = .10) or without it (z = .17). On the other hand, 77 was chosen 12.86% less often in the 70s than 7 among the single digits, which is a statistically significant difference, z = 2.01, p = .022. The difference between the two groups (12.20%) is statistically significant if a standard comparison of proportions is performed, z = 2.60, p = .0047.

GENERAL DISCUSSION

The four experiments support the notion that the predominance of 7 is due to a choice. The data are also compatible with the idea that the choice in tasks of this sort is motivated by the desire to appear to comply with the request of the experimenter, even when there is no utilitarian reason to do so. The experimenter's request is essentially a request for a spontaneous response, and the subject is placed in a paradoxical situation—only if he does not try to comply can he comply. But then his response might not appear to be in compliance because of its commonness or obviousness. So, if he wishes to appear to comply, the subject must carefully select his response and thus fail to comply. We believe that this is what subjects do.

Why does 7 appear spontaneous? Perhaps 7 is unique among the numbers from 0 to 9 because it has no multiples among these numbers, and yet it is itself not a multiple of any of these numbers. The numbers fall into groups: 2, 4, 6, 8 form one group; 3, 6, 9 form another. Only 0, 1, 5, 7 remain. One can rule out 0 and 1 for being endpoints, and perhaps 5 for being a traditional midpoint. This leaves us with 7 in the unique position of being, as it were, the "oddest" digit.

REFERENCES[a]

Dietz, P. A. Over onderbewuste voorkeur. Nederlandsche[3] tijdschrift voor psychologie, 1933, 1, 145–162.

Fodor, N. The psychology of numbers. Journal of Clinical Psychopathology, 1947, 8, 525–556; 628–654; 841–847.

Gardner, M. An astounding self-test of clairvoyance by Dr. Matrix. Scientific American, 1973, 229, 98–101.

Heywood, S. The popular number seven or number preference. Perceptual and Motor Skills, 1972, 34, 357–358.

Kish, L. Survey sampling. New York: Wiley, 1965.

Miller, G. A. The magical number seven plus or minus two: Some limits on our capacity for processing information. Psychological Review, 1956, 63, 81–97.

Simon, W. E. Number and color responses of some college students: Preliminary evidence for a "blue seven phenomenon." Perceptual and Motor Skills, 1971, 33, 373–374.

Simon, W. E., & Primavera, L. H. Investigation of the "blue seven phenomenon" in elementary and junior high school children. Psychological Reports, 1972, 31, 128–130.

[a]Normally presented beginning on a separate page of the manuscript.

Footnotes

A partial report on this investigation was presented at the 45th annual meeting of the Eastern Psychological Association, Philadelphia, April 18, 1974. Alice F. Healy did much to improve the clarity of this paper with her comments on various drafts.

Joseph Psotka is now at the Department of Psychology, University of Waterloo, Canada N2L 3G1.

Requests for reprints should be sent to Michael Kubovy, Department of Psychology, Yale University, New Haven, Connecticut 06520.

[1]Even so eminent a psychologist as George A. Miller has quite candidly admitted his attraction to 7 (1956, p. 96).

[2]We are grateful to the following students for their diligent data collection: Lon M. Berkeley, Debbie L. Davis, Cheryl A. Lewis, Peter E. Marshall, Jonathan T. Walker, Greg J. Wiber, and Walter R. Winning.

[3]Special thanks go to H. L. Roediger of Purdue University, to Jeff Carlson, Mary Weigand, and Edward Thompson of Southern Connecticut State College, to Anne Peplau of the University of California, Los Angeles, and to Robert P. Abelson, Barry P. Cook, James E. Cutting, Alice F. Healy, and Robert Rescorla at Yale University, for their collaboration in Experiments 2–4, and in studies preliminary to them.

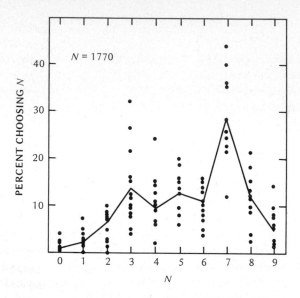

Figure 1. Frequency distribution for Experiment 1, with data from similar experiments.[b]

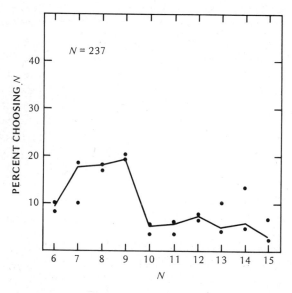

Figure 2. Frequency distribution for Experiment 2.

　　[b]Normally presented in a manuscript with one figure to a page.

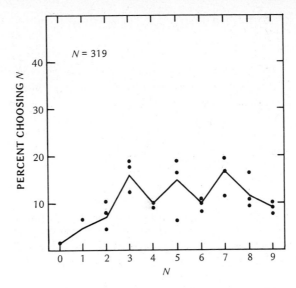

Figure 3. Frequency distribution for
Experiment 3.

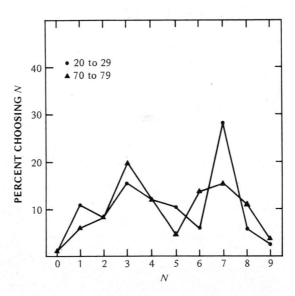

Figure 4. Frequency distribution for
responses in the 20s and 70s for
Experiment 4.

ORALLY PRESENTING A RESEARCH REPORT

Most research is communicated through written reports; however, the most current research is presented at psychological conventions and invited lectures. In most cases, the presentation of research papers at conventions follows the format of a written research report. This fact is understandable but unfortunate. The time limit for most paper-presentation sessions, about 15 to 20 min. per paper, does not allow a detailed presentation of methods and results. The object of presenting a paper at a convention is to let the listeners know what you are doing currently. This objective is not the same as for a written report. A 10-min. informal overview of the study, involving the research question, the subjects, the general procedures, and the most important results, is sufficient. Stick to a few main points and be redundant in presenting them.

If slide projectors are allowed, 35-mm slides of the research design, equipment, and graphs of the key results can be helpful. Slide shows are dangerous because you do not have time to solve mechanical, slide-projector problems (which seem to occur frequently at conventions) and because the viewing conditions for the audience are often abysmal (posts in the way, lighting too bright, and viewing screens placed so that only half of the audience can see them). As a more functional but costly alternative, you can prepare a several-page handout of the key information that would be presented in a slide show. It is difficult to project the size of the audience; but you should prepare more handouts than you expect to need. It is also difficult for you to keep the audience's attention when they have handouts to examine.

Most of us fear speaking in front of strange groups. One way we deal with these fears is to *read* research reports. There are few activities more boring and confusing than listening to a nervous person hurriedly read a lengthy research report. A better way to deal with this fear is to prepare and practice an informal presentation in which you do not read anything. When several students, graduate and undergraduate, are going to present papers at a convention, many psychology departments hold practice sessions that interested students and faculty attend. In addition to decreasing the magnitude of stage fright, the audience at practice sessions can provide helpful suggestions for improving the quality of the presentation. It sometimes helps if you remember that the audience knows you are nervous because most have had the same experience, and that the audience is really concerned about understanding the essence of your study rather than criticizing your work. Worrying about potential criticism of your study is a waste of time because there is usually little or no time for questions and answers, and most of the audience will be satisfied if they can just comprehend your report.

Several psychology departments organize annual, regional, undergraduate research conventions to which all undergraduate students in the area are invited. These departments send out bulletins noting dates and addresses for submitting potential reports. For either the professional convention or the undergraduate convention, it is useful to prepare a complete, formal, written report from which the orally presented material is derived. These formal written reports also can be duplicated for those who are really interested in your work and request a copy.

VALUES AND DIFFICULTIES OF PUBLICATION

Advantages of Publication

The transmission of information enhances scientific progress in several ways. Published research occasionally indicates *blind alleys* or fruitless approaches to a research problem that may be avoided by subsequent experimenters. It also reduces the likelihood of needless repetitions or *redundancy* by researchers who read the publications. The chief value of research publications is that they allow the possibility of *verification* and add to the systematic *body of knowledge* of a science. The results of experiments at one laboratory are used to supplement or clarify the results of experiments at another laboratory.

Methodological innovations (in equipment or procedures) are described in research reports. Research publications also serve a *historical* function. Human beings place a high value on identifying who was the first person to accomplish something. The date of receipt of manuscript and the date of first publication serve as official historical records in science.

Undergraduate Publication

Almost all serious science students dream about the day when they can point proudly to a published research study. Publishing as an undergraduate happens rather infrequently, but it does occur. Often undergraduate research projects are well done and provide significant information; with a little more work they can be submitted for publication. Instructors will help if asked. Publication while an undergraduate can greatly enhance your chances of being accepted into graduate or professional school. The fact that you carried out a publishable study as an undergraduate usually impresses graduate admission committees. So, if your goals include graduate education, you should seriously consider publication, especially in these times of high competition for admission to graduate education.

The Fickleness of Journal Editors and Reviewers

As a closing note, we present two letters from the editors of two different journals concerning the same research study submitted for publication. Both the *Journal of Abnormal Psychology* and the *Journal of Abnormal Child Psychology* are published in the United States and have international distribution. The recipients of these two letters felt that their future dealings with the journal editors would be unduly jeopardized if the censored material in the two letters were published. However, the letters are real and we do have permission to reprint them without identifying names. The first letter is from the *Journal of Abnormal Psychology*.

March 13, 197—

Dr. X
Department of Psychology
School Z

Dear Dr. X:

I have now had the opportunity to receive reviews of your article with [Dr. Y] on ["Title of the article"]. Both reviewers recommend that your article be rejected. Their remarks to the author are enclosed. I'm afraid I have to agree with their evaluation and reject your article.

Please be assured that we will be happy to receive further articles from you and your colleagues describing and evaluating your work with . . . children.

Sincerely yours,

The Editor

The same report was subsequently submitted to the *Journal of Abnormal Child Psychology,* and the editor responded with the following letter.

May 14, 197—

Dr. X
Department of Psychology
School Z

Dear Dr. X:

Your paper, co-authored with [Dr. Y, "Title of article"], has been accepted for publication in the *Journal of Abnormal Child Psychology.*

The reviewers have suggested a number of minor stylistic changes in the manuscript, but rather than bother you with these, I will edit the copy somewhat myself. You will have a chance to respond to any changes at the time you have the opportunity to correct the galley proofs.

Sincerely yours,

The Editor

We include these two letters to point out the inconsistency of reviewers across various journals. The content and purpose of a research article obviously can be misinterpreted by different readers. Moral of the story: if you have an article that you and your research advisor think makes a contribution to the field of psychology, submit it a few times. Maybe you will succeed in getting it published. Even if you do not, you will have achieved new knowledge, and perhaps the experience will motivate you to try another research study.

SUMMARY

1. Research results must be communicated to the research community so that they may be verified and be incorporated into the organized body of scientific knowledge.

2. The SQ3R method—survey, question, read, recite, and review—is a technique to facilitate reading difficult material such as research reports.

3. In reading research reports, you should read for understanding of the content, and you should critically analyze the research.

4. The second edition of the *Publication manual of the American Psychological Association* (1974) is the style and format reference for psychological research reports.

5. The general criteria for a technical research report include accuracy of information, including quotations; completeness of information; conciseness of style; and readability and clarity.

★6. The main elements of a research report format are: title, author's name and location, abstract or summary, introduction, method (including subjects, equipment, and procedure), results, conclusions, and references.

7. The objective of oral presentation is different from the objectives of written research reports. The brief, redundant presentation of the highlights of your study will suffice for an oral report. Written handouts of key information can be presented as a visual aid.

8. The advantages of publication include avoiding blind alleys, reducing the probability of needless redundancy, allowing the possibility of verification, adding to the body of scientific knowledge, describing methodological innovations, and providing an historical record.

9. Undergraduate publication in professional research journals does occur. In many cases the addition of one more control experiment or replication under improved control conditions will serve to make an undergraduate's study eligible for publication. In a few cases, a careful revision of the report is all that is necessary. Presentation of a research report at a professional convention or undergraduate convention is a form of publication achieved more easily than publication in a research journal.

10. The content, purpose, and control procedures in a given study can be viewed as adequate or inadequate by different reviewers. A research report inappropriate to one journal may be appropriate for another; rejection by one journal editor should not automatically preclude submission to another or even resubmission to the first.

SUGGESTED READINGS

American Psychological Association, Council of Editors. *Publication manual of the American Psychological Association* (2nd ed.). Washington, D. C.: Author, 1974.

Lorayne, H., & Lucas, J. *The memory book.* New York: Ballantine, 1974.

Payne, L. V. *The lively art of writing.* New York: Follett, 1965.

Schlosberg, H. Hints on presenting a paper at an APA convention. *American Psychologist,* 1956, *11,* 345–346.

Turabian, K. L. *A manual for the writers of term papers, theses, and dissertations* (3rd ed.). Chicago: Univ. of Chicago Press, 1967.

section four

Statistical Tools

16

The Inferential Process

Completing the data collection is not the final step in an experiment. We must interpret the data; we must decide whether the observed effect of the treatment is real or accidental. We also are concerned with generalizing the results from our sample to the population sampled. Inferential statistics is that branch of mathematics that assists decision-making and generalization under conditions of uncertainty. This chapter presents an elementary overview of the major steps in the inferential decision-making process.

The context in which inferential statistics is used by researchers is exemplified by the following research study, which was described in more detail in chapter 8. Traynham and Witte (1976) studied the effects of punishment on modifying color-meaning concepts in five-year-old children. Part of the study involved a randomized two-group design in which 20 children were randomly assigned to each group. The experimental group was punished by losing two pennies for guessing that a white animal was good, clean, smart, and so on, or for guessing that a black animal was ugly, wrong, naughty, and so on in a little story about a picture of two animals, one white and one black. There were 24 opportunities to guess, and the control group experienced the same procedure as the experimental group, except that the control group did not lose any pennies, regardless of the color they guessed.

The dependent measure was the number of times each subject responded to the story in a "conventional" manner, equating black with bad or white with good. The higher the score, the more conventionally biased the child's responses. At the end of the 24 trials, the mean number of conventional responses for the experimental group was 13.7, and the mean for the control group was 18.4. The experimental hypothesis was that the punishment procedures would reduce the frequency of conventional responses in the experimental group as compared to the control group. The means indicate that the experimental hypothesis appears to be supported; however, was a difference of 4.7 between the two means a sufficiently large difference for the experimenters to conclude that the experimental hypothesis was really supported? In other words, could the experimenters conclude that the difference was not due to chance and safely infer that for other samples from the same population, the same procedures would have a similar effect? The decision whether or not to generalize that the experimenters faced is an example of an inferential decision for which inferential statistics is helpful.

WHAT IS STATISTICS?

Statistics is a branch of applied mathematics used by scientists as a tool to make sense of observed data. After data are collected, we have two general statistical tasks: We must organize and summarize the data, and we must interpret the meaning of the data in relation to our experimental hypotheses. These two tasks correspond to the two major areas of statistics.

Descriptive and Inferential Statistics

Descriptive Statistics

Descriptive statistics deals with the organization and summarization of data. The general purpose and many of the techniques of descriptive statistics, such as graphing and calculating central-tendency measures, were described in chapter 5.

Summarizing and clearly presenting data are important statistical procedures. However, we are more interested in explanation and generalization than in mere description. The field of statistics corresponding to the area of interpreting the meaning of data and making legitimate generalizations from the data is called **inferential**

Inferential Statistics

statistics. Statistical inferences are appropriate to a research study when four conditions apply:

1. We have a defined *population* about which we are attempting to draw a general conclusion. In psychological research, the population (chapter 3) is a group of organisms sharing an attribute or set of attributes. For example, the population might be all current, full-time, undergraduate college students attending an institution belonging to the State University of New York system. The objective of our research is a general conclusion about an attribute of all members of the population. For example, we may be interested in the students' academic self-concepts.

2. The attribute of interest may have several dimensions and we may be concerned with only one dimension, or the attribute may have only one dimension. In either case, the population exhibits *variability* with respect to the dimension in question. Thus, the S.U.N.Y. students vary in their academic self-concepts, which is one dimension of a person's total self-concept. The variability or variance may be due to a large number of factors; the experiment is usually concerned with only one or two of these factors. We assume that most of the other factors are random sources of error variance in the observed data.

3. Our research project involves only a relatively small *sample* of the total population (chapter 3). This sample, a subset drawn from the population, must be representative and unbiased.

4. On the basis of the data obtained from the sample, we intend to make an inference about the specific attribute or dimensions of the attribute of the population. Since random variation contributes to individual differences in our population, no matter how carefully we select the sample, we expect that different samples from the population will differ from each other on the measure of the relevant attribute. Similarly, any sample will differ to some unknown degree from the population on the attributes that define the population. That is, we expect any single sample to be imperfectly representative of the population. Therefore, any generalization will be made with some degree of *uncertainty*. We can usually limit or at least specify the amount of uncertainty.

To summarize the preceding four conditions, inferential statistics is the area of statistics concerned with making generalizations about variable population attributes from sample data with a known degree of uncertainty about each generalization.

Parameter Estimation and Hypothesis Testing

Parameter Estimation

The area of inferential statistics has two main subareas: **Parameter estimation** is the area concerned with making a statistical inference about the value of a population parameter. As indicated in chapter 3, a *parameter* is a descriptive index of the distribution of a variable defining a population. For a given, defined population, a parameter is a *constant*. For example, the mean intelligence quotient (IQ) of all current, undergraduate, full-time S.U.N.Y. students is a constant.

We use the sample descriptive statistics as *estimates* of population parameters. This process is a form of the inductive process described in chapter 1. For example, we might find the mean sample IQ to be 125 and infer by induction that the population parameter is approximately 125, or that it is between 120 and 130.

Such an inductive inference is interesting, but is not usually considered as important as a theoretical explanation of why the parameter has such a value. We are usually more interested in testing experimental hypotheses that specify the relationship between two variables. **Hypothesis testing,** the second form of inferential statistics, is concerned with tests of theoretical deductions about specific, antecedent–consequent relationships in the population sampled. We use the tests to decide whether the observed data really support or only appear to support the experimental hypothesis. Before we develop the main concepts in parameter estimation and hypothesis testing, we will digress briefly to describe a frequency distribution called the normal distribution.

Hypothesis Testing (margin note)

THE NORMAL DISTRIBUTION

The development of statistical models has involved much use of the relative frequency distribution called the "normal" distribution or normal curve. As depicted in Figure 5.8 and in Figure 16.1, the mathematical function defining the normal curve yields a symmetrical, unimodal, bell-shaped distribution with most observations concentrated around the mode and with frequencies decreasing as the distance from the mode increases. *No empirically observed variable will be precisely normally distributed;* however, many empirical frequency distributions *approximate* the normal curve. It is often convenient to treat data *as if* they were normally distributed. Using the normal distribution as an abstract model, we *assume* that the frequency distribution of the values of a population variable is normal.

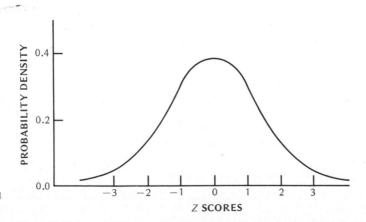

FIG. 16.1
The standard normal probability distribution or standardized normal curve.

z Score

In chapter 5, a standardized score or z score was defined as $(X - \overline{X})/S$. The standard normal curve is presented in Figure 16.1 because if we graph the normal curve with z on the abscissa instead of any random variable, several important properties of the normal curve immediately become apparent. As indicated in chapter 5, the mean and standard deviation of z scores are 0 and 1.0, respectively. If we consider the area under the curve in Figure 16.1 to be 100% of the area under the curve, we can examine various portions of it defined by values of z to see what percentage of the total distribution is contained within them. We find that approximately 68% of the area under the curve is located in the interval between −1 and +1 standard deviation of z values; approximately 95% is located in the interval between −2 and +2, and almost 100% is located in the interval between −3 and +3. These facts will be used in subsequent illustrations of inferential statistics.

STATISTIC AND PARAMETER ESTIMATION

Population parameters and sample statistics usually are not identical, but they are related in certain ways. If you know the population parameters, you can make intelligent statements about the sample statistics, and if you know the sample statistics you can make intelligence inferences about population parameters. This interrelation is very important for scientists.

Given the mean and standard deviation of a normally distributed population, we can make some fairly accurate statements about the nature of any sample drawn from that population. For example, assume that IQ scores are approximately normally distributed and that the standardized mean and standard deviation of an IQ test are 100 and 15, respectively. We expect about 68% of the people in any given sample to have IQ scores between 85 and 115, one standard diviation below and above the mean. This inference can be stated in several ways. If our sample size is one individual, we could predict that the person would have an IQ score falling between 85 and 115, with the knowledge that we would be right about 68% of the times we make such predictions. To increase our chances of being correct, we could expand the boundaries of our estimate. If we moved the boundaries, or *band width,* to include two standard deviations, IQ scores from 70 to 130, we would be correct about 95% of the time. A predictive accuracy of 998 times in 1000 could be attained by increasing the band width or confidence limits by another standard deviation to include IQ scores between 55 and 145.

As the boundaries, band width, or confidence interval is widened, the prediction is more likely to include any future observation, but at the same time the prediction will be less precise regarding the actual score. You must choose between a more precise numerical prediction or a prediction with a greater chance of being correct.

Sample Size

We can predict sample statistics more accurately than individual scores. The larger the sample size, the less likely is it that the sample will be unusual or unrepresentative of most of the population, and the more closely will the sample statistics reflect the population parameters. This trend reaches its ultimate when the sample becomes so large that it includes the entire population.

Beginning with known population parameters, it is relatively easy to predict sample statistics. However, most research projects involve the reverse inference: They are conducted in order to make inferences about unknown population parameters on the basis of statistics from a representative sample.

Just as we can make intelligent statements about sample statistics from known population parameters, so we can make informed statements about population parameters on the basis of known sample statistics. Our best single estimate of a population parameter is the sample statistic. If we have one sample, the best estimate of the population mean is the sample mean. For example, the mean number of conventional, "black is bad" or "white is good" responses by the control group in Traynham and Witte's (1976) study was 18.4 conventional responses out of a possible 24. The population was white, male and female, five-year-old, middle-class, private and public school kindergarten children in Fayetteville, Arkansas. The best single estimate of the mean number of conventional responses that would have been obtained from this population in 1974 is 18.4 conventional responses.

Using a reasoning process similar to that employed in predicting an individual's scores from known population parameters, we can assess the accuracy of our estimates of population parameters from sample statistics. For example, we can calculate the confidence with which we expect the band around the sample mean bounded by +1 and −1 sample standard deviations to include the population mean. Thus, it is possible to estimate the likely values of the population mean by calculating confidence limits around the sample statistic.

HYPOTHESIS TESTING

Hypothesis testing is part of common, daily decision-making. Assume that you are asleep in your home and are awakened by a noise. As you lie there tensely listening for more noises, you must decide whether the situation is dangerous or safe. Occasionally a noise in the night may obviously be in one category or the other. For example, a loud crash may be identified immediately as dangerous. On the other hand, most households are replete with noises created by the structure settling or reacting to temperature changes, by household equipment, or by the legitimate occupants of the house. In these cases, the noises are classified as safe. There is, however, a relatively large overlapping area in which a sound could belong to either classification. Your decision to investigate further, perhaps with weapon in hand, or to go back to sleep is sometimes erroneous.

The night-noise example contains most of the elements of the formal hypothesis-testing procedure used in making decisions about data; a main difference is that within the more formal procedure it is possible to provide a precise measure of the chance of being wrong.

Null and Experimental Hypotheses

The portion of the Traynham and Witte (1976) study described in the opening paragraphs of this chapter presented an example of a randomized, independent two-group design. Having collected data from the experimental and control groups, the experimenters were faced with deciding whether their manipulations of the indepen-

**Experimental vs.
Control Populations**

dent variable had any effect on the observed guessing behavior. If the treatment had no effect, the experimenters were essentially comparing two samples from a common population. If, on the other hand, the treatment did have some effect, the populations were now different for each group, and the scores of the treatment group should have shown some consistent difference introduced by the treatment. The problem is determining whether the observed difference between the groups is likely or unlikely to have occurred by chance for two samples from a common population.

Statistical Tests

Inferential statistical tests compare the observed difference between the sample statistics (for example, sample means) with some estimate of the likely differences if the samples had been drawn from the same population. If the observed difference is too great, you conclude that there was a real difference between the two samples. That is, you conclude that the two samples must belong to two populations (treatment and control) made different by the action of the independent variable.

Let us restate the night-noise decision in statistical decision terms. The category "safe noise" may be labeled the *null hypothesis* (abbreviated H_0). It means that there is *nothing* dangerous causing the noise, and that it is part of the normal night sounds for your house. The category "dangerous noise" includes a number of potential sources which are not usual to the house; in other words, there is *something* out of the ordinary there. The dangerous category may be labelled the *experimental hypothesis* (abbreviated H_1). You must choose between two overlapping distributions of possible sounds to decide whether the noise came from the collection of safe sounds, or if it came from an unusual, dangerous source (see Figure 16.2). Your only empirical basis for this decision is the set of sounds you normally hear at night. Therefore the decision can be restated, "Is the sound a normal night sound for your house?"

In many experiments, we do not have an opportunity to compile a long-term collection of normal or usual baseline data. However, most experiments include some

FIG. 16.2
Hypothesis testing in the night-noise example. There are two overlapping distributions: normal, safe house noises and unusual, dangerous noises. The shaded areas indicate the noises difficult to define.

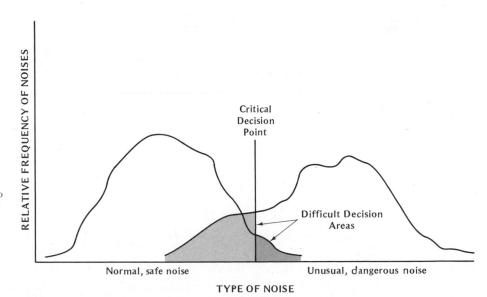

sort of control group. The control-group subjects are observed under "normal," zero-level treatment conditions. From the control group data, we then infer the "normal" parameters of the population. Instead of relying on a background experience of many nights spent in the house, it is possible to gain a parameter estimate on the basis of a single, control-group sample.

On the basis of the parameter estimated from the control group data, a prediction for the statistic of a second sample from the same population is established. The observed statistic from the experimental group's data is then compared to the predicted statistic. If there is little difference between the predicted and observed experimental group statistics, we conclude that the two samples probably came from the same population. If, on the other hand, there is a large enough difference, we conclude that the experimental group's scores must have been affected by the independent variable. Therefore the data from the experimental group come from a different treatment population.

In essence, the process involves making the tentative assumption that the treatment condition or independent variable has no effect. This assumption is known as a **null hypothesis** since it predicts *no* difference between the control and experimental groups' scores. We test the assumption that the null hypothesis is true. If it is unlikely that the experimental group data came from the control group population, then the experimental or alternative hypothesis that there is a real difference between the two groups is tentatively accepted. Rejecting the null hypothesis, we conclude that there is support for the experimental or alternative hypothesis.

Null Hypothesis

Types of Errors

Whether you decide that the experimental hypothesis is supported or rejected, you can be correct or in error (Table 16.1). You may decide correctly that the data support the null or the experimental hypothesis; you may decide incorrectly that the alternative hypothesis is supported (**Type I error**) or that the null hypothesis is supported (**Type II error**).

The probability of a Type I error, labeled α ("alpha"), is always specified *by the experimenter before* an experiment begins. The value of α reflects how confident you want to be in your decision making. The smaller the value of α, the less the chance of a

Type I Error
Type II Error

TABLE 16.1
Type I and Type II
Decision Errors

		Real World	
		No difference; the null hypothesis, H_0, is correct.	A real difference; the experimental hypothesis, H_1, is correct.
Experimenter's Decision	The data support the null hypothesis, H_0.	Correct decision (No error)	Type II error
	The data support the alternative hypothesis, H_1.	Type I error (Probability $= \alpha$)	Correct decision (No error)

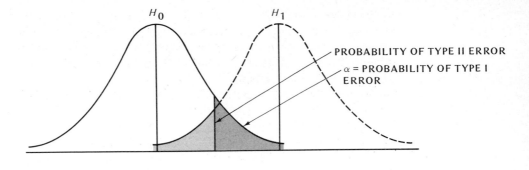

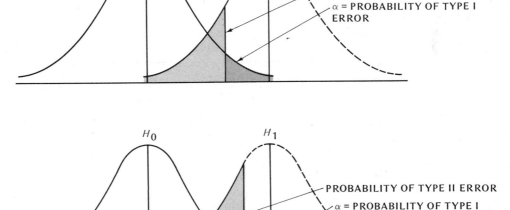

FIG. 16.3
The inverse relationship between the probability of Type I and Type II errors. H_0 is the distribution specified by the null hypothesis, and H_1 is the distribution expected on the basis of the experimental hypothesis. The two shaded areas represent the probability of a Type I and Type II error, respectively. The three pairs of distributions illustrate the effect of changing the level of α on the probability of a Type II error. Moving from the top drawing to the bottom, the probability of a Type I error decreases and the probability of a Type II error increases.

Level of Significance

Type I error. Alpha is often called the *level of significance* because it reflects the size or *significance* of the difference between experimental and control statistics needed to decide that the data support the experimental hypothesis. In most psychological research, α is .05 or less; this means that you are willing to risk the rejection of the null hypothesis, when it is true, 5 times out of 100. When $\alpha = .01$, you are willing to reject the null hypothesis falsely 1 time out of 100.

The relationship between the frequency distribution specified by the null hypothesis, the level of α, and the probability of a Type II error is depicted in Figure 16.3. One way to remember which error is a Type I error is to use the following memory aid: I is first; α is the first letter of the Greek alphabet and is associated with accepting the alternative or experimental hypothesis when it is false (note the italicized *a*s).

The significance level, or α, is *not* the probability of making a correct inference; rather, it is the probability of making a Type I error of rejecting the null hypothesis when it is really true. However, the ability to determine even this probability considerably increases the precision of our inferential conclusions.

In Traynham and Witte's (1976) study, α was set at .05. The experimental hypothesis was that the punishment procedure would decrease the mean number of conventional responses. That is, the mean for the experimental group was predicted to be less than the mean for the unpunished control group. The null hypothesis was that the two group means would differ only by chance. The control group's mean was 18.4; the estimated null population parameter was 18.4. As predicted, the experimental group's mean was smaller than the control group's mean. The experimental group mean was 13.7. Using the analysis of variance testing technique (Chapter 20), Traynham and Witte found that the experimental mean of 13.7 was unlikely to be sampled from a population with a mean of 18.4; the difference of 4.7 between the two means was unlikely to be due to chance factors. In other words, the probability that the difference was due to random, chance factors was less than α. The experimenters concluded that the punishment procedure did create a reliable change in the children's behavior. There was support for the hypothesis that if other samples from the population received the experimental treatment, these children also would be less likely to make conventional verbal guesses about which pictured animal was stupid, smart, naughty, or nice.

One- and Two-Tailed Tests

So far we have discussed hypothesis testing with experimental hypotheses that specify that there is some difference between the experimental and control group because of the treatment. A significant result in this case is any outcome that is unusual in terms of the null distribution. Either an unusually high or an unusually low performance by the experimental subjects provides a legitimate basis for rejecting the null hypothesis.

There are times, however, when the alternative hypothesis specifies that the difference will be in one direction. For example, in the Traynham and Witte (1976) study, the punished children were expected to be *less* conventional in their responses. When you have a hypothesis that specifies that the difference must be in a certain direction, if the experimental group's data is not in that direction (either not different or *more* conventional), then you know immediately that the data do not support the experimental hypothesis. If the experimental group's data are in the predicted direction, then only significantly low performance in that direction is sufficient to reject the null hypothesis. The use of a **two-tailed test** says that the experimenter is interested in *any* difference (either direction or either tail of the null distribution) created by the independent variable. A **one-tailed test,** on the other hand, is appropriate to experimental hypotheses that say the treatment effect will produce a difference in a single direction. Therefore Traynham and Witte used a one-tailed test.

The null and alternative hypotheses are stated in a subtly different way, depending on whether a one- or two-tailed test is used. In a two-tailed test, the null hypothesis calls for "no difference" between groups, while the alternative hypothesis predicts

One-Tailed and
Two-Tailed Tests

"a difference in either direction." In a one-tailed test, the alternative hypothesis is "a difference in a specific direction," while the null hypothesis is "not a difference in that direction." Implicit in the null hypothesis for the one-tailed test is the inclusion of a difference in the opposite direction.

Directional Hypotheses

The choice between one- and two-tailed statistical tests is dictated by the experimental hypothesis: one-tailed experimental hypotheses are called *directional hypotheses* and two-tailed experimental hypotheses are called *nondirectional hypotheses.*

Degrees of Freedom

We use the control and experimental data to estimate the parameter or parameters of the null distribution. This estimation process costs us in the sense that using the observed data to generate expected data puts restraints on the mathematical manipulations we can subsequently perform with the observed data. Certain statistical tests require the calculation of a number referred to as degrees of freedom *(df)*. The **degrees of freedom** number indicates how many of the total observed measures remain after the restrictions are imposed because of using the data to estimate parameters.

df

The following example provides a rough idea of the meaning of degrees of freedom. Suppose you are given the sum of a group of ten scores. In order to know what the ten scores are you need to be told only nine of the scores; the tenth score must be the number which, when added to the other nine, will make up the fixed sum. Calculating the sum and making it a constant (or parameter estimate) consumed the information in one of the scores. The other nine scores are free to vary, but after nine are established, the tenth must fill the known gap. The number of degrees of freedom is 9, the number of scores that are free to vary without such constraints. Notice that the number of degrees of freedom does not single out any specific score to become fixed. It is the last score in all possible orders of consideration.

SELECTING A STATISTICAL TEST

An overwhelming array of inferential statistical tests is available. These tests can be categorized in a number of ways, but a convenient division for this discussion is "classic" versus "exotic." The tests presented in the following chapters of this text are classic tests that have been used frequently by researchers in a wide variety of scientific disciplines. Several other classic tests are not represented here. Also not included are a large number of exotic statistical tests that are less frequently used, because of their structure, function, or obscurity.

Choosing the statistical test to apply is another aspect of the decision process. Two different statistical tests, if applied to the same data, will not necessarily yield identical statistical decisions. Sometimes differences are created by the calculational procedures. More frequently, two different tests utilize different amounts of the information contained in the data; this possibility was raised in the discussion of scales of

FIG. 16.4
A flow chart depicting the sequential decisions involved in selecting a statistical test. Only the sample of common, "classical" tests described in this text are included in the chart. The statistical analysis techniques are located in the boxes
[a]The "interocular trauma test" consists of looking at the data to see whether the prediction is or is not supported.

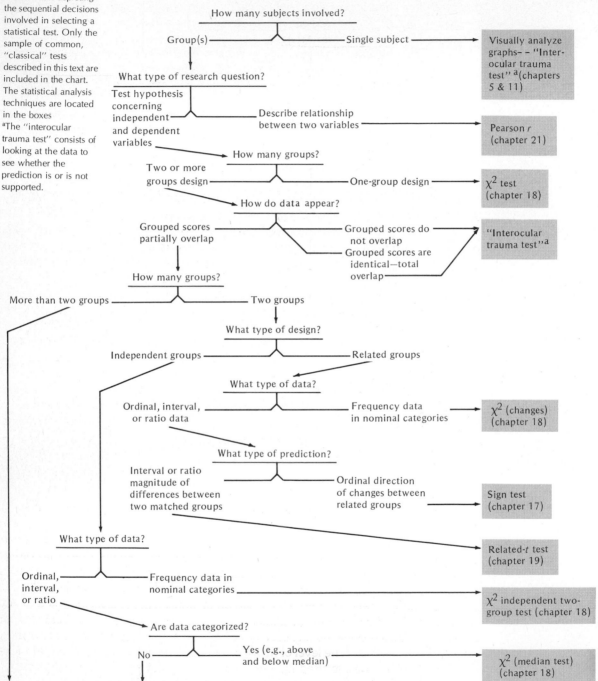

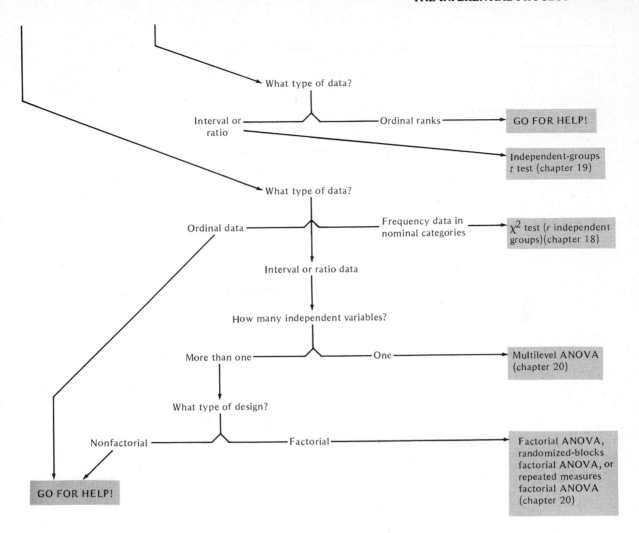

What type of data?

Interval or — Ordinal ranks — **GO FOR HELP!**
ratio

Independent-groups
_t_ test (chapter 19)

What type of data?

Ordinal data — Frequency data in — χ^2 **test (_r_ independent**
nominal categories **groups)(chapter 18)**

Interval or ratio data

How many independent variables?

More than one — One — **Multilevel ANOVA**
(chapter 20)

What type of design?

Nonfactorial — Factorial — **Factorial ANOVA,**
randomized-blocks
factorial ANOVA, or
repeated measures
factorial ANOVA
(chapter 20)

GO FOR HELP!

measurement in chapter 4. Finally, tests differ in their sensitivity to differences in central tendency, variability, or distribution shape.

To help in selecting among the statistical tests presented in this text, two guidelines are provided. Table 16.2 categorizes the tests presented in chapters 17–21 according to the level of measurement and the nature of the research design. The table is organized so that each test is located at the *lowest* level of measurement for which it is technically appropriate. Therefore the tests can be applied at the level indicated or any higher level of measurement. In applying the table, it is important to note that, in practice, the lines delineating any specific cell are often not as sharp and clear as they are in the printed form. The level of measurement is frequently subject to considerable argument, and the design used may not seem to fit precisely into any column. The table indicates only two criteria that may help the test-selection process.

Figure 16.4 uses a flow-chart approach to selecting a statistical test by asking a sequence of questions, with each answer eliminating some inappropriate tests until

TABLE 16.2
Matrix of Tests
Described in This
Text. A Test Can
Be Used with the
Level of
Dependent
Variable
Measurement
Indicated (Rows)
and All Greater
Levels

[1]ANOVA is a standard
abbreviation for
Analysis of Variance.

Level of Measurement of Data	Research Design				
	One-Group Designs (One Set of Scores)	Related Two-Group Designs (Two Related Sets of Scores)	Independent Two-Group Designs (Two Independent Sets of Scores)	Multilevel and Factorial Designs (Multiple Sets of Scores)	Correlation Coefficients (Two Related Sets of Scores)
Nominal	One-Group χ^2 (chapter 18)	Significance of changes χ^2 (chapter 18)	Two independent groups χ^2 (chapter 18)	r independent groups χ^2 (chapter 18)	
Ordinal		Sign test (chapter 17)	Median χ^2 (chapter 18)		
Interval or Ratio		Randomized-blocks ANOVA[1] (chapter 20) t test for related scores (chapter 19)	Multilevel ANOVA (chapter 20) Two independent samples t test (chapter 19)	ANOVA (chapter 20)	Pearson r (chapter 21)

finally the proper one is reached. Andrews, Klem, Davidson, O'Malley, and Rodgers (1974) present a much more detailed, 15-page "decision tree" including many "exotic" tests.

Although it may seem so, research is *not* the same thing as statistics. The application of inferential statistics gives the researcher a powerful tool for making decisions concerning data. All behavioral researchers are confronted with the problem of interpreting data. Is the difference observed between experimental scores and control scores a real difference, or is it just an accident? There are times when the data are so obvious that statistical tests are unnecessary. For example, if we hypothesize that a treatment condition should enhance the subjects' scores, and we find that the experimental group scores declined, it does not take statistical tests to tell us that the prediction was not supported. Similarly, if the experimental subjects performed three or four times better than any of the control subjects, then statistical tests only confirm our conviction that the treatment had an effect on behavior. Between these two extremes, inferential statistical tests help the decision process, but they do not take the place of an intelligent human being realistically evaluating the results.

SUMMARY

1. Statistics is an applied mathematical tool used for the summarization and interpretation of data.
2. Descriptive statistics deals with the organization and summarization of data. Inferential statistics deals with generalizing from sample data to population attributes with specified degrees of uncertainty.
3. A population is a group of organisms sharing defined attributes or sets of attributes. Populations vary in the dimension or dimensions of the attribute in question. Samples are subsets selected from the population. Different samples from a population are expected to differ from each other, and a sample from a population will not be perfectly representative of that population.
4. Parameter estimation is the inductive process of statistically estimating the value of a population parameter. A parameter is an index of the distribution of a variable defining a population.
5. Hypothesis testing is the process of testing a theoretical deduction about causal relationships in the population sampled.

6. The normal distribution is a theoretical, relative frequency distribution approximated by empirical frequency distributions.

7. Population parameters and sample statistics are related. Given the value of the population parameter, we can predict the value of sample score or statistic. The accuracy and precision of these predictions are inversely related. The larger the sample size, the more accurately the sample statistic reflects the population parameter.

8. Given a sample statistic, the best estimate of the population parameter is the value of the sample statistic.

9. In a two-group design, if the experimental treatment has no effect, then the two groups are two samples from a common population. If the experimental treatment does have an effect, then the experimental group represents a sample from a population that differs from the control group population as a function of the independent variable.

10. Inferential statistical tests compare observed differences between sample statistics with some estimate of the likely difference if the treatment has no effect. If the observed differences are too large relative to the expected, chance sampling differences, then the treatment is judged to have a real effect.

11. A null hypothesis is a negation of an experimental hypothesis. Usually the null hypothesis is a prediction that there will be no difference between groups.

12. Two types of decision errors can be made in testing null and experimental hypotheses: the Type I error of rejecting the null hypothesis when it is true, and the Type II error of rejecting the experimental hypothesis when it is correct. The probability of a Type I error is called α or the level of significance. The level of significance is set by the experimenter.

13. A one-tailed test is a statistical test in which the experimental hypothesis is directional. A two-tailed test is a statistical test in which the experimental hypothesis does not specify direction but simply states there will be some difference between the appropriate statistics.

14. The number of degrees of freedom is the number of sample scores that are free to vary within the constraints imposed by estimating population parameters in order to make statistical tests.

15. Statistical tests differ in (1) the calculation procedures, (2) the amount of information they use from the data scale, (3) the particular kinds of differences between population distributions to which they are most sensitive, (4) the type of research design for which they are appropriate, (5) the kind of null and experimental hypotheses to which they are relevant, (6) the size of the sample or samples involved, and (7) the form or type of data involved.

16. For some kinds of data, inferential statistical tests are not useful.

SUGGESTED READINGS

Edwards, A. L. *Statistical methods* (3rd ed.). New York: Holt, Rinehart and Winston, 1973.

Frank, H. *Introduction to probability and statistics: Concepts and principles.* New York: Wiley, 1974.

Hays, W. L. *Statistics for the social sciences* (2d ed.). New York: Holt, Rinehart and Winston, 1973.

Kirk, R. E. *Experimental design: Procedures for the behavioral sciences.* Belmont, Calif.: Brooks/Cole, 1968.

Kirk, R. E. (Ed.). *Statistical issues: A reader for the behavioral sciences.* Belmont, Calif.: Brooks/Cole, 1972.

McNemar, Q. *Psychological statistics* (4th ed.). New York: Wiley, 1969.

Steger, J. A. (Ed.). *Readings in statistics for the behavioral scientist.* New York: Holt, Rinehart and Winston, 1971.

17

The Sign Test: A Related-Sample Test

The sign test is a relatively simple test for differences between two related groups of scores. The data must be at least ordinal in nature and the differences between the related groups of scores can be sorted into pluses and minuses. This chapter provides several examples of how the sign test may be used.

The sign test gets its name from the fact that it uses plus and minus signs rather than raw test scores. It may be used with a one-group before–after design or with a two-matched-groups design; either design yields two groups of scores closely related to each other. There may be two scores from each subject (for example, a before-treatment or pretest measure and an after-treatment measure), or there may be two sets of scores from subjects who were carefully matched so as to control most secondary variables.

The sign test requires two sets of data at least ordinal in level (chapter 4); the scores from each subject or pair of subjects must be related in some way. For example, you may hypothesize that scores on an achievement test such as the Scholastic Aptitude Test can be increased by specific training. One way to get two sets of data is to pretest one group of students, give them a two-week cram course, and then test the students again to obtain an after-measure. If the after-measures are substantially different from the pretest measures, a sign test can provide a statistical test of the differences.

THE SIGN TEST: LOGIC AND METHOD

The data of interest in a sign test are the directions of the differences between the paired scores (+ or −). For example, suppose a person whose pretest score was 525 scored 550 after the cram course on the SAT. The magnitude of difference (25) is not a datum, only the sign of difference (+). If the after-measure had been lower than the before-measure, the sign of the difference would have been minus (−).

The null hypothesis (H_0) for the sign test is that the probability of either occurence (+ or −) is 50–50. (Other probability expectations could be used, but the calculation becomes cumbersome.) Therefore the null hypothesis becomes, "The probability of a plus is equal to the probability of a minus."

In the case of the sign test, an unusually high proportion of pluses or minuses indicates a deviation from this expected 50–50 distribution, and the precise probability of this deviation can be determined. You count the number of cases and the number of pluses or minuses. The precise probability of this particular combination of signs can then be obtained from a table (see Appendix D).

The other use of the sign test is best exemplified in the classic before–after research design. Suppose we were to measure the possible efficacy of a gasoline additive by recording the mileage of 12 automobiles before and after the additive was put in the tanks. The null hypothesis says that half the cars will get better mileage and half will get worse mileage. If all but one of the 12 cars showed an increase in gasoline mileage, we might have reason to purchase the additive. This result can be translated into the terms of the sign test by subtracting the first mileage figure from the second of each automobile and noting the direction (sign) of the difference. The observed results—11 pluses and 1 minus—are the data tested by the sign test. To find the probability under the null hypothesis of having 11 cars out of 12 get better mileage with the additive, read the following section and then turn to Appendix D.

USING THE SIGN-TEST TABLE

The procedure for the sign test is very simple. Count the total number of observations (N) and then count the occurrences of the less-frequent sign (x). In the car example, $N = 12$ and $x = 1$. (In this case x is equal to the number of minus signs.) Turn to Appendix D and locate the row and column which match these two critical numbers. Go across the top from 0 to column 1 (x), then go down the column until you come to the row corresponding to 12 (N). You will note that the tabled value is 003. The decimal point has been omitted from the table; the actual value should be read .003. That means that under the null hypothesis (chance), the probability of 11 cars out of 12 getting better mileage is .003. The probability .003 is so remote under the null, and so much less than our standard $\alpha = .05$, that we reject the null. You might want to notice that if 10 out of 12 cars had shown the improved mileage the probability would have been .019 (under column 2 and row 12), which also would have led us to reject the null.

The tabled values for the sign test are one-tailed; they give the probability for a difference that is in one predicted direction. If you wish to see whether there is any difference regardless of direction, you need a two-tailed test, and you must *double* the tabled values to take into account the other tail of the null distribution, regardless of its shape.

EXAMPLES

Suppose you are interested in the hypothesis that the direction of gaze reflects which hemisphere of the brain is dominant. Research indicates that the left hemisphere is primarily logical, while the right hemisphere is more intuitive in processing information. If a person looks right, the left hemisphere may be operating; looking left may utilize the right hemisphere. To test this hypothesis, ask subjects a question that could be answered either logically or impulsively (intuitively): "What would you do if you were given a million dollars?" You then observe in which direction your subjects' eyes shift as the question is being answered. The answers are categorized into logical ("Invest it") or impulsive ("Fly to Acapulco"). After the data are collected, you tabulate the direction of gaze and nature of the verbal response and mark whether each pairing agrees with the hypothesis $(+)$ or disagrees $(-)$. The data are shown in Table 17.1. (Note that your design is similar to a one-group before–after design.)

The right-hand column contains the data to be analyzed. Of the 22 total responses, 14 $(+)$ pairs of verbal response and direction of gaze supported the hypothesis. The other 8 pairs $(-)$ did not. Appendix D (row $N = 22$, column $x = 8$) shows that the probability of this occurrence by chance is .143. You are predicting agreement so your test is in one direction, a one-tailed test.

Since .143 is considerably above the standard .05 significance point, the experimental hypothesis cannot be accepted. The number of agreements between response and gaze probably was a chance event rather than a function of hemispherical dominance.

This example shows how signs can be derived by combining two different sets of scores. To obtain the sign to be tested we compared the direction of gaze with the nature of the answer. In this particular example the sign test also could have been applied to either the gaze data or the response category data. If such a test had been run, you would have been testing to see whether the responses (left or right, logical or impulsive) occurred equally often, without some factor favoring one or the other.

Consider another example. Assume that you want to decide which of two quadraphonic sound systems should be purchased. Both systems are set up in identical rooms, and 14 observers are asked to provide evaluative information by a complicated criterion procedure that results in a numerical summary score. The data are shown in Table 17.2. One observer couldn't make up his mind so the tied score (zero or no difference score), is discarded, resulting in $N = 13$. Ten scores are positive and three are negative. Since the table uses the less frequent sign, we enter Appendix D in

**TABLE 17.1
Hypothetical Data Comparing the Direction of Gaze and the Type of Verbal Response Given to the Question, "What Would You Do If You Were Given a Million**

Subject	Direction of Gaze	Response Category	Relation to Hypothesis
1	R	Logical	+
2	L	Logical	−
3	R	Impulsive	−
4	R	Logical	+
5	L	Impulsive	+
6	L	Impulsive	+
7	L	Impulsive	+
8	L	Logical	−
9	L	Impulsive	+
10	R	Logical	+
11	L	Logical	−
12	R	Logical	+
13	L	Impulsive	+
14	R	Impulsive	−
15	L	Logical	−
16	L	Impulsive	+
17	L	Impulsive	+
18	L	Impulsive	+
19	R	Impulsive	−
20	R	Logical	+
21	R	Logical	+
22	R	Impulsive	−

TABLE 17.2
Fourteen Subjects'
Evaluations of
Two Hi Fi Sets

Subjects	Set A	Set B	Sign of Difference
A	633	614	+
B	632	612	+
C	643	643	0
D	633	615	+
E	617	638	−
F	634	646	−
G	622	611	+
H	644	618	+
I	628	614	+
J	618	606	+
K	626	634	−
L	629	615	+
M	639	626	+
N	631	630	+

the $N = 13$ row and the $x = 3$ column. We find that the probability of this occurence is .046.

Although this probability appears to meet the .05 criterion, there is an important detail that you must consider. The tabled value is one-tailed, only giving the probability of set B being superior (more pluses than minuses). Since you are also interested in set A, you must include the possibility of the opposite results in your calculation. The probability of *one or the other* winning by a 3-to-10 margin is twice as great (.092). Since .092 is greater than the .05 criterion, the null hypothesis is accepted and the data show no real difference between the two systems.

ADVANTAGES AND LIMITATIONS

If the null hypothesis specifies a 50–50 probability, the sign test is very easy. However, when using the sign test you must be sure that each pair of scores is independent from each other pair of scores. When tabled values of N and x are exceeded it is sometimes difficult to determine the probability. If your level of measurement is greater than ordinal (an interval scale), you should consider using a t test (chapter 19) instead of a sign test.

SUMMARY

1. The sign test utilizes the sign of the difference (+ or −) between two related scores. Each pair of scores is independent of each other pair.
2. The sign test may be used in a before–after design or a matched design.
3. The sign test is easy to calculate and uses ordinal-level data.
4. If your data are at least interval in nature, we recommend using the t test.

SUGGESTED READING.

Siegel, S. *Nonparametric statistics.* New York: McGraw-Hill, 1956.

18

Chi-Square Tests

The chi-square (χ^2) test is one of the most popular statistical tests. The data must be frequencies in discrete categories. The calculations are easy to do and the statistical tables are easy to use. When your data are in frequency form, the chi-square test is the best method.

The χ^2 test is one of the classic inferential statistical tests. The major advantages of the test are that it is relatively easy to understand, fairly easy to calculate, and applicable to an extremely wide range of research situations.

There are several different tests that use the χ^2 distribution as a basis for statistical decision. The most common are the one-group test, the independent two-group test, and the related two-group test. In all cases the experimental hypothesis predicts a significant (non-chance) relationship between two or more variables. The data for the χ^2 tests are always frequencies or relative frequencies (proportions).

THE ONE-GROUP TEST

The one-group test is used to determine the significance of the correspondence between a set of sample frequencies and a set of theoretical frequencies. We collect data from a single sample and see whether it is distributed as some theory (the null hypothesis) suggests it should be. The two variables involved in such a study are (1) the response categories (using a nominal or greater level of measurement) and (2) the frequency with which the subjects fall into the categories.

Logic and Method

The χ^2 test is a test of the significance of the differences between the observed number of subjects and the expected number of subjects falling into each category. In **Frequency Data Only** the one-group χ^2 test, the null hypothesis states the proportion of subjects expected to fall into each category. When we know the size of the group, we can determine the expected frequencies by multiplying the expected proportions by the total sample size. Given a set of expected and observed frequencies, the χ^2 test is used to determine whether the observed differences between frequencies in each category are likely to have occurred if the null hypothesis is true.

The null hypothesis is tested with the following formula:

$$\chi^2 = \sum \left[\frac{(O - E)^2}{E} \right],$$

(18.1)

where O is the observed frequency in each category, E is the expected frequency in each category, and Σ indicates that the squared differences divided by E for *each* category should be summed across *all* categories. Note that the difference for each category must be squared and then divided by the expected frequency for *that* category. <u>If the differences between the observed and expected frequencies are small, then the resulting value for χ^2 will be small.</u> The larger the differences between the two sets of frequencies, the larger will be the value of χ^2. <u>In general, as the value of χ^2 increases, the likelihood of support for the null hypothesis decreases.</u> To determine the significance of the computed value of χ^2, it is compared with the tabled values in Appendix E. The appendix presents the probabilities for *critical values* of χ^2. For example, in the first row (one *df*), with the null assumed to be true, one would expect to obtain a value of χ^2 equal to or greater than 1.642 two times out of ten (.20). In other words, if the null is true, and with ten random samples of different subjects, by chance we would expect to calculate two values of χ^2 greater than 1.64.

Because χ^2 is the sum of the comparisons in all categories, the χ^2 distribution changes with the number of categories. Therefore we must compare our data with the χ^2 distribution according to the number of degrees of freedom (*df*). The number of *df* is determined by the number of categories or classes involved in a study. The *df* for the one-group χ^2 is equal to $k - 1$, wher k stands for the total number of categories used. That is,

$$df = k - 1. \tag{18.2}$$

Degrees of Freedom

If we have 20 people and two categories (for example, "yes" and "no" responses to a questionnaire), then if 10 people answer "yes," we know that the remaining 10 answered "no" and we have one *df*. With three categories and a fixed number of people sampled, as soon as we know the frequencies in two categories, we know the frequency in the third category. Therefore with three categories, there are only two categories free to vary or 2 *df*. With less than 30 *df*, you must use the correct theoretical distribution when evaluating a set of sample data. You must enter the χ^2 table in the row with the appropriate number of *df*. Beyond 30 *df*, there is little change in the critical values of χ^2.

Calculation Examples

One degree of freedom   Suppose you are asked by the local police chief to evaluate data concerning a crackdown on drunk drivers. The police have sent ten extra officers out on Friday and Saturday nights for one year to arrest and jail drunk drivers. They have collision data for at least one year prior to the crackdown program and for the experimental year. The data are the monthly tallies on all collisions. The baseline year and the experimental year data are shown in Table 18.1. The null hypothesis predicts no difference between years; the experimental hypothesis predicts a decrease in collisions due to increased enforcement.

$$\chi^2_{(1)} = \frac{(2047 - 1679.5)^2}{1679.5} + \frac{(1312 - 1679.5)^2}{1679.5} = 160.8$$

The equation shows the calculation of the χ^2 test. The $df = 2 - 1 = 1$ since we have only two categories (years). The subscript below χ^2 indicates the degrees of freedom. If you set your α level at .05, Appendix E yields a critical one-tailed value of 2.706. Since the value of χ^2 is greater than 2.706, you reject the null and accept the

TABLE 18.1   Hypothetical Number of Collisions (Observed in Top Half, Expected in Bottom Half)

Baseline Year	Experimental Year	Total
2047	1312	
		3359
1679.5	1679.5	

experimental hypothesis, that all other things being equal, the increased police enforcement reduced collisions.

Some maintain that with one degree of freedom a Yates correction for continuity should be used (see Walker and Lev, 1953).

Two degrees of freedom   There is considerable mystique surrounding a certain Colorado brew. Some people prize the beer so much that they bring cases home with them from vacation. Suppose a group of college students at a western college decides to test the experimental hypothesis, "College students prefer Coors over Olympia and Budweiser." The operational definition of "prefer" is a verbal statement that one beer is "best." Sixty students are polled; the results are presented in Table 18.2.

The null hypothesis would predict an equal number of choices of each type of beer (20, 20, and 20). The experimental hypothesis is that more students will choose Coors than choose Olympia or Budweiser. Alpha is set at .05. Applying Equation 18.2, we find that

$$\chi^2_{(2)} = \frac{(10 - 20)^2}{20} + \frac{(20 - 20)^2}{20} + \frac{(30 - 20)^2}{20} = \frac{100}{20} + 0 + \frac{100}{20} = 10, \, p < .05.$$

We have 2 df since k (number of categories) = 3; hence the subscript (2) in the equation. Since we have a directional prediction, we use a one-tailed test. Turning to Appendix E, we locate the number where the 2-df row and the one-tailed .05 column intersect. The one-tailed critical value of χ^2 at the .05 level with 2 df is 4.605. Since our obtained value of χ^2 exceeds 4.60, the data do not support the null hypothesis. The hypothetical data significantly support the experimental hypothesis.

THE INDEPENDENT TWO-GROUP TEST

The independent two-group test is used to determine the significance of the behavioral differences between two independent groups of subjects. We may have two or more

TABLE 18.2   Hypothetical Frequency of Beer Choice ($N = 60$). (Observed in Top Half, Expected in Bottom Half)

Budweiser	Olympia	Coors	Total
10	20	30	60
20	20	20	60

response categories. The test tells us whether two groups of subjects significantly differ in the proportion of each group falling into each category. The three variables involved in such a study are: (1) the response categories (nominal or greater level of measurement), (2) the two independent groups of subjects (independent variable), and (3) the *frequency* with which the subjects fall into the categories.

Logic and Method

The logic of the two-group test is the same as that of the one-group test, but the methods differ slightly. In the independent two-group test, the data are arranged in a two-by-k matrix or contingency table. We will have two rows (the two groups of subjects) and at least two columns (the response categories) of data.

Null Hypothesis

The calculation of the expected frequencies (E) is not quite as easy as in the one-group case. The *null hypothesis* most commonly states that the groups variable (rows) and response category variable (columns) are independent of each other. If the rows and columns are independent, then the probability of any subject falling into any cell of the contingency table is determined by multiplying the independent probabilities. The probability of a *row* is equal to the total number of subjects in the group (row) divided by the total number of subjects. The probability of a *column* is equal to the total number of responses in *that* column divided by the total number of subjects. Since we can only have *one response per subject,* these probabilities are always less than or equal to one. We multiply the probability of a row by the probability of a column in order to find the probability that any subject will fall into the cell consisting of the intersection of that row and that column. Since the E are frequencies, we must multiply the above probability of the cell by the total number of subjects in order to obtain the expected frequency for that cell. In practice, this is much simpler than it sounds. (See the calculational example.)

The *degrees of freedom* (df) for the independent two-group test is determined by the formula

$$df = (r - 1)(k - 1) \tag{18.3}$$

where r is the number of rows and k is the number of columns in the data matrix. In a two-by-two contingency table, there is only 1 df [$(2 - 1)(2 - 1) = 1$]. With a fixed number of subjects in each group, and with a given total number of responses in each category, as soon as the frequency in one cell of a two-by-two matrix is known, the frequencies in the remaining three cells are known. Since $(r - 1)$ always equals 1 in the two-independent-samples test, the df for the two-group test simplifies to $(k - 1)$.

Calculation Example

Three degrees of freedom   Suppose you are interested in measuring the effect of a potential eyewitness on the honesty of people. You select a relatively untraveled street and purposely drop an envelope on the sidewalk next to a mailbox. The envelope is addressed and stamped, but its open flap reveals a personal letter and a two-dollar bill. You observe and record people's reactions from a well-concealed observation point in a nearby building. For half of the "finders" there is no one else to

TABLE 18.3   Hypothetical Data of the Behavior of Subjects Who Found an Envelope with and without a Possible Witness Nearby

	Mailed letter and money	Kept letter and money	Kept money, mailed letter	Other
Witness present	12	5	3	18
No witness	7	8	11	13

half of the "finders" there is no one else to be seen in the vicinity; for the other half, a confederate of yours strolls down the street some distance behind the finder. You group the reactions of the finders into four categories: "dropped the letter and money into the mailbox," "pocketed the letter with the money," "took the money but mailed the letter," and "other." (Subjects in the "other" category usually appeared not to see the dropped envelope.) The data were tabulated into the categories according to the presence or absence of a potential witness, as shown in Table 18.3.

Now you can calculate row and column totals and compute expected scores for each cell in the table. The completed χ^2 frequency table is shown in Table 18.4. Expected scores, shown in the lower corner of each cell, are obtained by multiplying the column total by the row total for each cell and dividing by the grand total. For example, in the upper left cell expected frequency is $(19 \times 38)/77 \approx 9.4$; in the lower right cell it is $(31 \times 39)/77 \approx 15.7$.

From Equation 18.1 χ^2 is calculated as follows:

$$\chi^2 = \frac{(12 - 9.4)^2}{9.4} + \frac{(5 - 6.4)^2}{6.4} + \frac{(3 - 6.9)^2}{6.9} + \frac{(18 - 15.3)^2}{15.3}$$
$$+ \frac{(7 - 9.6)^2}{9.6} + \frac{(8 - 6.6)^2}{6.6} + \frac{(11 - 7.1)^2}{7.1} + \frac{(13 - 15.7)^2}{15.7}.$$
$$\chi^2 = \frac{6.8}{9.4} + \frac{2.0}{6.4} + \frac{15.2}{6.9} + \frac{7.3}{15.3} + \frac{6.8}{9.6} + \frac{2.0}{6.6} + \frac{15.2}{7.1} + \frac{7.3}{15.7}.$$
$$\chi^2 = .72 + .31 + 2.2 + .48 + .71 + .30 + 2.14 + .46.$$
$$\chi^2_{(3)} \approx 7.3.$$

You then compare the calculated χ^2 by entering Appendix E at the $df = 3$ row. Since the calculated χ^2 of 7.3 is less than the two-tailed critical value of 7.815 at the .05 level, we must conclude that there was no significant difference in the behavior of the subjects in the two conditions. Notice that the one-tailed test is inappropriate because there was no specific direction anticipated in the observed differences.

TABLE 18.4
χ^2 Frequency Table for Data in Table 18.3

	Mailed letter and money	Kept letter and money	Kept money, mailed letter	Other	Row totals
Witness present	12 / 9.4	5 / 6.4	3 / 6.9	18 / 15.3	38
No witness	7 / 9.6	8 / 6.6	11 / 7.1	13 / 15.7	39
Column totals	19	13	14	31	77 Grand Total

THE RELATED TWO-GROUP TEST

The related two-group χ^2 test is used when subjects serve as their own control or with a repeated-measures design. There must be two measures at the nominal or greater level of the behavior of each subject. Such a design might be a before–after design in which each subject is categorized or ranked before and after the introduction of some treatment (chapter 9). This χ^2 test is sometimes called the "McNemar test for the significance of changes" (Siegel, 1956).

Logic and Method

The data are arranged in a two-by-two contingency table of the general form presented in Table 18.5. The "no" and "yes" indicate the different responses.

Cells A and D represent subjects who changed their responses. Cells B and C represent those whose measure did not change. The *sum* of A and D is the total number of people that changed. The null hypothesis (H_0) is that half of these cases will change in one direction and half in the other. Since we are interested in only two cells, the usual χ^2 equation becomes

$$\chi^2 = \frac{(|A - D| - 1)^2}{A + D}, \tag{18.4}$$

where $|A - D|$ indicates that the sign of the difference between A and D is to be ignored. That is, if the difference between A and D is negative, ignore the negative sign and reduce the obtained difference by 1 before squaring. The *df* is always 1, since there are only two cells of interest. As before, use Appendix E to evaluate the significance of the obtained value.

Calculation Example

Suppose that a psychology professor has the theory that first-year college students generally view psychology positively. Furthermore, she hypothesizes that this positive emotional connotation decreases with exposure to the more statistical aspects of psychology. She decides to test this hypothesis with an introductory class of 40 students. First, she obtains a measure of each student's general attitude toward psychology during the first week of the course. She devotes the entire second week to a series of lectures on descriptive and inferential statistics. At the beginning of the third week, she obtains a second measure of each student's general attitude. The null

TABLE 18.5
General Form of Two-by-Two Table for Related Two-Groups χ^2 Test

		After	
		No	Yes
Before	Yes	A	B
	No	C	D

TABLE 18.6
The Hypothetical
Responses of a
Class to a
Questionnaire on
Their Attitudes
toward
Psychology

		After Statistics	
		Positive	Negative
Before Statistics	Negative	A　　4	B　　10
	Positive	C　　10	D　　16

hypothesis is that, of those students who change their attitude, one-half will change in the positive direction and one-half in the negative. She sets α at the .05 level. Suppose that the data in Table 18.6 were obtained.

Applying Equation 18.4, she finds that:

$$\chi^2 = \frac{(|4 - 16| - 1)^2}{16 + 4},$$

$$\chi^2 = \frac{(11)^2}{20},$$

$$\chi^2_{(1)} = 6.05.$$

There is 1 df. The tabled value of a one-tailed χ^2 at the .05 level with 1 df is 2.71. Since the obtained value of χ^2 exceeds 2.71, and the difference is in the predicted direction, she rejects H_0. She concludes that her hypothesis is supported by the data.

ADVANTAGES AND LIMITATIONS

The major advantage of the χ^2 tests is that they are frequently the only tests available for analyzing frequency data arranged in categories at the nominal level of measurement. A second advantage of the χ^2 tests is that they are comparatively easy to compute.

There are three major limitations or restrictions to the use of χ^2 tests. First, the data
Independent Data points *must be independent* of each other. In practice this means that you can have
Points only one response from each subject involved in the computation of χ^2. Therefore if there are several measures of each subject in an experiment, only one score (such as the rank of the mean of the subject's scores) can be used in χ^2 test. Second, the data
Frequency Data points *must be in frequency form.* The most common way in which this is achieved is by tallying the number of subjects that fall into a cell of a contingency table. Finally, the expected values for any cell of a contingency *must not be too small*. This restriction varies with the type of test: one-group, independent two-group, or related two-group.

One-group test When the df is 1 (the number of categories, $k = 2$), all of the E must be equal to or greater than 5. When the df are greater than 1 ($k > 2$), no more than 20% of the E can be less than 5 and no E can be less than 1. When $k > 2$, the categories can sometimes be meaningfully combined in order to satisfy the restriction on the size of E.

Independent two-group test   In the case of the two-by-two contingency table, if the total sample size (N) is greater than 40, there are no restrictions on the size of E. If N is between 20 and 40, all the E must be equal to or greater than 5. If N is less than about 20, the Fisher Exact Test (Siegel, 1956) should be used instead of χ^2. In the two-by-two χ^2 test, calculation Equation 18.5 should be used for a more accurate calculation of χ^2:

Fisher Exact Test

$$\chi^2 = \frac{N\left(|AD - BC| - \dfrac{N}{2}\right)^2}{(A + B)(C + D)(A + C)(B + D)} \tag{18.5}$$

where N is the total sample size; A, B, C, and D are the frequencies in the four quadrants of the two-by-two table; and $\left(|AD - BC| - \dfrac{N}{2}\right)$ indicates that the absolute value of the difference (ignoring the sign of the difference) should be reduced by $\dfrac{N}{2}$.

When there are more than two categories ($k > 2$), no more than 20% of the E can be less than 5 and no E can be less than 1. As before, it may be possible to combine categories *meaningfully* in order to meet this restriction. The combined categories must make sensible groups.

Related two-group test   If the expected frequency [½$(A + D)$] is less than 5, the sign test should be used.

SUMMARY

1. The chi-square (χ^2) test is easy to understand, easy to calculate, and applicable to a wide variety of situations.
2. The most common χ^2 tests are the one-group test, the independent two-group test, and the related two-group test.
3. The one-group test is used to determine the difference between a set of sample frequencies and a set of theoretical frequencies.
4. The one-group test may have from two to N categories.
5. The independent two-group test requires two or more response categories and two groups of subjects.
6. The related two-group test is used when subjects serve as their own controls and you have more than one measure on each subject.
7. Chi-square tests are frequently the only tests available for analyzing frequency data. The data points must be independent of each other.
8. In the case of a two-by-two contingency table, if the sample size is less than 20, you should use the Fisher Exact Test.

SUGGESTED READINGS

Lewis, D., & Burke, C. J. The use and misuse of the chi-square test. *Psychological Bulletin* 1949, *46,* 433–489.

Meyer, M. E. *A statistical analysis of behavior.* Belmont, Calif.: Wadsworth, 1976.

Siegel, S. *Nonparametric statistics.* New York: McGraw-Hill, 1956.

Walker, H. M., & Lev, J. *Statistical inference.* New York: Holt, Rinehart and Winston, 1953.

19

The *t* Tests

Often in psychological research, we obtain data at the interval or higher scale of measurement. When you desire to test the difference between two means from either two independent groups or two related groups, the *t* test gives a powerful technique.

The *t* tests are used with matched or independent two-group designs. The dependent variable must be measured at least at the interval level, since all the numerical information in the scores is utilized in the calculation of the *t*. The *t* test for independent groups is used to test whether the scores of two independent groups differ significantly. The *t* test for related groups is used to test whether the scores of two matched groups, or two measures of a single group (before–after design) differ significantly.

Standard Error   Although slightly different in calculation procedures, both versions of the *t* test use information in the data to generate a value known as the *standard error of the difference between the means*. The *t* statistic is the ratio of the observed mean difference between two sets of scores and the standard error of the difference between the means.

LOGIC

Sampling Distribution   When several sets of subjects are sampled from a population and measured on some variable, the distribution of the arithmetic means of the sample scores is called a **sampling distribution.** If the subjects are sampled randomly from the same population, the means also are random samples from the population. The mean of the

Grand Mean   sampling distribution (mean of means or **grand mean,** $\overline{Y}_G$) and the standard deviation of the means may be calculated. The standard deviation of the sampling distribution is

Standard Error of the Means   called the **standard error of the means ($S_{\overline{y}}$).**

Suppose we obtain five random samples from a population. The hypothetical means of each sample are presented in Table 19.1.

The grand mean of the sampling distribution is $\overline{Y}_G = \Sigma \overline{Y}/N = 15/5 = 3.0$. The variance of the sampling distribution is $S^2 = \Sigma(\overline{Y} - \overline{Y}_G)^2/N = 10/5 = 2.0$. The square root of the variance (S^2) yields the standard error for the five sample means. Therefore, $S_{\overline{y}} = \sqrt{2} \approx 1.4$. The standard error ($S_{\overline{y}}$) describes the variability of the sample means about $\overline{Y}_G$. With random samples, $S_{\overline{y}}$ is due to chance factors.

Usually, you do not sample a population repeatedly. Rather, you randomly sample one set of subjects from the population. If you use a two-group design, then you randomly assign the subjects from your sample to the two groups. Following the administration of an experimental treatment, you obtain the dependent scores for the

**TABLE 19.1
Sampling
Distribution from
Five Means**

$\bar{Y}$	$(\bar{Y} - \bar{Y}_G)$	$(\bar{Y} - \bar{Y}_G)^2$
5	2	4
4	1	1
3	0	0
2	−1	1
1	−2	4
$\Sigma = 15$	$\Sigma = 0$	$\Sigma = 10$

two groups. Using an interval measurement scale, you may calculate the mean $(\bar{Y})$ for each group. The difference between the two $\bar{Y}$s is presumably due to the independent variable. In order to decide whether the observed difference $(\bar{Y}_1 - \bar{Y}_2)$ is due to the independent variable or chance factors, you must be able to compare the difference to some estimate of the expected variance of randomly sampled means from the population.

**Estimate of
Standard Error of
Means**

The measure of the expected differences between randomly sampled means is obtained from the standard error of the means $(S_{\bar{y}})$. Since you did not sample repeatedly from the population, you must use some statistic to *estimate* $S_{\bar{y}}$. The value of $S_{\bar{y}}$ is estimated by dividing the square root of the unbiased variance of the sample by the square root of N (Equation 19.1).

$$S_y = \sqrt{\frac{s^2}{N}} = \frac{s}{\sqrt{N}}$$

(19.1)

If a distribution of scores is roughly bell-shaped, for a small sample of scores you are likely to underestimate the standard deviation of the distribution. Because extreme scores are relatively infrequent, they are less likely to appear in the sample. Consequently, a sample probably will have a narrower distribution. To correct for the inaccuracy caused by the smallness of the sample, an **unbiased estimate** of the variance of the population may be obtained by using the equation

**Unbiased Estimate
of Variance**

$$s^2 = \frac{\Sigma(Y - \bar{Y})^2}{N - 1},$$

(19.2)

where $\Sigma(Y - \bar{Y})^2$ is the sum of squared deviation scores of the sample distribution, N is the number of scores in the sample, and s^2 is the estimate of the variance of the population sampled. Note the difference between the formula for the unbiased estimate of the variance and the formula for a sample variance: the divisor is $N - 1$ instead of N. As mentioned earlier, the effect of subtracting 1 from N diminishes with increasing sample size, which reflects the increasing accuracy of large sample estimates.

Given two groups, with a mean and variance for each group, an estimate of the standard error of the *difference* between two means is obtained by combining the unbiased variances for each group ($s^2{}_1$ and $s^2{}_2$). The unbiased variances can be combined into one estimate by using Equation 19.3.

$$s_c^2 = \frac{\Sigma(Y_1 - \overline{Y}_1)^2 + \Sigma(Y_2 - \overline{Y}_2)^2}{N_1 + N_2 - 2} \tag{19.3}$$

The value s_c^2 is the **combined unbiased estimate** of the population variance, where

Standard Error of Difference between Means

Y_1, $\overline{Y}_1$, and N_1 refer to Group 1, and Y_2, $\overline{Y}_2$, and N_2 refer to Group 2.

The standard error of the difference between two means ($S\overline{y}_1 - \overline{y}_2$) is estimated by

$$S_{\overline{y}_1 - \overline{y}_2} = \sqrt{s_c^2 \left(\frac{1}{N_1} + \frac{1}{N_2}\right)} \tag{19.4}$$

where N_1 is the number of subjects in Group 1 and N_2 is the number of subjects in Group 2.

THE t TEST FOR TWO INDEPENDENT GROUPS

The independent t test is used to decide whether the difference between the means of two independent groups is likely on the basis of chance. The null hypothesis (H_0) is that the independent variable has no consistent effect on the behavior of the two groups of subjects. The difference between two $\overline{Y}$s randomly sampled from the same population should, on the average, be equal to zero ($\overline{Y}_1 - \overline{Y}_2 = 0$). The experimental hypothesis (H_1) is that the difference between the means is not zero ($\overline{Y}_1 - \overline{Y}_2 \neq 0$).

Method

The mean of the distribution of differences between randomly sampled means is zero. The t ratio is defined as the ratio of the observed difference between the means minus the expected difference (based on the H_0) divided by the standard error of the difference:

$$t = \frac{(\overline{Y}_1 - \overline{Y}_2) - 0}{S_{\overline{y}_1 - \overline{y}_2}} \tag{19.5}$$

The t ratio compares the difference between observed and expected variance to the estimate of chance variance. For a given value of $S_{\overline{Y}_1 - \overline{Y}_2}$, the larger the value of the numerator in Equation 19.5 the larger the value of t. For given values of N_1 and N_2, as the value of t increases, the probability of rejecting H_0 increases. All other things being equal, the greater the difference between the two means, the greater the likelihood of rejecting H_0 and accepting H_1.

The equation for calculating the independent *t* is derived from Equations 19.3, 19.4, and 19.5:

$$t = \frac{\overline{Y}_1 - \overline{Y}_2}{\sqrt{\left[\dfrac{\left(\dfrac{N_1 \Sigma Y_1^2 - (\Sigma Y_1)^2}{N_1}\right) + \left(\dfrac{N_2 \Sigma Y_2^2 - (\Sigma Y_2)^2}{N_2}\right)}{N_1 + N_2 - 2}\right]\left[\dfrac{1}{N_1} + \dfrac{1}{N_2}\right]}},$$

where $\overline{Y}_1$ is the mean of Group 1, N_1 is the size of Group 1, ΣY_1 is the sum of squared scores of Group 1, and $(\Sigma Y_1)^2$ is the square of the sum of the scores of Group 1. The subscript 2 refers to Group 2.

A calculated value of *t* is compared with the *critical values* listed in Appendix F. The left-hand column of Appendix F is labeled *df*. The *degrees of freedom (df)* for an independent two-sample test are the total number of subjects minus 2 ($df = N_1 + N_2 - 2$). The critical value of *t* depends on whether you use a one- or two-tailed test, on the value of *df*, and on the value of α. If the value you obtain for *t* is *equal to or greater than* the tabled critical value, then H_0 is rejected.

Calculation Example

Alpha Brain Waves

Biofeedback experimentation has caught the fancy of many psychology students. Of particular interest is brain-wave training that enables persons to emit a high proportion of "alpha brain waves" at will. The alpha brain wave is characteristic of a person who is physically relaxed and has a subjective sense of peace. It is defined as a wave of at least 10 μV in intensity, occurring at 8 to 12 cycles per second.

Suppose you hypothesize that alpha training can be facilitated by first teaching subjects some form of meditation. From a psychology class you randomly sample two groups: Group 1 is composed of 10 males, and Group 2 of 11 males. The biofeedback laboratory has made available to you an electroencephalograph (EEG), a machine that prints a record of brain-wave activity over time (Figure 19.1). From this record you will read the percentage of time a subject emits alpha brain waves.

You decide at random to pretrain Group 1 for 2 hrs. in a meditative technique that involves relaxation training, mental imagery, and silent repetition of certain phrases. Group 2 gets no special training. Afterwards, both groups are hooked up to the EEG machine in the same way and alpha training begins. Training consists of presenting a tone whenever a subject emits a brain wave in the alpha range. Your experimental hypothesis states that the group with meditative training will respond better to alpha training than the naive group (one-tailed prediction).

Each subject in both groups is given a 15-min. trial, and the percentage of time in alpha is recorded and converted to minutes. That is, a person who spent 66% of the time in alpha would get a score of 10 min. (.66 $\times$ 15 = 10). The data are at least interval in level; the results of the experiment are shown in Table 19.2. You decide that α is .001.

To test the data, you first must list the scores (Y) and the square of each score (Y^2). Then, as indicated in Table 19.2, you must sum each column to obtain the values of

FIG. 19.1
The electroencephalo-
graph (EEG) is recording
the brain wave activity
of a subject who is
undergoing
biofeedback training.
(Photograph by D. W.
Matheson.)

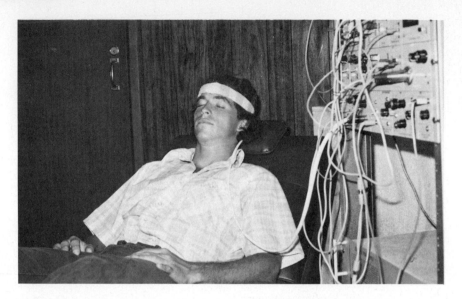

N, ΣY, and ΣY^2 for each group. Then the means of each group are calculated. When all these steps are completed, substitute the information into Equation 19.6. Note that ΣY_1^2, (1242) is *not* the same as $(\Sigma Y_1)^2$, $(110)^2$.

$$t = \frac{11.0 - 8.1}{\sqrt{\dfrac{\left[\dfrac{(10)(1242) - (110)^2}{10}\right] + \left[\dfrac{(11)(741) - (89)^2}{11}\right]}{10 + 11 - 2} \left[\dfrac{1}{10} + \dfrac{1}{11}\right]}}$$

To solve the equation for t, follow these steps:

1. Complete the operations required by the parentheses in the denominator. For example $(10)(1242) = 12420$, $(11)(741) = 8151$, $(110)^2 = 12100$, $(89)^2 = 7921$.
    The denominator of the t equation thus reduces to

$$\sqrt{\frac{\left[\dfrac{12420 - 12100}{10}\right] + \left[\dfrac{8151 - 7921}{11}\right]}{10 + 11 - 2} \left[\frac{1}{10} + \frac{1}{11}\right]}.$$

2. Complete the subtraction and addition within each set of brackets. For example, $12420 - 12100 = 320$, $8151 - 7921 = 230$, $1/10 + 1/11 = 21/110$.
    The t denominator is reduced to

$$\sqrt{\frac{[320/10] + [230/11]}{10 + 11 - 2} \left[\frac{21}{110}\right]}$$

TABLE 19.2
Number of Minutes Spent in an Alpha Brain-Wave State for Two Groups: Group 1 Received Special Meditative Training; Group 2 Did Not

Subject	Score (Y_1)	Y_1^2	Subject	Score (Y_2)	Y_2^2
A	10	100	K	6	36
B	8	64	L	7	49
C	12	144	M	10	100
D	13	169	N	9	81
E	9	81	O	6	36
F	12	144	P	7	49
G	14	196	Q	9	81
H	12	144	R	10	100
I	10	100	S	8	64
J	10	100	T	9	81
			U	8	64

$N_1 = 10$ $\Sigma Y_1^2 = 1242$ $N_2 = 11$ $\Sigma Y_2 = 89$ $\Sigma Y_2^2 = 741$
$\Sigma Y_1 = 110$

$\bar{Y}_1 = \Sigma Y_1 / N_1 = 11$
$\bar{Y}_2 = \Sigma Y_2 / N_2 = 8.1$

3. Complete the division within each bracket, and the addition or subtraction required. For example, $320/10 = 32$, $230/11 \approx 20.9$, $10 + 11 - 2 = 19$, $21/110 \approx .19$. The *t* denominator is reduced to

$$\sqrt{\left[\frac{32 + 20.9}{19}\right]} \, (.19).$$

4. Complete the addition and division within the brackets; for example,

$$32 + 20.9 = 52.9, \ 52.9 \div 19 \approx 2.78.$$

The *t* denominator becomes

$$\sqrt{2.78 \, (.19)}.$$

5. Complete the multiplication and compute the required square root. For example,

$$2.78 \times .19 \approx .53, \ \sqrt{.53} \approx .73.$$

The denominator of the *t* ratio ($S_{\bar{Y}_1 - \bar{Y}_2}$) is 0.73.
6. Complete the subtraction required in the numerator of the *t* ratio. For example, $11.0 - 8.1 = 2.9$. Therefore, the *t* ratio becomes

$$t = 2.9 \, .73 \approx 3.97.$$

Since you predicted that $\bar{Y}_1 > \bar{Y}_2$, you use a one-tailed test. The *df* $= 10 + 11 - 2 = 19$, and $\alpha = .001$. The critical value in Appendix F is 3.579. Since the obtained value of t (3.97) exceeds 3.579, H_0 is rejected ($t = 3.97$, $df = 19$, one-tailed $p < 0.001$). You therefore conclude that meditation training significantly facilitates alpha training. If you were to present your data in a journal format, you would state your conclusion like this: "Meditation training significantly facilitates alpha training, $t(19) = 3.97$, $p < .001$."

THE t TEST FOR TWO RELATED GROUPS

The second t test is used with matched-group designs or repeated-measures designs (before–after, one-group). In such designs, the *pairs* of scores are correlated in some way. The t test for related scores takes into account the correlation between paired measures in calculating the value of the standard error of the mean.

Method

The related t test is used to decide whether the difference between the means of two related groups is likely on the basis of chance. The difference between two means $(\overline{Y}_1 - \overline{Y}_2)$ is equal to the mean of the differences between the paired scores $(\overline{Y}_D)$. That is, $\overline{Y}_D = \overline{Y}_1 - \overline{Y}_2$. The null hypothesis is that the independent variable has no consistent effect on the behavior of the two groups of subjects: $\overline{Y}_D = 0$. The experimental hypothesis is that the difference between the means is not zero: $\overline{Y}_D \neq 0$.

The t ratio is defined as the ratio of the observed $\overline{Y}_D$ minus the expected $\overline{Y}_D$ (based on H_0) divided by the standard error of the differences:

$$t = \frac{\overline{Y}_D - 0}{S_D}.$$

(19.7)

For a given value of S_D, the larger the value of the numerator $(\overline{Y}_D - 0)$, the larger the value of t. All else being equal, the greater the difference between the scores of the two groups, the greater the likelihood of rejecting H_0 and accepting H_1.

The standard error of the mean difference is based on the variance of the difference between the *paired scores*. Equation 19.8 defines the standard error of the mean difference (S_D):

$$S_D = \sqrt{\frac{\Sigma(D_i - \overline{D})^2}{N(N - 1)}}.$$

(19.8)

In Equation 19.8, N is the number of *paired scores,* D_i is the difference between any pair of scores, and $\overline{D}$ is the average difference between paired scores ($\overline{D} = \overline{Y}_D$).

The formula for the related *t*, derived from Equations 19.7 and 19.8, is presented in Equation 19.9:

$$t = \frac{\overline{Y}_D}{\sqrt{\left[\dfrac{N\Sigma D^2 - (\Sigma D)^2}{N}\right]\left[\dfrac{1}{N(N-1)}\right]}} \qquad (19.9)$$

In Equation 19.9, $\overline{Y}_D$ is the mean of the difference scores, N is the number of paired scores, ΣD^2 is the sum of the squared difference scores, and $(\Sigma D)^2$ is the square of the sum of the difference scores.

A calculated value of *t* is compared with the *critical values* listed in Appendix F. The number of *degrees of freedom* equals the number of difference scores minus 1 ($df = N - 1$). If the obtained *t* value is *equal to or greater than* the critical value, then H_0 may be rejected.

Calculation Example

Suppose a high-school counselor thinks that anxiety-producing instructions will affect the achievement test scores of students. On the basis of IQ scores, the counselor obtains ten matched pairs of subjects (matched by correlated criterion). The students are all enrolled in college preparatory programs. One member of each pair is randomly assigned to Group A and the other to Group B. The two groups are placed in separate but similar rooms. Just before taking the achievement test, Group B is told that the test is a college entrance examination that will directly affect their chances of getting into college. Supposedly, the instructions will arouse anxiety in the students in Group B. Group A is told that the test is a practice test to help them discover which areas they should study in order to improve their chances of getting into college.

TABLE 19.3
Scores on Achievement Test for Matched Subjects

Pair of Subjects	Scores of Group A	Scores of Group B	Difference between Paired Scores $D_i = (Y_1 - Y_2)$	D_i^2
A	90	87	3	9
B	88	89	−1	1
C	93	91	2	4
D	94	92	2	4
E	88	86	2	4
F	87	84	3	9
G	89	90	−1	1
H	92	89	3	9
I	93	87	6	36
J	85	88	−3	9
$N = 10$	$\Sigma \overline{Y}_A = 899$	$\Sigma \overline{Y}_B = 883$	$\Sigma D = 16$	$\Sigma D^2 = 86$
	$\overline{Y}_A = 89.9$	$\overline{Y}_B = 88.3$	$\overline{Y}_D = 1.6$	

Because the counselor is not sure whether anxiety will increase or decrease the treatment scores, H_1 is two-tailed. The counselor arbitrarily sets $\alpha = .05$. The dependent variable is the performance of the two groups on the achievement test (measured as percentile scores). The counselor assumes that the test provides an interval scale. The counselor obtains the data shown in Table 19.3.

First the scores of each group are listed. Then the scores of one group are subtracted from the scores of the other and the differences (D_i) and (D_i^2) are listed. (It does not really matter which group is subtracted from which, so long as you are consistent and remember which way you subtracted.) As indicated in Table 19.3, the D_i and D_i^2 columns are summed. The sum of each group's scores provides a check on the subtraction procedures, since the difference between the two groups' sums must equal the sum of the differences. (The means of each group do *not* have to be calculated for the t test.) When these steps are complete, the information is substituted into Equation 19.9:

$$t = \frac{1.6}{\sqrt{\left[\dfrac{10(86) - (16)^2}{10}\right]\left[\dfrac{1}{10(10 - 1)}\right]}}.$$

To solve the equation for t, the following steps are performed:

1. Complete the operations required by the parentheses in the denominator. For example,

$$(10)(86) = 860, (16)^2 = 256,$$
$$(10 - 1) = 9, 10(9) = 90.$$

The denominator of the t equation then is reduced to

$$\sqrt{\left[\frac{860 - 256}{10}\right]\left[\frac{1}{90}\right]}.$$

2. Complete the subtraction and division within each set of brackets. For example,

$$\frac{604}{10} = 60.4; \frac{1}{90} \approx .011.$$

The t denominator is reduced to:

$$\sqrt{(60.4)(.011)}$$

3. Complete the multiplication within the square root sign and compute the square root. For example,

$$(60.4) \times (.011) \approx .66$$
$$\sqrt{.66} \approx .81.$$

The denominator of the *t* ratio (S_D) is .81.

4. The *t* ratio becomes

$$t = \frac{1.6}{.81} \approx 1.98.$$

The $df = N - 1 = 9$ (*pairs* of scores) and the two-tailed $\alpha = .05$. The critical value in Appendix F is 2.262. Since the obtained value of *t* (1.98) is less than the critical value, H_0 cannot be rejected ($t = 1.98$, $df = 9$, two-tailed $p > .05$). Therefore, the counselor concludes that the "anxiety-provoking instructions" did *not* have any significant differential effect on the subjects.

ADVANTAGES AND LIMITATIONS

While a little complicated to compute, the *t* tests take advantage of all the information presented by interval measurement to test differences between the means of two groups. The *t* tests are limited to comparing the means of only two groups. An experimenter may use multiple *t* tests to test the difference between any two groups in a multilevel or factorial experiment. The alpha level is inflated in a multiple *t* test; therefore multiple-comparison tests are usually preferred for multiple-group comparisons. Multiple-comparison tests (Kirk, 1968) based on the logic of the *t* test are specifically designed for multiple-group comparisons.

Independent Random Sampling

The independent two-group *t* test *demands* that the two groups be independent, random samples from a population. The assumptions of independence and randomness are met if the groups are sampled randomly and if subjects are assigned randomly to the two groups.

In order for the sample standard deviation to be a good estimate of the standard error of the mean, the population should be normally distributed. However, the assumption of normality of the population distribution is relatively unimportant, particularly if N_1 and N_2 are both greater than about 25 (Boneau, 1960).

In order for the two sample standard deviations to be combined into one estimate of the standard error of the mean, the populations from which both samples were derived should have approximately equal variances. Again, the assumption of equal population variance is relatively unimportant if the sample sizes are equal and both at least equal to 25 (Boneau, 1960). In general, if the sample sizes of the two groups are equal ($N_1 = N_2$), then as the sample size increases, extreme violations of the assumptions of normality and equal population variance have little effect on *t*. Slight differences in sample size have little effect as long as the smallest N is fairly large.

Random Assignment

The related two-group *t* test *demands* that each pair of subjects be randomly assigned to the two treatment groups. The assumptions of normality and equal population variance also apply to the related *t* test. As was the case with the independent *t* test, the assumptions are not very important with a fairly large number of pairs ($N > 25$).

The related *t* test is based on the differences between the scores of paired subjects. The difference scores are used in order to eliminate the correlation between the paired scores. Each pair contributes only one score (D) to the analysis. The use of only one score for each pair of subjects reduces the number of degrees of freedom (df) for the t test. If you look at Appendix F, you will note that the critical values of t increase as the df decrease. The use of the *related* t test with *independent* groups would lead to more frequent failures to reject H_0 when H_0 is false (Type II errors). For this reason the two sets of scores must be correlated in order to use the related t test legitimately. In addition, the correlation between the two groups should not be small. The correlation between the two groups must be large enough to offset the loss of df associated with using the related t test.

With both tests, as the sample size increases, the standard deviation of the means or mean differences becomes a better estimate of the standard error of the sampling distribution of means or mean differences. Also, as the sample size increases, the likelihood of detecting a small difference between means increases.

SUMMARY

1. The t tests may be used with matched or independent two-group designs.
2. The distribution of the means of several samples from a population is called a sampling distribution.
3. The standard deviation of a sampling distribution is called the standard error.
4. The combined standard errors from two distributions is called the standard error of the difference between means. This standard error is used as the denominator in a t test.
5. An independent t test for two groups is used to decide whether the observed difference between two means is likely on the basis of chance.
6. A t test for matched-group designs or repeated-measures designs tests the experimental hypothesis that the difference between the means of two related groups is not zero.
7. The t test takes advantage of all the information in the data from the two groups. The t test is limited to the comparison of only two groups.
8. The t test requires that the two groups be independent, random samples from a population.
9. Violations of the assumptions of the t test have little effect on t if the sample size is large enough.
10. As the sample size increases, the likelihood of detecting small differences increases.

SUGGESTED READINGS

Hays, W. L. *Statistics for social scientists* (2nd ed.). New York: Holt, Rinehart and Winston, 1973.

Jacobson, P. E. *Introduction to statistical measures for the social and behavioral sciences.* Hinsdale, Ill.: Dryden, 1976.

Kirk, R. E. *Experimental design: Procedures for the behavioral sciences.* Belmont, Calif.: Brooks/Cole, 1968.

Meyer, M. E. *A statistical analysis of behavior.* Belmont, Calif.: Wadsworth, 1976.

20

The Analysis of Variance

If your research design includes more than two groups of subjects, more than two levels of a treatment, or more than one independent variable, and you have an interval or greater level of measurement of the dependent variable, then the analysis of variance (ANOVA) may be appropriate. The F test is the critical statistic of an analysis of variance, and it may be used to good advantage with many different experimental designs. This chapter outlines directions for performing several forms of an analysis of variance.

When, after the "thrill" of designing your experiment, and the "agony" of getting your subjects assigned to groups, experimental settings, and various experimental treatments, you plan to evaluate your data it is important to choose the best statistical technique available. When you have two groups of subjects and are going to compare the two means of those groups, the obvious choice is the *t* test because of its various virtues. However, if you have more than two groups, the analysis of variance (abbreviated ANOVA) may be the best statistical technique available to you. As you learned in chapter 5, variance is a measure of dispersion in observed scores; and variance in dependent measure scores arises from three sources: subject factors, environmental factors, and experimentation factors. When an experimenter designs an experiment properly, subject factors or individual differences and experimentation factors are controlled, and any residual effects of these variables (uncontrolled sources of variation) are termed *error*. The environmental effects due to the manipulations of the independent variable are defined as *treatment effects,* and any other uncontrolled environmental effect not due to the independent variable is assumed to be error. In an *F* test you obtain the ratio comparing the variance due to the independent variable(s) with the error variance; then you look up this value, called the *F* ratio, in a table of critical values. The *F* test may be used with independent-groups or related-groups designs, and with factorial or repeated-measure factorial designs. We shall demonstrate how to do analysis of variance for these four designs, applied to the same hypothetical experiment.

Subject Factors
Environmental Factors
Experimentation Factors

Error

F Test

LOGIC AND METHOD

Regardless of the specific research design, the analytical model of the analysis of variance is constant; however, the specific details of the procedure depend on the type of research design. The following sections illustrate the ANOVA procedures with four designs (multilevel, randomized blocks, factorial, and split-plot).

To emphasize the common approach of ANOVA, the four designs are each illustrated with the identical raw data. That is, the dependent variable measures are identical, although they are analyzed into different variance components according to the design that supposedly led to the data. It is important to note that these data are hypothetical, and each design should be considered to be an independent experiment. The "coincidence" of identical numbers provides a convenient means of comparing the different designs and procedures.

**TABLE 20.1
Cooperation/
Competition
Game Presented
in a 2 × 2 Matrix**

		Jacks' Response	
		X	Y
Jill's Response	X	Jack wins 5¢ Jill wins 5¢	Jack wins 10¢ Jill wins 1¢
	Y	Jack wins 1¢ Jill wins 10¢	Jack wins 1¢ Jill wins 1¢

To set the stage, we must establish the hypothetical experiment. Assume that we are interested in some of the variables which cause children to cooperate or compete with other children. There are several "reward–cost" games that can be adjusted to provide a measure of competition and/or cooperation. For example, the 2 × 2 table, Table 20.1, shows a possible payoff matrix for two game players. If both children press button "X" they each win a nickel. If both press button "Y" they each win only a penny. If Jack presses "Y" when Jill presses "X," Jack wins a dime while Jill gets only a penny. With an outcome matrix of this type, it is reasonable to label an "X" button press a cooperative response while a "Y" button press is a competitive one.

MULTILEVEL DESIGN ($N = 18$ EXAMPLE)

If children observe other children (models) cooperating, they should be more likely to cooperate when they play the game. If they observe models competing, then they should be more likely to compete. To test this general modeling or imitation hypothesis, a three-group design is used with six children in each group. One group (A1) plays the game after watching the models compete; a second group (A2) plays the game without previously watching models; and a third group (A3) plays the game after watching the models cooperate. The dependent variable is the number of trials out of 15 on which the subjects cooperate. The dependent variable measures form a ratio scale (Chapter 5). The raw data are presented in Table 20.2. The research design in this portion of the example is a *multilevel design* (Chapter 10) with 18 girls randomly assigned in groups of 6 to 3 members.

**TABLE 20.2
Number of
Cooperative
Responses in
Modeling
Experiment:
Multilevel Three-
Group Design.**

	Groups			
1 *Competitive*	*2* *Control*	*3* *Cooperative*	*i* ΣY	$\overline{Y}_k$
3	8	7	18	6
6	8	10	24	8
6	11	10	27	9
5	6	10	21	7
7	7	10	24	8
9	8	13	30	10
$\overset{k}{\Sigma} Y = 36$	48	60	144	
$\overline{Y}_i = 6$	8	10	Grand Mean $= 8$	

We are concerned with determining if the data support the modeling hypothesis. The experimental hypothesis is that the mean cooperative response frequency for the cooperative group (A3) should be greater than the mean of the control group (A2), and the mean of the control group should be greater than the mean of the competitive group (A1). Symbolically, H_1 is $\overline{Y}_3 > \overline{Y}_2 > \overline{Y}_1$. The symbol $>$ means "greater than" as defined in Appendix A. The null hypothesis is that the means of the three groups should be equal. H_0 is $\overline{Y}_3 = \overline{Y}_2 = \overline{Y}_1$. The probability of a Type I error is set at .05 ($\alpha = .05$).

Between-Groups Variance

Within-Group Variance

It is assumed that the children would all have behaved essentially like the control group if they had been tested *prior to* watching the models. In other words, it is expected that there was no consistent *between-groups variance* at the time of, and as a result of, the random assignment to the three groups (chapter 2). Because of random error due to several possible sources, including individual differences, there is variance in the scores within each of the three groups. This *within-group variance* was expected to be similar for the three groups because of the random-assignment procedure. Another way of stating the experimental hypothesis is to say that *after* observing the models, the *between-groups* variance will be greatly increased while the *within-group* variance remains relatively stable. The null hypothesis in these terms is that the between-groups variance will remain unchanged by the experimental treatment. (H_0 is that before treatment, between-groups variance will be about zero and both between- and within-group variance will be unaffected by the treatment.)

Grand Mean

In the structural model for a multilevel design a subject's score (Y) is the sum of three parts: the mean score of all the subjects in the experiment ($\overline{Y}$), the effect of the independent variable (A_i), plus the effect of all the uncontrolled variance sources in the experiment, called error.

Sums of Squares

To calculate the between-groups and within-group variance you first must find the *sums of squares* associated with the total set of scores, the between-group means, and the within-group scores. The equation for the total sum of squares (total SS) is

$$\text{total } SS = \Sigma Y^2 - \frac{(\Sigma Y)^2}{N}, \tag{20.1}$$

where ΣY^2 is the sum of all scores squared, $(\Sigma Y)^2$ is the *square of the sum* of the scores, and N is the number of scores.

The equation for the sum of squares for the between-group means (treatment SS) is

$$\text{treatment } SS = \sum_{i}^{k} \frac{(\Sigma Y)^2}{N_k} - \frac{(\Sigma Y)^2}{N}, \tag{20.2}$$

where $\overset{k}{(\Sigma Y)^2}$ is the *square of the sum* of the scores in a treatment group, N_k is the number of scores in a treatment group, $(\Sigma Y)^2/N$ is defined for Equation 20.1, and the results of $\overset{k}{(\Sigma Y)^2}/N_k$ are summed across the three treatment levels before subtracting the value of $(\Sigma Y)^2/N$.

The equation for the within-group (within-subjects) sum of squares is

$$\text{within-subjects } SS = (\text{total } SS) - (\text{treatment } SS). \qquad (20.3)$$

Let us now return to our data. Squaring each of the 18 scores and summing the squares yields $\Sigma Y^2 = 1252$. Substituting the values of Table 20.2 into Equation 20.1, you obtain

$$\text{total } SS = 1252 - \frac{(144)^2}{18}$$
$$= 1252 - \frac{(20,736)}{18}$$
$$= 1252 - 1152$$
$$\text{total } SS = 100.$$

Substituting the values of Table 20.2 into Equation (20.2) yields

$$\text{treatment } SS = \left[\frac{36^2}{6} + \frac{48^2}{6} + \frac{60^2}{6}\right] - \frac{144^2}{18}$$
$$= \left[\frac{1296}{6} + \frac{2304}{6} + \frac{3600}{6}\right] - 1152$$
$$= (216 + 384 + 600) - 1152$$
$$= 1200 - 1152$$
$$\text{treatment } SS = 48.$$

Substituting the calculated values into Equation 20.3, you arrive at

$$\text{within-subjects } SS = 100 - 48 = 52.$$

Degrees of Freedom

Degrees of Freedom

The between and within variances are equal to the between and within sums of squares divided by the appropriate degrees of freedom (df). In general, the *degrees of freedom* for each variance term are equal to one less than the number of squared sums or scores upon which each variance is based. In the calculations of the treatment SS, three squared sums were involved (36^2, 48^2, 60^2), so there are $3 - 1 = 2$ df for the treatment SS. Similarly, in the case of the total SS, there were 18 squared scores, so there are $18 - 1 = 17$ df for the total SS. Within-subjects $df = $ total $df - $ treatment df; the df for the within-subjects SS is $17 - 2 = 15$.

Mean Squares

Mean Squares

The between and within variances are also called *mean squares*. The treatment mean square is $48/2 = 24$. The within-group mean square is $52/15 \approx 3.47$.

TABLE 20.3   Summary of Analysis of Variance for Modeling Experiment: Multilevel Design

Source of Variation	SS	df	Mean Square	F	p
Treatment	48	2	24.00	6.92	<.05
Within-subjects	52	15	3.47		
Total	100	17			

The *F test* of the modeling treatment effect is the ratio of the between-groups variance to the within-group variance. The null nypothesis is that there is no treatment effect; the three treatment groups were sampled from the same population, and therefore the means of the three treatment groups differ only by chance. The between-groups variance (treatment mean square) is an estimate of the variance due to random error plus the variance due to the modeling treatment. The within-group variance (within-subjects mean square) is an estimate of the variance due to random error. If there is no real treatment effect, then the F ratio should be close to 1.0; that is, if you divide random error by random error, the result will approximate 1.0. The experimental hypothesis is that the modeling conditions have a real effect on the cooperative behavior of nursery-school girls. If the experimental hypothesis is correct, the F ratio should be greater than 1.0.

The F ratio for the multilevel design was $F = 24/3.47 \approx 6.92$, with 2 df for the numerator and 15 df for the denominator. These calculations are summarized in Table 20.3.

Critical Values of F

The value of F is compared with the critical value of F in Appendix G. The appendix provides values for each combination of numerator (top row V_1) and denominator df (column V_2) and several levels of α. In the modeling study α is .05, df is 2 for the numerator (row V_1) and 15 for the denominator (column V_2). The critical value is 3.68. The probability of an F ratio as large as or larger than 6.92 is less than α. Therefore, you can conclude that the modeling treatment had significant effect on the cooperative behavior of the children. When writing the significant effect, use the format outlined in chapter 14: $F (2,15) = 6.92$, $p < .05$.

There is a real difference between at least one pair of the means of the treatment group. The significant F test, where there are more than two treatment groups, does not indicate which means are significantly different; it only indicates that there are some significant differences between means. You would normally apply a *multiple-comparison test* (Kirk, 1968) in order to find out which means differed.

Multiple Comparisons

Multiple
Comparisons

The t test is used to determine whether the difference between a specific pair of means is due to chance. Suppose you had chosen α to be a specific value, for example, .10. The level of α applies to the entire set of means, not just a specific pair. If the researcher applied the t test to *all possible pairs* of means in a multilevel design, then the probability of at least one Type I error becomes greater than α. The probability of at least one Type I error equals 1 minus the probability of no Type I errors. The probability of no Type I error in all comparisons equals the probability of no Type I error for one comparison, multiplied by the probability of no Type I error for another comparison, multiplied by the probability for the next, and so on. In symbolic form:

$$p\text{(at least one Type I error)} = 1 - [p(\text{no Type I}) \quad p(\text{no Type I}) \quad \ldots \quad p(\text{no Type I})]$$
$$= 1 - [(1 - a) \quad (1 - a) \quad \ldots \quad (1 - a)]$$
$$= 1 - (1 - a)^k,$$

$$(20.4)$$

where k is the number of comparisons of pairs of means. For example, if an α of .10 were used for the t test of all 10 possible comparisons of means ($k = 10$) when there are 5 group means in a 5-group multilevel design, the probability of *at least one* Type I error equals $1 - (1 - .10)^{10} = 1 - (.90)^{10} \approx .65$. Therefore there is a probability of .65 that at least one Type I error will occur among the 10 t tests. The solution to the problem of maintaining the probability of Type I error at the stated level of α is to divide the value of α by the number of multiple-comparison tests to be made. If k is 10 and α is .10, $\alpha/k = .01$ is the significance level for *any one* comparison of two means. In that case $1 - (1 - .01)^{10} = .10$, which is the stated level of α for the entire experiment (entire set of ten comparisons of five means).

In the case of the modeling experiment, α is .05 and k is 3 because there are three means and three possible comparisons of the three means taken in pairs. Suppose that you had predicted that the mean number of cooperative responses for the cooperation group would be greater than the mean of the control group and that the mean of the control group would be larger than the mean of the competition group ($\overline{Y}$ cooperation $> \overline{Y}$ control $> \overline{Y}$ competition). Dividing α by k you have $.05/3 \approx .017$. If you used .017 as the level of significance for each of the three t tests, the overall probability of a Type I error would be $1 - (1 - .017)^3 = .05$. However, the tabled values of t (Appendix F) do not contain a value of .017 for α. The closest tabled value of α is 0.02 for a two-tailed test or 0.01 for a one-tailed test. Since the predictions are one-tailed, you should use the value of 0.01 for the t tests. This choice is a conservative procedure, since α for all three t tests will be $1 - (1 - .01)^3 = 0.03$ instead of 0.05. The independent two-group t test (chapter 19) is applied to the three pairs of means. The value of the within-subjects mean square is equal to the average value (across the three possible pairs of groups) of

$$\frac{[\Sigma Y_1 - (\Sigma Y_1)^2] + [\Sigma Y_2^2 - (\Sigma Y_2)^2]}{N_1 + N_2 - 2},$$

$$(20.5)$$

where Y_1 and Y_2 are, first, the cooperative and control groups, then the cooperative and competitive groups, and finally the control and competitive groups.

The value of the within-subjects mean square is the best single estimate of variance due to random error. Therefore, it is substituted in Equation 19.6 to yield

$$t = \frac{\overline{Y}_1 - \overline{Y}_2}{\sqrt{M.S. \text{ within-subjects} \left(\frac{1}{N_1} + \frac{1}{N_2}\right)}} . \tag{20.6}$$

The difference between two pairs of means is 2 ($\overline{Y}$ cooperative $- \overline{Y}$ control: $\overline{Y}$ control $- \overline{Y}$ competitive) and the difference is 4 in the last possible pair ($\overline{Y}$ cooperative $- \overline{Y}$ competitive). The value of the t denominator is $\sqrt{3.47\ (2/6)} \approx 1.08$ in all three cases. Therefore, the resultant t values are:

cooperative vs. control t (10) $\approx$ 1.85, $p > .01$.
cooperative vs. competitive t (10) $\approx$ 3.70, $p < .01$.
control vs. competitive t (10) $\approx$ 1.85, $p > .01$.

The significant t for the comparison between the cooperative and competitive group means indicates that the statistical significance of the F value was due to the difference between those two group means. The prediction that they would differ was supported, but the two other predictions regarding the differences between the control group mean and the means of the other two groups, were not supported; a determination that can be made only with a multiple-comparison test.

RANDOMIZED-BLOCKS DESIGN

If each child experiences each of the three modeling conditions, then the research design is a *repeated-measures* design (chapter 9), a particular form of randomized-blocks design (chapter 8). Suppose you used 6 children instead of 18. Each child would first play the game under the control condition (no model) and then under the other two conditions (competitive and cooperative modeling) in random order. *The data in Table 20.2 remain the same, except that each row of data represents three scores from one of six girls.*

The structural model for the randomized-blocks design is $Y = (Y) + (A_i) + (S_k) +$ (error), where S_k refers to the average performance of each subject across the three modeling conditions.

Calculating F

The formulas and values for calculating the total SS and treatment SS remain the same (Equations 20.1 and 20.2). The sum of squares for between blocks (between subjects) is calculated from the sums at the right-hand margin of Table 20.2 by the formula

$$\text{blocks } SS = \sum^{k} \frac{\overset{i}{(\Sigma Y)^2}}{N_i} - \frac{(\Sigma Y)^2}{N},\tag{20.7}$$

where $\overset{i}{\Sigma}Y$ is the sum of scores for each block (subject), N_i is the number of scores for each block (subject), and $(\Sigma Y)^2/N$ is defined in Equation 20.1.

The formula for calculating the residual within-subjects variance (random error variance) is

$$\text{within-subjects } SS = (\text{total } SS) - (\text{treatment } SS) - (\text{blocks } SS).\tag{20.8}$$

Substituting the values from Table 20.2 yields

$$
\begin{aligned}
\text{blocks } SS &= \left[\frac{18^2}{3} + \frac{24^2}{3} + \frac{27^2}{3} + \frac{21^2}{3} + \frac{24^2}{3} + \frac{30^2}{3}\right] - 1152 \\
&= \left[\frac{324}{3} + \frac{576}{3} + \frac{729}{3} + \frac{441}{3} + \frac{576}{3} + \frac{900}{3}\right] - 1152 \\
&= (108 + 192 + 243 + 147 + 192 + 300) - 1152 \\
&= 1182 - 1152 \\
&= 30.
\end{aligned}
$$

$$\text{within-subjects } SS = 100 - 48 - 30$$

There are $6 - 1 = 5$ df for blocks and $17 - 2 - 5 = 10$ df for within subjects. The blocks mean square (blocks $M.S.$) equals blocks SS/blocks $df = 30/5 = 6$. The within-subjects mean square equals within-subjects SS/within-subjects $df = 22/10 = 2.2$. The F ratio for treatment is equal to the treatment $M.S.$/within-subjects $M.S. = 24/2.2 \approx 10.91$. These calculations are summarized in Table 20.4.

TABLE 20.4 Summary of Analysis of Variance of Modeling Experiment: Randomized-Blocks Design.

Source of Variation	SS	df	Mean Square	F	p
Treatment	48	2	24.00	10.91	<.05
Blocks	30	5	6.00		
Within-subjects	22	10	2.20		
Total	100	17			

Note. N = 6; *three scores obtained from each child.*

Multiple Comparisons

Although you conclude that the modeling treatment had a significant effect on the children's behavior, the F ratio again does not tell where the source of significance lies. The multiple-comparison techniques used with the multilevel design may also be used with the randomized-blocks design. In both cases, a strong reason for a one-tailed directional prediction must be available *before* the data are collected.

Equation 20.6 with the mean square within subjects is used; however, the denominator has changed, since within-subjects M.S. is now 2.2. The value of the t denominator in all three cases is $\sqrt{2.2\ (2/6)} = \sqrt{.73} = .85$. The resulting values of t are

cooperative vs. control $t\ (5) \approx 2.35$, $p > .01$
cooperative vs. competitive $t\ (5) \approx 4.70$, $p < .01$
control vs. competitive $t\ (5) \approx 2.35$, $p > .01$.

Related-Groups Design

Correlation between Repeated Scores

The df are 5 for each comparison because the randomized-blocks design is a related-groups design, using the same subjects under each pair of levels of the modeling treatment. The calculation of within-subjects M.S. takes into account the correlation between repeated scores, and each t test is calculated from six pairs of scores, so $df = 6 - 1 = 5$.

These results are the same as in the multilevel design; the cooperative-model group was significantly more cooperative then the competitive-model group. The control group did not significantly differ from either of the other two groups.

FACTORIAL DESIGN

Suppose you performed the modeling experiment using children of both sexes, so that a sex variable is added to the multilevel design. You have 9 males and 9 females ($N = 18$). Table 20.5 reformulates the data of Table 20.2 for this new factor. All possible

**TABLE 20.5
Raw Data of
Modeling
Experiment: 2 × 3
Factorial Design**

		Modeling Groups			
		A_1 (Competitive)	A_2 (Control)	A_3 (Cooperative)	$\underset{\Sigma}{i}$
B_1 (Male)		3	8	7	18
		6	8	10	24
		6	11	10	27
		$\underset{\Sigma}{k} = 15$	$\underset{\Sigma}{k} = 27$	$\underset{\Sigma}{k} = 27$	$\underset{\Sigma\Sigma}{i\ k} = 69$
B_2 (Female)		5	6	10	21
		7	7	10	24
		9	8	13	30
		$\underset{\Sigma}{k} = 21$	$\underset{\Sigma}{k} = 21$	$\underset{\Sigma}{k} = 33$	$\underset{\Sigma\Sigma}{i\ k} = 75$
		$\underset{\Sigma\Sigma}{j\ k} = 36$	$\underset{\Sigma\Sigma}{j\ k} = 48$	$\underset{\Sigma\Sigma}{j\ k} = 60$	$\underset{\Sigma\Sigma\Sigma}{i\ j\ k} = 144$

combinations of levels of sex and modeling conditions are included, so the design is a factorial design (chapter 10).

The level of significance for the modeling effect is .05. The level of significance for each of the two effects involving sex (sex effect and modeling-by-sex interaction effect) is $.05/2 = .025$.

Calculating F

The structural model for the factorial design is $Y = (\overline{Y}) + (A_i) + (B_j) + (AB_{ij}) +$ (error), where B_j refers to the sex groups and AB_{ij} refers to the interaction between sex and modeling conditions. The total SS and modeling treatment SS (now called modeling SS) are calculated the same way as in the multilevel design. The formula for the between-sex-groups sum of squares (abbreviated sex SS) is

Interaction

$$\text{sex } SS = \sum^{j} \frac{\overset{i\ k}{(\Sigma\Sigma Y)^2}}{N_{ik}} - \frac{(\Sigma Y)^2}{N}, \tag{20.9}$$

where $\overset{i\ k}{(\Sigma\Sigma Y)^2}$ is the *square of the sum* of all nine scores in each sex group, and N_{ik} is the number of scores in each sex group (9).

The sex-by-modeling interaction SS is

$$\text{sex-by-modeling } SS = \overset{i\ j}{\Sigma\Sigma} \left[\frac{\overset{k}{(\Sigma Y)^2}}{N_k} \right] - \frac{(\Sigma Y)^2}{N} - (\text{modeling } SS) - (\text{sex } SS), \tag{20.10}$$

where $\overset{k}{(\Sigma Y)}$ stands for the sum of all scores in any single cell of the design, which is then squared and divided by N_k, the number of subjects in each cell of the design (3). The within-subjects SS is calculated as before. The value of sex SS is

$$\text{sex } SS = \left[\frac{75^2}{9} + \frac{69^2}{9} \right] - \frac{144^2}{18}$$

$$= \left[\frac{5626}{9} + \frac{4761}{9} \right] - 1152$$

$$= (625 + 529) - 1152$$

$$\text{sex } SS = 1154 - 1152 = 2.$$

$$\text{sex-by-modeling } SS = \left[\frac{15^2}{3} + \frac{21^2}{3} + \frac{27^2}{3} + \frac{21^2}{3} + \frac{27^2}{3} + \frac{33^2}{3} \right] - 1152 - 2 - 48$$

$$= \left[\frac{225 + 441 + 729 + 441 + 729 + 1089}{3} \right] - 1202$$

$$\text{sex-by-modeling } SS = 1218 - 1202 = 16.$$

$$\text{within-subjects } SS = 100 - 48 - 2 - 16 = 34.$$

TABLE 20.6
Summary Table of
Analysis of
Variance:
Factorial Design
(N = 18, 9 Male, 9
Female)

Source of Variation	SS	df	Mean Square	F	p
Modeling	48	2	24.00	8.48	<.05
Sex	2	1	2.00	—	>.025
Sex-by-modeling	16	2	8.00	2.83	>.025
Within-Subjects	34	12	2.83		
Total	100	17			

The *df* for sex is $2 - 1 = 1$, for sex-by-treatment is $(3 - 1)(2 - 1) = 2$, and for within-subjects SS is $17 - 2 - 1 - 2 = 12$. The treatment M.S. is the same as before; sex M.S. $= 2/1 = 2$; sex-by-modeling M.S. $= 16/2 = 8$; within-subjects M.S. $= 34/12 \approx 2.83$. These calculations are summarized in Table 20.6.

Multiple Comparisons

The multiple-comparison technique used with the multilevel and randomized-blocks designs now may be applied to the modeling variable. The one-tailed predictions were $\overline{Y}$ cooperative $> \overline{Y}$ control $> \overline{Y}$ competitive. Equation (20.6) is used with the same mean differences in the numerator as before; however, the denominator is different, since within-subjects M.S. is now 2.83. The value of the *t* denominator in all three comparisons of the means is $\sqrt{2.83 \ (2/6)} \approx \sqrt{.94} \approx .97$. The resulting values of *t* are:

cooperative vs. control t (10) ≈ 2.06, $p > .01$
cooperative vs. competitive t (10) ≈ 4.12, $p < .01$
control vs. competitive t (10) ≈ 2.06, $p > .01$.

The same conclusion about modeling drawn before pertains here. In addition, there is no sex effect and no interaction of the treatment with sex. Contrary to your intuitive expectation, sex of child had no effect on cooperative behavior. The lack of an interaction with sex indicates that the modeling treatment generalized to both sexes. You actually did not have any a priori predictions about the sex effect and the sex-by-treatment interaction effect. Since neither of these effects was statistically significant, you *do not* apply a multiple-comparison test to the data.

FACTORIAL DESIGN WITH REPEATED MEASURES

Split-Plot Design

If each child experiences each of the three modeling conditions (repeated measures) and the design is otherwise like the factorial design discussed in the preceding section, then the design is a factorial design with repeated measures or a split-plot design (chapter 9). The data in Table 20.7 are the same as those in Table 20.5, except that each row of data points represents three scores for one of six children. As in the case of the factorial design, you make no prediction about the sex effect or sex-by-modeling group interaction effect. The null hypothesis is that there are no such effects; you are *exploring* whether they exist.

TABLE 20.7
Raw Data of
Modeling
Experiment: 2 × 3
Repeated-
Measures
Factorial Design

		A_1 (Competitive)	A_2 (Control)	A_3 (Cooperative)	$\overset{i}{\Sigma}$
		Modeling Groups			
B_1 (Male)	S_1	3	8	7	18
	S_2	6	8	10	24
	S_3	6	11	10	27
		$\overset{k}{\Sigma} = 15$	$\overset{k}{\Sigma} = 27$	$\overset{k}{\Sigma} = 27$	$\overset{i\ k}{\Sigma\Sigma} = 69$
B_2 (Female)	S_4	5	6	10	21
	S_5	7	7	10	24
	S_6	9	8	13	30
		$\overset{k}{\Sigma} = 21$	$\overset{k}{\Sigma} = 21$	$\overset{k}{\Sigma} = 33$	$\overset{i\ k}{\Sigma\Sigma} = 75$
		$\overset{j\ k}{\Sigma\Sigma} = 36$	$\overset{j\ k}{\Sigma\Sigma} = 48$	$\overset{j\ k}{\Sigma\Sigma} = 60$	$\overset{i\ j\ k}{\Sigma\Sigma\Sigma} = 144$

Note: N = 6, three male and three female; three scores were obtained for each subject. Data from Table 20.4.

Calculating F

Between-Subjects Mean Difference

The structural model for the factorial design with repeated measures is $Y = (\overline{Y}) + (A_i) + (B_j) + (AB_{ij}) + (S_k) + (\text{error})$, where S_k refers to the between-subjects mean difference. The total SS, modeling SS, sex SS, and sex-by-modeling SS are calculated as in the case of the factorial design. The formula for the between-subjects sum of squares (between-subjects SS) is

$$\text{Between-Subjects } SS = \overset{j\ k}{\Sigma\Sigma} \frac{(\overset{i}{\Sigma}Y)^2}{N_i} - \frac{(\Sigma Y)^2}{N} - (\text{sex } SS), \qquad (20.11)$$

where $\overset{i}{\Sigma}Y$ is the sum of the three repeated scores for each subject and N_i is the number of repeated measures (number of levels of A_i, since the subjects experience all levels of A_i).

The value of between-subjects SS is different from the previously calculated value of blocks SS because the effect of sex is removed from the blocks SS to yield the between-subjects SS:

within-subjects SS = (total SS) − (modeling SS)
− (sex SS) − (between-subjects SS) − (sex-by-modeling SS).

Applying the equation to the data in Table 20.7,

$$\text{between-subjects } SS = \left[\frac{18^2}{3} + \frac{24^2}{3} + \frac{27^2}{3} + \frac{21^2}{3} + \frac{24^2}{3} + \frac{30^2}{3} \right] - 1152 - 2$$

$$= 1182 - 1152 - 2 = 28.$$
within-subjects SS = 100 − 48 − 2 − 28 − 16 = 6.

The df for between subjects is 2(3 − 1) = 4; that is, there are 2 df for between subjects within each sex group. The df for within subjects is 17 − 1 − 4 − 2 − 2 = 8.

TABLE 20.8
Summary of Analysis of Variance: Repeated-Measures Factorial Design

Source of Variation	SS	df	Mean Square	F	p
Sex	2	1	2.00	—	>.025
Between-subjects	28	4	7.00		
Modeling	48	2	24.00	32.00	<.05
Sex-by-modeling	16	2	8.00	10.67	<.025
Within-subjects	6	8	0.75		
Total	100	17			

Dividing each *SS* term by the appropriate *df*, you obtain the values displayed in Table 20.8.

Interaction Effect

As in the preceding section, the level of significance was set at .025 for the sex effect and the sex-by-modeling interaction effect, and at .05 for the modeling effect.

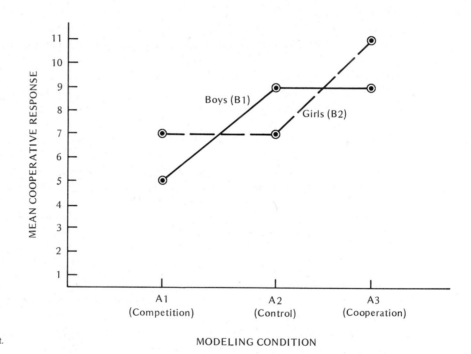

FIG. 20.1
Line graph of the modeling-ly-sex interaction in the factorial-design-with-repeated-measures version of the operation modeling experiment.

Between-Subjects Variance as an Error Term

The *F* ratio for sex is equal to sex mean square/between-subjects *M.S.* The *between-subjects* variance estimate represents the variance in average scores of the six subjects that is not accounted for by the difference between the sexes (residual random error). The sex variance estimate represents the variance due to random error for all six subjects plus the variance due to the difference between the average response of each sex. The *F* ratio for the modeling effect involves modeling *M.S.* divided by within-subjects *M.S.* The *F* ratio for the sex-by-modeling interaction involves sex-by-modeling *M.S.* divided by within-subjects *M.S.*

There is no significant sex effect. (To indicate that F is less than 1.0, the traditional practice is to place a horizontal dark line in a summary table.) The modeling effect is significant at $\alpha = .05$, as before, and the sex-by-modeling effect is significant at $\alpha = .025$ (from Table 20.8). The significant interaction can be seen in Figure 20.1. The effect of modeling depended on the sex of subject, even though there was no over-all-conditions sex difference in cooperation.

Multiple Comparisons

The multiple-comparison technique used with the randomized-blocks design may also be used with the modeling variable in the factorial design with repeated measures. As before, the df for each comparison is 6 pairs of scores minus 1 equals 5 df. Equation 20.6 is used with the same numerators as before, but the value of the denominator is $\sqrt{0.75\,(2/6)} = \sqrt{0.25} = .50$. The resulting values of t are:

cooperative vs. control t (5) = 4.0, $p < .01$
cooperative vs. competitive t (5) = 8.00, $p < .01$
control vs. competitive t (5) = 4.0, $p < .01$.

Subjects as Their Own Controls

In contrast to the results of the multilevel, randomized-blocks, and factorial analyses of variance, the predicted differences between all pairs of means were statistically significant in the factorial design with repeated measures. The use of subjects as their own controls and the inclusion of sex in the design as an independent variable controlled for a great amount of secondary and error variance. The estimate of variance due to random error decreased from 3.5 to 0.75. At the same time that the size of within-subjects SS decreased, the df for the estimate also decreased from 15 to

Loss of df

8. However, the loss in df was more than compensated for by the decrease in size of within-subjects SS (error). That is, the sex-by-modeling interaction source of variation and the variation due to average performance of each subject across repeated measures accounted for a large portion of the total variance. You can conclude that the three groups all responded as predicted, and that all three groups were significantly different from each other.

The sex-by-modeling interaction was also significant. However, since you had no strong reason for predicting the nature of the interaction *prior* to the experiment, the multiple-comparison technique using t tests is *not* appropriate for the 15 possible comparisons among the six mean cooperation scores in the six cells of the design (cooperative boys, cooperative girls, control boys, and so on). There are multiple-comparison tests for this kind of data; Kirk (1968) has the best integrated presentation of these tests.

ADVANTAGES AND LIMITATIONS

Like the t tests, the analysis of variance utilizes all of the numerical information in interval measurement to test differences between the means of two or more groups. The analysis of variance may be used with independent-groups and related-groups designs and is particularly appropriate to factorial designs or any design involving more than one independent variable.

There are many, many additional designs and combinations of designs for which the analysis-of-variance techniques and multivariate analysis-of-variance techniques have been developed. Multivariate analysis-of-variance designs accommodate two or more kinds of dependent measures from each subject, or two or more dependent measures of one kind from each subject. These techniques are frequently encountered in advanced statistical analysis or advanced research-design courses.

tion in applying analysis of variance to any design is that any score is the sum of the

A limitation in the analysis of variance is that the estimates of between-groups and within-group variance must be independent estimates. In theory, the scores must be sampled randomly from a normally distributed population of scores. In practice, the F distribution is relatively unaffected by moderate departures from population distribution normality.

A second limitation is that the "random errors" must be random and independent within each treatment level and across treatment groups. If subjects are randomly assigned to the levels of the indepenent variable and if other secondary sources of variance are controlled, these errors will be random and independent.

A basic assumption in applying analysis of variance to any design is that any score is the sum of the various effects involved in the linear model. The various estimates of random-error variance are averaged to yield the within-subjects estimate of random-error variance. That procedure is legitimate on the assumption that all within-group sources of variance are estimates of a common population error variance. In effect, it is assumed that the error variance within each group is homogeneous (S^2 error$_1$ = S^2 error$_2$ = S^2 error$_3$, and so on). The calculated values of each estimate seldom will be precisely equal. When the sample sizes for each group vary greatly, the actual values of S^2 error also vary greatly, then it is possible that the probabilities for the F ratio obtained from the F table are erroneous. When the sample sizes are equal, then there is probably little reason to suspect the obtained probabilities.

SUMMARY

1. If you have more than two groups of subjects and at least interval-level data, an analysis of variance and its corresponding statistical test, the F test, may be appropriate.
2. The F test is the ratio of the variation due to an independent variable (called between-variance) and variation due to error (called within-variance) or the ratio between an interaction of two independent variables and the within-variance.
3. The ratio of the between-variance and the within-variance is compared with a tabled value to see whether it is significant.
4. Analysis of variance may be used with several experimental designs. The most common are the multilevel independent-group design, the related-groups designs, and factorial designs with and without repeated measures.

5. Multilevel-design analysis of variance (ANOVA) yields a mean square for the treatment source of variation (the between-variance due to the independent variable) and a mean square for the error or within-subjects source of variance. The ratio of these two sources of variance is called the F ratio.
6. Multiple comparisons indicate which means of several groups are significantly different from each other.
7. Analysis of variance may be used with a randomized-blocks design when each subject experiences all of the treatments (repeated measures). The ANOVA allows the experimenter to partial out the variance due to subject differences (blocks), thus making the within-subjects error term smaller.
8. When an F test is used with a factorial design, interactions between two or more independent variables may be tested for significance, and multiple comparisons may be performed.
9. When repeated measures are utilized in a factorial design, two error terms result: between-subjects (used to test one independent variable) and within-subjects (used to test the other independent variable and the interaction).
10. ANOVA and its associated F tests are based on certain assumptions, but the test is strong and will still work if some of the assumptions are violated.

SUGGESTED READINGS

Kirk, R. E. *Experimental design: Procedures for the behavioral sciences.* Belmont, Calif.: Brooks/Cole, 1968.

Lee, W. *Experimental design and analysis.* San Francisco: Freeman, 1975.

Lindman, H. R. *Analysis of variance in complex experimental designs.* San Francisco: Freeman, 1974.

Winer, B. J. *Statistical principles in experimental design* (2nd ed.). New York: McGraw-Hill, 1971.

21

Correlation Coefficients and Correlation Studies

This chapter provides an elementary description of correlation coefficients and how to calculate a coefficient. The relationship between correlation and causation is discussed. Correlation coefficients are often misused and misinterpreted; the most common misuse is inferring causality when only correlational information is provided. The chapter concludes with a review of four kinds of correlation designs.

A correlation coefficient can be used to describe the relationship (chapter 2) between any two variables. As long as the measures can be logically paired, a correlation coefficient summarizes the relationship. The usual examples involve variables such as grades paired with IQ, reading speed paired with scores on a comprehension test, and scores on an extroversion–introversion scale paired with leadership tendencies. It is also legitimate to use a correlation coefficient to describe the relationship between grades and height, reading speed and ability to throw a baseball, and score on the introversion–extroversion scale and the total number of spots obtained by throwing two dice. In all of these examples, the pairing occurs because both measures are taken on the same person.

Numerical Value of r

A correlation coefficient describes in numerical form the degree and direction of relationship between two variables. The Pearson product-moment correlation coefficient (r) is the most frequently used measure of correlation; other coefficients approximate the Pearson r. The numerical value of a correlation ranges between $+1.00$ and -1.00. If there is no relationship between the variables, the value of r is zero. As the relationship between the two variables increases, the value of r increases from zero to plus or minus one. The *numerical value* of r describes the *strength* of the relationship between the two variables, and the *sign* describes the *direction*.

Sign of r

A correlation can be graphically portrayed by mapping the data points onto a scatterplot (chapter 5). Each data point represents a pair of scores on two variables. Each pair of scores is related in some way; the usual case in psychology involves two different measures of a subject's behavior. The values of each measure are arbitrarily assigned to the ordinate and abscissa of the scatterplot. If one of the measures represents an independent variable, it is assigned to the abscissa.

Perfect Correlation

A *perfect correlation* is depicted in Figure 21.1. The correlation is positive; large scores on measure X are associated with large scores on measure Y, and small scores on measure X are associated with small scores on measure Y. Each point in the graph represents the score of one subject on measure X and the score of the same subject on measure Y. A perfect correlation is also portrayed in Figure 21.2. The correlation in Figure 21.2 is negative; large scores on measure X are associated with small scores on measure Y, and small scores on measure X are associated with large scores on measure Y. Again, each point represents the score of one subject on measures X and

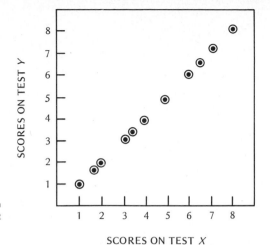

FIG. 21.1
Scatterplot of ordered pairs of scores for which the correlation is perfect and positive ($r = +1.00$).

Y. A *zero correlation* is presented in Figure 21.3. If there is a perfect correlation between two measures, you know a subject's score on the second measure when you know the subject's score on the first measure. If there is a zero correlation between two measures, knowledge of a subject's score on one measure gives you no information about the subject's score on the second measure.

The sign of r is related to the general trend of the plotted points in the graphs. A downward trend from left to right yields a negative value of r; an upward trend from **Line of Best Fit** left to right yields a positive value of r. The general trend is represented by a *straight line* drawn as close as possible to all the points, called the *line of best fit*. Other considerations being equal, the scatter-plot with the most widely dispersed points yields the smallest value of r. Therefore the value of r for Figure 21.4 is less than the value of r for Figure 21.5. The equation for calculating a Pearson r is presented in the next section.

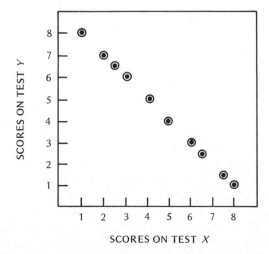

FIG. 21.2
Scatterplot of ordered pairs of scores for which the correlation is perfect and negative ($r = -1.00$).

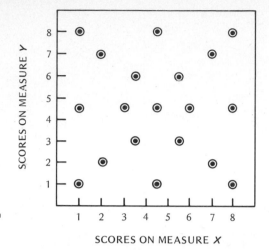

FIG. 21.3
Scatterplot of ordered pairs of scores for which the correlation is zero ($r = .00$).

There are two important factors that are easily overlooked when using the correlation coefficient. The first is that *r* is also appropriate to describe *lack of correlation*. The second is that a high correlation indicates that the two variables are related, but says *nothing about why* they are related. Unless causality is established by the experimental design, a correlational relationship should not be used to infer causality, no matter how plausible it appears. As an example, a high correlation between IQ and grades is often cited as evidence that intelligence leads to good school performance. It is also possible, however, to suggest that students who have learned good study habits also have learned the facts and skills to do well on an IQ test. In this case it is probable that both the measures of IQ and grades are caused by a common third variable. The fact remains that the correlation only indicates that there is a relationship and not that the relationship is causal.

The concept of correlation between measures was introduced in chapter 9, where related-groups designs are discussed. In related-groups designs certain sources of

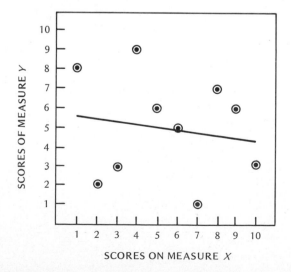

FIG. 21.4
Scatterplot of ordered pairs of scores for which *r* is approximately equal to −.15. The straight line in the figure is the line of best fit.

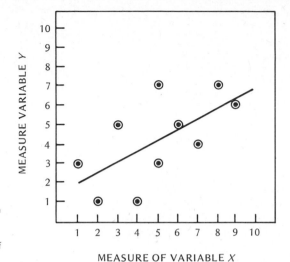

FIG. 21.5
Scatterplot of ordered pairs of scores for which *r* is approximately equal to +.62. The straight line is the line of best fit.

secondary variance are controlled in one of three ways: (1) the same subjects are used in two or more experimental groups, using repeated measures or subjects as their own control; (2) the subjects in two groups are matched on one or more criterion variables, as in a match-by-correlated-criterion design; or (3) groups, but not individual subjects, are matched on one or more criterion variables, as in a randomized-blocks design. In studies using these designs, correlation coefficients may or may not be calculated; however, the designs all involve the assumption that there is a substantial correlation either between two performance measures of a subject or between the behavioral measures of two matched subjects or groups. The sign or direction of the assumed correlation is not important, only size or strength of *r*.

Next we shall describe how to calculate one kind of correlation coefficient, simplifying the mathematical background.

THE PEARSON COEFFICIENT

Interval Scale

The Pearson product-moment correlation coefficient (*r*) is an index of the degree of *linear* relationship between two variables measured at the interval level. Several individuals are sampled and two measures are obtained from each individual. To determine the extent to which the two measures are related, a single statistic (*r*) is computed.

The equation for calculating *r* is

$$r = \frac{\Sigma XY - \dfrac{\Sigma X \Sigma Y}{N}}{\sqrt{\left[\Sigma X^2 - \dfrac{(\Sigma X)^2}{N}\right]\left[\Sigma Y^2 - \dfrac{(\Sigma Y)^2}{N}\right]}} \ , \tag{21.1}$$

**TABLE 21.1
Payoff Matrix for
a Two-Person
Game (the
Numbers 1 and 2
Represent the
Two Buttons)**

		Player B Chooses	
		1	2
Player A Chooses	1	Both Lose 20¢	B Pays A 50¢
	2	50¢ A Pays B	20¢ Both Win

where ΣXY is the sum of the products of the *paired* X and Y scores. Usually, each person's score on one measure (X) is multiplied by the person's score on the other measure (Y).

Suppose that a paper-and-pencil test of cooperativeness is given to a sample of 20 students. The scores constitute the first measure. The students also participate in a study of cooperative behavior. The study consists of a two-person game in which each person tries to win the most money. The two people playing the game each have a choice of pushing one of two buttons on each trial. The payoff matrix is presented in Table 21.1. For example, if A punches button 2 and B punches button 1, then A loses 50¢ and B wins 50¢. The only way that they can both win in the long run is for both of them to punch button 2. To make the game interesting, they cannot communicate verbally.

The second measure of "cooperation" is the frequency with which a student presses button 2. We can determine the correlation between the two measures of cooperation. The hypothetical data are presented in Table 21.2.

As indicated in Table 21.2, each column of numbers is added to produce $\Sigma X = 218$, $\Sigma Y = 180$, $\Sigma X^2 = 2614$, $\Sigma Y^2 = 1916$, and $\Sigma XY = 2081$. Each XY score is

**TABLE 21.2
Results of
Example
Experiment on
Cooperation**

Subject #	Cooperativeness Test Score (X)	Cooperation Study Score (Y)	X^2	Y^2	XY
1	10	6	100	36	60
2	12	8	144	64	96
3	16	14	256	196	224
4	7	9	49	81	63
5	8	10	64	100	80
6	10	7	100	49	70
7	14	6	196	36	84
8	20	12	400	144	240
9	13	11	169	121	143
10	11	15	121	225	165
11	10	3	100	9	30
12	9	8	81	64	72
13	11	10	121	100	110
14	8	4	64	16	32
15	10	5	100	25	50
16	16	13	256	169	208
17	8	11	64	121	88
18	7	2	49	4	14
19	6	10	36	100	60
20	12	16	144	256	192
Σ	218	180	2614	1916	2081
	ΣX	ΣY	ΣX^2	ΣY^2	ΣXY

Note. Σ = *sum.*

calculated by multiplying the X and Y scores of a specific subject in a given row. Applying Equation 21.1 to the data of Table 21.2, we find:

$$r = \frac{\Sigma XY - \dfrac{\Sigma X \Sigma Y}{N}}{\sqrt{\left[\Sigma X^2 - \dfrac{(\Sigma X)^2}{N}\right]\left[\Sigma Y^2 - \dfrac{(\Sigma Y)^2}{N}\right]}}$$

$$r = \frac{2081 - \dfrac{(218)(180)}{20}}{\sqrt{\left[2614 - \dfrac{(218)^2}{20}\right]\left[1916 - \dfrac{(180)^2}{20}\right]}}$$

Variance Is Zero or Positive

Note that ΣX^2 and $(\Sigma X)^2$ are two different numbers, $\Sigma X^2 = 2614$ and $(\Sigma X)^2 = 47{,}524$. Also, no variance can be negative; the result of the arithmetic within each bracket in the denominator *must be* equal to or greater than zero. The numerator can be a positive or a negative number. Simplifying the terms of the preceding equation, we find:

1. Multiplying ΣX and ΣY in the numerator, and squaring (ΣX) and (ΣY) in the denominator, yields

$$r = \frac{2081 - \dfrac{39{,}240}{20}}{\sqrt{\left[2614 - \dfrac{47{,}524}{20}\right]\left[1916 - \dfrac{32{,}400}{20}\right]}}$$

2. Dividing 39,240 by 20 in the numerator, and dividing 47,524 by 20 and 32,400 by 20 in the denominator yields

$$r = \frac{2081 - 1962}{\sqrt{(2614 - 2376.2)(1916 - 1620)}}$$

3. Performing the three subtractions yields

$$r = \frac{119}{\sqrt{(237.8)(296)}}$$

4. Multiplying 237.8 and 296 in the denominator yields

$$r = \frac{119}{\sqrt{70{,}388.8}}$$

5. Using a calculator to find the square root of 70,388.8 yields

$$r = \frac{119}{265.3}.$$

6. Dividing 119 by 265.3 yields

$$r \approx .45.$$

The correlation between the two measures is positive and is approximately equal to .45. The two measures are moderately, positively correlated. While the two tests are somewhat related, the size of r is not large, indicating that they probably measured different attributes. That is, the two kinds of "cooperation" measured by the two tests are not completely different from each other; however, the size of r indicates that the paper-and-pencil test measures a different kind of cooperation than the two-person game does.

Advantages and Limitations

One feature of the Pearson correlation coefficient is that the X scores and the Y scores need not be on the same measurement scale. The calculation process converts the X and Y values to standard scores (chapter 5).

Linear Relationship Another characteristic of the Pearson r is that it reflects the *linear* (straight-line) *relationship* between the two variables being correlated. As the scores deviate more and more from the straight line of best fit, the correlation coefficient decreases toward $r = .00$. A correlation coefficient of zero indicates that there is no overall linear trend to the data; in other words, there is no linear relationship between the values of the X and Y variables. Because the correlation coefficient reflects deviations from a straight line, any nonlinear relationship will yield a lower correlation coefficient. A statistic called the *correlation ratio* (Edwards, 1967, pp. 136–142; Hays, 1973, pp. 675–686) indexes the total linear and curvilinear relationships between two sets of scores. All applications of the Pearson r require the assumption that the relationship being measured is basically linear in nature.

Interpretations of r In addition to providing a shorthand expression for summarizing the direction and degree of relationship between two variables, the correlation coefficient provides the basis for a number of further interpretations (*see* McNemar, 1969, pp. 129–153). The correlation coefficient may be statistically tested for *significance* to determine whether or not the observed relationship is a result of random factors. Once the relationship between two variables is determined, values of one variable may be *predicted* from corresponding values of the other variable. The correlation coefficient allows you to state the *accuracy of predictions* by specifying the confidence limits of each prediction. If the correlated scores represent the independent and dependent variables in an experiment, the correlation coefficient allows you to state what *proportion of the variance* in the dependent variable is a result of variation of the independent variable.

Because the numerical notation for a correlation resembles a percentage figure, correlation coefficients are frequently misinterpreted. A correlation coefficient is *not a*

r ≠ %

percentage figure. You cannot interpret a correlation of .60 as indicating that two measures are 60% related. In addition, the interpretation of a given correlation coefficient depends on the sample size used to obtain the coefficient. The larger the sample size, the more reliable the coefficient. Without both the value of the coefficient and the number of observations, it is hard to tell what a coefficient means.

Test of the Significance of *r*

If subjects are randomly sampled from a population, then you are usually concerned with deciding whether the two variables are correlated in the population. That is, you test the null hypothesis that the population correlation coefficient is zero. The significance of *r* can be tested with the *t* test (chapter 19),

$$t = \frac{r}{\sqrt{1 - r^2}} (\sqrt{N - 2}) , \qquad (21.2)$$

df

where $df = N - 2$. The value of *r* in the cooperation example was ≈.45. Applying Equation 21.2, we find

$$t = \frac{.45}{\sqrt{1 - .45^2}} (\sqrt{20 - 2}) .$$

1. Squaring .45 and subtracting 2 from 20 yields

$$t = \frac{.45}{\sqrt{1 - .20}} (\sqrt{18}).$$

2. Subtracting .20 from 1 and using a calculator to determine the square root of 18 yields

$$t = \frac{.45}{\sqrt{.80}} (4.24).$$

3. Using a calculator to find the square root of .80 and multiplying .45 by 4.24 yields

$$t = \frac{1.91}{.89}.$$

4. Dividing 1.91 by .89 yields

$$t \approx 2.15.$$

With 18 *df,* and α at .05, the two-tailed *critical* value of *t* is 2.10 (Appendix F). Since the obtained value of *t* does exceed the tabled critical value, you conclude that the two variables are associated in the population, so that the population correlation coefficient is greater than zero. Since the value of *r* for the example exceeded 0.44, the obtained value of t exceeded the tabled critical value. In such a case we conclude that the two variables are positively associated in the population. We do not know the size of the population correlation coefficient; we just know that it is greater than zero in the population.

Goodness of Fit

skip this section

The t test of the significance of r is very similar to the t test used to test how well a straight line fits a set of plotted data points. The concept of the slope (b) of a straight line was discussed in chapter 5. The method of determining the value of b is presented in this section.

Usually, experimental data do not fall exactly on a straight line; however, the data points sometimes do seem to approximate a straight line. In such a case, you want to know precisely how well a straight line fits the the data; in other words, you want to know the **goodness of fit** of a straight line to the data. The attractiveness of a straight-line relationship is that it is the simplest form of functional relationship. All other factors being equal, the simplest description, explanation, or prediction is preferred.

Suppose a therapist is working with electively mute, autistic children. All of the children occasionally mutter unintelligible sounds, and the therapist wishes to increase the frequency of these sounds. She hopes that eventually the children will speak intelligible words, but first she must get them to vocalize on command. The therapist hypothesizes that, if the children are food-deprived and food-reinforced for making sounds, their rates of vocalizing will increase. She predicts that the rate of vocalization will increase linearly with the amount of food reinforcement and manipulates the amount of food reinforcement given five autistic children. After one week of training, the number of vocalizations in a single 5-min. period are recorded. The data are presented in Table 21.3.

The data are graphed in Figure 21.6. Each data point represents the value (X) of the independent variable assigned to a child and the dependent score (Y) of that child. In order to fit a straight line through the data points in Figure 21.6, the slope of the line of best fit must be calculated. The calculation proceeds according to the following steps:

1. Subtract the mean of the X scores (column II) from each X score ($x = X - \overline{X}$). These deviation scores are recorded in column IV of Table 21.3.
2. Similarly, the mean of the Y scores (column III) is subtracted from each Y score ($y = Y - \overline{Y}$). These deviation scores also are recorded in column IV of Table 21.3.
3. The deviation scores (x and y) are squared and recorded in column V of Table 21.3.
4. The corresponding x and y scores for each child are multiplied to provide the cross-products (xy) recorded in column VI. For example, child A had an x score of -6 and a y score of -3. The cross-product of -6 and -3 is 18, which is the first score in column VI.
5. The sums of the squared deviation scores (x^2 and y^2) are determined. In the example, $\Sigma x^2 = 90$ and $\Sigma y^2 = 34$. The sum of the crossed products is also determined. In the example, $\Sigma xy = 54$.

In Figure 21.6, the straight line the therapist is interested in is the line predicting the vocalizations of the children (Y) as a function of magnitude of food reinforcement (X).

**TABLE 21.3
Amount of Food
Reinforcement
and Number of
Verbalizations of
Five Autistic
Children.**

I Children	II Amount of Food Reinforcement in Grams X	III Number of Verbalizations per 5-Min. Period Y	IV Deviations from Means		V Squared Deviations		VI Cross-Products xy
			x	y	x²	y²	
A	1	2	−6	−3	36	9	18
B	4	3	−3	−2	9	4	6
C	7	4	0	−1	0	1	0
D	10	7	3	2	9	4	6
E	13	9	6	4	36	16	24
	Sum (Σ) = 35	25	0	0	90	34	54
	Mean (X̄) = 7	(Ȳ) 5					

The equation for the value of the slope (*b*) of the straight line relating *Y* to *X* is

Slope

$$b_{y.x} = \frac{\Sigma xy}{\Sigma x^2},$$ (21.3)

where $b_{y.x}$ is the slope of *y* on *x*, Σxy is the sum of cross-products, and Σx^2 is the sum of squared *x* deviation scores.

6. Substituting the values of Σxy and Σx^2 in Equation 21.3, the results are: $b_{y.x} = 54/90 = 0.60$.

In order to draw the straight line, you must use the equation for a straight line. In **Sample Regression Equation** the example, the equation is called the *sample regression equation of Y on X* and is

$$\widehat{Y} = \overline{Y} + b_{y.x}(X - \overline{X}),$$ (21.4)

where $\widehat{Y}$ is an estimated value of *Y* given the mean of the *Y* scores, the value of $b_{y.x}$,

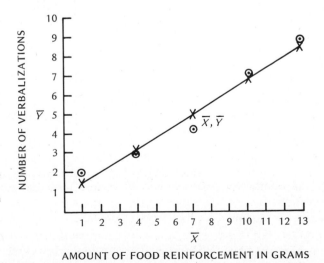

FIG. 21.6
A graph of the data points provided in columns II and III of Table 21.3. Each of the five circled points represents the score of a single child. The crossmarks on the straight line represent the five estimated values of Y.

AMOUNT OF FOOD REINFORCEMENT IN GRAMS

TABLE 21.4
Calculated Values
of $\hat{Y}$ and
Deviations from
Actual Scores ($d_{y.x}$
$= Y - \hat{Y}$).

Amount of Food Reinforcement in grams X	Actual Number of Verbalizations Y	Estimated Number of Verbalizations $\hat{Y}$	Deviations $Y - \hat{Y} = d_{y.x}$	Squared Deviations $d^2_{y.x}$
1	2	1.4	.6	.36
4	3	3.2	− .2	.04
7	4	5.0	−1.0	1.00
10	7	6.8	.2	.04
13	9	8.6	.4	.16

$$\Sigma d_{y.x} = 0.0 \quad \Sigma d^2_{y.x} = 1.60$$

and a given X deviation score ($x = X - \bar{X}$). The estimated Y values ($\hat{Y}$) are the points on the straight line that the therapist fits to her data. If Equation 21.4 is used, the straight line fit to the data is called the *line of best fit.* Using Equation 21.4, the straight line in Figure 21.6 was drawn. The value of $\bar{Y}$ is 5, the value of $\bar{X}$ is 7, and the value of $b_{y.x}$ is 0.60. Substituting these values in Equation 21.4, we have $\hat{Y} = 5 + 0.60 (X - 7)$. Algebraically, the equation may be simplified to $\hat{Y} = 0.8 + 0.60 (X)$. Now the values of X may be substituted into the equation to provide the points on the best-fit straight line. Thus, when $X = 1$, $\hat{Y} = 1.4$, when $X = 4$, $\hat{Y} = 3.2$, and so forth, as indicated in Table 21.4 and Figure 21.6.

Line of Best Fit

Test of fit The therapist now examines the line to see precisely how good a fit she has (Table 21.4). She uses the original values of X and Y, the estimated values, $\hat{Y}$, and the deviations of the obtained values from the estimated values ($Y - \hat{Y}$). These deviations are labeled $d_{y.x}$. Finally, the deviations are squared ($d^2_{y.x}$), and the sum of the squared deviations is calculated ($\Sigma d^2_{y.x}$). For the therapist's data, the sum of the squared deviations is $\Sigma d^2_{y.x} = 1.60$. This value represents the amount of squared error when fitting a straight line to the data.

The therapist's hypothesis (H_1) is that the frequency of verbalization will increase linearly with the amount of food reinforcement. Her null hypothesis (H_0) is that the independent and dependent variables are *not* linearly related. The two-tailed H_1 is that $b_{y.x}$ is greater than or less than zero and the relationship is linear, and H_0 is that $b_{y.x}$ is zero and the relationship is not linear. The therapist sets $\alpha = .01$. In order to test H_0, the therapist needs some unbiased estimate of the population variance of the deviations from the straight line of best fit.

The estimate is

$$s_{y.x}^{2} = \frac{\Sigma d_{y.x}^{2}}{(N - 2)},$$

where N is the number of paired X and Y scores. The estimated variance of the deviations from the best-fit line is used in the calculation of the standard deviation of the slope $b_{y.x}$. The equation for the standard deviation of the slope is

Standard Deviation
of the Slope

$$s_{b_{y.x}} = \sqrt{S_{y.x}^2 / \Sigma x^2} \tag{21.5}$$

In the autistic child example, $\Sigma d_{y.x}^2 = 1.60$, $N = 5$, and Σx^2 90. Substituting these values in the equation for the estimated variance,

$$s_{y.x}^2 = \frac{1.60}{(5-2)}.$$

Subtracting 2 from 5 yields 3, and dividing 1.60 by 3 yields

$$s_{y.x}^2 \approx .53.$$

Substituting the values of $s_{y.x}^2$ and Σx^2 into Equation 21.5, the therapist found

$$s_{b_{y.x}} = \sqrt{\frac{.53}{90}}.$$

Dividing .53 by 90 yields .006, so

$$s_{b_{y.x}} = \sqrt{0.006}.$$

Using a calculator to find the square root,

$$s_{b_{y.x}} \approx 0.077.$$

The t test of H_0 is

$$t = \frac{b_{y.x}}{s_{b_{y.x}}} \tag{21.6}$$

Degrees of Freedom

The value of $b_{y.x}$ was .60 and the value of $s_{b_{y.x}}$ was .077. Substituting these figures in Equation 21.6, the calculated value of t is $.60/.077 \approx 7.79$. The degrees of freedom for this t test are $df = N - 2$. In terms of the example, $df = 5 - 2 = 3$. The critical values of t are presented in Appendix F. The level of significance was set at .01 ($\alpha = .01$) and H_1 was a two-tailed prediction. The two-tailed critical value of t with $\alpha = .01$ and $df = 3$ is 5.84 (Appendix F). Since the calculated value of t exceeds 5.84, H_0 may be rejected (t (3) = 7.79, $p < .01$). The therapist concludes that the deviations from the straight line of best fit are due to chance and that there is a positive linear relationship between the amount of food reinforcement and frequency or rate of vocalization.

Note that this t test is a test of two hypotheses at once: the *goodness of fit* of a straight line to the data points, and the null hypothesis that the *population slope is zero*. When the t is significant and H_0 is rejected, then both the goodness of fit and nonzero-slope hypotheses are supported. The therapist can conclude that, in the population sampled, there is a positive linear relationship between amount of rein-

Ambiguity of Nonsignificant Test

forcement and amount of vocalization. However, if the calculated t were not significant, either the population slope is about zero (population r is zero) or the population relationship between the independent and dependent variables is not linear, or both parts of H_0 are correct.

Research example   Peggy Giffin, a student in one of our experimental psychology classes, was interested in the behavior of hospitalized mental patients. While visiting the local state hospital she became interested in a person diagnosed as a chronic catatonic schizophrenic. This man was 57 years of age and had been hospitalized for 36 years; he was capable of movement, but usually sat in one position all day.

Peggy wondered if there was some way she could get the man to engage in *some* behavior other than just sitting. At this time (1969), the hospital staff were excited about the potential use of behavior modification techniques in the hospital setting. She had read part of Ullman and Krasner's (1965) book, *Case Studies in Behavior Modification.* Since the hospital staff approved of the use of positive reinforcement techniques and since she had read about their use with severely disturbed patients, Peggy decided to try some form of positive reinforcement with her schizophrenic subject. At this point she had focused on a general class of dependent variable behavior, motor behavior, and on a general class of independent variable, positive reinforcement. She needed to define these variables more precisely. While observing the man, she noticed a set of building blocks on a card table in the day room. Since she had come to think of the man as childlike, she decided that the building blocks might provide a convenient, simple way to measure motor behavior: She could count the number of times he moved a block in a given time period. Reading the published case studies provided an idea for a means of providing positive reinforcement. Previous studies had shown verbal praise to be an effective reinforcer for certain behaviors. She decided to test the hypothesis that verbal praise and encouragement provided after the catatonic schizophrenic person made any hand or arm movement toward or with the blocks would lead to an increase in those movements over time.

Peggy tested the hypothesis over eight 30-min. sessions. For each session, the 13 building blocks were placed on a table in front of the man and Peggy began to build objects with them. Any appropriate hand or arm movement by the patient was reinforced verbally. The design was a single-subject, "B-only" design; the experimenter did not use a baseline period, but depended on prior staff reports about the subject to provide her "baseline" data. (She should have used at least an "A–B" design, chapter 11.)

The number of movements per session increased from 2 during the first session to 351 during the eighth session. The number of movements were plotted against the number of sessions and the slope of the line was calculated. The slope was tested by a t test against the null hypothesis of a population slope of zero and was found to be significant ($p < .001$).

The data indicated that verbal reinforcement was effective in modifying catatonic behavior. Because of individual differences among hospitalized persons, the specific method may not generalize to other patients. The success of this particular experiment gives rise to many questions: Is verbal reinforcement as effective as nonverbal reinforcement? Are female experimenters more effective with male patients? Would the same technique work with other patients? Would the experimenter's presence alone, without verbal reinforcement, have yielded the observed change in movement behavior? Were there any lasting changes in the schizophrenic person's behavior in other settings as a consequence of the block-building experience?

CAUSAL INFERENCES

To arrive at a causal inference, a researcher needs to have control of the variables in an experiment so that the observed relationship between independent and dependent variables can be assessed. In an experiment, most of the *reasonable* or *plausible,* potential causal variables will be controlled, usually by holding constant, so that the effects of only a few potential causal variables can be examined in one study. In contrast, a naturalistic study does not allow such extensive control and, therefore, causal inferences from naturalistic studies are very tenuous. A naïve researcher may draw false causal inferences from a naturalistic study, and even a sophisticated researcher may be drawn in fruitless pursuits by the results of naturalistic observation. For example, in a process called imprinting, a newly hatched bird becomes attached to and follows whatever moving object is nearby at hatching (Lorenz, 1952). Normally, of course, this moving object is a member of the same species. Also, of course, birds are observed to mate with their own species. However, the conclusion that the sex object of an adult bird is determined by the object on which it is imprinted is misleading because, in fact, the bird will probably mate with its own kind, no matter what it is imprinted on (Sluckin, 1965). Naturalistic observation discovers many such correlations that may or may not represent causality.

Correlation coefficients used either in experimental research projects or in correlational, naturalistic observation studies may aid legitimate causal inference. However, a great many correlational studies do not provide sufficient control for a causal inference. For example, the significant positive correlation between smoking and lung cancer leads many people to infer that smoking causes lung cancer. The fact that there is a relationship does not necessarily condemn cigarettes. As far as the coefficient is concerned, it is just as reasonable to infer that lung cancer causes smoking. The existence of a relationship between A and B does *not* allow you to make the inference that A causes B, or B causes A. The relationship itself may be caused by a third, unknown variable. It may be that hereditary or personality factors make individuals cancer-prone *and* predispose them to smoke cigarettes. No matter how plausible, no causal statement should be made until an *experimental study* is conducted. It must be demonstrated that controlled increases in frequency of cigarette smoking by a random sample of people leads to an increased probability of lung cancer. That has not been demonstrated. Experimental research has demonstrated a causal relationship between breathing cigarette smoke and lung cancer in dogs. Dogs are not human beings. People have generalized the conclusion of the dog research to human beings; however, that generalization *has not been experimentally tested.* The correlation remains, however, that nonsmokers are less likely to develop lung cancer.

To illustrate the problem of causality further, we list a few of the statements containing correlational information used by Clifton (1958) in his tongue-in-cheek essay entitled "The Dread Tomato Addiction." Clifton correlates a measure of one variable, eating or not eating tomatoes, with measures of several other variables. (The odd numbering reflects omissions from the quotation.)

1. Ninety-two point four percent of juvenile delinquents have eaten tomatoes.
3. Informers reliably inform that of all known American Communists, ninety-two point three percent have eaten tomatoes.
5. Those who object to singling out specific groups for statistical proof, require measurements within a total. Of those people born before the year 1800, regardless of race, color, creed or caste, and known to have eaten tomatoes, there has been one hundred percent mortality.
6. In spite of their dread addiction, a few tomato eaters born between [1850] and [1880] still manage to survive, but the clinical picture is poor—their bones are brittle, their movements feeble, their skin seamed and wrinkled, their eyesight failing, hair falling, and frequently they have lost all their teeth. (pp. 97–98)

Correlation coefficients are used in a variety of ways in research. The most common uses can be grouped into two general categories. The first category includes the use of correlation coefficients as secondary research tools. In this case, the coefficient is not a major, integral part of the research design. Included in the first category are:

1. The use of correlation coefficients to measure the effectiveness of control of secondary-variance sources.
2. The use of coefficients as the statistical dependent measure.
3. The use of coefficients to index the reliability and validity of the dependent measures.
4. The use of coefficients to index the magnitude of the relationship between independent and dependent variables.

These four uses will be briefly examined in the following four sections of this chapter.

The second major category includes research designs that depend on the use of correlation coefficients. The second category includes:

1. Some naturalistic research studies.
2. Cross-lagged correlation designs.
3. Research designs permitting or depending on covariance analysis.
4. Multivariate research designs.

These four types of design will be examined briefly in the last four sections of this chapter.

COEFFICIENTS AS SECONDARY TOOLS

Control of Secondary Variance

Matching designs and randomized-blocks designs are discussed in chapters 9 and 10. Matching subjects on a secondary criterion variable requires that the criterion variable be correlated with the dependent variable. Similarly, matching groups in blocks requires that the blocking variable be correlated with the dependent variable. If the correlation between the two variables is negligible, then a matching procedure is a waste of time and subjects. One way to find out whether matching would be useful is to sample randomly a group of subjects from the population and collect measures on the matching or blocking, and dependent variables from each subject. Given a high positive or negative correlation between the two measures, you know that some form of matching will be useful.

Correlation as a Dependent Variable

The effect of an independent variable on the *relationship* between *two* dependent variables may be of interest to you. In this case, the correlation between the two dependent variables can be treated as a dependent variable (see Jones, 1968). For example, you may wish to measure the effect of an audience on the subjects' task performance. The task involves placing pegs in a pegboard, and you record the number placed in a 1-min. period. You use a before–after two-group design. All persons are given a 1-min. before-measure of peg-placing ability while isolated. Control persons are then given a second isolated performance test. Members of an experimental group also are given a second 1-min. test, but must perform in front of a class. The observed before and after scores for each group, the two dependent variables, are shown in Figure 21.7. Notice that the same scores occur in the before and after measures of each group. In other words, the audience did not affect the performance of the experimental group considered *as a whole*. For both groups, the average score and the variance were the same on both the before and after measures. The lines connecting the before and after scores indicate the performance of each

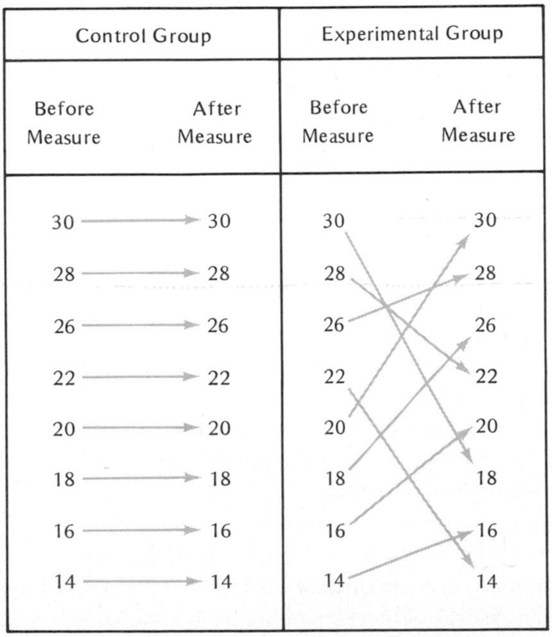

FIG. 21.7
Hypothetical peg-placing scores of the experimental and control groups on the before and after tests. The arrows indicate each person's two scores.

Control Group		Experimental Group	
Before Measure	After Measure	Before Measure	After Measure
30 → 30		30	30
28 → 28		28	28
26 → 26		26	26
22 → 22		22	22
20 → 20		20	20
18 → 18		18	18
16 → 16		16	16
14 → 14		14	14

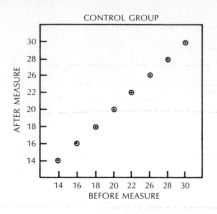

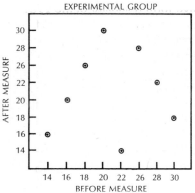

FIG. 21.8
Scatterplots of the number of pegs placed (dependent measures) in the before and after tests of each group in the hypothetical pegboard experiment. The correlation coefficients are 1.00 and .08 for the control and experimental groups, respectively.

individual. The controls scored the same on both tests ($r = 1.00$), while the presence of an audience disrupted the performance of the experimentals ($r \approx .08$). The scatterplot for each group is presented in Figure 21.8.

Measures of Reliability and Validity

In studies that use judges or raters to score the performance of subjects, you want the rating or scoring system to be reliable, so that when anyone uses the scoring system, generally consistent results will be obtained. One way of checking the reliability of the rating system is to have two or more raters use the system. If the correlation between the two sets of ratings is fairly high, then the system is considered reliable. In their study of verbal creativity, Maier, Julius, and Thurber (1967) used two raters to score the creativity of their subjects' stories. They obtained an *interrater reliability coefficient* of .80, which they considered to be sufficiently high.

In the study (chapter 10) of group insight and group desensitization in treating speech anxiety (Meichenbaum, Gilmore, & Fedoravicius, 1971), one of the dependent variables was a behavioral checklist of the performance of the subjects in a speech-giving situation. Two pairs of trained observers rated the presence or absence of 20 manifestations of anxiety during the first 4 min. of each speech by the subjects. The range of correlations bettwen the ratings by the pairs of observers was +.70 to

+.90. The median correlation was .85. The authors considered this figure to indicate the high reliability and objectivity of such measures.

Reliability

When psychologists use tests such as intelligence tests, they want them to be reliable. If a test is *reliable,* a subject will receive approximately the same score each time the person takes the test or an equivalent form of the test. When an applied psychologist uses a test such as an achievement test to make predictions about the *future* behavior of an individual, the psychologist wants to be fairly confident that the test is *valid.* That is, the test score should correlate with later measures of behavior. The reliability and validity of tests are described in terms of correlation coefficients. A high coefficient indicates either high reliability or high validity, depending on what variables are measured.

Validity

The Stanford-Binet Intelligence Scale is a widely used measure of general intellectual development. The alternative-form *reliability* of the 1937 revision of the Stanford-Binet was determined by administering the two forms of the test within one week or less to the same individuals (Terman & Merrill, 1960). Correlation coefficients were calculated for each set of paired scores. At ages 2½ and 5½ the reliability coefficients (correlation coefficients) ranged from +.83 to +.98, depending on the range of IQ scores and age range included in a sample of subjects. The older the subjects (14–18) and the lower the IQ (60–69), the higher the reliability (+.98). The correlation coefficients indicate the short-term stability of the IQ scores and the equivalence of the content of the two forms of the test. The IQ test scores are also quite stable over the elementary, high-school, and college period (Anastasi, 1976). The group test–retest correlation depends on the length of time between the two administrations of the test, for example, ten-year correlation = +.73, one-year correlation = +.83. The correlation between scores on an IQ test and scores on another measure of intellectual ability, such as school achievement, indicates the criterion-referenced *validity* of an IQ scale. The usual criterion measures include school grades, teacher ratings, or achievement test scores. The correlations between IQ scores and *concurrent criterion measures or future (predicted) criterion measures* range between +.40 and +.75 (Anastasi, 1976).

In chapter 3, validity was defined as the degree to which a measure actually reflects what it is supposed to measure. Reliability was defined as consistency of results, time after time. There the terms were used to describe sampling procedures; here we have applied them to testing. Test reliability is defined as consistency of scores on repeated testing. Test validity is defined in terms of value in predicting future performance or concurrent performance on another measure of the same attribute.

Measures of Magnitude of Causal Relationships

Most of the experimental research designs previously discussed involve the comparison of two or more groups of experimental subjects that are exposed to different levels of treatment, usually including a zero level. This general paradigm is usual for a behavioral experiment. The emphasis is on the *difference* produced by the treatment condition. A statistical test determines whether or not the differences are great enough to be considered "significant." (See chapter 16 for discussion of statistical significance.) If the experimental treatment does result in significant differences, then we infer that the treatment must have created the differences; there is some causal relationship between the treatment and the behavior.

Sometimes you are interested in a precise measure of the relationship between two variables. Instead of simply stating that the independent variable caused a difference in the measure of the dependent variable, you wish to specify in some numerical way the extent to which different levels of the independent variable affect the observed behavior. One such numerical description is provided by using a *linear regression coefficient.* The calculation of the regression coefficient follows the same procedure as the calculation of r when the sample standard deviations (chapter 5) are equal. However, the standard deviations are seldom equal, so regression coefficients or slopes usually are found by calculating the slope of the line of best fit.

CORRELATION STUDIES

Descriptive, Naturalistic Research

In some naturalistic studies the objective is to measure two naturally occurring nonmanipulated variables and summarize the relationship between the two with a correlation coefficient. The scores on variable X are paired in some way with the scores on variable Y. For example, you may correlate two measures of the subjects' behavior, the number of pages in term papers with the grades on the papers, or the number of trees on campuses with the academic standing of the colleges. Correlation coefficients may be used to describe the correlation between any two kinds of measures where the scores may be logically paired.

Correlational Studies

Certain variables can be evaluated only in correlational studies. For example, the personality traits and sociological characteristics associated with suicide cannot be studied with the experimental approach. After a person commits suicide, the researcher looks at historical records of the person's life (ex post facto). Sainsbury and Barraclough (1968) found that the suicide rates in 1959 of foreign-born United States citizens correlated highly ($r = +.87$) with the suicide rates of their countries of birth. Given the suicide rates of their native lands, you can predict which of two immigrants is more likely to commit suicide (for example, an Austrian immigrant is more likely to commit suicide than a person from Mexico).

The study cited in chapter 2 (Rodin & Rodin, 1972) established a correlation between student ratings of the teaching effectiveness of assistant instructors (subjective measure) and student performance (objective measure) on a set of 40 calculus problems. The correlation between the objective and subjective measures was equal to $-.75$. The graphed relationship between the two measures is presented in Figure 21.9. Gessner (1973) also conducted a study of the relationship between student ratings of instructors and student performance on an examination. In the study, the ten instructors were all involved in teaching parts of a single basic science course for sophomore premedical students. There were 23 subject areas in the course, and 78 students rated each subject area on a three-point scale (good, satisfactory, and unsatisfactory) in terms of (1) content and organization and (2) instructor's presentation. The students' learning was measured by the multiple-choice National Medical Board Examination given five weeks after the end of the class and by three departmental examinations used for grading purposes. The correlation between class performance on the national examination and student ratings of content and organization was $+.77$ and the correlation between national examination scores and student

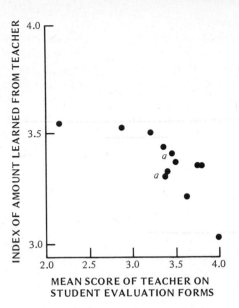

FIG. 21.9
Relationship between objective and subjective criteria of good teaching ($r = -.75$). The points labeled a are for two sections taught by the same instructor. (From "Student evaluations of teachers" by M. Rodin and B. Rodin, *Science,* 1972, *177,* 1164–1166. Copyright 1972 by the American Association for the Advancement of Science. Reprinted by permission.)

ratings of presentation was $+.69$. The scatterplot of the scores for the $.77$ correlation is presented in Figure 21.10. The correlations between performance on the departmental grading examinations and student ratings of content and organization ($r = +.11$) and student rating of presentation ($r = +.17$) were very low. The discrepancy between the results of the two teacher-evaluation studies may arise from the many

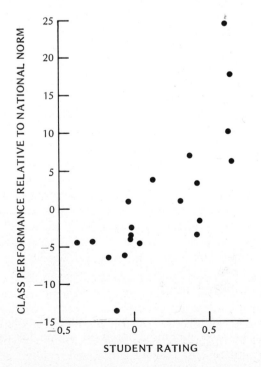

FIG. 21.10
Scatter diagram of class performance on a national normative examination in 20 subject areas of a course and of the student ratings of the content and organization of instruction in these subject areas ($r = 0.77$). (From "Evaluation of instruction" by P. K. Gessner, *Science,* 1973, *180,* 566–574. Copyright 1973 by the American Association for the Advancement of Science. Reprinted by permission.)

TABLE 21.5 Correlation Coefficient Results of the Correlational Study of the Relationship Between Lüscher's Color Test and Eysenck's Personality Inventory Test

Color Preference	Extroversion	Neuroticism
Gray	.29	−.01
Blue	.07	.39
Green	−.19	.31
Orange	.10	−.25
Yellow	.29	−.31
Violet	−.33	.18
Brown	−.01	−.11
Black	−.31	−.34

procedural differences between the two studies. The discrepancy indicates that correlational studies should be evaluated carefully before important decisions and generalizations are made (see Rodin, Frey, & Gessner, 1975).

The concluding example of a naturalistic correlational study is a brief description of an undergraduate student's project. Nancy Smith read about the Lüscher personality test based on liking for various colors (Lüscher, 1948, 1969). Lüscher maintains that knowing a person's color likes and dislikes can lead to successful prediction of personality traits. Smith decided to conduct a test of this theory in order to fulfill part of the experimental psychology class requirements.

She picked 20 female students from her dormitory to participate in the study. The students were given the Eysenck Personality Inventory Test, which provides measures of "extroversion–introversion" and degree of "neuroticism." Next, the students were given the Lüscher Color Test, which consists of eight colored squares arranged on white paper. Each student ranked the colors in order of preference. The tests were given one after the other to each student individually.

Smith constructed a scatterplot of the students' scores and determined the Pearson correlation coefficients. Extroversion–introversion and high–low neuroticism were correlated separately for each color. Since there were eight colors under each of the two personality traits, 16 correlation coefficients were calculated. The Pearson correlation coefficients for each set of color-preference scores and personality test scores are presented in Table 21.5. All the r values were too small to be significant, at $\alpha = .05$. The values of r appear to randomly vary around a correlation of zero. Since the correlations were not significant, it doesn't matter what the Lüscher test predicts in terms of personality type. The results of the study do not support the hypothesis that the two sets of scores would be related. Further research should consider using a personality test that would measure a larger number of personality traits and should involve more subjects. The attractiveness of the Lüscher test is its simplicity; however, Smith's study indicates that it may not have adequate validity.

Cross-Lagged Correlation Analysis

The cross-lagged correlation design is a nonexperimental design primarily used for exploratory purposes. Its most common use is to search for causal relationships between uncontrolled but measured variables. The purpose of a cross-lagged design is to attempt to reduce the number of plausible alternative explanations of a causal effect. The *minimal* elements of the design include (1) two different measures of behavior or dependent variables and (2) repeated measures of these two variables at two different points in time. The design is a *longitudinal* design in the sense that measures are taken on the same subject over at least two points in time, separated by weeks, months, or years. The two dependent variables measured at two times generate at least four measures (W_1, W_2, Y_1, and Y_2), and the combination of these four measures generates six correlation coefficients: ($r_{w_1 w_2}$, $r_{y_1 y_2}$, $r_{w_1 y_1}$, $r_{w_2 y_2}$, $r_{w_1 y_2}$, and $r_{w_2 y_1}$). The last two correlation coefficients are called *cross-lagged correlations* because they index the relationship between two different kinds of measures "lagged" or delayed over time. These symbols are included in Figure 21.11, a diagram of the cross-lagged correlation design.

Initially, statisticians thought that the comparison of the two cross-lagged correlation coefficients ($r_{w_1 y_2} - r_{w_2 y_1}$, called the **cross-lagged differential**) should provide determinative information about two competing causal hypotheses: either variable 1 causes variable 2, or variable 2 causes variable 1. If 1 caused 2, the cross-lagged differential should be positive ($r_{w_1 y_2} > r_{w_2 y_1}$), and if 2 caused 1, the cross-lagged differential should be negative ($r_{w_1 y_2} < r_{w_2 y_1}$). As indicated later in this section, the situation is not so simple (Rozelle & Campbell, 1969).

According to Kenny (1975), the cross-lagged analysis is essentially a test for spuriousness. **Spuriousness** means that the relationship between variables 1 and 2 is not due to the causal effects of either variable, but to the effect of a third variable which is not measured and usually unknown prior to the completion of a cross-lagged study. The spurious, third variable is a secondary variable in the sense that the researcher hypothesizes that there is a causal relationship between 1 and 2. The null hypothesis for a cross-lagged design is that the relationship between 1 and 2 is due to the unmeasured, spurious variable and that there is no direct causal relationship between 1 and 2. The null hypothesis essentially predicts that the cross-lagged differential will be zero; the two cross-lagged correlations will be equal within the limits of sampling error. If the null hypothesis is rejected, then you may examine the sign of the cross-lagged differential and the nature of the other correlation coefficient to see whether it is possible to determine the direction of the causal relationship between variables 1 and 2.

Longitudinal Design

Cross-Lagged Correlation

Cross-Lagged Differential

Spuriousness

FIG. 21.11
Schematic diagram of the cross-lagged correlation design. Behavior measures 1 and 2 are taken at time *W*; and then they are taken again at time *Y*. The six possible correlations among these four measurements are indicated by the lines connecting them and by the symbol *r* with appropriate subscripts.

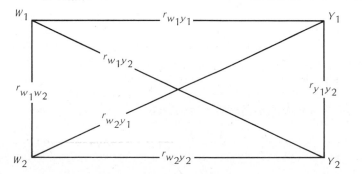

Research example The following briefly described study of the relationship between self-concept and social desirability illustrates the use of the cross-lagged design. If a self-report questionnaire personality-test item has an answer that indicates a positive description of oneself, there is a general response bias (chapter 14) toward choosing that socially desirable answer. Social desirability is supposedly a relatively enduring personality trait associated with defensiveness and the need for social approval. A person's general concept of self is also measured by self-report, personality inventories. These inventories tend to contain questions like, "I am popular" or "I am a bad person"; the person completing the questionnaire usually has two choices: "agree"/"true" or "disagree"/"false." The socially desirable answer to such questions is apparent. Measures of social desirability tend to have less obviously "correct" or positive self-description question-and-answer combinations. For example, it is not immediately apparent which answer is socially desirable for questions such as: "Are you always glad to cooperate?" and "Do you ever shout when you feel angry?" Arlin (1976) suggests that social desirability measures should be more stable indicators of defensiveness than self-concept measures because the social desirability questions have less obviously socially desirable answers.

Positive correlation coefficients between these two measures indicate that high self-concept scores tend to occur with high social desirability scores. Negative correlation coefficients indicate that persons with high self-concept scores tend to have low social desirability scores. Positive and negative correlations have been found in previous studies. In either case, the correlation coefficient cannot inform us whether the two variables are causally related. There are at least six possible rival hypotheses:

1. Increases in social desirability scores, the independent variable, cause increases in self-concept scores, the dependent variable.
2. Increases in social desirability scores cause *decreases* in self-concept scores.
3. Increases in self-concept scores, the independent variable, cause increases in social desirability scores, the dependent variable.
4. Increases in self-concept scores cause *decreases* in social desirability scores.
5. Both self-concept and social desirability scores are dependent variables caused by a third, unknown spurious variable.
6. Both self-concept and social desirability are independent variables that influence the dependent variable of self-report test-taking behavior.

At least three of these six rival hypotheses are *plausible.* Hypothesis 1 would be correct if social desirability scores measure defensiveness and approval need. Persons with high defensiveness would tend to inflate their self-concept scores. Hypothesis 3 would be correct if self-concept scores influence social desirability scores. Persons with a truly high self-concept would respond positively to all questions that are honestly if naively viewed as favorable to them. Hypothesis 4 could be correct if social desirability scores measure defensiveness and approval need. Persons with high self-concepts would have low defensiveness and would consequently have low social desirability scores. One way to begin to see which hypothesis or hypotheses are more likely to be correct is to examine the correlation between the two variables over time. Such a procedure requires a longitudinal study in which individuals are measured at least twice on both variables with a significant time period between the two measurement occasions.

Arlin (1976) conducted a cross-lagged correlation study of the relationship between self-concept and social desirability. He tested the rival hypotheses in the context of a laboratory school program that was intended, in part, to increase the self-concepts of children who were achieving below grade level and below the level that their IQ scores indicated they should achieve. Arlin reasoned that during the course of a complete academic year, the children would discover that the educators were trying to raise the children's self-concepts, and, as a consequence, the children's self-concept test scores should increase between September and May. On the other hand, the social desirability test should be more ambiguous to the children and, therefore, the social desirability scores should not change as much over the 9-mo. period. If Hypothesis 1 is correct, then September social desirability scores should predict May self-concept scores better than September self-concept scores predict May social desirability scores. In addition, the two kinds of measures should be significantly positively correlated in September and again in May. The initial null hypothesis of the design is Hypothesis 5, which suggests that a spurious variable exists.

The 57 pupils in the school were surrounded by four teachers and by full-time psychology and learning-disability specialists who worked with the children daily to provide academic and social success experiences. The professionals continuously and positively reinforced the fact that each child had worth, both as a student and as a person in general. The measures of self-concept and social desirability were administered before the therapeutic treatment and again 9 mo. later. The therapeutic treatment had a significant effect on the measure of self-concept; the students as a group gained almost 8 points between September and May. The children's social desirability scores did not change significantly; these scores were more stable across time as Arlin predicted.

The cross-lagged correlation coefficients and the other correlations are presented in Figure 21.12. The cross-lagged correlation of September social desirability scores

FIG. 21.12
Cross-lagged and other correlation coefficients between the Piers-Harris Self-Concept (SC) measure and the Children's Social Desirability (CSD) measure at two times. The asterisks indicate coefficients significant at α = .05. (From "Causal priority of social desirability over self-concept: A cross-lagged correlation analysis" by M. Arlin, *Journal of Personality and Social Psychology*, 1976, *33*, 267–272. Copyright 1976 by the American Psychological Association. Reprinted by permission.)

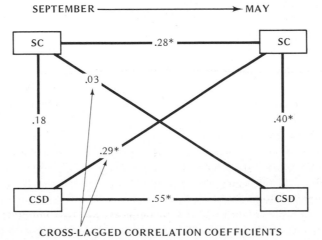

with May self-concept scores ($r = .29$) was significantly greater than the cross-lagged correlation of September self-concept scores with May social desirability scores. Thus, Hypothesis 1 that the social desirability variable is causally antecedent to the self-concept variable was supported. The null hypothesis, Hypothesis 5, was rejected. Also, as predicted, the correlations between the two kinds of measures in September and again in May were positive.

Arlin points out that the sample size was small and restricted to a particular population, and that the tests provided social desirability *scores* and self-concept *scores* that are not necessarily accurate measures of their corresponding personality constructs. While different children have different conceptions of social desirability, the group seemed to have a common conception of what the teachers and psychologists thought was socially desirable. Arlin notes that the assumption of a common conception of social desirability is crucial to the study.

Since the cross-lagged correlation of September self-concept score with May social desirability score is approximately zero, the results are not consistent with Hypothesis 3, that self-concept is causally prior to social desirability. Since there were positive correlations between the two sets of September measures and between the two sets of May measures, and since the September self-concept with May social desirability cross-lagged correlation was not negative, Hypothesis 4, that increases in self-concept would cause decreases in social desirability, was not supported. Among the three plausible alternative hypotheses at this point, the cross-lagged correlation analysis supports only Hypothesis 1.

The therapeutic treatment seems to have influenced the self-concept scores but not the social desirability scores of the children. If the therapeutic treatment had been examined only in terms of self-concept "gain" scores, a misleading conclusion would have resulted. In this particular study, it appears that the apparent "gain" in self-concept scores was at least in part due to the influence of the social desirability variable. Students with high social desirability scores were more affected by the treatment as measured by self-concept scores than students with low social desirability scores. The cross-lagged correlation analysis suggests that three variables interacted in the study: the therapeutic intervention, the social desirability personality measure, and the self-concept personality measure.

Advantages   The cross-lagged correlation design can be used with variables that cannot be manipulated (selection of values by the researcher and random assignment of subjects to conditions controlled by the researcher) for practical or ethical reasons. The design is well suited to detecting longitudinal cause–effect relationships that do not allow experimentation and in which initial small causal effects emerge as powerful causal effects over time.

Limitations   Two assumptions are important to the null hypothesis test of spuriousness. First, it is assumed that variables 1 and 2 are measured at the same time (simultaneous W measures and simultaneous Y measures). Besides the obvious limitation that the actual measurements must be as close to simultaneous as possible, this assumption also means that the measures cannot depend on the subject's recall of past experience, attitude, and so forth, and that the measures cannot be averages of several measures such as GPA or average weight over the last year.

Second, it is assumed that the causal processes are constant over the two points of measurement of the variables. There should be no change over the time of the two measurements in the strength and direction of the causal relationship between the variables. This assumption means that the cross-lagged correlation design is not appropriate for the study of the initiation of a *causal* effect or of behavior that changes with the stage of the subject (for example, social relationships of preadolescents vs. adolescents). Arlin's (1976) study does not violate this assumption, because the educational program was designed to change the self-concept scores, not the causal relationship between the measures of self-concept and social desirability.

Even when the above assumptions are met and a significant cross-lagged differential exists, there is still the problem of determining the source and direction of the causal relationship between the two measured variables. As indicated in Arlin's (1976) study, many plausible competing hypotheses may exist even when only two variables are measured twice each. In many cases, the cross-lagged analysis will only rule out a few of the alternative hypotheses, leaving some complex combination of hypotheses or several conflicting hypotheses still plausible.

A final limitation of a cross-lagged design is that, as a longitudinal design, it is very complex and requires much more time and expense than other designs.

Statistical analysis   The test of significance of the cross-lagged differential is beyond the scope of this text. Kenny (1975) describes the procedure.

Covariance Analysis

In chapter 20, the inferential statistical analysis technique known as analysis of variance (ANOVA) is briefly described. Analysis of covariance (ANCOVA) is a statistical technique that combines regression analysis with ANOVA. In addition to the manipulated independent variable and the measured dependent variable, one or more concomitant variables **(covariates)** are measured. Each covariate is a secondary variance source, *not* controlled by the researcher, that is believed to be related to the dependent variable. The essential purpose of ANCOVA is to "adjust" the dependent variable so as to statistically control the effects of the experimentally uncontrolled covariate source. In short, ANCOVA provides a means of *statistical control* of one or more covariates in order to reduce error variance and control a source of secondary variance.

ANOVA is designed to deal with experimentally manipulated independent variables that are qualitative variables measured at the nominal or ordinal level. Regression analysis is designed to deal with either experimentally manipulated or nonmanipulated, naturalistically observed independent variables that are quantitative variables measured at the interval or ratio level. ANCOVA links regression analysis with ANOVA because, in addition to the qualitative, experimentally manipulated independent variable, a nonmanipulated but quantitatively measured variable is incorporated into the analysis. The most elementary case involves a single dependent variable, a single independent variable, and a single covariate. This design is illustrated in Table 21.6.

In general, there are three conditions under which ANCOVA is employed. First, in an attempt to reduce some of the difficulties with a static-group comparison study (chapter 8), a researcher may have access to a covariate measure unaffected by the

ANCOVA

Covariates

Statistical Control

Static-Group Comparison with Covariate

TABLE 21.6 An Example of a Multilevel Design with Three Independent Groups and One Covariate

Group	Assignment	Covariate Measure	Treatment	After-Observation
1	R	C_1	—	Y_1
2	R	C_2	X_1	Y_2
3	R	C_3	X_2	Y_3

naturally occurring treatment and may subject the data to ANCOVA. The classic example of such a procedure is educational research, in which three classrooms are randomly assigned to one of three pedagogical treatment conditions. Because the students are not randomly assigned to classrooms and between-teacher differences are uncontrolled, it is probable that many preexisting sources of secondary variance, such as selection bias, maturation, experimental mortality, and the interaction of selection bias with the treatment (chapter 3), will influence the results. Frequently, intelligence or achievement test scores exist prior to the introduction of the treatment and you cannot use these data to match the groups. The *linear* relationship between the IQ scores (covariate) and the dependent variable can be calculated and used to adjust the dependent variable scores by removing the between-group IQ differences. This procedure does not solve all of the problems created by the use of nonrandom intact groups; any nonlinear effects of IQ and all unmeasured sources of variance are still free to bias the results. If several different covariates exist, each can be incorporated into the regression analysis and adjustment procedures (for example, IQ *and* achievement test scores). It is unlikely that a static-group comparison study will provide data that meet the assumptions of ANCOVA we shall describe; therefore this classic procedure is not recommended.

Randomized Designs with Before-Covariate

A second, more useful application may occur when a random assignment or matching design is employed. In a randomized-groups design, you may collect baseline or before-measures but not use that data to match groups. Subsequently, the covariate baseline data, unaffected by the treatment since it was collected prior to the administration of the treatment, can be used to adjust the after-scores with an ANCOVA procedure. Alternatively, you may match groups on a correlated criterion and have an additional before-measure on a second covariate. The measured covariate may be used in addition to the matching procedure to control statistically for between-group differences. For example, you may have an anxiety test and a stress-tolerance test administered at the onset of an experiment on the effect of social pressure on reaction time. The stress-tolerance test scores may be used to match people between groups, and the anxiety test scores may become a covariate in the ANCOVA of the dependent data.

Randomized Designs with Concurrent Covariate

Third, occasionally during the course of a study you may discover a variable that is a plausible source of difference between groups randomly assigned to treatments. For example, a research project involving several experimenters may be well started before you discover that there are differences in procedures between experimenters. If these differences are not related to the independent variable, but can *reasonably* be expected to affect the dependent variable, then you may be able to use ANCOVA to remove the linear effect of the procedural differences from the dependent data.

Limitations   There are a large number of assumptions and limitations to the use of ANCOVA.

1. Each source of error should be independent of every other source of error. In practice this means random assignment of subjects to groups is required.
2. The distribution of errors within each treatment group should be normal (chapter 16), and the error variance for each treatment group should be approximately equal across all groups. In practice this condition can be satisfactorily achieved by random assignment to groups of the same size.
3. The regression coefficients for each treatment group should be approximately equal across all groups. This assumption can be tested.
4. The deviations from the within-group regression lines should be distributed normally and independently with a population mean of zero and common variance. In practice this means that the data can be fitted adequately by a linear regression line or a nonlinear regression line, two different kinds of regression analysis. This assumption also can be tested.
5. The covariate is *not* a function of the independent variable. In practice this means that the covariate either is a before-measure, is measured after the treatment is administered but before it takes effect (for example, delayed drug effects), or is measured after the treatment is administered but we can unquestionably assume that the covariate is unaffected by the treatment (a very unlikely case).
6. Of course, a covariate measure must exist; it must not be manipulated; and it must be a secondary variance source.

Statistical control is not as effective as experimental control. Whenever possible, ANCOVA should be avoided in favor of matching designs or randomized-blocks designs. An additional disadvantage of ANCOVA includes the significant increase in computational complexity of the data analysis.

Statistical analysis   The details of the statistical analysis are beyond the scope of this text. Numerous texts provide the needed information, for example, Edwards (1972), Kirk (1968), and Winer (1971).

Comments   One can add more and more covariates to the analysis if they exist; however, there is a diminishing return as less and less of the dependent variance remains to be accounted for as each covariate is added. While ANCOVA does remove at least part of the effect of a secondary variance source that may be impossible to control by other methods, ANCOVA has a large number of restrictions on its use and must be employed with discretion.

Multivariate Analysis

Two of many possible types of multivariate analysis are briefly described in this section. The details of the statistical analysis are far beyond the scope and level of this text. This very brief section is included primarily to give a general idea of the meaning of terms that are more and more frequently encountered in research journals.

Multiple-Regression Analysis

Multiple-Correlation Analysis

Multiple-correlation or multiple-regression analysis is used when two or more variables are used to "predict" scores on a third criterion variable. If the predictor variables are manipulated independent variables, then the analysis is called **multiple-regression analysis.** If the predictor variables are measured at the interval or ratio level but are not manipulated independent variables, then the analysis is called **multiple-correlation analysis.** It is common in personality research to have two or more measures used to predict scores on a criterion variable. For example, scores on two or more subscales of the Minnesota Multiphasic Personality Inventory may be used to predict rate of recovery under therapeutic intervention in a mental hospital setting.

Multiple-correlation or multiple-regression analysis is a generalization of the Pearson correlation coefficient from the case of one independent or predictor variable correlated with one criterion or dependent variable to the case of two or more predictors correlated with one criterion. The mathematical manipulation of the data produces the equivalent of the Pearson r between the criterion and a linear combination of weighted scores on the predictor variables. The weights are chosen to maximize the value of R (the multiple-correlation coefficient). The null hypothesis is that the value of R is zero.

ANOVA is appropriate to research designs involving a single dependent variable measured at the interval or ratio level and one or more independent variables with two or more levels each measured at the nominal or ordinal level of measurement.

Multivariate Analysis of Variance (MANOVA)

Multivariate analysis of variance (MANOVA) is appropriate to the analysis of a design including one or more independent, manipulated variables of two or more levels each measured at the nominal or ordinal level and two or more dependent variables measured at the interval or ratio level. MANOVA is a generalization of ANOVA from the single dependent variable to the multiple dependent-variable situation. For example, a researcher may measure achievement test performance and "liking for school" in a factorial design involving the independent variables of bussing/nonbussing (randomly assigned), ethnic background, and parental income.

The mathematical manipulation of the data reduces the set of two or more dependent measures to a single variable that is a linear combination of the weighted dependent measures. The weights are chosen to maximize the F ratio (chapter 20) for each independent variable *or* for a particular independent variable. The analysis produces the equivalent of an F ratio for a single dependent measure, but tests the null hypothesis of no significant effect of an independent variable or interaction of two or more variables on any one or all dependent measures.

SUMMARY

1. Correlation coefficients may be used to describe numerically the relationship between any two variables that allow pairing of scores.
2. The Pearson product-moment correlation coefficient describes the degree and direction of linear relationship. The value of r varies from -1.00 to $+1.00$.
3. The strength or degree of relationship is indicated by the numerical value of r. The direction of relationship is indicated by the sign of r; a positive, direct relationship is

Questions

1. t-table - does not have df I need what to do?

2. x^2 - can I use it even tho I don't have 5 for expected

3. In Result section how do I express my interpretations? where do I talk about my α level?

4 discussion ~~stat~~ section

5. 1 table & 1 graph

1. chapter 21
2. Pat's book correlation
3. my notes

$(t = \frac{\text{calcula.}}{t}) P < .05).$

graphically depicted as an upward trend, and a negative, inverse relationship is depicted by a downward trend.

4. The Pearson r is used with two variables measured at the interval or ratio level. The Pearson r is *not* a percentage figure; it does not indicate the "percentage of relationship."

5. The significance of r is tested with the t test. The null hypothesis is that the population correlation coefficient (parameter) is zero.

6. One "goodness of fit" test is concerned with the degree to which a straight line fits observed data. A straight line relationship is the simplest function to describe the trend of data. The slope of the best-fit line is calculated in the process of fitting a straight line to data.

7. The goodness of fit of a straight line may be tested; the null hypothesis is that the population slope of the function relating the independent and dependent variables is zero. Failure to reject the null may mean that the population slope is close to zero, or that the relationship between the two variables is not linear, or both.

8. Correlation is *not* equivalent to causation. Correlation does *not* necessarily imply causation. The existence of a correlation between two variables *may* mean that A causes B or that B causes A. An experimental study with manipulated control of independent variables is necessary for causal inference. Naturalistic, correlational research does not allow the confidence about causal inference that experimental research allows. Naturalistic, correlational research does disclose interesting, potential causal relationships.

9. Correlation coefficients may be used as secondary statistical tools as part of a research study, or as a crucial aspect or objective of a research study.

10. In order for matching to be useful, the correlation between the matching and dependent variables must be nontrivial.

11. A correlation coefficient between two dependent variables can also be used as a dependent variable in research.

12. Reliability and validity are described in terms of correlation coefficients. Interrater reliability and test reliability occur when an individual gets approximately the same score each time the person is rated or takes a test, or takes alternate forms of a test. If a test score does a good job of predicting a future behavior, then the test has high predictive validity. If a test score correlates highly with another measure of the same or similar behavior, then the test has high criterion-referenced validity.

13. Regression coefficients may be used to measure the magnitude of the significant relationship between an experimentally manipulated independent variable and a dependent variable.

14. The objective of some naturalistic research studies is the description in numerical form of the relationship between two naturally occurring variables. Such a study is called a correlational study; the outcome of the study is a correlation coefficient.

15. The cross-lagged correlation design is a nonexperimental design consisting of at least two different behavioral measures repeated at two different points in time for the same subjects. The design is a longitudinal design involving the use of correlation coefficients between all possible combinations of measurements. The cross-lagged correlation coefficient indexes the relationship between two different kinds of measures with a time delay between the points of measurement.

16. The objective of cross-lagged analysis is to determine the causal priority of the two variables involved. The null hypothesis is that a spurious, noncausal relationship exists between the two variables; that is, the correlation between the two variables is caused by a third variable.

17. ANCOVA combines regression analysis with ANOVA. ANCOVA is used in an experimental study in which one or more secondary variables are measured. The linear relationship between the secondary variable or covariate and the dependent variable is determined.

ANCOVA statistically controls for the effect of the covariate by removing the linear effect of the covariate from the data.

18. The limitations and assumptions of ANCOVA include: (a) random assignment of subjects to groups is required; (b) groups should be approximately equal in size; (c) the regession coefficients for each treatment group should be approximately equal; (d) the relationship between the covariate and dependent variable should be linear; and (e) the covariate should not be related to the independent variable. Experimental control is preferable to statistical control.

19. In experimental research with two or more independent variables, the relationship between the independent variables and the dependent variable can be described by multiple-regression analysis. In a nonexperimental study with more than two variables measured, the relationship between the variables can be described by multiple-correlation analysis.

20. MANOVA is used with experimental research designs involving one or more independent variables with two or more levels each, and two or more dependent variables measured at the interval or ratio level.

SUGGESTED READINGS

Edwards, A. L. *Experimental design in psychological research* (4th ed.). New York: Holt, Rinehart and Winston, 1972.

Edwards, A. L. *Statistical methods* (3d ed.). New York: Holt, Rinehart and Winston, 1973.

Hays, W. *Statistics for the social sciences* (2d ed.). New York: Holt, Rinehart and Winston, 1973.

Jones, M. B. Correlation as a dependent variable. *Psychological Bulletin,* 1968, *70,* 69–72.

McNemar, Q. *Psychological statistics* (4th ed.). New York: Wiley, 1969.

Winer, B. J. *Statistical principles in experimental design* (2d ed.). New York: McGraw-Hill, 1971.

References

Adams, J. S. Toward an understanding of inequity. *Journal of Abnormal and Social Psychology,* 1963, *67,* 422–436.

Alder, H. L., & Roessler, E. B. *Introduction to probability and statistics* (3rd ed.). San Francisco: Freeman, 1964.

Allen, E. M. Why are research grant applications disapproved? *Science,* 1960, *132,* 1532–1534.

Althauser, R. P., & Rubin, D. The computerized construction of a matched sample. *The American Journal of Sociology,* 1970, *76,* 325–346.

American Psychological Association, Committee on Ethical Standards in Psychological Research. *Ethical principles in the conduct of research with human participants.* Washington, D.C.: Author, 1973.

American Psychological Association, Committee on Precautions and Standards in Animal Experimentation. *Principles for the care and use of animals.* Washington, D.C.: Author, 1971.

American Psychological Association, Council of Editors. Testing and public policy. *American Psychologist,* 1965, *20,* 857–993.

American Psychological Association. *Publication manual of the American Psychological Association* (2nd ed.). Washington, D.C.: Author, 1974.

Anastasi, A. *Psychological testing* (4th ed.). New York: Macmillan, 1976.

Anderson, B. F. *The psychology experiment: An introduction to the scientific method* (2nd ed.). Belmont, Calif.: Wadsworth, 1971.

Anderson, B. F. *Cognitive psychology: The study of knowing, learning and thinking.* New York: Academic Press, 1975.

Anderson, N. H. Scales and statistics: Parametric and nonparametric. *Psychological Bulletin,* 1961, *58,* 305–316.

Andrews, F. M., Klem, L., Davidson, T. N., O'Malley, P. M., & Rodgers, W. L. *A guide for selecting statistical techniques for analyzing social science data.* Ann Arbor, Mich.: Institute for Social Research, University of Michigan, 1974.

Arlin, M. Causal priority of social desirability over self-concept: A cross-lagged correlation analysis. *Journal of Personality and Social Psychology,* 1976, *33,* 267–272.

Aronson, E. *The social animal* (2nd ed.). San Francisco: Freeman, 1976.

Ausubel, D., & Sullivan, E. *Theories and problems of child development* (2nd ed.). New York: Grune & Stratton, 1970.

Axelrod, S. N., Hall, R. V., Weis, L., & Rohrer, S. Use of self-imposed contingencies to reduce the frequency of smoking behavior. In M. J. Mahoney & C. E. Thoresen (Eds.), *Self control: Power to the person.* Monterey, Calif.: Brooks/Cole, 1974.

Bachrach, A. J. *Psychological research: An introduction* (3rd ed.). New York: Random House, 1972.

Bandura, A., & Walters, R. H. *Social learning and personality development.* New York: Holt, Rinehart and Winston, 1963.

Barber, T. X. *Pitfalls in human research: Ten pivotal points.* New York: Pergamon, 1976.

Barber, T. X., & Silver, M. J. Fact, fiction, and the experimenter effect. *Psychological Bulletin Monographs,* 1968, *70,* (6, Pt. 2).

Barlow, D. H., & Hersen, M. Single-case experimental design: Uses in applied clinical research. *Archives of General Psychiatry,* 1973, *29,* 319–325.

Baron, R. A. The reduction of human aggression: A field study of the influence of incompatible reactions. *Journal of Applied Social Psychology,* 1976, *6,* 260–274.

Bartz, W. R. Personal communication, June, 1976.

Beach, F. A. The snark was a boojum. *American Psychologist,* 1950, *5,* 115–124.

Beauchamp, K. L. Drive and maintenance schedule (Doctoral dissertation, Claremont Graduate School, 1968). *Dissertation Abstracts,* 1969, *29,* 2644B–2645B. (University Microfilms No. 68–18, 254)

Beckwith, J., & Miller, L. Behind the mask of objective science. *The Sciences,* November/December 1976, pp. 16–19; 29; 31.

Bell, J. E. *A guide to library research in psychology.* Dubuque, Iowa: Brown, 1971.

Bergmann, G., & Spence, K. W. Operationism and theory in psychology. *Psychological Review,* 1941, *48,* 1–14.

Berkowitz, L. (Ed.). *Advances in experimental social psychology* (10 vols.). New York: Academic Press, 1964–1976.

Bickett, A. Personal communication, September–December, 1975.

Bijou, S. W., & Baer, D. M. The laboratory-experimental study of child behavior. In P. H. Mussen (Ed.), *Handbook of research methods in child development.* New York: Wiley, 1960.

Bijou, S. W., & Sturges, P. T. Positive reinforcers for experimental study with children—consumables and manipulatables. *Child Development,* 1959, *30,* 151–170.

Bitterman, M. E. Phyletic differences in learning. *American Psychologist,* 1965, *20,* 396–410.

Blomgren, G. W., & Scheuneman, T. W. *Psychological resistance to seat belts* (Research Project RR-115). Evanston, Ill.: Northwestern University Traffic Institute, 1961.

Blommers, P., & Lindquist, E. F. *Elementary statistical methods in psychology and education.* Boston: Houghton Mifflin, 1960.

Bloom, K., & Esposito, A. Social conditioning and its proper control procedures. *Journal of Experimental Child Psychology,* 1975, *19,* 209—222.

Bolles, R. *Theory of motivation.* New York: Harper & Row, 1967.

Boneau, C. A. The effects of violations of assumptions underlying the *t* test. *Psychological Bulletin,* 1960, *57,* 49—64.

Boring, E. G. Perspective: Artifact and control. In R. Rosenthal & R. L. Rosnow (Eds.), *Artifact in behavioral research.* New York: Academic Press, 1969.

Borkovec, T., Kaloupeck, D. G., & Slama, K. The facilitative effect of muscle tension-release in the relaxation treatment of sleep disturbance. *Behavior Therapy,* 1975, *6,* 302–309.

Bower, T. G. R. The visual world of infants. *Scientific American,* 1966, *215* (6), 80–92.

Bradburn, N. M. *N* achievement and father dominance in Turkey. *Journal of Abnormal and Social Psychology,* 1963, *67,* 464–468.

Brady, J. V. Ulcers in "executive" monkeys. *Scientific American,* 1958, *199* (4), 95–100.

Bridgman, P. W. *The logic of modern physics.* New York: Macmillan, 1927.

Bridgman, P. W. Remarks on the present state of operationalism. *Scientific Monthly,* 1954, *79,* 224–226.

Brown, R. *Social psychology.* New York: Free Press, 1965.

Bruner, J. S., Olver, R. R., Greenfield, P. M., Hornsby, J. R., Kenney, H. F., Maccoby, M., Modiano, N., Mosher, F. A., Olson, D. R., Potter, M. C., Reich, L. C., & Sonstroem, A. M. *Studies in cognitive growth.* New York: Wiley, 1966.

Buros, O. K. *The seventh mental measurements yearbook.* Highland Park, N.J.: Gryphon, 1972.

Caldwell, W. E., & Russo, F. An exploratory study of the effects of an A.C. magnetic field upon the behavior of the Italian honeybee (Apis millifica). *The Journal of Genetic Psychology,* 1968, *113,* 233–252.

Calfee, R. *Human experimental psychology.* New York: Holt, Rinehart and Winston, 1975.

Calhoun, J. B. Population density and social pathology. *Scientific American,* 1962, *206*(2), 139–148.

Campbell, D. T. Prospective: Artifact and control. In R. Rosenthal & R. L. Rosnow (Eds.), *Artifact in behavioral* research. New York: Academic Press, 1969.

Campbell, D. T., & Stanley, J. C. *Experimental and quasi-experimental designs for research.* Skokie, Ill. Rand McNally, 1963.

Candland, D. K. *Psychology: The experimental approach.* New York: McGraw-Hill, 1968.

Cantril, H. *Gauging public opinion.* Princeton: Princeton University Press, 1944.

Castaneda, A., & Fahel, L. S. The relationship between the psychological investigator and the public schools. *American Psychologist,* 1961, *16,* 201–203.

Christophersen, E. R., Arnold, C. M., Hill, D. W., & Quilitch, H. R. The home point system: Token reinforcement procedures for application by parents of children with behavior problems. *Journal of Applied Behavior Analysis,* 1972, *5,* 485–497.

Cialdini, R. B., & Mirels, H. L. Sense of personal control and attributions about yielding and resisting persuasion targets. *Journal of Personality and Social Psychology,* 1976, *33,* 395–402.

Clifton, M. The dread tomato addiction. *Outstanding Science Fiction,* February 1958, pp. 97–98.

Cofer, C. N., & Appley, M. H. *Motivation: Theory and research.* New York: Wiley, 1964.

Conant, J. B. *On understanding science: An historical approach.* New Haven: Yale University Press, 1947.

Coombs, C. H., Raiffa, H., & Thrall, R. M. Some views on mathematical models and measurement theory. *Pschological Review,* 1954, *61,* 132–144.

Cornsweet, T. N. *Visual perception.* New York: Academic Press, 1970.

Corso, J. F. *The experimental psychology of sensory behavior.* New York: Holt, Rinehart and Winston, 1967.

Cronbach, L. *Essentials of psychological testing* (3rd ed.). New York: Harper & Row, 1970.

Davidson, P. O., & Costello, C. G. *N = 1: Experimental studies of single cases.* New York: Van Nostrand Reinhold, 1969.

Day, R. *Human perception.* New York: Wiley, 1969.

Deese, J. *Psychology as science and art.* New York: Harcourt Brace Jovanovich, 1972.

Deese, J., & Hulse, S. H. *The psychology of learning* (3rd. ed.). New York: McGraw-Hill, 1967.

Dember, W. N. *The psychology of perception.* New York: Holt, Rinehart and Winston, 1960.

Denny, M. R., & Ratner, S. C. *Comparative psychology: Research in animal behavior* (Rev. ed.). Homewood, Ill.: Dorsey, 1970.

Dethier, V., & Stellar, E. *Animal behavior* (3rd ed.). Englewood Cliffs, N.J.: Prentice-Hall, 1969.

Dewsbury, D. A., & Rethlingshafer, D. (Eds.). *Comparative psychology: A modern approach.* New York: McGraw-Hill, 1973.

Diefenderfer, A. J. *Principles of electronic instrumentation.* Philadelphia: Saunders, 1972.

Dillon, P. C., Graham, W. K., & Aidells, A. L. Brainstorming on a "hot" problem: Effects of training and practice on individual and group performance. *Journal of Applied Psychology,* 1972, *56,* 487–490.

Dohrenwend, B. S., & Dohrenwend, B. P. (Eds.). *Stressful life events: Their nature and effects.* New York: Wiley, 1974.

Downing, G. *The massage book.* New York: Random House, 1972.

Edwards, A. L. *Statistical methods* (2nd ed.). New York: Holt, Rinehart and Winston, 1967.

Edwards, A. L. *The measurement of personality traits by scales and inventories.* New York: Holt, Rinehart and Winston, 1970.

Edwards, A. L. *Experimental design in psychological research* (4th ed.). New York: Holt, Rinehart and Winston, 1972.

Edwards, A. L. *Statistical methods* (3rd ed.). New York: Holt, Rinehart and Winston, 1973.

Eisenberg, J. F., & Dillon, W. S. *Man and beast: Comparative social behavior.* Washington, D.C.: Smithsonian, 1971.

Endler, N. S., Boulter, L. R., & Osser, H. (Eds.). *Contemporary issues in developmental psychology.* New York: Holt, Rinehart and Winston, 1968.

Fawl, C. L. Disturbances experienced by children in their natural habitats. In R. G. Barker (Ed.), *The stream of behavior.* New York: Appleton, 1963.

Ferguson, E. D. *Motivation: An experimental approach.* New York: Holt, Rinehart and Winston, 1976.

Ferster, C. B., & Perrott, M. C. *Behavior principles.* New York: Appleton, 1968.

Fisher, J. D., & Nadler, A. Effect of donor resources on recipient self-esteem and self-help. *Journal of Experimental Social Psychology,* 1976, *12,* 139–150.

Flavell, J. H. *The developmental psychology of Jean Piaget.* Princeton: Van Nostrand, 1963.

Fleischman, P. R., Israel, J. V., Burr, W. A., Hoaken, P. C. S., Thaler, O. F., Zucker, H. D., Hanley, J., Ostow, M., Lieberman, L. R., Hunter, F. M., Rinsker, H., Blair, S. M., Reich, W., Wiedeman, G. H., Pattison, E. M., & Rosenhan, D. L. Assorted letters in *Science,* 1973, *180,* 356–369.

Forgus, R. H., & Melamed, L. E. *Perception: A cognitive-stage approach* (2nd ed.). New York: McGraw-Hill, 1976.

Frank, H. *Introduction to probability and statistics: Concepts and principles.* New York: Wiley, 1974.

Frisch, K., von. *Bees—their vision, chemical senses, and language.* New York: Cornell University Press, 1950.

Furby, L. Interpreting regression toward the mean in developmental research. *Developmental Psychology,* 1973, *8,* 172–179.

Gaito, J. Statistical dangers involved in counterbalancing. *Psychological Reports,* 1958, *4,* 463–468.

Gay, W. I. (Ed.). *Methods of animal experimentation* (5 vols.). New York: Academic Press, 1965–1974.

Geldard, F. A. *The human senses* (2nd ed.). New York: Wiley, 1972.

Gentile, J. R., Roden, A. H., & Klein, R. D. An analysis-of-variance model for the intrasubject replication design. *Journal of Applied Behavior Analysis,* 1972, *5,* 193–198.

Gergen, K., & Marlow, D. *Personality and social behavior.* Reading, Mass.: Addison-Wesley, 1970.

Gessner, P. K. Evaluation of instruction. *Science,* 1973, *180,* 566–570.

Gibson, E. J. *Principles of perceptual learning and development.* New York: Appleton, 1969.

Gibson, J. J. *The senses considered as perceptual systems.* Boston: Houghton Mifflin, 1966.

Ginsberg, H., & Opper, S. *Piaget's theory of intellectual development: An introduction.* Englewood Cliffs, N.J.: Prentice-Hall, 1969.

Godstein, K. M., Taub, H. B., Caputo, D. V., & Silberstein, R. M. Child status and demographic variables as related to maternal child-rearing attitudes. *Perceptual and Motor Skills,* 1976, *42,* 87–97.

Goodall, J. My life among wild chimpanzees. *National Georgraphic,* 1963, *124,* 272–308.

Gottman, J. M., McFall, R. M., Barnett, J. T. Design and analysis of research using time series. *Psychological Bulletin,* 1969, *72,* 299–306.

Gottschalk, L. A., Serota, H. M., & Shapiro, L. F. *Psychological conflict and neuromuscular tension in life stress and bodily disease.* Baltimore: Williams & Wilkins, 1950.

Gregory, R. *Eye and brain: The psychology of seeing.* New York: McGraw-Hill, 1966.

Gregory, R. *The intelligent eye.* New York: McGraw-Hill, 1970.

Guilford, J. P. *Fundamental statistics in psychology and education* (4th ed.). New York: McGraw-Hill, 1965.

Guilford, J. P., & Fruchter, B. *Fundamental statistics in psychology and education* (5th ed.). New York: McGraw-Hill, 1973.

Haber, R. N. Discrepancy from adaptation level as a source of affect. *Journal of Experimental Psychology,* 1958, *56,* 370–375.

Haber, R. N. (Ed.). *Current research in motivation.* New York: Holt, Rinehart and Winston, 1966.

Haber, R. N., & Hershenson, M. *The psychology of visual perception.* New York: Holt, Rinehart and Winston, 1973.

Hall, R. V., Cristler, C., Cranston, S. S., & Tucker, B. Teachers and parents as researchers using multiple-baseline designs. *Journal of Applied Behavior Analysis,* 1970, *3,* 247–255.

Harlow, H. F. Love in infant monkeys. *Scientific American,* 1959, *200* (6), 68–74.

Harlow, H. F. The heterosexual affectional system in monkeys. *American Psychologist,* 1962, *17,* 1–9.

Harlow, H. F. Age-mate or peer affectional systems. In D. S. Lehrman, R. D. Hinde, & E. Shaw (Eds.), *Advances in the study of behavior* (Vol. 2). New York: Academic Press, 1969.

Hartmann, D. P. Forcing square pegs into round holes: Some comments on "An analysis of variance model for the intrasubject replication design." *Journal of Applied Behavior Analysis,* 1974, *7,* 635–638.

Hays, W. L. *Statistics for social scientists* (2nd ed.). New York: Holt, Rinehart and Winston, 1973.

Held, R., & Hein, A. Movement produced stimulation in the development of visually guided behavior. *Journal of Comparative and Physiological Psychology,* 1963, *56,* 872–876.

Hergenhahn, B. R. *An introduction to theories of learning.* Englewood Cliffs, N.J.: Prentice-Hall, 1976.

Herman, C. P. External and internal cues as determinants of the smoking behavior of light and heavy smokers. *Journal of Personality and Social Psychology,* 1974, *30,* 664–672.

Hersen, M., & Barlow, D. H. *Single case experimental designs: Strategies for studying behavior change.* New York: Pergamon, 1976.

Hess, E. H. Attitude and pupil size. *Scientific American,* 1965, *212*(4), 46–54.

Hilgard, E. R., & Bower, G. H. *Theories of learning* (4th ed.). New York: Appleton, 1974.

Hills, M. *Statistics for comparative studies.* London: Chapman & Hill, 1974.

Holmes, T. H., & Wolff, H. B. *Life situations, emotions and backache in life stress and bodily disease.* Baltimore: Williams & Wilkins, 1950.

Horton, D., & Turnage, T. *Human learning.* Englewood Cliffs, N.J.: Prentice-Hall, 1976.

Horvath, F. The effect of selected variables on interpretation of polygraph records. *Journal of Applied Psychology,* 1977, *62,* (2), 127–136.

Houston, J. P. *Fundamentals of learning.* New York: Academic Press, 1976.

Huff, D. *How to lie with statistics.* New York: Norton, 1954.

Hulse, S. H., Deese, J., & Egeth, H. E. *The psychology of learning* (4th ed.). New York: McGraw-Hill, 1975.

Hurlock, E. *Developmental psychology* (4th ed.). New York: McGraw-Hill, 1975.

Isaacson, R. L., Hutt, M. L., & Blum, M. L. *Psychology: The science of behavior.* New York: Harper & Row, 1965.

Ittleson, W. H. *Environment and cognition.* New York: Academic Press, 1973.

Jacobson, P. E. *Introduction to statistical measures for the social and behavioral sciences.* Hinsdale, Ill.: Dryden, 1976.

Jenni, D. A., & Jenni, M. A. Carrying behavior in humans: Analysis of sex differences. *Science,* 1976, *194,* 859–860.

Jensen, A. R., Kagan, J. S., Hunt, J. McV., Crowe, J. F., Bereiter, C., Elkind, D., Crowbach, L. J., & Brazziel, W. F. *Environment, heredity, and intelligence.* Cambridge, Mass.: Harvard Educational Review Reprint Series, No. 2, 1969.

Johnson, H. H., & Solso, R. L. *An introduction to experimental design in psychology: A case approach.* New York: Harper & Row, 1971.

Jones, F. P. Experimental methods in antiquity. *American Psychologist,* 1964, *19,* 419.

Jones, M. B. Correlation as a dependent variable. *Psychological Bulletin,* 1968, *70,* 69–72.

Jones, T. B., & Kamil, A. C. Tool-making and tool-using in the northern blue jay. *Science,* 1973, *180,* 1076–1078.

Jung, J. *Verbal learning.* New York: Holt, Rinehart and Winston, 1968.

Jung, J. Current practices and problems in the use of college students for psychological research. *Canadian Psychologist,* 1969, *10,* 280–290.

Jung, J. *The experimenter's dilemma.* New York: Harper & Row, 1971.

Kazdin, A. E. Methodological and assessment considerations in evaluating reinforcement programs in applied settings. *Journal of Applied Behavior Analysis,* 1973, *6,* 1—23.

Kazdin, A. E. *Behavior modification in applied settings.* Homewood, Ill.: Dorsey, 1975.

Kelley, H. H. *Attribution in social interaction.* New York: General Learning Press, 1971.

Kenny, D. A. Cross-lagged panel correlation: A test for spuriousness. *Psychological Bulletin,* 1975, *82,* 887–903.

Kerlinger, F. N. *Foundations of behavioral research* (2nd ed.). New York: Holt, Rinehart and Winston, 1973.

Kershner, R. B., & Wilcox, L. R. *The anatomy of mathematics.* New York: Ronald, 1950.

Kimble, G. A. *Hilgard and Marquis' conditioning and learning* (Rev. ed.). New York: Appleton, 1961.

Kimble, G. A. (Ed.). *Foundations of conditioning and learning.* New York: Appleton, 1967.

Kirk, R. E. *Experimental design: Procedures for the behavioral sciences.* Belmont, Calif.: Brooks/Cole, 1968.

Kirk, R. E. (Ed.). *Statistical issues: A reader for the behavioral sciences.* Belmont, Calif.: Brooks/Cole, 1972.

Klausmeier, H. G., Chatala, E. S., & Fryer, D. A. *Conceptual learning and development: A cognitive view.* New York: Academic Press, 1974.

Kling, J., & Riggs, L. (Eds.). *Woodworth/Schlosberg's experimental psychology* (3rd ed.). New York: Holt, Rinehart and Winston, 1971.

Klopfer, P. H. Behavioral aspects of habitat selection: The role of early experience. *Wilson Bulletin,* 1963, *75,* 15–22.

Koch, S. (Ed.). *Psychology: A study of a science* (6 vols.). New York: McGraw-Hill, 1959–1963.

Kovacs, R. M. *A manual of physical therapy.* Philadelphia: Lea & Febriger, 1944.

Kraus, H. *Principles and practices of therapeutic exercise.* Springfield, Ill.: C. C Thomas, 1949.

Krech, D., Rosenzweig, M., & Bennett, E. Relations between brain chemistry and problem-solving among rats in enriched and improverished environments. *Journal of Comparative and Physiological Psychology,* 1962, *55,* 801–807.

Kruskal, W. H., & Wallis, W. A. Use of ranks in one-criterion variance analysis. *Journal of the American Statistical Association,* 1952, *47,* 583–621.

Kubovy, M., & Psotka, J. The predominance of seven and the apparent spontaneity of numerical choices. *Journal of Experimental Psychology: Human Perception and Performance,* 1976, *2,* 291–294.

Kuhn, T. S. *The structure of scientific revolutions* (2nd ed.). Chicago: University of Chicago Press, 1970.

Lana, R. E. Pretest sensitization. In R. Rosenthal & R. L. Rosnow (Eds.), *Artifact in behavioral research.* New York: Academic Press, 1969.

Landon, P. B. The unimportance of experimenter-bias in sensory deprivation research. *Perceptual and Motor Skills,* 1976, *42,* 619–624.

Langer, J. *Theories of development.* New York: Holt, Rinehart and Winston, 1969.

Lawick-Goodall, J. van. Tool-using bird: The Egyptian vulture. *National Georgraphic,* 1968, *133,* 631–641.

Lee, W. *Experimental design and analysis.* San Francisco: Freeman, 1975.

Lehrman, D. S., Hinde, R. A., & Shaw, E. (Eds.). *Advances in the study of behavior* (7 vols.). New York: Academic Press, 1965–1976.

Leitenberg, H., Agras, W. S., & Thomson, L. A sequential analysis of the effect of selective positive reinforcement in modifying anorexia nervosa. *Behavior Research and Therapy,* 1968, *6,* 211–218.

Lenneberg, E. H. Understanding language without ability to speak: A case report. *Journal of Abnormal and Social Psychology,* 1962, *65,* 419–425.

Levinson, L. *Webster's unafraid dictionary.* New York: Collier, 1967.

Lewis, D., & Burke, C. J. The use and misuse of the chi-square test. *Psychological Bulletin,* 1949, *46,* 433–489.

Lewontin, R. C. The fallacy of biological determinism. *The Sciences,* March/April 1976, pp. 6–10.

Libby, W. F. Review of D. Irving, "The German atomic bomb." *Science,* 1968, *160,* 1975.

Lindman, H. R. *Analysis of variance in complex experimental designs.* San Francisco: Freeman, 1974.

Lindquist, E. F. *Design and analysis of experiments in psychology and education.* Boston: Houghton Mifflin, 1953.

Lindzey, G., & Aronson, E. (Eds.). *Handbook of social psychology* (Rev. ed., 5 vols). Cambridge, Mass.: Addison-Wesley, 1967–1969.

Lipsitt, L. L., & Spiker, C. C. (Eds.). *Advances in child development and behavior* (11 vols.). New York: Academic Press, 1963–1976.

Lorayne, H., & Lucas, J. *The memory book.* New York: Ballantine, 1974.

Lorenz; K. *King Solomon's ring.* New York: Crowell, 1952.

Lüscher, M. *The Lüscher color test* (I. A. Scott, ed. and trans.). New York: Random House, 1969. (Originally published, 1948.)

Lutzker, J. R. Reducing self-injurious behavior with a retardate in three classrooms by facial screening. Manuscript submitted for publication, 1977.

Maier, N. R. F., Julius, M, & Thurber, J. A. Studies in creativity: Individual differences in the storage and utilization of information. *American Journal of Psychology,* 1967, *80,* 492–519.

Maier, N. R. F., & Schneirla, T. C. *Principles of animal psychology.* New York: Dover, 1964.

Maier, R., & Maier, B. *Comparative animal behavior.* Belmont, Calif.: Brooks/Cole, 1970.

Malmo, R. B. *On emotions, needs and our archaic brain.* New York: Holt, Rinehart and Winston, 1975.

Malmstadt, H. V., Enke, C. G., & Toren, E. C. *Electronics for scientists.* New York: W. B. Benjamin, 1963.

Martin, I. Somatic reactivity. In H. J. Eysenck (Ed.), *Handbook of abnormal psychology.* London: Putnam, 1960.

Matheson, D. W., Edelson, R., Hiatrides, D., Newkirk, J., Twinem, K., & Thurston, S. Relaxation measured by EMG as a function of vibrotactile stimulation. *Biofeedback and Self-regulation,* 1976, *1,* 285–292.

McConnell, J. V. Comparative physiology: Learning in invertebrates. *Annual Review of Physiology,* 1966, *28,* 107–136.

McGill, T. E. (Ed.). *Readings in animal behavior.* New York: Holt, Rinehart and Winston, 1965.

McGinnies, E. *Social behavior: A functional analysis.* Boston: Houghton Mifflin, 1970.

McGuigan, F. *Experimental psychology: A methodological approach* (2nd ed.). Englewood Cliffs, N.J.: Prentice-Hall, 1968.

McGuire, W. J. Suspiciousness of experimenter's intent. In R. Rosenthal & R. Rosnow (Eds.), *Artifact in behavioral research.* New York: Academic Press, 1969.

McGuire, W. J. The yin and yang of progress in social psychology: Seven koan. *Journal of Personality and Social Psychology,* 1973, *26,* 446–456.

McNemar, Q. *Psychological statistics* (4th ed.). New York: Wiley, 1969.

Meditation and the mind. *Public Broadcasting System,* "NOVA" series #303, produced by WGBH-TV, Boston, Mass., 1976.

Mees, C. E. K. Scientific thought and social reconstruction. *Sigma Xi Quarterly,* 1934, *22,* 13–24.

Meichenbaum, D. H., Gilmore, T. B., & Fedoravicius, A. Group insight versus group desensitization in treating speech anxiety. *Journal of Counseling and Clinical Psychology,* 1971, *36,* 410–421.

Meyer, M. E. *A statistical analysis of behavior.* Belmont, Calif: Wadsworth, 1976.

Michael, J. Statistical inference for individual organism research: Mixed blessing or cure? *Journal of Applied Behavior Analysis,* 1974, *7,* 647–653.

Middlemist, R. D., Knowles, E. S., & Matter, C. F. Personal space invasions in the lavatory: Suggestive evidence for arousal. *Journal of Personality and Social Psychology,* 1976, *33,* 541–546.

Milgram, S. Behavioral study of obedience. *Journal of Abnormal and Social Psychology,* 1963, *67,* 371–378.

Milgram, S. Issues in the study of obedience: A reply to Baumrind. *American Psychologist,* 1964, *19,* 848–852.

Miller, N. E. Comments on theoretical models, illustrated by the development of a theory of conflict behavior. *Journal of Personality,* 1951, *20,* 82–100.

Mills, J. (Ed.). *Experimental social psychology.* New York: Macmillan, 1969.

Mosteller, F., Rourke, R. E. K., & Thomas, G. B., Jr. *Probability with statistical applications.* Reading, Mass.: Addison-Wesley, 1961.

Mullen, F. A. The school as a psychological laboratory. *American Psycchologist,* 1959, *14,* 53–56.

Murch, G. *Visual and auditory perception.* Indianapolis, Inc.: Bobbs-Merrill, 1973.

Mussen, P. H. (Ed) *Handbook of research methods in child development.* New York: Wiley, 1960.

Mussen, P. H. (Ed.). *Carmichael's manual of child psychology* (2nd ed.). New York: Wiley, 1970.

Myers, J. L. *Fundamentals of experimental design.* Boston: Allyn and Bacon, 1966.

Newsweek. The polls and the pols and the public. *Newsweek,* July 8, 1968, pp. 23–27.

Nunnally, J. C., Jr. *Psychometric theory.* New York: McGraw-Hill, 1967.

Nunnally, J. C., Jr. *Introduction to psychological measurement.* New York: McGraw-Hill, 1970.

Nuttin, J. M., Jr. *The illusion of attitude change.* New York: Academic Press, 1975.

Oppenheim, A. N. *Questionnaire design and attitude measurement.* New York: Basic Books, 1966.

Orne, M. T. Demand characteristics and the concept of quasi-controls. In R. Rosenthal & R. L. Rosnow (Eds.), *Artifact in behavioral research.* New York: Academic Press, 1969.

Ornstein, R. E. *The mind field.* New York: Grossman, 1976.

Osgood, C. E. *Method and theory in experimental psychology.* New York: Oxford University Press, 1953.

Palmer, R. R. *A history of the modern world* (2nd ed.). New York: Knopf, 1958.

Paul, G. L. Physiological effects of relaxation training and hypnotic suggestions. *Journal of Abnormal Psychology,* 1969.

Payne, L. V. *The lively art of writing.* New York: Follett, 1965.

Phelan, M. *Tactual perception in deaf and hearing children.* Unpublished manuscript, University of the Pacific, 1972.

Plutchik, R. *Foundations of experimental research* (2nd ed.). New York: Harper & Row, 1974.

Proshansky, H. M., Ittelson, W. H., & Rivlen, L. G. *Environmental psychology.* New York: Holt, Rinehart and Winston, 1970.

Realon, R. E. *Reinforcement and participant modeling in the modification of agoraphobia.* Unpublished manuscript, University of the Pacific, 1976.

Reese, H., & Lipsitt, L. (Eds.). *Experimental child psychology.* New York: Academic Press, 1970.

Resnick, J. H., & Schwartz, T. Ethical standards as an independent variable in psychological research. *American Psychologist,* 1973, *28,* 134–39.

Rodin, M., Frey, P. W., & Gessner, P. K. Student evaluation. *Science,* 1975, *187,* 555–559.

Rodin, M., & Rodin, B. Student evaluations of teachers. *Science,* 1972, *177,* 1164–1166.

Roethlisberger, F. J., & Dickson, W. J. *Management and the worker.* Cambridge, Mass.: Harvard University Press, 1939.

Rosenberg, M. J. The conditions and consequences of evaluation apprehension. In R. Rosenthal & R. L. Rosnow (Eds.), *Artifact in behavioral research.* New York: Academic Press, 1969.

Rosenhan, D. L. On being sane in insane places. *Science,* 1973, *179,* 250–258.

Rosenthal, R. *Experimenter effects in behavioral research.* New York: Appleton, 1966.

Rosenthal, R. Unintended communication of interpersonal expectation. *American Behavioral Scientist,* 1967, *10,* 24–26.

Rosenthal, R. Interpersonal expectations: Effects of the experimenter's hypothesis. In R. Rosenthal & R. L. Rosnow (Eds.), *Artifact in behavioral research.* New York: Academic Press, 1969.

Rosenthal, R., & Jacobson, L. *Pygmalion in the classroom: Teacher expectation and pupils' intellectual development.* New York: Holt, Rinehart and Winston, 1968.

Rosenthal, R., & Rosnow, R. L. (Eds.). *Artifact in behavioral research.* New York: Academic Press, 1969.(a)

Rosenthal, R., & Rosnow, R. L. The volunteer subject. In R. Rosenthal & R. L. Rosnow (Eds.), *Artifact in behavioral research.* New York: Academic Press, 1969.(b)

Rosenthal, R., & Rosnow, R. L. *Primer of methods for the behavioral sciences.* New York: Wiley, 1975.

Rosnow, R. L., Holper, H. M., & Gitter, A. G. More on the reactive effects of pretesting in attitude research: Demand characteristics or subject commitment? *Educational and Psychological Measurement,* 1973, *33,* 7–17.

Rozelle, R. M., & Campbell, D. T. More plausible rival hypotheses in the cross-lagged panel correlation technique. *Psychological Bulletin,* 1969, *71,* 74–80.

Rubin, D. The use of matched sampling and regression adjustment to remove bias in observational studies. *Biometrics,* 1973, *29,* 185–203.(a)

Rubin, D. Matching to remove bias in observational studies. *Biometrics,* 1973, *29,* 159–183. (b)

Ruch, F. L. Personality: Public or private? *Psychology Today,* October 1967, pp. 46; 58–61.

Runkel, P., & McGrath, J. *Research on human behavior: A systematic guide to method.* New York: Holt, Rinehart and Winston, 1972.

Sackett, G. P. The maturation and development of learning, motivated by change in light stimulation (Doctoral dissertation, Claremont Graduate School, 1963). *Dissertation Abstracts,* 1965, *26,* 1795. (University Microfilms No. 63-7751)

Sainsbury, P., & Barraclough, B. Differences between suicidal rates. *Nature,* 1968, *220,* 1252.

Sanford, F. H., & Capaldi, E. J. (Eds.). *Advancing psychological science* (Vol. 1). *Philosophies, methods, and approaches.* Belmont, Calif.: Wadsworth, 1964.

Scarboro, M. E., & Forehand, R. Effects of two types of response-contingent time-out on compliance and oppositional behavior of children. *Journal of Experimental Child Psychology,* 1975, *19,* 252–264.

Schlosberg, H. Hints on presenting a paper at an APA convention. *American Psychologist,* 1956, *11,* 345–346.

Schmidt-Koenig, K. Current problems in bird orientation. In D. S. Lehrman, R. A. Hinde, & E. Shaw (Eds.), *Advances in the study of behavior* (Vol. 1). New York: Academic Press, 1965.

Schwartz, M. L., & Hawkins, R. P. Application of delayed conditioning procedures to the behavior problems of an elementary school child. In R. Ulrich, T. Stachnik, & J. Mabry (Eds.), *Control of human behavior: From cure to prevention* (Vol. 2). Glenview, Ill.: Scott, Foresman, 1970.

Scott, W. A., & Wertheimer, M. *Introduction to psychological research.* New York: Wiley, 1962.

Searle, L. V. The organization of hereditary maze-brightness and maze-dullness. *Genetic Psychology Monographs,* 1949, *39,* 279–325.

Segall, M. H., Campbell, D. T., & Herskovitz, M. J. *The influence of culture on visual perception.* Indianapolis: Bobbs-Merrill, 1966.

Selltiz, C., Wrightsman, L. S., & Cook, S. W. Research methods in social relations (3rd ed.). New York: Holt, Rinehart and Winston, 1976.

Seven, M. Personal communication, February–May, 1964.

Sheridan, C. L. *Fundamentals of experimental psychology* (2nd ed.). New York: Holt, Rinehart and Winston, 1976.

Sidman, M. *Tactics of scientific research.* New York: Basic Books, 1960.

Sidowski, J. B. (Ed.). *Experimental methods and instrumentation in psychology.* New York: McGraw-Hill, 1966.

Sidowski, J. B., & Ross, S. (Eds.). Instrumentation in psychology. *American Psychologist,* 1969, *24,* 185–384.

Siegel, S. *Nonparametric statistics.* New York: McGraw-Hill, 1956.

Siekevitz, P. Recombinant DNA research: A Faustian bargain? *Science,* 1976, *194,* 256–257.

Siever, R. Science: Observational, experimental, historical. *American Scientist,* 1968, *56,* 70–77.

Silverman, I. *The human subject in the psychological laboratory.* New York: Pergamon, 1977.

Skinner, B. F. A case history in scientific method. *American Psychologist,* 1956, *11,* 221–233.

Skinner, B. F. Pigeons in a pelican. *American Psychologist,* 1960, *15,* 28–37.

Sloan, L. R., Love, R. E., & Ostrom, T. M. Political heckling: Who really loses? *Journal of Personality and Social Psychology,* 1974, *30,* 518–525.

Sluckin, W. *Imprinting and early learning.* Chicago: Aldine, 1965.

Solomon, R. L. An extension of control group design. *Psychological Bulletin,* 1949, *46,* 137–150.

Solomon, R. L., & Lessac, M. S. A control group design for experimental studies of developmental processes. *Psychological Bulletin,* 1968, *70,* 145–150.

Sommer, R. Hawthorne dogma. *Psychological Bulletin,* 1968, *70,* 592–595.

Sommer, R. *Personal space: The behavioral basis of design.* Englewood Cliffs, N.J.: Prentice-Hall, 1969.

Sommer, R. G. Guide to scientific instruments. *Science,* 1976, *194* (4267A).

Spence, K. W., & Spence, J. T. *The psychology of learning and motivation: Advances in research and theory* (10 vols.). New York: Academic Press, 1967–1976.

Sprafkin, J. N., Liebert, R. M., & Poulos, R. W. Effects of a pro-social televised example on children's helping. *Journal of Experimental Child Psychology,* 1975, *20,* 119–126.

Statistical inference for individual organism research. *Journal of Applied Behavior Analysis,* Monograph No. 4, 1975.

Steger, J. A. (Ed.). *Readings in statistics for the behavioral scientist.* New York: Holt, Rinehart and Winston, 1971.

Sterman, M. B. Neurophysiologic and clinical studies of sensorimotor EEG biofeedback training: Some effects on epilepsy. In L. Birk (Ed.), *Biofeedback: Behavioral medicine.* New York: Grune & Stratton, 1973.

Stevens, S. S. On the theory of scales of measurement. *Science,* 1946, *103,* 677–680.

Stevens, S. S. *Handbook of experimental psychology.* New York: Wiley, 1951.

Stevens, S. S. Problems and methods of psychophysics. *Psychological Bulletin,* 1958, *55,* 177–196.

Stevens, S. S. *Psychophysics.* New York: Wiley, 1975.

Stevenson, H. W., & Wright, J. C. Child psychology. In J. B. Sidowski (Ed.), *Experimental methods and instrumentation in psychology.* New York: McGraw-Hill, 1966.

Stilson, D. W. *Probability and statistics in psychological research and theory.* San Francisco: Holden-Day, 1966.

Stouffer, S. A. *Communism, conformity, and civil liberties.* Garden City, N.Y.: Doubleday, 1955.

Summers, G. *Attitude measurement.* Chicago: Rand McNally, 1970.

Sutcliffe, J. P. A general method of analysis of frequency data for multiple classification designs. *Psychological Bulletin,* 1957, *54,* 134–137.

Tate, M., & Clelland, R. C. *Nonparametric and shortcut statistics.* Danville, Ill.: Interstate, 1957.

Taylor, D. W., Festinger, L., Garner, W. R., Hebb, D. O., Hunt, H. F., Lawrence, D. H., Osgood, C. E., Skinner, B. F., & Wertheimer, M. Education for research in psychology. *American Psychologist,* 1959, *14,* 167–179.

Terman, L. M. & Merrill, M. A. *Stanford-Binet intelligence scale: Manual for the third revision, form L-M.* Cambridge, Mass: Riverside, 1960.

Thorpe, W. H. *Learning and instinct in animals* (2nd ed.). London: Methuen, 1963.

Townsend, J. C. *Introduction to experimental method.* New York: McGraw-Hill, 1953.

Traynham, R. N., & Witte, K. L. The effects of modifying color-meaning concepts on racial concept attitudes in five- and eight-year-old children. *Journal of Experimental Child Psychology,* 1976, *21,* 165–174.

Troland, L. *The fundamentals of human motivation.* New York: Hafner, 1967.

Tryon, R. C. Genetic differences in maze learning in rats. *Yearbook of the National Society for the Study of Education,* 1940, *39,* 111–119.

Turabian, K. L. *A manual for the writers of term papers, theses, and dissertations* (3rd ed.). Chicago: University of Chicago Press, 1967.

Turner, M. B. *Philosophy and the science of behavior.* New York: Appleton, 1967.

Ullmann, L. P., & Krasner, L. (Eds.). *Case studies in behavior modification.* New York: Holt, Rinehart and Winston, 1965.

Underwood, B. J. *Experimental psychology* (2nd ed.). New York: Appleton, 1966.

Urquhart, F. A. Found at last: The Monarch's winter home. *National Geographic,* 1976, *150,* 161–173.

Van Dyke, J. E., & Beauchamp, K. L. *The effects of effort and day of exposure on imprinting.* Paper presented at the meeting of the Western Psychological Association, Sacramento, April, 1975.

Vernon, M. *Human motivation.* New York: Cambridge University Press, 1969.

Wade, N. Animal rights: NIH cat sex study brings grief to New York museum. *Science,* 1976, *194,* 162–167.

Walker, H. M., & Hops, H. Increasing academic achievement by reinforcing direct academic performance and/or facilitative non-academic performance. *Journal of Educational Psychology,* 1976, *68,* 218–225.

Walker, H. M., & Lev, J. *Statistical inference.* New York: Holt, Rinehart and Winston, 1953.

Wallace, R. K., & Benson, H. The physiology of meditation. *Scientific American,* 1972, *226*(2), 85–90.

Warkany, J., & Takacs, E. Lysergic acid diethylamide (LSD): No teratogenicity in rats. *Science,* 1968, *159,* 731–732.

Weaver, W. *Lady Luck: The theory of probability.* Garden City, N.Y.: Doubleday, 1963.

Webb, E. J., Campbell, D. T., Schwartz, R. D., & Sechrest, F. *Unobtrusive measures: Nonreactive research in the social sciences.* Skokie, Ill.: Rand McNally, 1966.

Weber, L. J., & McLean, D. L. *Electrical measurement systems for biological and physical scientists.* Reading, Mass.: Addison Wesley, 1975.

Weiner, B. (Ed.). *Cognitive views of human motivation.* New York: Academic Press, 1974.

Weiss, J. M. Effects of coping behavior in different warning signal conditions on stress pathology in rats. *Journal of Comparative and Physiological Psychology,* 1971, *77,* 1–13. (a)

Weiss, J. M. Effects of punishing the coping response (conflict) on stress pathology in rats. *Journal of Comparative and Physiological Psychology,* 1971, *77,* 14–21. (b)

Weiss, J. M. Effects of coping behavior with and without a feedback signal on stress pathology in rats. *Journal of Comparative and Physiological Psychology,* 1971, *77,* 22–30. (c)

Willems, E. P., & Rausch, H. L. (Eds.). *Naturalistic viewpoints in psychological research.* New York: Holt, Rinehart and Winston, 1969.

Williams, J. E. *Color meaning test (CMT II): General information and manual of directions.* Unpublished manuscript, Wake Forest University, 1971.

Williams, J. E., Best, D. L., Boswell, D. A., Mattson, L. A., & Graves, D. J. Preschool racial attitude measurement II. *Educational and Psychological Measurement,* 1975, *35,* 3–18.

Winer, B. J. *Statistical principles in experimental design* (2nd ed.). New York: McGraw-Hill, 1971.

Woodmansee, J. J. Methodological problems in pupillographic experiments. *Proceedings of the 74th Annual Convention of the American Psychological Association,* 1966, *1,* 133–134.

Wright, H. *Recording and analyzing child behavior.* New York: Harper & Row, 1967.

Zucker, M. H. *Electronic circuits for the behavioral and biomedical sciences: A reference book of useful solid state circuits.* San Francisco: Freeman, 1969.

Zuckerman, M. Physiological measures of sexual arousal in the human. In N. S. Greenfield & R. A. Sternbach (Eds.), *Handbook of psychophysiology.* New York: Holt, Rinehart and Winston., 1972. (Reprinted from *Psychological Bulletin* 1971, *75,* 297–329.)

Appendices

APPENDIX A
Mathematical Symbols and Operations

GLOSSARY OF CONVENTIONAL MATHEMATICAL SYMBOLS USED IN THIS TEXT

	Symbol	Name	Operation	Examples
1.	$+$	addition	a plus b	$3 + 4 = 7$
2.	$-$	subtraction	a minus b	$5 - 3 = 2$
3.	$\times$	multiplication	a times b	$4 \times 5 = 20, 4 \cdot 5 = 20, 4(5) = 20$
4.	$\div$	division	a divided by b	$20 \div 5 = 4, 20/5 = 4, \dfrac{20}{5} = 4$
5.	$=$	equals	$a = b$	$3 = 3$
6.	$\approx$	approximately equals	$a \approx b$	$3.13 \approx 3.1$
7.	a^2	squaring	a times a	$5^2 = 25$
8.	$\sqrt{a}$	square root	inverse of squaring	$\sqrt{25} = 25$
9.	$<$	less than	a is less than b	$4 < 5$
10.	$>$	greater than	a is greater than b	$5 > 4$
11.	$\%$	percentage	a is 10% of b (frequency divided by the total and multiplied by 100)	10% of 50 = 5 $(5/50)100 = 10\%$
12.	$\cap$	intersection	a intersection b	all elements common to sets a and b
13.	Σ	summation	a_1 plus a_2 plus . . .	see below

ORDER OF OPERATIONS

Rule Sets of terms within parentheses or brackets are treated as a single number.

To prevent ambiguity when several operations are involved in one equation or formula, symbols and terms are grouped within parentheses or brackets. For example,

$$(3 + 5) + 2(7 - 3) = (8) + 2(4) = 8 + 8 = 16;$$
or
$$(4 + 6)/(6 - 2) = 10/4 = 2.5;$$
or
$$3[(7 - 1)/(8 - 5)] = 3(6/3) = 3(2) = 6.$$

If several overlapping sets of parentheses or brackets are involved in an equation, the innermost grouping of operations is completed first. The grouped operations are completed in sequence from the innermost to the outermost grouping.

IMPLIED MULTIPLICATION

Rule If numbers or symbols are enclosed in parentheses or brackets without any intervening signs or symbols, then multiply the numbers or symbols.

For example,

$$(3 + 2)(4 - 1) = (5)(3) = 15;$$

or

$$[2(6)/3][4 - 2] = (4)(2) = 8.$$

SUMMATION

The capital Greek letter sigma (Σ) is used to indicate summation. For example,

$$\sum_{i=1}^{n} X = \sum_{1}^{n} X = \Sigma X = X_1 + X_2 + \cdots + X_n$$

if there are four values of $X (N = 4)$, with $X_1 = 2$, $X_2 = 4$, $X_3 = 6$ and $X_4 = 8$, then

$$\sum^{4} X = 2 + 4 + 6 + 8 = 20$$

Rule 1 $\Sigma(X + Y) = \Sigma X + \Sigma Y$ where X and Y are both variables such that each value of X has a value of Y paired with it.

For example, if $X_1 = 2$, $X_2 = 4$, $X_3 = 6$, $X_4 = 8$, and $Y_1 = 1$, $Y_2 = 3$, $Y_3 = 5$, and $Y_4 = 7$, then

$$\Sigma(X + Y) = (2 + 1) + (4 + 3) + (6 + 5) + (8 + 7),$$
$$= (2 + 4 + 6 + 8) + (1 + 3 + 5 + 7),$$
$$\Sigma(X + Y) = 20 + 16 = 36.$$

Rule 2 $\Sigma(X - Y) = \Sigma X - \Sigma Y$ where X and Y are paired variables as above.

For example, if the same values of X and Y occur as in the previous example, then

$$\Sigma(X - Y) = (2 - 1) + (4 - 3) + (6 - 5) + (8 - 7),$$
$$= (2 + 4 + 6 + 8) - (1 + 3 + 5 + 7),$$
$$\Sigma(X - Y) = 20 - 16 = 4.$$

Rule 3 $\Sigma(X + C) = \Sigma X + nC$, where C is any constant and n is the number of scores summed.

For example, if $X_1 = 2$, $X_2 = 4$, $X_3 = 6$, and $X_4 = 8$, and $C = 2$, then

$$\Sigma(X + C) = (2 + 2) + (4 + 2) + (6 + 2) + (8 + 2),$$
$$= (2 + 4 + 6 + 8) + (2 + 2 + 2 + 2)$$
$$\Sigma(X + C) = 20 + 4(2) = 28.$$

Rule 4 $\Sigma(X - C) = \Sigma X - nC$, where C is any constant.
Rule 5 $\Sigma CX = C\Sigma X$, where C is any constant.

For example, if $C = 2$ and $X_1 = 2$, $X_2 = 4$, $X_3 = 6$, and $X_4 = 8$, then,

$$\Sigma CX = 2(2) + 2(4) + 2(6) + 2(8),$$
$$= 2(2 + 4 + 6 + 8),$$
$$\Sigma CX = 2(20) = 40.$$

Rule 6 $\Sigma(X/C) = (1/C)\Sigma X$, where C is any constant.

CALCULATION OF MEANS

Since the mean is $\Sigma X/n$, the preceding rules for summation have the following implications about arithmetic means.

Rule 1 $\overline{C} = C$, where C stands for a constant. That is, $\overline{C} = \Sigma C/n = nC/n = C$.

Rule 2 $\overline{CX} = C\overline{X}$, where X is a variable and C is any constant.

For example, if $X_1 = 2$, $X_2 = 4$, $X_3 = 6$, $X_4 = 8$, and $C = 2$, then

$$\overline{CX} = [2(2) + 2(4) + 2(6) + 2)8)]/4,$$
$$= [2(2 + 4 + 6 + 8)]/4,$$
$$\overline{CX} = (2)(20)/4 = 10.$$
$$\overline{X} = 20/4 = 5, \text{ and}$$
$$C\overline{X} = 2(5) = 10.$$

Rule 3 $\overline{X + C} = \overline{X} + C$, where X is a variable and C is any constant.

Rule 4 $\overline{X + Y} = \overline{X} + \overline{Y}$, where X and Y are variables.

For example, if $X_1 = 2$, $X_2 = 4$, $X_3 = 6$, $X_4 = 8$, and $Y_1 = 1$, $Y_2 = 3$, $Y_3 = 5$, and $Y_4 = 7$, then

$$\overline{X + Y} = \frac{(2 + 1) + (4 + 3) + (6 + 5) + (8 + 7)}{n = 4},$$

$$\overline{X + Y} = \frac{(2 + 4 + 6 + 8) + (1 + 3 + 5 + 7),}{4},$$

$$\overline{X + Y} = (20/4) + (16/4),$$

$$\overline{X + Y} = 5 + 4 = \overline{X} + \overline{Y} = 9.$$

ROUNDING NUMBERS

Rule 1   If the rightmost digit of a number to be "rounded" is less than 5, we discard the excess. If it is greater than 5, the number is rounded up to the next largest number.

For example, when rounding to whole numbers, if the decimal fraction is less than 0.5, then the decimal is discarded and the whole number is unchanged. If the decimal fraction is greater than 0.5, the whole number is increased by one unit and the decimal fraction is discarded (4.4 = 4, 4.7 = 5).

Rule 2   By arbitrary convention in the case that the rightmost digit is 5, if the number preceding the 5 to be dropped is an *even* number, then it is *not changed* when the 5 is discarded. If the number preceding the 5 is an *odd* number, then it is increased by one unit.

For example, 6.5 = 6, 7.5 = 8, 369.5 = 370, and 42.5 = 42.

SIGNIFICANT NUMBERS

There is much confusion about how many decimal places (significant figures) should be carried in a set of computations. Given that any set of data will contain error (including measurement error), it must be recognized that all data are approximations to the impossible ideal of errorless, perfectly measured scores. Furthermore, in any study the precision of measurement depends upon many factors, including the equipment used. If a set of data points is relatively imprecise, it makes no sense to carry many more significant figures in computations with the data than the number of significant figures in the original data. For example, if the data is time measured to the nearest whole second, then calculating the mean to be 1.237986 seconds is an absurd waste of time.

Rule   According to Edwards (1967), the best single principle is to carry along one or two more figures in various computations than there are in the original data. Then the final answer is rounded back to either the number of significant figures in the original data, or a reasonable number. A "reasonable number" is that number determined from conventional practice or the logic of the statistics. For example, conventional practice is to report correlation coefficients in two decimal places, to the nearest hundredth. If the original data is measured to one significant digit in whole numbers, then if you rounded back the calculated value of r to the nearest whole number, only three possible values of r could exist, -1, 0, or $+1$. The informational value of r is nearly eliminated by such a procedure. The only way to determine conventional practice (when rational analysis does not lead to an immediate answer) is to examine the research literature in psychological journals.

APPENDIX B Squares and Square Roots
of Numbers from 1 to 1000

Number	Square	Square Root	Number	Square	Square Root	Number	Square	Square Root	Number	Square	Square Root
1	1	1.000	31	9 61	5.568	61	37 21	7.810	91	82 81	9.539
2	4	1.414	32	10 24	5.657	62	38 44	7.874	92	84 64	9.592
3	9	1.732	33	10 89	5.745	63	39 69	7.937	93	86 49	9.644
4	16	2.000	34	11 56	5.831	64	40 96	8.000	94	88 36	9.695
5	25	2.236	35	12 25	5.916	65	42 25	8.062	95	90 25	9.747
6	36	2.449	36	12 96	6.000	66	43 56	8.124	96	92 16	9.798
7	49	2.646	37	13 69	6.083	67	44 89	8.185	97	94 09	9.849
8	64	2.828	38	14 44	6.164	68	46 24	8.246	98	96 04	9.899
9	81	3.000	39	15 21	6.245	69	47 61	8.307	99	98 01	9.950
10	1 00	3.162	40	16 00	6.325	70	49 00	8.367	100	1 00 00	10.000
11	1 21	3.317	41	16 81	6.403	71	50 41	8.426	101	1 02 01	10.050
12	1 44	3.464	42	17 64	6.481	72	51 84	8.485	102	1 04 04	10.100
13	1 69	3.606	43	18 49	6.557	73	53 29	8.544	103	1 06 09	10.149
14	1 96	3.742	44	19 36	6.633	74	54 76	8.602	104	1 08 16	10.198
15	2 25	3.873	45	20 25	6.708	75	56 25	8.660	105	1 10 25	10.247
16	2 56	4.000	46	21 16	6.782	76	57 76	8.718	106	1 12 36	10.296
17	2 89	4.123	47	22 09	6.856	77	59 29	8.775	107	1 14 49	10.344
18	3 24	4.243	48	23 04	6.928	78	60 84	8.832	108	1 16 64	10.392
19	3 61	4.359	49	24 01	7.000	79	62 41	8.888	109	1 18 81	10.440
20	4 00	4.472	50	25 00	7.071	80	64 00	8.944	110	1 21 00	10.488
21	4 41	4.583	51	26 01	7.141	81	65 61	9.000	111	1 23 21	10.536
22	4 84	4.690	52	27 04	7.211	82	67 24	9.055	112	1 25 44	10.583
23	5 29	4.796	53	28 09	7.280	83	68 89	9.110	113	1 27 69	10.630
24	5 76	4.899	54	29 16	7.348	84	70 56	9.165	114	1 29 96	10.677
25	6 25	5.000	55	30 25	7.416	85	72 25	9.220	115	1 32 25	10.724
26	6 76	5.099	56	31 36	7.483	86	73 96	9.274	116	1 34 56	10.770
27	7 29	5.196	57	32 49	7.550	87	75 69	9.327	117	1 36 89	10.817
28	7 84	5.292	58	33 64	7.616	88	77 44	9.381	118	1 39 24	10.863
29	8 41	5.385	59	34 81	7.681	89	79 21	9.434	119	1 41 61	10.909
30	9 00	5.477	60	36 00	7.746	90	81 00	9.487	120	1 44 00	10.954

Note: From A Simplified Guide to Statistics (4th ed.) by G. M. Smith. New York: Holt, Rinehart and Winston, 1962.

APPENDIX B (Continued)

Number	Square	Square Root	Number	Square	Square Root	Number	Square	Square Root	Number	Square	Square Root
121	1 46 41	11.000	151	2 28 01	12.288	181	3 27 61	13.454	211	4 45 21	14.526
122	1 48 84	11.045	152	2 31 04	12.329	182	3 31 24	13.491	212	4 49 44	14.560
123	1 51 29	11.091	153	2 34 09	12.369	183	3 34 89	13.528	213	4 53 69	14.595
124	1 53 76	11.136	154	2 37 16	12.410	184	3 38 56	13.565	214	4 57 96	14.629
125	1 56 25	11.180	155	2 40 25	12.450	185	3 42 25	13.601	215	4 62 25	14.663
126	1 58 76	11.225	156	2 43 36	12.490	186	3 45 96	13.638	216	4 66 56	14.697
127	1 61 29	11.269	157	2 46 49	12.530	187	3 49 69	13.675	217	4 70 89	14.731
128	1 63 84	11.314	158	2 49 64	12.570	188	3 53 44	13.711	218	4 75 24	14.765
129	1 66 41	11.358	159	2 52 81	12.610	189	3 57 21	13.748	219	4 79 61	14.799
130	1 69 00	11.402	160	2 56 00	12.649	190	3 61 00	13.784	220	4 84 00	14.832
131	1 71 61	11.446	161	2 59 21	12.689	191	3 64 81	13.820	221	4 88 41	14.866
132	1 74 24	11.489	162	2 62 44	12.728	192	3 68 64	13.856	222	4 92 84	14.900
133	1 76 89	11.533	163	2 65 69	12.767	193	3 72 49	13.892	223	4 97 29	14.933
134	1 79 56	11.576	164	2 68 96	12.806	194	3 76 36	13.928	224	5 01 76	14.967
135	1 82 25	11.619	165	2 72 25	12.845	195	3 80 25	13.964	225	5 06 25	15.000
136	1 84 96	11.662	166	2 75 56	12.884	196	3 84 16	14.000	226	5 10 76	15.033
137	1 87 69	11.705	167	2 78 89	12.923	197	3 88 09	14.036	227	5 15 29	15.067
138	1 90 44	11.747	168	2 82 24	12.961	198	3 92 04	14.071	228	5 19 84	15.100
139	1 93 21	11.790	169	2 85 61	13.000	199	3 96 01	14.107	229	5 24 41	15.133
140	1 96 00	11.832	170	2 89 00	13.038	200	4 00 00	14.142	230	5 29 00	15.166
141	1 98 81	11.874	171	2 92 41	13.077	201	4 04 01	14.177	231	5 33 61	15.199
142	2 01 64	11.916	172	2 95 84	13.115	202	4 08 04	14.213	232	5 38 24	15.232
143	2 04 49	11.958	173	2 99 29	13.153	203	4 12 09	14.248	233	5 42 89	15.264
144	2 07 36	12.000	174	3 02 76	13.191	204	4 16 16	14.283	234	5 47 56	15.297
145	2 10 25	12.042	175	3 06 25	13.229	205	4 20 25	14.318	235	5 52 25	15.330
146	2 13 16	12.083	176	3 09 76	13.266	206	4 24 36	14.353	236	5 56 96	15.362
147	2 16 09	12.124	177	3 13 29	13.304	207	4 28 49	14.387	237	5 61 69	15.395
148	2 19 04	12.166	178	3 16 84	13.342	208	4 32 64	14.422	238	5 66 44	15.427
149	2 22 01	12.207	179	3 20 41	13.379	209	4 36 81	14.457	239	5 71 21	15.460
150	2 25 00	12.247	180	3 24 00	13.416	210	4 41 00	14.491	240	5 76 00	15.492

APPENDIX B (Continued)

Number	Square	Square Root
241	5 80 81	15.524
242	5 85 64	15.556
243	5 90 49	15.588
244	5 95 36	15.620
245	6 00 25	15.652
246	6 05 16	15.684
247	6 10 09	15.716
248	6 15 04	15.748
249	6 20 01	15.780
250	6 25 00	15.811
251	6 30 01	15.843
252	6 35 04	15.875
253	6 40 09	15.906
254	6 45 16	15.937
255	6 50 25	15.969
256	6 55 36	16.000
257	6 60 49	16.031
258	6 65 64	16.062
259	6 70 81	16.093
260	6 76 00	16.125
261	6 81 21	16.155
262	6 86 44	16.186
263	6 91 69	16.217
264	6 96 96	16.248
265	7 02 25	16.279
266	7 07 56	16.310
267	7 12 89	16.340
268	7 18 24	16.371
269	7 23 61	16.401
270	7 29 00	16.432
271	7 34 41	16.462
272	7 39 84	16.492
273	7 45 29	16.523
274	7 50 76	16.553
275	7 56 25	16.583
276	7 61 76	16.613
277	7 67 29	16.643
278	7 72 84	16.673
279	7 78 41	16.703
280	7 84 00	16.733
281	7 89 61	16.763
282	7 95 24	16.793
283	8 00 89	16.823
284	8 06 56	16.852
285	8 12 25	16.882
286	8 17 96	16.912
287	8 23 69	16.941
288	8 29 44	16.971
289	8 35 21	17.000
290	8 41 00	17.029
291	8 46 81	17.059
292	8 52 64	17.088
293	8 58 49	17.117
294	8 64 36	17.146
295	8 70 25	17.176
296	8 76 16	17.205
297	8 82 09	17.234
298	8 88 04	17.263
299	8 94 01	17.292
300	9 00 00	17.321
301	9 06 01	17.349
302	9 12 04	17.378
303	9 18 09	17.407
304	9 24 16	17.436
305	9 30 25	17.464
306	9 36 36	17.493
307	9 42 49	17.521
308	9 48 64	17.550
309	9 54 81	17.578
310	9 61 00	17.607
311	9 67 21	17.635
312	9 73 44	17.664
313	9 79 69	17.692
314	9 85 96	17.720
315	9 92 25	17.748
316	9 98 56	17.776
317	10 04 89	17.804
318	10 11 24	17.833
319	10 17 61	17.861
320	10 24 00	17.889
321	10 30 41	17.916
322	10 36 84	17.944
323	10 43 29	17.972
324	10 49 76	18.000
325	10 56 25	18.028
326	10 62 76	18.055
327	10 69 29	18.083
328	10 75 84	18.111
329	10 82 41	18.138
330	10 89 00	18.166
331	10 95 61	18.193
332	11 02 24	18.221
333	11 08 89	18.248
334	11 15 56	18.276
335	11 22 25	18.303
336	11 28 96	18.330
337	11 35 69	18.358
338	11 42 44	18.385
339	11 49 21	18.412
340	11 56 00	18.439
341	11 62 81	18.466
342	11 69 64	18.493
343	11 76 49	18.520
344	11 83 36	18.547
345	11 90 25	18.574
346	11 97 16	18.601
347	12 04 09	18.628
348	12 11 04	18.655
349	12 18 01	18.682
350	12 25 00	18.708
351	12 32 01	18.735
352	12 39 04	18.762
353	12 46 09	18.788
354	12 53 16	18.815
355	12 60 25	18.841
356	12 67 36	18.868
357	12 74 49	18.894
358	12 81 64	18.921
359	12 88 81	18.947
360	12 96 00	18.974

APPENDIX B (Continued)

Number	Square	Square Root	Number	Square	Square Root	Number	Square	Square Root
361	13 03 21	19.000	391	15 28 81	19.774	421	17 72 41	20.518
362	13 10 44	19.026	392	15 36 64	19.799	422	17 80 84	20.543
363	13 17 69	19.053	393	15 44 49	19.824	423	17 89 29	20.567
364	13 24 96	19.079	394	15 52 36	19.849	424	17 97 76	20.591
365	13 32 25	19.105	395	15 60 25	19.875	425	18 06 25	20.616
366	13 39 56	19.131	396	15 68 16	19.900	426	18 14 76	20.640
367	13 46 89	19.157	397	15 76 09	19.925	427	18 23 29	20.664
368	13 54 24	19.183	398	15 84 04	19.950	428	18 31 84	20.688
369	13 61 61	19.209	399	15 92 01	19.975	429	18 40 41	20.712
370	13 69 00	19.235	400	16 00 00	20.000	430	18 49 00	20.736
371	13 76 41	19.261	401	16 08 01	20.025	431	18 57 61	20.761
372	13 83 84	19.287	402	16 16 04	20.050	432	18 66 24	20.785
373	13 91 29	19.313	403	16 24 09	20.075	433	18 74 89	20.809
374	13 98 76	19.339	404	16 32 16	20.100	434	18 83 56	20.833
375	14 06 25	19.363	405	16 40 25	20.125	435	18 92 25	20.857
376	14 13 76	19.391	406	16 48 36	20.149	436	19 00 96	20.881
377	14 21 29	19.416	407	16 56 49	20.174	437	19 09 69	20.905
378	14 28 84	19.442	408	16 64 64	20.199	438	19 18 44	20.928
379	14 36 41	19.468	409	16 72 81	20.224	439	19 27 21	20.952
380	14 44 00	19.494	410	16 81 00	20.248	440	19 36 00	20.976
381	14 51 61	19.519	411	16 89 21	20.273	441	19 44 81	21.000
382	14 59 24	19.545	412	16 97 44	20.298	442	19 53 64	21.024
383	14 66 89	19.570	413	17 05 69	20.322	443	19 62 49	21.048
384	14 74 56	19.596	414	17 13 96	20.347	444	19 71 36	21.071
385	14 82 25	19.621	415	17 22 25	20.372	445	19 80 25	21.095
386	14 89 96	19.647	416	17 30 56	20.396	446	19 89 16	21.119
387	14 97 69	19.672	417	17 38 89	20.421	447	19 98 09	21.142
388	15 05 44	19.698	418	17 47 24	20.445	448	20 07 04	21.166
389	15 13 21	19.723	419	17 55 61	20.469	449	20 16 01	21.190
390	15 21 00	19.748	420	17 64 00	20.494	450	20 25 00	21.213
						451	20 34 01	21.237
						452	20 43 04	21.260
						453	20 52 09	21.284
						454	20 61 16	21.307
						455	20 70 25	21.331
						456	20 79 36	21.354
						457	20 88 49	21.378
						458	20 97 64	21.401
						459	21 06 81	21.424
						460	21 16 00	21.448
						461	21 25 21	21.471
						462	21 34 44	21.494
						463	21 43 69	21.517
						464	21 52 96	21.541
						465	21 62 25	21.564
						466	21 71 56	21.587
						467	21 80 89	21.610
						468	21 90 24	21.633
						469	21 99 61	21.656
						470	22 09 00	21.679
						471	22 18 41	21.703
						472	22 27 84	21.726
						473	22 37 29	21.749
						474	22 46 76	21.772
						475	22 56 25	21.794
						476	22 65 76	21.817
						477	22 75 29	21.840
						478	22 84 84	21.863
						479	22 94 41	21.886
						480	23 04 00	21.909

APPENDIX B (Continued)

Number	Square	Square Root	Number	Square	Square Root	Number	Square	Square Root
481	23 13 61	21.932	511	26 11 21	22.605	541	29 26 81	23.259
482	23 23 24	21.954	512	26 21 44	22.627	542	29 37 64	23.281
483	23 32 89	21.977	513	26 31 69	22.650	543	29 48 49	23.302
484	23 42 56	22.000	514	26 41 96	22.672	544	29 59 36	23.324
485	23 52 25	22.023	515	26 52 25	22.694	545	29 70 25	23.345
486	23 61 96	22.045	516	26 62 56	22.716	546	29 81 16	23.367
487	23 71 69	22.068	517	26 72 89	22.738	547	29 92 09	23.388
488	23 81 44	22.091	518	26 83 24	22.760	548	30 03 04	23.409
489	23 91 21	22.113	519	26 93 61	22.782	549	30 14 01	23.431
490	24 01 00	22.136	520	27 04 00	22.804	550	30 25 00	23.452
491	24 10 81	22.159	521	27 14 41	22.825	551	30 36 01	23.473
492	24 20 64	22.181	522	27 24 84	22.847	552	30 47 04	23.495
493	24 30 49	22.204	523	27 35 29	22.869	553	30 58 09	23.516
494	24 40 36	22.226	524	27 45 76	22.891	554	30 69 16	23.537
495	24 50 25	22.249	525	27 56 25	22.913	555	30 80 25	23.558
496	24 60 16	22.271	526	27 66 76	22.935	556	30 91 36	23.580
497	24 70 09	22.293	527	27 77 29	22.956	557	31 02 49	23.601
498	24 80 04	22.316	528	27 87 84	22.978	558	31 13 64	23.622
499	24 90 03	22.338	529	27 98 41	23.000	559	31 24 81	23.643
500	25 00 00	22.361	530	28 09 00	23.022	560	31 36 00	23.664
501	25 10 01	22.383	531	28 19 61	23.043	561	31 47 21	23.685
502	25 20 04	22.405	532	28 30 24	23.065	562	31 58 44	23.707
503	25 30 09	22.428	533	28 40 89	23.087	563	31 69 69	23.728
504	25 40 16	22.450	534	28 51 56	23.108	564	31 80 96	23.749
505	25 50 25	22.472	535	28 62 25	23.130	565	31 92 25	23.770
506	25 60 36	22.494	536	28 72 96	23.152	566	32 03 56	23.791
507	25 70 49	22.517	537	28 83 69	23.173	567	32 14 89	23.812
508	25 80 64	22.539	538	28 94 44	23.195	568	32 26 24	23.833
509	25 90 81	22.561	539	29 05 21	23.216	569	32 37 61	23.854
510	26 01 00	22.583	540	29 16 00	23.238	570	32 49 00	23.875
						571	32 60 41	23.896
						572	32 71 84	23.917
						573	32 83 29	23.937
						574	32 94 76	23.958
						575	33 06 25	23.979
						576	33 17 76	24.000
						577	33 29 29	24.021
						578	33 40 84	24.042
						579	33 52 41	24.062
						580	33 64 00	24.083
						581	33 75 61	24.104
						582	33 87 24	24.125
						583	33 98 89	24.145
						584	34 10 56	24.166
						585	34 22 25	24.187
						586	34 33 96	24.207
						587	34 45 69	24.228
						588	34 57 44	24.249
						589	34 69 21	24.269
						590	34 81 00	24.290
						591	34 92 81	24.310
						592	35 04 64	24.331
						593	35 16 49	24.352
						594	35 28 36	24.372
						595	35 40 25	24.393
						596	35 52 16	24.413
						597	35 64 09	24.434
						598	35 76 04	24.454
						599	35 88 01	24.474
						600	36 00 00	24.495

APPENDIX B (Continued)

Number	Square	Square Root
601	36 12 01	24.515
602	36 24 04	24.536
603	36 36 09	24.556
604	36 48 16	24.576
605	36 60 25	24.597
606	36 72 36	24.617
607	36 84 49	24.637
608	36 96 64	24.658
609	37 08 81	24.678
610	37 21 00	24.698
611	37 33 21	24.718
612	37 45 44	24.739
613	37 57 69	24.759
614	37 69 96	24.779
615	37 82 25	24.799
616	37 94 56	24.819
617	38 06 89	24.839
618	38 19 24	24.860
619	38 31 61	24.880
620	38 44 00	24.900
621	38 56 41	24.920
622	38 68 84	24.940
623	38 81 29	24.960
624	38 93 76	24.980
625	39 06 25	25.000
626	39 18 76	25.020
627	39 31 29	25.040
628	39 43 84	25.060
629	39 56 41	25.080
630	39 69 00	25.100

Number	Square	Square Root
631	39 81 61	25.120
632	39 94 24	25.140
633	40 06 89	25.159
634	40 19 56	25.179
635	40 32 25	25.199
636	40 44 96	25.219
637	40 57 69	25.239
638	40 70 44	25.259
639	40 83 21	25.278
640	40 96 00	25.298
641	41 08 81	25.318
642	41 21 64	25.338
643	41 34 49	25.357
644	41 47 36	25.377
645	41 60 25	25.397
646	41 73 16	25.417
647	41 86 09	25.436
648	41 99 04	25.456
649	42 12 01	25.475
650	42 25 00	25.495
651	42 38 01	25.515
652	42 51 04	25.534
653	42 64 09	25.554
654	42 77 16	25.573
655	42 90 25	25.593
656	43 03 36	25.612
657	43 16 49	25.632
658	43 29 64	25.652
659	43 42 81	25.671
660	43 56 00	25.690

Number	Square	Square Root
661	43 69 21	25.710
662	43 82 44	25.729
663	43 95 69	25.749
664	44 08 96	25.768
665	44 22 25	25.788
666	44 35 56	25.807
667	44 48 89	25.826
668	44 62 24	25.846
669	44 75 61	25.865
670	44 89 00	25.884
671	45 02 41	25.904
672	45 15 84	25.923
673	45 29 29	25.942
674	45 42 76	25.962
675	45 56 25	25.981
676	45 69 76	26.000
677	45 83 29	26.019
678	45 96 84	26.038
679	46 10 41	26.058
680	46 24 00	26.077
681	46 37 61	26.096
682	46 51 24	26.115
683	46 64 89	26.134
684	46 78 56	26.153
685	46 92 25	26.173
686	47 05 96	26.192
687	47 19 69	26.211
688	47 33 44	26.230
689	47 47 21	26.249
690	47 61 00	26.268

Number	Square	Square Root
691	47 74 81	26.287
692	47 88 64	26.306
693	48 02 49	26.325
694	48 16 36	26.344
695	48 30 25	26.363
696	48 44 16	26.382
697	48 58 09	26.401
698	48 72 04	26.420
699	48 86 01	26.439
700	49 00 00	26.458
701	49 14 01	26.476
702	49 28 04	26.495
703	49 42 09	26.514
704	49 56 16	26.533
705	49 70 25	26.552
706	49 84 36	26.571
707	49 98 49	26.589
708	50 12 64	26.608
709	50 26 81	26.627
710	50 41 00	26.646
711	50 55 21	26.665
712	50 69 44	26.683
713	50 83 69	26.702
714	50 97 96	26.721
715	51 12 25	26.739
716	51 26 56	26.758
717	51 40 89	26.777
718	51 55 24	26.796
719	51 69 61	26.814
720	51 84 00	26.833

APPENDIX B (Continued)

Number	Square	Square Root	Number	Square	Square Root	Number	Square	Square Root	Number	Square	Square Root
721	51 98 41	26.851	751	56 40 01	27.404	781	60 99 61	27.946	811	65 77 21	28.478
722	52 12 84	26.870	752	56 55 04	27.423	782	61 15 24	27.964	812	65 93 44	28.496
723	52 27 29	26.889	753	56 70 09	27.441	783	61 30 89	27.982	813	66 09 69	28.513
724	52 41 76	26.907	754	56 85 16	27.459	784	61 46 56	28.000	814	66 25 96	28.531
725	52 56 25	26.926	755	57 00 25	27.477	785	61 62 25	28.018	815	66 42 25	28.548
726	52 70 76	26.944	756	57 15 36	27.495	786	61 77 96	28.036	816	66 58 56	28.566
727	52 85 29	26.963	757	57 30 49	27.514	787	61 93 69	28.054	817	66 74 89	28.583
728	52 99 84	26.981	758	57 45 64	27.532	788	62 09 44	28.071	818	66 91 24	28.601
729	53 14 41	27.000	759	57 60 81	27.550	789	62 25 21	28.089	819	67 07 61	28.618
730	53 29 00	27.019	760	57 76 00	27.568	790	62 41 00	28.107	820	67 24 00	28.636
731	53 43 61	27.037	761	57 91 21	27.586	791	62 56 81	28.125	821	67 40 41	28.653
732	53 48 24	27.055	762	58 06 44	27.604	792	62 72 64	28.142	822	67 56 84	28.671
533	53 72 89	27.074	763	58 21 69	27.622	793	62 88 49	28.160	823	67 73 29	28.688
734	53 87 56	27.092	764	58 36 96	27.641	794	63 04 36	28.178	824	67 89 76	28.705
735	54 02 25	27.111	765	58 52 25	27.659	795	63 20 25	28.196	825	68 06 25	28.723
736	54 16 96	27.129	766	58 67 56	27.677	796	63 36 16	28.213	826	68 22 76	28.740
737	54 31 69	27.148	767	58 82 89	27.695	797	63 52 09	28.231	827	68 39 29	28.758
738	54 46 44	27.166	768	58 98 24	27.713	798	63 68 04	28.249	828	68 55 84	28.775
739	54 61 21	27.185	769	59 13 61	27.731	799	63 84 01	28.267	829	68 72 41	28.792
740	54 76 00	27.203	770	59 29 00	27.749	800	64 00 00	28.284	830	68 89 00	28.810
741	54 90 81	27.221	771	59 44 41	27.767	801	64 16 01	28.302	831	69 05 61	28.827
742	55 05 64	27.240	772	59 59 84	27.785	802	64 32 04	28.320	832	69 22 24	28.844
743	55 20 49	27.258	773	59 75 29	27.803	803	64 48 09	28.337	833	69 38 89	28.862
744	55 35 36	27.276	774	59 90 76	27.821	804	64 64 16	28.355	834	69 55 56	28.879
745	55 50 25	27.295	775	60 06 25	27.839	805	64 80 25	28.373	835	69 72 25	28.896
746	55 65 16	27.313	776	60 21 76	27.857	806	64 96 36	28.390	836	69 88 96	28.914
747	55 80 09	27.331	777	60 37 29	27.875	807	65 12 49	28.408	837	70 05 69	28.931
748	55 95 04	27.350	778	60 52 84	27.893	808	65 28 64	28.425	838	70 22 44	28.948
749	56 10 01	27.368	779	60 68 41	27.911	809	65 44 81	28.443	839	70 39 21	28.965
750	56 25 00	27.386	780	60 84 00	27.928	810	65 61 00	28.460	840	70 56 00	28.983

Number	Square	Square Root	Number	Square	Square Root	Number	Square	Square Root	Number	Square	Square Root
841	70 72 81	29.000	871	75 86 41	29.513	901	81 18 01	30.017	931	86 67 61	30.512
842	70 89 64	29.017	872	76 03 84	29.530	902	81 36 04	30.033	932	86 86 24	30.529
843	71 06 49	29.034	873	76 21 29	29.547	903	81 54 09	30.050	933	87 04 89	30.545
844	71 23 36	29.052	874	76 38 76	29.563	904	81 72 16	30.067	934	87 23 56	30.561
845	71 40 25	29.069	875	76 56 25	29.580	905	81 90 25	30.083	935	87 42 25	30.578
846	71 57 16	29.086	876	76 73 76	29.597	906	82 08 36	30.100	936	87 60 96	30.594
847	71 74 09	29.103	877	76 91 29	29.614	907	82 26 49	30.116	937	87 79 69	30.610
848	71 91 04	29.120	878	77 08 84	29.631	908	82 44 64	30.133	938	87 98 44	30.627
849	72 08 01	29.138	879	77 26 41	29.648	909	82 62 81	30.150	939	88 17 21	30.643
850	72 25 00	29.155	880	77 44 00	29.665	910	82 81 00	30.166	940	88 36 00	30.659
851	72 42 01	29.172	881	77 61 61	29.682	911	82 99 21	30.183	941	88 54 81	30.676
852	72 59 04	29.189	882	77 79 24	29.698	912	83 17 44	30.199	942	88 73 64	30.692
853	72 76 09	29.206	883	77 96 89	29.715	913	83 35 69	30.216	943	88 92 49	30.708
854	72 93 16	29.223	884	78 14 56	29.732	914	83 53 96	30.232	944	89 11 36	30.725
855	73 10 25	29.240	885	78 32 25	29.749	915	83 72 25	30.249	945	89 30 25	30.741
856	73 27 36	29.257	886	78 49 96	29.766	916	83 90 56	30.265	946	89 49 16	30.757
857	73 44 49	29.275	887	78 67 69	29.783	917	84 08 89	30.282	947	89 68 09	30.773
858	73 61 64	29.292	888	78 85 44	29.799	918	84 27 24	30.299	948	89 87 04	30.790
859	73 78 81	29.309	889	79 03 21	29.816	919	84 45 61	30.315	949	90 06 01	30.806
860	73 96 00	29.326	890	79 21 00	29.833	920	84 64 00	30.332	950	90 25 00	30.822
861	74 13 21	29.343	891	79 38 81	29.850	921	84 82 41	30.348	951	90 44 01	30.838
862	74 30 44	29.360	892	79 56 64	29.866	922	85 00 84	30.364	952	90 63 04	30.854
863	74 47 69	29.377	893	79 74 49	29.883	923	85 19 29	30.381	953	90 82 09	30.871
864	74 64 96	29.394	894	79 92 36	29.900	924	85 37 76	30.397	954	91 01 16	30.887
865	74 82 25	29.411	895	80 10 25	29.916	925	85 56 25	30.414	955	91 20 25	30.903
866	74 99 56	29.428	896	80 28 16	29.933	926	85 74 76	30.430	956	91 39 36	30.919
867	75 16 89	29.445	897	80 46 09	29.950	927	85 93 29	30.447	957	91 58 49	30.935
868	75 34 24	29.462	898	80 64 04	29.967	928	86 11 84	30.463	958	91 77 64	30.952
869	75 51 61	29.479	899	80 82 01	29.983	929	86 30 41	30.480	959	91 96 81	30.968
870	75 69 00	29.496	900	81 00 00	30.000	930	86 49 00	30.496	960	92 16 00	30.984

APPENDIX B (Continued)

Number	Square	Square Root
961	92 35 21	31.000
962	92 54 44	31.016
963	92 73 69	31.032
964	92 92 96	31.048
965	93 12 25	31.064
966	93 31 56	31.081
967	93 50 89	31.097
968	93 70 24	31.113
969	93 89 61	31.129
970	94 09 00	31.145
971	94 28 41	31.161
972	94 47 84	31.177
973	94 67 29	31.193
974	94 86 76	31.209
975	95 06 25	31.225
976	95 25 76	31.241
977	95 45 29	31.257
978	95 64 84	31.273
979	95 84 41	31.289
980	96 04 00	31.305

Number	Square	Square Root
981	96 23 61	31.321
982	96 43 24	31.337
983	96 62 89	31.353
984	96 82 56	31.369
985	97 02 25	31.385
986	97 21 96	31.401
987	97 41 69	31.417
988	97 61 44	31.432
989	97 81 21	31.448
990	98 01 00	31.464
991	98 20 81	31.480
992	98 40 64	31.496
993	98 60 49	31.512
994	98 80 36	31.528
995	99 00 25	31.544
996	99 20 16	31.559
997	99 40 09	31.575
998	99 60 04	31.591
999	99 80 01	31.607
1000	100 00 00	31.623

APPENDIX C   Random Numbers

COLUMN NUMBER

Row	00000 01234	00000 56789	11111 01234	11111 56789	22222 01234	22222 56789	33333 01234	33333 56789
				1st Thousand				
00	23157	54859	01837	25993	76249	70886	95230	36744
01	05545	55043	10537	43508	90611	83744	10962	21343
02	14871	60350	32404	36223	50051	00322	11543	80834
03	38976	74951	94051	75853	78805	90194	32428	71695
04	97312	61718	99755	30870	94251	25841	54882	10513
05	11742	69381	44339	30872	32797	33118	22647	06850
06	43361	28859	11016	45623	93009	00499	43640	74036
07	93806	20478	38268	04491	55751	18932	58475	52571
08	49540	13181	08429	84187	69538	29661	77738	09527
09	36768	72633	37948	21569	41959	68670	45274	83880
10	07092	52392	24627	12067	06558	45344	67338	45320
11	43310	01081	44863	80307	52555	16148	89742	94647
12	61570	06360	06173	63775	63148	95123	35017	46993
13	31352	83799	10779	18941	31579	76448	62584	86919
14	57048	86526	27795	93692	90529	56546	35065	32254
15	09243	44200	68721	07137	30729	75756	09298	27650
16	97957	35018	40894	88329	52230	82521	22532	61587
17	93732	59570	43781	98885	56671	66826	95996	44569
18	72621	11225	00922	68264	35666	59434	71687	58167
19	61020	74418	45371	20794	95917	37866	99536	19378
20	97839	85474	33055	91718	45473	54144	22034	23000
21	89160	97192	22232	90637	35055	45489	88438	16361
22	25966	88220	62871	79265	02823	52862	84919	54883
23	81443	31719	05049	54806	74690	07567	65017	16543
24	11322	54931	42362	34386	08624	97687	46245	23245

Note: From "Randomness and random sampling numbers," by M. G. Kendall and B. B. Smith, *Journal of the Royal Statistical Society,* 1938, *101,* 147–166. Reprinted by permission of the Royal Statistical Society.

APPENDIX C (Continued)

COLUMN NUMBER

2nd Thousand

Row	00000 01234	00000 56789	11111 01234	11111 56789	22222 01234	22222 56789	33333 01234	33333 56789
00	64755	83885	84122	25920	17696	15655	95045	95947
01	10302	52289	77436	34430	38112	49067	07348	23328
02	71017	98495	51308	50374	66591	02887	53765	69149
03	60012	55605	88410	34879	79655	90169	78800	03666
04	37330	94656	49161	42802	48274	54755	44553	65090
05	47869	87001	31591	12273	60626	12822	34691	61212
06	38040	42737	64167	89578	39323	49324	88434	38706
07	73508	30908	83054	80078	86669	30295	56460	45336
08	32623	46474	84061	04324	20628	37319	32356	43969
09	97591	99549	36630	35106	62069	92975	95320	57734
10	74012	31955	59790	96982	66224	24015	96749	07589
11	56754	26457	13351	05014	90966	33674	69096	33488
12	49800	49908	54831	21998	08528	26372	92923	65026
13	43584	89647	24878	56670	00221	50193	99591	62377
14	16653	79664	60325	71301	35742	83636	73058	87229
15	48502	69055	65322	58748	31446	80237	31252	96367
16	96765	54692	36316	86230	48296	38352	23816	64094
17	38923	61550	80357	81784	23444	12463	33992	28128
18	77958	81694	25225	05587	51073	01070	60218	61961
19	17928	28065	25586	08771	02641	85064	65796	48170
20	94036	85978	02318	04499	41054	10531	87431	21596
21	47460	60479	56230	48417	14372	85167	27558	00368
22	47856	56088	51992	82439	40644	17170	13463	18288
23	57616	34653	92298	62018	10375	76515	62986	90756
24	08300	92704	66752	66610	57188	79107	54222	22013

APPENDIX C (Continued)

COLUMN NUMBER

3rd Thousand

Row	00000 01234	00000 56789	11111 01234	11111 56789	22222 01234	22222 56789	33333 01234	33333 56789
00	89221	02362	65787	74733	51272	30213	92441	39651
01	04005	99818	63918	29032	94012	42363	01261	10650
02	98546	38066	50856	75045	40645	22841	53254	44125
03	41719	84401	59226	01314	54581	40398	49988	65579
04	28733	72489	00785	25843	24613	49797	85567	84471
05	65213	83927	77762	03086	80742	24395	68476	83792
06	65553	12678	90906	90466	43670	26217	69900	31205
07	05668	69080	73029	85746	58332	78231	45986	92998
08	39302	99718	49757	79519	27387	76373	47262	91612
09	64592	32254	45879	29431	38320	05981	18067	87137
10	07513	48792	47314	83660	68907	05336	82579	91582
11	86593	68501	56638	99800	82839	35148	56541	07232
12	83735	22599	97977	81248	36838	99560	32410	67614
13	08595	21826	54655	08204	87990	17033	56258	05384
14	41273	27149	44293	69458	16828	63962	15864	35431
15	00473	75908	56238	12242	72631	76314	47252	06347
16	86131	53789	81383	07868	89132	96182	07009	86432
17	33849	78359	08402	03586	03176	88663	08018	22546
18	61870	41657	07468	08612	98083	97349	20775	45091
19	43898	65923	25078	86129	78491	97653	91500	80786
20	29939	39123	04548	45985	60952	06641	28726	46473
21	38505	85555	14388	55077	18657	94887	67831	70819
22	31824	38431	67125	25511	72044	11562	52379	82268
23	91430	03767	13561	15597	06750	92552	02391	38753
24	38635	68976	25498	97526	96458	03805	04116	63514

APPENDIX C (Continued)

COLUMN NUMBER

4th Thousand

Row	00000 01234	00000 56789	11111 01234	11111 56789	22222 01234	22222 56789	33333 01234	33333 56789
00	02490	54122	27944	39364	94239	72074	11679	54082
01	11967	36469	60627	83701	09253	30208	01385	37482
02	48256	83465	49699	24079	05403	35154	39613	03136
03	27246	73080	21481	23536	04881	89977	49484	93071
04	32532	77265	72430	70722	86529	18457	92657	10011
05	66757	98955	92375	93431	43204	55825	45443	69625
06	11266	34545	76505	97746	34668	26999	26742	97516
07	17872	39142	45561	80146	93137	48924	64257	59284
08	62561	30365	03408	14754	51798	08133	61010	97730
09	62796	30779	35497	70501	30105	08133	00997	91970
10	75510	21771	04339	33660	42757	62223	87565	48468
11	87439	01691	63517	26590	44437	07217	98706	39032
12	97742	02621	10748	78803	38337	65226	92149	59051
13	98811	06001	21571	02875	21828	83912	85188	61624
14	51264	01852	64607	92553	29004	26695	78583	62998
15	40239	93376	10419	68610	49120	02941	80035	99317
16	26936	59186	51667	27645	46329	44681	94190	66647
17	88502	11716	98299	40974	42394	62200	69094	81646
18	63499	38093	25593	61995	79867	80569	01023	38374
19	36379	81206	03317	78710	73828	31083	60509	44091
20	93801	22322	47479	57017	59334	30647	43061	26660
21	29856	87120	56311	50053	25365	81265	22414	02431
22	97720	87931	88265	13050	71017	15177	06957	92919
23	85237	09105	74601	46377	59938	15647	34177	92753
24	75746	75268	31727	95773	72364	87324	36879	06802

APPENDIX C (Continued)

COLUMN NUMBER

5th Thousand

Row	00000 01234	00000 56789	11111 01234	11111 56789	22222 01234	22222 56789	33333 01234	33333 56789
00	29935	06971	63175	52579	10478	89379	61428	21363
01	15114	07126	51890	77787	75510	13103	42942	48111
02	03870	43225	10589	87629	22039	94124	38127	65022
03	79390	39188	40756	45269	65959	20640	14284	22960
04	30035	06915	79196	54428	64819	52314	48721	81594
05	29039	99861	28759	79802	68531	39198	38137	24373
06	78196	08108	24107	49777	09599	43569	84820	94956
07	15847	85493	91442	91351	80130	73752	21539	10986
08	36614	62248	49194	97209	92587	92053	41021	80064
09	40549	54884	91465	43862	35541	44466	88894	74180
10	40878	08997	14286	09982	90308	78007	51587	16658
11	10229	49282	41173	31468	59455	18756	08908	06660
12	15918	76787	30624	25928	44124	25088	31137	71614
13	13403	18796	49909	94404	64979	41462	18155	98335
14	66523	94596	74908	90271	10009	98648	17640	68909
15	91665	36469	68343	17870	25975	04662	21272	50620
16	67415	87515	08207	73729	73201	57593	96917	69699
17	76527	96996	23724	33448	63392	32394	60887	90617
18	19815	47789	74348	17147	10954	34355	81194	54407
19	25592	53587	76384	72575	84347	68918	05739	57222
20	55902	45539	63646	31609	95999	82887	40666	66692
21	02470	58376	79794	22482	42423	96162	49491	17264
22	18630	53263	13319	97619	35859	12350	14632	87659
23	89673	38230	16063	92007	59503	38402	76450	33333
24	62986	67364	06595	17427	84623	14565	82860	57300

APPENDIX D Cumulative Probabilities of Observed *x* for a Given N in the Binomial and Sign Tests [a]

N	x 0	1	2	3	4	5	6	7	8	9	10	11	12	13	14	15
5	031	188	500	812	969	°										
6	016	109	344	656	891	984	°									
7	008	062	227	500	773	938	992	°								
8	004	035	145	363	637	855	965	996	°							
9	002	020	090	254	500	746	910	980	998	°						
10	001	011	055	172	377	623	828	945	989	999	°					
11		006	033	113	274	500	726	887	967	994	°	°				
12		003	019	073	194	387	613	806	927	981	997	°	°			
13		002	011	046	133	291	500	709	867	954	989	998	°	°		
14		001	006	029	090	212	395	605	788	910	971	994	999	°	°	
15			004	018	059	151	304	500	696	849	941	982	996	°	°	°
16			002	011	038	105	227	402	598	773	895	962	989	998	°	°
17			001	006	025	072	166	315	500	685	834	928	975	994	999	°
18			001	004	015	048	119	240	407	593	760	881	952	985	996	999
19				002	010	032	084	180	324	500	676	820	916	968	990	998
20				001	006	021	058	132	252	412	588	748	868	942	979	994
21				001	004	013	039	095	192	332	500	668	808	905	961	987
22					002	008	026	067	143	262	416	584	738	857	933	974
23					001	005	017	047	105	202	339	500	661	798	895	953
24					001	003	011	032	076	154	271	419	581	729	846	924
25						002	007	022	054	115	212	345	500	655	788	885

[a] The value of *x* = *r* or *N* − *r*, whichever is smaller. The table contains one-tailed probabilities under H_0 when $P = Q = .5$. Double the tabled probability values for a two-tailed test. Decimal points are omitted to save space.

*1.0 or approximately 1.0

Note: From *Statistical Inference* by H. M. Walker and J. Lev. Copyright 1953 by Holt, Rinehart and Winston. Reprinted by permission of Holt, Rinehart and Winston.

APPENDIX E Critical Values of $\chi^2 = \sum \frac{(O-E)^2}{E} \geq 0$

one-tail

Degrees [a] of Freedom df	one-tail p = .25 two-tail p = .50	.15 .30	.10 .20	.05 .10	.025 .05	.01 .02	.005 .01
1	.455	1.074	1.642	2.706	3.841	5.412	6.635
2	1.386	2.408	3.219	4.605	5.991	7.824	9.210
3	2.366	3.665	4.642	6.251	7.815	9.837	11.341
4	3.357	4.878	5.989	7.779	9.488	11.668	13.277
5	4.351	6.064	7.289	9.236	11.070	13.388	15.086
6	5.348	7.231	8.558	10.645	12.592	15.033	16.812
7	6.346	8.383	9.803	12.017	14.067	16.622	18.475
8	7.344	9.524	11.030	13.362	15.507	18.168	20.090
9	8.343	10.656	12.242	14.684	16.919	19.679	21.666
10	9.342	11.781	13.442	15.987	18.307	21.161	23.209
11	10.341	12.899	14.631	17.275	19.675	22.618	24.725
12	11.340	14.011	15.812	18.549	21.026	24.054	26.217
13	12.340	15.119	16.985	19.812	22.362	25.472	27.688
14	13.339	16.222	18.151	21.064	23.685	26.873	29.141
15	14.339	17.322	19.311	22.307	24.996	28.259	30.578
16	15.338	18.418	20.465	23.542	26.296	29.633	32.000
17	16.338	19.511	21.615	24.769	27.587	30.995	33.409
18	17.338	20.601	22.760	25.989	28,869	32.346	34.805
19	18.338	21.689	23.900	27.204	30.144	33.687	36.191
20	19.337	22.775	25.038	28.412	31.410	35.020	37.566
21	20.337	23.858	26.171	29.615	32.671	36.343	38.932
22	21.337	24.939	27.301	30.813	33.924	37.659	40.289
23	22.337	26.018	28.429	32.007	35.172	38.968	41.638
24	23.337	27.096	29.553	33.196	36.415	40.270	42.980
25	24.337	28.172	30.675	34.382	37.652	41.566	44.314
26	25.336	29.246	31.795	35.563	38.885	42.856	45.642
27	26.336	30.319	32.912	36.741	40.113	44.140	46.963
28	27.336	31.391	34.027	37.916	41.337	45.419	48.278
29	28.336	32.461	35.139	39.087	42.557	46.693	49.588
30	29.336	33.530	36.250	40.256	43.773	47.962	50.892

[a]For different values of df, the table contains one- and two-tailed critical values of χ^2 under H_0. For values of df greater than 30, the expression $\sqrt{2\chi^2} - \sqrt{2(df) - 1}$ may be used as a normal deviate (z) with unit standard error.

Note: Abridged from Table III of *Statistical methods for research workers* by R. A. Fisher (Edinburgh: Oliver & Boyd Ltd. Reprinted by permission of the author and publishers.)

APPENDIX F One- and Two-Tailed Critical

Values of t

df	one-tailed $p = 0.4$ two-tailed $p = 0.8$	0.25 0.5	0.1 0.2	0.05 0.1	0.025 0.05	0.01 0.02	0.005 0.01	0.001 0.002
1	0.325	1.000	3.078	6.314	12.706	31.821	63.657	318.31
2	.289	0.816	1.886	2.920	4.303	6.965	9.925	22.326
3	.277	.765	1.638	2.353	3.182	4.541	5.841	10.213
4	.271	.741	1.533	2.132	2.776	3.747	4.604	7.173
5	0.267	0.727	1.476	2.015	2.571	3.365	4.032	5.893
6	.265	.718	1.440	1.943	2.447	3.143	3.707	5.208
7	.263	.711	1.415	1.895	2.365	2.998	3.499	4.785
8	.262	.706	1.397	1.860	2.306	2.896	3.355	4.501
9	.261	.703	1.383	1.833	2.262	2.821	3.250	4.297
10	0.260	0.700	1.372	1.812	2.228	2.764	3.169	4.144
11	.260	.697	1.363	1.796	2.201	2.718	3.106	4.025
12	.259	.695	1.356	1.782	2.179	2.681	3.055	3.930
13	.259	.694	1.350	1.771	2.160	2.650	3.012	3.852
14	.258	.692	1.345	1.761	2.145	2.624	2.977	3.787
15	0.258	0.691	1.341	1.753	2.131	2.602	2.947	3.733
16	.258	.690	1.337	1.746	2.120	2.583	2.921	3.686
17	.257	.689	1.333	1.740	2.110	2.567	2.898	3.646
18	.257	.688	1.330	1.734	2.101	2.552	2.878	3.610
19	.257	.688	1.328	1.729	2.093	2.539	2.861	3.579
20	0.257	0.687	1.325	1.725	2.086	2.528	2.845	3.552
21	.257	.686	1.323	1.721	2.080	2.518	2.831	3.527
22	.256	.686	1.321	1.717	2.074	2.508	2.819	3.505
23	.256	.685	1.319	1.714	2.069	2.500	2.807	3.485
24	.256	.685	1.318	1.711	2.064	2.492	2.797	3.467
25	0.256	0.684	1.316	1.708	2.060	2.485	2.787	3.450
26	.256	.684	1.315	1.706	2.056	2.479	2.779	3.435
27	.256	.684	1.314	1.703	2.052	2.473	2.771	3.421
28	.256	.683	1.313	1.701	2.048	2.467	2.763	3.408
29	.256	.683	1.311	1.699	2.045	2.462	2.756	3.396
30	0.256	0.683	1.310	1.697	2.042	2.457	2.750	3.385
40	.255	.681	1.303	1.684	2.021	2.423	2.704	3.307
60	.254	.679	1.296	1.671	2.000	2.390	2.660	3.232
120	.254	.677	1.289	1.658	1.980	2.358	2.617	3.160
∞	.253	.674	1.282	1.645	1.960	2.326	2.576	3.909

Note: Abridged from Table 12 of the *Biometrika Tables for Statisticians* (Vol. 1, ed. 1), edited by E. S. Pearson and H. O. Hartley. Reproduced by permission of E. S. Pearson and the trustees of *Biometrika*.

APPENDIX G Probabilities of Values of the F Ratio for Specified Values of α Numerator df (v_1), and Denominator df (v_2)

$a = 0.05$

v_2 \ v_1	1	2	3	4	5	6	7	8	9	10	12	15	20	24	30	40	60	120	∞
1	161.4	199.5	215.7	224.6	230.2	234.0	236.8	238.9	240.5	241.9	243.9	245.9	248.0	249.1	250.1	251.1	252.2	253.3	254.3
2	18.51	19.00	19.16	19.25	19.30	19.33	19.35	19.37	19.38	19.40	19.41	19.43	19.45	19.45	19.46	19.47	19.48	19.49	19.50
3	10.13	9.55	9.28	9.12	9.01	8.94	8.89	8.85	8.81	8.79	8.74	8.70	8.66	8.64	8.62	8.59	8.57	8.55	8.53
4	7.71	6.94	6.59	6.39	6.26	6.16	6.09	6.04	6.00	5.96	5.91	5.86	5.80	5.77	5.75	5.72	5.69	5.66	5.63
5	6.61	5.79	5.41	5.19	5.05	4.95	4.88	4.82	4.77	4.74	4.68	4.62	4.56	4.53	4.50	4.46	4.43	4.40	4.36
6	5.99	5.14	4.76	4.53	4.39	4.28	4.21	4.15	4.10	4.06	4.00	3.94	3.87	3.84	3.81	3.77	3.74	3.70	3.67
7	5.59	4.74	4.35	4.12	3.97	3.87	3.79	3.73	3.68	3.64	3.57	3.51	3.44	3.41	3.38	3.34	3.30	3.27	3.23
8	5.32	4.46	4.07	3.84	3.69	3.58	3.50	3.44	3.39	3.35	3.28	3.22	3.15	3.12	3.08	3.04	3.01	2.97	2.93
9	5.12	4.26	3.86	3.63	3.48	3.37	3.29	3.23	3.18	3.14	3.07	3.01	2.94	2.90	2.86	2.83	2.79	2.75	2.71
10	4.96	4.10	3.71	3.48	3.33	3.22	3.14	3.07	3.02	2.98	2.91	2.85	2.77	2.74	2.70	2.66	2.62	2.58	2.54
11	4.84	3.98	3.59	3.36	3.20	3.09	3.01	2.95	2.90	2.85	2.79	2.72	2.65	2.61	2.57	2.53	2.49	2.45	2.40
12	4.75	3.89	3.49	3.26	3.11	3.00	2.91	2.85	2.80	2.75	2.69	2.62	2.54	2.51	2.47	2.43	2.38	2.34	2.30
13	4.67	3.81	3.41	3.18	3.03	2.92	2.83	2.77	2.71	2.67	2.60	2.53	2.46	2.42	2.38	2.34	2.30	2.25	2.21
14	4.60	3.74	3.34	3.11	2.96	2.85	2.76	2.70	2.65	2.60	2.53	2.46	2.39	2.35	2.31	2.27	2.22	2.18	2.13
15	4.54	3.68	3.29	3.06	2.90	2.79	2.71	2.64	2.59	2.54	2.48	2.40	2.33	2.29	2.25	2.20	2.16	2.11	2.07
16	4.49	3.63	3.24	3.01	2.85	2.74	2.66	2.59	2.54	2.49	2.42	2.35	2.28	2.24	2.19	2.15	2.11	2.06	2.01
17	4.45	3.59	3.20	2.96	2.81	2.70	2.61	2.55	2.49	2.45	2.38	2.31	2.23	2.19	2.15	2.10	2.06	2.01	1.96
18	4.41	3.55	3.16	2.93	2.77	2.66	2.58	2.51	2.46	2.41	2.34	2.27	2.19	2.15	2.11	2.06	2.02	1.97	1.92
19	4.38	3.52	3.13	2.90	2.74	2.63	2.54	2.48	2.42	2.38	2.31	2.23	2.16	2.11	2.07	2.03	1.98	1.93	1.88
20	4.35	3.49	3.10	2.87	2.71	2.60	2.51	2.45	2.39	2.35	2.28	2.20	2.12	2.08	2.04	1.99	1.95	1.90	1.84
21	4.32	3.47	3.07	2.84	2.68	2.57	2.49	2.42	2.37	2.32	2.25	2.18	2.10	2.05	2.01	1.96	1.92	1.87	1.81
22	4.30	3.44	3.05	2.82	2.66	2.55	2.46	2.40	2.34	2.30	2.23	2.15	2.07	2.03	1.98	1.94	1.89	1.84	1.78
23	4.28	3.42	3.03	2.80	2.64	2.53	2.44	2.37	2.32	2.27	2.20	2.13	2.05	2.01	1.96	1.91	1.86	1.81	1.76
24	4.26	3.40	3.01	2.78	2.62	2.51	2.42	2.36	2.30	2.25	2.18	2.11	2.03	1.98	1.94	1.89	1.84	1.79	1.73
25	4.24	3.39	2.99	2.76	2.60	2.49	2.40	2.34	2.28	2.24	2.16	2.09	2.01	1.96	1.92	1.87	1.82	1.77	1.71
26	4.23	3.37	2.98	2.74	2.59	2.47	2.39	2.32	2.27	2.22	2.15	2.07	1.99	1.95	1.90	1.85	1.80	1.75	1.69
27	4.21	3.35	2.96	2.73	2.57	2.46	2.37	2.31	2.25	2.20	2.13	2.06	1.97	1.93	1.88	1.84	1.79	1.73	1.67
28	4.20	3.34	2.95	2.71	2.56	2.45	2.36	2.29	2.24	2.19	2.12	2.04	1.96	1.91	1.87	1.82	1.77	1.71	1.65
29	4.18	3.33	2.93	2.70	2.55	2.43	2.35	2.28	2.22	2.18	2.10	2.03	1.94	1.90	1.85	1.81	1.75	1.70	1.64
30	4.17	3.32	2.92	2.69	2.53	2.42	2.33	2.27	2.21	2.16	2.09	2.01	1.93	1.89	1.84	1.79	1.74	1.68	1.62
40	4.08	3.23	2.84	2.61	2.45	2.34	2.25	2.18	2.12	2.08	2.00	1.92	1.84	1.79	1.74	1.69	1.64	1.58	1.51
60	4.00	3.15	2.76	2.53	2.37	2.25	2.17	2.10	2.04	1.99	1.92	1.84	1.75	1.70	1.65	1.59	1.53	1.47	1.39
120	3.92	3.07	2.68	2.45	2.29	2.17	2.09	2.02	1.96	1.91	1.83	1.75	1.66	1.61	1.55	1.50	1.43	1.35	1.25
∞	3.84	3.00	2.60	2.37	2.21	2.10	2.01	1.94	1.88	1.83	1.75	1.67	1.57	1.52	1.46	1.39	1.32	1.22	1.00

Note: Abridged from Table 18 of *Biometrika tables for statisticians* (Vol. 1, ed. 3), edited by E. S. Pearson and H. O. Hartley. Reprinted by permission of E. S. Pearson and the trustees of *Biometrika*.

APPENDIX G (Continued)

$\alpha = 0.025$

v_2 \ v_1	1	2	3	4	5	6	7	8	9	10	12	15	20	24	30	40	60	120	∞
1	647.8	799.5	864.2	899.6	921.8	937.1	948.2	956.7	963.3	968.6	976.7	984.9	993.1	997.2	1001	1006	1010	1014	1018
2	38.51	39.00	39.17	39.25	39.30	39.33	39.36	39.37	39.39	39.40	39.41	39.43	39.45	39.46	39.46	39.47	39.48	39.49	39.50
3	17.44	16.04	15.44	15.10	14.88	14.73	14.62	14.54	14.47	14.42	14.34	14.25	14.17	14.12	14.08	14.04	13.99	13.95	13.90
4	12.22	10.65	9.98	9.60	9.36	9.20	9.07	8.98	8.90	8.84	8.75	8.66	8.56	8.51	8.46	8.41	8.36	8.31	8.26
5	10.01	8.43	7.76	7.39	7.15	6.98	6.85	6.76	6.68	6.62	6.52	6.43	6.33	6.28	6.23	6.18	6.12	6.07	6.02
6	8.81	7.26	6.60	6.23	5.99	5.82	5.70	5.60	5.52	5.46	5.37	5.27	5.17	5.12	5.07	5.01	4.96	4.90	4.85
7	8.07	6.54	5.89	5.52	5.29	5.12	4.99	4.90	4.82	4.76	4.67	4.57	4.47	4.42	4.36	4.31	4.25	4.20	4.14
8	7.57	6.06	5.42	5.05	4.82	4.65	4.53	4.43	4.36	4.30	4.20	4.10	4.00	3.95	3.89	3.84	3.78	3.73	3.67
9	7.21	5.71	5.08	4.72	4.48	4.32	4.20	4.10	4.03	3.96	3.87	3.77	3.67	3.61	3.56	3.51	3.45	3.39	3.33
10	6.94	5.46	4.83	4.47	4.24	4.07	3.95	3.85	3.78	3.72	3.62	3.52	3.42	3.37	3.31	3.26	3.20	3.14	3.08
11	6.72	5.26	4.63	4.28	4.04	3.88	3.76	3.66	3.59	3.53	3.43	3.33	3.23	3.17	3.12	3.06	3.00	2.94	2.88
12	6.55	5.10	4.47	4.12	3.89	3.73	3.61	3.51	3.44	3.37	3.28	3.18	3.07	3.02	2.96	2.91	2.85	2.79	2.72
13	6.41	4.97	4.35	4.00	3.77	3.60	3.48	3.39	3.31	3.25	3.15	3.05	2.95	2.89	2.84	2.78	2.72	2.66	2.60
14	6.30	4.86	4.24	3.89	3.66	3.50	3.38	3.29	3.21	3.15	3.05	2.95	2.84	2.79	2.73	2.67	2.61	2.55	2.49
15	6.20	4.77	4.15	3.80	3.58	3.41	3.29	3.20	3.12	3.06	2.96	2.86	2.76	2.70	2.64	2.59	2.52	2.46	2.40
16	6.12	4.69	4.08	3.73	3.50	3.34	3.22	3.12	3.05	2.99	2.89	2.79	2.68	2.63	2.57	2.51	2.45	2.38	2.32
17	6.04	4.62	4.01	3.66	3.44	3.28	3.16	3.06	2.98	2.92	2.82	2.72	2.62	2.56	2.50	2.44	2.38	2.32	2.25
18	5.98	4.56	3.95	3.61	3.38	3.22	3.10	3.01	2.93	2.87	2.77	2.67	2.56	2.50	2.44	2.38	2.32	2.26	2.19
19	5.92	4.51	3.90	3.56	3.33	3.17	3.05	2.96	2.88	2.82	2.72	2.62	2.51	2.45	2.39	2.33	2.27	2.20	2.13
20	5.87	4.46	3.86	3.51	3.29	3.13	3.01	2.91	2.84	2.77	2.68	2.57	2.46	2.41	2.35	2.29	2.22	2.16	2.09
21	5.83	4.42	3.82	3.48	3.25	3.09	2.97	2.87	2.80	2.73	2.64	2.53	2.42	2.37	2.31	2.25	2.18	2.11	2.04
22	5.79	4.38	3.78	3.44	3.22	3.05	2.93	2.84	2.76	2.70	2.60	2.50	2.39	2.33	2.27	2.21	2.14	2.08	2.00
23	5.75	4.35	3.75	3.41	3.18	3.02	2.90	2.81	2.73	2.67	2.57	2.47	2.36	2.30	2.24	2.18	2.11	2.04	1.97
24	5.72	4.32	3.72	3.38	3.15	2.99	2.87	2.78	2.70	2.64	2.54	2.44	2.33	2.27	2.21	2.15	2.08	2.01	1.94
25	5.69	4.29	3.69	3.35	3.13	2.97	2.85	2.75	2.68	2.61	2.51	2.41	2.30	2.24	2.18	2.12	2.05	1.98	1.91
26	5.66	4.27	3.67	3.33	3.10	2.94	2.82	2.73	2.65	2.59	2.49	2.39	2.28	2.22	2.16	2.09	2.03	1.95	1.88
27	5.63	4.24	3.65	3.31	3.08	2.92	2.80	2.71	2.63	2.57	2.47	2.36	2.25	2.19	2.13	2.07	2.00	1.93	1.85
28	5.61	4.22	3.63	3.29	3.06	2.90	2.78	2.69	2.61	2.55	2.45	2.34	2.23	2.17	2.11	2.05	1.98	1.91	1.83
29	5.59	4.20	3.61	3.27	3.04	2.88	2.76	2.67	2.59	2.53	2.43	2.32	2.21	2.15	2.09	2.03	1.96	1.89	1.81
30	5.57	4.18	3.59	3.25	3.03	2.87	2.75	2.65	2.57	2.51	2.41	2.31	2.20	2.14	2.07	2.01	1.94	1.87	1.79
40	5.42	4.05	3.46	3.13	2.90	2.74	2.62	2.53	2.45	2.39	2.29	2.18	2.07	2.01	1.94	1.88	1.80	1.72	1.64
60	5.29	3.93	3.34	3.01	2.79	2.63	2.51	2.41	2.33	2.27	2.17	2.06	1.94	1.88	1.82	1.74	1.67	1.58	1.48
120	5.15	3.80	3.23	2.89	2.67	2.52	2.39	2.30	2.22	2.16	2.05	1.94	1.82	1.76	1.69	1.61	1.53	1.43	1.31
∞	5.02	3.69	3.12	2.79	2.57	2.41	2.29	2.19	2.11	2.05	1.94	1.83	1.71	1.64	1.57	1.48	1.39	1.27	1.00

APPENDIX G (Continued)

$$\alpha = 0.01$$

ν_2 \ ν_1	1	2	3	4	5	6	7	8	9	10	12	15	20	24	30	40	60	120	∞
1	4052	4999.5	5403	5625	5764	5859	5928	5982	6022	6056	6106	6157	6209	6235	6261	6287	6313	6339	6366
2	98.50	99.00	99.17	99.25	99.30	99.33	99.36	99.37	99.39	99.40	99.42	99.43	99.45	99.46	99.47	99.47	99.48	99.49	99.50
3	34.12	30.82	29.46	28.71	28.24	27.91	27.67	27.49	27.35	27.23	27.05	26.87	26.69	26.60	26.50	26.41	26.32	26.22	26.13
4	21.20	18.00	16.69	15.98	15.52	15.21	14.98	14.80	14.66	14.55	14.37	14.20	14.02	13.93	13.84	13.75	13.65	13.56	13.46
5	16.26	13.27	12.06	11.39	10.97	10.67	10.46	10.29	10.16	10.05	9.89	9.72	9.55	9.47	9.38	9.29	9.20	9.11	9.02
6	13.75	10.92	9.78	9.15	8.75	8.47	8.26	8.10	7.98	7.87	7.72	7.56	7.40	7.31	7.23	7.14	7.06	6.97	6.88
7	12.25	9.55	8.45	7.85	7.46	7.19	6.99	6.84	6.72	6.62	6.47	6.31	6.16	6.07	5.99	5.91	5.82	5.74	5.65
8	11.26	8.65	7.59	7.01	6.63	6.37	6.18	6.03	5.91	5.81	5.67	5.52	5.36	5.28	5.20	5.12	5.03	4.95	4.86
9	10.56	8.02	6.99	6.42	6.06	5.80	5.61	5.47	5.35	5.26	5.11	4.96	4.81	4.73	4.65	4.57	4.48	4.40	4.31
10	10.04	7.56	6.55	5.99	5.64	5.39	5.20	5.06	4.94	4.85	4.71	4.56	4.41	4.33	4.25	4.17	4.08	4.00	3.91
11	9.65	7.21	6.22	5.67	5.32	5.07	4.89	4.74	4.63	4.54	4.40	4.25	4.10	4.02	3.94	3.86	3.78	3.69	3.60
12	9.33	6.93	5.95	5.41	5.06	4.82	4.64	4.50	4.39	4.30	4.16	4.01	3.86	3.78	3.70	3.62	3.54	3.45	3.36
13	9.07	6.70	5.74	5.21	4.86	4.62	4.44	4.30	4.19	4.10	3.96	3.82	3.66	3.59	3.51	3.43	3.34	3.25	3.17
14	8.86	6.51	5.56	5.04	4.69	4.46	4.28	4.14	4.03	3.94	3.80	3.66	3.51	3.43	3.35	3.27	3.18	3.09	3.00
15	8.68	6.36	5.42	4.89	4.56	4.32	4.14	4.00	3.89	3.80	3.67	3.52	3.37	3.29	3.21	3.13	3.05	2.96	2.87
16	8.53	6.23	5.29	4.77	4.44	4.20	4.03	3.89	3.78	3.69	3.55	3.41	3.26	3.18	3.10	3.02	2.93	2.84	2.75
17	8.40	6.11	5.18	4.67	4.34	4.10	3.93	3.79	3.68	3.59	3.46	3.31	3.16	3.08	3.00	2.92	2.83	2.75	2.65
18	8.29	6.01	5.09	4.58	4.25	4.01	3.84	3.71	3.60	3.51	3.37	3.23	3.08	3.00	2.92	2.84	2.75	2.66	2.57
19	8.18	5.93	5.01	4.50	4.17	3.94	3.77	3.63	3.52	3.43	3.30	3.15	3.00	2.92	2.84	2.76	2.67	2.58	2.49
20	8.10	5.85	4.94	4.43	4.10	3.87	3.70	3.56	3.46	3.37	3.23	3.09	2.94	2.86	2.78	2.69	2.61	2.52	2.42
21	8.02	5.78	4.87	4.37	4.04	3.81	3.64	3.51	3.40	3.31	3.17	3.03	2.88	2.80	2.72	2.64	2.55	2.46	2.36
22	7.95	5.72	4.82	4.31	3.99	3.76	3.59	3.45	3.35	3.26	3.12	2.98	2.83	2.75	2.67	2.58	2.50	2.40	2.31
23	7.88	5.66	4.76	4.26	3.94	3.71	3.54	3.41	3.30	3.21	3.07	2.93	2.78	2.70	2.62	2.54	2.45	2.35	2.26
24	7.82	5.61	4.72	4.22	3.90	3.67	3.50	3.36	3.26	3.17	3.03	2.89	2.74	2.66	2.58	2.49	2.40	2.31	2.21
25	7.77	5.57	4.68	4.18	3.85	3.63	3.46	3.32	3.22	3.13	2.99	2.85	2.70	2.62	2.54	2.45	2.36	2.27	2.17
26	7.72	5.53	4.64	4.14	3.82	3.59	3.42	3.29	3.18	3.09	2.96	2.81	2.66	2.58	2.50	2.42	2.33	2.23	2.13
27	7.68	5.49	4.60	4.11	3.78	3.56	3.39	3.26	3.15	3.06	2.93	2.78	2.63	2.55	2.47	2.38	2.29	2.20	2.10
28	7.64	5.45	4.57	4.07	3.75	3.53	3.36	3.23	3.12	3.03	2.90	2.75	2.60	2.52	2.44	2.35	2.26	2.17	2.06
29	7.60	5.42	4.54	4.04	3.73	3.50	3.33	3.20	3.09	3.00	2.87	2.73	2.57	2.49	2.41	2.33	2.23	2.14	2.03
30	7.56	5.39	4.51	4.02	3.70	3.47	3.30	3.17	3.07	2.98	2.84	2.70	2.55	2.47	2.39	2.30	2.21	2.11	2.01
40	7.31	5.18	4.31	3.83	3.51	3.29	3.12	2.99	2.89	2.80	2.66	2.52	2.37	2.29	2.20	2.11	2.02	1.92	1.80
60	7.08	4.98	4.13	3.65	3.34	3.12	2.95	2.82	2.72	2.63	2.50	2.35	2.20	2.12	2.03	1.94	1.84	1.73	1.60
120	6.85	4.79	3.95	3.48	3.17	2.96	2.79	2.66	2.56	2.47	2.34	2.19	2.03	1.95	1.86	1.76	1.66	1.53	1.38
∞	6.63	4.61	3.78	3.32	3.02	2.80	2.64	2.51	2.41	2.32	2.18	2.04	1.88	1.79	1.70	1.59	1.47	1.32	1.00

Glossary

Parenthetical numbers following the term indicate the page of the text where it is introduced. Italics indicate that the word or phrase is defined elsewhere in the Glossary.

A–B design *(176)*   A *single-subject design* involving a *baseline period* (A), followed by a treatment period (B), during which the experimental treatment is administered to the subject. Essentially a *correlational* design.

A–B–A design *(177)*   A *single-subject design* involving a *baseline period* (A), followed by a treatment period (B), during which the experimental treatment is administered, followed by a *reversal period* (A) in which the baseline condition is reinstated.

Additive relationship *(156)*   A relationship between two independent variables that do not interact in affecting behavior. An interaction between two independent variables as reflected in the dependent measure is called a nonadditive relationship.

Alpha level *(327)*   The probability of a *Type I error*. See *Level of significance*.

ANCOVA *(373)*   Analysis of covariance. An *inferential statistical* technique involving the analysis of *variance* combined with a linear adjustment for one secondary source of individual differences. The adjustment procedure is based on the correlation between a preexisting, *covariate* measure and the *dependent variable*.

ANOVA *(329)*   Analysis of variance. A sophisticated and powerful statistical technique for evaluating the *main effects* and interactions in a multiple-treatment design.

Artifact *(243)*   A source of *secondary variance* that is a result of the research process itself.

Attribute *(56)*   A characteristic that can be identified and measured.

Available samples *(50)*   The most frequently used sampling technique in behavioral research, consisting of choosing to include as subjects those easily available to the researcher. This sampling procedure is justified by the philosophical stance that imperfect *data* will have to do when the perfect sample cannot be attained.

Bar graph *(69)*   A method of summarizing and presenting *data* in graphic form. The heights of various columns represent the frequency of various measurement categories. See *histogram*.

Baseline Measure *(174)*   The measurement of behavior in a *single-subject design* prior to the administration of *treatment* in order to establish a reference point for evaluating the effectiveness of the treatment. A "before" measure.

Before–after static group comparison design *(121)*   A relatively weak independent two-group design in which the experimenter cannot assign the subjects to the experimental and control groups. The opportunity to pretest the subjects in the groups provides a reference point for comparing the changes due to *treatment* and assessing the equality of the two groups.

Before–after two-group design *(126)*   An independent two-group design in which the subjects are also administered a pretest prior to the *treatment* condition.

Before–match–after design *(137)*   A *related two-group research design* that involves pretesting the subjects and using the scores to create matched groups.

Bellwether sample   (49)   A sampling technique in which elements in the sample are selected for their history of accurately reflecting the characteristics of the population.

Between-groups variance   (106)   The difference observed in the numerical *data* between two groups in an experiment. Between-groups variance is comprised of *primary variance* and *secondary variance.*

Bias   (36)   Any procedure or factor, deliberate or accidental, that consistently lessens the accuracy of the measurement procedure.

Biased selection   (38)   Any sampling procedure that disproportionately favors the inclusion or causes the exclusion of some elements in the *population*. Biased selection results in *secondary variance.*

Blocking variable   (159)   A measure taken on subjects in order to categorize them for assignment to experimental and control groups. Since blocking does not match subjects on a subject-by-subject basis, it is considered an independent-groups procedure.

Bogus pipeline   (257)   A procedure for controlling subjects' responding to demand characteristics, where the subjects believe that any lying will be detected by physiological measurements.

Carry-over   (113)   The *secondary variance* that occurs when the treatment administered to the subject early in an experiment affects the measures of the behavior of the subject when exposed to another treatment later in the same experiment.

Causal inference   (361)   The conclusion that the changes in one *independent variable* directly bring about changes in a *dependent variable.*

Central tendency   (72)   A *descriptive statistic* describing the typical or average score in a distribution of *data.* Usually the measures of central tendency are the *mean,* the *median,* or the *mode.*

Changing-criterion design   (179)   A *single-subject design* in which the administration of the treatment is contingent on the behavior of the subject, and the behavioral criterion is shifted according to the progress of the subject. Also known as *shaping.*

Chi square tests (χ^2)   (307)   The *inferential statistical* tests that analyze the observed frequencies compared to the expected (theoretical) frequencies within various categories.

Class intervals   (68)   A descriptive, data-organization procedure in which performance along a continuous variable is divided into discrete intervals, or discrete measures are grouped into categories or classes.

Conceptual hypothesis   (14)   The step in the inductive-deductive reasoning process where a specific hypothesis is derived from the theory. The conceptual hypothesis lacks coordinating, *operational definitions.*

Confounding   (38)   A term used to describe the operation of variables in an experiment that confuse the interpretation of the data. If the *independent variable* is confounded with an uncontrolled *secondary variable,* the experimenter cannot separate the effects of the two variables on the dependent measure.

Conservative arrangement   (45)   A relatively weak method of controlling a source of *secondary variance.* The experiment is arranged in such a way that if a *secondary variable* is in operation it will decrease the magnitude of the *primary variance* attributable to the *independent variable.*

Constant   (21)   A measure of an attribute that does not change. The opposite of a *variable.*

Continuous Variable   (57)   A *variable* that does not fall into discrete categories but exists along a continuum of infinitely small, perceptually inseparable units.

Contrived-natural-environment study   (97)   A research procedure in which the subject is placed in an artificial situation for the sake of observation, but the situation resembles a natural environment as much as possible. Zoos are often good examples of contrived natural environments.

Control   (37)   Maintaining constancy of conditions; calibrating measuring tools; manipulating behavior; and establishing research procedures designed to maximize *primary variance,* limit *secondary variance* and minimize *error variance.*

Control group   (37)   A group as identical as possible to the experimental group except for the experience of the treatment condition. See *experimental group.*

Correlation coefficient   (348)   A descriptive statistic that numerically describes the degree and direction of relationship between two variables.

Correlational study   (98)   A research procedure that involves the simultaneous or sequential measurement of two or more variables in order to determine the degree of relationship between them. Because there are no clear *independent* and *dependent variables* in a correlational study, causal relationships cannot be established.

Counterbalanced experimental conditions design   (112)   A multiple-treatment design that presents two or more *independent variables* in sequential alternation to partially control for effects created by the order of presentation of the treatments.

Covariance analysis   (373)   See ANCOVA.

Covariate   (373)   A secondary variable measured but not manipulated or otherwise controlled in a study. Usually a covariate is a pretest or organismic measure of the subjects.

Cross-lagged correlational analysis   (363)   A *statistical analysis* technique involving the calculation of *correlation coefficients* between two variables measured both before and after the administration of a treatment in a *longitudinal study.* The "cross-lagged correlation coefficients" index the relationship between the before measure on one variable and the after measure on the other variable.

DRO design (Differential Reinforcement of Other)   (178)   A single-subject design (A–B–C–B) in which the A–B sequence is followed by a period (C) in which reinforcement is administered for behavior *other* than the original target behavior. If the original target behavior tends to return to the baseline (A) level, the hypothesis that there is a contingent relationship between reinforcement and consequent change in behavior is supported.

Data   (56)   The raw material for research conclusions; the numbers generated by the measurement process of determining how many units of a particular dimension are present at a particular moment in time.

Data-analysis error   (47)   Any error in the data-analysis procedure ranging from choice of the wrong statistical test to arithmetical error, which results in an inappropriate research conclusion.

Debriefing   (251)   The procedure for informing a human subject of the actual intent of an experiment after the session and assessing the subject's suspiciousness of intent to deceive. Debriefing is required if the subject was seriously misled during participation in the experiment.

Deduction   (10)   The process by which broad general statements are examined and logically manipulated to derive a relatively specific hypothesis. Deduction is necessary for deriving a *conceptual hypothesis* from a *theory.*

Degrees of freedom (df)   (297)   A statistical term used to describe the amount of information remaining in the *data* after certain information has been extracted and used in the data-analysis procedure. The number of degrees of freedom is related to the sample size or the number of categories or classes in which *frequency data* are sorted.

Dependent variable   (21)   In behavioral research: measures of behavior.

Deprivation schedules   (219)   A procedure for motivating animals to perform in a research setting. It typically involves food deprivation, with food as a reward in the research task.

Descriptive statistics   (289)   Graphical, tabular, and numerical techniques for organizing and summarizing *data.*

Desensitization therapy   (147)   A process for eliminating a phobic response. This is usually accomplished by presenting successively larger amounts of the feared stimulus but never allowing them to become large enough to precipitate the response.

Directional prediction (297) An inferential procedure for increasing the power of the research decision process. If the researcher is sure that the treatment will change behavior in a specific direction, the entire power of the *inferential statistical* procedure can be focused in the specified direction. Also known as a *one-tailed test.*

Discrete variable (57) The measures of a discrete variable exist as counts of discriminable units. The opposite of a *continuous variable.*

Double blind (41) A control procedure where neither the subject nor the experimenter knows whether the subject is in the treatment or the control condition.

Duration data (63) A measure of behavior using time as the measuring standard. Examples of duration data might be delay, response time, and interresponse interval.

EEG (321) Electroencephalograph, a reading of the electrical activity of the brain.

Elimination of secondary variable (40) A control procedure involving removing the *secondary variable* from the research setting.

<u>*Empirical*</u> *(9)* Based on observation of external, physical events.

Environmental variable (21) Any *attribute* of the environment that may affect the subject's behavior.

Error variance (30) Unpredictable, inconsistent variations in the measures of behavior.

Ethics (227) The professional and humane responsibilities the experimenter bears on behalf of subjects and colleagues.

Ex-post-facto design (118) A nonexperimental research procedure involving measuring the effect of the uncontrolled treatment after it has occurred.

Experimental contamination (39) Sources of *secondary variance* that are caused by the experimental procedure itself.

Experimental group (37) The group of subjects that receive the treatment condition. See *control group.*

Experimental hypothesis (12) The precise statement of the question being investigated by the experiment. A clearly stated, specific explanation of an event's occurrence.

Experimental mortality (39) The loss of *data* sources during the research process, usually due to the loss of subjects. A source of *secondary variance* in that there is a differential loss between experimental groups.

Experimental observation (94) The observation of events under controlled, experimental conditions. Contrast to *naturalistic observation.*

Experimentation factors (107) Sources of *variance* created by the research setting and research process. See *experimental contamination.*

Experimenter effect (248) Changes in the recorded scores of the subject due to the experimenter. Experimenter effects may range from biased recording of data to subtly manipulating the subject's behavior.

Experimenter expectancy bias (250) A type of *experimenter effect.* A source of *secondary variance* where the experimenter unconsciously, subtly cues the subjects so that the *data* supports the *experimental hypothesis.*

Explanation (15) One of the goals of the scientific method, which retraces a causal chain by beginning with the consequent events and working backward in time to the appropriate antecedent conditions.

External validity (38) The generalizability of research results to other situations and populations.

Extreme values (31) A procedure for maximizing *primary variance* by selecting the most compelling levels of the *independent variable.* In most basic experiments, this involves comparing the treatment *(experimental group)* with zero level of treatment *(control group).*

F *test* *(330)* A sophisticated statistical test that can accommodate multiple-treatment-design data. See *ANOVA*.

Factorial design *(150)* A research design that involves two or more *independent variables* being used simultaneously.

Field study *(97)* A *naturalistic* research procedure involving the collection of behavioral data in the natural setting without experimental manipulation.

Frequency data *(62)* A behavioral measurement procedure that involves counting the number of behaviors occurring in a set of categories.

Frequency distribution *(62)* A method of summarizing *data* by showing the number of cases falling within a series of specified categories or intervals.

Frequency polygon *(71)* A graphical means of summarizing a *frequency distribution*. The intervals are arranged along the abcissa and the frequency in each of the intervals is measured along the ordinate with the data line connecting the adjacent points.

Frequency table *(67)* A tabular presentation of *data* in which the cells represent the categories and the numerals indicate the frequency of occurrence within that category.

Function *(26)* A special case of a *relationship* between the *independent* and *dependent variables,* where one and only one value of the dependent variable is found for each and every value of the independent variable.

Generalization *(50)* The process of applying the *sample* results obtained in an experiment to the *population* sampled, including populations of subjects, *dependent variables,* procedures, and experimenters.

Goodness of fit *(356)* A statistical procedure for determining how close the *data* points come to a specified line or function.

Halo effect *(255)* The tendency of human evaluators, based on past observation of the subjects, to score the performances of subjects higher than the scores they would receive in a strictly objective procedure.

Hawthorne effect *(246)* A change in observed behavior attributable directly to the fact that the subjects are aware that *data* are being collected.

Histogram *(69)* A graphical means of summarizing data by using the heights of bars to reflect the frequencies of occurrence within the measured categories. See *bar graph*.

History effects *(39)* The effects of all events, except the *independent variable,* occurring between the before and after measures.

Holding constant *(41)* A means of controlling a source of *secondary variance* by not allowing it to vary during the *data*-collection process.

Hypothesis testing *(290)* An application of *inferential statistical* procedures to decide whether or not the observed *data* support the *experimental hypothesis*.

Hypothetico-deductive *(10)* The ongoing scientific process of collecting information from various sources, combining and organizing it into a theoretical framework, and drawing specific predictions for further experimental tests.

Idea log book *(194)* A means of preserving spontaneous research ideas as they occur by recording them in a journal or diary.

Independent variable *(21)* In an experimental study, the variable that is manipulated by the experimenter. Also called the *treatment*.

Individual differences *(38)* The subject's source of *secondary variance* due to the consistent, differential effects of *maturation, sequence effects, biased selection, statistical regression,* and the confounded interaction of two or more sources of *secondary variance*. The inconsistent effect of intrinsic individual differences between subjects produces *error variance*.

Individual position *(72)* A *descriptive statistic* that describes in a single numerical value the position of an individual relative to the group.

Induction (10) A logical process by which several specific cases are summarized into a general rule.

Inferential process (289) The process of determining whether the data from a specific experiment can be generalized to a larger population.

Inferential statistics (289) The field of statistics concerned with the *inferential process.*

Intact groups (221) The practice of drawing subjects for research purposes from groups that are already formed. Since intact groups are not created by random selection, they form a dubious basis for establishing representative groups for generalization purposes.

Intensity data (62) A measure of behavior that involves the strength of the response.

Interaction (30) An interaction between two variables occurs when changing the values of one alters the effects of the other.

Interaction effect (45) The measure of the interaction between two or more *independent variables* and the *dependent variable.*

Internal validity (244) An evaluation of the accuracy of the data obtained from an experiment. Internal validity is accomplished when the *secondary* and *error variables* are adequately controlled so that the interpretation of the effect of the *independent variable* is clear.

Interval scale (60) A *measurement scale* in which the distance between numbers contains meaningful information. The interval scale by definition includes *nominal* and *ordinal* information, and an arbitrary zero point.

Level of significance (295) A precise probability value adopted by the researcher for rejecting the *null hypothesis* when true, and consequently, falsely accepting the *experimental hypothesis.*

Levinson's Law (233) "If anything can possibly go wrong, it will." See *Murphy's Law.*

Likert scale (101) A paper and pencil procedure for measuring attitudes by asking the subject to locate himself or herself along one or more dimensions. The typical Likert scale involves five or seven choices on each item.

Line graph (81) A graphical means of summarizing data that uses lines to indicate trends, *relationships, central tendencies, scatter,* and so on.

Line of best fit (358) A line on a graph that best summarizes the data points distributed on the same graph. Usually the line of best fit is a straight line and "good fit" is determined by mathematical rules. See *goodness of fit.*

Linear relationship (354) A straight line that summarizes the *relationship* between two variables.

Longitudinal studies (96) A study of the behavior of one or more subjects over a period of time.

Main effect (151) In *factorial designs,* the *variance* that can be attributed to each *independent variable* exclusively. The average effect of an *independent variable.*

Match by correlated criterion (134) A means of matching the subjects in the experimental and control groups on the basis of a *covariate measure* that is related to the *independent variable.*

Matching (42) A procedure for controlling *secondary variance* by making treatment groups numerically equivalent on a measure of the secondary variable.

Maturation (38) An *organismic,* secondary source of *variance* related to the amount of time that the subjects spend in the experimental situation, or between before and after measures.

Mean (75) A measure of *central tendency* that is the arithmetical average of a set of scores.

Mean square (333) A value used in the calculation of the *F-test.* A figure representing the average squared deviation from the group mean. Also known as the *between-groups variance* or the *within-group variance.*

Measurement (55) The process of assigning numbers to events or behaviors according to rules.

Measurement error (46) A source of *secondary* and *error variance* due to inaccuracies in the measurement procedure.

Measurement scale (58) A specific empirical measurement procedure and the rules for assigning numbers to the observed behavior.

Median (73) A measure of *central tendency* appropriate to an *ordinal scale* of measurement. The median is that point in a distribution above which 50% of the scores lie and below which 50% lie.

Mode (73) A measure of *central tendency* appropriate to a *nominal scale* of measurement. The mode is the most frequently occurring score in a distribution.

Model (11) A framework used in the theoretical phase of the *inductive-deductive* process. An abstract set of assumptions, logic, and rules not identified with empirical events.

Multilevel design (146) A research design that incorporates several levels of an *independent variable*.

Multiple-baseline design across behaviors (180) A *single-subject design* that focuses a treatment condition on two or more behaviors in a sequential A–B format. The treatment is applied to each new behavior as control is established for a prior behavior.

Multiple-baseline design across settings (185) A *single-subject design* in which the treatment condition is administered to the same subject in several environmental settings. Essentially, several *A–B designs* are run in sequence with a subject, with the treatment introduced in each new setting as control is established in the prior setting.

Multiple-baseline design across subjects (185) An extension of the *single-subject A–B design,* in which the same treatment is administered to several subjects in sequence. Essentially, each new subject represents a replication of the original experiment, with each subject being exposed to treatment (B) after control is demonstrated for the prior subject.

Multiple comparison (334) A supplement to the analysis of variance *(ANOVA, F test)* involving a significant *main effect*. The researcher can determine which of the specific group means were significantly different from each other when more than two levels of the *independent variable* exist.

Multiple correlation analysis (376) A statistical procedure used to determine the relationship between two or more measured, uncontrolled variables and a criterion measure.

Multiple regression analysis (376) A statistical procedure used to determine the relationship between two or more *independent variables* and a criterion measure.

Multivalent research (33) A research procedure that includes many levels of a variable in one study.

Multivariate analysis (375) A statistical procedure that examines several variables simultaneously. Multivariate analysis can be used in multiple-treatment designs where there are several *independent variables* correlated with a criterion variable, or in designs that utilize multiple *dependent-variable* measures.

Murphy's Law (233) "If anything can possibly go wrong it will." See *Levinson's Law*.

Natural environment studies (97) Research, both experimental and naturalistic, that is conducted in the natural or "home" setting of the subject.

Naturalistic observation (94) A nonexperimental procedure of observing the behavior of the subjects in their natural environment. Contrast with *experimental observation*.

Nominal scale (59) The weakest scale of measurement. The name or number assigned in the measurement process represents only the classification name of the behavioral category assigned.

Normal distribution (290) The unimodal, symmetrical, bell-shaped distribution observed when the variable being measured is a function of a sequence of random events.

Null hypothesis *(294)* The statistical hypothesis that the *treatment* has no effect on behavior. The null hypothesis is proposed in the *inferential statistical* process in order to provide a basis for making probability statements about the observed results. In order to find support for the effectiveness of the treatment, the null hypothesis must be rejected.

One- and two-tail tests *(296)* A procedure for concentrating the power of a *hypothesis-testing* statistical procedure. If the experimenter has strong reason to believe that the *treatment* will change the behavior only in a specific direction, the researcher can then use a one-tailed test. The two-tailed test is used if a directional effect of the treatment cannot be predicted.

One-group before–after design *(109)* The *one-group design* that includes a control measure of the subjects' behavior prior to the administration of the *treatment,* which is compared with a measure of the subjects' behavior during or after the treatment.

One-group design *(108)* A research design that involves measurement of the behavior of a single group of subjects.

One-shot case study *(108)* A nonexperimental research procedure in which a single measure of the behavior of a group of subjects is collected, usually after the occurrence of some natural "treatment" event.

Operational definition *(13)* A means of clearly defining theoretical concepts in concrete terms for empirical observation. The *independent* and *dependent variables* are described by the operations necessary to produce or measure them.

Optimal values *(32)* A control procedure for maximizing *primary variance* (the effect of an *independent variable*) by selecting values of the independent variable that have been shown to be most likely to produce the largest *treatment effect.*

Ordered lists *(68)* A tabular means of summarizing numerical data by presenting them in rank order.

Ordinal scale *(59)* A scale of measurement in which the symbols or numbers assigned both name and rank-order the variable along the dimension measured.

Organismic variables *(21)* Physiological or psychological characteristics of the subject that may be measured.

Outside influences *(39)* *Secondary variance* sources that can influence the behavior being measured. Environmental factors occurring between pre- and post-measures, causing a differential loss of subjects between groups, producing differences in time or place of testing between groups, or any other factor affecting groups differentially.

Parameter *(47)* A descriptive characteristic (*mean, standard deviation,* and so on) of a population.

Parameter estimation *(289)* The *inferential statistical* procedure of estimating the descriptive characteristics of a population *(parameters)* from the *descriptive statistics* of the sample.

Pearson product-moment correlation coefficient *(351)* A *descriptive statistic* that numerically summarizes the degree and direction of *relationship* between two *variables.*

Percentile rank *(78)* A *descriptive statistic* indicating individual position by indicating the percentage of the scores that fall below the particular score being described.

Pilot study *(202)* A tentative, incomplete experiment that provides information for a more formal research study.

Placebo *(41)* The apparent administration of a *treatment* without the presumed key component needed for an effect. A placebo effect indicates a source of *secondary variance* due to the administration procedures surrounding the treatment rather than to the treatment itself.

Population *(47)* The group that contains all of the organisms for which explanations of behavior are tested in a given research study. Subjects from the population are *sampled* for research measurement, and the results of the research are then *generalized* to the population sampled.

Prediction   (9)   One element of the scientific process of describing the *relationship* between antecedent variables and consequent events. Prediction works forward in time, beginning with measuring the antecedent variables and then anticipating the measures of the consequent events.

Pretest sensitization   (39)   A type of *secondary variance* source in which a before-measure prior to treatment affects the subjects' responses to the *treatment*.

Primary variance   (29)   Changes in the measure of the *dependent variable* (behavior) that are due to the *independent variable*. Also known as the *treatment effect*.

Public observation   (9)   One of the restrictions on the scientific research process; to be scientific, the *data* must be publically observable.

Quasi-experimental research   (95)   A research procedure that may have some elements of control but leaves many sources of *secondary variance* uncontrolled. Does not involve the manipulation of an *independent variable*. See *naturalistic observation*.

Quota sample   (49)   A restricted sampling procedure involving sampling subjects according to one or more known characteristics of the *population*.

Random assignment   (42)   A method of assigning subjects to the groups of an experiment with all subjects having an equal chance to be in any group. Random assignment frequently employs a *table of random numbers,* although other unbiased procedures (flipping a coin) are legitimate.

Random sample   (49)   A sampling procedure whereby all individuals in the *population* are available to be sampled, and the selection of the sample is totally unbiased among these individuals.

Randomization   (43)   A procedure by which a variable may be selected, assigned, or scheduled, in a completely unbiased manner. Randomization involves the use of the *table of random numbers* so that no predictable sequence can be established.

Randomized-blocks design   (129)   An independent two-group design by which subjects are first categorized and then the subjects within each category are randomly assigned to the research groups.

Randomized-blocks factorial design   (159)   A combination of a *randomized-blocks design* and a *factorial design*. The design procedure involves conducting the research as in a *randomized-blocks design,* but then analyzing the data taking the blocking variable into account.

Randomized factorial design   (151)   A multiple-treatment design that includes all possible combinations of the levels of two or more *independent variables*. Usually each combination forms a condition to which at least two subjects are exposed. Subjects are *randomly assigned* to conditions.

Randomized two-group design   (123)   An independent two-group design in which the subjects are *randomly assigned* to the experimental and control groups.

Range   (75)   A measure of variation designating the numerical distance between the upper real limit of the highest score and the lower real limit of the lowest score.

Rank   (78)   A measure of individual position achieved by listing the number of other scores above or below the target score.

Ratio scale   (60)   A powerful scale of measurement in which all the arithmetic characteristics of the numeral assigned are reflected within the measurement process. The scale includes a real, nonarbitrary zero point, so that ratios of numbers assigned are meaningful.

Reactive effects of experimental arrangement   (39)   A source of *secondary variance* in which the characteristics of the research process affect the scores of the subjects. Decreases the *external validity* of the research.

Real limits   (69)   A measurement convention by which the boundary betwen two adjacent numerical categories is precisely defined.

Regression toward the mean (38) The statistical process by which those individuals with extreme scores on a first measure tend to get scores closer to the mean of the distribution on subsequent measurements.

Related two-group design (134) Two-group designs that include *matching* the subjects in the *experimental* and *control* groups on a subject-by-subject basis.

Relationship (25) A set of paired values of the *independent* and *dependent variables.* More generally, any set of paired values from two variables. See *function.*

Reliability (48) A statement about the degree of consistency of a measurement technique. Reliable techniques yield similar measures upon repeated measurement under similar conditions.

Repeated-measures factorial design (163) A multiple-treatment research design including a *factorial* design and a repeated-measures, time-series design. All possible combinations of all levels of two or more variables are included in the design, and each subject experiences all levels of at least one variable. Also called a *split-plot design.*

Repeated-measures multilevel design (148) Multilevel research design combined with a repeated-measures or *time-series design.* All subjects experience all levels of at least one variable.

Replication (20) Repeating the scientific observation procedures exactly, or as exactly as possible.

Representative sample (48) A sample that accurately reflects the characteristics of the population.

Research design (95) A plan for measuring target behavior. Choosing a research design involves attempting to anticipate and control the sources of *variance* that affect the measured behavior. A research design includes the assignment of subjects to levels of the *independent variables* and the *operational definition* of the *dependent variables.*

Research ethics (227) The moral rules and expectations that guide the behavior of a researcher. Ethical guidelines derive from being a member of the human race, a member of the scientific community, and an individual interacting with others, both animal and human.

Reversal (174) A control procedure in a *single-subject* design in which a *treatment effect,* after having been introduced and measured, is then removed to measure the effect of loss.

Sample (47) A subset of a *population.*

Sample bias (48) Any sampling procedure that produces a sample not representative of the characteristics of the *population.*

Sample regression equation (357) The statistical equation that estimates the values of the *dependent variable* given the value of the *independent variable,* the *mean* of the independent scores, and the *slope* of the *best fit* straight line.

Scatter plot (80) A graphical means of summarizing the measured relationship between two *variables* by representing the paired observations on the two variables as points at the appropriate coordinates on the graph.

Secondary variance (29) Changes in the measure of behavior that are not due to the *independent variable* but consistently affect the behavior measured.

Self-fulfilling prophecy (250) A tendency for individuals who hold a hypothesis to preferentially make observations that support the hypothesis.

Sequence effects (38) Changes in behavior that can be measured during, and be directly attributable to, the on-going research process. A source of *secondary variance.* See *testing effects.*

Serendipity (27) An attitude that allows "lucky" research accidents to be capitalized upon by the researcher.

Several values *(32)* A means of clarifying the effect of the *independent variable* by selecting several different levels of treatment. See *multivalent research.*

Sham operation *(41)* A control procedure used in surgical research where the control subjects are subjected to all the surgical procedures except removal of the target tissue or injection of the crucial substance.

Shaping *(179)* A behavior-modification term where the administration of a reinforcement depends upon the performance of the subject, but the criterion is progressively changed to demand higher levels of performance as the training continues. See *changing-criterion design.*

Simple effects *(152)* In a *factorial design* experiment, the effect of the levels of one *independent variable* under each level of the other independent variable.

Single blind *(41)* A control procedure in which the experimenter measuring the behavior does not know whether the subject being measured is a member of the experimental or the control group. See *double blind.*

Single-subject design *(172)* A research design that measures the effects of a treatment on a single subject.

Skewed distribution *(71)* A distribution that is assymetrical, there being an unusual concentration of scores either above or below the mean.

Slope *(87)* A graphing term that describes the rate of change in the measure of behavior across the levels of the *independent variable.*

Solomon four-group design *(165)* A research design that simultaneously measures and controls for the treatment effect and the effect of administering a pretest.

Split-plot design *(161)* A *repeated-measures factorial design.*

Spuriousness *(369)* A measured relationship between two variables that is not effected by either but by some third variable.

Standard deviation *(77)* A *descriptive statistic* that numerically summarizes the average amount of variation about the *mean* of a distribution of scores.

Standard deviation of the slope *(358)* The error term for determining how well the data can be fitted to a straight line.

Standard error of the mean *(318)* A statistic that numerically summarizes the expected variation of *means* when the *null hypothesis* is correct. The *standard deviation* of the sample means about the mean of the sample means.

Standard score *(78)* An individual-position *descriptive statistic.* The target score is compared to the entire group in terms of the ratio of the difference from the *mean* and the *standard deviation.*

Static-group comparison *(118)* Nonexperimental research procedure that compares two or more existing groups after the uncontrolled occurrence of a "treatment."

Statistic *(47)* A description of data obtained from a sample.

Statistical control *(373)* A method of measuring or controlling for sources of *secondary variance* by statistical corrections applied to the measures of the *dependent variable.*

Statistical regression *(38)* A statistical phenomenon whereby extreme scores from a subject tend to *regress towards the mean* (become less extreme) upon remeasurement of the same subject.

Statistical tests *(293)* Mathematical procedures for comparing observed differences between sample statistics with some estimate of the likely differences if the *null hypothesis* is correct.

Subject factors *(29)* Factors peculiar to the subjects that may affect the outcome of an experiment. For example, the heredity, history, or present state of a subject may influence the *variance* in the observed data.

Subjects as their own controls *(42)* The practice of obtaining the control measures from the same subjects that provide the treatment measures. *Single-subject designs, one-group designs,* and *repeated-measures designs* use subjects as their own controls.

Systematizing (44)   A method of controlling *secondary variance* by including the secondary variable as an *independent variable* in the research study.

Table of random numbers (43)   A series of the digits from zero through nine arranged in a totally unpredictable order.

Taming (220)   A procedure often required in infrahuman research in order to reduce *subject effects as* sources of *secondary variance* during the actual experiment.

Testing effects (38)   Sources of *secondary variance* caused by the measurement process itself. Testing effects occur when a pretest affects the measure on the post-test. See sequence effects.

Theoretical constructs (28)   Statements in a theory that symbolize or label the connection between the measured antecedent events and the consequent events.

Theory (13)   An internally consistent system that summarizes the *data* from the past and can be used to provide predictions to be tested in the future. A *model* with coordinating, *operational definitions.*

Three-way interaction (85)   The most complicated interaction that can occur in a *factorial design* involving three different *independent variables.* The effect of variable A depends on the levels of variable B and variable C.

Time-of-testing effects (39)   Differences in the measured behavior of groups of subjects that can be attributed to differences between groups in the time at which their behaviors were measured.

Time-series design (110)   A research design that involves multiple measures of one group of subjects over a prescribed period of time. Multiple before and after measures are taken.

Treatment (39)   The *independent variable* in an experiment.

Treatment effect (38)   Another term for *primary variance.*

Two-by-two matrix (63)   A table for organizing *data.* The table has two dimensions, rows and columns, and each dimension has two levels. The combination of two rows and two columns produces a table with four cells or quadrants. Two-by-two matrices may also be used to indicate the groups involved in a 2 × 2 *factorial design.*

Two-way interaction (84)   The dependent *variance* that is the result of the simultaneous operation of two *independent variables.* The effect of one variable is dependent on the level of the other variable.

Type I error (294)   The erroneous rejection of the *null hypothesis.*

Type II error (294)   The erroneous acceptance of the *null hypothesis.*

Unbiased variance estimate (319)   The statistical procedure that allows a more accurate estimate of the population variance on the basis of the sample variance.

Unobtrusive measures (100)   Observation and measurement procedures specifically selected not to interfere with the natural behavior or enter the conscious awareness of the subject.

Validity (47)   An indication of the accuracy of a measure in terms of how well the measurements correspond to reality.

Variability (75)   A *descriptive statistic* that provides an estimate of the degree of scatter of the data.

Variable (21)   Any factor that can be measured and can change.

Variance (29)   A measure of variability. The average squared deviation of individual scores from the group mean.

Within-group variance (29)   The variability measured in the scores from a group of subjects that all receive the same treatment. Within-group variance is another term for *error variance;* the uncontrolled, inconsistent variation between measures.

Yoked-control group design (140) A *related-groups design* that matches the subjects according to the pattern of treatment experienced. This pattern is usually dictated by the behavior of the subject in the experimental group and imposed on the corresponding subject in the control group. The difference between experimental and control subjects is that the behavior of the experimental subject controls the rate of occurrence of the treatment while the control subject receives the treatment contingent on the experimental subject's behavior.

Index of Names

INDEX OF NAMES

Index of Subjects

INDEX OF SUBJECTS

RESEARCH DESIGNS

	MATCHED RANDOM ASSIGNMENT (Experimental Designs)			
	One Dependent Measure per Subject		Two Dependent Measures per Subject	
	Two levels of the independent variable actually included	More than two levels for one or more independent variables	Two levels of the independent variable actually included	More than two levels for one or more independent variables
More than one independent variable and no covariate				
One independent variable and one covariate	MATCH–BY–CORRELATED–CRITERION CHAPT. 9	THREE–OR–MORE–GROUPS MATCH–BY–CORRELATED–CRITERION		
One independent variable and no covariate	YOKED CONTROL–GROUP CHAPT. 9	THREE–OR–MORE–GROUPS YOKED CONTROL–GROUP	TWO–GROUP BEFORE–MATCH–AFTER CHAPT. 9	MULTILEVEL WITH PRE-TEST, MATCH ON PRETEST CHAPT. 10
One or more un-manipulated treatment conditions				

NUMBER OF MANIPULATED INDEPENDENT VARIABLES AND MEASURED COVARIATES*

* A covariate is a secondary variance source, not experimentally manipulated or controlled, but measured by the researcher.